推古论今辩东西

TUIGULUNJIN BIAN DONGXI

中山大学哲学系复办60周年庆贺文集·逻辑学、科学哲学卷

张伟　张清江　主编

中山大學出版社
SUN YAT-SEN UNIVERSITY PRESS
·广州·

图书在版编目（CIP）数据

推古论今辩东西．逻辑学、科学哲学卷/张伟，张清江主编．—广州：中山大学出版社，2020. 11
（中山大学哲学系复办60周年庆贺文集）
ISBN 978－7－306－07052－4

Ⅰ. ①逻…　Ⅱ. ①张…　②张…　Ⅲ. ①逻辑学—文集　②科学哲学—文集　Ⅳ. ①B－53

中国版本图书馆CIP数据核字（2020）第219837号

出 版 人：王天琪
策划编辑：嵇春霞
责任编辑：熊锡源
封面设计：曾　斌
责任校对：周昌华
责任技编：何雅涛
出版发行：中山大学出版社
电　　话：编辑部020－84110771，84110283，84111997，84110771
　　　　　发行部020－84111998，84111981，84111160
地　　址：广州市新港西路135号
邮　　编：510275　　传　　真：020－84036565
网　　址：http：//www. zsup. com. cn　E-mail：zdcbs@ mail. sysu. edu. cn
印 刷 者：佛山家联印刷有限公司
规　　格：787mm×1092mm　1/16　21. 5印张　398千字
版次印次：2020年11月第1版　2020年11月第1次印刷
定　　价：78. 00元

中山大学哲学系复办60周年庆贺文集

主　编　张　伟　张清江

编　委（按姓氏笔画排序）

　　　　马天俊　方向红　冯达文　朱　刚　吴重庆

　　　　陈少明　陈立胜　周春健　赵希顺　徐长福

　　　　黄　敏　龚　隽　鞠实儿

中山大学哲学系复办60周年庆贺文集

总　序

中山大学哲学系创办于 1924 年，是中山大学创建之初最早培植的学系之一。1952 年逢全国高校院系调整而撤销建制，1960 年复办至今。先后由黄希声、冯友兰、傅斯年、朱谦之、杨荣国、刘嵘、李锦全、胡景钊、林铭钧、章海山、黎红雷、鞠实儿、张伟等担任系主任。

早期的中山大学哲学系名家云集，奠立了极为深厚的学术根基。其中，冯友兰先生的中国哲学研究、吴康先生的西方哲学研究、朱谦之先生的比较哲学研究、李达先生与何思敬先生的马克思主义哲学研究、陈荣捷先生的朱子学研究、马采先生的美学研究等，均在学界产生了重要影响，也奠定了中山大学哲学系在全国的领先地位。

日月其迈，逝者如斯。迄于今岁，中山大学哲学系复办恰满一甲子。60 年来，哲学系同仁勠力同心、继往开来，各项事业蓬勃发展，取得了长足进步。目前，我系是教育部确定的全国哲学研究与人才培养基地之一，具有一级学科博士学位授予权，拥有国家重点学科 2 个、全国高校人文社会科学重点研究基地 2 个。2002 年教育部实行学科评估以来，稳居全国高校前列。2017 年，中山大学哲学学科成功入选国家“双一流”建设名单，我系迎来了跨越式发展的重要机遇。

近年来，中山大学哲学学科的人才队伍不断壮大，且越来越呈现出年轻化、国际化的特色。哲学系各位同仁研精覃思、深造自得，在各自的研究领域均取得了丰硕的成果，不少著述产生了国际性影响，中山大学哲学系已逐渐发展成为全国哲学研究的重镇之一。

为庆祝中山大学哲学系复办60周年，我系隆重推出“中山大学哲学系复办60周年庆贺文集”，主要收录哲学系在职教师（包括近年来加盟我系的充满活力的博士后和专职科研人员）的代表性学术论文。本文集共分五卷，依据不同学科各自定名如下：

逻辑、历史与现实（马克思主义哲学卷）

什么是经典世界（中国哲学卷）

面向事情本身之思（外国哲学、伦理学卷）

推古论今辩东西（逻辑学、科学哲学卷）

经史之间的思想与信仰（宗教学、美学卷）

文集的编撰与出版，也是我系教师学术成果的一个集中展示，代表了诸位学者近年来的学术思考，在此谨向学界同仁请益，敬希教正。

“中山大学哲学系复办60周年庆贺文集”的出版，得到中山大学出版社的鼎力支持，在此谨致以诚挚谢意！

中山大学哲学系

2020年6月20日

目　录

Preservation of Semantic Properties in Collective Argumentation: The Case of Aggregating Abstract Argumentation Frameworks①

Weiwei Chen[1] Ulle Endriss[2]

1 *Institute of Logic and Cognition and Department of Philosophy Sun Yat-sen University*, *China*

2 *ILLC*, *University of Amsterdam*, *The Netherlands*

1. Introduction

Formal argumentation theory provides tools for modelling both the arguments an agent may wish to employ in a debate and the relationships that hold between such arguments②. This applies both to human agents and to intelligent software agents. In the widely used model of *abstract argumentation*, introduced in the seminal work of Dung③, we abstract away from the internal structure of arguments and only model whether or not one argument *attacks* another argument. Thus, arguments are vertices in a directed graph, with edges representing attacks. This is a useful perspective when we require a high-level understanding of how different arguments relate to each other. When several agents engage in a debate, they may differ on their assessment of some of the arguments and their relationships. How best to model such scenarios of

① This is an extended version of a paper first presented at TARK-2017. W. Chen, & U. Endriss, Preservation of semantic properties during the aggregation of abstract argumentation frameworks, in *Proceedings of the 16th Conference on Theoretical Aspects of Rationality and Knowledge* (*TARK*), 2017, pp. 118 – 133. We would like to thank Sirin Botan, Umberto Grandi, Ronald de Haan, Zoi Terzopoulou, and Shengyang Zhong for numerous enlightening discussions on this material and the anonymous TARK and Artificial Intelligence reviewers for their constructive feedback.

② P. E. Dunne, T. J. M. Bench-Capon, *Proceedings of the 1st International Conference on Computational Models of Argument* (*COMMA*), IOS Press, 2006; T. J. M. Bench-Capon, P. E. Dunne, Argumentation in artificial intelligence, *Artificial Intelligence*, 2007, 171, pp. 619 – 641; P. Besnard, A. Hunter, *Elements of Argumentation*, MIT Press, 2008; I. Rahwan, G. R. Simari (Eds.), *Argumentation in Artificial Intelligence*, Springer, 2009; S. Modgil, N. Oren, F. Toni (Eds.), *Proceedings of the 1st International Workshop on Theory and Applications of Formal Argumentation* (TAFA), Springer, 2012.

③ P. M. Dung, On the acceptability of arguments and its fundamental role in nonmonotonic reasoning, logic programming and n-person games, *Artificial Intelligence*, 1995, 77, pp. 321 – 358.

collective argumentation is a question of considerable interest, not only in AI. Over the past decade or so, several authors have started to contribute to its resolution①.

Specifically, when agents differ on their assessment of which attacks between the arguments are in fact justified, i. e., when they put forward different *attack-relations*, we may wish to *aggregate* these individual pieces of information to obtain a global view. In this paper we analyse the circumstances under which a given *aggregation rule* will *preserve* relevant properties of the individual attack-relations, particularly properties that relate to the various *semantics* that have been proposed for abstract argumentation. For example, if all agents agree that argument A is *acceptable*, either because it is not attacked by any other argument or because it can be successfully defended against any such attack, then we would like A to also be considered acceptable relative to the attack-relation returned by our aggregation rule. Thus, *argument acceptability* is an example for a property that, ideally, should be preserved under aggregation. Our objective is to analyse what kind of simple aggregation rules can guarantee that this will be the case. Our approach is grounded in *social choice theory*, the formal study of collective decision making②. In particular,

① See, e. g., S. Coste-Marquis, C. Devred, S. Konieczny, M. - C. Lagasquie-Schiex, P. Marquis, On the merging of Dung's argumentation systems, *Artificial Intelligence*, 2007, 171, pp. 730 – 753; F. A. Tohmé, G. A. Bodanza, G. R. Simari, Aggregation of attack relations: A social-choice theoretical analysis of defeasibility criteria, in *Proceedings of the 5th International Symposium on Foundations of Information and Knowledge Systems* (*FoIKS*), Springer, 2008, pp. 8 – 23; M. Caminada, G. Pigozzi, On judgment aggregation in abstract argumentation, *Journal of Autonomous Agents and Multiagent Systems*, 2011, 22, pp. 64 – 102; I. Rahwan, F. A. Tohmé, Collective argument evaluation as judgement aggregation, in *Proceedings of the 9th International Conference on Autonomous Agents and Multiagent Systems* (*AAMAS*), IFAAMAS, 2010, pp. 417 – 424; J. Leite, J. Martins, Social abstract argumentation, in *Proceedings of the 22nd International Joint Conference on Artificial Intelligence* (*IJCAI*), 2011, pp. 2287 – 2292; P. E. Dunne, P. Marquis, M Wooldridge, Argument aggregation: Basic axioms and complexity results, in *Proceedings of the 4th International Conference on Computational Models of Argument* (*COMMA*), IOS Press, 2012, pp. 129 – 140; J. Delobelle, S. Konieczny, S. Vesic, On the aggregation of argumentation frameworks, in *Proceedings of the 24th International Joint Conference on Artificial Intelligence* (*IJCAI*), 2015, pp. 2911 – 2917; S. Airiau, E. Bonzon, U. Endriss, N. Maudet, J. Rossit, Rationalisation of profiles of abstract argumentation frameworks: Characterisation and complexity, *Journal of Artificial Intelligence Research* (*JAIR*), 2017, 60, pp. 149 – 177; G. A. Bodanza, F. A. Tohmé, M. R. Auday, Collective argumentation: A survey of aggregation issues around argumentation frameworks, *Argument & Computation*, 2017, 8, pp. 1 – 34; W. Chen, U. Endriss, Aggregating alternative extensions of abstract argumentation frameworks: Preservation results for quota rules, in *Proceedings of the 7th International Conference on Computational Models of Argument* (*COMMA*), IOS Press, 2018.

② K. J. Arrow, A. K. Sen, K. Suzumura (Eds.), *Handbook of Social Choice and Welfare*, North-Holland, 2002; W. Gaertner, *A Primer in Social Choice Theory*, *LSE Perspectives in Economic Analysis*, Oxford University Press, 2006; F. Brandt, V. Conitzer, U. Endriss, J. Lang, A. D. Procaccia (Eds.), *Handbook of Computational Social Choice*, Cambridge University Press, 2016.

we apply the so-called *axiomatic method* [1] and make use of recent results on *graph aggregation* [2].

Related work. Coste-Marquis et al. [3] were the first to address the question of how best to aggregate several abstract argumentation frameworks, but without making explicit reference to social choice theory. Instead, they focus on a family of sophisticated aggregation rules that minimise the *distance* between the input argumentation frameworks and the output argumentation framework.

Tohmé et al. [4] were the first to explicitly use social choice theory to analyse the aggregation of argumentation frameworks. Their focus is on the preservation of the *acyclicity* of attack-relations under aggregation. Acyclicity is an important property in the context of abstract argumentation, because it greatly simplifies the evaluation of arguments (in an acyclic argumentation framework, it is unambiguous which arguments to accept and which to reject). Tohmé et al. show that *qualified majority rules* will always preserve this property. [5]

Bodanza and Auday [6] were the first to give a completely general definition of an aggregation rule mapping any set of individual argumentation frameworks into a collective argumentation framework. In contrast to this, all earlier authors restrict attention to specific aggregation rules or specific classes of aggregation rules. Bodanza and Auday compare two different scenarios of collective argumentation that both combine abstract argumentation with social choice theory. In the first scenario, we assume that every agent reports an argumentation framework and we need to find a

---

[1] A. K. Sen, Social choice theory, in K. J. Arrow, M. D. Intriligator (Eds.), *Handbook of Mathematical Economics*, volume 3, North-Holland, 1986, pp. 1073 – 1181; W. Thomson, On the axiomatic method and its recent applications to game theory and resource allocation, *Social Choice and Welfare*, 2001, 18, pp. 327 – 386; U. Endriss, Logic and social choice theory, in A. Gupta, J. van Benthem (Eds.), *Logic and Philosophy Today*, volume 2, College Publications, 2011, pp. 333 – 377.

[2] U. Endriss, U. Grandi, Graph aggregation, *Artificial Intelligence*, 2017, 245, pp. 86 – 114.

[3] S. Coste-Marquis, C. Devred, S. Konieczny, M. -C. Lagasquie-Schiex, P. Marquis, On the merging of Dung's argumentation systems, *Artificial Intelligence*, 2007, 171, pp. 730 – 753.

[4] F. A. Tohmé, G. A. Bodanza, G. R. Simari, Aggregation of attack relations: A social-choice theoretical analysis of defeasibility criteria, in *Proceedings of the 5th International Symposium on Foundations of Information and Knowledge Systems (FoIKS)*, Springer, 2008, pp. 8 – 23.

[5] A qualified majority rule accepts a given attack between two arguments if (*i*) a majority of the agents accept that attack and (*ii*) none of a subset of the agents with a special status (the right to "veto") reject it.

[6] G. A. Bodanza, M. R. Auday, Social argument justification: Some mechanisms and conditions for their coincidence, in *Proceedings of the 10th European Conference on Symbolic and Quantitative Approaches to Reasoning with Uncertainty (ECSQARU)*, Springer, 2009, pp. 95 – 106.

good way of aggregating this input into a single collective argumentation framework. This is the scenario we study in this paper. In the other scenario, every agent is presented with the same argumentation framework but reports a (possibly) different set of arguments she considers acceptable given that argumentation framework, i. e., every agent reports her own *extension* of the common argumentation framework. This latter scenario—which is equally interesting but technically very different from the one we investigate here—has later been studied in more depth by a number of authors, including Caminada and Pigozzi① and Rahwan and Tohmé②, as well as the present authors③. Other authors, such as Gabbay and Rodrigues④ and Delobelle et al.⑤, work with models that are hybrids between these two scenarios. In these hybrid models each agent comes equipped an individual argumentation framework, but we also have access to some additional information to exploit during aggregation. For instance, for Delobelle et al. this additional information specifies the argumentation semantics adopted by all agents, which allows the mechanism performing the aggregation to compute extensions for all agents, which can then feed into the aggregation process.

While Tohmé et al.⑥ had made the important step of introducing the methodology of social choice theory into the study of collective argumentation, their work in fact was largely a study *within* social choice theory that made little reference to the specifics of the domain of argumentation, the only exception being the focus on

---

① M. Caminada, G. Pigozzi, On judgment aggregation in abstract argumentation, *Journal of Autonomous Agents and Multiagent Systems*, 2011, 22, pp. 64 – 102.

② I. Rahwan, F. A. Tohmé, Collective argument evaluation as judgement aggregation, in *Proceedings of the 9th International Conference on Autonomous Agents and Multiagent Systems (AAMAS)*, IFAAMAS, 2010, pp. 417 – 424.

③ W. Chen, U. Endriss, Aggregating alternative extensions of abstract argumentation frameworks: Preservation results for quota rules, in *Proceedings of the 7th International Conference on Computational Models of Argument (COMMA)*, IOS Press, 2018.

④ D. M. Gabbay, O. Rodrigues, An equational approach to the merging of argumentation networks, *Journal of Logic and Computation*, 2013, 24, pp. 1253 – 1277.

⑤ J. Delobelle, A. Haret, S. Konieczny, J. -G. Mailly, J. Rossit, S. Woltran, Merging of abstract argumentation frameworks, in *Proceedings of the 15th International Conference on Principles of Knowledge Representation and Reasoning (KR)*, 2016, pp. 33 – 42.

⑥ F. A. Tohmé, G. A. Bodanza, G. R. Simari, Aggregation of attack relations: A social-choice theoretical analysis of de-feasibility criteria, in *Proceedings of the 5th International Symposium on Foundations of Information and Knowledge Systems (FoIKS)*, Springer, 2008, pp. 8 – 23.

the property of acyclicity. A few years later, Dunne et al. ① succeeded in bringing abstract argumentation and social choice theory closer together by defining several preservation requirements on aggregation rules that directly refer to the semantics of the argumentation frameworks concerned. This includes the requirement that an argument that is acceptable to all individual agents should also be acceptable in the argumentation framework returned by the aggregation rule ("credulous σ-acceptance unanimity") and the requirement specifying that, when all agents agree on what the acceptable arguments are, then this agreement should be preserved under aggregation ("σ-unanimity"). ② The focus of their technical contribution, however, is on analysing the computational complexity of deciding whether a given aggregation rule has a given property, rather than on the axiomatic method. In follow-up work, Delobelle et al. ③ establish for several concrete rules whether or not they satisfy the preservation requirements introduced by Dunne et al. ④.

In further related work, employing a similar model and making more explicit use of the axiomatic method of social choice theory to analyse scenarios of collective argumentation, Li⑤ discusses a variant of Sen's famous Paradox of the Paretian Liberal⑥ in the context of aggregating abstract argumentation frameworks. He shows that granting some agents "expert rights", i. e., the right to autonomously decide on certain attack relations that are within the scope of their special expertise, is incompatible with basic efficiency requirements when we require aggregation rules that

---

① P. E. Dunne, P. Marquis, M. Wooldridge, Argument aggregation: Basic axioms and complexity results, in *Proceedings of the 4th International Conference on Computational Models of Argument (COMMA)*, IOS Press, 2012, pp. 129–140.

② Dunne et al. (see P. E. Dunne, P. Marquis, M Wooldridge, Argument aggregation: Basic axioms and complexity results, in *Proceedings of the 4th International Conference on Computational Models of Argument (COMMA)*, IOS Press, 2012, pp. 129–140) refer to these requirements as "axioms", while we prefer to distinguish axioms (normative properties of aggregation rules that typically encode some notion of fairness) from the "collective rationality" requirement that certain properties of argumentation frameworks should be preserved under aggregation.

③ J. Delobelle, S. Konieczny, S. Vesic, On the aggregation of argumentation frameworks, in *Proceedings of the 24th International Joint Conference on Artificial Intelligence (IJCAI)*, 2015, pp. 2911–2917.

④ P. E. Dunne, P. Marquis, M Wooldridge, Argument aggregation: Basic axioms and complexity results, in *Proceedings of the 4th International Conference on Computational Models of Argument (COMMA)*, IOS Press, 2012, pp. 129–140.

⑤ N. Li, A paradox of expert rights in abstract argumentation, *Social Choice and Welfare* (In press).

⑥ A. K. Sen, The impossibility of a Paretian liberal, *The Journal of Political Economics*, 1970, 78, pp. 152–157.

always return an argumentation framework that has at least one stable extension.

While Endriss and Grandi① explicitly mention abstract argumentation as a possible domain of application for the model of graph aggregation they develop, they do not present any technical results related to argumentation.

Let us also briefly mention a small number of contributions a little further afield. Bonzon and Maudet② define an *interaction protocol* for agents intent on persuading each other about the acceptability of a given argument and compare the outcomes of such persuasion dialogues with the results obtained by applying an aggregation rule to the argumentation frameworks initially held by these agents. Leite and Martins③ introduce *social abstract argumentation frameworks*, which are abstract argumentation frameworks enriched with a function mapping each argument to the numbers of agents voting in favour and against it. In particular the enriched model proposed by Eĝilmez et al.④, which also allows for votes in favour of and against attacks, bears some relation to the scenario we study here. For instance, if an aggregation rule aggregates individual positions separately on each individual attack (i. e., if it satisfies the axiom of *independence* to be introduced in the sequel), then we can use such an enriched social abstract argumentation framework as an intermediate form of representation. Airiau et al.⑤ introduce the concept of the *rationalisability* of a profile of argumentation frameworks. A profile is rationalisable if the diversity of views it contains can be explained in terms of (i) an underlying factual argumentation framework shared by all agents and (ii) everyone's individual preferences. Thus, their work is concerned with understanding what kind of profiles a good aggregation rule should be able to deal with, rather than with aggregation itself.

For a detailed review of research on collective argumentation beyond this small

① U. Endriss, U. Grandi, Graph aggregation, *Artificial Intelligence*, 2017, 245, pp. 86 – 114.

② E. Bonzon, N. Maudet, On the outcomes of multiparty persuasion, in *Proceedings of the 10th International Conference on Autonomous Agents and Multiagent Systems* (*AAMAS*), IFAAMAS, 2011, pp. 47 – 54.

③ J. Leite, J. Martins, Social abstract argumentation, in *Proceedings of the 22nd International Joint Conference on Artificial Intelligence* (*IJCAI*), 2011, pp. 2287 – 2292.

④ S. Eĝilmez, J. Martins, J. Leite, Extending social abstract argumentation with votes on attacks, in *Proceedings of the 2nd International Workshop on Theory and Applications of Formal Argumentation* (*TAFA*), Springer, 2014, pp. 16 – 31

⑤ S. Airiau, E. Bonzon, U. Endriss, N. Maudet, J. Rossit, Rationalisation of profiles of abstract argumentation frameworks: Characterisation and complexity, *Journal of Artificial Intelligence Research* (*JAIR*), 2017, 60, pp. 149 – 177.

selection we refer to the recent survey by Bodanza et al. ①.

Contribution. Our first contribution is the formulation of a clear and simple model for the axiomatic study of the preservation of semantic properties during the aggregation of attack-relations over a common set of arguments. Our technical results delineate how fundamental axiomatic properties of aggregation rules interact with such preservation requirements. These results range from characterisation theorems that indicate what kind of aggregation rule can satisfy certain combinations of desiderata, to impossibility theorems that show that only aggregation rules that are clearly unacceptable from an axiomatic point of view (namely, so-called dictatorships) can preserve the most demanding semantic properties.

In terms of methodology, we show how techniques originally developed for the more general domain of graph aggregation② can be applied in the context of abstract argumentation. At the same time, we identify a number of properties of graphs that are of interest in the specific context of abstract argumentation that cannot be analysed with existing techniques and the novel technique we develop to handle these properties—which we call *k-exclusive properties*—likely will find future application in other domains where graphs need to be aggregated.

Finally, while we restrict attention to the aggregation of argumentative positions that can be modelled using Dung's system of abstract argumentation, the idea of collective argumentation is more general than that and we believe that our approach can, at least in principle, be extended to richer models of argumentation that also account for the internal structure of arguments. This is important, given that—despite the enormous popularity and widespread use of Dung's model in the literature on argumentation in AI and other disciplines③—there is broad consensus that the expressive power of this model

① G. A. Bodanza, F. A. Tohmé, M. R. Auday, Collective argumentation: A survey of aggregation issues around argu-mentation frameworks, *Argument & Computation*, 2017, 8, pp. 1 – 34.

② U. Endriss, U. Grandi, Graph aggregation, *Artificial Intelligence*, 2017, 245, pp. 86 – 114.

③ P. E. Dunne, T. J. M. Bench-Capon, *Proceedings of the 1st International Conference on Computational Models of Argument* (*COMMA*), IOS Press, 2006; T. J. M. Bench-Capon, P. E. Dunne, Argumentation in artificial intelligence, *Artificial Intelligence*, 2007, 171, pp. 619 – 641; I. Rahwan, G. R. Simari (Eds.), Argumentation in *Artificial Intelligence*, Springer, 2009; S. Modgil, N. Oren, F. Toni (Eds.), *Proceedings of the 1st International Workshop on Theory and Applications of Formal Argumentation* (*TAFA*), Springer, 2012.

is limited and can only account for certain high-level aspects of argumentation①.

Paper overview. The remainder of this paper is organised as follows. Section 2 is a brief review of relevant concepts from the theory of abstract argumentation. Section 3 introduces our model and Section 4 presents our technical results on the preservation of semantic properties of argumentation frameworks under aggregation. We conclude in Section 5 with a brief summary of the insights obtained as well as suggestions for future work. This includes opportunities for applying our approach to richer models of argumentation than Dung's classical model of abstract argumentation as well as applying some of the methodological tools we develop, particularly regarding the analysis of k-exclusive graph properties, in other domains of aggregation—possibly unrelated to the study of argumentation.

2. Abstract Argumentation

In this section we recall some of the fundamentals of the model of abstract argumentation as originally introduced by Dung②. An *argumentation framework* is a pair $AF = \langle Arg, \rightharpoonup \rangle$, where Arg is a finite set of *arguments* and $\rightharpoonup$ is an irreflexive binary relation on Arg. ③ If $A \rightharpoonup B$ holds for two arguments A, $B \in Arg$, we say that A *attacks* B. The internal structure of individual arguments and thus the reasons for why one argument attacks or does not attack another are explicitly left unspecified in this model of argumentation. This approach has both advantages and disadvantages, which have been discussed at length in the literature④.

Attacking and defending arguments. Let us introduce some further notation and terminology. We use the term *attack* to refer to an element $att \in Arg \times Arg$ of an

---

① M. Caminada, L. Amgoud, On the evaluation of argumentation formalisms, *Artificial Intelligence*, 2007, 171, pp. 286 – 310; H. Prakken, An abstract framework for argumentation with structured arguments, *Argument and Computation*, 2010, 1, pp. 93 – 124; S. Modgil, Revisiting abstract argumentation frameworks, in *Proceedings of the 2nd International Workshop on Theory and Applications of Formal Argumentation* (*TAFA*), Springer, 2014, pp. 1 – 15.

② P. M. Dung, On the acceptability of arguments and its fundamental role in nonmonotonic reasoning, logic programming and n-person games, *Artificial Intelligence*, 1995, 77, pp. 321 – 358.

③ Neither the finiteness nor the irreflexivity assumption are crucial for our results, but they simplify exposition and clearly are natural for most applications.

④ See, e. g., M. Caminada, L. Amgoud, On the evaluation of argumentation formalisms, *Artificial Intelligence*, 2007, 171, pp. 286 – 310; H. Prakken, An abstract framework for argumentation with structured arguments, *Argument and Computation*, 2010, 1, pp. 93 – 124; S. Modgil, Revisiting abstract argumentation frameworks, in *Proceedings of the 2nd International Workshop on Theory and Applications of Formal Argumentation* (*TAFA*), Springer, 2014, pp. 1 – 15.

attack-relation ($\rightharpoonup$) $\subseteq Arg \times Arg$. That is, these are the "individual arrows" in $\langle Arg, \rightharpoonup \rangle$, For a set of arguments $\Delta \subseteq Arg$ and an argument $B \in Arg$, we say that Δ *attacks* B, denoted as $\Delta \rightharpoonup B$, if $A \rightharpoonup B$ holds for some argument $A \in \Delta$. We write $\Delta + = \{B \in Arg \mid \Delta \rightharpoonup B\}$ for the set of arguments attacked by Δ. We further say that Δ *defends* the argument $B \in Arg$, if $\Delta \rightharpoonup A$ holds for all arguments $A \in Arg$ such that $A \rightharpoonup B$. The *characteristic function* of AF is defined as the function $fAF: 2^{Arg} \rightarrow 2^{Arg}$ that maps any given set of arguments $\Delta \subseteq Arg$ to the set of arguments defended by Δ:

$$fAF(\Delta) = \{B \in Arg \mid \Delta \text{ defends } B\}$$

Semantics. Given an argumentation framework AF, the question arises which arguments to accept. For example, we may not want to accept two arguments that attack each other. A *semantics* specifies which sets of arguments can be accepted together for a given argumentation framework. Any such set of arguments is called an *extension* of AF under the semantics in question. For all the definitions of specific choices of semantics that follow, consider an arbitrary but fixed argumentation framework $AF = \langle Arg, \rightharpoonup \rangle$, and a set of arguments $\Delta \subseteq Arg$. The following notions of conflict-freeness and admissibility play a central role in these definitions. We say that Δ is *conflict-free*, if there exist no arguments $A, B \in \Delta$ such that $A \rightharpoonup B$; and Δ is called *admissible* if it is conflict-free and defends every single one of its members. We are going to work with six different types of semantics, which are amongst the most widely studied abstract argumentation semantics in the literature. The first four of them were introduced by Dung① in his original paper. The remaining two semantics were introduced more recently, by Caminada② and Dung et al. ③, respectively. ④

---

① P. M. Dung, On the acceptability of arguments and its fundamental role in nonmonotonic reasoning, logic programming and n-person games, *Artificial Intelligence*, 1995, 77, pp. 321 –358.

② M. Caminada, Semi-stable semantics, in *Proceedings of the* 1*st International Conference on Computational Model of Argument* (*COMMA*), IOS Press, 2006, pp. 121 – 130.

③ P. M. Dung, P. Mancarella, F. Toni, Computing ideal sceptical argumentation, *Artificial Intelligence*, 2007, 171, pp. 642 – 674.

④ Note that what we call the *ideal extension* is called the *maximal ideal set* in the original paper by Dung et al. (see P. M. Dung, P. Mancarella, F. Toni, Computing ideal sceptical argumentation, *Artificial Intelligence*, 2007, 171, pp. 642 –674). This change in terminology is in line with the more recent literature (see P. Baroni, M. Caminada, M. Giacomin, An introduction to argumentation semantics, *Knowledge Engineering Review*, 2011, 26, pp. 365 –410).

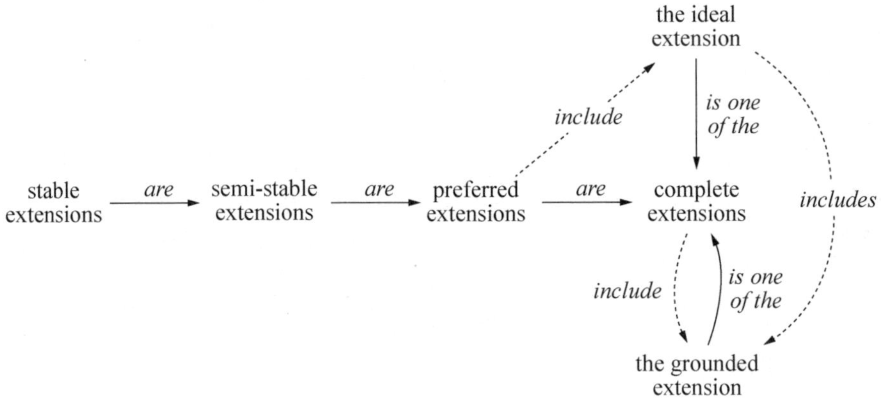

Figure 1: Relationships between argumentation semantics.

Definition 1. A ***stable extension*** of AF is a conflict-free set Δ of arguments in Arg that attacks all other arguments B ∈ Arg \ Δ, i. e., $\Delta \cup \Delta^{+} = \text{Arg}$.

Definition 2. A ***preferred extension*** of AF is an admissible set of arguments in Arg that is maximal with respect to set inclusion.

Definition 3. A ***complete extension*** of AF is an admissible set of arguments in Arg that includes all of the arguments it defends.

Definition 4. A ***grounded extension*** of AF is a least fixed point of its characteristic function fAF.

Definition 5. A ***semi-stable extension*** of AF is a complete extension Δ of AF for which $\Delta \cup \Delta^{+}$ is maximal with respect to set inclusion.

Definition 6. An ***ideal extension*** of AF is an admissible subset of the intersection of all preferred extensions that is maximal with respect to set inclusion.

The research community has produced several tools to automatically compute the extensions for a given argumentation framework under these semantics. One such tool is CONARG①. ②

Relationships between different semantics. Let us briefly recall some well-

① S. Bistarelli, F. Santini, ConArg: A constraint-based computational framework for argumentation systems, in *Proceedings of the 23rd IEEE International Conference on Tools with Artificial Intelligence* (*ICTAI*), IEEE, 2011, pp. 605 – 612.

② As several of the proofs in this paper rely on constructions involving certain argumentation frameworks having certain extensions, to provide an additional level of verification of the correctness of these proofs, we have used CONARG to recompute the relevant extensions.

*known facts about these different semantics and how they relate to each other*①. The set of stable extensions may be empty for a given argumentation framework, while there always exists at least one extension under each of the other five semantics. Unlike the other four semantics, there always are exactly one grounded extension and exactly one ideal extension. However, these extensions may be empty. We can compute the grounded extension Δ by initialising Δ with the empty set θ and then repeatedly executing the program $\Delta: =fAF(\Delta)$, until no more changes occur. Thus, the grounded extension is nonempty if and only if there is at least one argument that is not attacked at all. The ideal extension is always a (not necessarily proper) superset of the grounded extension. All stable extensions are also semi-stable extensions, and all semi-stable extensions are also preferred extensions. As the ideal extension is a subset of every preferred extension, it also is a subset of every semi-stable and every stable extension. The grounded, the ideal, and all preferred extensions are also complete extensions. Indeed, the grounded extension is the (unique) complete extension that is minimal with respect to set inclusion, while every preferred extension is a (not necessarily unique) complete extension that is maximal with respect to set inclusion. Furthermore, the grounded extension is a subset of every complete extension, and thereby also a subset of every preferred, every semi-stable, and every stable extension. Most of these relationships are summarised in Figure 1. Finally, any extension under any of the six semantics considered here is admissible and thus also conflict-free.

Example 1. *Consider an argumentation framework* $AF = \langle Arg, \rightharpoonup \rangle$ *with an isolated cycle of length* 3. *Thus,* $(\rightharpoonup) \supseteq \{A \rightharpoonup B; B \rightharpoonup C; C \rightharpoonup A\}$ *for three arguments* $A, B, C \in Arg$ *and there are no further attacks on either* A, B, *or* C. *Then none of* A, B, *and* C *can be part of a complete extension* Δ: *if we include two or more of them in* Δ, *then* Δ *is not conflict-free; if we include just one of them in* Δ, *then* Δ *does not defend itself. Hence, by the relationships between the different semantics shownin Figure* 1, *none of* A, B, *and* C *can be part of an extension under any of the other five semantics either. We are going to make use of this kind of reasoning—which also works for longer isolated odd-length cycles—everal times in this paper.* Δ

An interesting question is under what circumstances the extensions determined by different semantics coincide. Probably the clearest example for when they do

① P. Baroni, M. Caminada, M. Giacomin, An introduction to argumentation semantics, *Knowledge Engineering Review*, 2011, 26, pp. 365 – 410.

coincide is the case of argumentation frameworks with an *acyclic* attack-relation: if $\rightharpoonup$ does not include any cycles, then the grounded extension coincides with the ideal extension and it is the only stable extension, the only semi-stable extension, the only preferred extension, and the only complete extension. Indeed, for an acyclic $\rightharpoonup$ it is entirely uncontroversial which arguments to accept. A condition of this kind that is weaker than acyclicity is what is known as *coherence* in the literature①: the argumentation framework AF is called *coherent* if every preferred extension of AF is stable, i. e., if the two semantics coincide.

3. The Model

Fix a finite set Arg of arguments and a set $N = \{1,\ldots,n\}$ of n *agents*. Suppose each agent $i \in N$ supplies us with an argumentation framework $AF_i = \langle Arg, \rightharpoonup_i \rangle$, reflecting her individual views on the status of possible attacks between arguments. Thus, we are given a *profile* of attack-relations $\rightharpoonup = (\rightharpoonup 1, \ldots, \rightharpoonup n)$. ② What would be a good method of aggregating these individual argumentation frameworks to arrive at a single argumentation framework that appropriately reflects the views of the group as a whole? This is the central question we address in this paper. An *aggregation rule* is a function $F: (2^{Arg \times Arg})^n \rightarrow 2^{Arg \times Arg}$ mapping any given profile of attack-relations into a single attack-relation. Thus, we are interested in understanding what makes a good aggregation rule.

Example 2. *The first aggregation rule that comes to mind is the majority rule: include attack $A \rightharpoonup B$ in the outcome if and only if a (weak) majority of the individual agents do. If we apply this rule to the profile shown in Figure 2, then we obtain the argumentation framework consisting of the three attacks $A \rightharpoonup B$, $B \rightharpoonup C$, and $C \rightharpoonup A$.*

---

① P. M. Dung, On the acceptability of arguments and its fundamental role in nonmonotonic reasoning, logic programming and n-person games, *Artificial Intelligence*, 1995, 77, pp. 321 – 358.

② Note that we assume that all agents report an attack-relation over *the same* set of arguments *Arg*. As argued by Coste-Marquis et al. (see S. Coste-Marquis, C. Devred, S. Konieczny, M. -C. Lagasquie-Schiex, P. Marquis, On the merging of Dung's argumentation systems, *Artificial Intelligence*, 2007, 171, pp. 730 – 753), generalisations, where different agents may be aware of different subsets of *Arg*, are possible and interesting, but—in line with most existing work in the area—we shall not explore them here.

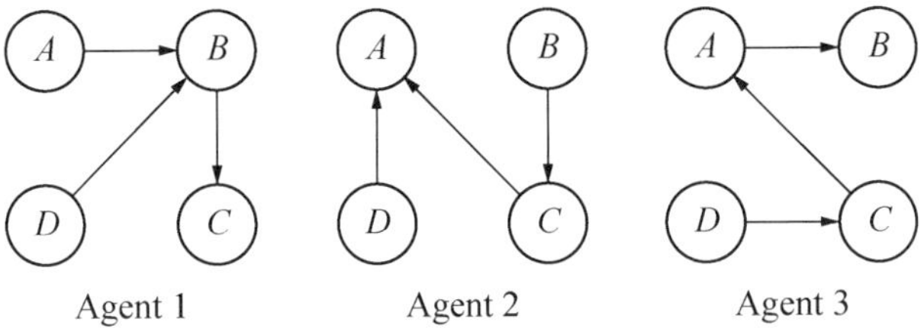

Figure 2: Example for a profile with $Arg = \{A, B, C, D\}$.

Section overview. In the remainder of this section we first define a number of *specific aggregation rules*. We then define several *properties of aggregation rules*, usually referred to as *axioms*, and briefly discuss which of the rules defined satisfy which of these properties. Finally, we review several *properties of argumentation frameworks*, particularly properties relating to their semantics, and formulate the question of whether a given rule will *preserve* such a property when all individual agents report argumentation frameworks that satisfy the property in question.

3.1 Specific aggregation rules

Recall that an aggregation rule is a function F, mapping any given profile $\rightharpoonup = (\rightharpoonup 1, \ldots, \rightharpoonup n) \in (2\ Arg \times Arg)\ n$ of attack-relations on Arg to a single attack-relation $F(\rightharpoonup) \subseteq Arg \times Arg$. We sometimes write $(A \rightharpoonup B) \in F(\rightharpoonup)$ for $(A, B) \in F(\rightharpoonup)$. We use $N^{\rightharpoonup}_{att} := \{i \in N \mid att \in (\rightharpoonup i)\}$ to denote the set of supporters of the attack att in profile $\rightharpoonup$.

We now introduce two families of aggregation rules, the *quota rules* and the *oligarchic rules*. These are simple rules that are adaptations of well-known rules used in the social choice literature, particularly in judgment aggregation① and graph aggregation②.

Definition 7. *Let* $q \in \{1, \ldots, n\}$. *The* **quota rule** Fq *with quota* q *accepts all those attacks that are supported by at least* q *agents*:

$$Fq(\rightharpoonup) = \{att \in Arg \times Arg \mid \#N^{\rightharpoonup}_{att} \geqslant q\}$$

The weak majority rule is the quota rule Fq with $q = [\frac{n+1}{2}]$ and the strict majority rule is the quota rule Fq with $q = [\frac{n+1}{2}]$. Two further quota rules are also

① D. Grossi, G. Pigozzi, *Judgment Aggregation: A Primer*, *Synthesis Lectures on Artificial Intelligence and Machine Learning*, Morgan & Claypool Publishers, 2014.

② U. Endriss, U. Grandi, Graph aggregation, *Artificial Intelligence*, 2017, 245, pp. 86–114.

of special interest. The unanimity rule only accepts attacks that are supported by everyone, i. e. , this is Fq with $q = n$. The nomination rule is the quota rule Fq with $q = 1$. Despite being a somewhat extreme choice, the nomination rule has some intuitive appeal in the context of argumentation, as it reflects the idea that we should take seriously any conflict between arguments raised by at least one member of the group

Definition 8. *Let* $\mathfrak{C} \in 2^N \setminus \{\varnothing\}$ *be a nonempty coalition of agents. The* ***oligarchic rule*** $F_{\mathfrak{C}}$ *accepts all those attacks that are accepted by all members of* $\mathfrak{C}$:

$$F_{\mathfrak{C}}(\rightharpoonup) = \{att \in Arg \times Arg \mid \mathfrak{C} \subseteq N_{att}^{\rightharpoonup}\}$$

Thus, any member of the oligarchy $\mathfrak{C}$ can *veto* an attack from being accepted. Observe that the unanimity rule can also be characterised as the oligarchic rule $F_{\mathfrak{C}}$ with $\mathfrak{C} = N$. A subclass of the oligarchic rules are the *dictatorships*. The dictatorship of dictator $i \in N$ is the oligarchic rule $F_{\mathfrak{C}}$ with $\mathfrak{C} = \{i\}$. Thus, under a dictatorship, to compute the outcome, we simply copy the attack-relation of the dictator. Intuitively speaking, oligarchic rules, and dictatorships in particular, are unattractive rules, as they unfairly exclude everyone not in $\mathfrak{C}$ from the decision process.

Some rules combine features of the quota rules and the oligarchic rules. For example, we may choose to accept an attack only if it is accepted by (i) a weak majority of all agents and (ii) a small number of distinguished agents to which we want to give the right to veto the acceptance of attacks. Such rules (sometimes called *qualified majority rules*) are certainly more attractive than the oligarchic rules, but they are still unfair in the sense of granting some agents more influence than others.

Definition 9. *Agent* $i \in N$ *has* ***veto powers*** *under aggregation rule* F, *if* $F(\rightharpoonup) \subseteq (\rightharpoonup_i)$ *for every profile* $\rightharpoonup$.

Thus, under an oligarchic rule $F\mathfrak{C}$ the agents in $\mathfrak{C}$, and only those, have veto powers. With the exception of the unanimity rule, under which all agents have veto powers, a quota rule does not grant veto powers to any agent.

3. 2 Axioms: Properties of aggregation rules

Next, we introduce several basic *axioms*, each of which encodes an intuitively desirable property of an aggregation rule F. All of these axioms are direct adaptations of axioms formulated in the literature on graph aggregation①, which in turn are very

① U. Endriss, U. Grandi, Graph aggregation, *Artificial Intelligence*, 2017, 245, pp. 86 – 114.

similar to axioms used in both the literature on judgment aggregation[①] and that on preference aggregation[②].

Definition 10. *An aggregation rule F is said to be* **anonymous**, *if* $F(\rightharpoonup) = F(\rightharpoonup_{\pi(1)}, \cdots, \rightharpoonup_{\pi(n)})$ *holds for all profiles* $\rightharpoonup = (\rightharpoonup_1, \dots, \rightharpoonup_n)$ *and all permutations* $\pi: N \to N$.

Definition 11. *An aggregation rule F is said to be* **neutral**, *if* $N^{\rightharpoonup}_{att} = N^{\rightharpoonup}_{att'}$ *implies* $att \in F(\rightharpoonup) \Leftrightarrow att' \in F(\rightharpoonup)$ *for all profiles* $\rightharpoonup$ *and all attacks att, att'.*

Definition 12. *An aggregation rule F is said to be* **independent**, *if* $N^{\rightharpoonup}_{att} = N^{\rightharpoonup'}_{att}$ *implies* $att \in F(\rightharpoonup) \Leftrightarrow att \in F(\rightharpoonup')$ *for all profiles* $\rightharpoonup, \rightharpoonup'$ *and all attacks att.*

Definition 13. *An aggregation rule F is said to be* **monotonic**, *if* $N^{\rightharpoonup}_{att} \subseteq N^{\rightharpoonup'}_{att}$ *(together with* $N^{\rightharpoonup}_{att} = N^{\rightharpoonup'}_{att}$ *for all attacks* $att' \neq att$*) implies* $att \in F(\rightharpoonup) \Rightarrow att \in F(\rightharpoonup')$ *for all profiles* $\rightharpoonup, \rightharpoonup'$ *and all attacks att.*

Definition 14. *An aggregation rule F is said to be* **unanimous**, *if* $F(\rightharpoonup) \supseteq (\rightharpoonup_1) \cap \cdots \cap (\rightharpoonup_n)$ *holds for all profiles* $\rightharpoonup = (\rightharpoonup_1, \dots, \rightharpoonup_n)$.

Definition 15. *An aggregation rule F is said to be* **grounded**, *if* $F(\rightharpoonup) \subseteq (\rightharpoonup_1) \cup \cdots \cup (\rightharpoonup_n)$ *holds for all profiles* $\rightharpoonup = (\rightharpoonup_1, \dots, \rightharpoonup_n)$.

Anonymity is a symmetry (and thus fairness) requirement regarding agents, and neutrality is a symmetry requirement regarding attacks. Independence expresses that whether an attack is accepted should only depend on its supporters. Monotonicity says that additional support for an accepted attack should never cause it to be rejected. Unanimity postulates that an attack supported by everyone must be accepted, while groundedness means that only attacks with at least one supporter can be collectively accepted. [③]

Observe that all quota rules and all oligarchic rules are easily seen to be unanimous, grounded, neutral, independent, and monotonic. [④] The quota rules

---

① D. Grossi, G. Pigozzi, *Judgment Aggregation: A Primer*, *Synthesis Lectures on Artificial Intelligence and Machine Learning*, Morgan & Claypool Publishers, 2014.

② W. Gaertner, *A Primer in Social Choice Theory*, *LSE Perspectives in Economic Analysis*, Oxford University Press, 2006.

③ Note that, in line with the existing literature in argumentation theory on the one hand and social choice theory on the other, we use the term "grounded" in two unrelated ways (grounded extensions *vs.* grounded aggregation rules).

④ Thus, in particular the unanimity rule satisfies the unanimity axiom, but so do all other quota and oligarchic rules. Note that, while the unanimity axiom requires that all unanimously accepted attacks need to be returned by an aggregation rule, the unanimity rule returns *only* those unanimously accepted attacks.

furthermore are also anonymous. In fact, it is not difficult to adapt a well-known result from judgment aggregation due to Dietrich and List[①] to our setting, so as to see that the quota rules are *the only* aggregation rules that satisfy all of these six axioms (refer to Endriss and Grandi[②] for a formulation of this result in the context of graph aggregation).

Note that, if an aggregation rule F is independent, then we can represent it by listing for every potential attack $att = (A \rightharpoonup B)$ the coalitions of agents that would be sufficient to get that attack accepted if exactly the members of that coalitions were to support it. Formally, if F is independent, then for every attack $att \in Arg \times Arg$ there exist a family of coalitions $W_{att} \subseteq 2^N$ such that for every profile $\rightharpoonup$ it is the case that $att \in F(\rightharpoonup)$ if and only if $N^{\rightharpoonup}_{att} \in W_{att}$. The elements of W_{att} are called winning coalitions. If F is both independent and neutral, then the family of winning coalitions must be the same for all attacks, i. e., in that case there exists a single family $W \subseteq 2^N$ such that for every profile $\rightharpoonup$ and every attack att it is the case that $att \in F(\rightharpoonup)$ if and only if $N^{\rightharpoonup}_{att} \in W$.

3. 3 Preservation of semantic properties of argumentation frameworks under aggregation

Typically, agents will disagree on whether certain attacks between arguments in *Arg* are in fact justified (if not, aggregation becomes trivial). But even when they disagree on the details, there may be high-level agreement on certain features. For example, maybe all agents agree that, under a particular semantics, argument A is acceptable. Whenever we observe such agreement on semantic features in a profile, we would like those features to be preserved under aggregation. Thus, for our example, under the same semantics, we would like A to be acceptable also in the argumentation framework computed by our aggregation rule. In other words, we are interested in the preservation of properties of argumentation frameworks (i. e., of the attack-relations that define them) under aggregation.

An example for a property is antisymmetry (i. e., the absence of mutual attacks between arguments). Another example is the existence of an argument that is not attacked by any other argument. But in some cases, what we are really interested in

---

① F. Dietrich, C. List, Judgment aggregation by quota rules: Majority voting generalized, *Journal of Theoretical Politics*, 2007, 19, pp. 391 – 424.

② U. Endriss, U. Grandi, Graph aggregation, *Artificial Intelligence*, 2017, 245, pp. 86 – 114.

is the preservation of entire collections of properties. For example, for every argument A, we may want the acceptability of A under a certain semantics to be preserved under aggregation.

Formally, an *AF-property* $P \subseteq 2^{Arg \times Arg}$ is simply the set of all attack-relations on *Arg* that satisfy P. But in the interest of readability, we write $P(\rightharpoonup)$ rather than $(\rightharpoonup) \in P$. A *collection of AF-properties* $\mathcal{P}$ is a set of such AF-properties. Typically, the elements of $\mathcal{P}$ will be indexed by either the arguments $A \in Arg$ or the sets $\Delta \subseteq Arg$. Technically, every single AF-property P can also be thought of as a collection of AF-properties, namely $\mathcal{P} = \{P\}$.

Definition 16. *Let F be an aggregation rule and let* $\mathcal{P}$ *be a collection of AF-properties. We say that F preserves* $\mathcal{P}$, *if for every profile* $\boldsymbol{\rightharpoonup}$ *and every AF-property* $P \in \mathcal{P}$ *we have that* $P(\rightharpoonup_i)$ *being the case for all agents* $i \in N$ *implies* $P(F(\boldsymbol{\rightharpoonup}))$.

Thus, F preserves the single AF-property P if for every profile $\boldsymbol{\rightharpoonup}$ we have that $P(\rightharpoonup_i)$ being the case for all agents $i \in N$ implies $P(F(\boldsymbol{\rightharpoonup}))$. This notion of preservation (of a single property) is known under the name of *collective rationality* in other parts of social choice theory①.

Properties of interest. We now review the specific AF-properties for which we study preservation in this paper. Two of them we have already introduced in Section 2, namely *acyclicity* and *coherence*. Recall that these are attractive properties, because—if satisfied by an argumentation framework— they ensure that several different semantics will coincide and result in the same recommendations about which arguments to accept, thereby making decisions less controversial.

Both the grounded and the ideal semantics are attractive for two reasons. First, they encode a notion of scepticism in the sense of only accepting arguments we can have high confidence in the literature ②. Second, unlike the other extensions we have defined, the grounded and the ideal extension are always unique. On the downside, that unique extension may be empty, i. e., these semantics will sometimes not suggest any arguments to be accepted. Thus, argumentation frameworks that satisfy the AF-property of *nonemptiness of the grounded extension* or

① K. J. Arrow, *Social Choice and Individual Values*, 2nd ed., John Wiley and Sons, 1963. First edition published in 1951; C. List, P. Pettit, Aggregating sets of judgments: An impossibility result, *Economics and Philosophy*, 2002, 18, pp. 89 – 110; U. Endriss, U. Grandi, Graph aggregation, *Artificial Intelligence*, 2017, 245, pp. 86 – 114.

② P. Baroni, M. Caminada, M. Giacomin, An introduction to argumentation semantics, *Knowledge Engineering Review*, 2011, 26, pp. 365 – 410.

nonemptiness of the ideal extension are of particular interest.

Collections of properties of interest. Next, we turn to collections of AF-properties we may wish to preserve. Let $A \in Arg$ be one of the arguments under consideration. Then, for any given argument-tation framework, A may or may not belong to the grounded extension. Thus, every $A \in Arg$ defines an AF-property, namely the property of membership of A in the grounded extension, i. e., of acceptance of A under the grounded semantics. This in itself would be too narrow a property to be of much interest for our purposes. However, what is of interest is whether membership is preserved for *all* arguments. We say that F *preserves argument acceptability under the grounded semantics*, if it is the case that, for all arguments $A \in Arg$, whenever A belongs to the grounded extension of $\langle Arg, \rightharpoonup_i \rangle$ for all agents $i \in N$, then A also belongs to the grounded extension of $\langle Arg, F(\rightharpoonup) \rangle$. Thus, argument acceptability under the grounded semantics is a collection of AF-properties, consisting of one AF-property for every argument $A \in Arg$. The collection of AF-properties of *argument acceptability under the ideal semantics* is defined accordingly.

For the stable, semi-stable, preferred, and complete semantics, we require a more refined definition, given that extensions under these semantics need not be unique. We say that F *preserves credulous argument acceptability under the stable semantics*, if it is the case that, for all arguments $A \in Arg$, whenever A belongs to *some* stable extension of $\langle Arg, \rightharpoonup_i \rangle$ for all agents $i \in N$, then A also belongs to *some* stable extension of $\langle Arg, F(\rightharpoonup) \rangle$. Analogously, F *preserves sceptical argument acceptability under the stable semantics*, if it is the case that, for all arguments $A \in Arg$, whenever A belongs to *all* stable extensions of $\langle Arg, \rightharpoonup_i \rangle$ for all agents $i \in N$, then A also belongs to *all* stable extensions of $\langle Arg, F(\rightharpoonup) \rangle$. The corresponding concepts for the semi-stable, the preferred, and the complete semantics are defined accordingly. All of these are also collections of AF-properties, one for every argument $A \in Arg$.

Rather than just preserving the acceptability status of a single argument, we may also be interested in preserving entire extensions. For example, we say that F *preserves extensions under the stable semantics*, if it is the case that, for all sets $\Delta \subseteq Arg$, whenever Δ is a stable extension of $\langle Arg, \rightharpoonup_i \rangle$ for all agents $i \in N$, then Δ is also a stable extension of $\langle Arg, F(\rightharpoonup) \rangle$. So this again concerns the preservation of a collection of AF-properties, one for every set $\Delta \subseteq Arg$. The corresponding concept can be defined analogously for the other five semantics.

Similarly, we say that F *preserves conflict-freeness*, if it is the case that, for all sets $\Delta \subseteq Arg$, whenever Δ is conflict-free in $\langle Arg, \rightharpoonup_i \rangle$ for all agents $i \in N$, then Δ is also conflict-free in $\langle Arg, F(\rightharpoonup) \rangle$. Finally, *preservation of admissibility* is defined accordingly.

Summary. To summarise, we have identified the following AF-properties that, in case all agents agree on one of them being satisfied, we would like to see preserved under aggregation:

acyclicity and *coherence* (reducing semantic ambiguity),

nonemptiness of the grounded extension and the ideal extension (enabling a sceptical approach to argument evaluation),

argument acceptability under different semantics (allowing for agreement on arguments even in the face of disagreement on the attacks between them), and the property of a set *being an extension* under different semantics or of being either *conflict-free* or *admissible* (also allowing for semantic agreement despite disagreement on attacks).

The latter two items concern collections of AF-properties (rather than single AF-properties), one for every argument $A \in Arg$ and every set $\Delta \subseteq Arg$, respectively.

Example 3. *Consider again the profile of Figure 2 and recall that the (weak or strict) majority rule will return the argumentation framework with $A \rightharpoonup B$, $B \rightharpoonup C$, and $C \rightharpoonup A$. Thus, the majority rule does not preserve acyclicity.* ① *What about some of the other AF-properties? The grounded extension of AF1 is $\{A, C, D\}$, that of AF 2 is $\{B, D\}$, that of AF 3 is $\{A, D\}$, and that of the majority outcome is $\{D\}$. Thus, preservation of the property of nonemptiness of the grounded extension is not violated by this particular example, given that the grounded extension of the majority outcome is nonempty. Preservation of argument acceptability under the grounded semantics also is not violated: the only argument contained in the grounded extension of all three individual argumentation frameworks is D, and D is also included in the extension of the argumentation framework returned by the majority rule. Of course, this is not to say that these two properties might not be violated for other profiles. Finally, observe that also preservation of being the grounded extension is not violated by this example, given that the three agents do not agree on the grounded extension to begin with.*

---

① This observation is closely related to the famous *Condorcet Paradox* in the theory of preference aggregation [see I. McLean, A. B. Urken (Eds.), *Classics of Social Choice*, University of Michigan Press, 1995].

While we believe that this is the first time that the notion of preservation of a semantic property has been developed systematically in the literature on collective argumentation, there are—as already noted in the introduction—some specific instances of this idea that have been discussed in earlier work, notably by Dunne et al. ① These authors define the notions of an aggregation rule preserving the nonemptiness of certain extensions (termed " σ -weak nontriviality" by Dunne et al.), of extension preservation (" σ -unanimity"), and of preserving either credulous or sceptical argument acceptability (" ca_σ -unanimity" and " sa_σ -unanimity", respectively). A few years earlier, Tohmé et al. ② furthermore studied the preservation of acyclicity during the aggregation of argumentation frameworks.

4. Preservation Results

In this section we present our results on the preservation of semantic properties under aggregation. This includes both positive and negative results: some properties can be preserved by intuitively appealing aggregation rules, while others require us to use rules that give veto powers or even dictatorial powers to some of the agents. Most of our results have the following form: if we look for an aggregation rule F that satisfies a certain combination of axioms and if we would like F to preserve a certain AF-property P (or a certain collection P of AF-properties), then F must belong to a certain family of aggregation rules.

Section overview. We begin with two very simple properties, namely conflict-freeness and admissibility. As we are going to see, the requirement of preserving admissibility is closely related to the neutrality axiom and this connection allows us to derive neutrality (rather than having to assume it for several subsequent results). We then cover, in turn, results pertaining to the preservation of argument acceptability, extension preservation, preservation of the nonemptiness of uniquely determined extensions, and acyclicity and coherence.

4.1 Conflict-freeness, admissibility, and the neutrality axiom

Recall that a set of arguments is called conflict-free if it does not contain two

① P. E. Dunne, P. Marquis, M. Wooldridge, Argument aggregation: Basic axioms and complexity results, in *Proceedings of the 4th International Conference on Computational Models of Argument* (*COMMA*), IOS Press, 2012, pp. 129-140.

② F. A. Tohmé, G. A. Bodanza, G. R. Simari, Aggregation of attack relations: A social-choice theoretical analysis of defeasibility criteria, in *Proceedings of the 5th International Symposium on Foundations of Information and Knowledge Systems* (*FoIKS*), Springer, 2008, pp. 8-23.

arguments for which it is the case that the first attacks the second. Our first result demonstrates that this most basic property of sets of arguments is preserved under essentially all reasonable aggregation rules.

Theorem 1. *Every aggregation rule F that is grounded preserves conflict-freeness.*

Proof. Let F be an aggregation rule that is grounded. Consider any set $\Delta \subseteq Arg$ and any profile $\rightharpoonup = (\rightharpoonup_1, \ldots, \rightharpoonup_n)$ such that Δ is conflict-free in $\langle Arg, \rightharpoonup_i \rangle$ for all $i \in N$. For the sake of contradiction, assume Δ is *not* conflict-free in $\langle Arg, F(\rightharpoonup) \rangle$, i. e., there exist two arguments $A, B \in \Delta$ such that $(A \rightharpoonup B) \in F(\rightharpoonup)$. Due to the groundness of F, there then must be at least one agent $i \in N$ such that also $A \rightharpoonup_i B$, i. e., Δ is not conflict-free in $\langle Arg, \rightharpoonup_i \rangle$ either. But this contradicts our assumption.

Next, we turn to admissibility. Recall that a set of arguments is admissible if it is conflict-free and defends all of its members. Before we establish our main result regarding the preservation of admissibility, we are going to prove a lemma that unveils an interesting connection between admissibility and the neutrality axiom. It shows that every unanimous, grounded, and independent aggregation rule that preserves admissibility must be neutral. This lemma is similar in spirit to the *Contagion Lemma* in the literature on preference aggregation, which shows that any independent and Pareto efficient preference aggregation rule that preserves the transitivity of the input must be neutral①. In fact, we are first going to prove a more general lemma that shows that this implication holds not only for admissibility but for every collection of AF-properties of a certain type. This more general lemma is similar to a recent result by Endriss and Grandi [24, Lemma 12], which—when adapted to our terminology—states that any unanimous, grounded, and independent aggregation rule F that preserves some AF-property P must be neutral whenever P belongs to what they call the family of *contagious* properties. We now adapt this notion of contagiousness to collections of properties. ②

---

① A. K. Sen, Social choice theory, in: K. J. Arrow, M. D. Intriligator (Eds.), *Handbook of Mathematical Economics*, volume 3, North-Holland, 1986, pp. 1073 – 1181.

② We stress that contagiousness is a meta-property—a property of (collections of) properties—that serves as a purely technical device we use in some of our proofs. It is of interest to the study of argumentation only in so far as one can show that semantic properties of argumentation frameworks (such as admissibility) that are of direct demonstrable interest to argumentation theory turn out to be properties that are contagious. As we are going to see, this indeed is the case. Analogous considerations apply to the meta-properties of implicativeness, disjunctiveness, and k-exclusiveness to be introduced in the sequel.

Definition 17. *A collection* $\mathcal{P}$ *of AF-properties is called contagious if, for every distinct arguments* A, B, $C \in Arg$, *there exist a property* $P \in \mathcal{P}$ *and a set* $Att \subseteq Arg \times Arg$ *of attacks such that* $\langle Arg, Att \cup S \rangle$ *with* $S \subseteq \{A \rightharpoonup B, B \rightharpoonup C\}$ *satisfies* P *if and only if* $S \neq \{B \rightharpoonup C\}$.

Thus, $\mathcal{P}$ is contagious if for every triple of arguments A, B, $C \in Arg$ we can find an AF-property P in the collection $\mathcal{P}$ such that satisfaction of P requires that $B \rightharpoonup C$ implies $A \rightharpoonup B$ (at least if the rest of the argumentation framework looks as specified by Att). A single AF-property P is contagious if $\mathcal{P} = \{P\}$ is.[①] This choice of terminology is intended to convey the idea that—in the context of Att and assuming you would like to satisfy P —accepting arguments is "contagious", given that accepting $B \rightharpoonup C$ forces you to also accept $A \rightharpoonup B$.

Lemma 2. *For* $|Arg| \geqslant 3$, *any unanimous, grounded, and independent aggregation rule* F *that pre-serves some contagious collection* $\mathcal{P}$ *of AF-properties must be neutral.*

Proof. Suppose $|Arg| \geqslant 3$, let $\mathcal{P}$ be a contagious collection of AF-properties, and let F be an aggregation rule that is unanimous, grounded, and independent and that preserves $\mathcal{P}$. Due to being independent, F can be described in terms of one family of winning coalitions W_{att} for every potential attack $att \in Arg \times Arg$. To show that F is neutral, we must prove that $W_{att} = W_{att'}$ for any two attacks att, $att' \in Arg \times Arg$. Now consider any three (distinct) arguments A, B, $C \in Arg$. We are going to prove $W_{B \rightharpoonup C} \subseteq W_{A \rightharpoonup B}$. As A, B, and C have been chosen arbitrarily, it then follows that $W_{att} = W_{att'}$ for all att, $att' \in Arg \times Arg$. To see this, suppose that $att = (\alpha \rightharpoonup \beta)$ and $att' = (\alpha' \rightharpoonup \beta')$. Then repeated application of the reasoning pattern we are about to establish yields $W_{\alpha \rightharpoonup \beta} \subseteq W_{\beta' \rightharpoonup \alpha} \subseteq W_{\alpha' \rightharpoonup \beta'}$ as well as $W_{\alpha' \rightharpoonup \beta'} \subseteq W_{\beta \rightharpoonup \alpha'} \subseteq W_{\alpha \rightharpoonup \beta}$, and thus $W_{\alpha \rightharpoonup \beta} = W_{\alpha' \rightharpoonup \beta'}$.

So pick an arbitrary coalition $\mathfrak{C} \in W_{B \rightharpoonup C}$. Due to $\mathcal{P}$ being contagious, for our choice of A, B, and C there exist a property $P \in \mathcal{P}$ and a set $Att \subseteq Arg \times Arg$ such that $\langle Arg, Att \cup S \rangle$ with $S \subseteq \{A \rightharpoonup B, B \rightharpoonup C\}$ satisfies P if and only if $S \neq \{B \rightharpoonup C\}$. Construct a profile $\rightharpoonup$ in which exactly the agents in $\mathfrak{C}$ report the attack-relation $Att \cup \{A \rightharpoonup B, B \rightharpoonup C\}$ and all others report Att. Thus, in this profile all individual attack-relations satisfy P. As F preserves P, the outcome $F(\rightharpoonup)$ must satisfy P as well. Due to the unanimity and groundedness of F, $F(\rightharpoonup)$ must be of

① This definition of contagiousness of a single property P is a special case of the more complex definition given by Endriss and Grandi (see U. Endriss, U. Grandi, Graph aggregation, *Artificial Intelligence*, 2017, 245, pp. 86 - 114). We do not require the greater generality of the original definition for our purposes here.

the form $Att \cup S$ with $S \subseteq \{A \rightharpoonup B, B \rightharpoonup C\}$. Due to $\mathfrak{C}$ being a winning coalition, we furthermore must have $(B \rightharpoonup C) \in F(\rightharpoonup)$. This, together with the fact that $F(\rightharpoonup)$ must satisfy P means that we must have $(A \rightharpoonup B) \in F(\rightharpoonup)$ as well. But this means that coalition $\mathfrak{C}$ succeeded in getting attack $A \rightharpoonup B$ accepted, i. e., $\mathfrak{C}$ must be a winning coalition also for this attack. Thus, we have succeeded in deriving $\mathfrak{C} \in W_{A \rightharpoonup B}$ and are done.

Lemma 3. *For* $|Arg| \geqslant 3$, *any unanimous, grounded, and independent aggregation rule F that pre-serves admissibility must be neutral.*

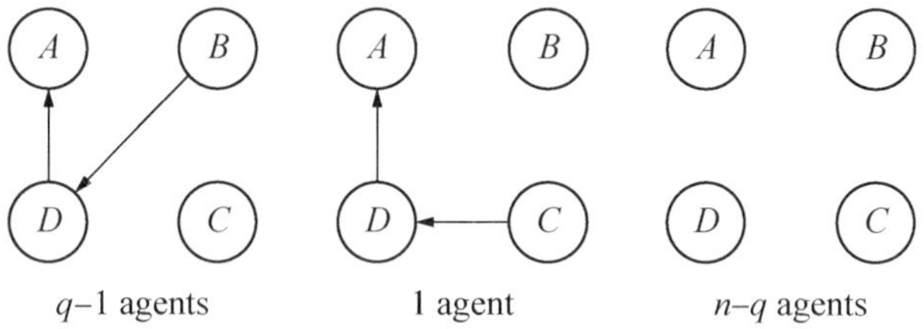

Figure 3: Profile used in the proof of Theorem 4.

Proof. The claim follows from Lemma 2, provided we can show that admissibility is a contagious collection of AF-properties. So consider any distinct A, B, $C \in Arg$. With reference to Definition 17, let P be the property of the set $\{A, C\}$ being admissible and let Att be the empty set of attacks. Now consider the four argumentation frameworks of the form $\langle Arg, Att \cup S \rangle$ with $S \subseteq \{A \rightharpoonup B, B \rightharpoonup C\}$. By the definition of admissibility, the only argumentation framework of this kind that does not satisfy P is the one we get for $S = \{B \rightharpoonup C\}$. This concludes the proof.

We are now ready to state our main result regarding the preservation of admissibility. It is significantly less broad than Theorem 1, our result for the preservation of conflict-freeness, but it still clearly is a positive result. It shows that there exists a reasonable rule that preserves the admissibility of arbitrary sets of arguments.

Theorem 4. *For* $|Arg| \geqslant 4$, *the only unanimous, grounded, anonymous, independent, and monotonic aggregation rule F that preserves admissibility is the nomination rule.*

Proof. We first show that the nomination rule indeed preserves admissibility. So let F be the nomi-nation rule. Consider any set $\Delta \subseteq$ Arg and any profile $\rightharpoonup = (\rightharpoonup_1, \ldots, \rightharpoonup_n)$ such that Δ is admissible in $AF_i = \langle Arg, \rightharpoonup_i \rangle$ for all $i \in N$. For the sake of contradiction, assume Δ is not admissible in $\langle Arg, F(\rightharpoonup) \rangle$, i. e., there is an *argument* $A \in \Delta$ that, in $F(\rightharpoonup)$, is attacked by an argument $B \in Arg \setminus \Delta$ and there does not exist a $C \in \Delta$ such that $(C \rightharpoonup B) \in F(\rightharpoonup)$. As $(B \rightharpoonup A) \in F(\rightharpoonup)$ and as F is grounded, we must have $B \rightharpoonup_i A$ for some $i \in N$. And as there does not exist a $C \in \Delta$ such that $(C \rightharpoonup A) \in F(\rightharpoonup)$, given the definition of the nomination rule, there cannot exist an argument $C \in \Delta$ such that $C \rightharpoonup_i A$ for that same agent i. Hence, Δ is not admissible in AF_i, in contradiction to our original assumption.

We still need to show that there can be no other aggregation rule than the nomination rule that preserves admissibility and that satisfies all of the axioms mentioned in the statement of Theorem 4. Let F be a unanimous, grounded, independent, and monotonic aggregation rule that preserves admissibility. By Lemma 3, we know that F is also neutral. So, the claim is equivalent to the claim that for $|Arg| \geqslant 4$, the only unanimous, grounded, anonymous, neutral, independent, and monotonic aggregation rule F that preserves admissibility is the nomination rule. By the characterisation result for quota rules due to Dietrich and List① in the context of judgment aggregation, which has been adapted to graph aggregation by Endriss and Grandi② and which we have briefly recalled near the end of Section 3. 2, this claim is equivalent to the claim that *no quota rule Fq* with a quota $q > 1$ always preserves admissibility. So let us prove this.

Consider the generic profile shown in Figure 3 (and note that $q > 1$ ensures $q-1 > 0$, i. e., there is at least one agent of the first kind). The set $\{A, B, C\}$ is admissible in all argumentation frameworks in such a profile. But when we aggregate using a quota rule Fq with a quota $q > 1$, we obtain an argumentation framework with a single attack $D \rightharpoonup A$, which means that A cannot be part of any admissible set. Hence, no such rule can preserve admissibility.

4. 2 Credulous and sceptical argument acceptability

Recall that an argument is credulously accepted under a given semantics if it is a member of at least one extension under that semantics. It is sceptically accepted if it is a member of every extension. In the case of the grounded and the ideal semantics, the notions of credulous and sceptical acceptability coincide. We are going to

① F. Dietrich, C. List, Judgment aggregation by quota rules: Majority voting generalized, *Journal of Theoretical Politics*, 2007, 19, pp. 391 - 424.

② U. Endriss, U. Grandi, Graph aggregation, *Artificial Intelligence*, 2017, 245, pp. 86 - 114.

demonstrate that preserving credulous or sceptical acceptability of an argument when using a "simple" aggregation rule is impossible, unless we are willing to use a dictatorship. This is true under any of the six semantics. To prove this result—and some of those that follow—we are going to use a technique developed by Endriss and Grandi① for the more general framework of graph aggregation, which in turn was inspired by the seminal work on preference aggregation of Arrow②. It amounts to showing that, under certain assumptions, the families of winning coalitions defining an aggregation rule must form an ultrafilter. The technique developed by Endriss and Grandi, however, greatly simplifies the process of deriving such results. We only need to show that the properties preserved under aggregation are of a certain type.

Using our present terminology, Endriss and Grandi③ show that, for argumentation frameworks with three or more arguments, any aggregation rule that satisfies certain basic axioms and that is supposed to preserve some AF-property P must be a dictatorship—at least in case P belongs to what they call the family of *implicative* and *disjunctive* properties. Let us first adapt these two concepts to our needs.

Definition 18. *An AF-property P is called implicative if there exist a set $Att \subseteq Arg \times Arg$ of attacks and three individual attacks att_1, att_2, $att_3 \in Arg \times Arg \setminus Att$ such that $\langle Arg, Att \cup S \rangle$ with $S \subseteq \{att_1, att_2, att_3\}$ satisfies P if and only if $S \neq \{att_1, att_2\}$.*

Definition 19. *An AF-property P is called disjunctive if there exist a set $Att \subseteq Arg \times Arg$ of attacks and two individual attacks att_1, $att_2 \in Arg \times Arg \setminus Att$ such that $\langle Arg, Att \cup S \rangle$ with $S \subseteq \{att_1, att_2\}$ satisfies P if and only if $S \neq \varnothing$.*

Thus, an implicative property P requires that, in the context of Att, accepting att_1 and att_2 implies accepting att_3 (and all seven patterns of acceptance consistent with that requirement are possible). A disjunction AF-property P requires that, given Att, we must accept at least one of att_1 and att_2 (and all three patterns of acceptance consistent with that requirement are possible). ④ We call a collection P of

① U. Endriss, U. Grandi, Graph aggregation, *Artificial Intelligence*, 2017, 245, pp. 86 – 114.

② K. J. Arrow, *Social Choice and Individual Values*, 2nd ed., John Wiley and Sons, 1963. First edition published in 1951.

③ U. Endriss, U. Grandi, Graph aggregation, *Artificial Intelligence*, 2017, 245, pp. 86 – 114, Theorem 18.

④ Our definitions of implicativeness and disjunctiveness are special cases of the more general definitions given by Endriss and Grandi (see U. Endriss, U. Grandi, Graph aggregation, *Artificial Intelligence*, 2017, 245, pp. 86 – 114). They simplify exposition and are sufficient for our purposes here.

AF-properties implicative if it includes at least one implicative property. Disjunctive collections of properties are defined analogously. Note that these definitions are different in nature from the definition of contagiousness. Contagiousness requires *every* $P \in \mathcal{P}$ to satisfy certain requirements, and those requirements concern *all* triples A, B, $C \in Arg$, while for both implicativeness and disjunctiveness we merely have to find a single pattern of the relevant kind. For this reason, we are able to directly reuse the results of Endriss and Grandi[①] regarding implicativeness and disjunctiveness here, while we had to prove Lemma 2 from scratch.

With all the relevant definitions now in place, we can formally restate the result of Endriss and Grandi[②] using our present terminology as follows:

Let $\mathcal{P}$ be a collection of AF-properties that is both implicative and disjunctive. Then, for $|Arg| \geqslant 3$, any unanimous, grounded, neutral, and independent aggregation rule F that preserves $\mathcal{P}$ must be a dictatorship.

We are now ready to state and prove our result on the preservation of argument acceptability.[③] It relies on the following lemma, the proof of which can be found in the appendix. Like the proof of Lemma 3, it is a simple application of Lemma 2.

Lemma 5. *Let $\mathcal{P}$ be the collection of AF-properties representing either credulous or sceptical argument acceptability under either the grounded, the ideal, the complete, the preferred, the semi-stable, or the stable semantics. Then, for $|Arg| \geqslant 4$, any unanimous, grounded, and independent aggregation rule F that preserves $\mathcal{P}$ must be neutral.*

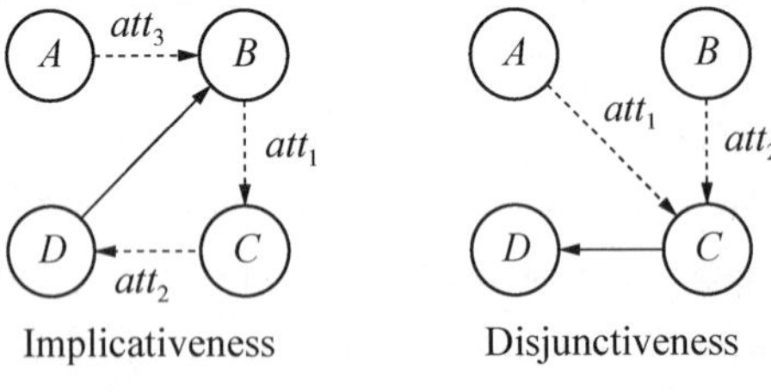

Figure 4: Scenarios used in the proof of Theorem 6.

① U. Endriss, U. Grandi, Graph aggregation, *Artificial Intelligence*, 2017, 245, pp. 86 – 114.

② U. Endriss, U. Grandi, Graph aggregation, *Artificial Intelligence*, 2017, 245, pp. 86 – 114, Theorem 18.

③ Recall that for the grounded and the ideal semantics, the notions of credulous and sceptical acceptability coincide, i. e., for them the formulation of the theorem could be simplified, by simply speaking of "argument acceptability".

Theorem 6. *Let P be the collection of AF-properties representing either credulous or sceptical argument acceptability under either the grounded, the ideal, the complete, the preferred, the semi-stable, or the stable semantics. Then, for* | Arg | ≥4, any unanimous, grounded, and independent aggregation rule F that preserves P must be a dictatorship.

Proof. Let Arg = {A, B, C, D, ...}, let be one of the twelve collections of AF-properties of interest (credulous or sceptical acceptability under one of the six semantics), and let *F* be defined as in the statement of the theorem. By Lemma 5, *F* must also be neutral. Thus, by the aforementioned result of Endriss and Grandi①, we are done if we can show that each of the twelve instances of *P* is both implicative and disjunctive.

Let us first prove implicativeness. Suppose we are interested in the acceptability of argument *C*. Let $Att = \{D \rightharpoonup B\}$, $att_1 = (B \rightharpoonup C)$, $att_2 = (C \rightharpoonup D)$, and $att_3 = (A \rightharpoonup B)$. This scenario is sketched in the lefthand part of Figure 4. Now consider the argumentation frameworks of the form $\langle Arg, Att \cup S\rangle$ with $S \subseteq \{att_1, att_2, att_3\}$. If $S \subseteq \{att_2, att_3\}$, then *C* is not attacked by any other argument. If $S = \{att_1\}$ or $S = \{att_1, att_3\}$, then *C* is defended by *D*, which is not attacked by any other argument. If $S = \{att_1, att_2, att_3\}$, then *C* is defended by *A*, which is not attacked by any other argument. Thus, in all of these seven cases, either *C* is not attacked by any other argument or it is defended by an argument that is not attacked by any other argument. This implies that *C* must be part of the grounded extension. Hence, *C* is both credulously and sceptically accepted under each of the six semantics. On the other hand, if $S = \{att_1, att_2\}$, then $\{B, C, D\}$ forms an isolated odd-length cycle. This means that *C* is neither credulously nor sceptically acceptable under any of the six semantics. We have thus found a set of attacks *Att* and three individual attacks att_1, att_2, and att_3 such that $P(Att \cup S)$ if and only if $S \neq \{att_1, att_2\}$, where *P* is either the property of credulous or of sceptical acceptability of *C* under either one of the six semantics. Hence, the collection *P*, which includes *P*, is implicative.

Next, we show disjunctiveness. Suppose we are interested in the acceptability of *D*. Let $Att = \{C \rightharpoonup D\}$, $att_1 = (A \rightharpoonup C)$, and $att_2 = (B \rightharpoonup C)$. This scenario is depicted on the righthand side of Figure 4. Consider all argumentation frameworks

---

① U. Endriss, U. Grandi, Graph aggregation, *Artificial Intelligence*, 2017, 245, pp. 86 – 114, Theorem 18.

$\langle Arg, Att \cup S\rangle$ with $S \subseteq \{att_1, att_2\}$. If $S = \{att_1\}$, then D is defended by A. If $S = \{att_2\}$, then D is defended by B. If $S = \{att_1, att_2\}$, then D is defended by both A and B. In all three cases, D is defended by some argument that is not attacked by any other argument. This implies that D must be part of the grounded extension and thus both credulously and sceptically accepted under all six semantics. However, if $S = \varnothing$, then D is attacked by C and not defended by any other argument, which means that D is neither credulously nor sceptically acceptable under any of the six semantics. To summarise, we have seen that $P(Att \cup S)$ if and only if $S \neq \varnothing$, where P is the property of credulous or of sceptical acceptability of D under either one of the six semantics. Hence, P is a disjunctive collection of AF-properties.

Recall that Theorem 6 applies only when $|Arg| \geqslant 4$. This covers all cases of practical interest, but from a purely technical point of view one might still wonder whether the theorem could be strengthened to $|Arg| \geqslant 3$. We conjecture that the bound on the cardinality of Arg used in Theorem 6 and all similar bounds in later theorems are sharp, but we have no been able to verify this conjecture in all cases. Only in some cases are there obvious counterexamples. For example, we know that for $|Arg| = 3$ argument acceptability under the grounded semantics is preserved by the strict majority rule,[①] which of course satisfies the three axioms mentioned in Theorem 6.

4.3 The property of being an extension

Next, we turn to the property of a given set of arguments being an extension under one of the six semantics. We obtain impossibility results for five out of the six semantics and—somewhat surprisingly—a positive result for the stable semantics. Our impossibility results differ very subtly for the grounded and the ideal semantics on the one hand, and the complete, the preferred, and the semi-stable semantics on the other. In all five cases, they show that the preservation of extensions is impossible by means of a "simple" aggregation rule, unless we are willing to use a dictatorship.

Theorem 7. *For $|Arg| \geqslant 4$, any unanimous, grounded, and independent aggregation rule F that preserves either grounded or ideal extensions must be a*

---

① To see this, suppose $Arg = \{A, B, C\}$ and focus on the acceptability of C. If C is part of the grounded extension for all individual argumentation frameworks, then in each of them either C is not attacked at all or it is defended by a third argument that is itself not attacked. In the latter case, w. l. o. g., suppose C is attacked by B, which is attacked by A, which is not attacked by any argument. Thus, if there is a strict majority for $B \rightharpoonup C$, then there also must be a strict majority for $A \rightharpoonup B$. Hence, either C is not attacked in the outcome, or it is defended successfully.

dictatorship.

Theorem 8. *For* $|Arg| \geqslant 5$, *any unanimous, grounded, and independent aggregation rule F that preserves either complete, preferred, or semi-stable extensions must be a dictatorship.*

Proofs of both theorems can be found in the appendix. They employ the same technique as for the proof of Theorem 6: we first show that the relevant collections of AF-properties are contagious (to be able to apply Lemma 2) and then that they are both implicative and disjunctive (to be able to apply the result of Endriss and Grandi[①]).

Note that Theorem 7 and Theorem 8 differ with respect to the number of arguments required for the result to apply. Again, we do not know whether all of these bounds are sharp, but we do know that the same proof technique cannot be used to lower the bounds stated in the theorems. For instance, for Theorem 8 the same kind of proof does not go through for $|Arg| \geqslant 4$. To verify this, we have written a computer program that enumerates all relevant scenarios involving four arguments and found that we cannot establish the conditions for implicativeness in this manner. On the other hand, we also know that neither the strict majority rule nor any other quota rule can be used to construct a counter-example to Theorem 7 for $|Arg| = 3$.[②] So, while we still conjecture the bound stated in that theorem to be sharp, proving that it is by finding a counterexample is more difficult in this case than it is for Theorem 6.

Interestingly, for the preservation of stable extensions we obtain a much more positive result:

Proposition 9. *The nomination rule preserves stable extensions.*

Proof. Let F be the nomination rule. Consider any set $\Delta \subseteq$ Arg and any profile $\rightharpoonup = (\rightharpoonup_1, \ldots, \rightharpoonup_n)$ such that Δ is stable in $\langle Arg, \rightharpoonup_i \rangle$ for all $i \in N$. According to Theorem 1, given that F is grounded, F preserves conflict-freeness. Thus, Δ is conflict-free in $\langle Arg, F(\rightharpoonup) \rangle$.

---

① U. Endriss, U. Grandi, Graph aggregation, *Artificial Intelligence*, 2017, 245, pp. 86 – 114.

② For example, to see that the strict majority rule does not preserve grounded extensions in all cases when $|Arg| = 3$ (even though, as we have seen, it does preserve acceptability of individual arguments under the grounded semantics), consider the profile with two agents where the first agent reports $\{A \rightharpoonup B, B \rightharpoonup C\}$ and the second reports $\{C \rightharpoonup B, B \rightharpoonup A\}$. Both individual grounded extensions are equal to $\{A, C\}$, but the strict majority outcome is the argumentation framework without any attacks and thus has the grounded extension $\{A, B, C\}$.

What remains to be shown is that Δ attacks every argument $B \in Arg \setminus \Delta$. In case $\Delta = Arg$, the claim holds vacuously. Otherwise, consider an arbitrary argument $B \in Arg \setminus \Delta$. We need to show that B is attacked by some argument in Δ in $F(\rightharpoonup)$. Take the argumentation framework $AF_i = (Arg, \rightharpoonup_i)$ for some $i \in N$. As Δ is stable in AF_i by assumption, there exists an argument $A \in \Delta$ such that $A \rightharpoonup_i B$. As F is the nomination rule, we also get $(A \rightharpoonup B) \in F(\rightharpoonup)$ as claimed.

4.4 Nonemptiness of thegrounded and the ideal extension

We have seen that preserving the grounded extension and the ideal extension is impossible for simple yet reasonable aggregation rules (see Theorem 7). What about the seemingly less demanding requirement of at least preserving nonemptiness of the unique extension defined by each one of these two semantics? First, the bad news is that for the ideal semantics this intuition fails and the same kind of impossibility prevails.

Theorem 10. *For* $|Arg| \geq 4$, *any unanimous, grounded, and independent aggregation rule* F *that preserves nonemptiness of the ideal extension must be a dictatorship.*

We prove Theorem 10 in the appendix by showing that nonemptiness of the ideal extension is an AF-property that is contagious, implicative, and disjunctive.

For the grounded semantics, however, we can do better. For instance, it is easy to check that the unanimity rule preserves nonemptiness of the grounded extension. Still, as we shall see next, we cannot do *much* better: only rules that grant veto powers to some agents will work. Recall that the grounded extension is nonempty if an only if at least one argument is not attacked by any other argument. Thus, this AF-property is about the *absence* of attacks, while the technique we employed to prove Theorem 7 (and all other impossibility results we have encountered so far) exploits the *presence* of certain attacks (to see this, recall the definitions of implicativeness and disjunctiveness). We are now going to present our preservation result regarding the nonemptiness of the grounded extension as a corollary to a more general theorem about the preservation of AF-properties that require the absence of certain attacks. We first define a suitable meta-property.

Definition 20. *Let* $k \in \mathbb{N}$. *An AF-property* P *is called k-exclusive if there exist* k *distinct attacks* $att_1, \ldots, att_k \in Arg \times Arg$ *such that (i)* $\{att_1, \ldots, att_k\} \subseteq (\rightharpoonup)$ *for no attack-relation* $\rightharpoonup$ *with* $P(\rightharpoonup)$, *and (ii) for every* $S \nsubseteq \{att_1, \ldots, att_k\}$ *there exists an attack-relation* $\rightharpoonup$ *such that* $S \subseteq (\rightharpoonup)$ *and* $P(\rightharpoonup)$.

Thus, you cannot accept all_k attacks, but you should be able to accept any proper subset of them. We call of collection P of AF-properties k-exclusive if at least one property $P \in P$ is k-exclusive. ① We are able to prove the following powerful theorem (recall that n is the number of agents in N).

Theorem 11. *Let $k \geqslant n$ and let P be an AF-property that is k-exclusive. Then under any neutral and independent aggregation rule F that preserves P at least one agent must have veto powers.*

Proof. Let $k \geqslant n$, let P be an AF-property that is k-exclusive, and let F be an aggregation rule that is neutral and independent. We need to show that, if F preserves P, then F must give some agents the power to veto the collective acceptance of attacks.

First, observe that, if an aggregation rule F is both neutral and independent, then there exists a (single) family of winning coalitions $W \subseteq 2^N$ such that, for all profiles $\rightharpoondown$ and all potential attacks $att \in Arg \times Arg$, the following relationship holds:

$$att \in F(\rightharpoondown) \qquad \text{if and only} \qquad \text{if } N_{att}^{\rightharpoondown} \in W$$

Recall that $i \in N$ having veto powers under F means that $F(\rightharpoondown) \subseteq (\rightharpoondown_i)$ for every profile $\rightharpoondown$. Let us show that an agent $i \in N$ has veto powers, if she is a member of all winning coalitions:

$$i \in \bigcap_{\mathfrak{C} \in W} \mathfrak{C} \textit{ implies } \mathrm{F}(\rightharpoondown) \subseteq (\rightharpoondown_i) \textit{ for all profiles } \rightharpoondown$$

If $\bigcap_{\mathfrak{C} \in W} \mathfrak{C} = \varnothing$, then the above claim holds vacuously. Otherwise, take any attack $att \in F(\rightharpoondown)$. As att got accepted, $N_{att}^{\rightharpoondown}$ must be a winning coalition, i. e., $N_{att}^{\rightharpoondown} \in W$ and therefore $i \in N_{att}^{\rightharpoondown}$. But this is just another way of saying $att \in (\rightharpoondown_i)$, so we are done.

Next, we are going to show that the fact that F preserves the k-exclusive AF-property P implies that the intersection of any k winning coalitions must be nonempty:

$$\mathfrak{C}_1 \cap \cdots \cap \mathfrak{C}_k \neq \varnothing \text{ for all } \mathfrak{C}_1, \ldots, \mathfrak{C}_k \in W$$

For the sake of contradiction, assume there do exist winning coalitions $\mathfrak{C}_1, \ldots, \mathfrak{C}_k \in W$ such that $\mathfrak{C}_1 \cap \cdots \cap \mathfrak{C}_k \neq \varnothing$. We construct a profile $\rightharpoondown = (\rightharpoondown_1, \ldots, \rightharpoondown_n)$ with $P(\rightharpoondown i)$ for all $i \in N$ as follows: for every $j \in \{1, \ldots, k\}$, exactly the agents in $\mathfrak{C}_j$ accept attack $attj$ (for all other attacks, it is irrelevant which agents accept them). As, by our assumption, no agent is a member of all k winning

① We include this generalisation of the definition of k-exclusiveness for the sake of completeness, even though, in this paper, we only apply the concept of k-exclusiveness to single AF-properties.

coalitions, no agent accepts all k attacks, so this construction indeed is possible for a k-exclusive property such as P. However, as each of the k attacks is supported by a winning coalition, they all get accepted, i. e., $\{att_1, \ldots, att_k\} \subseteq F(\rightharpoonup)$, meaning that the outcome does *not* satisfy P. Thus, we have found a contradiction to our assumption of F preserving P and are done.

Let us briefly recap where we are at this point. We know that F is characterised by a family of winning coalitions W. We also know that $\mathfrak{C}_1 \cap \cdots \cap \mathfrak{C}_k \neq \varnothing$ for all $\mathfrak{C}_1, \ldots, \mathfrak{C}_k \in W$. We need to show that some agents have veto powers, and we know that this is the case if we can prove that $\mathfrak{C}^{(1)} \cap \cdots \cap \mathfrak{C}^{(l)} \neq \varnothing$, where $\{\mathfrak{C}^{(1)}, \ldots, \mathfrak{C}^{(l)}\}$ is some enumeration of the coalitions in W. Thus, we are done, if we can show that $\mathfrak{C}_1 \cap \cdots \cap \mathfrak{C}_k \neq \varnothing$ for all $\mathfrak{C}_1, \ldots, \mathfrak{C}_k \in W$ implies $\mathfrak{C}^{(1)} \cap \cdots \cap \mathfrak{C}^{(l)} \neq \varnothing$. We are going to prove the contrapositive, namely that the following holds for *some* $\mathfrak{C}_1, \ldots, \mathfrak{C}_k \in W$:

$$\mathfrak{C}^{(1)} \cap \cdots \cap \mathfrak{C}^{(l)} = \varnothing \text{ implies } \mathfrak{C}_1 \cap \cdots \cap \mathfrak{C}_k = \varnothing$$

In other words, we need to show that in case the intersection of *all* winning coalitions is empty, then so is at least one intersection of just k winning coalitions.

Recall that we have assumed $k \geqslant n$. We construct a set $W \subseteq W'$ of k (or fewer) winning coalitions as follows. Initially, set $W' := \varnothing$. Then, for every j from 1 to l in turn, add $\mathfrak{C}^{(j)}$ to W' if and only if the following condition is satisfied:①

$$(\mathfrak{C}^{(j)} \cap \bigcap_{\mathfrak{C} \in W'} \mathfrak{C}) \nsubseteq (\bigcap_{\mathfrak{C} \in W'} \mathfrak{C})$$

Thus, every additional $\mathfrak{C}^{(j)}$ is selected only if it causes the removal of at least one further agent from the intersection. As there are only n agents, we therefore will pick at most n coalitions. Hence, we will indeed arrive at a family W' of n or fewer—and thus certainly at most k—winning coalitions, the intersection of which is empty. This completes the proof.

We note that, unlike for impossibility theorems such as Theorem 6, for Theorem 11 (and the results we are going to prove in the sequel by reference to this theorem), it is not possible to remove the neutrality axiom from the set of assumptions and to instead derive neutrality using independence and the requirement of preserving P. Indeed, it is easy to construct counter-examples. One such counter-example is the rule that always rejects all attacks except for $A \rightharpoonup B$, on which it

---

① By convention, let $\bigcap_{\mathfrak{C} \in \varnothing} \mathfrak{C} = N$, i. e., the intersection of *no* winning coalitions is defined as the universe N of *all* agents.

decides by majority. This rule is independent and does not grant veto powers to any of the agents, yet it guarantees preservation of any k-exclusive AF-property. ①

Let us now return to the issue of the preservation of the nonemptiness of the grounded extension. It suffices to show that this AF-property is an $|Arg|$-exclusive property to obtain the following result.

Theorem 12. *If* $|Arg| \geqslant n$, *then under any neutral and independent aggregation rule F that preserves nonemptiness of the grounded extension at least one agent must have veto powers.*

Proof. To obtain the claim as a corollary to Theorem 11, we need to show that the property of an argumentation framework having a nonempty grounded extension is a k-exclusive AF-property for $k = |Arg|$. Recall that having a nonempty grounded extension is equivalent to the property of having at least one argument that is not attacked by any other argument. We are going to show that the latter property is k-exclusive for $k = |Arg|$.

So let $k = |Arg|$. If $k = 1$, then the claim holds vacuously. So, w. l. o. g., assume that $k > 1$. Take an arbitrary enumeration $\{A^{(1)}, \ldots, A^{(k)}\}$ of Arg and consider the set of attacks $\{att_1, \ldots, att_k\}$ with $att_i = (A^{(i)} \rightharpoonup A^{(i+1)})$ for $i < k$ and $att_k = (A^{(k)} \rightharpoonup A^{(1)})$. Clearly, this set of attacks meets our requirements: (i) if $\{att_1, \ldots, att_k\} \subseteq (\rightharpoonup)$, then $\rightharpoonup$ does not have the property of leaving at least one argument without an attacker and (ii) for every $S \nsubseteq \{att_1, \ldots, att_k\}$ there exists an attack-relation $\rightharpoonup$ with $S \subseteq (\rightharpoonup)$, namely S itself, that does leave one or more arguments without an attacker.

We note that it is not difficult to prove that the converse of Theorem 12 holds as well: all rules that grant veto powers to at least one agent preserve nonemptiness of the grounded extension. To see this, observe that, if we start with an argumentation framework with a nonempty grounded extension (and thus at least one unattacked argument) and remove some of the attacks, then the grounded extension will remain nonempty (as that same argument remains unattacked). Therefore, as long as at least one agent with veto powers submits an argumentation framework in which at least one argument is unattacked, the same will be true for the outcome.

---

① For $k > 1$, this holds vacuously, as the outcome will at most include the single attack $A \rightharpoonup B$. For $k = 1$ and if the attack of interest is $att_1 = (A \rightharpoonup B)$, then no individual agent is allowed to accept att_1, so it will not be collectively accepted either. Note that this construction crucially depends on the aggregation rule violating the neutrality axiom.

4.5 Acyclicity and coherence

The final group of AF-properties for which we wish to analyse the conditions under which they can be preserved under aggregation are properties that guarantee that several of the argumentation semantics agree on what arguments are (credulously or sceptically) acceptable. Recall that acyclicity guarantees that all six semantics agree with the grounded semantics and thus unambiguously define which arguments to accept. Also recall that coherence is a weaker property that ensures that the stable, the semi-stable, and the preferred semantics coincide. It is defined as the AF-property of every preferred extension being a stable extension (the rest follows from the known relationships between these three semantics).

Acyclicity is a prime example for a *k*-exclusive property, so we immediately obtain the following result as another simple corollary to Theorem 11. ①

Theorem 13. *If* $|Arg| \geqslant n$, *then under any neutral and independent aggregation rule F that preserves acyclicity at least one agent must have veto powers.*

For the sake of completeness, the straight for ward proof is given in the appendix. We note that, just as for Theorem 12, the converse of Theorem 13 is immediately seen to hold as well, i. e., all aggregation rules that grant veto powers to some agents clearly preserve acyclicity. This includes the qualified majority rules studied by Tohmé et al. ②.

Finally, regarding the preservation of the coherence of argumentation frameworks, we obtain the following impossibility result.

Theorem 14. *For* $|Arg| \geqslant 4$, *any unanimous, grounded, and independent aggregation rule F that preserves coherence must be a dictatorship.*

Thus, somewhat surprisingly, even though acyclicity is a stronger property than

---

① Theorem 13 was anticipated in the work of Tohmé et al. (see F. A. Tohmé, G. A. Bodanza, G. R. Simari, Aggregation of attack relations: A social-choice theoretical analysis of defeasibility criteria, in *Proceedings of the 5th International Symposium on Foundations of Information and Knowledge Systems (FoIKS)*, Springer, 2008, pp. 8–23), who make a similar claim, but without appealing to the neutrality axiom. We stress that Theorem 13 cannot be strengthened by dropping neutrality from the set of assumptions. Indeed, there are rules that preserve acyclicity, that are independent (but not neutral), and that do not give veto powers (regarding all potential attacks) to any of the agents. An example, for $N = \{1, 2\}$ and $Arg = \{A, B\}$, is the rule that accepts $A \rightharpoonup B$ if at least one agent does and that accepts $B \rightharpoonup A$ if both agents do.

② F. A. Tohmé, G. A. Bodanza, G. R. Simari, Aggregation of attack relations: A social-choice theoretical analysis of defeasibility criteria, in *Proceedings of the 5th International Symposium on Foundations of Information and Knowledge Systems (FoIKS)*, Springer, 2008, pp. 8–23.

coherence, it is easier to preserve under aggregation. The proof of Theorem 14 canbe found in the appendix. It amounts to showing that coherence is an AF-property that is contagious, implicative, and disjunctive, i. e., this is yet another application of the technique of Endriss and Grandi①.

5. Conclusion

Using avariety of techniques, we have attempted to paint a clear picture of the capabilities and limitations of simple aggregation rules regarding the preservation of properties related to the semantics of abstract argumentation frameworks. While the significance of this issue and the promise of social choice theory for its resolution have previously been emphasised in the work of several authors②, this is the first systematic analysis of its kind. Our results show that only the most basic of properties, namely conflict-freeness, is preserved by essentially all rules. More demanding properties require either the nomination rule, a rule granting some agents veto powers, or a rule that is dictatorial. Thus, the rules imposed on us by these results range from the positive, to the highly restrictive, to the clearly unacceptable.

We stress that these results only apply to *simple* rules, in particular, to rules that satisfy the axiom of independence. Using aggregation rules that are independent has the advantage that we can focus on one attack at a time when we determine the outcome, thereby simplifying the process of aggregation in both conceptual and computational terms. On the other hand, requiring independence clearly limits the design space for aggregation rules we can explore and prevents us from incorporation complex dependencies in the aggregation process. An alternative route, the one chosen by Coste-Marquis et al. ③, is to use distance-based rules (which violate

① U. Endriss, U. Grandi, Graph aggregation, *Artificial Intelligence*, 2017, 245, pp. 86 – 114.

② F. A. Tohmé, G. A. Bodanza, G. R. Simari, Aggregation of attack relations: A social-choice theoretical analysis of defeasibility criteria, in *Proceedings of the 5th International Symposium on Foundations of Information and Knowledge Systems (FoIKS)*, Springer, 2008, pp. 8 – 23; P. E. Dunne, P. Marquis, M Wooldridge, Argument aggregation: Basic axioms and complexity results, in *Proceedings of the 4th International Conference on Computational Models of Argument (COMMA)*, IOS Press, 2012, pp. 129 – 140 ; J. Delobelle, S. Konieczny, S. Vesic, On the aggregation of argumentation frameworks, in *Proceedings of the 24th International Joint Conference on Artificial Intelligence (IJCAI)*, 2015, pp. 2911 – 2917 ; G. A. Bodanza, F. A. Tohmé, M. R. Auday, Collective argumentation: A survey of aggregation issues around argumentation frameworks, *Argument & Computation*, 2017, 8, pp. 1 – 34.

③ S. Coste-Marquis, C. Devred, S. Konieczny, M. -C. Lagasquie-Schiex, P. Marquis, On the merging of Dung's argumentation systems, *Artificial Intelligence*, 2007, 171, pp. 730 – 753.

independence). Such rules can be designed so as to guarantee specific properties of the outcome, so the question of preservation does not arise. On the downside, distance-based rules are computationally intractable①. We also stress that our results are based on the assumption that all agents report attack-relations over a single *common* set of arguments. Richer models, where different agents may choose to put forward of different sets of arguments②, are clearly of great interest as well and should be studied in future work. Finally, we stress that our results apply to one specific and highly *abstract* model of argumentation only③, albeit one that that has been exceptionally well received by the scientific community. Future work should also be directed at understanding to what extent our approach can be applied to models other than Dung's classical model of abstract argumentation. Natural candidates for such models are, first and foremost, those that are relatively close to Dung's model, such as bipolar abstract argumentation systems④ or Bench-Capon's value-based argumentation frameworks⑤. In the long run, we recommend to attempt also going beyond such abstract models of argumentation and to consider structured forms of argumentation that account for the internal logical structure of individual arguments and thereby come closer to accurately modelling features of argumentation found in debates occurring in the real world⑥.

At the methodological level, we believe that Theorem 11, which shows that simple rules that preserve k-exclusive properties must give some agents veto powers,

---

① S. Konieczny, J. Lang, P. Marquis, DA2 merging operators, *Artificial Intelligence*, 2004, 157, pp. 49 - 79; E. Hemaspaandra, H. Spakowski, J. Vogel, The complexity of Kemeny elections, *Theoretical Computer Science*, 2005, 349, pp. 382 - 391; U. Endriss, U. Grandi, D. Porello, Complexity of judgment aggregation, *Journal of Artificial Intelligence Research* (*JAIR*), 2012, 45, pp. 481 - 514.

② See, e. g., S. Coste-Marquis, C. Devred, S. Konieczny, M. -C. Lagasquie-Schiex, P. Marquis, On the merging of Dung's argumentation systems, *Artificial Intelligence*, 2007, 171, pp. 730 - 753; S. Airiau, E. Bonzon, U. Endriss, N. Maudet, J. Rossit, Rationalisation of profiles of abstract argumentation frameworks: Characterisation and complexity, *Journal of Artificial Intelligence Research* (*JAIR*), 2017, 60, pp. 149 - 177.

③ P. M. Dung, On the acceptability of arguments and its fundamental role in nonmonotonic reasoning, logic programming and n-person games, *Artificial Intelligence*, 1995, 77, pp. 321 - 358.

④ C. Cayrol, M. Lagasquie-Schiex, Bipolar abstract argumentation systems, in I. Rahwan, G. R. Simari (Eds.), *Argumentation in Artificial Intelligence*, Springer, 2009, pp. 65 - 84.

⑤ T. J. M. Bench-Capon, Persuasion in practical argument using value-based argumentation frame-works, *Journal of Logic and Computation*, 2003, 13, pp. 429 - 448.

⑥ See, e. g., P. Besnard, A. Hunter, *Elements of Argumentation*, MIT Press, 2008; H. Prakken, An abstract framework for argumentation with structured arguments, *Argument and Computation*, 2010, 1, pp. 93 - 124.

is of particular interest as it likely will find application also beyond the confines of abstract argumentation, in the same way as the results of Endriss and Grandi① on contagious, implicative, and disjunctive properties can be applied to a range of domains of graph aggregation. Also of some methodological interest are our simplified forms of the meta-properties of contagiousness, implicativeness, and disjunctiveness originally due to Endriss and Grandi and our observation that these meta-properties can not only be applied to single properties of graphs but also to collections of properties. For contagiousness, in particular, this makes a significant difference, as a collection of properties can be contagious even if no single property in that collection is contagious.

Staying with the theme of methodology for a moment, the techniques we have employed to prove impossibility theorems reduce the task of finding a proof to the task of identifying suitable scenarios that show that a given property (or collection of properties) is contagious, implicative, disjunctive, or k-exclusive. Once such a scenario is found, presenting and verifying the proof is routine, but finding such a scenario can be difficult. In some cases we have found these scenarios with the help of a computer program (the same program we used to verify that our techniques cannot be used to lower the bounds on the number of arguments for the theorems reported in Section 4.3) and in some cases we have verified the correctness of the constructions on which our proofs rely using an existing tool for computing extensions of abstract argumentation frameworks②. This suggests that there is room for applying automated reasoning tools in this domain, an approach that recently has been used very successfully in several other areas of computational social choice③. Investigating this point further constitutes another promising direction for future work.

Finally, there are natural opportunities for investigating application scenarios of our work. One such scenario has been presented in recent work by Shi et al.④, who

---

① U. Endriss, U. Grandi, Graph aggregation, *Artificial Intelligence*, 2017, 245, pp. 86 – 114.

② S. Bistarelli, F. Santini, ConArg: A constraint-based computational framework for argumentation systems, in *Proceedings of the 23rd IEEE International Conference on Tools with Artificial Intelligence (ICTAI)*, IEEE, 2011, pp. 605 – 612.

③ C. Geist, D. Peters, Computer-aided methods for social choice theory, in U. Endriss (Ed.), *Trends in Computational Social Choice*, AI Access, 2017, pp. 249 – 267.

④ C. Shi, S. Smets, F. R. Vel'azquez-Quesada, Argument-based belief in topological structures, in *Proceedings of the 16th Conference on Theoretical Aspects of Rationality and Knowledge (TARK)*, 2017, pp. 489 – 503.

propose an approach for modelling an agent's beliefs in which *beliefs are grounded in arguments*. If one were to attempt to extend this model to also allow for the representation of groups of agents as well as their beliefs and pieces of evidence for those beliefs, then it may be possible to use our techniques to analyse aggregation rules for selecting the beliefs and the supporting evidence for the group. As a second example for a promising scenario of application, it would be interesting to investigate the *strategic incentives* of agents who are reporting an argumentation framework to an aggregation rule and whose objective might be to get a certain argument accepted. ① This problem is similar to the problem of strategic manipulation in voting②. Recall that it is well-known that strategy-proofness is closely linked to the independence axiom in voting③, meaning that the insights regarding independent aggregation rules collected in this paper may well be of direct relevance to such an investigation.

6. Appendix: Remaining Proofs

In this appendix we present the proofs omitted from the body of the paper. They all have the same structure: they show that a given collection of semantic AF-properties of interest has certain meta-properties, which allows us to apply certain more general results. Only the first proof for each meta-property is included in the body of the paper.

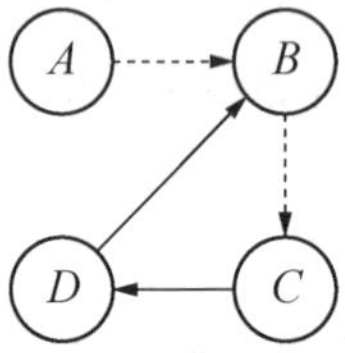

Figure 5: Scenario used in the proof of Lemma 5.

① Prior work has dealt with a related but different question connecting abstract argumentation and game theory (see I. Rahwan, K. Larson, Argumentation and game theory, in I. Rahwan, G. R. Simari (Eds.), *Argumentation in Artificial Intelligence*, Springer, 2009, pp. 321 – 339): We are given a fixed argumentation framework. Every agent can report a subset of the available arguments. We then restrict the given argumentation framework to the union of the sets of arguments reported by the agents and apply an argumentation semantics to select an extension. What are the incentives of an individual agent to not report an argument she in fact is aware of?

② A. D. Taylor, *Social Choice and the Mathematics of Manipulation*, Cambridge University Press, 2005.

③ U. Endriss, Logic and social choice theory, in A. Gupta, J. van Benthem (Eds.), *Logic and Philosophy Today*, volume 2, College Publications, 2011, pp. 333 – 377.

Proof of Lemma 5 (*neutrality lemma for argument acceptability*)

Suppose $|Arg| \geqslant 4$. Let P be the collection of AF-properties representing either credulous or sceptical argument acceptability under either the grounded, the ideal, the complete, the preferred, the semi-stable, or the stable semantics. The claim follows from Lemma 2 if we can show that P is contagious. So consider any three arguments A, B, $C \in Arg$. As $|Arg| \geqslant 4$, we can pick a fourth argument $D \in Arg$. Let $Att = \{C \rightharpoonup D, D \rightharpoonup B\}$ and consider the four argumentation frameworks of the form $\langle Arg, Att \cup S\rangle$ with $S \subseteq \{A \rightharpoonup B, B \rightharpoonup C\}$. They are indicated in Figure 5. Now focus on the acceptability of argument C. If $S = \varnothing$ or $S = \{A \rightharpoonup B\}$, then C is not attacked by any other argument and thus a member of the grounded extension and thereby credulously and sceptically accepted under all six semantics. If $S = \{A \rightharpoonup B, B \rightharpoonup C\}$, then C is defended by A, which is not attacked by any other argument. Hence, C is a member of the grounded extension and thereby credulously and sceptically accepted under all six semantics also in this case. If $S = \{B \rightharpoonup C\}$, on the other hand, we obtain an isolated odd-length cycle including C, which means that C is not part of any extension under any of the six semantics. Hence, both credulous and sceptical acceptability of C is an AF-property of the kind we require, under all of the six semantics.

Proof of Theorem 7 (*extension preservation for the grounded and ideal semantics*)

Suppose $|Arg| \geqslant 4$. Let P be either the collection of AF-properties representing a given set of arguments being the grounded extension or that of a given set of arguments being the ideal extension. We need to show that P is contagious, implicative, and disjunctive in both cases.

Contagiousness. Consider any four arguments A, B, C, $D \in Arg$. Suppose we are interested in the property of $\{A, C, D\}$ being the grounded or the ideal extension. We define Att as follows:

$$Att = \{C \rightharpoonup B\} \cup \{D \rightharpoonup X \mid X \in Arg \setminus \{A, B, C, D\}\}$$

Consider the argumentation frameworks of the form $\langle Arg, Att \cup S\rangle$ with $S \subseteq \{A \rightharpoonup B, B \rightharpoonup C\}$. They are indicated in the leftmost part of Figure 6. The reader may verify that for $S \neq \{B \rightharpoonup C\}$, both the grounded and the ideal extension indeed are $\{A, C, D\}$: these are the arguments that are either successfully defended or not attacked at all, while B is not. On the other hand, for $S = \{B \rightharpoonup C\}$, both the grounded and the ideal extension are $\{A, D\}$. Thus, P is contagious.

Implicativeness. Let $Arg = \{A, B, C, D, \ldots\}$. We focus on $Arg \setminus \{C\}$ as the subset of arguments that may (or may not) form the grounded or the ideal extension. We define $Att = \{B \rightharpoonup C, D \rightharpoonup C\}$, $att_1 = (C \rightharpoonup D)$, $att_2 = (C \rightharpoonup B)$, and $att_3 = (A \rightharpoonup C)$. This scenario is depicted in the middle part of Figure 6. Consider all argumentation frameworks of the form A $F = \langle Arg, Att \cup S\rangle$ with $S \subseteq \{att_1, att_2, att_3\}$. The reader may verify that, indeed, for $S \neq \{att_1, att_2\}$ both the grounded and the ideal extension are equal to $Arg \setminus \{C\}$. On the other hand, for $S = \{att_1, att_2\}$ both of them are equal to $Arg \setminus \{B, C, D\}$. Thus, P is implicative.

Disjunctiveness. Let $Arg = \{A, B, C, D, \ldots\}$. We again focus on $Arg \setminus \{C\}$ as the subset of arguments that may (or may not) form the grounded or the ideal extension. We define $Att = \{C \rightharpoonup D\}$, $att_1 = (A \rightharpoonup C)$, and $att_2 = (B \rightharpoonup C)$. This is shown on the righthand side of Figure 6. Consider argumentation frameworks $AF = \langle Arg, Att \cup S\rangle$ with $S \subseteq \{att_1, att_2\}$. As the reader can easily verify, if $S \neq \varnothing$, then $Arg \setminus \{C\}$ is both the grounded and ideal extension of AF. But if $S = \varnothing$, then $Arg \setminus \{D\}$ is both the grounded and the ideal extension. Thus, P is disjunctive. □

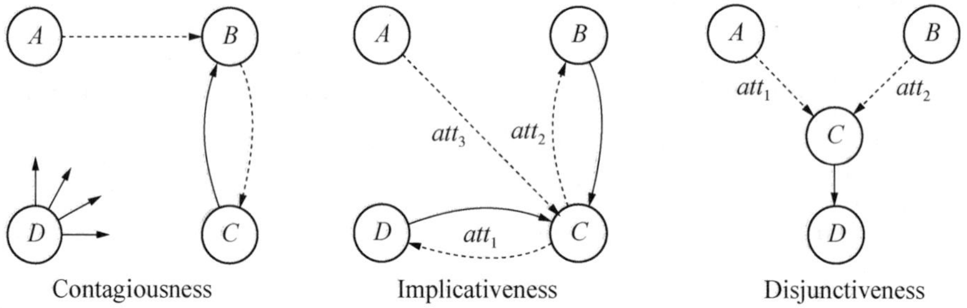

Figure 6: Scenarios used in the proof of Theorem 7.

Proof of Theorem 8 (*extension preservation for the complete, preferred, and semi-stable semantics*) Suppose $|Arg| \geqslant 5$. Let P be the collection of AF-properties representing a given set of arguments being an extension under either the complete, the preferred, or the semi-stable semantics. We need to show that P is contagious, implicative, and disjunctive in all three cases.

Contagiousness. We first consider the case of complete extensions. Consider any five arguments $A, B, C, D, E \in Arg$. Let $Arg \setminus \{B, D, E\}$ be the set of arguments of interest. We define $Att = \{D \rightharpoonup B, D \rightharpoonup E, E \rightharpoonup D\}$. Now consider the argumentation frameworks of the form $\langle Arg, Att \cup S\rangle$ with $S \subseteq \{A \rightharpoonup B, B \rightharpoonup C\}$.

This scenario is depicted in the upper lefthand corner of Figure 7. If $S \neq \{B \rightharpoonup C\}$, then $Arg \setminus \{B, D, E\}$ is a complete extension. But if $S = \{B \rightharpoonup C\}$, then it is not, because C is attacked but not defended by A or any other argument in the set. Thus, being a complete extension is contagious.

Next, we consider the case of preferred and semi-stable extensions, where contagiousness can be established even for $|Arg| \geqslant 4$. So consider four arguments A, B, C, $D \in Arg$. Let $Arg \setminus \{A, B, C, D\}$ be the set of interest, i. e., we ask whether it is possible that none of our four distinguished arguments will get accepted. We define $Att = \{A \rightharpoonup B, B \rightharpoonup C, C \rightharpoonup A, C \rightharpoonup D\}$. Now consider the argumentation frameworks of the form $\langle Arg, Att \cup S \rangle$ with $S \subseteq \{B \rightharpoonup D, D \rightharpoonup A\}$. This scenario is shown in the lower lefthand corner of Figure 7. If $S \neq \{D \rightharpoonup A\}$, then no subset of $\{A, B, C, D\}$ other than \ is admissible. Hence, in these three cases, $Arg \setminus \{A, B, C, D\}$ is the only preferred extension, and thus also the only semi-stable extension. However, for $S = \{D \rightharpoonup A\}$ the set $Arg \setminus \{A, B, C, D\}$ is not a preferred extension (and thus also not a semi-stable extension), because its superset $Arg \setminus \{A, C\}$ is admissible as well. Thus, being either a preferred or a semi-stable extension is contagious.

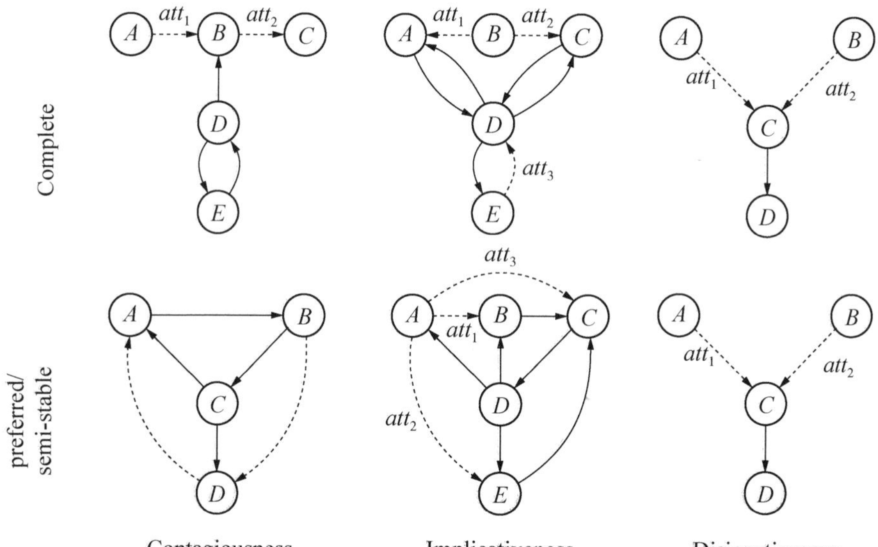

Figure 7: Scenarios used in the proof of Theorem 8.

Implicativeness. Let $Arg = \{A, B, C, D, E, \ldots\}$. We again start with the case of complete extensions. We focus on the set $Arg \setminus \{A, C, D, E\}$ as a possible complete extension. Define $Att = \{A \rightharpoonup D, D \rightharpoonup A, C \rightharpoonup D, D \rightharpoonup C, D \rightharpoonup E\}$, $att_1 = (B \rightharpoonup A)$, $att_2 = (B \rightharpoonup C)$, and $att_3 = (E \rightharpoonup D)$. This scenario is shown in the middle of the top row in Figure 7. Now consider the eight argumentation frameworks of the form $\langle Arg, Att \cup S\rangle$ with $S \subseteq \{att_1, att_2, att_3\}$. In all eight cases, B is part of every complete extension, because it is not attacked. If $S \neq \{att_1, att_2\}$, then (as far as our five distinguished arguments are concerned) it is possible to accept only B, i. e., $Arg \setminus \{A, C, D, E\}$ is a complete extension. But for $S = \{att_1, att_2\}$, we also must accept D, because it is successfully defended by B. Hence, being a complete extension is implicative.

Next, we turn to the preferred and the semi-stable semantics. Let $Arg \setminus \{A, B, C, D, E\}$ be the set of arguments under consideration. Define $Att = \{B \rightharpoonup C, D \rightharpoonup A, D \rightharpoonup B, D \rightharpoonup E, C \rightharpoonup D, E \rightharpoonup C\}$, $att_1 = (A \rightharpoonup B)$, $att_2 = (A \rightharpoonup E)$, and $att_3 = (A \rightharpoonup C)$. This situation is sketched in the middle of the bottom row in Figure 7. We again consider the eight argumentation frameworks $\langle Arg, Att \cup S\rangle$ with $S \subseteq \{att_1, att_2, att_3\}$. First, consider the seven argumentation frameworks with $S \neq \{att_1, att_2\}$. The reader may verify that none of the nonempty and conflict-free subsets of $\{A, B, C, D, E\}$ is admissible. Hence, $Arg \setminus \{A, B, C, D, E\}$ is the only preferred extension (and thus also the only semi-stable extension) for any of these seven argumentation frameworks. On the other hand, if $S = \{att_1, att_2\}$, then $\{A, C\}$ is admissible and thus $Arg \setminus \{A, B, C, D, E\}$ cannot be either preferred or semi-stable. Hence, both being a preferred extension and being a semi-stable extension are implicative collections of AF-properties.

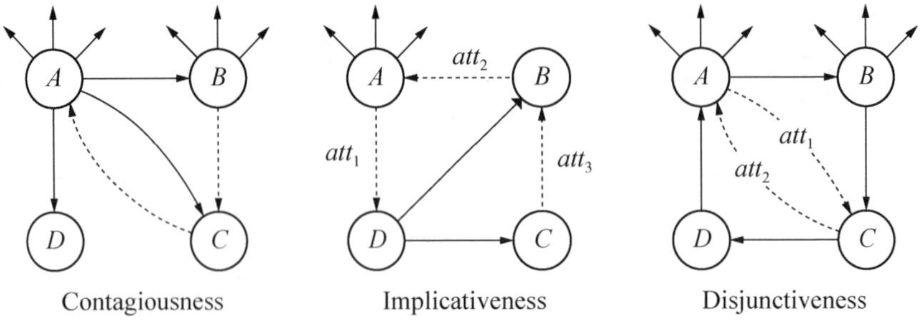

Figure 8: Scenarios used in the proof of Theorem 10.

Disjunctiveness. To prove disjunctiveness of P we can use the same construction as in the proof of Theorem 7 in all three cases. To see that this is possible, it is sufficient to observe that the argumentation frameworks used in the proof are all acyclic, i. e., all our semantics coincide with the grounded semantics. Observe that this means that disjunctiveness holds even for $|Arg| \geqslant 4$.

Proof of Theorem 10 (*preservation of nonemptiness of the ideal extension*)

Suppose $|Arg| \geqslant 4$. We need to show that nonemptiness of the ideal extension is an AF-property that is contagious, implicative, and disjunctive. ①

Contagiousness. Fix four arguments A, B, C, $D \in Arg$. We define the set Att of attacks as follows:

$$\begin{aligned} Att = & \{A \rightharpoonup B, A \rightharpoonup C, A \rightharpoonup D\} \cup \\ & \{A \rightharpoonup X \mid X \in Arg \setminus \{A, B, C, D\}\} \cup \\ & \{B \rightharpoonup X \mid X \in Arg \setminus \{A, B, C, D\}\} \end{aligned}$$

Now consider the four argumentation frameworks $\langle Arg, Att \cup S\rangle$ with $S \subseteq \{B \rightharpoonup C, C \rightharpoonup A\}$. This scenario is depicted in the leftmost part of Figure 8. If $S = \{C \rightharpoonup A\}$, then the only preferred extension is $\{A\}$. Hence, in these cases, the ideal extension is $\{A\}$ as well and thus nonempty. But if $S = \{C \rightharpoonup A\}$, then there are two preferred extensions, namely $\{A\}$ and $\{B, C, D\}$. As their intersection is empty, the ideal extension must be empty as well. Thus, nonemptiness of the ideal extension is a contagious AF-property.

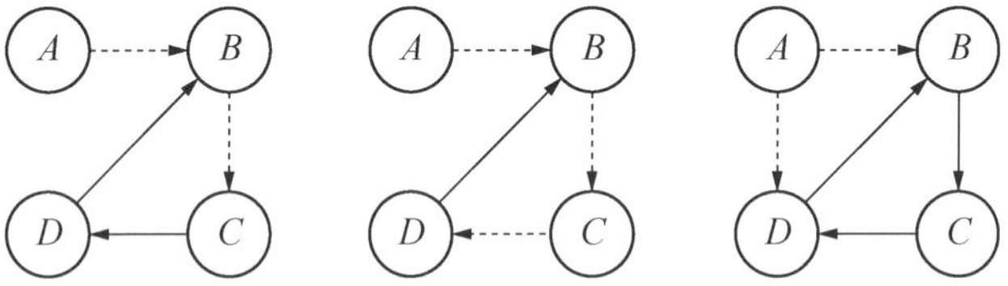

Figure 9: Scenarios used in the proof of Theorem 14.

Implicativeness. Let $Arg = \{A, B, C, D, \dots\}$. We define Att as follows:

$$Att = \{D \rightharpoonup B, D \rightharpoonup C\} \cup \{A \rightharpoonup X \mid X \in Arg \setminus \{A, B, C, D\}\}$$

Furthermore, let $att_1 = (A \rightharpoonup D)$, $att_2 = (B \rightharpoonup A)$, and $att_3 = (C \rightharpoonup B)$. This scenario is shown in the middle part of Figure 8. Now consider the eight argumentation frameworks of the form $\langle Arg, Att \cup S\rangle$ with $S \subseteq \{att_1, att_2, att_3\}$.

① Note that this is the first time we are proving this for a single AF-property rather than a collection of properties.

Whenever $S \neq \{att_1, att_2\}$, there is only a single preferred extension and A is part of it. Hence, the ideal extension is a superset of $\{A\}$ and thus nonempty. But if $S = \{att_1, att_2\}$, then the only preferred extension is the empty set and thus the ideal extension is empty as well. Hence, nonemptiness of the ideal extension is an implicative AF-property.

Disjunctiveness. Let $Arg = \{A, B, C, D, \ldots\}$. We define Att as follows:

$$Att = \{A \rightharpoonup B, B \rightharpoonup C, C \rightharpoonup D, D \rightharpoonup A\} \cup \{A \rightharpoonup X \mid X \in Arg \setminus \{A, B, C, D\}\} \cup \{B \rightharpoonup X \mid X \in Arg \setminus \{A, B, C, D\}\}$$

Furthermore, let $att_1 = (A \rightharpoonup C)$ and $att_2 = (C \rightharpoonup A)$. This scenario is shown on the righthand side of Figure 8. Now consider the four argumentation frameworks of the form $\langle Arg, Att \cup S\rangle$ with $S \subseteq \{att_1, att_2, att_3\}$. If $S \neq \varnothing$, then the only preferred extension is $\{B, D\}$, which is also the ideal extension. On the other hand, for $S = \varnothing$ the preferred extensions are $\{A, C\}$ and $\{B, D\}$, meaning that the ideal extension is empty. Thus, nonemptiness of the ideal extension is a disjunct-tive AF-property.

Proof of Theorem 13 (*preservation of acyclicity*)

The claim holds vacuously for $|Arg| = 1$. So, w. l. o. g., let us assume that $|Arg| > 1$. Acyclicity is an AF-property that is k-exclusive for every $k \in \{2, \ldots, |Arg|\}$. To see this, consider the case where the attack relations $\{att_1, \ldots, att_k\}$ form a cycle, and observe that the shortest (proper) cycle has length 2, while the longest cycle visits every vertex exactly once and thus has length $|Arg|$. The claim now follows from Theorem 11.

Proof of Theorem 14 (*preservation of coherence*)

Recall that an argumentation framework is coherent if all its preferred extensions are also stable extensions. Suppose $|Arg| \geqslant 4$. We need to show that coherence is an AF-property that is contagious, implicative, and disjunctive.

Contagiousness. Fix four arguments $A, B, C, D \in Arg$. Let $Att = \{C \rightharpoonup D, D \rightharpoonup B\}$. Now consider the argumentation frameworks of the form $\langle Arg, Att \cup S\rangle$ with $S \subseteq \{A \rightharpoonup B, B \rightharpoonup C\}$. This scenario is depicted on the lefthand side of Figure 9. If $S = \varnothing$, then $Arg \setminus \{D\}$ is the only preferred and the only stable extension. If $S = \{A \rightharpoonup B\}$ or $S = \{A \rightharpoonup B, B \rightharpoonup C\}$, then $Arg \setminus \{B, D\}$ is the only preferred and the only stable extension. Hence, each of these three argumentation frameworks is coherent. On the other hand, if $S = \{B \rightharpoonup C\}$, then $\{B, C, D\}$ forms an isolated odd-length cycle. Then $Arg \setminus \{B, C, D\}$ is the only preferred extension, which however is not stable. Hence, this argumentation framework is not coherent. In conclusion, we have shown that coherence is a contagious AF-property.

Implicativeness. Let $Arg = \{A, B, C, D, \ldots\}$. We define $Att = \{D \rightharpoonup B\}$, $att_1 = (B \rightharpoonup C)$, $att_2 = (C \rightharpoonup D)$, and $att_3 = (A \rightharpoonup B)$. This scenario is shown in the middle of Figure 9 and is identical to the scenario used in the proof of Theorem 6. Now consider the eight argumentation frameworks $\langle Arg, Att \cup S \rangle$ with $S \subseteq \{att_1, att_2, att_3\}$. If $S \subseteq \{att_1, att_3\}$, then the only preferred extension is $Arg \setminus \{B\}$, which is also stable. If $S = \{att_2\}$, then the only preferred extension is $Arg \setminus \{D\}$, which again is also stable. If $S = \{att_2, att_3\}$ or $S = \{att_1, att_2, att_3\}$, then the only preferred extension is $Arg \setminus \{B, D\}$, which once again also is stable. Thus, in all seven cases we obtain coherent argumentation frameworks. However, if $S = \{att_1, att_2\}$, then the only preferred extension is $Arg \setminus \{B, C, D\}$, which is not stable. So in this case, coherence is violated. Hence, coherence is an implicative AF-property.

Disjunctiveness. Let $Arg = \{A, B, C, D, \ldots\}$. We define $Att = \{B \rightharpoonup C, C \rightharpoonup D, D \rightharpoonup B\}$, $att_1 = (A \rightharpoonup B)$, and $att_2 = (A \rightharpoonup D)$. This scenario is shown on the righthand side of Figure 9. Now consider the four argumentation frameworks $\langle Arg, Att \cup S \rangle$ with $S \subseteq \{att_1, att_2\}$. If $S = \{att_1\}$ or $S = \{att_1, att_2\}$, then the only preferred extension is $Arg \setminus \{B, D\}$, which is also stable. If $S = \{att_2\}$, then the only preferred extension is $Arg \setminus \{C, D\}$, which again is also stable. Thus, in all three cases every preferred extension is stable. On the other hand, if $S = \varnothing$, then the only preferred extension is $Arg \setminus \{B, C, D\}$, which is not stable. Hence, coherence is a disjunctive AF-property.

《墨经》分科研究方法省思[①]

何 杨

《墨经》包括《墨子》之《经上》《经下》《经说上》《经说下》四篇[②]，由约180条经文和相应的说文构成[③]。其书素称难解，自汉迄明，研习者极少。西晋鲁胜注《墨经》，今仅存其序。清中叶毕沅注《墨子》，认为《墨经》“讹错独多，不可句读”[④]。清末，因受西学影响，不少学者尝试从数学、力学、光学、逻辑学等学科视角对《墨经》中的相关条目展开研究，进而开启了分科解读《墨经》的研究范式，影响至今。[⑤]

分科研究使得曾经几不可读的《墨经》得到了丰富的诠释，促进了近现代中国的墨学复兴。然而，该方法以后出外来的学科观念审视《墨经》，研究者常常篡改原文，以合己意。诚如沈有鼎所言：“过去诂解《墨经》的人，除了早期的几位如孙诒让等不计以外，余者常常望文生义，先构成了一个主观成见，于是利用《墨经》一书脱误本来极多这话作为理由，任意改窜《墨经》的文字来适合自己的成见。”[⑥] 时至今日，《墨经》诸多条目的解释依然是众说纷纭、莫衷一是。虽然影响对《墨经》原文的理解的因素很多，但是研究方法至关重要。本文拟对这种分科治墨的研究方法予以考察，进而探究《墨经》研究的合理方法，以推动墨学的进一步发展。

---

① 本文原刊《现代哲学》2018年第5期。另本文受国家社会科学基金项目（16CZX053）资助。

② 一般而言，《墨经》（或称《墨辩》）有广狭二分，本文所指为狭义《墨经》。若为广义《墨经》，还包括《墨子》中的《大取》《小取》。

③ 经文和说文原本分列，因此，后人根据个人理解引说就经时，有极少数条目有经无说或有说无经。

④ 毕沅注：《墨子》，载任继愈主编：《墨子大全》第11册，北京图书馆出版社2002年影清乾隆四十九年（1784）毕氏灵岩山馆刻本，第249页。

⑤ 关于墨学史的总体情况可参阅郑杰文：《中国墨学通史》，人民出版社2006年版。关于近现代墨学复兴详情可参阅崔清田：《显学重光》，辽宁教育出版社1997年版；张斌峰：《近代〈墨辩〉复兴之路》，山西教育出版社1999年版；张永春：《清代墨学与中国传统思想学术的近代转型》，黄山书社2014年版。

⑥ 沈有鼎：《墨经的逻辑学》序，中国社会科学出版社1980年版，第1－2页。此外，沈有鼎所言《墨经》为广义《墨经》。

一、《墨经》分科研究的历史回顾

一般认为，邹伯奇（1819—1869）较早注意到《墨经》含有来自西方的科学知识①。邹伯奇本人对于天文、数学、物理、地理等学科均有研究，所著《学计一得·论西法皆古所有》（1844）认为《墨经》含有西洋数学（如"《经上》云'圜，一中同长也'即《几何》言'圜面惟一心，圜界距心皆等'之意"）、重学（即力学，如"《经说下》'招负衡木'一段"）、视（即光学，如"《经下》'临鉴而立'；'一小而易，一大而正'数语"）等知识。②

邹伯奇的观点得到了友人陈澧（1810—1882）的进一步阐发。陈澧引用《几何原本》《海岛算经》和《九章算术》刘徽注等文献解读《墨经》算法；引证《墨经》条目表明"西洋人制镜之巧，不过窪、突二法，而墨子已知之"；提出《经说下》"'挈，有力也'，'引，无力也'，疑即西人起重之法"③。其后，出现了不少以数学、力学、光学等自然科学知识诠释《墨经》的著述，例如：张自牧的《瀛海论》（1876）与《蠡测卮言》（1878）、殷家儁《格物补笺》（1876）、冯澂《光学述墨》（1894）、王仁俊《格致古微》（1896），等等。

作为校释《墨子》的集大成之作，孙诒让的《墨子间诂》（1895 年初本，1910 年定本）在注释《墨经》时，援引了邹伯奇、陈澧等人的见解，亦采西方科学知识解读《墨经》。此外，他还注意到《墨经》的逻辑学说。1897 年，他致信梁启超："尝谓《墨经》，楬举精理，引而不发，为周名家言之宗。窃疑其必有微言大例，如欧士论理家雅里大得勒之演绎法，培根之归纳法，及佛氏之因明论者。"④

1904 年，梁启超在《新民丛报》第 3 年第 1、2、3 号连载《墨子之论理学》，采用西方传统逻辑研究《墨子》，认为"墨子所谓辩者，即论理学也"，"《墨子》全书殆无一处不用论理学之法则，至专言其法则之所以成立者，则

---

① 持此观点者颇多，可参阅梁启超：《〈墨经通解〉序》，《墨子学案》附录三，《饮冰室合集》专集之三十九，第 8 册，中华书局 1989 年版，第 84－85 页；栾调甫：《二十年来之墨学》，载《墨子研究论文集》，人民出版社 1957 年版，第 140 页；陈柱：《历代墨学述评》，载《墨学十论》，商务印书馆 1928 年版，第 189－190 页；A. C. Graham，Later Mohist Logic，Ethics and Science，The Chinese University Press，1978，pp. 70－71。

② 邹伯奇：《学计一得》，《邹徵君遗书》，载戴念祖主编：《中国科学技术典籍通汇·物理卷》第一分册，河南教育出版社 1995 年版，第 1012 页。

③ 陈澧：《东塾读书记》卷十二《诸子书》，载黄国声主编：《陈澧集》（贰），上海古籍出版社 2008 年版，第 241－242 页。

④ 孙诒让：《与梁卓如论墨子书》，载《籀廎述林》，中华书局 2010 年版，第 382 页。

惟《经说上》《经说下》《大取》《小取》《非命》诸篇为特详"[①]。后来，梁启超借鉴胡适等人的研究成果，撰写了《墨子学案》（1921）和《墨经校释》（1922）。在其看来，逻辑学为《墨经》中最重要的部分，"《经》中论名学原理者约居四之一，其他亦皆用'名学的'之演绎归纳而立义者也"[②]。与《墨子之论理学》相比，《墨子学案》第七章《墨家之论理学及其他科学》对墨家逻辑的论述显得更为详实，此外还基于《墨经》条目阐述形学（几何）、物理学、经济学等学科思想；而《墨经校释》则常借助来自西方的自然科学和社会科学知识予以诠释。

与梁相似，胡适偏重于对墨家逻辑的发掘。其博士论文《先秦名学史》（1917 年写成，1922 年出英文版）及据此完成的《中国哲学史大纲（卷上）》（1919，后于 1930 年改名为《中国古代哲学史》）对于《墨经》的知识论和逻辑学都作了较为详细的论说，此外也例举了《墨经》中有关算学、形学、光学、力学、心理学、人生哲学、政治学、经济学等内容的条目。[③] 当然，清末民初，还有更多学者注重《墨经》逻辑的阐发，如章太炎的《诸子学略说》（1906）和《原名》（1909）、章士钊《逻辑指要》（1917 年写成，1943 年出版）等。

由上可见，梁启超、胡适等学者均已注意到《墨经》所含的各种学科知识。其后，张纯一《墨学分科》（1923）明确采用分科治学的方法整理《墨子》。他将墨学分为教育、政治、宗教三纲，并作细化。（1）教育：教育学、算学、形学、微积分、物理学、力学、机械学、测量学、地圆说、热学、光学、声学、医药学、生物进化说、生理卫生学、心理学、唯识学、他心通、气象学、论理学、伦理学；（2）政治：政治哲学、法理学、理财学、军事学；（3）宗教学。在其看来，广义《墨经》为"墨子用教高材生者"[④]，因此这六篇文献（尤其是《墨经》）是其论证墨家教育类学科的核心文献。此外，也引证《墨经》条目论述墨家的政治哲学、法理学、理财学、宗教学。

更进一步，则是集中处理《墨经》，将各条目依照学科分类予以整理。较早者有张其锽《墨经通解》（1931），该书认为《经上》"上列言性行、修为、

---

① 梁启超：《墨子之论理学》，《子墨子学说》附录，《饮冰室合集》专集之三十七，第 8 册，中华书局 1989 年版，第 56 页。

② 梁启超：《墨经校释 · 读墨经余记》，《饮冰室合集》专集之三十八，第 8 册，中华书局 1989 年版，第 7 页。

③ 参见胡适：《中国古代哲学史》，载欧阳哲生编：《胡适文集》（6），北京大学出版社 2013 年 2 版，第 274－275 页。

④ 张纯一：《墨学分科》，载任继愈主编：《墨子大全》第 28 册，北京图书馆出版社 2003 年影 1923 年排印本，第 617 页。

政治之义，下列言名数质力及人群相用、宇宙相推之理”；《经下》次序“错无可理”，乃“以类为次，关于言辩学者得半，置于上列；关于言修身、心理、政治、经济、数理、天学、光学、重学者得半，置于下列”。[①]

其后，谭戒甫《墨经分类译注》（1957年成书，1981年出版）将《墨经》分成十二类：名言类、自然类、数学类、力学类、光学类、认识类、辩术类、辩学类、政法类、经济类、教学类、伦理类。与之类似，孙中原《〈墨经〉分类译注》（2006）亦分十二类：世界观、认识论、逻辑学、方法论、历史观、经济学、政治学、伦理学、数学、力学物理学和简单机械学、光学、心理学，其中前八类属于哲学和社会科学，后四类属于自然科学。台湾学者陈癸淼《墨辩研究》（1977）则将广义《墨经》分成七类：伦理学、知识论、逻辑思想、辩论学、宇宙观、科学（包括力学、化学、数学、光学、经济学）、论人。[②]

综上可见，近现代《墨经》研究的主要方法是：基于来自于西方的学科分类观念进行分科研究。由诸多研究成果来看，该方法的确促进了墨学（尤其是《墨经》）的复兴。不过，我们也看到各家分类多有差异，以下谨以分科颇为明显的研究为代表，讨论分科研究的方法问题。

二、《墨经》分科研究的方法讨论

对于清末民初的学者来说，发掘《墨经》中的数学、力学、光学、逻辑学等学科思想，常常受到学术救国等实用价值取向影响。[③] 撇开这种取向不论，由于是将《墨经》置于来自西方的近现代学科框架之中，因此有助于《墨经》与近现代学术接轨，便于今人初步了解《墨经》。正如陈癸淼所言：“将同性质、同范畴之各条加以组织，然后以现代学术之眼光作一综述，使此二千余年前之古代学术能纲举目张，并以新面孔呈现于现代人之眼前。”[④] 孙

---

① 张其锽：《墨经通解》叙，载任继愈主编：《墨子大全》第39册，北京图书馆出版社2003年影1931年独志堂印本，第11－12页。

② 除上所述，20世纪中叶以来还有一大批著述研究《墨经》中的各种自然科学与人文社会科学，例如：沈有鼎《墨经的逻辑学》（1954—1955年连载于《光明日报》，1980年结集出版）、葛瑞汉 *Later Mohist Logic, Ethics and Science*（1978）、陈孟麟《墨辩逻辑学》（1979初版，1983修订）、方孝博《墨经中的数学和物理学》（1983）、杨向奎《墨经数理逻辑》（1993）、周云之《墨经校注今译研究——墨经逻辑学》（1993）、梅荣照《墨经数理》（2003），等等。限于篇幅，此不赘述。

③ 相关讨论可参阅张永春：《清代墨学与中国传统思想学术的近代转型》，黄山书社2014年版，第125－155页；何杨：《胡适的中国古代逻辑史研究》，《兰州大学学报》（社会科学版）2017年第2期，第93－99页。

④ 陈癸淼：《墨辩研究》，载《名家与名学：先秦诡辩学派研究》，台湾学生书局2010年版，第230页。

中原亦言："本书的分类，只是为了便利读者在理解时，更容易同现代和西方的知识系统接轨。这是古为今用和洋为中用的一种努力。"① 如果说《墨经》研究旨在面向现代、古为今用，那么将准确理解的近现代学术恰当地用于《墨经》研究，有其合理之处。不过，理解《墨经》文本的原意仍是这种研究不可忽视的前提条件。实际上，诸多分科研究者亦以准确理解文本为己任。

然而，中国古代文本的原意和来自于西方的近现代学科知识或难以兼顾，如梁启超指出研究《墨经》时"借材于域外之学以相发，亦可有意外创获"，但是"标异太过，任情涂附，则以凿汩智，求深益晦，其失又不止如啖赵之狎侮仲尼、荆舒之唐突仓颉而已"。② 实际上，由于《墨经》的作者及其所处时代并无来自西方的近现代学术分科观念，更不会依照近现代学科观念来编排诸条目，因此，如果根据后出外来的学术分科观念审视《墨经》，并且未能证明这些学科与《墨经》学说是同类性质的学问，那么《墨经》的文本顺序难免打乱、其文字难免篡改、其文义难免附会。分科研究将部分文本（如所谓的"光学"类条目）从其所隶属的整体文本（如《墨经》或《墨子》）中抽取出来，在研究时可能导致研究者只集中处理相关内容的条目，而忽略这些条目的上下文，忽略这些条目与其他条目之间的关联，忽略《墨经》条目与其他《墨子》篇章的联系，进而脱离整体文本语境以及文本所处的历史文化背景，而主要依靠现代学科知识进行理解与评价，从而容易出现任意比附的情况。对此，汪奠基曾批评道：

> 《墨经》的科学思想，主要是从实际经验总结得来的。它的许多定义，如"平、中、直、圜、方"等等，都是以当时百工习用的经验为根据的。……近人更有用现代物理学、力学和光学等来解释景、鉴、力、负、挈诸概念的，如果作为帮助了解《墨经》的参考材料说，这样作也未尝不可，但说这种解释就是《墨经》的认识，那就比附失真了。我们认为《墨经》的科学是战国时代的科学。如果一一用近代科学概念或术语附会起来，那不仅无益于《墨经》本身的逻辑认识，而且对古代科学历史本来面目，将会大加损害。③

① 孙中原：《〈墨经〉分类译注》，载《中国逻辑研究》，商务印书馆2006年版，第549页。

② 梁启超：《〈墨经通解〉叙》，载任继愈主编：《墨子大全》第39册，北京图书馆出版社2003年影1931年独志堂印本，第85页。

③ 汪奠基：《中国逻辑思想史料分析》（第一辑），中华书局1961年版，第285－286页。

从具体研究成果来看，分科研究的明显表现有二：一是《墨经》诸条目原有次序的改变，二是大量原文的篡改。

针对表现一，研究者的常见辩护是《墨经》原文本无严格次序，例如，陈癸淼说："墨辩各条之次序均无义理上及文理上之连贯性。"① 谭戒甫也说："《墨经》各条的意义原有一些是前后连贯的，尤其特殊的如光学八条就是顺序排列着；但其它大部分却都是散开的。"② 不过，上述观点实际上是依据后世学者对《墨经》的主观理解。与之相反，有些学者尝试不改变原有次序，而给予具有连贯性的体系化解读。例如，伍非百将《经上》主旨视为"正名"，依次分为散名和专名两编；《经下》主旨为"立说"，依次分为"名辩本论""名理遗说""名辩问题"三编。每编又依次分成数章③。此外，杨宽、汪奠基、曾昭式等也都主张不改变原文次序④。

从分科研究者内部来看，亦有研究者主张存有次序，如张其锽认为"《墨经》分列，当有义例"，上列、下列各有类别⑤。当然，为了符合其观点，他对部分条目的次序作了调整，如将《经上》第 3 条"体，分于兼也"和第 4 条"必，不已也"对换，因其对条目"体"作如下解读："分析为物理数学之奥，故次言之。"⑥ 此外，即便是分科研究者通常也会承认部分条目存在次序，例如：《经上》第 3 – 6 条（即知、虑、知、恕）、第 7 – 9 条（即仁、义、礼）；《经说下》的"光学"条目；等等。由此看来，《墨经》作者并非完全随意编排条目。那么，何以部分条目有次序，部分条目却无次序？是原本如此，还是研究者未能把握古人的用意呢？对此，分科研究者需要给出合理的解释。

---

① 陈癸淼：《墨辩研究》，载《名家与名学：先秦诡辩学派研究》，台湾学生书局 2010 年版，第 229 – 230 页。

② 谭戒甫：《墨经分类译注》自序，中华书局 1981 年版，第 3 页。

③ 伍非百：《墨辩解故·新考定墨子辩经目录》，载《中国古名家言》，中国社会科学出版社 1983 年版，第 7 – 16 页。

④ 参见杨宽：《墨经哲学》，载《杨宽古史论文集》，上海人民出版社 2003 年版，第 525 – 650 页；汪奠基：《中国逻辑思想史料分析》（第一辑）第七章"墨辩的逻辑科学思想分析"，中华书局 1961 年版，第 266 – 401 页；曾昭式：《先秦逻辑新论》第五章"《经上》《经说上》《经下》《经说下》释义"，科学出版社 2018 年版，第 214 – 262 页。关于《墨经》诸条目的连贯性和整体性的解读，将另文探讨。

⑤ 张其锽：《墨经通解》叙，载任继愈主编：《墨子大全》第 39 册，北京图书馆出版社 2003 年影 1931 年独志堂印本，第 11 – 12 页。

⑥ 张其锽：《墨经通解》叙，载任继愈主编：《墨子大全》第 39 册，北京图书馆出版社 2003 年影 1931 年独志堂印本，第 27 页。

针对表现二，其常见辩护是《墨经》原文本就存在讹、脱、衍等诸多错误[①]。虽然原文在历代传抄过程中，的确会发生错误。但是，以此为理由，在无文献版本依据的情况下，主要依靠研究者个人学识（尤其是来自西方的近现代学科知识），采用理校方法校改原文，很容易产生新的错误。梁启超就意识到了这种困难，一方面指出“此经因传写之值乱及讹谬太甚，若拘拘焉望文生义，则必有‘举烛尚明’‘孝经八十宗’之失，故宜以大胆运锐眼，力求本来面目于今本行墨之外”；另一方面又强调“稍掉以轻心，则指鹿为马，移张冠李，厚诬作者，治丝益棼”[②]。从实际校释成果来看，应该多属后者。因此，早在1931年，陈寅恪就曾批评：“今日之墨学者，任何古书古字，绝无依据，亦可随其一时偶然兴会，而为之改移，几若善博者能呼卢成卢，喝雉成雉之比。”[③]

试以“光学”条目为例。姑且不论条目次第、条目划分、标点断句等问题，仅从文字校改方面考察，若以《道藏》本《墨子》为原文依据，通常都对这部分文字进行了或大或小的修改。例如，张其锽、梁启超、谭戒甫、孙中原都认为有八条“光学”类条目，对这八条，张其锽全都作了修改[④]，而其他三位则修改了其中七条[⑤]。与上述四位不同的是，张纯一认为有一条说文可以分成三条，其中两条并无经文，从而认为“光学”条目有十条，并修改了五条[⑥]。虽然校改文字的原因繁多，但是基于西方的光学知识理解《墨经》条目，是其中的一个重要原因，如谭戒甫在校改时常引光学理论为据，校改原文的理由在于与“今光学理不合”[⑦]。

综上所论，采用来自于西方的近现代学科观念研究《墨经》固然有助于今人初步了解《墨经》的基本内容，但是从对文本固有含义的理解来看，该

---

① 参见梁启超：《墨经校释》自序，《饮冰室合集》专集之三十八，第8册，中华书局1989年版，第1-2页；陈癸淼：《墨辩研究》，载《名家与名学：先秦诡辩学派研究》，台湾学生书局2010年版，第229页；孙中原：《〈墨经〉分类译注》，载《中国逻辑研究》，商务印书馆2006年版，第548页。

② 梁启超：《〈墨经通解〉叙》，载任继愈主编：《墨子大全》第39册，北京图书馆出版社2003年影1931年独志堂印本，第85页。

③ 陈寅恪：《冯友兰中国哲学史上册审查报告》，载《金明馆丛稿二编》，生活·读书·新知三联书店2015年3版，第280页。

④ 张其锽：《墨经通解》，载任继愈主编：《墨子大全》第39册，北京图书馆出版社2003年影1931年独志堂印本，第226-240页。

⑤ 梁启超：《墨经校释》，《饮冰室合集》专集之三十八，第8册，中华书局1989年版，第66-69页；谭戒甫：《墨经分类译注》，中华书局1981年版，第64-84页；孙中原：《〈墨经〉分类译注》，载《中国逻辑研究》，商务印书馆2006年版，第637-641页。

⑥ 张纯一：《墨学分科》，载任继愈主编：《墨子大全》第28册，北京图书馆出版社2003年影1923年排印本，第639-641页。

⑦ 参见谭戒甫：《墨经分类译注》，中华书局1981年版，第70、75、80、83页。

方法依然存在诸多问题。

三、关于《墨经》研究方法的思考

关于如何研究中国古代文本，鞠实儿等曾以《九章算术注》为例，提出和实施了一套本土化研究程式，其特点是“拒绝使用任何当时当地不存在的元素来解读和解释文本”[①]。在笔者看来，该程式要义有二：其一，基于文献学、汉语言文字学的研究，获取需要解释的文本材料；其二，基于文本形成的社会文化语境解释文本。应该说，要义一为各门中国传统学问研究的共识，要义二所言“社会文化语境”主要包括“影响文本生成的社会文化事件和作者所使用的本土概念、方法和学说等”[②]，该概念需要根据具体文本进一步澄清。以下，拟结合该本土化研究程式谈谈《墨经》的研究方法。

首先，有必要完成一部《墨子》（包括《墨经》）的集校集释，为后续研究提供文献基础。对此，栾调甫在总结20世纪初期的墨学研究时就曾指出：“《墨子》既无善本，旧校亦多误谬。宜聚诸本，重为校勘，分别章句，刊定读本。次则旧注多疏，且复依违不决。宜合诸家，重为考辨，定所弃取，纂为集注。”[③] 迄今为止，通常还是公认孙诒让《墨子间诂》在《墨子》校释方面的权威地位，然而孙诒让所见版本有限，而且对于《墨经》的校释所获不多，从而存有不足。因此，后来有不少学者对其进行补正。其中，尤其值得一提的是吴毓江的《墨子校注》（1944），该书在搜集版本方面收获颇丰。在《墨经》注释方面常常引作代表的还有高亨的《墨经校诠》（1958），不过，实际上，此书改字甚多。相比于孙诒让、吴毓江等人所处的时代，今天所能掌握的《墨经》版本显然更多，例如，严灵峰《无求备斋墨子集成》（1975）收录了20世纪60年代之前的90余种墨学著作；《墨子大全》（2002—2004）则收录2003年前的300余种墨学著作，尤其是第一编收录明清版本30余种。关于集释，近现代以来注释颇多，需要注意甄别优劣，阐明注释的依据及其合理性，并根据观点异同进行分类处理。

其次，《墨经》各条目的论说往往较为简略，然其作为墨家的经典要义，在《墨子》其他篇章中也多有体现。实际上，《墨经》所述内容不仅多次出现在《墨经》中，而且也出现在其他《墨子》篇章中。因此，有必要基于整本

① 鞠实儿、张一杰：《中国古代算学史研究新途径——以刘徽割圆术本土化研究为例》，载《哲学与文化》2017年第6期，第26页。

② 鞠实儿、张一杰：《中国古代算学史研究新途径——以刘徽割圆术本土化研究为例》，载《哲学与文化》2017年第6期，第26页。

③ 栾调甫：《二十年来之墨学》，载《墨子研究论文集》，人民出版社1957年版，第146页。

《墨子》来解读各条目，将《墨经》置于《墨子》一书的文本语境之中，在其他篇章中寻找《墨经》诸条目诠释的合理性依据（正因如此，以上提出应给《墨子》作集校集释），此即一些学者所言的“以《墨》证《墨》”[①]、“让《墨经》自己来注释自己”[②]。以《经上》第1条“故”为例，其说文中的“体”“端”等术语在《墨经》其他条目中皆有论述，如第二条为“体”，并举“尺之端”为证；第七条为“仁，体爱也”，此外还有“端，体之无序而最前者也”（《墨子·经上》）、“端，是无同也”（《墨子·经说上》）、“尺，前于区穴而后于端，不夹于端与区内”（《墨子·经说上》）等等。此外，从论证方法上看，《墨子》诸篇应该也有所关联。墨子在《非命》诸篇提出的三表/法也为《墨子》其他篇章所共用，虽然《墨经》诸条目都较为简略，但并非缺乏论证，如《墨经》常用“若”字标明例证，《经下》则常以“说在”标明理由。如果将三表/法和《墨经》的论证结合起来考察，将不仅有助于《墨经》的校释，也有助于对三表/法本身的认识[③]。

值得一提的是，除了传世文献，有不少出土文献与墨家存有关联，如信阳长台关楚简《申徒狄》、上博简《容成氏》、清华简《鬼神之明》等，而其他出土文献对于解读《墨经》条目亦有帮助，如裘锡圭曾参考马王堆汉墓帛书、银雀山汉墓竹简等出土文献解读条目“佴”“詷”“廉”“令”。[④]

再次，《墨经》所讨论的术语与话题也为相近时代所共同讨论，如故、类、知、辩、仁、义、礼、信、忠、孝、名实、同异、坚白、无厚等皆为战国诸子所讨论，因此，有必要结合这些相近时代的文献予以研究。例如，关于“坚白”之说，不仅《墨经》多次论及［如“坚白，不相外也”（《墨子·经上》）、“坚白，说在因”（《墨子·经下》）、“坚白之撄相尽”（《墨子·经说上》）、“无坚得白，必相盈也”（《墨子·经说下》）等］，而且其他诸子也多有论说，最为典型的是《公孙龙子·坚白论》，此外还有“离坚白，若悬寓”（《庄子·天地》）、“合同异，离坚白”（《庄子·秋水》）、“以坚白同异之辩相訾”（《庄子·天下》）、“坚白同异之察，入焉而溺”（《荀子·礼论篇》）、“坚白无厚之词章，而宪令之法息”（《韩非子·问辩》）、“坚白之察，无厚之辩外矣”（《吕氏春秋·审分览·君守》）等等。

最后，除了术语、话题的相关性，《墨经》思想也与相近时代其他文献相

---

① 杨宽：《墨经哲学》，载《杨宽古史论文集》，上海人民出版社2003年版，第528页。

② 沈有鼎：《墨经的逻辑学》序，中国社会科学出版社1980年版，第2页。

③ 参见何杨：《论证实践与中国逻辑史研究》，《逻辑学研究》2017年第3期，第151页。

④ 裘锡圭：《〈墨经〉“佴”“詷”“廉”“令”四条校释》，载《裘锡圭学术文集》第四卷，复旦大学出版社2015年版，第423－429页。

关，这也就是要将《墨经》置于更大的社会文化语境之中。不妨回到本文所讨论的分科治墨方法，虽然我们难以在先秦时期找到来自于西方的近现代学科观念，但是这并不表示先秦时人就没有对学问进行分类。例如，《周礼·地官》谈及六艺（礼、乐、射、御、书、数），《论语·先进》谈及孔门四科（德行、言语、政事、文学）。墨子则提出了与孔门四科类似的三分，即“能谈辩者谈辩，能说书者说书，能从事者从事”（《墨子·耕柱》）。其中，谈辩相似于言语、说书相似于文学、从事相似于政事。因此，若能结合先秦时人的学问分类（尤其是墨家的三分）研治《墨经》，或可对其作出更贴近固有含义的理解。当然，这还有待进一步的工作。

四、结语

综上所论，从墨学复兴的维度来看，近现代以来的分科研究的确功不可没，但从理解文本固有含义的维度来看，分科研究则存在诸多问题（如根据来自西方的近现代学科知识改变条目次第、轻易校改原文等）。实际上，从一个多世纪的《墨经》研究情况来看，对于如何理解《墨经》，最为重要的是引说就经、旁行、牒字等体例的发现，而非光学、力学、逻辑学等学科知识的发掘。如今的《墨经》研究应该回到原典，在其形成的社会文化语境中，基于《墨子》文本内证和相近时代相关文献的互证，予以本土解释。

语言学转向为什么是必然的[①]

黄　敏

对于语言学转向与分析哲学的关系，许多人表示了怀疑。[②] 如果从描述的角度看，分析哲学确实与语言哲学渐行渐远。[③] 但是，若要把握分析哲学的基本精神，似乎还找不到比“语言学转向”更好的解释。这里，我们希望了解的不是哲学史事实，而是哲学史的内在机理。我们希望理解，为什么会有分析哲学这样一种哲学形态，并希望获得一种哲学解释，而不是像普莱斯顿[④]那样，从社会角度来解释分析哲学这种社会 - 历史现象。我们希望给出的解释是修正性的，试图弄清分析哲学应该是怎样的，而不仅是它实际上是怎样的。对于一个尚且活着的传统来说，这样的探究当然不仅仅具有历史价值。

对于语言学转向的最佳表述仍然是达米特给出的。按照这种表述，语言学转向意味着接受语言的优先性论题，即

> （1）对思想的哲学解释可以通过对语言所做出的哲学解释获得；
> （2）只能用这种方式得到全面的解释。[⑤]

这里的“思想”就是指陈述句的意义。在达米特看来，弗雷格是语言学转向的完成者。弗雷格在《算术基础》中反对对逻辑做出心理主义解释，

---

① 本文是国家社科基金后期项目“意向性视野中的意义理论”（批准号 16FZX032）的阶段性成果。

② Hans-Johann Glock, *What Is Analytic Philosophy?* Cambridge University Press, 2008, p. 18; Aaron Preston, *Analytic Philosophy: The History of an Illusion*, Continuum International Publishing Group, 2007, p. 2.

③ John Searle, *Intentionality: An Essay in the Philosophy of Mind* (Cambridge University Press, 1983) 是一个非常突出的例子。关于这一趋势的描述，参见［英］哈克：《分析哲学：内容、历史与走向》，载陈波主编：《分析哲学——回顾与反省》，四川教育出版社 2001 年版，第 50 页以下；以及江怡：《论分析哲学运动中的三大转变》，载《中国社会科学》2016 年第 12 期，第 26 - 27 页。

④ Aaron Preston, *Analytic Philosophy: The History of an Illusion*, Continuum International Publishing Group, 2007.

⑤ ［英］达米特：《分析哲学的起源》，王路译，上海译文出版社 2005 年版，第 4 页。

并利用语境原则来达到这一目的。达米特认为，《算术基础》的出版标志着语言学转向的开始，它为弗雷格赢得了分析哲学创始人（grandfather）的殊荣。①

达米特对语言学转向的解释可以引向关于知识论的一个深刻洞见，它表明弗雷格的工作在何种意义上改变了哲学的基本面貌。按语言的优先性论题，语言学转向的关键就在于把知识（思想就是知识的内容）当作一种语言现象，而不是心理现象。须知，自笛卡尔开创近代哲学以来，知识首先就被理解成观念，从而被理解成心理现象，而这一点决定了哲学家们思考知识问题的框架。循此，我们就可以领会到优先性论题的深意——它会改变我们理解知识的方式，而这是基础框架层级的改变，它构成真正的进步。

但是，达米特的思路并未向这个方向推进——他没有把语言学转向与知识论的一般形态联系起来，而是与语言哲学在整个哲学领域中的地位相联系。这里的区别在于，如果语言学转向对知识论一般形态的转变起作用，那么分析哲学与近代哲学之间的连续性就可以得到很好的解释。从而，分析哲学的革命之处也就能得到很好的解释。而如果仅仅是把语言学转向与语言哲学的崛起联系起来，那就不仅难以解释为什么语言突然重要起来了，而且，随着语言哲学让位于心灵哲学，分析传统的真实身份也就暧昧不明了。

对于语言学转向的另外一种成型的解释是哈克给出的。在他看来，语言学转向与人们对理解的追求联系在一起。理解主要体现在概念而不是知识上，这样，概念问题与事实问题之间的区分，也就成为分析哲学的主要成就。这种区分在前期维特根斯坦关于言说与显示的区分上，以及在后期维特根斯坦的哲学治疗观中，得到了最完全的体现。② 哈克的解释完全跳过了弗雷格，而把语言学转向与维特根斯坦联系在一起。我们当然可以把维特根斯坦看作语言学转向的顶点，但是，跳过弗雷格，就让我们完全不清楚语言学转向为什么会发生。如果情况就像哈克所想的那样，哲学本来就应该围绕概念问题展开，那么我们就无法弄清，语言学转向为何没有早些发生。

我们这里要给出的解释则从达米特和哈克都忽略的一个要素开始，那就是由弗雷格发起，罗素与维特根斯坦都加以接受的逻辑主义计划开始。逻辑主义

---

① ［英］达米特：《分析哲学的起源》，王路译，上海译文出版社 2005 年版，第二章。

② 参见 Peter Hacker, *Analytic Philosophy: Beyond the Linguistic Turn and Back Again*, edited by Michael Beaney, The Analytic Turn, New York: Routledge, 2007; Peter Hacker, *The Linguistic Turn in Analytic Philosophy*, in *The Oxford Handbook of The History of Analytic Philosophy*, edited by Michael Beaney, Oxford, 2013。关于哈克的这种哲学观的讨论，可以参见胡欣诣：《“语言转向”已成过去了吗？——哈克与威廉姆森之争》，载《哲学分析》2012 年第 5 期，第 121 – 138 页。陈嘉映对于语言学转向也持有相似的理解，参见陈嘉映：《语言转向之后》，载《江苏社会科学》2009 年第 5 期，第 26 – 33 页。

计划是连接近代哲学与分析哲学的桥梁，它可以同时解释分析哲学为何从一种知识论研究开始，以及语言为何会在分析哲学家那里如此重要。[①]

接下来，本文第一节说明近代哲学的知识论架构；第二节说明逻辑主义计划与这一架构的关系，而语境原则，则作为实现逻辑主义计划的途径而被引入；第三节则说明，语境原则如何促成了语言学转向，进而如何拒斥了心理主义；第四节则说明语言学转向的最终依据。

1. 观念理论

近代哲学实际上把知识论作为观念理论（theory of idea）来加以讨论。这样做就预先假定了，知识以观念的形态存在，而观念是一种心理学实体。观念理论与"观念论"（idealism）没有关系。在笛卡尔之后，把观念理解为心理学实体的这种意义应当是最为基础的。虽然在德国古典哲学那里，尤其是在黑格尔那里，"观念"已经完全脱离了这一最初的意义，但这并不影响人们理解知识所使用的基本架构。这种架构就是由上述预设所决定的。

按照观念理论来理解，知识就是心灵中的一种观念，这种观念表征了所知道的事物，从而，心灵通过拥有观念来知道观念所表征的事物。这种表征功能对观念来说是本质性的，至于观念本身是什么，则受制于这种表征功能。因此，观念常常被理解为表象。[②] 这种理解的结果是，人们会用谈论事物的方式来谈论观念。比如人们会说有白色的观念等。笛卡尔通过设计怀疑论来打破观念与事物间的相似关系，但后来又利用上帝来加以修复。贝克莱则认为，如果事物与观念不相似，那么事物将是不可理解的。

这就产生了一个效果，人们会像谈论关于事物的知识一样，来谈论关于观念的知识。按照上述模式，这将在心灵中引入表征了观念的观念，即一种二阶的观念。但是，笛卡尔论证道，我们关于观念的知识是不可怀疑的，我们不需要借助其他东西的担保，就能够知道观念——我们直接知道观念；与此不同，我们关于事物的知识则是间接的。这样一来也就免除了二阶观念的必要。这种直接知识与间接知识的划分，导致了近代哲学中标志性的二元论，即心与物的区分，或者说，内与外的区分。直接知识是通过内省获得的。内省与普通感官知觉相似，区别只在于它朝向心灵"内部"。

近代哲学家还基本上共享这样一个看法：知识论研究的任务就是讨论，如

---

① 斯鲁格强调了逻辑主义的重要性，不过是从先验哲学角度，而没有处理它与语言学转向的关系。参见［美］斯鲁格：《弗雷格》，江怡译，中国社会科学出版社 1989 年版。

② Descartes, *The Philosophical Writings of Descartes*, Vol. Ⅱ, trans. by John Cottingham et al, Cambridge, 1984, pp. 25 – 26.

何以这些直接知识为基础，使间接知识，尤其是关于心灵之外的事物的知识获得辩护。这就是基础主义的知识论计划，它要求划分基础的和上层的知识领域，并让上层知识通过基础知识获得辩护。这个任务其实就等于要解决笛卡尔所设置的关于外部世界的怀疑论。人们认为，在这一点上，笛卡尔没有获得成功。尽管如此，笛卡尔还是通过设置怀疑论，通过区分可以怀疑的东西和不容怀疑的东西，而建立了思考知识的框架。

这个框架有一个很重要的特征：由于知识被“落实”到心理学实体上，心灵与观念之间的认识论关系同时又是存在物之间的关系。有时人们设想，观念像盒子里的东西一样被盛放在心灵中，而更多的想象则是，观念就像可供观看的图像一样矗立在心灵之眼面前。这种存在物间的关系被认为实现了心灵与其直接认识的观念之间的那种被称为“知道”的关系。心灵与观念间的认识论关系与形而上学关系的这种重合，就自然而然地让人们认为，就像腺体分泌体液一样，心灵也会分泌知识。知识的认识论特性因而就会受制于心灵的生理－心 理特性，由此自然而然引向了知识论上的自然主义，按照这种自然主义观点，知识的可靠性将通过心理学原理或者生理学原理来得到保证。①

当按照物与物的关系来想象知识变得自然，由于心灵是特殊的存在物，人们就会倾向于把心灵与观念的关系想成特殊物的关系。比如，人们会认为，同一个观念不会同时存在于两个心灵中，这与同一只台球不可能同时在两张台球桌上滚过一样。由于心灵与观念间的这种关系同时又是一种知识论关系，人们就会认为，就“直接知道”这种关系而言，观念是私人性的，没有心灵会直接知道其他心灵中的观念。这种私人性不仅会建立在不同心灵之间，甚至也会在处于不同瞬间的同一心灵之间。作为特殊物，不同瞬间的观念是不同的，于是它们与同一个心灵建立的关系也是不同的。这意味着，当前的这个心灵不会直接知道其他瞬间的观念。

直接知识的这种私人性与瞬间性意味着，回忆与关于他人心理状态的知识与关于外部世界的知识一样，只有在解决了怀疑论问题以后才能得到保障。怀疑论所施加的这种理论压力非常巨大。我们将会看到，这种压力压垮了观念理论的知识论架构本身。

2. 逻辑主义与语境原则

逻辑主义计划的目标就是在纯粹逻辑的基础上论证算术知识，也就是说，把算术还原成逻辑。弗雷格的逻辑主义计划虽然被公认失败了，但他为这个计

---

① Descartes, *The Philosophical Writings of Descartes*, Vol. Ⅰ, trans. by John Cottingham et al, Cambridge, 1984, p. 165ff.

划所做出的准备工作，却真正建立了现代意义上的数理逻辑。[①] 弗雷格为这种逻辑所做出的理论阐述虽然不成系统，但其理论深度和洞察力却让人印象深刻。

很容易看出，逻辑主义计划是基础主义观点的产物。这里，逻辑知识被认为是基础，弗雷格希望从中导出算术知识。逻辑主义计划的这种特性使其从属于近代哲学，也就是说，从属于以知识论为第一哲学的近代哲学形态。作为分析哲学的初始形态，逻辑主义计划的这一特性表明了分析哲学与近代哲学之间的连续性，从而为分析哲学的建立赋予了知识论上的动机。后面我们会看到，这种动机对于我们理解语言学转向以及分析哲学是如何起作用的。

逻辑主义计划的最初形成与 19 世纪中期的数学发展状况有关。非欧几何的诞生引发了对于数学基础的思考。人们意识到数学证明的不严格性对于理解数学基础来说构成了障碍，而这种不严格性又与数学证明中的诉诸直觉相关。对数学严格性的追求是把算术还原成逻辑的直接动因[②]，而逻辑就成为把直觉驱逐出算术的终极武器。而对于还原计划的实施，则一方面让弗雷格得以构造出第一个现代意义上的数理逻辑系统，另一方面让他得以思考推理的本质。这种思考产生了丰硕的哲学果实。

数学证明的严格性与符号的使用有关。按照莱布尼茨的“通用文字”设想，严格的论辩应该采取符号演算的方式进行。论辩的双方把观点和推理步骤写成符号的形式，然后按照规则来进行符号演算，这种演算就是一种严格的推理。这个设想的关键是，在演算的过程中，符号的意义不起作用，人们只需辨别符号本身即可。对符号的识别取决于人们是如何使用符号的，因此，对于有语言能力的人来说，对符号的错误识别是不可能的，符号演算过程的严格性也由此得到保证。

弗雷格用一种巧妙的方式来达到用符号保证推理严格性的目的，这种方式就是为符号定义概念内容。简单说来，符号的概念内容就是“对逻辑推理有价值的东西”[③]，为了弄清这种有价值的东西是什么，需要仔细观察一下什么是逻辑推理。

逻辑推理实际上是命题之间的一种连接关系，沿着这种连接关系，我们可以从一个命题过渡到另一个命题。从这个角度看，符号的概念内容，作为对逻

① 但弗雷格的逻辑观与当代的逻辑观存在着足够大的区别，参见 Warren Goldfarb，Frege's conception of logic，*The Cambridge Companion to Frege*，edited by Michael Potter and Tom Ricketts，University of Cambridge，2010，pp. 63 – 85。

② 参见 Paul Benacerraf，Frege：The Last Logicist，in *Midwest Studies in Philosophy* Vol. 6，1981。

③ Gottlob Frege，Begriffsschrift，in *The Frege Reader*，edited and translated by Michael Beaney，Routledge，1997，p. 49.

辑推理有价值的东西，其价值就应当是使这种连接得以建立。不妨看这样一个推理（这里用箭头表示实质蕴涵）：

$p \rightarrow q$；$q \rightarrow r$；由此推出 $p \rightarrow r$。

在这个推理中，符号“p”“q”以及“r”对于推理有价值的地方在于，它们分别是两个命题符号中共同的东西。比如，“p”是“$p \rightarrow q$”与“$p \rightarrow r$”共同的东西，而它本身具体表示什么，则是不重要的。这样，符号“p”的概念内容，就是“$p \rightarrow q$”与“$p \rightarrow r$”这两个命题符号所表达的命题内容中共同的东西。当不同的概念内容用不同符号来表示，我们就能通过操作符号来进行推理。由于符号所表示的内容仅仅作为不同命题间共同的东西起作用，这些符号所表达的，也就是推理的模式。当把其中的“p”“q”“r”这样的命题符号换成自然语言中的句子，我们就得到具体的推理，它们的有效性由推理模式保证。

这就与自然推理不同。自然推理依据所使用的词语意义进行，我们通过了解词语所表示的东西是什么，来判断推理是否有效。如果对于词语所指之物所知不同，那么，对于有些人来说能够成立的推理，对另外一些人来说就不会成立。这样的推理是不严格的，原因是它诉诸直觉。诉诸直觉的推理是否有效，取决于所指之物实际上是怎样的。比如，我们能否从三角形两条中线交点的位置推论出另外两条中线交点的位置，取决于三角形的三条中线是否交于一点，而后者则由三角形的特性决定。在诉诸直觉的推理中，推理的有效性建立在非语言性的事实上，而严格的推理，其严格性则仅仅取决于语言。

诉诸直觉的推理与符号推理的区别有着巨大的理论价值，而这种价值只有在基础主义背景下才体现出来。基础主义所理解的辩护，必须能够在怀疑论情境中起作用，必须是为怀疑论者所接受的辩护。一般而言，这里的怀疑论针对的是关于所辩护那个命题或那一类命题。但是，诉诸直觉的推理由于需要事先拥有关于对象的知识，而为怀疑论者所不能接受。因此，作为辩护基础的逻辑，就必须排除直觉，完全采取符号推理的形式。

当然，这并不意味着一定要使用人工语言来进行推理。严格性所要求的仅仅是，所有对于推理有价值的东西都必须表现在符号中。自然语言也是一种符号，因此，自然语言只要能够达到这种要求，用自然语言进行的推理，也是严格的。

基于上述对于严格性的理解，要让逻辑在逻辑主义计划中起作用，就必须能够对比如数学命题这样的非逻辑命题运用推理模式，从而得到严格的辩护。

正是这种可运用性，要求语境原则对于意义来说普遍成立，也就是说，要求“只能在句子语境中探究词语的意义”①。

“在句子语境中探究词语的意义”，就是把词语意义理解为对句子意义所做出的贡献，而那些没有作出这种贡献的部分，则不是所需要关注的意义②。这种理解方式是对概念内容这个概念加以提炼的结果。词语的概念内容就是词语对于句子所参与的推理产生影响的那部分内容，而这部分内容是不同的句子内容中重合的部分。因此，词语的概念内容是对句子内容进行“切分”得到的，这种“切分”表现了句子所参与推理的模式。语境原则要求，只能把这些“切分”出来的东西当作词语的意义，而无需考虑据说也是通过词语表达的其他内容。

只能在句子语境中探究词语的意义，这看起来是一种方法论的指导原则，它说明我们该如何分析词语的意义，以便用适于严格推理的形式来表示句子。然而，这个原则完全可以理解成表述了意义这个概念的本质，理解成意义的形而上学特性。这还是在逻辑主义背景下理解的结果。在这个背景下，如果我们拥有相应的知识，那么，考虑到怀疑论者的要求，这些知识就应当能够以严格推理为基础加以辩护，而这就意味着，这些知识必须能够以满足严格推理要求的方式表述，也就是说，相应词语的意义要满足语境原则。

语境原则所说的实际上是，词语的意义就其能够表达知识而言，必须是由句子语境所决定的。这就是说，句子意义在逻辑上优先于词语的意义，词语意义接受句子语境的约束。

这种优先性意味着，我们不可能脱离句子语境来确定词语的意义。假设能够这么做，那么我们就能够在句子语境之外，从而在辩护语境之外（只有句子才能参与辩护，而词语不能），来确定词语的意义。这样一来，在句子语境之内确定的意义也就必须与在其外确定的意义相同才行。但是，确定这种意义上的相同总是需要对象的事实来支持，而这也是怀疑论者所不能接受的。

比如，假定我们在辩护中使用了“启明星早晨位于东方”这个句子，这个句子可以视为确定了“启明星”一词的意义，而这个词又通过其他方式确定了意义，比如确定了“启明星”表示傍晚位于西方的那颗星。这时，要借助那个句子为在后面那种方式中关于启明星的谈论做出辩护，就需要一个新的

---

① Gottlob Frege, *The Foundations of Arithmetic: A Logical-methematical Enquiry into the Concept of Number*, 2nd revised edition, trans. by J. L. Austin, New York: Harpers & Brothers, 1960, p. 22.

② 弗雷格把意义区分为涵义与指称，因此语境原则相应地也要在这两种层次上分别解释。但是，在提出语境原则时他的这个区分还没有做出，我们这里也就不考虑这个区分。

事实，即早晨位于东方的那颗星到了傍晚转移到了西方。

当然，在为关于启明星的 A 命题做出辩护时，我们一般可以借助关于它的 B 事实。在所辩护的是关于特定对象的知识时，这常常是被允许的。但是，在一般性的哲学分析中，比如在为自然数进行逻辑分析时，我们关注的是一类事物的本性，这时，这类情况是不允许的。

这样，借助逻辑主义的知识论动机，我们得以理解为何会有语境原则。语境原则是贯彻可辩护性要求的结果。

3. 语境原则与语言学转向

贯彻语境原则的结果就是促成语言学转向，即建立语言之于意义（思想）的逻辑优先性。

语境原则看起来形成了一个循环：为了确定词语的意义，我们需要先确定句子的意义，但是，确定句子意义，又要借助词语的意义。看起来，这个循环会让我们无法确定词语和句子任何一方的意义。然而，这个循环只不过意味着，我们必须一同确定那些词语的意义。

句子是词语通过特定的关系结合而成的结构，因此，在确定特定词语的意义之前，句子仅仅作为一种结构出现。为了实现句子的知识论价值，这些结构被赋予了特定的语义学功能。比如，弗雷格就为完整的陈述句赋予了函项结构，并区分出主目和函项词，从而为之确定相应的意义类型。句子的这种结构是作为句法特征出现的，因为，在被赋予特定的意义之前，填充这种结构的只能是句法实体，是纯粹语言性的东西。比如，在弗雷格的语言系统中，我们有名称和概念词这样的句法实体。照这样的理解，语境原则就等于说，在句子的句法结构就位了以后，才能赋予词语以意义。由于句子的具体意义在这之后才能确定，我们最终得到的就是句法结构（进而语言）之于（词语和句子的）意义的逻辑优先性。

语境原则的这种内涵被弗雷格给予了充分的重视。[1] 在《算术基础》中，他把语境原则当作拒斥心理主义的首要途径。[2] 19 世纪中期的德语哲学家试图把逻辑（以及整个知识论的基础）建立在心理学的基础上，这种做法在《算术基础》以及《思想》中遭到了猛烈的抨击。

---

① 有哲学家认为弗雷格后来放弃了语境原则，对此，哈克在《语义整体论：弗雷格与维特根斯坦》（载涂纪亮主编：《语言哲学名著选辑》，生活·读书·新知三联书店 1988 年版，第 35－66 页）中给予了驳斥。

② Gottlob Frege, *The Foundations of Arithmetic: A Logical-methematical Enquiry into the Concept of Number*, 2nd revised edition, trans. by J. L. Austin, New York: Harpers & Brothers, 1960, p. 22.

但是，弗雷格究竟在何种意义上拒斥心理主义，达米特和斯鲁格对此却存在不同看法。在达米特看来，弗雷格是一边站在实在论一边反对心理主义，因为他用心理表象来解释知识[①]；而在斯鲁格看来，他则是站在康德先验论反对自然主义，这种自然主义学说希望通过对心理学的经验研究来建立逻辑[②]。不过，达米特在说弗雷格的目的是捍卫知识的客观性的同时又补充说，由于坚持在句子语境中确定词语意义，而这等于也要在句子语境中确定词语所指称的对象，弗雷格所说的客观性，不是体现为对象的独立存在的那种客观性，而是体现为关于对象的陈述所拥有的真值。[③]

若要给出一种哲学的解释，那就自然希望把这两种看法综合到一起。这种综合的工作到下一节才会结束，这里先起个头。

语境原则相当于给出了一种整体论语义学，它主张词项的意义要在与其他词项的连接中确定。这种整体论语义学可以说构成了康德先验哲学的一部分，因为这种先验哲学包含了一种概念理论，它把概念之间的连接关系当作本质性的规定，而先验哲学则把这种概念的连接当作概念具有表征能力的前提条件。如果这样理解，那么斯鲁格所说的弗雷格对于自然主义的不满，也就在于自然主义错误地以为概念间这种连接可以通过经验建立起来。于是，在批评心理主义时，弗雷格就可以重复康德对经验主义的批判。在这种意义上，经验主义的弊端就要通过贯彻语境原则来加以避免，因为经验本身就是独立于语言的，而语境原则把这种不诉诸语言的概念连接排除在外。

如果弗雷格在达米特的那种意义上理解客观性，那么他对心理主义的指责就不应该停留于表象的主观性上，而在于由于他诉诸心理实体来解释意义时，让知识内容脱离了句子，从而脱离了辩护。而鉴于语境原则与关于知识的辩护要求已经建立起来的那种联系，语境原则可以在何种意义上避免心理主义带来的主观性，也就容易理解了。

接下来就需要论证，当用心理实体来解释意义时，确实也就让知识内容不可能进入辩护。这个论证是由维特根斯坦最终给出的，它可以视为语言学转向的主论证。

4. 私人语言与观念理论

哈克虽然不恰当地忽视了弗雷格，但他还是正确地看到，语言学转向是在

---

① ［英］达米特：《弗雷格——语言哲学》，黄敏译，商务印书馆 2017 年版，第 899 – 900 页。

② ［美］斯鲁格：《弗雷格》，江怡译，中国社会科学出版社 1989 年版，第一、二章。

③ ［英］达米特：《弗雷格——语言哲学》，黄敏译，商务印书馆 2017 年版，第 40 – 41 页，第 470 – 475 页。

维特根斯坦那里完成的。弗雷格为语言学转向定了基调，但并未从哲学上发展它，是维特根斯坦把这个基调发展成了强有力的主旋律——在他笔下，整个哲学的任务就是语言分析。由于忽视了维特根斯坦与弗雷格之间的承接关系[①]，哈克未能看到语言学转向的深层机制。

维特根斯坦为语言学转向提供的关键构件，就是私人语言论证。这个论证从观念理论的基本假设中导出了不可接受的结论，从而在否定观念理论的同时，肯定了语言之于意义的优先性。[②]

按照观念理论的基本假设，知识是一种观念。这意味着，用语言来表达知识，就是利用符号与观念的对应关系，来让人们从符号追溯到相应的观念。这里，符号的意义就是与之形成固定的对应关系的观念。这种对应或许是通过"任意的安排"建立的[③]，或许是通过某种习惯建立[④]。由于观念是一种心理学实体，从而独立于语言而存在，与符号建立对应关系的，也就是事先确定好的东西。维特根斯坦的论证表明，这样理解语言与其意义的关系，将使得意义成为不能表达的东西。

维特根斯坦建议读者考虑这样一种情况：假设我（读者自己）为自己的一种感觉做一份日记，用一个特定的记号来表示这种感觉的出现，然后每当这种感觉出现，就在日记本上写下那个记号。[⑤] 这是一种私人的感觉日记，这一情境的设置恰好与观念理论相一致。我自己先让符号与感觉对应起来，以此确定符号的意义，此后，就使用这个符号来记录感觉的出现。维特根斯坦对这种私人日记的评论是这样的：当我为符号下定义时，我会把注意力集中在那种感觉上，这样做要"使我将来能正确回忆起这种联系，但在这个例子里我全然没有是否正确的标准"[⑥]。在没有正确与否的标准的情况下，我们只能说，对符号的定义失败了，我不能用这种方式来记录我的感觉。

为了看出维特根斯坦是如何达到这个结论的，不妨设想，我用"E"这个符号来表示这种感觉。后来又出现了一种感觉，我觉得就是当初对应于"E"的那种感觉，于是就在日记本上写下"E"这个符号。这就是私人日记的场

---

① 关于这种关系，参见 Michael Beaney, *Wittgenstein and Frege*, *A Companion to Wittgenstein*, John Wiley & Sons, Ltd., 2017, pp. 74 – 91。

② 这个论证很可能是针对罗素的亲知理论。这种亲知理论明确承认知觉知识的私人性，参见 Bertrand Russell, *The Problems of Philosophy*, Oxford, 1912, ch. V。然而，亲知理论分享了观念理论的基本假设，我们很容易就可以把这个论证看作是针对观念理论的。

③ ［英］洛克：《论人类的认识》（旧译《人类理解论》），胡景钊译，上海人民出版社 2017 版，第 384 页。

④ ［英］休谟：《人性论》，关文运译，商务印书馆 1980 年版，第 33 页。

⑤ ［奥地利］维特根斯坦：《哲学研究》，陈嘉映译，上海人民出版社 2001 年版，第 258 节。

⑥ ［奥地利］维特根斯坦：《哲学研究》，陈嘉映译，上海人民出版社 2001 年版，第 258 节。

景。维特根斯坦建议我们考虑这样一个问题：我该如何判断我记录得是否正确呢？也就是说，我该如何判断当前出现的那种感觉就是被当作意义赋予了“E”的那种感觉呢？看来我需要回忆一下在为“E”下定义时出现的感觉是什么。现在，问题来了——只有正确地回忆起当初的感觉，我才能运用这个定义，但是，要确保回忆正确，我必须已经正确地回忆起当初的感觉，因为，回忆得正确与否，是通过与回忆起的那种感觉对比来确定的。这个循环使得以前在符号与感觉之间建立的对应关系不可能充当正确使用符号的标准。

显然，论证的着力点不像艾耶尔（1998 年）以为的那样，是记忆的可靠性，而是运用标准时陷入的循环。① 在后面的段落中，维特根斯坦多次提示这种循环的存在。② 为了解决这一问题，维特根斯坦建议把不同的符号在特定的使用活动中连接起来，从而让我们有独立的标准，来判断那种感觉是否真的出现。③ 当然，由于是用在为符号赋予意义的场合，这种连接也就不是符号的意义之间的连接，而是符号与符号之间的通过使用活动达成的连接。这种整体论的特点让我们想起语境原则，这可以算是语境原则的一个推广版本。

进一步可以看出，私人定义之所以会陷入循环，是因为来自于辩护的压力。符号“E”使用得正确与否，是需要辩护的。这种辩护需要符号之间的结合，这种结合为“E”的使用正确与否提供了标准。与此同时，这种结合作为辩护的先决条件，要求承诺整体论。

应当说，定义本身是无需辩护的。当科学家把巴黎标准尺的长度定义为一米时，他不需要为这种定义进行辩护。但是，如果标准尺的长度可以单独地确定，那么在将其定义为一米时，也就需要考虑其长度变化的可能性，从而也就需要一种标准，来确定其长度是否发生了变化。在定义一米是多长时，我们需要这样的标准，来确保当初确实把一个确定的长度定义为一米。这个标准随后要被用来判断是否正确地使用了“一米”这个词。辩护的需要来自定义项的独立性。

我们可以用原子振动的波长来充当标准，也可以用别的，比如光在某个时间段走过的距离。无论用什么来衡量标准尺长度是否发生变化，这个标准已经先就与“一米”这个词语联系了起来。无论标准尺的实际长度是多少，这种联系必须已经建立。如果我们把标准尺的实际长度当作是“一米”这

---

① ［英］艾耶尔：《可能有一种私人语言吗?》，载［美］A. P. 马蒂尼奇编，牟博等译：《语言哲学》，商务印书馆 1998 年版，第 873 – 886 页。

② ［奥地利］维特根斯坦：《哲学研究》，陈嘉映译，上海人民出版社 2001 年版，259、265、268 节。

③ ［奥地利］维特根斯坦：《哲学研究》，陈嘉映译，上海人民出版社 2001 年版，270 节。

个词的意义，那么先于定义建立的上述联系也就属于语言，或者说，属于使用语言的行为。因此，通过维特根斯坦的论证得以建立的，是语言之于意义的优先性。

私人语言论证击中了观念理论的要害。它可以看作对观念理论的归谬论证。首先，考虑到在辩护语境中我们仍然需要接受怀疑论的前提，在观念理论框架下，对语言作出定义时所能够使用的就只能是免予怀疑的知识，即直接知识。但是，既然直接知识具有瞬时性和私人性，不同时刻以及不同人的观念之间就是相互独立的。这样我就来到了私人感觉日记的场景中，从而有义务为符号的使用正确与否作出辩护。但是，如论证所示，我没有判断正确与否的标准，因此最初给出的定义是无效的。

至于对观念理论的主观主义理解和经验主义理解，则可以看出汇聚到了一起。从主观主义角度理解，观念以表象的形式出现，由此理解的知识强烈地依赖于内省方法，而从自然主义的角度理解观念理论，则观念是来自于外部世界刺激产生的结果，因此知识本质上可以用自然科学来处理。在这两种情况下，观念的私人性与瞬间性都将成立，这使其导向同一种后果。

表面上看，对自然主义的理解借助了自然科学来解释观念，而既然自然科学是公共可观察的、拥有恒常基础的东西，观念似乎也就摆脱了私人性与瞬间性。但是，这只是调转了看问题的视角。自然主义者之所以以为可以利用自然科学来处理知识，只是因为他在观念理论所要求的第一人称视角与自然科学天然的第三人称视角之间来回切换。这种切换并未改善我们对知识的理解。在观念理论那里，心灵与观念间的关系具有双重性，它们同时是存在物间的形而上学关系与主体－对象间的知识论关系。造成观念的私人性与瞬间性的是这种双重性，而自然主义并未消除这种双重性。自然主义者希望利用关于心灵的自然科学成果来解释知识，就相当于用存在物间的形而上学关系来解释知识论关系。但是，只有当我们带着这种自然科学解释回到心灵自身的第一人称视角，我们才能确信这是对知识的解释。这样我们就恢复了上述双重性，而私人性与瞬间性仍将主导我们对于知识的理解。

一旦拒绝把知识理解为观念，自然的选择就是，把知识与语言联系起来，从而将其理解为语言能力的一种运用。这当然不是说，知识的存在要以任何特定语言的存在作为前提，而是说，只有结合语言能力，我们才能获得对知识的一种合乎要求的理解。这种要求就是，知识必须是可以辩护的，而这种所要求的辩护最终将追溯到人们对于语言的使用。

知识论转向提升了哲学思考的层次，这是因为笛卡尔通过怀疑论所提出的辩护问题成为了提出哲学观点前必须解决的问题。当哲学家给出某种哲学知识时，实际上也就是在宣称自己知道这些知识，而笛卡尔的问题则是，哲学家们有什么资格认为自己知道这些。与知识论转向相比，语言学转向（或“语言转向”）进一步提升了哲学思考的层次。这是因为，想要解决辩护问题，以对知识与辩护拥有恰当的理解为前提才有可能，而这种恰当的理解要通过语言学转向才能获得。

智能机器的道德问题研究

黄子瑶　徐嘉玮

一、智能机器的新兴及其伦理挑战

2016 年 9 月 20 日，美国交通部发布了全球第一份关于自动驾驶汽车的政策性文件《联邦自动驾驶汽车政策》（*Federal Automated Vehicles Policy*），这标志着自动驾驶汽车正式从专业技术领域走向公共事务领域，相关的产业、管理、法律、道德等方面的讨论已被提上日程。事实上，自动驾驶汽车自 20 世纪 80 年代至今已经历了 30 余年的开发过程，而这项技术之所以迟迟未能投入市场，除了技术尚且不成熟之外，在伦理方面遇到困难也是一个重要的原因。毕竟，开车不仅仅是一项技术活，同时也是一种道德实践。一个合格的司机除了需要熟练掌握驾车技术之外，还需要掌握许多规章制度、驾驶规范和行车礼仪。当在道路上发生了事故和争执的时候，我们还需要判断当事人的对错并明确责任的归属。因此，解决了驾车技术问题只是开发自动驾驶汽车的第一步—— 尽管是至关重要的一步——接下来还需要克服自动驾驶汽车所带来的道德和法律上的挑战。

自动驾驶汽车并非唯一的新兴智能机器。近数十年来，随着自动化技术、人工智能和机器人行业的长足发展，已经有许多不同种类的智能机器走进了我们的生活，并且在工业生产、科学考察、灾难救援、军事行动和网络服务等领域扮演着越来越重要的角色。然而，如同自动驾驶汽车一样，智能机器在为人们带来经济效益和生活品质的同时，也引发了人们对机器道德的担忧——机器会不会给人类带来危害？应该如何处理机器引发的事故？如何能让机器遵守人类制订的道德规范？回应这些担忧不仅是技术人员的职责，哲学从业者也有义务承担这项工作，对机器的道德属性做一般的考察。

放眼历史，智能机器面临伦理挑战的境况与 20 世纪六七十年代医学和生命科学的境遇相似，当时，器官移植、基因工程、遗传筛查、安乐死等新技术开始投入应用，于是它们所涉及的道德问题受到了普遍重视，并引发了广泛争论。但是，争论并未使医学和生命科学停滞发展，相反，挑战最终转换成了机遇，产生了极具生命力的跨领域合作学科——生命伦理学。有鉴于此，我们有理由相信：第一，随着自动化、人工智能等技术的发展，对智能机器的道德属性进行研究是一个必然趋势；第二，这种研究最终也会产生一个富有生命力的跨领域合作学科——机器伦理学。

目前，国内外学者对机器伦理学的研究仍处于起步阶段，相关讨论主要集中于两个基本问题：第一个问题是机器的道德主体性问题，它关注的是机器原则上是否可能对它的行为负道德责任，并且如果回答是肯定的话，接受这样一个人工道德主体（artificial moral agent，简称“AMA”）需要满足哪些条件。第二个问题是机器的道德行动机制的设计问题，亦即应当采取什么样的设计思路来设计并制造机器，它才能够合乎道德地行动。本文接下来的两节将分别讨论这两个问题。

二、道德主体性问题

与传统伦理学的研究对象——人的道德实践相比，自动驾驶汽车等智能机器的道德实践具有显著的特殊性：第一，机器行为是由人为设计的计算过程所决定的，这不是自然的因果过程，从而使得机器行为区别于一般的意外或自然灾害；第二，机器行为在很大程度上不由其使用者来决定，这使得机器不同于传统意义上的工具；第三，对于具有广泛适用性、需处理复杂情况的机器——尤其是拥有学习能力的机器——设计师和制造商很难或原则上不可能准确预料机器行为，或是对机器行为进行控制。这种特殊性导致传统的道德责任归属不适用于智能机器。以自动驾驶汽车为例，如果一种具有较高可靠性的自动驾驶汽车违背了行车礼仪或者造成了交通事故，那么将事件视作意外、要求乘客负责或要求设计师负责的做法都不能让人信服。因此，有必要考虑一种看似荒诞的解决方案：让汽车为自己造成的事故负责。

要机器为自己的行为负责，前提是机器可能具有道德主体性。这意味着机器的行为是自由的，因为仅当机器的行为是自由的，将道德责任归属于机器的做法才是合理的。传统道德哲学关于道德责任归属的讨论围绕着自由与必然之间的关系而展开，并在此基础上发展出了三种不同的立场：主张决定论与自由意志之间存在矛盾的不相容论观点，主张二者不矛盾的相容论观点，以及斯特劳森所主张的不考虑二者间关系的反应态度学说（也称斯特劳森式相容论）。接下来我们将分别考察这三种立场，看看它们是否容许机器的道德主体性。

在三种立场中，所谓相容论和不相容论都是针对决定论和自由行动之间的关系而言的。其中，决定论指的是一种主张“凡事皆有因”的观点，认为世界上任何事情都有先前就存在的、充分的原因。至于自由行动，不同学者会有不同的理解，不过最为常见的理解方式是：一个人的一次行动是自由的，仅当他原本能够采取其他行动。随着近几十年来自然科学——尤其是心理学和神经科学——取得日益丰硕且令人瞩目的成果，我们很难对决定论提出严肃的质疑。但如果我们承认决定论，那么一种明显的张力就会出现在决定论和自由行动之间，而这种张力就是不相容论的立足点。

不相容论认为决定论与自由行动是矛盾的：如果决定论是真的，那么任何行动都不是自由的；如果存在自由的行动，那么决定论就不是真的。因此，在承认决定论的基础上，不相容论很容易走向道德责任的怀疑论。不相容论的这一立场通常可以通过下面这组余地论证（Leeway Argument）[①] 来表明：

（1）如果一个人无法采取其他行动，那么它所做出的任何行动都是不自由的。

（2）如果决定论是真的，那么任何行动都有充分的原因，从而是必然发生的。

（3）因此，如果决定论是真的，那么人的任何行动都是不自由的。

根据余地论证，结合前面关于决定论和自由意志的概念分析，我们可以得出结论：人不是道德主体。同样，如果将余地论证的适用范围扩大到机器，那么我们也可以推出类似的结论：机器没有道德主体性。事实上，即便不承认决定论是真的，我们也可以论证机器不具有道德主体性。这是因为，机器的任何行动都是由在先的内在计算状态决定的，而计算状态本质上是有内容的因果角色。因此，机器的任何行动都存在在先的、充分的原因。模仿余地论证，我们可以绕开决定论，构造一个新的论证来否证机器的道德主体性：

（4）如果一台机器无法采取其他行动，那么它所做出的任何行动都是不自由的。

（5）机器的任何行动都有充分的原因，从而是必然发生的。

（6）因此，机器的任何行动都是不自由的。

因此，站在不相容论的立场上，人和机器都不会被认为是道德主体，并且机器的道德主体地位比人的道德主体地位更加脆弱，AMA 在原则上是不可能的。除了余地论证之外，道德责任怀疑论还会采取若干其他论证，如诉诸道德主体对其行为的终极控制的终极性论证（Ultimacy Argument）等。[②] 这些论证与余地论证大同小异，这里不再赘述。

在不相容论的阵营中，除了道德责任怀疑论之外，还有后果论观点（consequentialist view）。后果论观点也被称为“后果相容论”，主张即便决定

---

① 程炼：《伦理学导论》，北京大学出版社 2008 年版，第 23 页；M. McKenna，D. Pereboom，*Free Will：A Contemporary Introduction*，New York & London：Routledge，2016，p. 147。

② R. Kane，*The Significance of Free Will*，New York：Oxford University Press，Inc.，1998，pp. 112 – 115.

论与自由行动不相容，但是它仍然与道德主体性相容，因为道德责任归属的合理性不在于行动的自由，而在于它无可替代的社会效用。① 根据后果论观点，如果对机器进行道德责任归属具有无可替代的社会效用，那么这么做就是合理的。这个假言命题的前提是否为真呢？其实，机器伦理学的出现就已经回答了这个问题。正是我们对 AMA 日渐增加的需求导致了机器伦理学的诞生，因此，根据后果相容论的观点，机器伦理学的存在本身就论证了机器的道德主体性。②

与不相容论相对，相容论重新诠释了“自由”概念，主张所谓“自由行动”并不意味着行动没有原因，而是说人的心理状态构成了行动的充分原因，即如果一个人决定要做出一个行动，那么这个人就会这么做。③ 从认知的角度说，这意味着人必须拥有一套行动决策机制，这套认知机制能够独立地作为原因决定人的行动。如此一来，“一个人无法采取其他行动”除了可能是由于他的行动是不自由的以外，还可能仅仅意味着他决定了要做出这次行动，余地论证的前提（1）便不再为真。从而，即便决定论是真的，人的行动仍然存有自由的可能。

对于一台智能机器而言，拥有一套行动决策机制，并且这套行动决策机制决定了它的行动无疑是可能的。毋宁说，现如今的许多智能机器都是这样设计的。使人的行动变得不自由的许多因素，如疾病和受迫等，对机器的影响反而有所降低，并且可以预期，尤其人很容易由于自身安全或利益受到威胁而被迫做出某些行动，但只要我们不为机器设计相关机制，它就不可能被强迫。由此我们可以得到推论：在相容论立场上，将一台智能机器接受为 AMA 是可能的。

除了关于决定论与自由意志的传统讨论之外，斯特劳森所提出的道德责任的反应态度学说也有巨大的影响力，它与传统讨论的本质区别在于放弃了关于如何合理地进行道德责任归属的先验研究，转向关于如何解释人的道德责任归属行为的经验研究，从而建立了一种对道德责任的主观性理解。斯特劳森认为，道德责任归属本质上是对合适的主体表达反应态度，同时，当行动仅仅是

---

① 胡靖波：《斯特劳森的道德责任理论与合理性问题》（硕士学位论文），中山大学2016年，第2页。

② 扬波利斯基（Roman V. Yampolisky）对此表达了不同的看法，认为尝试让机器进行伦理决策来确保其行为合乎道德是错误的研究方向。相反，他主张我们应该发展一种新科学：人工智能主体的安全工程学，参见 R. V. Yampolisky, Artificial Intelligence Safety Engineering: Why Machine Ethics Is a Wrong Approach, in V. C. Müller (ed.), *Philosophy and Theory of Artificial Intelligence*, Berlin & Heidelberg: Springer-Verlag GmbH, 2013。

③ 程炼：《伦理学导论》，北京大学出版社 2008 年版，第 27－30 页；A. J. Ayer, Freedom and Necessity, in *Philosophical Essays*, London & Basingstoke: The Macmillan Press Ltd., 1954, p. 282。

出于无心之失，或者主体缺乏基本的道德能力的时候，道德责任可以被免除。[①] 因此，一台机器如果要成为斯特劳森式的 AMA，一方面，它必须首先加入到一个社交圈子当中，并且为了使得圈子里的其他成员对他产生社会情绪；另一方面，与相容论的情况相同，这台机器必须具备道德行动机制以提供基本的道德能力，从而使得它的道德责任不会被免除。

反应态度学说虽然在某种意义上能够描绘未来智能机器过上道德的生活时的场景，但是并没有告诉我们为什么应该接受智能机器的道德主体性。这与反应态度学说的描述本性有关。斯特劳森曾经就人的道德责任归属行为的合理性的不可辩护性提出了三点理由：反应态度是自然的；反应态度独立于信念系统；对合理性的辩护是一个内部问题。[②] 然而，这三点理由不仅争议重重，并且都不适用于机器。因此，反应态度学说无法单独地回答智能机器的道德主体性问题，它只能充当相容论回答的有益补充。

综上所述，一台智能机器的道德主体地位的接受标准由以下三个条件构成：第一，这台机器能够通过内在的行动决策机制来产生行动；第二，我们在决定论和自由意志问题上采取相容论立场；第三，公众社会情绪普遍地接纳这类机器为道德共同体的一部分。这意味着，接受智能机器的道德主体地位在理论上是可能的。

然而在现实中，智能机器的道德主体地位在未来相当长一段时间内将继续受到质疑。这是因为，第一，通过机器的计算过程实现现有的伦理学框架下的道德决策存在技术困难，复杂而灵活的人类道德准则难以使用数字化程序简单表达。第二，虽然近几十年已经出现了诸如《剪刀手爱德华》《底特律：化身为人》等许多强调机器具有心智的可能性、呼吁对人形智能机器一视同仁的艺术作品，但是主流观点依然认为人和机器存在本质不同，机器难以被社会情绪接纳为道德共同体的一部分。第三，即便我们接受机器的道德主体地位，也很难因为机器行为的正当或不正当对它们进行奖励或惩罚，因为机器对奖惩并不敏感，通常意义上的奖惩对促进机器道德而言并无帮助。责任和奖惩的分离也体现了机器伦理学与传统伦理学的差异。这种差异意味着，一旦我们承认机器是道德主体，我们的立法司法、组织管理和社会治理等活动都不得不做出重大改变。

---

① 胡靖波：《斯特劳森的道德责任理论与合理性问题》（硕士学位论文），中山大学 2016 年，第 5 页。

② 胡靖波：《斯特劳森的道德责任理论与合理性问题》（硕士学位论文），中山大学 2016 年，第 10－15 页。

三、道德行动机制设计问题

机器道德和人的情况有一点显著不同，那就是无论我们最终认为机器的道德主体性是可能的还是不可能的，我们都可以继续讨论如何设计机器使机器遵守道德规范，这体现了机器伦理学诸议题的独立性。与自动驾驶汽车等智能机器在技术方面日臻完善所不同步的是，现在对如何设计 AMA 的讨论仍然处于讨论该采取哪种设计思路的最初阶段，还远未涉及如何实现设计方案的技术细节问题。要分辨出哪种设计思路最为合理，我们有必要先对所有可能的设计思路做一番考察。

目前已有学者对 AMA 的设计思路进行过分类，其中以穆尔（James H. Moor）和沃勒克等人（Wendell Wallach et al.）的分类最具代表性。穆尔将 AMA 的设计思路分为两类：一类是隐式设计：机器的行动能力被设计为合乎道德（穆尔称它“以支持伦理行为的方式被编程了”）；另一类是显式设计：机器在决定其行为的计算过程中出现了明确的道德判断。[①] 沃勒克等人则将 AMA 的设计思路分作下行设计与上行设计两类：下行设计是让机器的行动决策从一组特定的普遍伦理学理论出发，结合特定的情境而导出不同的结果的设计思路；上行设计则是让机器的行动决策具有某种表现的度量，通过多种试错技术不断调整机器的行为表现，最终使它接近或超越某个标准的设计思路。[②]

穆尔和沃勒克等人的分类法是相互独立的。从认知的角度说，显式/隐式的分类依据是机器是否具有道德决策机制（即包含“好”“正确”“应该”等伦理表征的计算系统），上行/下行的分类依据是机器是否具有学习机制。两种分类法相结合便可以区分显式上行、显式下行、隐式上行和隐式下行共计四种 AMA 设计思路。但是，沃勒克等人的分类法是不彻底的，所谓的上行设计仍然包含了两种截然不同的设计思路。根据沃勒克等人的表述，上行设计是通过学习使机器“接近或超越某个标准”，如果这个“标准”是事先设定的，那么这种上行设计其实是伪装成上行设计的下行设计，它区别于未事先设定标准的、机器在与环境互动的过程中根据环境反馈不断调整自身所遵循的道德准则

---

① J. H. Moor, The Nature, Importance and Difficulty of Machine Ethics, *IEEE Intelligent System*, 2006, 21 (4), pp. 19 – 20, 穆尔将 AMA 分作“隐式道德主体”和“显式道德主体”两类。这种命名方式具有误导性，它容易让人以为这一分类是对道德主体性的分类；而事实上，穆尔的分类依据是机器道德行动机制的设计思路。因此，为了避免混淆，本文用“隐式设计”和“显式设计”来指称穆尔所说的隐式道德主体和显式道德主体的道德行动机制设计。

② W. Wallach, C. Allen, I. Smit, Machine Morality: Bottom-up and Top-down Approaches for Modelling Human Moral Faculties, *AI & Society*, 2008, 22 (4), pp. 568 – 569.

的上行设计。我们可以通过两类智能机器来说明两种上行设计的区别：以近几年声名鹊起的人工智能围棋程序“阿尔法围棋”（Alpha Go）和前些年在网络上流行过一段时间的聊天机器人“小黄鸡”为例。在机器伦理方面，这两类智能机器所采用的都是隐式上行设计，我们期望 Alpha Go 遵守不悔棋等棋德，期望“小黄鸡”遵守不说脏话等社交礼仪。但是在投入使用一段时间后，Alpha Go 仍然恪守棋德，但“小黄鸡”却开始说起了脏话。这就是环境互动对两类道德行动机制设计产生的不同影响。为了刻画这种差异，同时为了与沃勒克的分类法相区别，我们依据机器行为所遵循的道德准则是否敏感于环境反馈区分动态设计和静态设计，或者依据机器行为是否遵循事先设定的固定不变的道德准则称之为经验设计和先天设计，这是两种等价表述。一个下行设计必是静态设计，但一个上行设计既可能是静态设计，也可能是动态设计。

<table>
<tr><td></td><td></td><td colspan="3">是否具有学习机制?</td></tr>
<tr><td></td><td></td><td>否/下行设计</td><td colspan="2">是/上行设计</td></tr>
<tr><td rowspan="2">是否具有道德决策机制?</td><td>是/显式设计</td><td>显式下行：机器拥有固化的道德准则和道德决策机制</td><td>静态显式上行：机器拥有道德学习机制，在投入使用前完成训练</td><td>动态显式上行：机器拥有道德学习机制，在投入使用后继续发挥作用</td></tr>
<tr><td>否/隐式设计</td><td>隐式下行：机器的行动机制设计体现了特定道德准则</td><td>静态隐式上行：机器拥有体现了特定道德准则的非道德学习机制</td><td>动态隐式上行：机器拥有不体现特定道德准则的非道德学习机制</td></tr>
<tr><td></td><td></td><td colspan="2">否/静态设计</td><td>是/动态设计</td></tr>
<tr><td></td><td></td><td colspan="3">是否敏感于环境反馈?</td></tr>
</table>

图 3－1　三种分类法①的相互关系示意图

尽管穆尔和沃勒克等人的分类法在技术上都很有见地，但它们都没有把不同设计思路作为道德行动机制设计的实质差异。这一点可以从道德行动机制设计的经典案例“机器人学三定律”中看出来。机器人学三定律是美国科幻小说作家阿西莫夫（Isaac Asimov）在作品《我，机器人》（*I*，*Robot*）中提出的机器人必须遵守的三个道德准则②：

第一，机器人不得伤害人，也不得见人受到伤害而袖手旁观；

第二，机器人应服从人的一切命令，但不得违反第一定律；

第三，机器人应保护自身安全，但不得违反第一、第二定律。

在小说中，机器人学三定律总是因为信息不充足、概念定义不明确等各种

① 三种分类法所划分的都是基础设计思路，在此基础上，不同设计思路可以相互组合以形成更为复杂的道德行动机制设计。

② ［美］艾·阿西莫夫：《我，机器人》，国强、赛德、程文译，科学普及出版社 1981 版，第 1 页。

各样的原因而无法实行，机器伦理学的公认观点也认为机器人学三定律不是通用机器人道德行动机制设计的正确思路。运用动态/静态之分进行分析，能够帮助我们找到机器人学三定律问题所在：机器人学三定律的失败在于，它作为一种事先设定好目标的静态设计，无法在人类面对的原本的复杂道德实践情境中展现出足够的灵活性。与之相比，显式/隐式之分和上行/下行之分也都做不到这一点。这是因为，一个遵照三定律行动的机器人既可以知道这些准则，也可以不知道这些准则；它对三定律的遵循既可以是三定律在它的认知系统中固化的结果，也可以是通过学习机制训练的结果。也就是说，一个遵循三定律的通用机器人所采用的设计可以是显式上行、显式下行、隐式上行和隐式下行四种设计中的任何一种，显式/隐式之分和上行/下行之分都无助于我们分析出机器人学三定律的缺陷。因此，对于讨论智能机器的道德行动机制设计而言，动态/静态之分比显式/隐式之分和上行/下行之分更加重要。

通过将机器人学三定律的失败推广到整个机器伦理学领域，沃勒克等人认为，任何类似于阿西莫夫的机器人学三定律的静态设计都是不可能成功的。他们提出了三点理由：第一，伦理学并没有找到可应用于静态设计的普遍伦理学理论；第二，即便存在这样的理论，其原理往往是高度抽象的，以致于人和机器都不知道怎么样在现实中实现它；第三，人类社会原本就处于不断变化的过程中，所以如果伦理学原理不是高度抽象的，那么它一定会在面临种种新情况时陷入困难和争执当中，并且我们的立法、司法等机关事实上就是为了处理这些频频出现的新状况而设立的。① 沃勒克等人对静态设计的三点批评意见都基于一个重要前提：AMA 的道德实践应该与人相似——因为与人相似，所以，AMA 所需要处理的道德问题领域与人类相同；人类没有的普遍伦理法则，机器也一定不会有；人类社会不断出现的道德纠纷和伦理观念的变更，也一定会出现在机器身上——总而言之，因为人类的道德判断是动态的，所以智能机器也应该采取动态设计。事实上，沃勒克等人的这一看法是极为自然和常见的，普通大众甚至不少学者对人工智能的看法仅仅停留于“与人类智能相似”这一点上。并且，往往是成熟度越高、技术性越强的学科领域，越是执着于在人工智能上复刻人类智能的做法。当然，人工智能决不能与人类智能一点都不像，否则我们就没有把握说这种“人工智能”确实体现了某种智能。可是，这种相似性是不是非得具体到每一个技术细节里头去呢？答案是否定的。

一方面，对“智能”概念的分析表明智能行动具有多样性。在逻辑行为主义的概念框架里，“智能”通常是外延定义的，例如赖尔通过“聪明”“机

① W. Wallach, C. Allen, I. Smit, Machine Morality: Bottom-up and Top-down Approaches for Modelling Human Moral Faculties, *AI & Society*, 2008, 22 (4), pp. 571 -575.

敏”“谨慎”等词汇来刻画“智能”的含义。[①] 有学者指出，智能概念“强调的是行事方式，即行动所具备的某种风格或方法”[②] 也就是说，智能仅仅是数量众多的行为模式构成的类，它并不涉及除了表层结构之外的任何因素。在认知主义的概念框架里，“智能”一词的适用范围已大大扩展，人类智能被宽泛地刻画为加工来自环境的信息输入并将之用于解决问题的实践。认知主义往往通过计算机的运作方式来理解人类心智，因此，如果说人类活动体现了智能的话，那么任何能够与外界互动的计算机原则上都或多或少地具备智能。此外，认知主义将个人水平的认知能力解释为亚人水平心理机制运作的结果，二者之间是功能角色和实现者的关系，而功能角色存在多重实现的可能。这表明人工智能与人类智能的相似性只需要限制在行为模式的相似性，而行为模式的实现机制是多样的，人工智能的实现机制完全可以与人类智能不同。

另一方面，当代最成功的人工智能设计并没有预设人工智能与人类智能在实现机制上的相似性。我们再以 Alpha Go 为例。Alpha Go 事先考察大量棋谱，而后在对局中通过预测后几步走棋的可能性并评估这些可能性所带来的胜率，配合特定的计算装置来决定接下来的走棋。这种决定落子的方法要求大量的计算和存储操作，对于人类棋手来说是不可能完成的任务。2016 年 3 月，Alpha Go 在对局中击败韩国职业选手李世石，一举成名；2017 年 5 月，Alpha Go 以 3∶0 的战绩横扫围棋世界冠军柯洁，标志着人工智能棋手完成了对人类棋手的全面超越。没有理由认为 Alpha Go 的棋艺没有体现出智能，而 Alpha Go 的成功也就意味着成功的人工智能并不需要彻底地模仿人类智能，实现人工智能的机制完全可以不同于人类智能，并达到与人类智能相同甚至更高的高度。

所以，沃勒克等人在设计问题上的最大失误，就是忽略了人工智能的多样性和人类智能的多重可实现性。也许对于沃勒克等人最为关心的那些最终将会与人极为相似的机器人而言，动态设计确实体现出相较于静态设计充分的优越性，但是，这种机器人并不是人工智能的全部，也不是 AMA 的全部。如果一台机器被设计处理的问题领域是高度限定的，那么这台机器所需要处理的伦理问题也是十分有限的，因此找到可应用于静态设计的伦理学原理仍然是可能的。

要判断一台机器究竟适合静态设计还是动态设计，我们必须结合这台机器的功能和它打交道的问题领域来进行判断。大体上，一台机器所要执行的功能越是简单，所需处理的问题越是有限，那么它的道德行动机制就越是适合静态设计；相反，功能复杂、任务繁重的机器则更适合动态设计。不过，这个标准

① Gilbert Ryle, *The Concept of Mind*, London & New York: Routledge, 2009, pp. 14 - 15.

② 郁振华：《论能力之知：为赖尔一辩》，载《哲学研究》2010 年第 10 期，第 72 页。

既不是精确的，也不是绝对的。它只是表明了，无论是静态设计还是动态设计，都是 AMA 可能的设计思路。机器的道德行动机制的设计方法是多样的，我们不能简单地认为一类设计思路就比另一类设计思路更出色。

四、结语

随着科学技术不断发展，智能机器在生产生活中的参与程度不断加深，未来智能机器的开发和制造必定会遭遇越来越多的伦理挑战，机器伦理学将在智能机器的研发中扮演越来越重要的角色，越来越多的学者将会加入到智能机器道德问题的研究和讨论中。不过，机器伦理学的意义并不止于此。正如穆尔所说，我们需要重视机器伦理学的研究工作的理由之一，是“通过编程或者教育让一台机器合乎道德地行动，有助于我们更好地理解伦理学”①。在这个意义上，机器伦理学是一项采用了设计立场的传统伦理学研究。如果有朝一日我们解决了机器伦理学的两个基本问题并实现了 AMA，那么我们对人类心智中的道德认知机制和人所遵从的道德规范的认识也必定会再上一个台阶。

① J. H. Moor, The Nature, Importance and Difficulty of Machine Ethics, *IEEE Intelligent System*, 2006, 21 (4), p. 21.

休谟问题的不可解性与归纳的局部辩护[①]

鞠实儿

一、导论

一般说来，科学研究有两个主要目的：发现关于世界的假说和评价这些假说。所谓的科学研究活动的理性重建指：建立科学家实现其研究目标的合理的规则或方法论系统。科学家的直接感性知识受到时空限制，而科学假说却远远超出人的观察和实验范围。因此，如果存在科学方法，那么它们必须能够像归纳法那样来处理知识。这个结论立即遭遇来自休谟问题的巨大挑战。在演绎论证中，如果前提为真，那么结论不可能为假，这是因为结论的内容没有超出前提。反之，归纳论证具有放大性，它的结论的内容超出了前提。那么归纳论证必然保真吗？这就是休谟（Hume）问题或归纳的一般形式。

在论述休谟问题时，韦斯利·萨尔蒙（Wesley Salmon）和沃尔夫冈·施太格缪勒（Wolfgang Stegmuller）已经指出，休谟问题所关注的是所有的放大性论证，而不是一个仅与枚举法有关的特殊归纳形式，并且它与假说评价方法的合理性有关，但与发现无关[②]。我赞同他们的大部分观点。但是，若要阐明科学发现方法的认知合理性和逻辑合理性，则休谟问题也同样与发现假说的方法有关（参见本文第五节的讨论）。因此，是否存在合理的科学方法取决于休谟问题的解决。

在本文中，我并不试图如同人们反复所做的那样，用各种不同的途径对休谟问题给出正面的或反面的回答。而是要证明：首先，休谟问题在逻辑范围内不可解，或在逻辑中没有方法对它做出正面或反面的解答；其次，我将在逻辑学的范围之外，给出局部合理性概念和归纳的局部辩护方法（LJI），并以此说

---

① 本文由李章吕、任晓明译自 Shier Ju., The Unsolvability of Hume's Problem and the Local Justification of Induction, *Epistemologia* XVI, 1993, pp. 77 – 96。鞠实儿对译文进行了校订，并对原文中若干错漏进行了文字上的修订。

② W. Salmon, *The Foundations of Scientific Inference*, Pittsburgh: University of Pittsburgh Press, 1967, pp. 3 – 23; W. Stegmuller, The Problem of Induction: Hume's Challenge and the Contemporary Answers, in *Collected Papers on Epistemology. Philosophy of Science and History of Philosophy*, Vol. 2, Dordrecht: Reidel, 1977, pp. 68 – 136.

明归纳法的合理性可以得到局部辩护、拒斥或悬置；最后，我将给出科学研究的局部归纳重建程序。

二、对波普尔解决休谟问题办法的批评

在本文中，归纳论证是指结论内容超出前提内容的论证，即放大性论证。关于归纳的合理性，休谟已经指出：

> 说到过去的经验则我们不能不承认它所给我们的直接的确定的报告，只限于我们所认识的那些物象和认识发生时的那个时期，但是这经验为什么可以扩展到将来，扩展到我们所见仅在貌相上相似的别的物象？这正是我所欲坚持的一个问题。①

这个问题构成休谟问题的原初形式。显然，它涉及归纳论证的前提和结论之间的保真关系，因而是一个逻辑问题。本节将表明：波普尔并没有能够在逻辑学的范围内对休谟问题做出反面的解答。这就是说，他没能使用正确的演绎论证从真前提得出这样的结论：归纳推理不具保真性。

休谟关于这个问题的解决方法具有双重性。他认为，我们既不能演绎地证明归纳论证具有保真性，否则它本身就是演绎的，也不能归纳地证明它的保真性，否则就会陷入恶性循环。② 因此，他明确地说，要想在逻辑层面上正面解决这个问题是不可能的。虽然，他并未讨论在逻辑范围内反面解答休谟问题的可能性。但是，他继而从心理主义的角度来回答问题：

> 在这里，我们的确发现了一个非常清楚的命题，即便它不是一个真命题，但至少在看到两个物象的持续会合之后，我们可以断言……当一个物象出现之后，我们仅仅根据习惯来期待另一个物象的出现……因此，根据经验得来的所有推理都是习惯的结果，而不是理性的结果。③

因此，休谟指出，该问题可以在心理学范围内得到正面解答。波普尔（Popper）沿着休谟的道路来解决归纳问题：“我认为，休谟指出归纳法不能获

① D. Hume, An Enquiry Concerning Human Understanding, 1776, in *The Philosophical Works*, T. H. Green (eds.), Aalen: Scientia Verlag, 1964.

② 参见 D. Hume, An Enquiry Concerning Human Understanding, 1776, in *The Philosophical Works*, T. H. Green (eds.), Aalen: Scientia Verlag, 1964, p. 30。

③ D. Hume, An Enquiry Concerning Human Understanding, 1776, in *The Philosophical Works*, T. H. Green (eds.), Aalen: Scientia Verlag, 1964, pp. 37 – 38.

得逻辑的辩护，这一点是完全正确的。”① 因此，波普尔接受了休谟的第一个结论，即归纳问题在逻辑学范围内不可能有正面解答。但是，波普尔却尝试着超越休谟。他指出：

归纳原理必然是一个综合陈述，也就是说，否定它并不会导致自相矛盾，因而在逻辑上是可能的。……我依然认为，一个归纳原理……必然导致逻辑不一致。②

因此，波普尔提出了他反对归纳论证的第二个观点：在逻辑学范围内，休谟问题的反面解答是可能的。不仅如此，为反对休谟的心理主义解答，波普尔继续说道：

不仅某些经验事实不支持休谟，而且存在决定性的纯逻辑的论据反对他的心理学理论。……休谟的心理学归纳理论将导致无穷倒退。③

因此，波普尔的第三个观点是，在心理学范围内对归纳进行辩护是不可能的。为了赢得反对归纳法的战役，波普尔最后一步是：建立证伪主义理论来代替科学方法论中的归纳法或归纳论证模式。

我接受波普尔的第一个结论，虽然它与休谟的观点完全相同——但我并不赞同他的另外三个观点。事实上，波普尔似乎从来没有对休谟问题在逻辑范围内反面解决的可能性做出真正的证明。如果上述结论确实曾被证明为真，那么他必定能够在不借助经验假设的条件下证明这一命题：归纳必定导致逻辑矛盾。但他所有的努力只是表明：归纳辩护要么导致无穷倒退，要么导致先验论。与此同时，他还引用了一些反例，借此说明归纳法如枚举法是不可靠的。

但是，导致无穷倒退的论证或陷入循环的论证不同于自相矛盾的论证。证明中的无穷倒退和循环只是表明：所关注命题无法得到恰当证明或辩护，并且它的真值也无法通过这种方式来确定。但是，所关注命题的证明导致矛盾，则说明该命题是假的，并且，根据排中律，我们可以断定这个命题的否定是真的。类似地，如果为了证明某个命题为真，我们必须假定一个先天综合命题作为前提；这也只是表明，我们无法找到一个合理的或可接受的方法来证明该命题为真。但是，这并不能证明该命题是假的。

不过，波普尔走得更远。他的另一个著名论断是：归纳原则容易导致矛盾。考虑一个典型的归纳论证：根据枚举法，从“所有已知的天鹅都是白的”

---

① K. Popper, *Conjectures and Refutations*, London: Routledge & Kegan Paul, 1963, p. 42.

② K. Popper, *The Logic of Scientific Discovery*, New York: Basic Books, 1959, pp. 1 – 4.

③ K. Popper, *Conjectures and Refutations*, London: Routledge & Kegan Paul, 1963, p. 45.

可以推出“所有的天鹅都是白的”。但是，当发现一只黑天鹅时，这一新证据将证明上述全称命题是假的，我们就会因此认为“并非所有的天鹅都是白的”为真。因为“所有的天鹅都是白的”和“并非所有的天鹅都是白的”构成了一对矛盾。上述归纳论证合逻辑地被否定了。但是，这个典型论证却有一个无法克服的困难。从逻辑的观点看，新证据或枚举法应该对这对矛盾负责。为什么我们只把责任归咎于枚举法呢？事实上，根据波普尔所接受的“观察渗透理论”学说，仅当预设一系列辅助性假说时，我们才可以安全地把观察陈述看做真的。但是，当我们尝试着为这些辅助性假说进行辩护时，另外一系列的观察陈述和辅助假说又将被引进，这无疑将导致无穷倒退。因此，从逻辑的观点看，我们可以得出如下结论：上文所提到的矛盾不能成立，相应的归纳论证没有被反驳。

进一步，波普尔提出了两个理由来反驳休谟的心理主义辩护：其一，存在与休谟联想主义心理学不相容的经验事实；其二，心理学解决方案将导致无穷倒退这一逻辑事实。但是，正如上文所述，经验事实无法反驳归纳法，并且辩护过程中出现的无穷倒退也无法证伪被辩护的命题。因此，波普尔并没有证明归纳不具有保真性。

最后，在逼真性概念的基础上，波普尔提出了评价理论的一个标准。但是，这种评价方法却面临着一个困境。根据这个标准，理论 T_2 比理论 T_1 更逼近于真，当且仅当：（1）T_2 的真内容超过了 T_1，（2）T_1 的假内容超过了 T_2。但是，哪些内容构成了这个理论的真内容，这是根据对该理论进行的实验或观察来确定的。假定这些实验和观察是在时刻 t_0 进行的，如果这种方法对该理论在时刻 t_0 后的行为没有提供任何评价，那么它对于现实世界就没有任何指导作用，因而它是无用的；如果这种方法对该理论在时刻 t_0 后的行为提供某种评价的话，它无疑属于波普尔所拒斥的归纳论证。这一困境表明，归纳主义幽灵隐藏在波普尔的理论方法之中。总之，波普尔确实没有能够在逻辑范围内拒斥归纳法的合理性。

三、休谟问题的不可解性

现在，进一步的问题是：事实上是否存在逻辑正确的方法可推导出休谟问题的反面解答，即归纳论证不具保真性。在我看来这是不可能的，正如不可能存在正确的逻辑方法可推导出休谟问题的正面解答。

令 p_1，……，p_n，q 是归纳论证的一般形式，其中 p_1，……，p_n 是前提，q 是结论。如果存在一个正确的逻辑方法可以从前提推导出上述结论的否定或非 q，那么，我们就说归纳论证不具保真性，也就是说，在逻辑范围内休谟问题有一个反面的解答。由于仅有两种逻辑推导方法，即归纳法和演绎法。所以，如果居然可以从上述归纳论证的前提推出非 q，那么必采用归纳法或演绎法。为了方便起见，根据演绎证明的前提的组成，把它分为三类：D_1为前提中只包含逻辑公理的证明；D_2为前提中除包含逻辑公理外，至少还包含一个经验假设的证明；D_3为前提仅包含数学公理的证明。不难看出，那些更复杂的演绎证明都可以还原为上述三种简单的证明形式。因此，我只考虑这三种简单的情况。另一方面，根据归纳法的使用情况，我们可以将归纳式“证明”分为两类：I_1为运用一种归纳论证进行自我反驳，I_2为运用一种归纳论证反驳其它归纳论证。下面，我将分别检验这些证明形式，最终表明没有一种可用来反驳归纳论证的合理性。

首先，让我们考虑演绎证明。

D_1：假定归纳论证的前提与结论一致。在此假定下不可能存在一个演绎证明使得 p_1，……，p_n；非 q。如果上述假定不成立，矛盾将被视为合法，进而任何结论都将成为可接受的，故上述假定不可缺失。因此不存在有效的 D_1 型演绎证明可以推翻归纳论证。

D_2：设 H 是经验陈述，且有演绎证明 H，p_1，……，p_n；非 q。如所公认，一个证明是可接受的，当且仅当其前提为真并且证明有效，又设该证明有效。现在我们来分析该证明的前提。首先，假定 H 是一个全称条件句。那么除非 H 确定为真，否则我们就没有理由接受非 q。但是，这一确定性的追求本身就蕴含着无穷倒退。其次，假设 H 是一个单称命题且为 q 的一个反例。但是，将数学或逻辑反例等同于经验反例是不合适的，因为数学的或逻辑的反例由数学公理或逻辑公理构造出来，具有分析性。但是，正如我们在第二部分所看到的那样，经验反例是实验和观察的结果，并且预设了一系列经验假设，正是借助这些经验假设，那些反例为真。因此，一个数学或逻辑的反例能够证伪一个命题。相形之下，除非事先将这些假设视为先验的，单纯凭借经验反例无法证伪一个命题。因此，试图通过 D_2 型演绎证明对休谟问题做出反面解答，将导致无穷倒退或先验论，因而归于失败。

D_3：设 M 是一个数学理论，且有演绎证明 M，p_1，……，p_n；非 q。如果 p_1，……，p_n，q 被解释成数学公式和符号串，那么上述证明表明：归纳论证的形式结构与 M 不一致。但是，这并不能成为反驳归纳论证的充分条件。因为，不能排除该数学理论不适合于表达归纳论证的可能性。类似地，如果 p_1，…… ，p_n，q 被解释成经验科学命题；那么该证明的结论是不可接受的，除非假定 M 真实地或者恰当地描述了经验世界。在数学理论中，纯数学命题的真值可根据数学公理来判定，而 M 相对于经验世界的真实性或恰当性由这两者之间的关系来确定。因此，上述证明是否是可接受的取决于 M 的经验真实性或恰当性。于是，我们从 D_3 绕了一圈又回到了 D_2。

其次，我们考虑归纳法。

I_1：如果一个归纳论证不借助其他原则就可以实行自我反驳，则必然导致悖论；因而论证 I_1 无效。进一步，如果需要借助其他假设才能实行自我反驳，那么这些假设必须被证明为真。显然，这将导致了一个无穷倒退。

I_2：如果我们使用一个归纳论证来反驳另一个归纳论证，那么，我们必须相信前一个归纳论证是合理的。但是我们先前已经说明：归纳问题正面解答不可能。因此，无论如何 I_1 和 I_2 都是失败的。

最后，我的观点可以用更直接的方式加以证明。让我们从一个问题开始：当我们说“归纳论证不必然保真”时，确切意思是什么呢？包括波普尔在内的大多数人都会说，我们的意思是：或许某一归纳论证迄今为止所得结论尚未被证明为假。但是，存在一个逻辑可能的世界，在那个世界中这些结论是假的。现在，一个进一步的问题出现了：这个逻辑可能世界事实上可能吗？换句话说，这个逻辑可能世界有可能成为现实世界吗？有三种可能性：其一，如果相信存在这类可能性，那就对未来做出了某种假设，并用以决定归纳论证是否具有保真性，这本身就接受了某种归纳论证；其二，如果不相信这类可能性，那么在这样一个逻辑可能世界中讨论归纳论证的保真性，这只能是一个没有意义的逻辑游戏；其三，如果无法判定上述问题的答案，那就应该说：归纳论证是否具有保真性是不可判定的。因此，休谟问题的反面解答在逻辑上是不可能的。

根据以上所述，对归纳的反驳，如同对它的辩护一样——或者导致无穷倒退，或者导致先验论——我们不可能合乎逻辑地证明归纳论证不具有保真性。因此，部分地借助于休谟本人关于归纳合理性的讨论，本文证明了休谟问题的不可解原理（UHP）：在逻辑学范围内，休谟问题的反面解决与正面解决同样是不可能的。在下一节，本文将在 UHP 的基础上，提出新的归纳辩护方案。

四、归纳的局部辩护方案

本文中，所谓归纳合理性辩护是指：制定一系列合理性标准，根据归纳推理是否满足这些标准来证明它的合理性。为了规避休谟问题所导致的严重困难，我们将放弃整体的或纯逻辑范围内的归纳辩护，转而进行一种局部的辩护。① 博格丹指出：“归纳是可以被局部辩护的。”所谓局部辩护就是“根据语

① J. Bogdan, *Local Induction*, Dordrecht: Reidel, 1973, p. 9.

言的句法和语义特征而进行的语言选择，以及相对于初始证据或背景知识、主体效用和偏好等进行的概率评价”。这就是最早的关于归纳的局部辩护（LJI）思想的表述。

但是，上述观点似乎从来没有得到详细的说明和论证。根据上一节对休谟问题不可解原理的讨论可知，在归纳的辩护中，逻辑学是中立的。因此，如果可能的话，归纳合理性的判据或标准可从背景知识或非逻辑因素中选取。进一步，同样根据关于上述原理的讨论，归纳论证本身既不是自相矛盾也不是逻辑有效，那么非逻辑因素能够被用来进行归纳辩护。因此，在非逻辑因素的基础上归纳的局部辩护是可能实现的。现在，我试图给出局部合理性概念，它是归纳局部辩护的基础。

定义 1：一个命题 H 是局部合理或局部可接受的，当且仅当它满足下列三个条件之一：（1）H 是一个逻辑定理；（2）（a）H 和非 H 都不是逻辑定理；并且（b）在背景知识 B 中，存在命题 B_1，使得 H 是 B_1 的后承或 B_1 是 H 的后承，但 B 中不存在 B_2，使得非 H 是 B_2 的后承或非 B_2 是 H 的后承；（3）H 是满足条件（1）或（2）的命题的逻辑后承。在这里，B 由经验知识（BE）、价值信念（BV）和形式知识（BF）即逻辑和数学知识构成。

定义 2：一个命题 H 是局部不合理或局部不可接受的，当且仅当它满足下列三条件之一：（1′）非 H 是一个逻辑定理；（2′）H 满足（2）（a），但 B 中存在一个 B_1 且使得非 H 是 B_1 的后承或非 B_1 是 H 的后承；（3′）H 是满足条件（1′）或（2′）的命题的后承。

定义 3：一个命题 H 是局部不可判定的，当且仅当它满足下列两条件之一：（1″）H 不满足定义 1，并且也不满足定义 2；（2″）H 是满足（1″）的命题的逻辑后承。

上述三个定义就构成了局部合理性理论（LRT）。LRT 的核心观念是：对于非逻辑定理的命题，提出包含非逻辑因素的判据，确定该命题是否局部可接受、局部不可接受、或局部不可判定。首先，如果 H 与 B 不一致，那么，根据（2′）可知，LRT 拒斥 H；这就意味着，LRT 拒绝与事实相矛盾命题。其次，如果 B 中成员是 H 为真的充分或必要条件，那么，根据（2）LRT 接受 H。这就意味着 LRT 接受得到事实支持的命题。最后，如果逻辑公理和背景知识对 H 的真值保持中立，LRT 只能将 H 悬置起来。值得一提的是：当 H 满足定义 1 时，它相对于 B 无可怀疑，此时，不可能存在任何逻辑或非逻辑理由能用来反对被 LJI 判定为局部合理的命题。因此，LRT 具有可靠性。

尽管 LRT 中的合理性（可接受）、不合理性（不可接受）和不可判定性概念与逻辑学中的相应概念有所不同，但是，它们还是与逻辑学、数学和经验科学所蕴含的合理性概念相一致。首先，根据（1）和（1′），LRT 不允许逻辑矛盾存在，这与逻辑学相容。其次，所有的演绎系统，比如逻辑、数学和物理学系统等，都是建立在一些未经证明的公理之上。为什么这些公理具有可接受性呢？最主要的理由是：它们可以从其他系统推出，比如某些生物学公理就是物理学定理，或者它们的逻辑推论与 B 中的某些假设是相容的。事实上，一个逻辑系统被看作恰当的或合理的，仅当某些已被接受的推理规则可从该系统的公理推出。类似地，在数学中，当某个数学理论的定理与我们关于世界抽象结构的观点不相符时，该数学理论避免被拒绝的唯一途径是：修改该理论，使两者相吻合。因此，逻辑的、数学的和经验科学的合理性都是通过如同局部合理性理论（LRT）所描述的方式得到辩护的。

进一步，LRT 为我们提供了一种新的归纳辩护方法。根据 LRT，休谟问题可以表述为：归纳论证具有局部保真性吗？或者，假定一个归纳论证的前提局部可接受，那么它的结论也是局部可接受的吗？假设归纳论证的规则可表达为条件句，例如著名的枚举归纳法可表达为：如果已观察到的 A 中有 m/n 是 B，那么在长时段内 A 是 B 的相对频率是 m/n。

令 p_1，……，p_n是归纳论证的前提，例如：已观察到的天鹅中的 m/n 是黑的。利用三段论规则，从归纳推理规则和前提可推出结论；例如：天鹅中 m/n 是黑的。根据以上案例分析，利用枚举归纳法则，可以得到一个枚举归纳论证：已观察到的天鹅中有 m/n 是黑的，因此，在长时段内天鹅中的黑天鹅的相对频率 m/n。根据定义 1 中的第（3）条和 LRT 框架下的休谟问题的提法，一个归纳论证的结论是局部合理的，仅当归纳论证规则被局部辩护。由此可以明确判定依据某归纳规则构造的归纳论证是否具有局部合理性。因此，若要对归纳论证做辩护，就要对归纳论证的规则做辩护。然而，存在一系列非逻辑等值的归纳推理规则。因此，我们不可能使用一种统一的方法同时对所有的规则进行辩护。不仅如此，相对于某个固定的 B 来说，某些规则可能是局部合理的，某些却不是。因此，根据 LRT，所要做的并不是简单地对归纳规则自身进行辩护，而是要澄清，使它们分别成为合理、不合理或不可判定的条件。

为了展示归纳的局部辩护方法（LJI），让我们试着对枚举归纳规则的局部合理性进行辩护。假定我们抛某个硬币 n 次，出现正面的次数为 m_1，出现反面的次数为 n－m_1。根据规则，在长时段内出现正面的相对频率是 m_1/n，出现反面的相对频率是（n－m_1）/n。然而，我们能确定除了出现正面和反面这两种情况之外就不会出现第三种情况吗？例如：该硬币会不会侧立着呢？如果不能确定这一点，那么就不能否认第三种情况出现的可能性，就如我们不能否认上述两种情况发生的可能性那样。显然，在此条件下，上述归纳推理是不可接受的。事实上，沙克尔已经指出：使用这条规则的必要条件是列举实验的所有可能结果。① 更一般地说，所有那些可以用数学概率来解释的归纳法则都必须满足上述条件。否则，我们就不可能构建样本空间和用概率度量归纳不确定性。值得一提的是：也许正如沙克尔所说的那样，对于任何上述条件不成立的试验，或许应该用一种非分布变量，例如潜在惊奇来描述其不确定性。

假定上述条件都已经满足了，另一个众所周知的问题却出现了：相对频率具有稳定性吗？如果不是（正如大多数人所承认的那样），那就不存在所谓的“长时段内的相对频率”。对这个问题的肯定回答构成了应用这条规则的必要条件。但是，这问题涉及描述一个随机装置未来的行为，即世界齐一性。解决它就是回答休谟问题。因此，它在逻辑学范围内不可解。以下，我将修改赖欣巴哈为这一规则做辩护的方法。为了回避休谟问题，赖欣巴哈从实用主义的立场为枚举法则辩护。其辩护过程可以概述为：（1）世界要么是齐一的要么不是；（2）如果世界是齐一的，那么枚举归纳法就成立；（3）如果某个归纳法成立，那么世界就是齐一的；因此，如果某个归纳法成立，那么枚举归纳法就是成立的。② 根据前提（3），赖欣巴哈的解决方案预先假定世界的齐一性在于：世界的行为可以通过使用某种归纳方法 X 进行预测。但是，X 并没有提到任何关于世界的性质。因此，他的方法可以让我们安全地假设：除去上述预测所展现的齐一性，世界混乱而无序。③ 所以，枚举法的唯一作用就是预测 X 的成功，而并没有告诉我们任何关于世界的知识。因此，相对频率的稳定性是没有经过任何解释而被预设了的一个预设。枚举法是否比 X 更合理？这依然没有定论。然而，LJI 可以克服这些困难。事实上，BE 可接受或者不可接受。如果是，则可运用它做出可接受的选择；如果不是，则不能做出可接受的选择。为了生存，我们必须做出可接受的选择。所以，接受 BE 对于我们的生存是必须的。这样一来，从 BV 中的一个生存信念和 LRT 出发，我们已经证明了 BE 是局部合理的了。因此，如果可以通过 LRT 从 BE 推出相对频率的稳定性性—— 正如它在概率论的应用场合中被广泛接受的那样——这里似乎就没有任何经验理由可以反对枚举归纳了。（否则，其它满足概率演算公理的归纳法则，比如先验法则、主观方法等，就应该被看作是测量试验或假设不确定性的候选方法了。）

除经验知识和价值观念之外，归纳论证原则的局部合理性还受到论证所涉

① G. Shackle, A Scheme of Economic Theory, 1965, p. 49.

② 参见 H. Reichenbach, On the justification of induction, *Journal of Philosophy*, 1940, 37 (4), pp. 97 - 103。

③ 参见 B. Skyrms, *Choice & Chance*, Encino (CA): Dickenson Publishing Company, 1966。

句子的形式特征的限制。假设归纳法则由二元函数 P［H，E］来表示，其中，H 和 E 分别表示假设和证据。H 可以是全称的也可以是特称的，它可以被认为描述了个体事件（individual event）或一般事件（average event）。但是，与一般事件不同，对个体事件不能进行重复检验——正如大多数人所接受的那样——个 体事件的不确定性不能通过枚举法来度量。因此，成功运用枚举归纳法则的必要条件是：H 表达一个一般事件。

根据以上所述，如果 H 描述的是一般事件，同时，在 LJI 和 LRT 框架下，根据给定的 B 可以确定：穷竭地列举了关于 H 的试验的所有可能结果，长时段内相对频率具有稳定性，以及 B 中不存在与枚举规则相矛盾的元素。由此，枚举归纳法被辩护为局部合理。或许有人会认为：上述辩护受制于 B，可能忽略某些支持或反对枚举归纳法则的因素，因此，这不是一个成功的辩护。但是，如果真出现这样的情况，批评者就有责任罗列出那些被忽略掉的因素。不过，到那时候我需要做的只是：修改背景知识 B，继续进行局部辩护。虽然从逻辑的观点看，LJI 并非绝对可靠，但是，相对于 B 而言，LJI 的结论无可反驳。

现在，我将概述 LJI 程序：（1）列举所有已知的归纳法则；（2）列举 B 中所有可用于辩护或反驳这些归纳法则的因素；（3）确定一组因素，试图对某个规则进行局部辩护。如果上述步骤都完成了，那么清单中的所有规则都得到了局部辩护；最后结果是：它们或局部合理、局部不合理或局部不可判定。

观察上述程序，我们可以发现一个有趣的现象：假定有 n 个因素与归纳法则的合理性相关，那么可构建一个 n 元组，使得每个因素或它的否定两者之中必有一个出现在其中。令所有这样的 n 元组构成一个集合。显然，会出现这样的情况：存在该集合的一个子集，某个已知归纳法相对于该子集中的某个 n 元组成员得到辩护。不过，也可能会出现这样的情况：对于该子集在上述集合中的补集而言，没有一个已知归纳法相对于该补集的成员得到辩护。所以，接下来的问题就是：哪一个归纳法则对应于该补集中的成员呢？换句话说，哪一种法则可以相对于该补集中的成员得到辩护呢？因此，与元素周期表在发现新元素中的作用类似，该子集展示的是未知归纳规则的性质，并且为进一步发现和研究新的归纳法指明方向。

五、科学研究的局部归纳重建

根据上述结论，休谟问题的局部解决办法已经建立，借助它归纳论证可以得到局部辩护。因此，我们可以利用局部合理的归纳法，对科学研究活动进行合理的归纳重建。在本节，我将给出一个科学研究的局部归纳重建程序。

正如我们在本文开篇所说，科学研究可以分为两部分，即科学假说的发现和评价。评价一个科学假说就是在给定证据的基础上评估它的可靠程度。一般说来，评价假说的过程分为两个阶段：（1）先验评价阶段：根据提出假说时所具有的背景知识 B 和证据，对假说进行评价；（2）后验评价阶段：通过构造假说检验收集证据，对假说进行评价。在本文中，科学发现是指：首次提出具有一定合理性的假说。但它不是简单地等同于产生一个没有认识论意义的新思想。由此，科学发现就包含了新假说产生和评价两个方面。然而，评价的两个阶段中究竟哪一个与科学发现相关呢？一方面，在提出假说时，科学家 X 可以依据他此时具有的 B，实行先验评价，以满足科学发现的需要。因此，科学发现过程中的评价应该是先验的。事实上，如果此时采用后验评价，那么对任何一个新提出的假说都要构造检验进行评价。但是，这不具有可行性。另一方面，从可计算性的观点看，使用先验评价来约束假说发生过程，以避免组合式的激增是必要的。总之，科学发现的过程必须包含一个假说产生过程和一个假说先验评价过程。上述结论可以严格地表示为：

令 X 是一个科学家，X 在时刻 t_i时的背景知识为 Bxt_i，X 的评价函数是 Px［H，E］，其中 $i > 0$。

定义 4：在时刻 t_j，X 提出假说 H 的标准是，H 不属于 Bxt_i，其中 $j > i$。

定义 5：令 b 是阈值，$b > 0$；E 是证据。在时刻 t_j，X 关于 H 的可靠性或接受 H 的先验标准是 Px［H，E］$> b$，其中，E 属于 Bxt_i。

定义 6：在时刻 t_j，X 发现假说 H，当且仅当，在时刻 t_j，X 提出假说 H 同时满足定义 4 和定义 5。

根据定义 5 和 LJI，我们有可能建立一个局部合理的具有假说评价功能的归纳论证或程序。但是，我们同样有可能建立一个具有假说发现功能的归纳推理或程序吗？如果回答是肯定的，那么发现方法或程序结构是什么呢？令 E 是 Bxt_i 中的初始数据，H 是时刻 t_j 发生程序输入 E 后输出的结果。因此，从逻辑的观点看，发生程序是一个归纳推理。同时，如果把 E 和 H 看作是前提和结论的话，那么可以借助局部合理归纳方法对 H 进行评价。因此，发现程序的结构是：它由归纳发生程序和归纳评价程序两者构成。现在，一个严峻的问题是：X 提出假说 H 时，Bxt_i 提供初始数据 E 是否能成为评价 H 的有效证据？波普尔认为，只有那些新颖的可检验后承的才有可能为假说提供证据支持。如果这是正确的，那么与发现相关的先验评价就是不可能的。但这种观点过于狭隘，以至于不能给证据支持提供一个完整的描述。事实上，H 的评价应该在关于它的所有知识的基础上进行。如果认为只有那些对 H 的新颖的可检验后承才有可能提供证据的话，那么，假说 H 发生时输入归纳发生程序的数据 E 以

及 Bxt_j 中其他成员，就会被系统地忽略而不能成为证据。因此，由新颖后承检验和假说发生时所输入的数据所提供的都是有效的证据。不过，正如尼古拉斯所指出的那样，同样的信息不能既提供发生支持，又提供后承检验支持。① 由此，科学发现可以通过局部合理的归纳论证或程序来进行重建。最后，从定义 6 可知，科学发现可以通过一个生成程序和一个评价程序来实现，并按下述次序运行：前者生成一个假说，后者评价前者所生成的假说。事实上，从 20 世纪 80 年代中期开始，人工智能领域的学者就已经意识到了机器学习中生成和评价之间的关系。②

在上述讨论的基础上，我们现在可以给出科学研究中的局部归纳重建程序了：（1）运用 LJI 方法，从 B 出发来为归纳进行局部辩护；（2）在具有局部合理性的归纳逻辑的基础上重建假说评价方法；（3）运用局部合理的评价方法来约束假说发生程序的输出结果，使得由科学发现程序给出的假说具有局部合理性。尽管我不认为我的程序已经完全刻画了人类的科学研究行为，但是，它可以为人工智能领域中的研究，特别是为机器学习和不确定性条件下的推理的研究提供一种研究方法。

---

① T. Nickles, Lakatosian Heuristic and Epistemic Support, *British Journal for the Philosophy of Science*, 1987, 38, p. 189.

② R. Michalski, Understanding the Nature of Learning, *Machine Learning*, 1986, 2, pp. 1 – 43.

Dynamic Consistency in Incomplete Information Games under Ambiguity

Hailin Liu, Wei Xiong

1. Introduction

Many economic situations of interest involve interactive decision making under uncertainty in which the participants have only partial information about the payoff relevant aspects of the circumstance. In his seminal contribution, Harsanyi① proposes to model such strategic situations by introducing incomplete information games. The basic picture of Harsanyi's game model goes like this. There is a fundamental state space that includes all the possibilities of the players' relevant characteristics. And the players possess different private information about the situation in which they interact. Nevertheless, it is assumed that all the players in the game employ a *single*, *common* prior to represent their beliefs about the states before having received any private information. Upon the arrival of new information about the states, each player is required to revise her initial belief by applying Bayes' rule. ② As a final step, each player is asked to choose a strategy that maximizes her expected utility with respect to this updated probability distribution and her belief about the other players' strategy choices, which is called the player's *best response*. The requirement of being best response to each other's choice thus gives rise to the most commonly used solution concept for Bayesian games knowns as *Bayesian Nash equilibrium*. Such a framework provides a powerful tool for analyzing strategic situations involving differences of private information among the players, which has a wide range of applications in

---

① J. C. Harsanyi, Games with incomplete information played by "Bayesian" players, Part Ⅰ, *Manag. Sci.*, 1967/68, 14, pp. 159 – 182; J. C. Harsanyi, Games with incomplete information played by "Bayesian" players, Part Ⅱ, *Manag. Sci.*, 1967/68, 14, pp. 320 – 334; J. C. Harsanyi, Games with incomplete information played by "Bayesian" players, Part Ⅲ, *Manag. Sci.*, 1967/68, 14, pp. 486 – 502.

② Such a game model is commonly known as "Bayesian" game exactly due to its use of Bayes' rule for updating players' beliefs in the light of new information.

various domains such as auction, mechanism design and jury voting. ①

An important feature of Bayesian Nash equilibrium is that it ensures the so-called *dynamic consistency* property, which has been extensively discussed in the context of sequential decision making. ② Roughly speaking, dynamic consistency requires that an optimal contingent plan of action will remain optimal when new information is updated. In the context of Bayesian games, this implies that, upon the receipt of private information, the players would not want to revise their planned actions that they deem as optimal when evaluated from the *ex ante* perspective. As a matter of fact, within the framework of Bayesian games, there is no need to distinguish between *ex ante* and *interim* Bayesian Nash equilibrium, since it makes no difference whether the players evaluate their strategies using the *ex ante* or *interim* versions of expected utility maximization. Such an equivalence result is not surprising at all, for expected utility model does satisfy dynamic consistency due to the law of iterated expectations. The intuition behind the law of iterated expectation lies in the fact that a (joint) probability distribution can be decomposed into expressions involving its conditional and marginal distribution. As we shall see, this decomposition property plays a critical role in the latter discussion concerning dynamic consistency in the context of non-expected utility.

It is important to note, however, that Harsanyi's theory of Bayesian games relies heavily on the assumption of the existence of a single common prior representing

---

① D. Fudenberg, J. Tirole, *Game Theory*, Cambridge, MA: MIT Press, 1991; M. J. Osborne, *An Introduction to Game Theory*, New York, NY: Oxford University Press, 2004.

② P. J. Hammond, Consequentialist foundations for expected utility, *Theory Decis*, 1988, 25, pp. 292 - 297; T. Seidenfeld, Decision theory without "Independence" or without "Ordering": What is the difference?, *Econ. Philos.*, 1988, 4, pp. 267 - 290; M. J. Machina, Dynamic consistency and non-expected utility models of choice under uncertainty, *J. Econ. Lit.*, 1989, 27, pp. 1622 - 1668; E. Karni, Z. Safra, Behaviorally consistent optimal stopping rules, *J. Econ. Theory*, 1990, 51, pp. 391 - 402; E. F. McClennen, *Rationality and Dynamic Choice: Foundational Explorations*, Cambridge: Cambridge University Press, 1990; E. Karni, D. Schmeidler, Atemporal dynamic consistency and expected utility, *J. Econ. Theory*, 1991, 54, pp. 401 - 408.

all the players' initial beliefs. [①] This assumption seems extremely implausible in many real world situations. Furthermore, a number of researchers have cast doubt on the adequacy of modelling uncertainty using a single probability distribution in a variety of contexts. Knight[②] raises questions about the suitability of probabilistic characterization of uncertainty in certain situations, which leads to the important distinction between risk and uncertainty. Since the seminal work of Ellsberg[③], many authors have convincingly argued that the representation of uncertainty in terms of a single precise probability function is not only practically unrealistic but also normatively insufficient in many situations[④]. Motivated by this, a vast literature has developed on extending expected utility theory to accommodate the Ellsberg paradox by modelling uncertainty through a set of probabilities rather than a precise probability distribution[⑤]. In light of these, it is natural to think that the common prior assumption in Bayesian games should be relaxed as well in order to accommodate Ellsberg-type uncertainty, which constitutes the primary motivation of the current work.

In this paper, we take the view that due to limited information a player may not be able to identify a unique probability for representing her belief about the states, which thus should be depicted as a set of probability distributions instead. Based on this view, we present a general model of incomplete information games, which

---

① An alternative but equivalent way of formulating Bayesian games is to assume that its basic primitives are the beliefs of all the players given their private information. see J. C. Harsanyi, Games with incomplete information played by "Bayesian" players, Part Ⅰ, *Manag. Sci.*, 1967/68, 14, pp. 159 – 182; J. C. Harsanyi, Games with incomplete information played by "Bayesian" players, Part Ⅱ, *Manag. Sci.*, 1967/68, 14, pp. 320 – 334; J. C. Harsanyi, Games with incomplete information played by "Bayesian" players, Part Ⅲ, *Manag. Sci.*, 1967/68, 14, pp. 486 – 502. As Harsanyi points out, however, such beliefs can be regarded as conditional probability distributions derived from a prior probability measure.

② F. H. Knight, *Risk, Uncertainty, and Profit*, Boston, MA: Houghton Miffin Company, 1921.

③ D. Ellbsberg, Risk, ambiguity, and the Savage axioms, *Q. J. Econ.* 1961, 75, pp. 643 – 649.

④ H. Kyburg, *Epistemology and Inference*, Minneapolis: University of Minnesota Press, 1983; I. Levi, On indeterminate probabilities, *J. Philos.*, 1974, 71, pp. 391 – 418; I. Levi, *The Enterprise of Knowledge*, Cambridge: MIT Press, 1980; P. Walley, *Statistical Reasoning with Imprecise Probabilities*, New York: Chapman and Hall, 1994.

⑤ I. Gilboa, D. Schmeidler, Maxmin expected utility with non-unique prior, *J. Math. Econ.*, 1989, 18, pp. 141 – 153; D. Schmeidler, Subjective probability and expected utility without additivity, *Econometrica*, 1989, 57, pp. 571 – 587; T. Seidenfeld, M. J. Schervish, J. B. Kadane, Decisions without ordering, in W. Sieg (Ed.), *Acting and Reflecting*, Dordrecht: Kluwer Academic Publishers, 1990, pp. 143 – 170; T. Seidenfeld, M. J. Schervish, J. B. Kadane, A representation of partially ordered preferences, *Ann. Stat.*, 1995, 23, pp. 2168 – 2217; P. Walley, *Statistical Reasoning with Imprecise Probabilities*, New York: Chapman and Hall, 1994.

extends the traditional framework of Bayesian games to include Ellsberg-type ambiguity. Following the pioneer work of Kajii and Ui ①, we assume that each player's perception of uncertainty about the states is modelled by a compact set of probability measures, instead of a single common probability distribution. Moreover, we allow for the possibility that different players may have different initial beliefs, which can be represented by uncommon sets of probability distributions. We also adopt the principle of Γ-maximin as the decision rule used by all the players. ② Similarly to Kajii and Ui's approach, we propose to study equilibrium concepts in which each player chooses the optimal action in the sense of maximizing the minimum expected utility for each realization of her private signal. In this sense, our model constitutes only a minor departure from the standard approach to games with incomplete information.

Nevertheless, our model differs from the model introduced by Kajii and Ui③ in the following respects. Kajii and Ui assume that each player is endowed with an updating rule for determining their posterior beliefs, whereas we allow for any set of well-defined posterior functions to represent players' updated beliefs. In view of this, our model is a bit more general than the one developed by Kajii and Ui④. In addition, it has two advantages over their game model. First, our approach avoids the ongoing controversy concerning the right updating rule under ambiguity, as the theoretical literature on dynamic choices under ambiguity has not yet reached a consensus on which updating rule is most plausible for the modelling of ambiguity through a set of probabilities. Second, it also facilitates the discussion about the relationship between priors and posteriors, which turns out to be crucial for establishing the central result of this paper (see Section 4).

---

① A. Kajii, T. Ui, Incomplete information games with multiple priors, *Jpn. Econ. Rev.*, 2005, 56, pp. 332 – 351.

② The use of Γ-maximin to decision making under severe uncertainty can be traced back to at least A. Wald, *Statistical Decision Functions*, New York: John Wiley, 1950 and L. Hurwicz, Optimality criteria for decision making under ignorance, *Cowles Commission Discussion Paper*, 1951. I. Gilboa, D. Schmeidler, Maxmin expected utility with non-unique prior, *J. Math. Econ.*, 1989, 18, pp. 141 – 153 supply it with an axiomatic foundation.

③ A. Kajii, T. Ui, Incomplete information games with multiple priors, *Jpn. Econ. Rev.*, 2005, 56, pp. 332 – 351.

④ A. Kajii, T. Ui, Incomplete information games with multiple priors, *Jpn. Econ. Rev.*, 2005, 56, pp. 332 – 351.

It has already been shown (see for instance Refs. ①) that, non-expected utility decision makers are expected to violate the requirement of dynamic consistency when uncertainty is represented by a set of probability measures. It thus should come as no surprise that the concepts of *ex ante* and *interim* Γ-*maximin equilibrium* generally do not coincide in the current framework. Indeed, as Kajii and Ui② have rightly recognized, an *ex ante* Γ-maximin equilibrium may specify strategies that are not components of any *interim* Γ-maximin equilibrium. In this paper, we reinforce this point by showing an example (see the main example of Section 3) in which the set of *ex ante* Γ-maximin equilibria of the game is disjoint from the one of its *interim* Γ-maximin equilibria. This thus implies that dynamic consistency does not hold in the present framework and these two equilibrium concepts should be treated differently.

In view of violations of dynamic consistency, Kajii and Ui③ suggest to sidestep this problem by focusing merely on the interim equilibrium concept. It should be remarked that, however, the counterintuitive phenomenon of aversion to cost-free information may occur when the condition of dynamic consistency is violated. ④ From a normative point of view, such a behavior seems quite problematic, which is often used as an argument against non-expected utility theories (see for example⑤).

The main objective of this paper is then to determine under what conditions these two equilibrium concepts become equivalent in the present game-theoretic framework, which in turn guarantees the property of dynamic consistency. The crucial condition comes from the work of Epstein and Schneider⑥, which they call "*rectangularity*". The rectangularity condition is concerned with the relation between the set of priors and posteriors, which can be regarded as a generalization of the decomposition

---

① L. G. Epstein, M. Le Breton, Dynamically consistent beliefs must be Bayesian, *J. Econ. Theory*, 1993, 61, pp. 1 – 22; R. Sarin, P. Wakker, Dynamic choice and nonexpected utility, *J. Risk Uncertain.*, 1998, 17, pp. 87 – 120.

② A. Kajii, T. Ui, Incomplete information games with multiple priors, *Jpn. Econ. Rev.*, 2005, 56, pp. 332 – 351.

③ A. Kajii, T. Ui, Incomplete information games with multiple priors, *Jpn. Econ. Rev.*, 2005, 56, pp. 332 – 351.

④ P. Wakker, Non-expected utility as aversion to information, *J. Behav. Decis. Mak.*, 1988, 1, pp. 169 – 175; L. G. Epstein, M. Le Breton, Dynamically consistent beliefs must be Bayesian, *J. Econ. Theory*, 1993, 61, pp. 1 – 22.

⑤ N. I. Al-Najjar, J. Weinstein, The ambiguity aversion literature: a critical assessment, *Econ. Philos.*, 2009, 25, pp. 249 – 284.

⑥ L. G. Epstein, M. Schneider, Recursive multiple priors, *J. Econ. Theory*, 2003, 113, pp. 1 – 31.

property of a probability measure. Informally speaking, rectangularity requires that every element in the set of priors can be factorized into its marginal and an *arbitrary* conditional distribution in the set of posterior probabilities. Epstein and Schneider① prove that in the single-agent dynamic choice setting rectangularity implies dynamic consistency. Motivated by the discussion on independence concepts for imprecise probability models②, we relax the rectangu-larity condition by demanding that only those extreme probability distributions in the set of priors satisfy such a factorization property. Under this weaker assumption, we establish that the *ex ante* and *interim* Γ-maximin equilibrium concepts coincide in the framework of incomplete information games under ambiguity, which constitutes the central result of our paper.

There is a small but growing literature that attempts to extend the framework of Nash equilibrium to the context of ambiguity in which players' uncertainty can be represented by imprecise probabilities rather than a single probability distribution. Dow and Werlang③ introduce an equilibrium concept for two-player normal form games in which players' beliefs about the opponents' strategy choices are represented by non-additive probabilities and players are Choquet expected utility maximizers. Eichberger and Kelsey④ extend Dow and Werlang's equilibrium concept to normal form games with n-player and discuss some mathematical properties of this concept. By employing the multiple priors model introduced by Gilboa and Schmeidler⑤ to represent players' uncertainty, Klibanoff⑥ and Lo⑦ provide two different equilibrium-type solution concepts for normal form games with any finite number of players. Nau⑧ extends the notion of coherence to non-cooperative games by

① L. G. Epstein, M. Schneider, Recursive multiple priors, *J. Econ. Theory*, 2003, 113, pp. 1 – 31.

② F. G. Cozman, Sets of probability distributions, independence, and convexity, *Synthese*, 2012, 186, pp. 577 – 600.

③ J. Dow, S. Werlang, Nash equilibrium under Knightian uncertainty: breaking down backward induction, *J. Econ. Theory*, 1994, 64, pp. 305 – 324.

④ J. Eichberger, D. Kelsey, Non-additive beliefs and strategic equilibria, *Games Econ. Behav.*, 2000, 30, pp. 183 – 215.

⑤ I. Gilboa, D. Schmeidler, Maxmin expected utility with non-unique prior, *J. Math. Econ.*, 1989, 18, pp. 141 – 153.

⑥ P. Klibanoff, Uncertainty, *Decision and Normal Form Games*, MIT, Mimeo, 1994.

⑦ K. C. Lo, Equilibrium in beliefs under uncertainty, *J. Econ. Theory*, 1996, 71, pp. 443 – 484.

⑧ R. Nau, Imprecise probabilities in non-cooperative games, in F. Coolen, G. de Cooman, T. Fetz, M. Oberguggenberger (Eds.), *Proceedings of the 7th International Symposium on Imprecise Probabilities: Theories and Applications*, Innsbruck, Austria, 2011, pp. 297 – 306.

employing the concept of lower and upper previsions to model the beliefs of the players. It is worth mentioning that all of these papers consider only normal form games with complete information. Thus, the critical issue of dynamic consistency does not even arise in these frameworks.

The framework of incomplete information games provides a relatively simple structure for discussing the issue of dynamic consistency, when uncertainty in games is represented by a set of probability distributions. However, not too much work has been done on the generalization of incomplete information games to include ambiguity. Most of the existing literature on this topic focuses merely on how to apply the framework of incomplete information games to examine auctions. For instance, Salo and Weber①, Lo②, and Bose et al. ③ study auctions as incomplete information games, where participants are allowed to be modelled as non-expected utility decision makers. In the theoretical category, Epstein and Wang④ and Kajii and Ui⑤ have developed formal frameworks that deal with the modelling of uncertainty through sets of probability distributions in incomplete information games. Yet, these works do not investigate under what condition dynamic consistent behavior would always occur. By generalizing the characterization result of Epstein and Schneide⑥ in the setting of single-agent dynamic choices, we provide a sufficient condition under which dynamic consistency is always assured in the framework of incomplete information games under ambiguity.

The rest of the paper is organized as follows. In Section 2 we provide a general game-theoretic framework that allows for the modelling of uncertainty through a set of probability distributions. In Section 3 we briefly characterize general properties of the equilibrium concepts that we propose, and also present an example that illustrates the difference between *ex ante* and interim equilibrium concepts within the current framework. In Section 4 we discuss the main result that ensures dynamic consistency

---

① A. Salo, M. Weber, Ambiguity aversion in first-price sealed-bid auctions, *J. Risk Uncertain.*, 1995, 11, pp. 123 – 137.

② K. C. Lo, Sealed bid auctions with uncertainty averse bidders, *Econ. Theory*, 1998, 12, pp. 1 – 20.

③ S. Bose, E. Ozdenoren, A. Pape, Optimal auctions with ambiguity, *Theor. Econ.*, 2006, 1, pp. 411 – 438.

④ L. G. Epstein, T. Wang, Beliefs about beliefs without probabilities, *Econometrica*, 1996, 64, pp. 1343 – 1373.

⑤ A. Kajii, T. Ui, Incomplete information games with multiple priors, *Jpn. Econ. Rev.*, 2005, 56, pp. 332 – 351.

⑥ L. G. Epstein, M. Schneider, Recursive multiple priors, *J. Econ. Theory*, 2003, 113, pp. 1 – 31.

in incomplete information games under ambiguity. Section 5 concludes with a brief discussion about possible extensions of the current work.

2. The Framework

In this section, we present a model of strategic interaction under ambiguity with incomplete information as proposed in Kajii and Ui①. The basic idea of such a model is to generalize the standard framework of Bayesian games developed by Harsanyi② to include ambiguity concerning payoff structures. More precisely, we assume that each player's belief about the states is depicted by a non-empty set of priors rather than a single common prior. For ease of exposition we restrict ourselves to incomplete information games with finitely many players, actions, and states.

We follow the standard model of a Bayesian game, where each player is endowed with a partition of a finite state space that represents her private information. There is a finite set Ω of states and a finite set I of players. Each player i receives some private information concerning the states, which is summarized by a signal function τ_i. Denote with T_i the range of the signal function τ_i, which is often called the *type* set of player i. Any type $t_i \in T_i$ can be interpreted as a signal privately received by player i at the interim stage. Given a state $\omega \in \Omega$, the unique signal observed by player i at ω is denoted by $\tau_i(\omega)$.

After observing a signal $t_i \in T_i$, each player i is asked to choose a pure action from the set A_i of options available to her. We write $\Delta(A_i)$ for the set of mixed actions of player i. ③ As usual, a strategy of player i is defined as a mapping from her signals to actions, i. e., $\sigma_i: T_i \mapsto \Delta(A_i)$. The set of all strategies for player i is denoted Σ_i, and the set of all strategy profiles is denoted $\Sigma := \Pi_{i \in I} \Sigma_i$ with typical element $\sigma = (\sigma_1, \cdots, \sigma_I)$. In particular, denote with S_i and S the set of all pure strategies for player i and the set of all pure strategy profiles respectively. The probability with which player i chooses the action $a_i \in A_i$ after observing the signal t_i according to σ_i is denoted $\sigma_i(a_i | t_i)$. By convention σ_{-i} stands for a strategy profile of players other than

① A. Kajii, T. Ui, Incomplete information games with multiple priors, *Jpn. Econ. Rev.*, 2005, 56, pp. 332 – 351.

② J. C. Harsanyi, Games with incomplete information played by "Bayesian" players, Part Ⅰ, *Manag. Sci.*, 1967/68, 14, pp. 159 – 182; J. C. Harsanyi, Games with incomplete information played by "Bayesian" players, Part Ⅱ, *Manag. Sci.*, 1967/68, 14, pp. 320 – 334; J. C. Harsanyi, Games with incomplete information played by "Bayesian" players, Part Ⅲ, *Manag. Sci.*, 1967/68, 14, pp. 486 – 502.

③ Given a set X, we denote the set of all probability distributions on X by $\Delta(X)$.

player i in which every player $j \neq i$ plays as in σ. For notational convenience, we also denote with $\sigma(a \mid t) = \Pi_{i \in I} \sigma_i(a_i \mid t_i)$ the probability of action profile a is chosen when a profile t of signals is realized, and likewise for $\sigma_{-i}(a_{-i} \mid t_{-i}) = \Pi_{j \neq i} \sigma_j(a_j \mid t_j)$.

As in the Bayesian game model, players' payoffs depend not only upon the choice made by the players but also upon the private signals concerning the states revealed to them. Similarly, our model assumes that each player's preference ordering is represented by a von Neumann-Morgenstern utility function① $u_i : A \times \Omega \mapsto \mathbb{R}$.

So far our descriptions of the game are the same as the usual specifications of Bayesian game. Our major departure from the standard model lies in the way of representing players' initial beliefs about the states. Differently from the traditional framework of Bayesian games, in this work we do not assume that there is a single common prior over the states. Instead, the current game model allows for the possibility that players' beliefs about the states are represented by possibly uncommon sets ofprobabilities. To be more specific, it is assumed in our model that there is a non-empty, closed, and convex set $P_i \subseteq \Delta(\Omega)$ for player $i \in I$, which characterizes player i's initial beliefs concerning the states. In addition, we require that there is no null signal, i. e., $p(\tau_i^{-1}(t_i)) > 0$ for all $t_i \in T_i, p \in P_i$, and $i \in I$. Obviously, if each set P_i is a singleton for each $i \in I$ and they coincide, then the current game model collapses back into the traditional model of Bayesian game.

In order to complete the description of the model, we have to include an additional component that depicts each player's belief about the states after a certain signal is observed. There are two different ways to achieve such a purpose. One way is to take some updating rule for players as primitive, which specifies how to derive the posterior beliefs from a set of prior probabilities. This is the approach adopted in Kajii and Ui②. To define the notion of an updating rule, we first need to identify the set of conditional probabilities derived from a set of priors. Given an arbitrary $p \in P$ and $t_i \in T_i$, we write $p(\cdot \mid t_i) \in \Delta(\Omega)$ the conditional probability over Ω defined in the standard way: for all $E \subseteq \Omega$,

$$p(E \mid t_i) = \frac{p(E \cap \tau_i^{-1}(t_i))}{p(\tau_i^{-1}(t_i))} \tag{1}$$

① J. von Neumann, O. Morgenstern, *Theory of Games and Economic Behavior*, Princeton, NJ: Princeton University Press, 1944.

② A. Kajii, T. Ui, Incomplete information games with multiple priors, *Jpn. Econ. Rev.*, 2005, 56, pp. 332 - 351.

And denote with $P_i(t_i) = \{p(\cdot|t_i) \in \Delta(\Omega) | p \in P_i\}$ the set of conditional probability distributions when the signal t_i is revealed to player i. An updating rule $\Phi_i: T_i \mapsto 2^{P_i(t_i)}$ for player i is a function that prescribes a subset of $P_i(t_i)$ for every $t_i \in T_i$. As discussed in Gilboa and Schmeidler①, there are several reasonable methods for updating a set of probabilities given an observation. However, there is no agreement in the literature which one is the appropriate updating procedure among them. Here we shall consider the following two relatively more established updating rules. The first one is commonly known as the full Bayesian updating rule②, which can be regarded as a natural generalization of the standard Bayes rule: for all $t_i \in T_i$,

$$\Phi_i^{FB}(t_i) = P_i(t_i) \tag{2}$$

The other rule is closely related to the work of Dempster③ and Shafer④, which is often called the maximum likelihood updating rule, as described below: for all $t_i \in T_i$,

$$\Phi_i^{ML}(t_i) = \{q(\cdot|t_i) \in P_i(t_i): q \in \arg\max_{p \in P_i} p(\tau_i^{-1}(t_i))\} \tag{3}$$

It is easy to verify that both $\Phi_i^{FB}(t_i)$ and $\Phi_i^{ML}(t_i)$ are nonempty, closed, and convex for all $t_i \in T_i$, provided that the set P_i is assumed to be nonempty, closed, and convex.

An alternative way is to assume posteriors to be primitives of the model the same as the priors but without imposing any particular relation between them. Such an approach is a bit more general than the previous one, since it even allows the set of posterior probabilities to include ones that cannot be identified as a conditional probability of any priors in the set of priors. Moreover, it sidesteps the controversial issue concerning the appropriate updating procedure under ambiguity. Instead of arguing for a particular updating rule, one can investigate what kind of relationship between priors and posteriors is right for establishing a certain result. In view of these advantages, we shall pursue such an approach in this paper. More precisely, we assume in the current model that each player i is endowed with a posterior function $\Phi_i: T_i \mapsto 2^{\Delta(\Omega)}$ that satisfies the following two conditions: (1) $\Phi_i(t_i)$ is nonempty,

① I. Gilboa, D. Schmeidler, Updating ambiguous beliefs, *J. Econ. Theory*, 1993, 59, pp. 33-49.

② R. Fagin, J. Halpern, A new approach to updating beliefs, in *Proceedings of the 6th Conference on Uncertainty in AI*, New York: Elsevier, 1990, pp. 317-325.

③ A. P. Dempster, Upper and lower probabilities induced by a multivalued mapping, *Ann. Math. Stat.*, 1967, 38, pp. 325-339.

④ G. Shafer, *A Mathematical Theory of Evidence*, Princeton, NJ: Princeton University Press, 1976.

closed, and convex for all $t_i \in T_i$; (2) $q(\tau_i^{-1}(t_i)) = 1$ for all $q \in \Phi_i(t_i)$ and $t_i \in T_i$. The latter condition basically states that the information revealed by the signal t_i is correct, that is, given t_i player i knows that one of the states in $\tau_i^{-1}(t_i)$ occurs. We shall discuss below how these two alternative approaches are related to each other.

In summary, an incomplete information game under ambiguity can be formally defined as follows.

Definition 2.1. *An* **incomplete information game under ambiguity** *is a tuple* $G = \langle I, \Omega, (A_i, T_i, \tau_i, P_i, \Phi_i, u_i)_{i \in I} \rangle$ *where*

a set of players $I = \{1, 2, \ldots, I\}$,

a set of states $\Omega = \{\omega_1, \omega_2, \ldots, \omega_n\}$,

a set of actions A_i *for each player* $i \in I$,

a set of signals or types T_i *and a signal function* $\tau_i : \Omega \mapsto T_i$ *for each player* i $\in$ I,

a nonempty, closed, and convex set P_i *of priors for each player* $i \in I$, *where each prior* $p \in P_i$ *on* Ω *satisfies* $p(\tau_i^{-1}(t_i)) > 0$ *for all* $t_i \in T_i$ *and* $i \in I$,

a posterior function $\Phi_i : T_i \mapsto 2^{\Delta(\Omega)}$ *for each player* $i \in I$ *such that* (*i*) $\Phi_i(t_i)$ *is nonempty, closed, and convex for all* $t_i \in T_i$, *and* (*ii*) $q(\tau_i^{-1}(t_i)) = 1$ *for all* $q \in \Phi_i(t_i)$ *and* $t_i \in T_i$,

a utility function $u_i : A \times \Omega \mapsto \mathbb{R}$ *for each player* i, *where* A *is the product of the action set* A_i*'s.*

Following the standard interpretation, an incomplete information game under ambiguity is played as follows. At the beginning of the game, each player i holds a belief concerning how a state $\omega \in \Omega$ is realized. After the realization of the state, player i does not observe the state but receives a signal $\tau_i(\omega)$ that provides her with some incomplete information about the state. Then player i is asked to choose an action, whose utility depends on her own action, the actions chosen by other players as well as the state. Unlike in the traditional Bayesian game model, however, we assume that each player has not only partial information about the other players, but also may be uncertain about nature's move in choosing the states. And we assume that this kind of uncertainty is represented by a set of probability distributions over the states. Such an approach to strategic interaction allows us to deal with any state of insufficiencies in players' information about the state, including complete ignorance. And we also assume that the whole structure of an incomplete information game under ambiguity as described above is commonly known among the players.

Once it is assumed that players' prior and posterior beliefs are modelled using sets of probabilities, it is necessary to replace the principle of maximizing expected utility with some generalized decision criterion, since the expected utility is no longer precise and becomes an interval instead. As far as single-agent decision making is concerned, several decision rules such as *Γ-maximin*[1], *E-admissibility*[2], and *maximality*[3] have been proposed in the literature as possible generalizations of expected utility maximization.[4] There is, however, no general agreement among decision theorists as to which is the right rule for judging rational decisions when uncertainty is expressed by a closed convex set of probability functions. Among these suggested criteria, the decision rule Γ-maximin generalizes the principle of maximizing expected utility by simply taking the lower expected utility, thereby inducing a complete order on the decision set. More precisely, according to the principle of Γ-maximin, a rational decision maker should choose an option to maximize the minimum expected value with respect to a convex set of probabilities. Such a criterion for decision making under uncertainty seems suitable for describing decision makers who are uncertainty averse, as it always takes the worst possible expected value as the base for maximization. In this paper we adopt the principle of Γ-maximin as the intended decision rule for evaluating players' strategies in incomplete information games under ambiguity.

Although incomplete information games are one-stage strategic games, one may distinguish between two different stages when considering the evaluation of players' strategies, which are commonly known as the *ex ante* and *interim* stage. In order to illustrate the difference, let us consider an incomplete information game under ambiguity. In the *ex ante* stage, the players are assumed to know each other's prior beliefs about the states while have not yet learnt any information about the states. That

---

① I. Gilboa, D. Schmeidler, Maxmin expected utility with non-unique prior, *J. Math. Econ.*, 1989, 18, pp. 141 – 153.

② I. Levi, On indeterminate probabilities, *J. Philos.*, 1974, 71, pp. 391 – 418.

③ P. Walley, *Statistical Reasoning with Imprecise Probabilities*, New York: Chapman and Hall, 1994.

④ For a detailed comparison between these criteria see M. J. Schervish, T. Seidenfeld, J. B. Kadane, I. Levi, Extensions of expected utility theory and some limitations of pairwise comparisons, in J. M. Bernard, T. Seidenfeld, M. Zaffalon (Eds.), *Proceedings of the 3rd International Symposium on Imprecise Probabilities and Their Applications*, Lugano, Switzerland, Waterloo: Carleton Scientific, 2003, pp. 496 – 510; T. Seidenfeld, A contrast between two decision rules for use with (convex) sets of probabilities: T-maximin versus E-admissibility, *Synthese*, 2004, 140, pp. 69 – 88; M. Troffaes, Decision making under uncertainty using imprecise probabilities, *Int. J. Approx. Reason.*, 2007, 45, pp. 17 – 29.

is, the players can only evaluate their strategies based on the prior probabilities without observing any private signals. In this case, one can compute player i's expected payoff under a mixed strategy profile σ given $p \in P_i$ using the following formula:

$$\mathbb{E}_i^A(\sigma \mid p) = \sum_{\omega \in \Omega} \sum_{a \in A} p(\omega)\sigma(a \mid \tau_i(\omega))u_i(a,\omega). \tag{4}$$

We shall call $\mathbb{E}_i^A(\sigma \mid p)$ player i's *ex ante expected payoff* under the strategy profile σ given the prior p. By contrast, in the interim stage, each player is informed of her private signal but not the other players' signals about the states, and thus can evaluate her strategies in the light of this new information. This means that after observing t_i player i can use the posteriors in $\Phi_i(t_i)$ to assess her strategies. Given a mixed strategy profile σ and $q \in \Phi_i(t_i)$, one can calculate player i's expected payoff in the interim stage according to the following formula:

$$\mathbb{E}_i^I(\sigma \mid q) = \sum_{\omega \in \Omega} \sum_{a \in A} q(\omega \mid t_i)\sigma(a \mid \tau_i(\omega))u_i(a,\omega). \tag{5}$$

Similarly, we shall call $\mathbb{E}_i^I(\sigma \mid q)$ player i's *interim expected payoff* under the strategy profile σ given the posterior q when t_i is observed. It can be seen from Eq. (4) and Eq. (5) that the key difference between the notions of *ex ante* and interim maximin payoff lies in the part of beliefs about the states used in the evaluation. In the former case the prior beliefs are used to evaluate the strategies, whereas in the latter case the assessment of the strategies is given based on the posterior beliefs after the signals are observed.

Now we are in a position to define solution concepts using these two different ways of computing expected payoffs to players' strategies. Like in standard Bayesian games, the solution concepts defined here require that each player's conjecture regarding the other players' behaviors should be correct, that is, players' conjectures coincide with the components specified in the equilibrium profile. As mentioned above, we assume that all the players employ the principle of Γ-maximin as their decision rule. Thus, our solution concepts require that each player chooses a strategy in order to maximizes her minimum *ex ante* or interim expected payoffs. We first define a solution concept based on the notion of *ex ante* expected payoff described above.

Definition 2.2. *A strategy profile σ^* is an* **ex ante Γ-maximin equilibrium** *for an incomplete information game G if for each $i \in I$*

$$\min_{p \in P_i} \mathbb{E}_i^A(\sigma_i^*, \sigma_{-i}^* \mid p) \geqslant \min_{p \in P_i} \mathbb{E}_i^A(\sigma_i, \sigma_{-i}^* \mid p) \tag{6}$$

for all $\sigma_i \in \Sigma_i$.

In a similar fashion, we can formally define an equilibrium concept for the interim case as follows.

Definition 2.3. *A strategy profile* σ^* *is an* **interim Γ-maximin equilibrium** *for an incomplete information game G if for each* $i \in I$ *and* $t_i \in T_i$

$$\min_{q \in \Phi_i(t_i)} \mathbb{E}_i^I(\sigma_i^*, \sigma_{-i}^* | q) \geqslant \min_{q \in \Phi_i(t_i)} \mathbb{E}_i^I(\sigma_i, \sigma_{-i}^* | q) \tag{7}$$

for all $\sigma_i \in \Sigma_i$.

Note that this interim equilibrium concept corresponds to the notion of *mixed equilibrium* introduced by Kajii and Ui①, provided that the posterior functions are derived from the prior probabilities using the updating rule presupposed in their framework. Kajii and Ui mainly focused on the notion of mixed equilibrium and established its existence. However, they did not investigate further the properties of this solution concept including its relationship with Bayesian Nash equilibrium and the *ex ante* equilibrium concept. To complete the investigation, we will study in the next section more about the equilibrium concepts introduced above and their relationship.

It is also worth pointing out that in the traditional framework of Bayesian games the *ex ante* and interim equilibrium concepts do coincide with each other. More precisely, a strategy is an *ex ante* Bayesian Nash equilibrium if and only if it is an interim Bayesian Nash equilibrium. The main reason behind this result is that the expected utility maximization respects the law of iterated expectations. Such a feature is called *dynamic consistency* in the literature of decision theory, which roughly says that if an option is optimal after learning new information, then it is also the best plan of actions in the *ex ante* case. We shall formally define it later. In view of this result, there is no need to distinguish between these two equilibrium concepts in Bayesian games. In the present framework, however, the interim Γ-maximin equilibrium concept often differs from the notion of *ex ante* Γ-maximin equilibrium, since the principle of Γ-maximin does not obey the law of iterated expectations. As we will see in the next section, the set of interim Γ-maximin equilibria can even be disjoint from the set of *ex ante* Γ-maximin equilibria in some incomplete information game under ambiguity.

---

① A. Kajii, T. Ui, Incomplete information games with multiple priors, *Jpn. Econ. Rev.*, 2005, 56, pp. 332–351.

3. Properties of Equilibrium Concepts

This section is mainly devoted to exploring general properties of equilibrium concepts introduced in the previous section. Among other things, we present below an example of an incomplete information game under ambiguity which has a unique solution using either *ex ante* or interim Γ-maximin equilibrium, but where these solutions are not identical. Using the same example, we also show that, in contrast to the *ex ante* Γ-maximin equilibrium, the interim Γ-maximin equilibrium does not coincide with a Bayesian Nash equilibrium under any single probability in the (common) set of posterior probability distributions. This is in the same spirit as in decision making under uncertainty that an option that is admissible according to Γ-maximin may not be Bayesian admissible. ①

It has become standard practice in every game-theoretic framework to provide an existence result for the proposed solution concept. Thus we first show that both *ex ante* and interim Γ-maximin equilibria exist in every incomplete information game under ambiguity. These results depend crucially upon the properties of the sets of priors and posteriors, which play a key role in characterizing the best response correspondences.

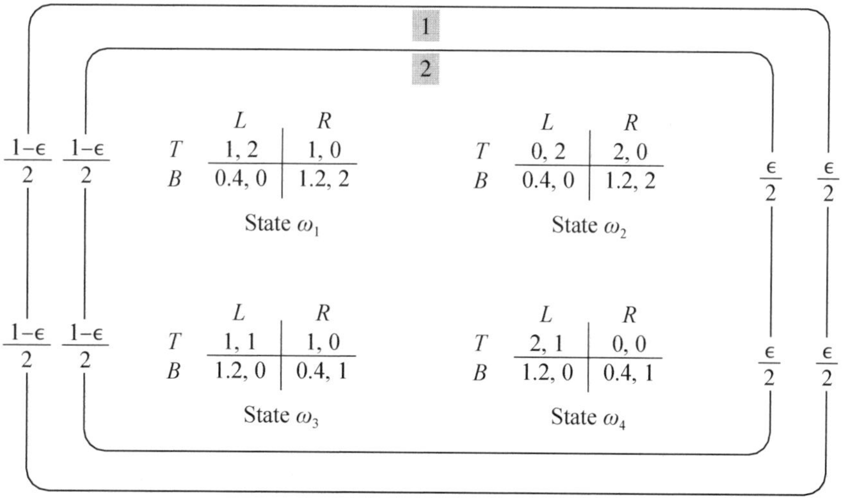

Fig. 1 An incomplete information game under ambiguity

① See T. Seidenfeld, A contrast between two decision rules for use with (convex) sets of probabilities: Γ-maximin versus E-admissibility, *Synthese*, 2004, 140, pp. 69-88 for a detailed discussion on the comparison between different criteria for decision making under uncertainty when uncertainty is depicted by a set of probability distributions.

Proposition 3. 1. *Every finite incomplete information game under ambiguity G has at least one ex ante* Γ *-maximin equilibrium, and also has at least one interim* Γ *-maximin equilibrium.*

Note that the definition of *ex ante* Γ -maximin equilibrium is reduced to that of *ex ante* Bayesian Nash equilibrium when the set P_i of priors is the same singleton for all $i \in I$. And the same result holds for interim Γ -maximin equilibrium when the set $\Phi_i(t_i)$ is a singleton for all $i \in I$ and $t_i \in T_i$. Since *ex ante* and interim Bayesian Nash equilibrium coincide, it follows that the concepts of *ex ante* and interim Γ -maximin equilibrium are equivalent to each other under these conditions in the present framework.

Nevertheless, in incomplete information games under ambiguity with a common set of priors, the *ex ante* Γ -maximin equilibrium exhibits a closer relation to the Bayesian Nash equilibrium in comparison with the interim Γ -maximin equilibrium. To be a bit more specific, every *ex ante* Γ -maximin equilibrium can be justified as a Bayesian Nash equilibrium using some prior in the set of priors, whereas this generally does not hold for interim Γ -maximin equilibrium. We state this general result in the following proposition.

Proposition 3. 2. *Let G be an incomplete information game with a common set P of priors. If a strategy profile* σ^* *is an ex ante* Γ *-maximin equilibrium for G, then there exists some prior* $p \in P$ *such that* σ^* *is a Bayesian Nash equilibrium for the game* G', *where* G' *is the modified game that replaces the set P in G with* $\{p\}$.

Proof. This result can be easily established based on the observation that, from the *ex ante* perspective, an incomplete information game under ambiguity can be transformed into a normal form game in the traditional sense.

The above result is not surprising, since we can apply the standard techniques to transform an incomplete information game under ambiguity into a traditional strategic form game using the lower expected payoffs. Proposition 3. 2 shows that, although σ^* is an *ex ante* Γ -maximin solution to an incomplete information game under ambiguity, it can be viewed as a Bayesian Nash equilibrium for a Bayesian game with the right prior. According to this result, it is always possible to find at least one prior such that the *ex ante* Γ -maximin equilibrium behavior is consistent with expected utility maximization given that prior. This implies that, from the *ex ante* perspective, an outsider who can only observe the actual strategy choices in an incomplete information game under ambiguity will not be able to distinguish ambiguity averse players from Bayesian players.

Proposition 3. 2 also raises the questions as to whether this result holds in the interim case as well. The following example shows that the answer to this question is "No". Such an example also serves as a nice illustration of our game-theoretic framework and the solution concepts introduced in the previous section.

Example 3. 3. Consider the game structure shown in Fig. 1. In this game, there are two players and four possible states, i. e. , $I = \{1,2\}$ and $\Omega = \{\omega_1, \omega_2, \omega_3, \omega_4\}$. The action set of player 1 is given by $A_1 = \{T, B\}$ and that of player 2 is given by $A_2 = \{L, R\}$.

Suppose that both players in this game are uncertain about nature's move in choosing the state. Unlike a traditional Bayesian game, however, the present game model allows players' uncertainty to be represented by sets of probabilities. More specifically, assume that both players' prior beliefs about the states are represented by the following common set of priors over the states.

$$P = \bigcup_{\varepsilon \in [0.1, 0.9]} \left\{ p \in \Delta(\Omega) : p(\omega_1) = p(\omega_3) = \frac{1-\varepsilon}{2}, p(\omega_2) = p(\omega_4) = \frac{\varepsilon}{2} \right\}. \tag{8}$$

	L	R
TT	$1, {}^3/_2$	$1, 0$
TB	$1.1 - {}^{\varepsilon}/_2, 1$	$0.7 + {}^{\varepsilon}/_2, {}^1/_2$
BT	$0.7 + {}^{\varepsilon}/_2, {}^1/_2$	$1.1 - {}^{\varepsilon}/_2, 1$
BB	$0.8, 0$	$0.8, {}^3/_2$

Fig. 2 strategic form of the game in Fig. 1

After the realization of the state chosen by nature, the players receive only partial information about the state. In this game, player 1 observes two signals while player 2 only observe one signal. Formally, let $T_1 = \{t_1, t_1'\}$ and $T_2 = \{t_2\}$. And the players' signal functions satisfy the following conditions:

$$\begin{aligned} \tau_1(\omega_1) &= \tau_1(\omega_2) = t_1 \\ \tau_1(\omega_3) &= \tau_1(\omega_4) = t_1' \\ \tau_1(\omega_k) &= t_2, \textit{for } k = 1,2,3,4. \end{aligned} \tag{9}$$

In words, if t_1' is observed, player 1 learns that either state ω_1 or ω_2 occurs, while if t_1' is observed, player 1 learns that either state ω_3 or ω_4 occurs. By contrast, player 2 is informed of no additional information about the state at the interim stage. Given these signals, it seems natural to consider the following sets of conditional probability distributions as representation of player 1's posterior beliefs regarding the states.

$$\begin{aligned}\Phi_1(t_1) &= \bigcup_{\varepsilon\in[0.1,0.9]}\{q\in\Delta(\Omega):q(\omega_1)=1-\varepsilon,q(\omega_2)=\varepsilon\}\\ \Phi_1(t_1') &= \bigcup_{\varepsilon\in[0.1,0.9]}\{q\in\Delta(\Omega):q(\omega_3)=1-\varepsilon,q(\omega_4)=\varepsilon\}.\end{aligned} \tag{10}$$

It is easy to see that these sets can be viewed as posterior probabilities derived from the set of priors by applying the full Bayesian updating rule to P, that is, $\Phi_1(t_1) = \Phi_1^{FB}(t_1)$ for all $t_1\in T_1$. Since player 2 does not obtain any further information, her posterior belief about the state does not change, i. e., $\Phi_2(t_2) = P$.

Furthermore, the players' preference ordering over strategy profiles relative to the states are assumed to be represented by von Neumann-Morgenstern payoff functions. The payoffs for the players in the states are depicted as shown in Fig. 1. As usual, we assume that the game structure, the prior probabilities, the posterior probabilities, and the range of ε are all common knowledge among the players. And suppose that each player models the other player as a decision maker who employs the principle of Γ-maximin as the decision rule under ambiguity.

What should the players choose under such a strategic situation involving both incomplete information and ambiguity? To answer this question, we need to distinguish between the *ex ante* and interim analyses of this incomplete information game under ambiguity. As hinted above, they may produce different recommendations for solving the same game, as opposed to the identical analyses in the traditional Bayesian games. It is thus important to keep in mind that one should carefully distinguish the interim analysis from the *ex ante* one in the presence of ambiguity. In order to illustrate this important point, let us examine the above game from both the *ex ante* and interim perspectives.

To solve the game from the *ex ante* perspective, we can transform the game into its *ex ante* strategic form, since it is assumed that the players use the principle of Γ-maximin to evaluate their strategies, which does generate an ordering. Recall that in the current game model a strategy of a player needs to specify a choice for every possible signal that she would receive. Thus player 1 has four pure strategies: TT, TB, BT, and BB, whereas player 2 has only two pure strategies L and R. Using the set of priors P given in Eq. (8), we can then calculate the lower expected payoffs under all the strategy profiles. As an example, the *ex ante* expected payoff to player 1 under the strategy profile (TB, L) with respect to ε can be calculated as follows:

$$\mathbb{E}_1^A(TB, L) = \frac{1-\varepsilon}{2} \times 1 + \frac{\varepsilon}{2} \times 0 + \frac{1-\varepsilon}{2} \times 1.2 + \frac{\varepsilon}{2} \times 1.2$$

$$= 1.1 - \frac{\varepsilon}{2}$$

Similarly, we can calculate the *ex ante* expected payoffs to the players under all the other strategy profiles. This way the computation gives rise to the strategic form game shown in Fig. 2 where $\varepsilon \in [0.1, 0.9]$.

Given the range of ε, it is easy to verify that player 1's strategy TT always yields a higher minimum expected payoff than any other pure strategy does, no matter what player 2 chooses to play. As a Γ-maximin decision maker, player 1 should thus choose the pure strategy TT. Anticipating on this conjecture, player 2 should respond optimally by playing the pure strategy L. By applying the Γ-maximin decision rule, our analysis leads to (TT, L) as the unique solution to this game, and it thus constitutes the unique *ex ante* maximin equilibrium for the incomplete information game under ambiguity depicted in Fig. 1. It is important to note that the outcome associated with this unique equilibrium is $(1, \frac{3}{2})$, where the first number denotes the payoff to player 1.

To illustrate Proposition 3.2, consider for instance the case where $\varepsilon = 0.4$. In this case, the game described in Example 3.3 is then reduced to a standard Bayesian game. In a similar fashion, one can transform the Bayesian game into its strategic form, which turns out to be the game depicted in Fig. 2 by setting $\varepsilon = 0.4$. It is easy to check that the strategy profile (TT, L) is indeed a Nash equilibrium for that strategic form game, and thus it is a Bayesian Nash equilibrium for the original Bayesian game. This means that the *ex ante* Γ-maximin equilibrium can be rationalized as a Bayesian Nash equilibrium using some prior in the set of priors. Hence, it is impossible for an outside observer to tell from a player's actual strategy choice whether the player is uncertainty averse or not. It could be the case that the player is actually a Bayesian player who maximizes her expected utility with respect to that particular prior.

Now let us analyze the game in Fig. 1 from an interim perspective. Notice first that at the interim stage player 1 learns more information about the states than player 2 does, since the signals player 1 receives can provide additional information about the states. To be a bit more specific, player 1 can distinguish state ω_1 and ω_2 from state ω_3 and ω_4 using her two signals, whereas such information is not available to player 2. As mentioned above, player 1's posterior belief about the state is assumed to be represented by the sets of conditional probability distributions described in Eq. (10).

We claim that, under these conditions, there is a *unique* interim Γ-maximin equilibrium in pure strategy for the above game. To establish this, consider first the situation when player 1 observes the signal t_1. If player 2 chooses action L, the interim payoffs of player 1 given action T and B are

$$\mathbb{E}_1^I((T,L)\mid t_1,\varepsilon) = 1-\varepsilon$$

$$\mathbb{E}_1^I((B,L)\mid t_1,\varepsilon) = 0.4.$$

And if player 2 chooses action R, the interim payoffs of player 1 given T and B are

$$\mathbb{E}_1^I((T,R)\mid t_1,\varepsilon) = 1+\varepsilon$$

$$\mathbb{E}_1^I((B,R)\mid t_1,\varepsilon) = 1.2.$$

Given $\varepsilon \in [0.1, 0.9]$, it is clear that player 1's action B maximizes the minimum interim payoffs in both cases. Due to the symmetry of player 1's payoff structure, one can easily verify that player 1's action B maximizes the minimum interim payoffs, when player 1 observes the signal t_1'. To sum up, according to the principle of Γ-maximin, player 1 should always play the action B, regardless of the signal received by her and the pure strategy chosen by player 2. Player 2, anticipating on this supposed choice of player 1, will strictly prefer to choose action R, since it is the unique best response to player 1's strategy (B,B). This thus shows that the strategy profile $((B,B),R)$ forms the unique interim Γ-maximin equilibrium in pure strategy for the game in Fig. 1.

Recall that the only *ex ante* Γ-maximin equilibrium for this game is the strategy profile (TT,L), which is totally different from $((B,B),R)$, the only interim Γ-maximin equilibrium in pure strategy. This means that, using the Γ-maximin decision rule, the *ex ante* and interim analysis of an incomplete information game under ambiguity may produce rather different recommendation for the players. In the traditional Bayesian games, *ex ante* and interim Bayesian Nash equilibrium always coincide, which implies that new information received at the interim stage would not affect the analysis in terms of Bayesian Nash equilibrium. However, this generally is not the case in incomplete information games under ambiguity, since players' new information at the interim stage may play a substantial role in solving the game. Hence, one has to distinguish between the *ex ante* and interim stage when studying games in the current framework.

It is interesting to note that the discrepancy between *ex ante* and interim Γ-maximin equilibrium in games under study is somewhat related to the counterintuitive phenomenon called *dilation*① in decision theory. The phenomenon of dilation describes cases where conditioning on new information increases one's imprecision about certain event, contrary to common sense. To be a bit more precise, dilation happens when an interval probability for some event E is strictly contained in the interval probability of E conditional on *every* element of some information partition.

A phenomenon similar to dilation of sets of probabilities occurs in the present example, which perhaps causes the equivalence relationship between *ex ante* and interim equilibrium to break down. Notice that, before observing any signal, player 1's *ex ante* payoff from playing the strategy TT is *determinate*, regardless of the action adopted by player 2. However, when either t_1 or t'_1 is observed, player 1's interim payoffs from choosing the strategy TT become *indeterminate*, regardless of the action selected by player 2. In other words, player 1's initial evaluation of the strategy TT becomes less precise no matter which signal she receives in the interim stage. With more information about the states, player 1 is even more uncertain about the assessment of the strategy TT, which contradicts our intuition. It seems natural to think that this surprising phenomenon perhaps causes the usual relationship between *ex ante* and interim equilibrium analysis to break down in the current framework. Thus it would be an interesting project to study whether this is indeed the case in incomplete information games under ambiguity, which we shall pursue elsewhere in detail.

In addition to illustrating the nonequivalence of *ex ante* and interim Γ-maximin equilibrium in incomplete information games under ambiguity, the above example also brings out another important point that, contrary to *ex ante* Γ-maximin equilibrium, certain interim Γ-maximin equilibria cannot be justified as a Bayesian Nash equilibrium for any probability in the set of posterior probability distribution. To see this, consider the unique interim Γ-maximin equilibrium in pure strategy $((B, B), R)$ for this game. We argue that this strategy profile cannot be a Bayesian Nash

① T. Seidenfeld, L. Wasserman, Dilation for sets of probabilities, *Ann. Stat.*, 1993, 21, pp. 1139 – 1154.

equilibrium for any Bayesian game based on the posteriors given in Eq. (10). Fix a value of ϵ, we can transform the Bayesian game shown in Fig. 1 into a strategic form game. One can easily verify that it is identical to the game depicted in Fig. 2. Due to the equivalence between *ex ante* and interim analyses using Bayesian Nash equilibrium, it suffices to show that, given any value of $\epsilon \in [0.1, 0.9]$, the strategy profile $((B,B),R)$ does not form a Bayesian Nash equilibrium for this game. This directly follows from the fact that player 1's strategy *BB* is strictly dominated by the strategy *TT*. Hence, there exists no rational model, in the sense of expected utility maximization, for the interim Γ-maximin equilibrium $((B,B),R)$ in this example.

One immediate consequence from such an observation is that an outside observer may be able to distinguish Γ-maximin players from Bayesian players, provided that players are assumed to make decisions based on the interim analysis. In contrast to *ex ante* Γ-maximin equilibrium, interim Γ-maximin equilibrium can make a rather different prediction of how the game will be played from the one made by Bayesian Nash equilibrium. In view of this, it seems fair to say that the notion of interim Γ-maximin equilibrium contains a richer behavioral content than that of *ex ante* Γ-maximin equilibrium does when using imprecise probabilities to model uncertainty in interactive situations involving incomplete information.

4. Rectangularity and Dynamic Consistency

We now proceed to examine the conditions under which the *ex ante* and interim Γ-maximin equilibrium are equivalent to each other in games under study. We have already learnt from the foregoing example that such an equivalence relationship between them does not hold in general. It is well established in the literature that *dynamic consistency* can be restored in dynamic choice problems under uncertainty given the rectangularity condition introduced by Wakai① and Epstein and Schneider②. Roughly speaking, dynamic consistency requires that if, no matter what a decision maker learns, she prefers option f to option g, then she should prefer f to g before learning anything. As it appears, dynamic consistency is closely related to the aforementioned question concerning the equivalence. It is thus not

① K. Wakai, *Linking Behavioral Economics, Axiomatic Decision Theory and General Equilibrium Theory*, Ph. D. Dissertation, Connecticut Yale University, 2002.

② L. G. Epstein, M. Schneider, Recursive multiple priors, *J. Econ. Theory*, 2003, 113, pp. 1 – 31.

surprising that the rectangularity condition may play a critical role in establishing the required result. As a matter of fact, our main result in this section shows that the rectangularity condition, suitably adapted to the present framework, is sufficient to guarantee the equivalence of *ex ante* and interim Γ-maximin equilibrium.

The question under investigation is conceptually an issue concerning the relationship between players' *ex ante* and interim beliefs, which are assumed to be represented by sets of probability distributions in the current framework. We introduce below some notions about how the sets of priors and posteriors are related. As a starting point, it is natural to require that any probability in the set of posteriors for a player is a conditional probability obtained from some priors in the set of priors.

Definition 4.1. *Given a posterior function Φ_i, we say that the set of priors P_i is* ***Bayesian consistent*** *with Φ_i if for every t_i and $q \in \Phi_i(t_i)$, there exists a prior $p \in P_i$ such that $p(E \mid t_i) = q(E)$ for all $E \subseteq \Omega$.*

In words, this definition says that the set of priors should be large enough in order to identify each element in $\Phi_i(t_i)$ as a conditional probability derived from the Bayes' rule for any t_i. Intuitively, this condition demands that the relationship between the sets of priors and posteriors should respect the Bayes' rule as a special case. It is then straightforward to define a stronger requirement that is closely related to the full Bayesian updating rule.

Definition 4.2. *Given a posterior function Φ_i, we say that the set of priors P_i is fully Bayesian consistent with Φ_i if P_i is Bayesian consistent with Φ_i, and for all $p \in P_i$, if $p(\tau_i^{-1}(t_i)) > 0$, then $p(\cdot \mid t_i) \in \Phi_i(t_i)$ for all $t_i \in T_i$.*

Recall that in our framework the conditional probability $p(\cdot \mid t_i)$ is always well-defined, for we assume that there is no null signal, i. e., $p(\tau_i^{-1}(t_i)) > 0$ for every $t_i \in T_i$. It is easy to verify that P_i is fully Bayesian consistent with Φ_i if and only if Φ_i is updated based on P_i using the full Bayesian updating rule, i. e., $\Phi_i(t_i) = \Phi_i^{FB}(t_i)$ for all $t_i \in T_i$. In other words, the condition of fully Bayesian consistency requires that player i should be able to justify her posterior function using the generalized Bayesian updating rule operated on the set of priors. Nevertheless, such a requirement is still not strong enough to guarantee the equivalence of *ex ante* and interim Γ-maximin equilibrium in the current framework, as demonstrated by the example of Section 3. Hence, we have to impose some further restrictions on the relation between priors and posteriors in order to ensure the equivalence.

As pointed out by Epstein and Schneider①, the law of iterated expectations plays a key role in establishing dynamic consistency of the expected utility model, and it is satisfied by expected utility model mainly because every probability measure can be decomposed into its conditionals and marginals. One may thus wonder whether dynamic consistency holds for non-expected utility model under uncertainty whenever a restriction similar to the familiar decomposition condition is imposed. In the context of decision making using sets of probabilities, this leads to the idea of requiring a corresponding decomposition of the initial set of priors in terms of its induced sets of conditionals and marginals, which goes back at least to the work of Sarin and Wakker②. Such a requirement is now widely known as rectangularity condition in the literature. Below we present an instance of the rectangularity condition proposed by Epstein and Schneider③, which is suitably adapted to the present framework.

Definition 4.3. Given a posterior function Φ_i, we say that the set of priors P_i is *rectangular* with Φ_i if it holds that

$$P_i = \left\{ \sum_{t_i \in T_i} p(\tau_i^{-1}(t_i)) \, \Phi_i(t_i) : p \in P_i \right\}. \tag{11}$$

As indicated above, the rectangularity condition basically says that player i's set of priors can be constructed by recursively combining its marginals with *all* the posterior probability distributions in the set of posteriors. In order to satisfy this condition, one usually needs to make sure that the set of priors P_i is large enough to include those probability distributions that are obtained from combining its marginal and measures other than its own induced conditionals. Clearly, if P_i and $\Phi_i(t_i)$ are singletons for all $t_i \in T_i$, this condition is reduced to the usual decomposition condition. In this sense the rectangularity condition can be viewed as a generalization of the decomposition property of a single probability measure.

It is important to note that the rectangularity property introduced above is closely related to the *marginal extension* ④, which is a generalization of the law of iterated

① L. G. Epstein, M. Schneider, Recursive multiple priors, *J. Econ. Theory*, 2003, 113, pp. 1-31.

② R. Sarin, P. Wakker, Dynamic choice and nonexpected utility, *J. Risk Uncertain.*, 1998, 17, pp. 87-120.

③ L. G. Epstein, M. Schneider, Recursive multiple priors, *J. Econ. Theory*, 2003, 113, pp. 1-31.

④ See P. Walley, *Statistical Reasoning with Imprecise Probabilities*, New York: Chapman and Hall, 1994, Section 6.72; E. Miranda, G. de Cooman, Marginal extension in the theory of coherent lower previsions, *Int. J. Approx. Reason.*, 2007, 46 (1), pp. 188-225; E. Miranda, M. Zaffalon, G. de Cooman, Conglomerable natural extension, *Int. J. Approx. Reason.*, 2012, 53 (8), pp. 1200-1227.

expectations to lower previsions.① Because what Walley calls a coherent lower prevision is a lower expectation functional: it is the lower envelope of the expectations with respect to a closed convex set of probability measures. As mentioned above, dynamic consistency in decision problems depends crucially on the law of iterated expectations. It is thus natural to expect that the rectangularity property as well as the marginal extension is central to dynamic consistency when representing uncertainty using sets of probability distributions, as we shall reveal later.

In order to understand better the rectangularity property, let us consider the Ellsberg-type decision problem in a dynamic setting②.

Example 4.4. Suppose that a decision maker is facing an urn with 30 red balls and 60 blue or green balls. At time t_0, a ball is drawn from the urn at random. The state space consists of possible colors of the ball, i.e., $\Omega = \{R, B, G\}$. Without knowing the color of the ball drawn, the decision maker is asked to choose between two lotteries f and g, where f represents the lottery that pays \$100 if a blue or green ball is drawn, and \$0 otherwise, and where g denotes the lottery that pays \$100 if a red or green ball is drawn, and \$0 otherwise. At time t_1, the decision maker is first told whether the ball drawn is green or not, and then needs to decide whether to keep the lottery chosen at t_0, or to switch to the other lottery.

How should the decision maker choose in this example? Epstein and Schneider③ suggest that the decision maker may typically choose according to the following preference ranking. At time t_0, the decision maker prefers lottery f to lottery g. When the decision maker knows that the ball is not green, she will decide to switch, that is, she will prefer g to f conditional on knowing that the ball is not green. When the color of the ball is revealed to be green, the decision maker is indifferent between keeping and switching, since she wins the bet either way. These preference rankings clearly violate the requirement of dynamic consistency, since the decision maker prefers lottery f to lottery g, while she would rank g at least as good as f no matter what information is revealed.

Using the Γ-maximin decision rule, one may consider the following sets of priors P_0 and of posteriors P_1 to support the preferences described above:

---

① We thank the editor and an anonymous reviewer for pointing out this affinity.

② L. G. Epstein, M. Schneider, Recursive multiple priors, *J. Econ. Theory*, 2003, 113, pp. 1-31.

③ L. G. Epstein, M. Schneider, Recursive multiple priors, *J. Econ. Theory*, 2003, 113, pp. 1-31.

$$
\begin{aligned}
P_0 &= \left\{p = (\frac{1}{3}, p_B, \frac{2}{3} - p_B) : p_B \in [\frac{1}{6}, \frac{1}{2}]\right\}, \\
P_1(\{R,B\}) &= \left\{q = (\frac{\frac{1}{3}}{\frac{1}{3} + p_B}, \frac{p_B}{\frac{1}{3} + p_B}, 0) : p_B \in [\frac{1}{6}, \frac{1}{2}]\right\}, \qquad (12) \\
P_1(\{G\}) &= \{q = (0,0,1)\}.
\end{aligned}
$$

It is clear that P_1 can be regarded as the posterior functions updated on P_0 using the full Bayesian updating rule. As mentioned above, these preference rankings does not satisfy the requirement of dynamic consistency. Thus it is not surprising that the set of prior P_0 violates the rectangularity condition, given that P_1 is specified in Eq. (12).

In order to restore dynamic consistency, one can replace P_0 by the rectangular set of priors P'_0 described as follows to represent the decision maker's initial beliefs about the states:

$$
P'_0 = \left\{p = (\frac{1}{3}\frac{\frac{1}{3} + p'_B}{\frac{1}{3} + p_B}, p_B\frac{\frac{1}{3} + p'_B}{\frac{1}{3} + p_B}, \frac{2}{3} - p'_B) : \frac{1}{6} \leqslant p_B, p'_B \leqslant \frac{1}{2}\right\}. \qquad (13)
$$

Epstein and Schneider① have shown that the rectangularity condition implies dynamic consistency. Given that P'_0 is rectangularity with P_1, it immediately follows that the decision maker's preference must be dynamically consistent. One can easily verify that, according to the principle of Γ-maximin, g is preferred to f under P'_0, which reverses the preference ranking under P_0. It is debatable whether or not this change would be reasonable for Γ-maximin decision makers. It seems that this approach restricts the decision maker's *ex ante* preference by placing a stringent requirement on the set of priors. Nevertheless, this is the price one needs to pay in order to ensure dynamic consistency for the multiple priors model.

It is interesting to note that if P'_0 is updated in the light of new information with either the full Bayesian updating rule or the maximum likelihood updating rule, then the derived sets of conditional probabilities are both identical to P_1. This turns out to be true in general when the set of priors is rectangular. We thus state this result as a proposition in the following:

Proposition 4. 5. *Suppose that the set of priors P_i is both fully Bayesian consistent*

① L. G. Epstein, M. Schneider, Recursive multiple priors, *J. Econ. Theory*, 2003, 113, pp. 1-31.

and rectangular with posterior function Φ_i. *Then the full Bayesian updating rule and the maximum likelihood updating rule coincide, i. e.,* $\Phi_i(t_i) = \Phi_i^{FB}(t_i) = \Phi_i^{ML}(t_i)$ *for all* $t_i \in T_i$.

This result provides important insight into the connection between the current approach and Kajii and Ui's approach, where the updating rule is taken as a primitive instead. When the rectangularity condition is satisfied, however, we do not need to specify which updating rule between the two rules introduced above is actually used by the players to derive their posterior beliefs. If one interprets the updating rules as different attitudes toward uncertainty in the light of new information, then this result implies that the rectangularity condition does not allow to take into account the differences between them.

Before we continue, we wish to emphasize that, in order to satisfy the rectangularity condition, *every* element of the prior set P_i is required to be decomposed in the form of Eq. (11). In this sense, the rectangularity condition is a straightforward and direct generalization of the decomposition property in the precise case. This is a rather stringent requirement, which becomes problematic in the presence of convexity. In view of this, it seems natural to consider the following intuitive generalization, which requires that only those extreme points in P_i satisfy the decomposition property. In order to distinguish between these two ways of generalizing the decomposition property, we shall call the one defined in Definition 4.3 the *complete* rectangularity condition, and the one introduced below the *extreme-points* rectangularity condition.

Definition 4.6. *Given a posterior function* Φ_i, *we say that the set of priors* P_i *is extreme-points rectangular with* Φ_i *if it holds that*

$$ext(P_i) = \left\{ \sum_{t_i \in T_i} p(\tau_i^{-1}(t_i))\, \Phi_i(t_i) : p \in ext(P_i) \right\}, \tag{14}$$

where $ext(P_i)$ *denotes the set of extreme points of the prior set* P_i.

It is obvious that the extreme-points rectangularity condition is much weaker than the complete rectangularity condition. Furthermore, those who are familiar with the literature on independence concepts for the theory of sets of probability measures will easily recognize that this is similar to the important distinction between complete and strong independence.① In fact, the notion of extreme-points rectangularity is

① See F. G. Cozman, Sets of probability distributions, independence, and convexity, *Synthese*, 2012, 186, pp. 577 – 600 for a comprehensive review of different independence concepts in the literature.

motivated exactly by such a distinction. ①

Now let us turn to the main issue of this section, which is concerned with conditions under which the *ex ante* and interim Γ-maximin equilibrium are equivalent. As explained in Section 1, dynamic consistency in traditional Bayesian games is mainly due to the property that a probability distribution can be decomposed into its conditionals and marginals. Thus it is natural to expect that the *ex ante* and interim analysis of incomplete information games become identical once the rectangularity condition is satisfied. In fact, we show below that the equivalence of *ex ante* and interim Γ-maximin equilibrium holds, provided that all the players' sets of priors are extreme-points rectangular, which is weaker than the complete rectangularity condition.

Proposition 4.7. *Let G be an incomplete information game under ambiguity. Suppose that* P_i *is extreme-points rectangular for all* $i \in I$*. Then a strategy profile* σ^* *is an ex ante Γ-maximin equilibrium for G if and only if* σ^* *is an interim Γ-maximin equilibrium for G.*

The proof of Proposition 4.7 uses the fact that an expectation function achieves its minimum at the extreme points of a (closed and convex) set of probability distributions. ② Based on this, we thus only need to pay attention to those extreme probabilities, since all the players are assumed to be Γ-maximin decision makers.

Of course, we can easily establish the same equivalence result under the stronger condition of complete rectangularity, which directly follows from Proposition 4.7. We record this observation in the following corollary.

Corollary 4.8. *Let G be an incomplete information game under ambiguity. Suppose that* P_i *is completely rectangular for all* $i \in I$*. Then a strategy profile* σ^* *is an ex ante Γ-maximin equilibrium for G if and only if* σ^* *is an interim Γ-maximin equilibrium for G.*

Proof. This result follows readily from Proposition 4.7 and the observation that the extreme-points rectangularity condition is much weaker than the complete rectangularity condition.

---

① We are grateful to Teddy Seidenfeld for directing us to the literature on this topic.

② P. Walley, *Statistical Reasoning with Imprecise Probabilities*, New York: Chapman and Hall, 1994, Theorem 3.6.2.

5. Discussion and Conclusion

The main contribution of this paper lies in the characterization of a sufficient condition under which the equivalence of *ex ante* and interim equilibrium concepts for incomplete information games under ambiguity holds true. We adapted the framework of incomplete information games under ambiguity due to Kajii and Ui①, where a player's perception of uncertainty is allowed to be represented by a set of probability distributions over the states. As indicated above, it is not surprising that players tend to exhibit dynamic inconsistent behavior in this game-theoretic framework. It is often argued that dynamic consistency is plausible enough and should be treated as a normative requirement of rational decision making in the dynamic setting. In addition, it is also crucial for the theory of games to be able to make sensible recommendation for policy analysis involving sequential features.

Nevertheless, the existing literature including the work of Kajii and Ui② has not yet characterized conditions under which dynamic consistency is warranted in the framework of incomplete information games under ambiguity. Our paper fills this much-needed gap by identifying the sufficient condition for the equivalence between *ex ante* and interim Γ-maximin equilibrium. This in turn ensures that each player's equilibrium behavior is always dynamic consistent. The key to this main result is to generalize the decomposition property in the precise case to accommodate the modelling of uncertainty through a set of probability distributions. In this sense, our paper not only completes Kajii and Ui's analysis on incomplete information games under ambiguity, but also offers a counterpart of the equivalence result in the traditional framework of Bayesian games.

Besides the work by Kajii and Ui③, the literature on decision making using imprecise probabilities contains certain results that are parallel to ours. First of all, Epstein and Schneider④ on the characterization of dynamic consistency in dynamic decision problems has greatly inspired and influenced the current work, which

---

① A. Kajii, T. Ui, Incomplete information games with multiple priors, *Jpn. Econ. Rev.*, 2005, 56, pp. 332 - 351.

② A. Kajii, T. Ui, Incomplete information games with multiple priors, *Jpn. Econ. Rev.*, 2005, 56, pp. 332 - 351.

③ A. Kajii, T. Ui, Incomplete information games with multiple priors, *Jpn. Econ. Rev.*, 2005, 56, pp. 332 - 351.

④ L. G. Epstein, M. Schneider, Recursive multiple priors, *J. Econ. Theory*, 2003, 113, pp. 1 - 31.

essentially extends their result to the context of incomplete information games under ambiguity. Due to the two-stage game structure, we do not investigate the issue of dynamic consistency under the long-terms dynamics of beliefs, which has been studied by Epstein and Schneider①. This issue is worthy of future investigation by considering games with a richer dynamic structure.

The current work is also similar in spirit to Grünwald and Halpern②, which studies the relationship between the rectangularity property and time consistency (a stronger requirement than dynamic consistency), albeit in a different context motivated by questions in decision theory and artificial intelligence. Their work is essentially intended to address how one should update her beliefs in decision problems when her beliefs are represented by a set of probability distributions. To examine this issue, they propose to model a decision problem as a game between the agent and a bookie, and assume that the decision maker employs the minimax criterion as the decision rule. They show that conditioning is the right updating rule under the rectangularity condition. By contrast, we have undertaken in this paper a formal analysis of dynamic consistency in genuine games, where two players together with Nature are involved, and the players are assumed to use Γ-maximin to make decisions when uncertainty is represented by sets of probabilities. Although these two approaches consider different decision rules, they both demonstrate that the rectangularity condition plays a key role in establishing dynamic consistency. This seems to suggest that rectangularity may imply dynamic consistency under a wide variety of decision criteria.

As mentioned previously, the rectangularity property is intimately related to Walley's notion of marginal extension, which generalizes the law of iterated expectations to lower previsions. Zaffalon and Miranda③ demonstrate that dynamic consistency when suitably reformulated in terms of lower previsions holds under the marginal extension. This result is essentially parallel to the one by Epstein and Schneider④, which considers dynamic consistency in decision problems when uncertainty is represented by a set of probability distributions. In this sense, the

---

① L. G. Epstein, M. Schneider, Recursive multiple priors, *J. Econ. Theory*, 2003, 113, pp. 1 -31.

② P. D. Grünwald, J. Y. Halpern, Making decisions using sets of probabilities: updating, time consistency, and calibration, *J. Artif. Intell. Res.*, 2011, 42 (1), pp. 393 -426.

③ M. Zaffalon, E. Miranda, Desirability and the birth of incomplete preferences, arXiv: 1506.00529, 2015.

④ L. G. Epstein, M. Schneider, Recursive multiple priors, *J. Econ. Theory*, 2003, 113, pp. 1 -31.

current study complements these works by extending the result on dynamic consistency to the case of incomplete information games under ambiguity.

We conclude with a discussion of possible directions for future work. An interesting project of future work is concerned with the issue of value of information in games. As discussed by Osborne①, Bayesian players may rationally pay to avoid learning cost-free information, which is quite counterintuitive. It thus seems natural to investigate to what extent such a phenomenon would also occur in the current game model. We think that this phenomenon can happen in incomplete information games under ambiguity even under a weaker condition. This investigation is closely related to the topic of value of commitment in such games. It is possible to show that the value of commitment can be restored in the context of games under ambiguity, where ambiguity is represented by sets of probability distributions.

It is well known that the framework of incomplete information games has a wide range of applications to multiple fields such as auctions and jury voting. A straightforward line of future research is then to apply the game-theoretic framework developed in this paper to those domains. It also seems to study whether the main result of this paper can be used to shed light on issues relating to auctions and jury voting.

Acknowledgements

The authors would like to thank Teddy Seidenfeld and Kevin Zollman for various helpful discussions and insightful suggestions that helped to shape the final manuscript. The authors also wish to thank the editor and two anonymous reviewers for their valuable comments on our manuscript. Wei Xiong's research was supported by the Major Project of Key Research Institute of Chinese Ministry of Education (No. 14JD720001).

Appendix A. Proofs

Proposition 3. 1. *Every finite incomplete information game under ambiguity G has at least one ex ante* Γ *-maximin equilibrium, and also has at least one interim* Γ*-maximin equilibrium.*

Proof. In this proof, we focus on the existence of an interim Γ -maximin equilibrium. Nevertheless, the existence of an *ex ante* Γ -maximin equilibrium can be

① M. J. Osborne, *An Introduction to Game Theory*, New York, NY: Oxford University Press, 2004.

proved in a similar way. Following the standard method for establishing the existence of a Nash equilibrium, we formulate the existence problem as the search of a fixed point of a suitably constructed correspondence.

Note first that the underlying state space Ω, the type space T_i and the action set A_i are all finite. It thus follows that each Σ_i is non-empty, compact, and convex. Hence, their product set Σ is non-empty, compact, and convex.

For every mixed strategy profile $\sigma_{-i} \in \Sigma_{-i}$, let $B_i(\sigma_{-i})$ denote player i's interim Γ-maximin best response against σ_{-i}, that is,

$$\begin{aligned} B_i(\sigma_{-i}) &= \bigcap_{t_i \in T_i} B_i(\sigma_{-i}|t_i) \\ &= \bigcap_{t_i \in T_i} \{\sigma_i \in \Sigma_i : \sigma_i(t_i) \in \arg\max_{\sigma_i \in \Sigma_i} \min_{q \in \Phi_i(t_i)} \mathbb{E}_i^I(\sigma_i, \sigma_{-i}|q)\}. \end{aligned}$$

And we define the correspondence from Σ to Σ such that for all $\sigma \in \Sigma$,

$$B(\sigma) = \prod_{i \in I} B_i(\sigma_{-i}).$$

To apply the Kakutani's fixed point theorem, we need to prove that the correspondence $B(\sigma)$ satisfies all the required conditions, i. e., that it is non-empty, convex, compact-valued, and upper-hemicontinuous. It suffices to show that for each $i \in I$ and $t_i \in T_i$ the correspondence $\sigma_{-i} \mapsto B_i(\sigma_{-i}|t_i)$ is non-empty, convex, compact-valued, and upper-hemicontinuous.

First, we argue that this correspondence is non-empty, compact-valued, and upper-hemicontinuous. To establish this claim, recall that the set of states and each player i's set of actions are finite. It follows that $\mathbb{E}_i^I(\sigma_i, \sigma_{-i}|q)$ is continuous in $(\sigma_i, \sigma_{-i}, q)$. Moreover, it is assumed that $\Phi_i(t_i)$ is compact. This means that $\min_{q \in \Phi_i(t_i)} \mathbb{E}_i^I(\sigma_i, \sigma_{-i}|q)$ is the minimum of a continuous function over a compact set $\Phi_i(t_i)$. It then follows that $\min_{q \in \Phi_i(t_i)} \mathbb{E}_i^I(\sigma_i, \sigma_{-i}|q)$ is continuous in (σ_i, σ_{-i}) as well. By Berge's maximum theorem, the correspondence $\sigma_{-i} \mapsto B_i(\sigma_{-i}|t_i)$ is upper-hemicontinuous, non-empty and compact-valued.

In order to apply Kakutani's theorem, it remains to show that $B_i(\sigma_{-i}|t_i)$ is convex-valued. Note that $\mathbb{E}_i^I(\sigma_i, \sigma_{-i}|q)$ is continuous in $(\sigma_i, \sigma_{-i}, q)$ and $\Phi_i(t_i)$ is convex. It thus follows that the minimization of $\mathbb{E}_i^I(\sigma_i, \sigma_{-i}|q)$ is concave on Σ_i. Hence, we have that $B_i(\sigma_{-i}|t_i)$ is convex-valued.

Given these results, it follows from the definition that the correspondence $B(\sigma)$ satisfies the assumptions of Kakutani's fixed point theorem, which immediately implies the existence of a fixed point, $\sigma^* \in B(\sigma^*)$. Therefore, we can conclude that every incomplete information game has an interim Γ-maximin equilibrium.

Proposition 4. 5. *Suppose that the set of priors P_i is both fully Bayesian consistent and rectangular with posterior function Φ_i. Then the full Bayesian updating rule and the maximum likelihood updating rule coincide, i. e., $\Phi_i(t_i) = \Phi_i^{FB}(t_i) = \Phi_i^{ML}(t_i)$ for all $t_i \in T_i$.*

Proof. To establish this result, note first that $\Phi_i(t_i) = \Phi_i^{FB}(t_i)$ for P_i is fully Bayesian consistent with the posterior function Φ_i. Now fix an arbitrary type $t_i' \in T_i$. Let p_i^* denote the prior probability such that

$$p_i^* \in \arg\max_{p \in P_i} p(\tau_i^{-1}(t_i')).$$

Let $p_i(\cdot \mid t_i)$ be an arbitrary element of $\Phi_i^{FB}(t_i)$. It then follows from the definition of rectangularity that

$$p_i^* = \sum_{t_i \in T_i} p_i^*(\tau_i^{-1}(t_i))\, p_i(\cdot \mid t_i).$$

Meanwhile, we also have that

$$p_i^* = \sum_{t_i \in T_i} p_i^*(\tau_i^{-1}(t_i))\, p_i^*(\cdot \mid t_i).$$

Hence, it must be the case that $p_i^*(\cdot \mid t_i) = p_i(\cdot \mid t_i)$. This implies that $\Phi_i^{FB}(t_i) = \Phi_i^{ML}(t_i)$, which concludes the proof.

Proposition 4. 6. *Let G be an incomplete information game under ambiguity. Suppose that P_i is extreme-points rectangular for all $i \in I$. Then a strategy profile σ^* is an ex ante Γ-maximin equilibrium for G if and only if σ^* is an interim Γ-maximin equilibrium for G.*

Proof. Let us begin with two preliminary remarks. First, it is assumed in the current framework that each player i's initial and updated beliefs are represented by closed and convex sets of probability distributions. More precisely, both P_i and $\Phi_i(t_i)$ are closed and convex for all $t_i \in T_i$. Second, it has been shown that minima of expectations are attained at the extreme points of a closed and convex set of probability measures.① It thus follows from these facts that only the extreme probabilities play a role in determining the Γ-maximin equilibria for a given game.

For the direction of (**interim⇒ex ante**), assume that the strategy profile σ^* is an interim Γ-maximin equilibrium. By definition, we have that, for any $i \in I$ and $t_i \in T_i$, the following condition holds for any arbitrary $\sigma_i \in \Sigma_i$:

① P. Walley, *Statistical Reasoning with Imprecise Probabilities*, New York: Chapman and Hall, 1994, Theorem 3. 6. 2.

$$\min_{q \in \Phi_i(t_i)} \mathbb{E}_i^I(\sigma_i^*, \sigma_{-i}^* | q) \geqslant \min_{q \in \Phi_i(t_i)} \mathbb{E}_i^I(\sigma_i, \sigma_{-i}^* | q). \quad \text{(A. 1)}$$

Fix an arbitrary $\sigma_i \in \Sigma_i$. For each $i \in I$ and $t_i \in T_i$, let

$$p_i^* \in \arg\min_{p \in P_i} \mathbb{E}_i^A(\sigma_i^*, \sigma_{-i}^* | p),$$

$$p_i' \in \arg\min_{p \in P_i} \mathbb{E}_i^A(\sigma_i, \sigma_{-i}^* | p),$$

$$\text{and } q_i'(\cdot | t_i) \in \arg\min_{q \in \Phi_i(t_i)} \mathbb{E}_i^I(\sigma_i, \sigma_{-i}^* | t_i).$$

It must be the case that both p_i^* and p'_i are extreme points of P_i. Now fix an arbitrary $q_i(\cdot | t_i)$. Recall from the assumption that P_i is extreme-points rectangular. Then by the definition of extreme-points rectangularity we have that

$$p_i^* = \sum_{t_i \in T_i} p_i^*(\tau_i^{-1}(t_i)) q_i(\cdot | t_i),$$

$$p_i' = \sum_{t_i \in T_i} p_i^*(\tau_i^{-1}(t_i)) q_i'(\cdot | t_i).$$

Next, we show that the minimum of the *ex ante* Γ-maximin expected payoff to player i is attained by playing σ_i^* given the strategy profile σ_{-i}^*. To see this, let us find out the minimum of player i's *ex ante* Γ-maximin expected payoff under σ^*, as shown below.

$$\begin{aligned}
&\min_{p \in P_i} \mathbb{E}_i^A(\sigma_i^*, \sigma_{-i}^* | p) \\
= &\sum_{\omega \in \Omega} \sum_{a_i \in A_i} \sum_{a_{-i} \in A_{-i}} u_i(a_i, a_{-i}, \omega) \sigma_i^*(a_i | \tau_i(\omega)) \sigma_{-i}^*(a_{-i} | \tau_{-i}(\omega)) p_i^*(\omega) \\
= &\sum_{\omega \in \Omega} \sum_{a_i \in A_i} \sum_{a_{-i} \in A_{-i}} u_i(a_i, a_{-i}, \omega) \sigma_i^*(a_i | \tau_i(\omega)) \sigma_{-i}^*(a_{-i} | \tau_{-i}(\omega)) \sum_{t_i \in T_i} p_i^*(\tau_i^{-1}(t_i)) q_i(\omega | t_i) \\
= &\sum_{t_i \in T_i} p_i^*(\tau_i^{-1}(t_i)) \sum_{\omega \in \tau_i^{-1}(t_i)} \sum_{a_i \in A_i} \sum_{a_{-i} \in A_{-i}} u_i(a_i, a_{-i}, \omega) \sigma_i^*(a_i | \tau_i(\omega)) \sigma_{-i}^*(a_{-i} | \tau_{-i}(\omega)) q_i(\omega | t_i).
\end{aligned}$$

According to the supposition, σ^* is an interim Γ-maximin equilibrium. By definition, we have that:

$$\min_{q \in \Phi_i(t_i)} \mathbb{E}_i^I(\sigma_i^*, \sigma_{-i}^* | q) \geqslant \min_{q \in \Phi_i(t_i)} \mathbb{E}_i^I(\sigma_i, \sigma_{-i}^* | q).$$

It further follows from the way of calculating player i's *ex ante* expected payoff that

$$\min_{p \in P_i} \mathbb{E}_i^A(\sigma_i^*, \sigma_{-i}^* | p)$$

$$\geqslant \sum_{t_i \in T_i} p_i^*(\tau_i^{-1}(t_i)) \sum_{\omega \in \tau_i^{-1}(t_i)} \sum_{a_i \in A_i} \sum_{a_{-i} \in A_{-i}} u_i(a_i, a_{-i}, \omega) \sigma_i(a_i | \tau_i(\omega)) \sigma_{-i}^*(a_{-i} | \tau_{-i}(\omega)) q_i'(\omega | t_i)$$

$$= \sum_{\omega \in \Omega} \sum_{a_i \in A_i} \sum_{a_{-i} \in A_{-i}} u_i(a_i, a_{-i}, \omega) \sigma_i(a_i | \tau_i(\omega)) \sigma_{-i}^*(a_{-i} | \tau_{-i}(\omega)) \sum_{t_i \in T_i} p_i^*(\tau_i^{-1}(t_i)) q_i'(\omega | t_i)$$

$$= \sum_{\omega \in \Omega} \sum_{a_i \in A_i} \sum_{a_{-i} \in A_{-i}} u_i(a_i, a_{-i}, \omega) \sigma_i(a_i | \tau_i(\omega)) \sigma_{-i}^*(a_{-i} | \tau_{-i}(\omega)) p_i'(\omega)$$

$$= \min_{p \in P_i} \mathbb{E}_i^A(\sigma_i, \sigma_{-i}^* | p).$$

Note that the strategy σ_i used in these inequalities is arbitrarily chosen. Given the above inequality, it is clear that the requirement of *ex ante* Γ-maximin equilibrium is satisfied. Therefore, we can conclude that the strategy profile σ^* is an *ex ante* Γ-maximin equilibrium.

For the opposite direction, namely, (Ex Ante $\Rightarrow$ Interim), we prove by contraposition. Suppose that the strategy profile σ^* is not an interim Γ-maximin equilibrium. According to the definition, we know that the strategy σ^* does not yield the highest minimum expected payoff for a certain player. More precisely, for some $i \in I$, there exists a strategy σ_i such that for some $t_i' \in T_i$,

$$\min_{q \in P_i(t_i')} \mathbb{E}_i^I(\sigma_i^*, \sigma_{-i}^* | q) < \min_{q \in P_i(t_i')} \mathbb{E}_i^I(\sigma_i, \sigma_{-i}^* | q). \tag{A.2}$$

Next let us define a strategy of player i in the following way:

$$\sigma_i' = \begin{cases} \sigma_i(t_i) & \text{if } t_i = t_i' \\ \sigma_i^*(t_i) & \text{if } t_i \in T_i \setminus \{t_i'\} \end{cases}.$$

In a similar fashion, we are interested in those probabilities that achieve the minimum expectations under different strategy profiles. So let:

$$p_i^* \in \arg\min_{p \in P_i} \mathbb{E}_i^A(\sigma_i^*, \sigma_{-i}^* | p),$$

$$p_i' \in \arg\min_{p \in P_i} \mathbb{E}_i^A(\sigma_i', \sigma_{-i}^* | p),$$

$$q_i^*(\cdot | t_i') \in \arg\min_{q \in \Phi_i(t_i')} \mathbb{E}_i^I(\sigma_i^*, \sigma_{-i}^* | q).$$

It implies from the second remark made at the beginning of this proof that these two prior probabilities p_i^* and p_i' are the extreme points of the set P_i.

According to the assumption that P_i is extreme-points rectangular, we then have that

$$p_i' = \sum_{t_i \in T_i} p_i^*(\tau_i^{-1}(t_i)) q_i^*(\cdot | t_i).$$

We show below that σ^* cannot be an *ex ante* Γ-maximin equilibrium by examining its minimum *ex ante* maximin expected payoff to player i. To elaborate, we have that

$$\min_{p\in P_i} \mathbb{E}_i^A(\sigma_i',\sigma_{-i}^*|p)$$

$$= \sum_{\omega\in\Omega}\sum_{a_i\in A_i}\sum_{a_{-i}\in A_{-i}} u_i(a_i,a_{-i},\omega)\sigma_i'(a_i|\tau_i(\omega))\,\sigma_{-i}^*(a_{-i}|\tau_{-i}(\omega))\,p_i'(\omega)$$

$$= \sum_{\omega\in\tau_i^{-1}(t_i)}\sum_{a_i\in A_i}\sum_{a_{-i}\in A_{-i}} u_i(a_i,a_{-i},\omega)\sigma_i'(a_i|\tau_i(\omega))\,\sigma_{-i}^*(a_{-i}|\tau_{-i}(\omega))\sum_{t_i\in T_i} p_i^*(\tau_i^{-1}(t_i))\,q_i^*(\omega|t_i)$$

$$= \sum_{t_i\in T_i} p_i^*(\tau_i^{-1}(t_i))\sum_{\omega\in\tau_i^{-1}(t_i)}\sum_{a_i\in A_i}\sum_{a_{-i}\in A_{-i}} u_i(a_i,a_{-i},\omega)\sigma_i'(a_i|\tau_i(\omega))\,\sigma_{-i}^*(a_{-i}|\tau_{-i}(\omega))\,q_i^*(\omega|t_i)$$

$$= \sum_{t_i\in T_i\setminus\{t_i'\}} p_i^*(\tau_i^{-1}(t_i))\sum_{\omega\in\tau_i^{-1}(t_i)}\sum_{a_i\in A_i}\sum_{a_{-i}\in A_{-i}} u_i(a_i,a_{-i},\omega)\,\sigma_i^*(a_i|\tau_i(\omega))\,\sigma_{-i}^*(a_{-i}|\tau_{-i}(\omega))\,q_i^*(\omega|t_i)$$

$$+ p_i^*(\tau_i^{-1}(t_i'))\sum_{\omega\in\tau_i^{-1}(t_i')}\sum_{a_i\in A_i}\sum_{a_{-i}\in A_{-i}} u_i(a_i,a_{-i},\omega)\sigma_i(a_i|\tau_i(\omega))\,\sigma_{-i}^*(a_{-i}|\tau_{-i}(\omega))\,q_i^*(\omega|t_i').$$

Since σ^* is not an interim Γ-maximin equilibrium, it follows from the condition given in (A.2) that

$$\min_{p\in P_i} \mathbb{E}_i^A(\sigma_i',\sigma_{-i}^*|p)$$

$$> \sum_{t_i\in T_i\setminus\{t_i'\}} p_i^*(\tau_i^{-1}(t_i))\sum_{\omega\in\tau_i^{-1}(t_i)}\sum_{a_i\in A_i}\sum_{a_{-i}\in A_{-i}} u_i(a_i,a_{-i},\omega)\,\sigma_i^*(a_i|\tau_i(\omega))\,\sigma_{-i}^*(a_{-i}|\tau_{-i}(\omega))\,q_i^*(\omega|t_i)$$

$$+ p_i^*(\tau_i^{-1}(t_i'))\sum_{\omega\in\tau_i^{-1}(t_i')}\sum_{a_i\in A_i}\sum_{a_{-i}\in A_{-i}} u_i(a_i,a_{-i},\omega)\,\sigma_i^*(a_i|\tau_i(\omega))\,\sigma_{-i}^*(a_{-i}|\tau_{-i}(\omega))\,q_i^*(\omega|t_i')$$

$$= \sum_{t_i\in T_i} p_i^*(\tau_i^{-1}(t_i))\sum_{\omega\in\tau_i^{-1}(t_i)}\sum_{a_i\in A_i}\sum_{a_{-i}\in A_{-i}} u_i(a_i,a_{-i},\omega)\,\sigma_i^*(a_i|\tau_i(\omega))\,\sigma_{-i}^*(a_{-i}|\tau_{-i}(\omega))\,q_i^*(\omega|t_i)$$

$$= \sum_{\omega\in\Omega}\sum_{a_i\in A_i}\sum_{a_{-i}\in A_{-i}} u_i(a_i,a_{-i},\omega)\,\sigma_i^*(a_i|\tau_i(\omega))\,\sigma_{-i}^*(a_{-i}|\tau_{-i}(\omega))\,p_i'(\omega)$$

$$\geqslant \min_{p\in P_i} \mathbb{E}_i^A(\sigma_i^*,\sigma_{-i}^*|p),$$

which implies that σ^* is not an *ex ante* Γ-maximin equilibrium, as required.

Hence, we have shown that a strategy profile is an *ex ante* Γ-maximin equilibrium if and only if it is an interim Γ-maximin equilibrium, provided that the prior sets are all extreme-points rectangular.

On Formalizing Causation Based on Constant Conjunction Theory

Hu Liu, Xuefeng Wen

1. Introduction

The ability of building causal relations is fundamental for us in understanding the world in everyday life. Not surprisingly, causation has been one of the core concepts in philosophical study since antiquity. Since formal logic was founded, logicians have put a number of philosophical concepts under formal investigations, yielding various branches of non-classical logic. Causation has also been formalized in logic. ① As far as we know, however, no work has been done in formalizing the concept of causation based on constant conjunction theory (a. k. a. regularity theory). In this paper, we formalize constant conjunction and causation with the help of a linear temporal logic.

Constant conjunction theory (CCT, henceforth) had been the dominant theory in philosophy for a long time. It explains causation with a central pre-theoretic intuition that an effect is something that always accompanies its cause. Unsurprisingly, it still has found support in scientific discoveries, such as Pavlov's laws of conditioning and

---

① D. Lewis, Causation, *The Journal of Philosophy*, 1973, 70 (17), pp. 556 – 567; F. von Kutschera, Causation. *Journal of Philosophical Logic*, 1993, 22 (6), pp. 563 – 588; F. Lin, Embracing causality in specifying the indeterminate effects of actions, in *Proceedings of the 13th National Conference on Artificial Intelligence*, CA: Morgan Kaufmann, 1996, pp. 1985 – 1991; M. Xu, Causation in branching time (I): Transitions, events and causes, *Synthese*, 1997, 112 (2), pp. 137 – 192; N. McCain, & H. Turner, Causal theories of action and change, in *Proceedings of the 14th National Conference on Artificial Intelligence*, CA: Morgan Kaufmann, 1997, pp. 460 – 465; M. Thielscher, Ramification and causality, *Artificial Intelligence*, 1997, 89 (1 – 2), pp. 317 – 364; C. Schwind, Causality in action theories. *Electronic Articles in Computer and Information Science*, 1999, 4 (4), pp. 27 – 50; L. Giordano, A. Martelli, & C. Schwind, Ramification and causality in a modal action logic, *Journal of Logic and Computation*, 2000, 10 (5), pp. 625 – 662; J. Pearl, *Causality: Models, Reasoning, and Inference*, Cambridge, UK: Cambridge University Press, 2000; D. Zhang, & N. Foo, Epdl: A logic for causal reasoning, in *Proceedings of the 17th International Joint Conference on Artificial Intelligence*, CA: Morgan Kaufmann, 2001, pp. 131 – 136; L. Giordano, & C. Schwind, Conditional logic of actions and causation, *Artificial Intelligence*, 2004, 157 (1 – 2), pp. 239 – 279; J. Y. Halpern, & J. Pearl, Causes and explanations: A structural-model approach. Part I: Causes, *The British Journal for The Philosophy of Science*, 2005, 56 (4), pp. 843 – 887.

Hebbian neural networks.[①] However, CCT has virtually vanished from philosophical discussions in decades, until very recently, some philosophers have directed their attention back to this account of causation. See for example, Graßhoff & May[②], Hall[③], and Beebee[④], and also Mackie[⑤] for an earlier attempt. See also Baumgartner[⑥] for replies to criticisms against CCT, and Baumgartner[⑦] for an application of CCT in a coincidence analysis in deterministic causal structures. As argued by Baumgartner[⑧], there are several advantages of CCT over other theories of causation:

> [U]nlike e. g. counterfactual accounts regularity theories straight-forwardly handle cases of overdetermination. As against interventionist or manipulatory accounts, analyses of causation in terms of regularities do not run the risk of being anthropocentric. Contrary to probabilistic accounts, regularity theories are not compromised by paradoxical data as, for instance, generated in cases of Simpsons Paradox. Finally, while transference theories treat a fundamental type of causal process, transference processes, as conceptually primitive and thus do not attempt to provide a reductive analysis of causation, regularity accounts, properly conceived, offer the promising prospect of explicating the cause-effect relation C or at least one among possibly several types of cause-effect relations C in entirely non-causal terms.

Unlike its overwhelming opponent, the so-called counterfactual theory whose

---

① D. O. Hebb, *The Organization of Behavior: A Neuropsychological Theory*, Mahwah, NJ: Lawrence Erlbaum, 2002.

② G. Graßhoff, & M. May, Causal regularities, in W. Spohn, M. Ledwig, and M. Esfeld, (eds.), *Current Issues in Causation*. Paderborn, Germany: Mentis, 2001, pp. 85 – 114.

③ N. Hall, Two concepts of causation, in J. Collins, N. Hall, and L. A. Paul (eds.), *Causation and Counterfactuals*, Cambridge, MA: MIT Press, 2004, pp. 225 – 276.

④ H. Beebee, Does anything hold the universe together? *Synthese*, 2006, 149 (3), pp. 509 – 533.

⑤ J. L. Mackie, *The Cement of the Universe: A Study of Causation*, New York: Oxford University Press, 1974.

⑥ M. Baumgartner, Regularity theories reassessed, *Philosophia*, 2008, 36 (3), pp. 327 – 354.

⑦ M. Baumgartner, Uncovering deterministic causal structures: A boolean approach, *Synthese*, 2009, 170 (1), pp. 71 – 96.

⑧ M. Baumgartner, Regularity theories reassessed, *Philosophia*, 2008, 36 (3), pp. 327 – 354.

logical frameworks have been well-studied[①], logical theories of CCT have been missed in literature. It is our purpose of this paper to start such researches.

Why is the formalization of CCT interesting? Firstly, unlike other theories of causation, like counterfactual theory, CCT is an extensional theory. Hence, it is more natural to be embedded in the standard extensional logical framework (augmented with a time structure). A logic of causation based on CCT need not assume metaphysical concepts like possible worlds and similarity between possible worlds, which are usually required in the logic of causation based on counterfactual theory. These metaphysical concepts are highly controversial.

Secondly, with a logic for CCT in hand, we can get more explicit properties and consequences of CCT and thus can evaluate the theory better. Moreover, with a less metaphysically burdened framework, we can formalize many other theories of causationin it. In this way, we are hopeful to get deeper understanding of these theories and thus the notion of causation.

There are plenty of controversies about causation in philosophy. The present paper concerns a formal framework for an existing philosophical theory. We will try to be involved as little as possible in philosophical debate. For this purpose, we shall first settle several conceptual bases that are assumed in the paper.

We follow the standard view that causation is a relation between two objects, one called cause and the other effect. We introduce a binary causal operator C to formalize this relation. A formula $C(\alpha, \beta)$ means that α causes β.

Another standard view of causation is that objects related as causes and effects are events.[②] There is also considerable support for facts instead of events as the causal relata.[③] We will take the event view in our presentation, where propositional variables represent atomic events, and arbitrary formulas represent complex events. For this, we assume that there exist certain atomic events, based on which complex events are built by connectives $\neg$, $\vee$, and so on. It would make no difference if we understand the logic as a causal logic for facts. The formal framework is the same.

Many philosophers, as well as most ordinary persons, would agree that causation is closely related to the concept of time, in that a cause is no later than its

① D. Lewis, Causation, *The Journal of Philosophy*, 1973, 70 (17), pp. 556 – 567.

② D. Lewis, Events, *Philosophical Papers*, 1986, 2, pp. 241 – 269.

③ D. H. Mellor, *The Facts of Causation*, London: Routledge, 1995.

effects. This is taken to be a distinction between general conditionals and causal conditionals, for a general conditional statement does not require a temporal order. Some philosophers, including Kant[①], argued for simultaneous causation. See Mellor (1995)[②] for more details and replies to simultaneous causation. There has been a relatively new debate in philosophy about backward causation, supported by Dummett[③] and rebutted by Flew[④] and Black[⑤].

We follow the line of epistemic causation, or psychological causation[⑥], which started from Hume, and had been the dominant theory until decades ago. Hume stated his constant conjunction explanation of causation with the famous first definition: "We may define a cause to be an object, followed by another, and where all the objects similar to the first are followed by objects similar to the second."[⑦] According to Hume, causal statements are empirical, and the idea of causation is derived from human's experience. Causation is just a simplification for the convenience of the mind. CCT opposes both simultaneous causation and backward causation. Thus, we assume a cause always precedes its effects.

Hume's definition is for causation of particular events. A causal relation between α and β is derived from the fact that β did follow α, and all occurrences of events of type α (or in Hume's words, events similar to α) were followed by occurrences of events of type β (events similar to β). The present logic is meant to apply to causal generalizations, not to causation in particular cases. We deal with general causal statements like "events of type α cause events of type β".

For causal generalizations, the second part of Hume's definition suffices. We say that α *constantly conjoins* with β, if we have observed that after each occurrence of an α event, an occurrence of a β event was present. Each such pair of occurrences of

---

① I. Kant, *Critique of Pure Reason*, English edition, 2nd impression, translated by Smith, N. K. Macmillan, 1933.

② D. H. Mellor, *The Facts of Causation*, London: Routledge, 1995.

③ A. E. Dummett & A. Flew, Symposium: Can an effect precede its cause? *Proceedings of the Aristotelian Society*, Supplementary Volumes, 1954, 28, pp. 27-62.

④ A. E. Dummett & A. Flew, Symposium: Can an effect precede its cause? *Proceedings of the Aristotelian Society*, Supplementary Volumes, 1954, 28, pp. 27-62.

⑤ M. Black, Why cannot an effect precede its cause? *Analysis*, 1956, 16 (3), pp. 49-58.

⑥ J. Williamson, Causality, in *Handbook of Philosophical Logic* (second edition), Vol. 14, The Netherlands: Springer, 2006, pp. 95-126.

⑦ D. Hume, *An Enquiry Concerning Human Understanding: A Critical Edition*, English edition, edited by T. L. Beauchamp, New York: Oxford University Press, 2000, sec. Ⅶ.

events is an evidence that α constantly conjoins with β (also an evidence that α causes β). We will simply say that α occurs at t, or α is true at t, with the intended meaning that an event of type α occurs at t.

Let $t < u$ mean that time point t precedes time point u. Suppose that α occurred at t, and β occurred at u with $t < u$. Clearly, for this pair of occurrences of α and β to be a legitimate evidence of α causing β, there should be a constraint on the length of time between t and u. Even though we have observed that after each thunder, a year later it snows, we would not build a causal relation that thundering causes snowing. The time period is too long for a thunder to be influential. The principle of closeness, or contiguity, between cause and effect is an indispensable part of CCT, and is also crucial in a formal framework for this type of causation.

The question is how long it should be for a pair of occurrences of events to be contiguous, and therefore a legitimate evidence. This measurement has not been a subject in philosophy. It should not depend on effects. It is a measurement that how long the influence of a cause lasts. A massive event such as an earthquake should have a longer *effect period* than a minor event such as I eating my breakfast. Different causes may have different lengths of influence. This is almost all we can say about the measurement. There shall be no systematical way to determine an effect period for each object, partially because it is a matter of our psychological perspectives of objects.

We will not concern ourselves with the lengths of effect periods in this paper. We will work with a general linear time structure, in which for each event α, its effect period is modeled by a binary relation R_α. At time point t, those points in $R_\alpha(t) = \{u \mid R_\alpha tu\}$ are considered contiguous to t with respect to α. Any β that occurs at some point in $R_\alpha(t)$ is considered contiguous to the occurrence of α at t. An arbitrary binary relation is not suitable for the concept of effect period. We shall impose the following restrictions on R_α:

(1) A cause can only affect the future, which requires that $R_\alpha tu$ implies $t < u$.

(2) A cause's influence lasts for a period, i. e. time points under the influence of an occurrence of α should be uninterrupted, which requires that if $R_\alpha tu$ and $t < s < u$ then $R_\alpha ts$.

Causation is not guaranteed by constant conjunction. There are plenty of examples that two objects are constantly conjoined, whereas they are not causally linked. For the simplest example, consider a tautology α (or anything having always been true in the past), which by no mean can be a cause or an effect. However, if some β with a non-empty effect period happened in the past, α would certainly occur in the effect periods of every instance of occurrence of β. We cannot take this constant conjunction as a causation. Something should be done in distinguishing causal relations from those non-causal constant conjunction relations. This, however, is where a philosophical debate is inevitable. We will try to avoid the disputation by only setting the minimal conditions that a concept of causation should satisfy (see the next section). The corresponding logic will be called the *minimal causal logic*. We will discuss other plausible conditions in Section 3, which correspond to extensions of the minimal logic.

Our logic is a direct formalization of the constant conjunction explanation of causation. All causal relations are directly built from the observations of the past. The real process, however, may be much more complicated. For example, as the famous idea of theory-laden observation suggested①, theories are indispensable part of observations. A real process may involve the influence of the background knowledge. This, or other types of complications, are not discussed in this paper.

Our logic is built on linear time structures. Basically, there are two types of logics of time, first-order (or high-order) style and modal style. Both are reasonable ways to handle time and they are closely related to each other. The first-order approach is in general more expressive and more succinct. The modal approach has caught much attention. It is better in computational cost, and arguably closer to natural language. The first-order approach is external: sentences of the logic are evaluated with respect to whole structures. The modal approach is internal: formulas are evaluated at individual time points. We prefer the modal approach not only because of its popularity, but also because an internal perspective is more suitable for our purpose. The truth value of a causal statement $C(\alpha,\beta)$ depends on what have happened in the past of the *current* point. The evaluation has to be at a given current point. See Hodkinson & Reynolds (2007)② for more discussion on the two approaches.

Constant conjunction is a type of learning mechanism. Machine learning has been

① N. R. Hanson, *Patterns of Discovery: An Inquiry into the Conceptual Foundations of Science*, Cambridge, UK: Cambridge University Press, 1958.

② I. Hodkinson, & M. Reynolds, Temporal logic, in P. Blackburn, van J. Benthen, and F. Wolter (eds.), *Handbook of Modal Logic*, Amsterdam, The Netherlands: Elsevier, 2007, pp. 655 – 720.

intensively studied in AI with quite different views and techniques. These are algorithmic rather than logical. However, they may share some motivation with the current causal logic. The closest area to the current one is the so-called Reinforcement Learning①, where algorithms are designed to learn the effects of actions from observations, so as to take "right" actions to maximize some notion of rewards. Its focus is on finding a balance between exploration (observations) and exploitation (current knowledge). In this paper, we assume that observation is always prior to the current knowledge, which means that we unconditionally change our causal knowledge according to what we have observed. A trade-off between knowledge and observation would be an interesting topic in future research. Techniques in reinforcement learning may help for this purpose.

The remainder of the paper is structured as follows. The next section presents the minimal causal logic, including its axiomatization. Section 3 is on various extensions of the minimal causal logic by imposing conditions on either models or semantics. Also, we discuss the transitivity of causation and the inus condition in this section. In section 4 we compare the current logic with existing causal logics. We conclude the paper by suggesting some future work.

2. The minimal Causal Logic

2.1. Syntax

The alphabet of *causal logic* (CL) consists of a countable set $P = \{p, q, \ldots\}$ of propositional variables, Boolean connectives $\neg$ and $\vee$, temporal operators G and H, a binary causal operator C, and effect operators $\Box_\alpha$, one for each formula α.

Let $\alpha, \beta, \varphi, \psi$ range over arbitrary formulas. The set F of formulas is constructed as follows:

$$\varphi ::= p \mid \neg \varphi \mid \varphi \vee \psi \mid G\varphi \mid H\varphi \mid \Box_\alpha \varphi \mid C(\alpha, \beta)$$

Other Boolean connectives are defined as usual. Let $\bot =_{df} p \wedge \neg p$, $\top =_{df} \neg \bot$, $F\varphi =_{df} \neg G \neg \varphi$, $P\varphi =_{df} \neg H \neg \varphi$, and $\Diamond_\alpha \varphi =_{df} \neg \Box_\alpha \neg \varphi$.

Temporal operators have their usual meanings. $G\varphi$ says that it will always be the case that φ; $H\varphi$ says that it has always been the case that φ. Correspondingly, $F\varphi$ ($P\varphi$) states that it will be (was) the case at some future (past) point that φ. The effect operators $\Box_\alpha$ characterize the effect period of α. Formulas of the form $\Box_\alpha \varphi$ state

① R. S. Sutton, *Reinforcement Learning: An Introduction*, Cambridge, MA: The MIT Press, 2001.

that φ is true throughout the effect period of α. Formulas of the form $C(\alpha,\beta)$ are called *causal formulas* with intended meaning that α causes β.

We usually use α and β in causal formulas and φ and ψ outside causal formulas. This is only for a clear representation. All of α, β, φ and ψ represent arbitrary formulas.

We choose a general syntax in which arbitrary formulas can occur in a causal formula. This may not be appropriate in some cases. Consider the formula $C(Fp,q)$, which says that an occurrence of p in the future causes q. This causal relation depends on what will happen in the future, which contradicts the basic idea of CCT that causal relations should only depend on the past experience. We can restrict the syntax in an obvious way to exclude such cases. For the sake of simplicity, however, we keep the current one.

2. 2. Model

Definition 2. 1. *A (causal) model is a tuple* $\mathfrak{M} = (T, <, \{R_\alpha \mid \alpha \in F\}, V)$ *defined as follows:*

(i) *T is a non-empty set of (time) points.*

(ii) *$<$ is a linear order on T, i. e. $<$ is irreflexive ($\forall x \neg(x < x)$), transitive ($\forall xyz(x < y \wedge y < z \rightarrow x < z)$), and trichotomic ($\forall xy(x < y \vee x = y \vee y < x)$).*

(iii) *$V: P \rightarrow 2^T$ is a valuation function that assigns to each $p \in P$ a set of points at which p is true.*

(iv) *Each R_α is a binary relation on T (probably empty) such that*

(a) *$R_\alpha tu$ implies that $t < u$,*

(b) *$R_\alpha tu$ implies that $R_\alpha tv$ for all v such that $t < v < u$.*

$R_\alpha(t) = \{u \mid R_\alpha tu\}$ is called α's effect period at t. Any $u \in R_\alpha(t)$ is called an effect point with respect to α at t.

The time structure is for a concept of psychological time. It is the time that we perceive. We may consider the structure as a history of human beings, so that causal relations being built are from the perspective of human beings, or may consider the structure as a history of some agent's personal experience, so that causal relations being built are from the perspective of the agent.

We will write (t,u) for $\{s \mid t < s < u\}$. Similarly, we write $[t,u)$, $(t,u]$ and $[t,u]$ for their obvious meanings. Definition 2. 1 (iv - a) states that effect points are always in the future; Definition 2. 1 (iv - b) says that if u is contiguous to t, so are any points in (t,u). $u \in R_\alpha(t)$ means that u is contiguous to t with respect to α. If α is true at t and β is true at u, this occurrence of β is contiguous to this occurrence of α, and the pair is considered an evidence that α causes β.

2. 3. Semantics

Constant conjunction is a simple notion with a clear intuition. It, however, also has subtlety. Intuitively, α constantly conjoins with β, if, in the past, after any occurrence of α, some β occurred within α's effect period. This statement is not sound in a special case, as pictured in Figure 1.

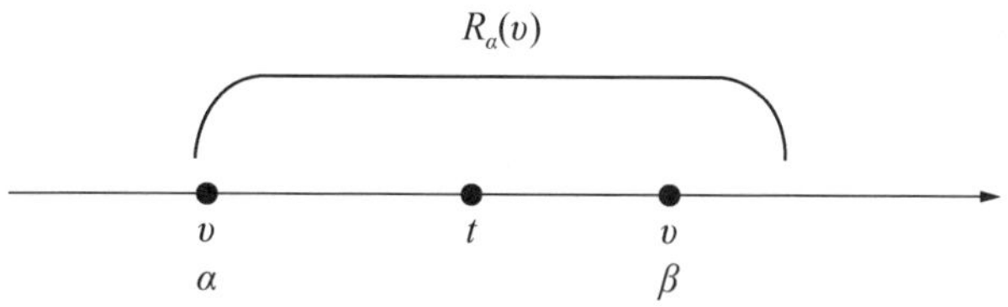

Fig. 1 The definition of data points.

There are three points u, t, v with $u < t < v$, and $t, v \in R_\alpha(u)$. Let t be the current point. Suppose α holds at u, and β does not hold at any $s \in (u,t)$. It seems a counterexample to α constantly conjoining with β at t, because α occurred at u, but β did not contiguously follow from the point of view at t. However, it is possible that there is a future point v, also within the effect period $R_\alpha(u)$, at which β holds. Thus, u cannot be a counterexample. The point is that, we cannot determine at t whether a β contiguously follows the occurrence of α at u. This suggests the definition of data points.

Given a point t and a formula α, let the set of *data points*

$$D(t,\alpha) = \{u \mid u < t, \textit{ and } v < t \textit{ for all } v \in R_\alpha(u)\}.$$

Thus, $D(t,\alpha)$ consists of those points at which, from the point of view of the current point, the effect period has been over.

On the other hand, even though non-data points cannot be counterexamples, they can be evidences, as shown in Figure 2. t is still the current point. u is not a data point with respect to α at t. Suppose that there was a $s \in (u,t)$ at which β is true. Then the pair of occurrences of α (at u) and β (at s) is a legitimate evidence of the constant conjunction, even this α's effect period has not been totally observed. What will happen after t is irrelevant in this case, because we have already observed a β after this α.

Definition 2.2. $\mathfrak{M}, t \models_C \varphi$ *denotes that* φ *is true at point t in causal model* $\mathfrak{M}$*, which is defined as follows*:

$\mathfrak{M}, t \models_C p$ *iff* $t \in V(p)$, *where* $p \in P$.

$\mathfrak{M}, t \models_C \neg \varphi$ *iff* $\mathfrak{M}, t \not\models_C \varphi$

$\mathfrak{M}, t \models_C \varphi \vee \psi$ *iff* $\mathfrak{M}, t \models_C \varphi$ *or* $\mathfrak{M}, t \models_C \psi$.

$\mathfrak{M}, t \models_C G\varphi$ *iff for all u with* $t < u$, $\mathfrak{M}, u \models_C \varphi$.

$\mathfrak{M}, t \models_C H\varphi$ *iff for all u with* $u < t$, $\mathfrak{M}, u \models_C \varphi$.

$\mathfrak{M}, t \models_C \Box_\alpha \varphi$ *iff for all u with* $R_\alpha tu$, $\mathfrak{M}, u \models_C \varphi$.

$\mathfrak{M}, t \models_C C(\alpha, \beta)$ *iff the following holds*:

(i) *For each* $u \in D(t, \alpha)$ *with* $\mathfrak{M}, u \models_C \alpha$, *there is a v such that* $R_\alpha uv$ *and* $\mathfrak{M}, v \models_C \beta$.

(ii) *There exist* u, v *such that* $u < t$, $v < t$, $R_\alpha uv$, $\mathfrak{M}, u \models_C \alpha$, *and* $\mathfrak{M}, v \models_C \beta$.

(iii) *There exists a* $u < t$ *with* $\mathfrak{M}, u \not\models_C \alpha$.

(iv) *There exists a* $v < t$ *with* $\mathfrak{M}, v \not\models_C \beta$.

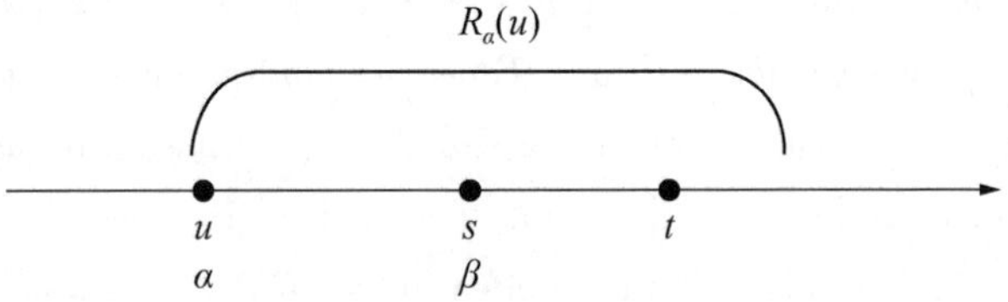

Fig. 2 A nondata point evidence.

In the semantic clause for C, the first two conditions state the constant conjunction between α and β. Condition (i) is to the effect that there has been no *counterexample* to $C(\alpha, \beta)$. Condition (ii) says that there has been some *evidence* of $C(\alpha, \beta)$. The last two conditions exclude any invariably true formulas to be either cause or effect. We take these two as the basic conditions that distinguish causal relations from non-causal constant conjunction relations. To sum up, α causes β if both statements have not been invariable true in the past, and no counterexample to it has been observed, and some evidence of it has been observed.

We sometimes write $t \models_C \varphi$ for $\mathfrak{M}, t \models_C \varphi$. A formula φ is true in a model $\mathfrak{M}$ (denoted by $\mathfrak{M} \models_C \varphi$) if $\mathfrak{M}, t \models_C \varphi$ for all points t in $\mathfrak{M}$. φ is valid (denoted by $\models_C \varphi$) if $\mathfrak{M} \models_C \varphi$ for all models $\mathfrak{M}$. φ is satisfiable if there is a model $\mathfrak{M}$ and a point t such that $\mathfrak{M}, t \models_C \varphi$. Given a class of models M, $M \models_C \varphi$ if $\mathfrak{M} \models_C \varphi$ for all models $\mathfrak{M} \in$ M. Notions like $t \models_C \Gamma$, where Γ is a set of formulas, are similarly defined.

The causal operator is not a normal binary modality. It is neither "$\Diamond$-type" nor "$\Box$-type". The semantic clause (i) is a $\forall$-$\exists$ statement. It is easy to check that neither the K axiom $C(\alpha \to \beta_1, \beta_2) \to (C(\alpha,\beta_1) \to C(\beta_1,\beta_2))$, nor the necessity rules $\alpha / C(\alpha,\beta)$ and $\beta / C(\alpha,\beta)$ hold.

Though the primary relations in the model are only for characterizing temporal operators and effect operators, the causal operator C is not definable by the rest.

Theorem 2. 3. *C is not definable by G, H, and $\{\Box_\alpha | \alpha \in F\}$.*

Proof. Suppose otherwise. Let $C(p,q) =_{df} \chi$, where χ is a formula with no occurrence of C.

Let $\mathfrak{M}$ be a model pictured in Figure 3, which contains a points u with proper past points, and after u, there is an integer line with their usual order.

Let the model satisfy the following:

(1) $u \models_C p$ and $0 \models_C C(p,q)$.

(2) $R_p(u) = \{i \mid i \in \mathbb{Z}, i < 2\}$.

(3) $R_\alpha(i) = \varnothing$ for all integers i and all formulas α.

(4) $i \models_C \neg q$ for all integers i.

(5) All integers agree on all propositional variables, i. e. for all i, $j \in \mathbb{Z}$ and all $p \in P$, $i \in V(p)$ iff $j \in V(p)$.

The definition is sound because u is not a p-data point at 0 so that it is not a counterexample to $C(p,q)$ at 0. Let the model $\mathfrak{M}'$ have the same definition as $\mathfrak{M}$ except that $R'_p(u) = \{i' \mid i' \in \mathbb{Z}, i' < 0\}$.

We have $\mathfrak{M}', 0' \models_C \neg C(p,q)$ because u is now a p-data point at $0'$ and is a counterexample to $C(p,q)$. Then we have $\mathfrak{M}, 0 \models_C \chi$ and $\mathfrak{M}', 0' \not\models_C \chi$. It is sufficient to show that for any formula φ with no occurrence of C, $\mathfrak{M}, 0 \models \varphi$ iff $\mathfrak{M}', 0' \models_C \varphi$.

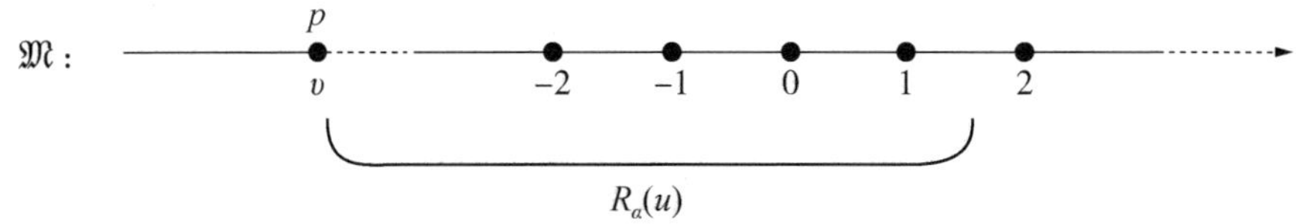

Fig. 3. The independency of *C*.

Let Z be the relation between the two models defined as follows:

For any non-integer pointst, Z is one-one so that tZt'.

(ⅰ) For integer points, Z is total, i. e. iZj' for all integers i and j'.

(ⅱ) It is a routine to check that Z is a bisimulation. Thus, 0 and $0'$ satisfy exact the same set of formulas with no occurrence of C.

Lemma 2. 4. $\models_C \neg C(\alpha,\beta) \wedge PC(\alpha,\beta) \rightarrow G\neg C(\alpha,\beta)$.

Proof. Suppose $t \models_C \neg C(\alpha,\beta)$ and $t \models_C PC(\alpha,\beta)$. Then there is a $u < t$ with $u \models_C C(\alpha,\beta)$, i. e. all the four conditions for $C(\alpha,\beta)$ in Definition 2. 2 hold at u. Because $u < t$, conditions (ⅱ) - (ⅳ) must also hold at t. Because $C(\alpha,\beta)$ is false at t, condition (i) must fail at t, i. e. there is a data point $v \in D(t,\alpha)$ such that v is a counterexample to $C(\alpha,\beta)$ at t. Clearly, v is also a counterexample to $C(\alpha,\beta)$ at all s with $t < s$. Then $s \models_C \neg C(\alpha,\beta)$. Thus, $t \models_C G\neg C(\alpha,\beta)$.

Lemma 2. 4 states that once we lose a causal relation, we will lose it forever. This is because losing it means that we found a counterexample to the causal relation. According to the lemma, the distribution of a causal statement $C(\alpha,\beta)$ along a time line is quite ordered. There are only five cases, as shown in Figure 4:

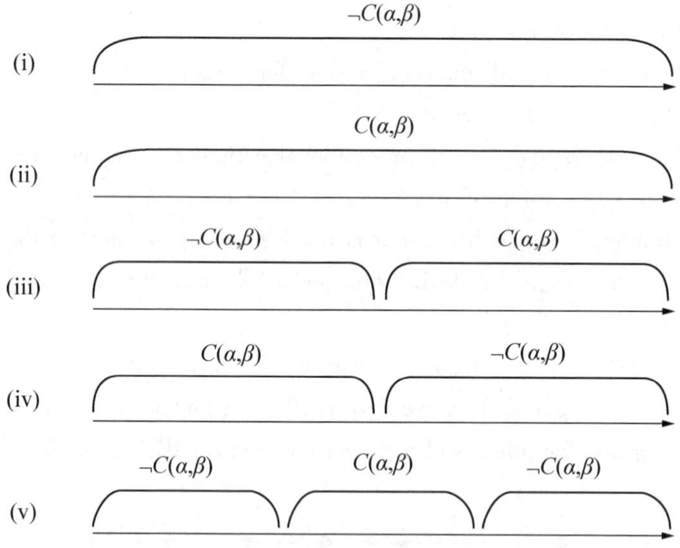

Fig. 4. The distributions of causal formulas.

(i) is the case that the causal relation does not hold throughout the structure. (ii) is the case that the causal relation always holds. (iii) is the case that the causal relation holds after some time point.

In case (ii) and case (iii), $C(\alpha,\beta)$ will always hold once it has been built. This indicates that no counterexample to the causal relation occurs anywhere. In this sense, $C(\alpha,\beta)$ can be considered as an *objective* causal relation. Though causation is an epistemic concept here, we may define the "objectivity" of causation as this *never observing a counterexample*.

(iv) and (v) are cases that the causal relation has been built, but will be found false by observing some counterexample. By Lemma 2.4, $C(\alpha,\beta)$ can never be recovered thereafter.

Case (ii) and (iv) seem unrealistic because the causal relation $C(\alpha,\beta)$ comes from nowhere. In real world, we shall start with $\neg C(\alpha,\beta)$, and build $C(\alpha,\beta)$ by collecting enough and proper data. (ii) and (iv) can be eliminated by assuming that there is a starting time point, at which no causal formula can be true according to the semantics.

The rest three cases classify causal relations into three types: Those *objective* causal relations that once was built and will always be held, as in (iii); those *false* causal relations that can never be built, as in (i); and those *delusive* causal relations that once was built, but will be removed later, as in (v).

2.4. Axiomatization

In the axiomatization, for characterizing non-temporal operators $\Box_\alpha$ and C, we will use name formulas to distinguish time points. For this purpose, Gabbay's general irreflexivity rule① suffices. Let $name(\psi) = \psi \wedge G\neg\psi$. In any transitive and trichotomic frame, if $name(\psi)$ is true at some point t, then it must be false at all other points. Thus, $name(\psi)$ acts as a name of t, and is called a *name formula*. For reference, the hybrid logic is another way of using nominals, which in its objective language contains atoms that each is interpreted as a name of a state. ②

The minimal causal logic C consists of the following axioms and rules:

(*Prop*) Propositional tautologies,

(K) $G(\varphi\to\psi)\to(G\varphi\to G\psi), H(\varphi\to\psi)\to(H\varphi\to H\psi)$,
$\Box_\alpha(\varphi\to\psi)\to(\Box_\alpha\varphi\to\Box_\alpha\psi)$,

(Re) $\varphi\to GP\varphi$, $\varphi\to HF\varphi$,

(4) $G\varphi\to GG\varphi$,

(.3$_r$) $(F\varphi\wedge F\psi)\to F(\varphi\wedge F\psi)\vee F(\varphi\wedge\psi)\vee F(\psi\wedge F\varphi)$,

---

① D. M. Gabbay, I. Hodkinson, & M. Reynolds, *Temporal Logic: Mathematical Foundations and Computational Aspects*, Vol. 1, New York: Oxford University Press, 1994.

② C. Areces, & B. Cate, Hybrid logics, in P. Blackburn, F. Wolter, and van J. Benthem (eds.), *Handbook of Modal Logic*, Amsterdam, The Netherlands: Elsevier, 2006, pp. 821 – 868.

(. 3_l) $(P\varphi \wedge P\psi) \to P(\varphi \wedge P\psi) \vee P(\varphi \wedge \psi) \vee P(\psi \wedge P\varphi)$,

(EP) $\Box_\alpha \varphi \wedge \Diamond_\alpha name(\psi) \to G(Fname(\psi) \to \varphi)$,

(EF) $\Diamond_\alpha \varphi \to F\varphi$,

(C) $name(\psi) \to [C(\alpha,\beta) \leftrightarrow P\neg \alpha \wedge P\neg \beta \wedge H(\neg \Diamond_\alpha name(\psi) \wedge \alpha \to \Diamond_\alpha \beta) \wedge P(\alpha \wedge \Diamond_\alpha(Fname(\psi) \wedge \beta))]$,

(*MP*) $\dfrac{\varphi, \varphi \to \psi}{\psi}$,

(*RN*) $\dfrac{\varphi}{G\varphi}, \dfrac{\varphi}{H\varphi}, \dfrac{\varphi}{\Box_\alpha \varphi}$,

(*IRR*) $\dfrac{\langle\rangle_1(\varphi_1 \wedge \dots \wedge \langle\rangle_m(\varphi_m \wedge name(p))\dots) \to \varphi}{\langle\rangle_1(\varphi_1 \wedge \dots \wedge (\langle\rangle_m \varphi_m)\dots) \to \varphi}$,

where p does not occur anywhere except in the displayed $name(p)$, and each $\langle\rangle_1 \cdots \langle\rangle_m$ is either F or P or $\Diamond_\alpha$ for some α.

Notions of proof ($\vdash_C \varphi$) and deduction ($\Gamma \vdash_C \varphi$) are defined as usual. The system contains the temporal logic for linear orders. The *axiom of effect period* (EP) guarantees that an effect period is an uninterrupted chain. The name formula in (EP) is to identify an effect point, say u. The consequent of (EP) says that any point lies between the current point and u is also an effect point. The *axiom of effect future* (EF) guarantees that an effect period is in the future. The *axiom of causation* (C) is a direct formalization of the semantic clause for operator C. Again, we need a name formula in the axiom to identify the current point in which $C(\alpha,\beta)$ is evaluated.

It is left open to us whether the irreflexivity rule add new theorems to the logic, i. e. whether it is an equivalent system if we remove (IRR) from C. In general, little has been known on the problem that whether there are natural criteria deciding such rules' redundancy over given deductive systems. ①

Soundness of the system is checked as usual.

Theorem 2. 5. (*Soundness*) *For any formula* φ, if $\vdash_C \varphi$ *then* $\models_C \varphi$.

A set of formulas Γ is (C-) consistent if $\Gamma \vdash_C \varphi \wedge \neg \varphi$ for no φ. A formula φ is consistent if $\{\varphi\}$ is. Γ is (C-) maximal consistent if it is consistent and any proper superset of it is inconsistent. The (C-) canonical model is defined as usual as a tuple $\mathfrak{M}^c = (T^c, <^c, \{R^c_\alpha | \alpha \in F\}, V^c)$ such that T^c is the set of maximal consistent sets, $t <^c u$ iff $\varphi \in u$ for all $G\varphi \in t$, $R^c_\alpha tu$ iff $\varphi \in u$ for all $\Box_\alpha \varphi \in t$, and $t \in V^c(p)$ iff p

---

① Y. Venema, Derivation rules as anti-axioms in modal logic, *The Journal of Symbolic Logic*, 1993, 58 (3), pp. 1003 – 1034.

$\in t$. We say that t and u are connected if either $u <^c t$ or $t <^c u$. It is direct from the definition that if $name(\psi) \in t$ then $name(\psi) \notin u$ for any u that connects with t. It follows that $name(\psi) \in t$ implies that t is an irreflexive point.

For any $T \subseteq T^c$, let $\mathfrak{M}^c | T$ be the submodel of $\mathfrak{M}^c$ induced by T. That is, $\mathfrak{M}^c | T = (T, <, \{R_\alpha | \alpha \in F\}, V)$, where $< = <^c \cap (T \times T)$, $R_\alpha = R^c_\alpha \cap (T \times T)$, and $V(p) = V^c(p) \cap T$ for all $p \in P$.

Definition 2.6. *A subset $T \subseteq T^c$ is called saturated if the following holds:*

(i) *For any $t \in T$, if $F\varphi \in t$, then there is a $u \in T$ such that $t <^c u$ and $\varphi \in u$.*

(ii) *For any $t \in T$, if $P\varphi \in t$, then there is a $u \in T$ such that $u <^c t$ and $\varphi \in u$.*

(iii) *For any $t \in T$, if $\Diamond_\alpha \varphi \in t$, then there is a $u \in T$ such that $R^c_\alpha tu$ and $\varphi \in u$.*

Definition 2.7. *A maximal consistent set is called witnessing if it contains some name formula. A subset $T \subseteq T^c$ is called witnessing if every member of T is witnessing. In the case that T is saturated (and/or witnessing), we say that $\mathfrak{M}^c | T$ is saturated (and/or witnessing).*

Lemma 2.8. *Let $T \subseteq T^c$ be saturated and witnessing. Then for any $t, u \in T$ with $name(\psi) \in t$ for some formula ψ, $u \in D(t,\alpha)$ in $\mathfrak{M}^c | T$ iff $u < t$ and $\neg \Diamond_\alpha name(\psi) \in u$.*

Proof. Suppose $u \in D(t,\alpha)$ in $\mathfrak{M}^c | T$. By the definition of data points, $u < t$. Also, $v < t$ for all $v \in R_\alpha(u)$. Because T is witnessing, $name(\psi) \notin v$ for all such v. Because T is saturated, $\neg \Diamond_\alpha name(\psi) \in u$.

Suppose $u < t$ and $\neg \Diamond_\alpha name(\psi) \in u$. By axiom (EF), $R^c_\alpha \subseteq <^c$. It follows that $R_\alpha \subseteq <$. Then for all $v \in R_\alpha(u)$, $u < v$. By temporal axioms, $\mathfrak{M}^c$ is non-branching, therefore $\mathfrak{M}^c | T$ is no-branching. Then by $u < v$ and $u < t$, we have that $v = t$, $v < t$, or $t < v$. Clearly $v \neq t$ because $name(\psi) \notin v$. We also have $t \not< v$. Suppose otherwise that $t < v$. We show that $R^c_\alpha ut$, and therefore $\Diamond_\alpha name(\psi) \in u$, which contradicts the assumption. It suffices to show that for any $\Box_\alpha \varphi \in u$, $\varphi \in t$. Let $\Box_\alpha \varphi \in u$. Since v is witnessing, $name(\chi) \in v$ for some χ. Then $\Diamond_\alpha name(\chi) \in u$. By axiom (EP), $G(Fname(\chi) \to \varphi) \in u$. Then $Fname(\chi) \to \varphi \in t$. By $t < v$, $Fname(\chi) \in t$. Then $\varphi \in t$. We conclude that $v < t$. It follows that $u \in D(t,\alpha)$.

Lemma 2.9. *If T is saturated and witnessing, then for any $t \in T$ and any formula φ, $\mathfrak{M}^c | T, t \models_C \varphi$ iff $\varphi \in t$.*

Proof. The proof is by induction on φ. We only check the case for C operator. As T is witnessing, let $name(\psi) \in t$.

Suppose $\mathfrak{M}^c|T,t \vDash_C C(\alpha,\beta)$. Then by definition we have the followings:

(i) For each $u \in D(t,\alpha)$ in $\mathfrak{M}^c|T$ such that $\mathfrak{M}^c|T,u \vDash_C \alpha$, there is a $v \in R_\alpha(u)$ such that $\mathfrak{M}^c|T,v \vDash_C \beta$.

(ii) There exist $u,v \in T$ such that $u < t$, $v < t$, $R_\alpha uv$, $\mathfrak{M}^c|T,u \vDash_C \alpha$, and $\mathfrak{M}^c|T,v \vDash_C \beta$.

(iii) There exists a $u < t$ with $\mathfrak{M},u \nvDash_C \alpha$.

(iv) There exists a $v < t$ with $\mathfrak{M},v \nvDash_C \beta$.

By (i), Lemma 2.8, and the inductive hypothesis, for each u in T with $u < t$, $\neg \Diamond_\alpha name(\psi) \in u$, and $\alpha \in u$, there is a $v \in R_\alpha(u)$ with $\beta \in v$. By the definition of the canonical model, for each u in T with $u < t$, $\neg \Diamond_\alpha name(\psi) \wedge \alpha \rightarrow \Diamond_\alpha \beta \in u$. Because $\mathfrak{M}^c|T$ is saturated, $H(\neg \Diamond_\alpha name(\psi) \wedge \alpha \rightarrow \Diamond_\alpha \beta) \in t$.

By (ii) and the inductive hypothesis, there exist $u,v \in T$ such that $u < t$, $v < t$, $R_\alpha uv$, $\alpha \in u$, and $\beta \in v$. Then $Fname(\psi) \in v$. Then $\alpha \wedge \Diamond_\alpha(F\,name(\psi) \wedge \beta) \in u$. Then $P(\alpha \wedge \Diamond_\alpha(F\,name(\psi) \wedge \beta)) \in t$.

By (iii) and (iv), $P\neg \alpha \wedge P\neg \beta \in t$. Then by axiom (C), $C(\alpha,\beta) \in t$. The other direction is similarly proved.

Lemma 2.10. *Let T be saturated and witnessing, and $t \in T$. Let $\mathfrak{M}^c|T_t$ be the submodel of $\mathfrak{M}^c|T$ generated by t. Then $\mathfrak{M}^c|T_t$ is a causal model.*

Proof. By the temporal axioms, $\mathfrak{M}^c$ is transitive and non-branching. Clearly $\mathfrak{M}^c|T$ is also transitive and non-branching, and therefore $\mathfrak{M}^c|T_t$ is transitive and trichotomic. For each $u \in \mathfrak{M}^c|T_t$, because $name(\psi) \in u$ for some ψ, u is an irreflexive point. Then $\mathfrak{M}^c|T_t$ is a linear order.

Let $<$ and R_α denote the respective relations in $\mathfrak{M}^c|T_t$. If $R^c_\alpha \subseteq <^c$, then $\mathfrak{M}^c|T_t$ will inherit this property, i. e. $R_\alpha \subseteq <$. To show that $R^c_\alpha \subseteq <^c$, let $R^c_\alpha uv$, and $G\varphi \in u$. It suffices to show that $\varphi \in v$. By $G\varphi \in u$ and axiom (EF), $\Box_\alpha \varphi \in u$. By $R^c_\alpha uv$, $\varphi \in v$.

Suppose $R_\alpha uv$ and $u < s < v$. We have to show that $R_\alpha us$. Because R_α and $<$ is respective restrictions from R^c_α and $<^c$, $R^c_\alpha uv$ and $u <^c s <^c v$. Let $\Box_\alpha \psi \in u$. Since v is witnessing, $name(\chi) \in v$ for some χ. Then $\Diamond_\alpha name(\chi) \in u$. By axiom (EP), $G(Fname(\chi) \rightarrow \psi) \in u$. Then $Fname(\chi) \rightarrow \psi \in s$. We have $Fname(\chi) \in s$ because $s <^c v$. Then $\psi \in s$. Then, $R^c_\alpha us$. Thus, $R_\alpha us$

Lemma 2.11. *Given a consistent formula φ, there is a saturated and witnessing* set T of maximal consistent sets, such that $\varphi \in \Gamma$ *for some* $\Gamma \in T$.

Proof. The proof is by a zigzag construction developed by Gabbay[①]. The full proof is in the Appendix.

Theorem 2. 12. (*Completeness of C*) *For any formula* φ, if $\models_C \varphi$ *then* $\vdash_C \varphi$.

Proof. It is sufficient to show that any consistent formula is satisfiable in a causal model. Let φ be a consistent formula. Then by Lemma 2. 11, there is a saturated and witnessing set T with $\varphi \in \Gamma$ for some $\Gamma \in T$. By Lemma 2. 10, $\mathfrak{M}^c | T_\Gamma$ is a causal model. Because $\mathfrak{M}^c | T$ is saturated and witnessing, $\mathfrak{M}^c | T_\Gamma$ is saturated and witnessing. By Lemma 2. 9, $\mathfrak{M}^c | T_\Gamma, \Gamma \models_C \varphi$.

3. Extensions of the Minimal Causal Logic

3. 1. Extensions by conditions on models.

In this section, we consider possible extensions of the minimal causal logic for various concepts of causation. Extensions are obtained by imposing more conditions on either causal models or the semantic definition.

The study of various conditions on time structures is a routine in temporal logic. Some of them are particularly interesting for the current logic. Because of the epistemic limitation of human beings, it is reasonable to assume that (psychological) time has a starting point ($\exists x \forall y (x \leqslant y)$), which corresponds to the axiom $H \perp \vee PH \perp$. At the starting point, no causal relation can be built, because no data has been observed. With this condition, cases (ii) and (iv) in Figure 3 are eliminated.

The effect period of an event is modelled by a binary relation. The length of an effect period is not expressible in the general linear time. Thus, we cannot say in the model that, for example, the same event always has the same length of effect period at all points. In order to enrich our framework with this apparatus, instead of general linear time, we may work with real number time or natural number time, in which the notion of length is natural. We may assign a fixed number to each event as the length of its effect period.

Another interesting topic is to extend the logic with a notion of causal degree by counting the number of instances of evidences of causal relations. We may say that we have confidence in a causal relation with the degree 100 if there have been a hundred

---

① D. M. Gabbay, I. Hodkinson, & M. Reynolds, *Temporal Logic: Mathematical Foundations and Computational Aspects*, Vol. 1, New York: Oxford University Press, 1994, p. 210.

instances of evidences of this causal relation. In this way, we can compare reliability of causal relations by their degrees. Again, for this purpose, we have to work with a time structure in which we can count numbers, such as natural number time.

We can already say something about effect periods in general linear time. For two events α and β, that β's influence lasts longer than α's can be modeled by $R_\alpha \subset R_\beta$. Intuitively, equivalent formulas denote the same event, so that the effect period of equivalent formulas should be the same. Formally, if α and β are equivalent then $R_\alpha = R_\beta$. We may add this condition to the model. It shall be noted that this condition only makes sense when we assume a type of logical omniscience. Effect period is an epistemic notion. The effect period of an event depends on our psychological perspectives of the event. Therefore, by assuming this condition, we assume that we always know the equivalence of α and β if they actually are.

The effect period of some complex formula may be relevant to the effect periods of its components. We think it is reasonable to assume that $R_{\alpha \vee \gamma} = R_\alpha \cup R_\gamma$. With this assumption, the formula

$$C(\alpha,\beta) \wedge C(\gamma,\beta) \wedge P\neg(\alpha \vee \gamma) \rightarrow C(\alpha \vee \gamma,\beta)$$

will be valid, which represents a plausible property of causation (see Section 4).

On the other hand, it seems implausible that the effect period of $\alpha \wedge \beta$ depends on effect periods of α and β. A massive event with a long effect period, like an earthquake, may be viewed as an agglomeration of smallish events each with a tiny effect period, like a motion of a grain of sand. There seems no way to compute an effect period of the earthquake from the effect period of the sand moving.

Following this, we should not determine the effect period of $\neg\alpha$ by the effect period of α. Otherwise, because $\alpha \wedge \beta = \neg(\neg\alpha \vee \neg\beta)$, the effect period of $\alpha \wedge \beta$ can be reduced.

It is natural to assume that, for each occurrence of α, we know where the influence of this occurrence ends. It requires that a non-empty effect period is always a right closed interval, i. e. if $R_\alpha(t) \neq \varnothing$ then $R_\alpha(t) = (t,s]$ for some s. With this condition, the following plausible formula becomes valid:

$$\neg C(\alpha,\beta) \wedge PC(\alpha,\beta) \rightarrow P(C(\alpha,\beta) \wedge G\neg C(\alpha,\beta)).$$

The formula states that if an existing causal relation is removed, then we know where it is removed.

3. 2. Extensions by conditions on semantics

In the minimal causal logic, besides the basic conditions for constant conjunction, the extra condition is that invariably true formulas are neither causes nor effects. More conditions may be added to distinguish causal relations from those non-causal constant conjunction relations. The question is, which ones? There does not exist a single *right* answer to the question. We present two possible candidates.

The first is motivated by the manipulablity theory of causation. According to the theory, a cause α is the one that, when its status is changed, will change the status of its effects. We may require that occurrences of α *did* change the status of β. For, even if $\alpha \wedge \beta$ was true at some point u, and β followed at some contiguous point v, it may not be enough to say that this is an evidence that α causes β. Because β already held at u, its occurrence at v may be caused by nothing: it is just because β's status did not change from u to v. Thus, we may require that a positive evidence to $C(\alpha,\beta)$ is a point at which $\alpha \wedge \neg \beta$ held, and β contiguously followed. In this case α does make a difference on the truth value of β. This condition is along the line of a weak manipulablity theory called interventionism, which uses manipulation as a feature of causation without claiming that it is more fundamental than causation.

Formally, let the logic C' be obtained from the minimal causal logic by changing the item (ii). in Definition 2. 2 to the following:

(ii') There exist u,v such that $u < t$, $v < t$, $R_\alpha uv$, $\mathfrak{M},u \models_C \alpha \wedge \neg \beta$, and $\mathfrak{M}$, $v \models_C \beta$.

A complete system for C' is obtained from system C by replacing the axiom (C) with the following one:

$$(C') \qquad name(\psi) \rightarrow [C(\alpha,\beta) \leftrightarrow P\neg \alpha \wedge P\neg \beta \wedge H(\neg \Diamond_\alpha name(\psi) \wedge \alpha \rightarrow \Diamond_\alpha \beta) \wedge P(\alpha \wedge \neg \beta \wedge \Diamond_\alpha(Fname(\psi) \wedge \beta))].$$

In the minimal causal logic, for a causal formula $C(\alpha,\beta)$ to be true, some (*positive*) evidence and no counterexample should present. For another candidate of extensions of the minimal logic, we may also require some *negative* evidence for a causal formula to be true. That is, instances that α did not occur, and β did not contiguously follow. It is in this case more likely that it is α that causes β.

Formally, we add the following item to the semantic clause of C in Definition 2. 2:

(v) There is a $u \in D(t,\neg \alpha)$ such that $R_{\neg\alpha}(u) \neq \varnothing$, $\mathfrak{M},u \models_C \neg \alpha$, and for all $v \in R_{\neg\alpha}(u)$, $\mathfrak{M},v \models_C \neg \beta$.

In a word, this notion of causation needs three conditions: some positive evidence, some negative evidence, and no counterexample. We call this logic C''.

For this semantics, a complete system C'' is obtained from the system C by replacing the axiom (C) with the following one:

(C'') $name(\psi) \rightarrow [C(\alpha,\beta) \leftrightarrow P\neg\alpha \wedge P\neg\beta \wedge H(\neg\Diamond_{\alpha} name(\psi) \wedge \alpha \rightarrow \Diamond_{\alpha}\beta) \wedge P(\alpha \wedge \Diamond_{\alpha}(Fname(\psi) \wedge \beta)) \wedge P(\neg\Diamond_{\neg\alpha} name(\psi) \wedge \Diamond_{\neg\alpha} T \wedge \neg\alpha \wedge \Box_{\alpha}\neg\beta)]$.

Logics C' and C'' can be combined in an obvious way. Let the logic C''' be obtained from the minimal causal logic by changing the item (ii) in Definition 2.2 to (ii'), and adding the following:

(v') There is a $u \in D(t,\neg\alpha)$ such that $R_{\neg\alpha}(u) \neq \varnothing$, $\mathfrak{M},u \models_C \neg\alpha \wedge \neg\beta$, and for all $v \in R_{\neg\alpha}(u)$, $\mathfrak{M},v \models_C \neg\beta$.

A complete system C''' with respect to this semantics can be obtained by replacing the axiom (C) with (C'''):

(C''') $name(\psi) \rightarrow [C(\alpha,\beta) \leftrightarrow P\neg\alpha \wedge P\neg\beta \wedge H(\neg\Diamond_{\alpha} name(\psi) \wedge \alpha \rightarrow \Diamond_{\alpha}\beta) \wedge P(\alpha \wedge \neg\beta \wedge \Diamond_{\alpha}(Fname(\psi) \wedge \beta)) \wedge P(\neg\Diamond_{\neg\alpha} name(\psi) \wedge \Diamond_{\neg\alpha} T \wedge \neg\alpha \wedge \neg\beta \wedge \Box_{\alpha}\neg\beta)]$.

In the minimal causal logic, it is possible that (1) for some point t, $t \models_C C(\alpha,\beta) \wedge C(\neg\alpha,\beta)$, and (2) for some point u, $u \models_C C(\alpha,\beta) \wedge C(\alpha,\neg\beta)$. They are unrealistic statements about causation. Contradictory events cannot both be causes of the same effect, and also cannot both be effects of the same cause. It can be verified that (1) is eliminated in C'', whereas (2) holds in all of C', C'' and C'''.

In practice, when we state a causal relation, like "short-circuit causes catching a fire", it usually assumes that "catching fire" occurs much less than "not catching fire". The latter is a routine that almost occurs at all situations. For such objects we do not look for a cause. This suggests a possible solution to (2) by distinguishing accidental events from the routines. We leave it for future research.

3.3. Transitivity

The transitivity of causation coincides with commonsense notions of causation, and fits with some explanatory practices. On the other hand, there have been quite a few counterexamples to the transitivity of causation (see Hall① for counterexamples and Lewis② for defensive replies).

---

① N. Hall, Causation and the price of transitivity, *The Journal of Philosophy*, 2000, 97 (4), pp. 198 – 222.

② D. Lewis, Causation as influence, in J. D. Collins, E. J. Hall, and L. A. Paul (eds.), *Causation and Counterfactuals*, Cambridge, MA: The MIT Press, 2004, pp. 75 – 106.

Causation in our minimal logic is not transitive: $C(\alpha,\beta) \wedge C(\beta,\gamma) \rightarrow C(\alpha,\gamma)$ is not valid. A transitive notion of causation can be obtained in an obvious way, as what David Lewis did in his counterfactual theory: It is simply by taking the transitive closure of the causal relations.

A *causal chain* from α to β at a time point t is a finite sequence $\alpha, \gamma_1, \dots, \gamma_n, \beta$ such that $t \models_C C(\alpha, \gamma_1), t \models_C C(\gamma_1, \gamma_2), \dots, t \models_C C(\gamma_n, \beta)$. Let C^* be the transitive causal operator. Then,

$t \models_C C^*(\alpha,\beta)$ if and only if there is a causal chain from α to β at t.

Theorem 3.1. *C^* is not definable in the minimal causal logic.*

Proof. Suppose otherwise. Let $C^*(p,q) =_{df} \chi$, where χ is a formula in the minimal causal logic. Construct a model $\mathfrak{M}_1$ with no starting point such that at a point t, the followings hold:

(1) $\mathfrak{M}_1, t \not\models_C C^*(p,q)$.

(2) p and q are not invariably true in the past of t.

(3) There are some points u, v in the past of t such that $\mathfrak{M}_1, u \models_C p$ and $\mathfrak{M}_1, v \models_C q$.

(4) u in (3) is a data point in $D(t,p)$.

(5) $R_r = \varnothing$ for any r that does not occur in χ.

(6) $R_p(s) \neq \varnothing$ for all points s.

Let r be any propositional variable that does not occur in χ. Let V_1 be the valuation function of $\mathfrak{M}_1$. A model $\mathfrak{M}_2$ is the same as $\mathfrak{M}_1$, except that we change the definitions of R_r and the valuation function on r as follows:

(1′) r is false at some point in the past of t.

(2′) For each data point $u \in D(t,p)$ with $\mathfrak{M}_2, u \models_C p$, let $\mathfrak{M}_2, v \models_C r$ for some $v \in R_p(u)$. This is sound because $R_p(u)$ is not empty.

(3′) Pick up a single point v in the past of t with $\mathfrak{M}_2, v \models_C q$, pick up an s in the past of v, and let $R_r sv$ and $\mathfrak{M}_2, s \models_C r$. This is sound because the model has no starting point.

By (2), (4) and (2′), $\mathfrak{M}_2, t \models_C C(p,r)$. By (2), (1′) and (3′), $\mathfrak{M}_2, t \models_C C(r,q)$. Then $\mathfrak{M}_2, t \models_C C^*(\alpha,\beta)$. We have that $\mathfrak{M}_1, t \not\models_C \chi$ and $\mathfrak{M}_2, t \models_C \chi$. However, because r does not occur in χ, we also have $\mathfrak{M}_1, t \models_C \chi$ if and only if $\mathfrak{M}_2, t \models_C \chi$.

The point in the proof is that, unlike in the minimal causal logic, the truth value of $C^*(p,q)$ depends on values of propositional variables other than p and q.

Similar arguments can show that C^* is not definable in the extended causal logics C', C'', and C'''.

3. 4. INUS condition

Mackie① has developed a sophisticated theory of causation along the line of CCT. The so-called INUS condition (Insufficient and Non-redundant parts of Unnecessary but Sufficient Causes) is better illustrated by his example that a short-circuit causes a house's catching fire. First, the short-circuit is not a sufficient condition for the fire. It is a number of conditions, including the short-circuit, the presence of inflammable materials, the absence of a suitably placed sprinkler, and so on, that constitute a sufficient condition for the house's catching fire. Second, though the complex condition is sufficient, it is not necessary because the fire could have started in other ways. Therefore, the short-circuit is an *inus* condition in the meaning that it is an insufficient but non-redundant part of a condition which is itself unnecessary but sufficient for the fire.

Causes in this paper are not INUS conditions. When $C(\alpha,\beta)$ holds, α is a sufficient condition for β, in the sense that α itself can bring about β. α may not be a necessary condition for β, because it is possible that $C(\gamma,\beta)$ holds for some other cause γ. Thus, α is an *us* condition (unnecessary but sufficient condition) for β. It is possible to define an INUS condition in the current framework. For this purpose, it suffices to define the non-redundant parts of a cause α.

Let $CNF(\alpha)$ be a conjunctive normal form of α such that $CNF(\alpha)$ contains only symbols occurring in α, and there is no repeated conjunct. The restriction is to guarantee that $CNF(\alpha)$ contains no redundant part. Let $\gamma_i \in CNF(\alpha)$ denote that γ_i is a conjunct in $CNF(\alpha)$. Then we say that γ is a *non-redundant part* of α if there are $\gamma_1,\ldots,\gamma_n \in CNF(\alpha)$ such that $\gamma = \gamma_1 \wedge \ldots \wedge \gamma_n$. An INUS type causal operator C^i can be defined as follows:

$t \models_C C^i(\gamma,\beta)$ *iff* γ *is a non-redundant part of some* α *such that* $t \models_C C(\alpha,\beta)$.

We have that

Theorem 3. 2. *C^i is not definable in the minimal causal logic.*

Proof. The proof is similar to the proof of Theorem 3. 1, by showing that the

---

① J. L. Mackie, Causes and conditions, *American Philosophical Quarterly*, 1965, 2 (4), pp. 245 – 264.

truth value of $C^i(p,q)$ is not totally determined by the truth values of p and q.

4. Related Work

Branching time is a time structure where the past is always linear, while the future may be branching. Von Kutschera ① and Xu ② have defined a notion of causation in branching time. Though the frameworks in the two proposals are different in technical details, they share the basic intuition. Their basic idea is that an event e is a cause of an event e' if the occurrence of e guarantees the occurrence of e'. The focus is on defining "guarantee" by a type of historical necessity: Roughly speaking, it means that e's occurrence in any history makes sure an occurrence of e' in that history. This understanding of causation is apparently different from ours based on CCT, since CCT does not concern what will happen in the future, whether it is deterministic or indeterministic. Causation is totally determined by the (linear) past. Thus, linear time, instead of branching time, is sufficient for characterizing CCT. Another important difference is that events are primitive in our logic, whereas they define events from the underlying time structure. It shall be noted that though the famous STIT theory③ has a branching time structure, using the notion of undivided histories, it concerns the abilities of agents rather than causation.

Reasoning about actions and changes is one of the oldest topics in logical AI, and is still an active research area. A notion of causation is normally required in the formalisms of actions, because their effects are what we concern about actions. For an incomplete list, there are Dynamic Logic, Situation Calculus, Event Calculus, Fluent Calculus, Features and Fluents, etc. Though most work in these areas take causation as an implicit notion behind their formal frameworks, some do focus on properties of causation itself. The logic in Lin ④ remains in the framework of classical logic. It introduces a special predicate "*Caused*" which can only be applied to

---

① F. von Kutschera, Causation. *Journal of Philosophical Logic*, 1993, 22 (6), pp. 563 - 588.

② M. Xu, Causation in branching time (I): Transitions, events and causes, *Synthese*, 1997, 112 (2), pp. 137 - 192.

③ N. Belnap, & M. Perloff, Seeing to it that: A canonical form for agentives, *Theoria*, 1988, 54 (3), pp. 175 - 199.

④ F. Lin, Embracing causality in specifying the indeterminate effects of actions, in *Proceedings of the 13th National Conference on Artificial Intelligence*, CA: Morgan Kaufmann, 1996, pp. 1985 - 1991.

atoms. McCain & Turner [①] defines a notion that a formula is a consequence of a given causal theory, which is a set of causal laws in the form of $\varphi \Rightarrow \psi$. Thielscher[②] presents an interesting method of deriving causal rules automatically from given influence information. The simplest example is, given a constraint $p \vee q$ and the influence information $(p,q) \in I$, which means that p might possibly influence q, we can generate a causal law "$\neg p$ causes q". Schwind[③] gives several criteria of causation by which existing formalisms are examined. Giordano *et al*. [④] defines a dynamic logic for actions and causality in which causality is expressed by a unary operator read as "caused". Also with a dynamic logic, Zhang & Foo [⑤] proposes to treat direct effects and propagated effects of actions in a unified framework by using propositions as modalities. Pearl[⑥] and Halpern & Pearl[⑦] define causal relations in structural equation models based on the counterfactual theory of causation. They concern more about model theory properties than a logical theory. The list can be longer without being exhausted.

The focus of these works in AI is not to defend some notion of causation in philosophy. It is to invent formalisms, with as least cost as possible, to solve fundamental problems of AI in actions. The most concerned problem are the *frame problem* (the persistency of facts after an action has been applied), the *ramification problem* (the propagated effects after an action has been applied), and the *qualification problem* (all the necessary conditions before an action can be applied). Not surprisingly, they admit some implausible statements about causation. For

---

① N. McCain, & H. Turner, Causal theories of action and change, in *Proceedings of the* 14*th National Conference on Artificial Intelligence*, CA: Morgan Kaufmann, 1997, pp. 460 – 465.

② M. Thielscher, Ramification and causality, *Artificial Intelligence*, 1997, 89 (1 – 2), pp. 317 – 364.

③ C. Schwind, Causality in action theories. *Electronic Articles in Computer and Information Science*, 1999, 4 (4), pp. 27 – 50.

④ L. Giordano, A. Martelli, and C. Schwind, Ramification and causality in a modal action logic, *Journal of Logic and Computation*, 2000, 10 (5), pp. 625 – 662.

⑤ D. Zhang, & N. Foo, Epdl: A logic for causal reasoning, in *Proceedings of the* 17*th International Joint Conference on Artificial Intelligence*, CA: Morgan Kaufmann, 2001, pp. 131 – 136.

⑥ J. Pearl, *Causality: Models, Reasoning, and Inference*, Cambridge, UK: Cambridge University Press, 2000.

⑦ J. Y. Halpern, and J. Pearl, Causes and explanations: A structural-model approach. Part Ⅰ: Causes, *The British Journal for the Philosophy of Science*, 2005, 56 (4), pp. 843 – 887.

example, *Lin*[①], McCain & Turner[②] and Giordano *et al.*[③] admit monotonicity of causal relations, i. e. from φ causing ψ infer that $\varphi \wedge \chi$ causes ψ.

David Lewis's counterfactual theory is the most popular philosophical theory of causation in decades.[④] Though Lewis's analysis of causation is impressive in its philosophical subtlety, the logical theory of counterfactuals, the so-called conditional logic[⑤], can hardly be considered as a causal logic. In the logic, the formula $\alpha > \beta$ is to state that β is counterfactually depended on α. If we read $\alpha > \beta$ as that α causes β, some axioms of the logic would be counterintuitive, such as $\alpha > \alpha$, $\alpha \wedge \beta \rightarrow (\alpha > \beta)$ and $(\alpha > \beta) \rightarrow (\alpha \rightarrow \beta)$.

As a remedy, Giordano & Schwind[⑥] defined a causal logic (called AC) by choosing those axioms of Lewis's logic that represent wanted properties of causation, and omitting those unwanted axioms, including the three we mentioned. AC has a similarity with our logic, but also has fundamental differences. AC admits that a tautology is caused by everything, i. e. whenever β is a tautology, $\vdash \alpha > \beta$. They want to keep this formula because it is derivable from a basic inference rule of conditional logic which they want to keep: If $\vdash \beta \rightarrow \gamma$ then $\vdash (\alpha > \beta) \rightarrow (\alpha > \gamma)$. The rule in general is not valid in our logic. Instead, it can be checked that a restrictive version of the rule is valid, i. e. if $\vdash_C \beta \rightarrow \gamma$ then $\vdash_C C(\alpha,\beta) \wedge P\neg\gamma \rightarrow C(\alpha,\gamma)$. This valid rule in our logic, we think, is more suitable as a rule of a causal logic than the general rule in conditional logic.

AC has the axiom $(\alpha > \beta) \wedge (\gamma > \beta) \rightarrow (\alpha \vee \gamma > \beta)$, which is not valid in the minimal causal logic. The axiom seems right about causation. We have shown in Section 3. 1 that if we assume $R_{\alpha\vee\gamma} = R_\alpha \cup R_\gamma$, then a restrictive version of the axiom will be valid in our logic, i. e. $C(\alpha,\beta) \wedge C(\gamma,\beta) \wedge P\neg(\alpha \vee \gamma) \rightarrow C(\alpha \vee \gamma, \beta)$. The difference is that we state in the premise that $\alpha \vee \gamma$ is not invariably true in the past. Again, we think it is a more suitable axiom for the interaction between

① F. Lin, Embracing causality in specifying the indeterminate effects of actions, in *Proceedings of the 13th National Conference on Artificial Intelligence*, CA: Morgan Kaufmann, 1996, pp. 1985 – 1991.

② N. McCain, and H. Turner, Causal theories of action and change, in *Proceedings of the 14th National Conference on Artificial Intelligence*, CA: Morgan Kaufmann, 1997, pp. 460 – 465.

③ L. Giordano, A. Martelli, and C. Schwind, Ramification and causality in a modal action logic, *Journal of Logic and Computation*, 2000, 10 (5), pp. 625 – 662.

④ D. Lewis, Causation, *The Journal of Philosophy*, 1973, 70 (17), pp. 556 – 567.

⑤ D. Lewis, *Counterfactuals*, Oxford, UK: Blackwell, 1973, chapter 6.

⑥ L. Giordano, and C. Schwind, Conditional logic of actions and causation, *Artificial Intelligence*, 2004, 157 (1 – 2), pp. 239 – 279.

causal relation and disjunction.

As for the interaction between causal relation and conjunction, we think in general there should be no connection between the two, because the effect period of a conjunction should not depends on its conjuncts. AC abandons the valid formula in conditional logic, $\alpha > \beta \rightarrow (\alpha \wedge \gamma) > \beta$. Nevertheless, it introduces a weaken formula: $\neg (\alpha > \neg \gamma) \wedge (\alpha > \beta) \rightarrow ((\alpha \wedge \gamma) > \beta)$. They argue for the formula for its usefulness in describing interactions among actions and facts. However, it still suffers from those counterexamples to $\alpha > \beta \rightarrow (\alpha \wedge \gamma) > \beta$: *rain* causes *wet* but *rain* $\wedge$ *umbrella* does not.

AC admits an axiom $(\gamma > \alpha) \wedge (\gamma > (\alpha > \beta)) \rightarrow (\gamma > \beta)$, which is not valid in the minimal causal logic. Its invalidity in the minimal causal logic is not a surprise, because what we formalize in the minimal causal logic are causal relations directly from our observations. We can extend the logic to deal with such indirect causal knowledge. The logic with the transitive causal operator C^* in Section 3. 3 is an example of such extensions. The formula $C(\gamma,\alpha) \wedge C(\gamma,C(\alpha,\beta)) \rightarrow C(\gamma,\beta)$ states an ability of us to deduce indirect causal relations from the existing ones. We can use it to extend our logic in a similar way as we did in Section 3. 3

5. Conclusion

We give a formal framework for causation based on constant conjunction theory. Causal relation is expressed as a binary operator C. We investigate properties of C with the help of a linear temporal logic. Causal statements are evaluated in a linear time, where their truth values are determined by what has been in the past. We present the minimal causal logic, which is mainly a direct formalization of the concept of constant conjunction by Hume. We discuss its extensions by assuming more conditions on models and semantics. There remain a lot to be investigated, partially because the concept of causation is itself bewildering. It is open to arguments that which conditions should be applied, so that the concept of causation being formalized can satisfy, loosely speaking, some philosophical standard.

The degree of causation is one of the important topics that is not explored in the paper. Such degree theory will be different from the probabilistic theory of causation. A probabilistic causeα is such that α's occurrence increases the probability of the effect β. The expected degree theory for the current framework would mainly concern the reliability of causal relations: If we have observed more instances of evidences to a causal relation, we will have more confidence in it.

Proper extensions of the logics in this paper can serve for an agent and multi-agent theory. For this, we may look upon a linear time model as an agent's perspective of what have happened along time. An agent builds or removes a causal relation according to herexperiences as instances of evidences or counterexamples being observed. Things could be more interesting in the case of multi-agent systems. We may let each agent has her own model, which is a linear time model represents her past experience. Thus different agents may possess different causal knowledge. Or, we may let agents only have incomplete observations of what have really happened. One way to do this is to assign a subset of the set of the past points to each agent as her observations.

6. Acknowledgments

This research is supported by A Foundation for the Author of National Excellent Doctoral Dissertation of PR China (FANEDD 2007B01) and Guangdong 12th Five-Year Planning Fund of Philosophy and Social Science, and partially supported by the MOE Key Project of Philosophy and Social Sciences (No. 10JZD0006).

Appendix A: Proof of Lemma 2.11.

The proof method is due to Gabbay *et al.* ①. We adapt it for our framework and adopt the notational convention in Blackburn *et al.* ② to make the proof more readable.

A tree (N, A) is defined as usual such that N is the set of nodes, and A is the set of arcs. A path in (N, A) is a sequence of nodes $(t_1, \ldots, t_m)$ such that (t_i, t_{i+1}) is an arc for $1 \leqslant i < m$.

Definition A.1. *A network is a tuple* $N = (N, A, d, f)$ *such that* (N, A) *is a finite tree*; d *labels each arc* (u, v) *of the tree with a member in* $\{F, P\} \cup \{\Diamond_\alpha | \alpha \in F\}$; f *labels each node of the tree with a finite, non-empty and consistent set of formulas.*

---

① D. M. Gabbay, I. Hodkinson, and M. Reynolds, *Temporal Logic: Mathematical Foundations and Computational Aspects*, Vol. 1, New York: Oxford University Press, 1994.

② M. Black, Why cannot an effect precede its cause? *Analysis*, 1956, 16 (3), pp. 49 - 58; P. Blackburn, M. De Rijke, and Y. Venema, *Modal Logic*, Cambridge, UK: Cambridge University Press, 2001.

A network $N' = (N', A', d', f')$ *is an extension of a network* $N = (N, A, d, f)$ *if* $N \subseteq N'$, $A = A' \cap N \times N$, $d(u,v) = d'(u,v)$ *for any* $u, v \in N$, *and* $f(u) \subseteq f'(u)$ *for any* $u \in N$.

Let $\lambda(u) = \bigwedge f(u)$. *Let* $S(u)$ *be the set of successors of* u.

A network N *is coherent if for any non-leaf node* u *and any* $v \in S(u)$, $d(u,v)\lambda(v) \in f(u)$.

Definition A. 2. *Let* $N = (N, A, d, f)$ *be a network*, u *a node in the network and* φ *a formula. Let* t *be the root of the network. Let* $(u_1, \ldots, u_m)$ *where* $u_1 = t$ *and* $u_m = u$ *be the path from* t *to* u. *Let* $N_{\varphi,u} = (N, A, d, f_{\varphi,u})$ *be defined as follows:*

(1) *For any node* v *that does not occur in the path* $(u_1, \ldots, u_m)$, $f_{\varphi,u}(v) = f(v)$.

(2) $f_{\varphi,u}(u) = f(u) \cup \{\varphi\}$.

(3) *For each* $1 \leqslant n < m$, $f_{\varphi,u}(u_n)$ *is inductively defined as that*

$f_{\varphi,u}(u_n) = f(u_n) \cup \{d(u_n, u_{n+1})\lambda_{\varphi,u}(u_{n+1})\}$, *where* $\lambda_{\varphi,u}(u_{n+1}) = \bigwedge f_{\varphi,u}(u_{n+1})$.

$N_{\varphi,u}$ is a structure obtained from N by adding the formula φ to the label of u and making corresponding changes to other nodes, so that if N is coherent, so is $N_{\varphi,u}$. In general, $N_{\varphi,u}$ may not be a network. The label of some node in $N_{\varphi,u}$ may be inconsistent set of formulas.

Lemma A. 3. *Given a coherent network* $N = (N, A, d, f)$, *a node* u *in the network and a formula* φ, *either* $N_{\varphi,u}$ *or* $N_{\neg\varphi,u}$ *is a coherent network.*

Proof. Suppose otherwise that neither $N_{\varphi,u}$ nor $N_{\neg\varphi,u}$ is a coherent network. Let t be the root of the network. Let $(u_1, \ldots, u_m)$ be the path from t to u. The coherency of both $N_{\varphi,u}$ and $N_{\neg\varphi,u}$ is direct by the definition. Then neither of them is networks. There must exist an i, $1 \leqslant i \leqslant m$, such that $f_{\varphi,u}(u_i)$ is inconsistent, and must exist a j, $1 \leqslant j \leqslant m$ such that $f_{\neg\varphi,u}(u_j)$ is inconsistent. Note that in normal modal logic, if a formula ψ is inconsistent, so is $\Diamond\psi$. Because F, P and $\Diamond_\alpha \vdash$ are standard diamonds, for all $k \leqslant i$ and all $l \leqslant j$, $f_{\varphi,u}(u_k)$ and $f_{\neg\varphi,u}(u_l)$ are inconsistent. Then there is an n such that both $f_{\varphi,u}(u_n)$ and $f_{\neg\varphi,u}(u_n)$ are inconsistent. For simplicity, let $\Diamond_i$ stand for $d(u_i, u_{i+1})$. Then

$$\vdash_C \lambda(u_n) \to \neg \Diamond_n(\lambda(u_{n+1}) \wedge \Diamond_{n+1}(\ldots \wedge \Diamond_{m-1}(\lambda(u_m) \wedge \varphi)\ldots)). \quad (A1)$$

$$\vdash_C \lambda(u_n) \to \neg \Diamond_n(\lambda(u_{n+1}) \wedge \Diamond_{n+1}(\ldots \wedge \Diamond_{m-1}(\lambda(u_m) \wedge \neg\varphi)\ldots)). \quad (A2)$$

By A1 and A2, we will have

$$\vdash_C \lambda(u_n) \to \neg \Diamond_n(\lambda(u_{n+1}) \wedge \Diamond_{n+1}(\ldots \to \Diamond_{m-1} \lambda(u_m)\ldots)). \quad (A3)$$

By the coherency of N, we will have

$$\vdash_C \lambda(u_n) \to \Diamond_n(\lambda(u_{n+1}) \wedge \Diamond_{n+1}(\cdots \to \Diamond_{m-1}\lambda(u_m)\cdots)). \qquad (A4)$$

It follows that $\lambda(u_n)$ is inconsistent and N is not a network.

Definition A. 4. *In a network N, a D1 defect is a pair $(u, F\varphi)$ such that $F\varphi \in f(u)$ and there is no $v \in S(u)$ with $d(u,v) = F$ and $\varphi \in f(v)$; a D2 defect is a pair $(u, P\varphi)$ such that $P\varphi \in f(u)$ and there is no $v \in S(u)$ with $d(u,v) = P$ and $\varphi \in f(v)$; a D3 defect is a pair $(u, \Diamond_\alpha \varphi)$ such that $\Diamond_\alpha \varphi \in f(u)$ and there is no $v \in S(u)$ with $d(u,v) = \Diamond_\alpha$ and $\varphi \in f(v)$; a D4 defect is a pair (u,φ) such that neither $\varphi \in f(u)$ nor $\neg\varphi \in f(u)$; a D5 defect is a node u such that $name(\psi) \notin u$ for any formula ψ.*

Lemma A. 5. *For any defect of a coherent network N, there is a coherent extension of N that lacks the defect.*

Proof. Let $N = (N, A, d, f)$. We show each type of defects is repairable.

Suppose that $(u, F\varphi)$ is a D1 defect. Let v be an arbitrary node that is not in N. Let $N' = (N', A', d', f')$ be such that $N' = N \cup \{v\}$, $A' = A \cup \{(u,v)\}$, $d' = d \cup \{(u,v), F\}$, and $f' = f \cup \{v, \{\varphi\}\}$. φ is consistent because $F\varphi$ is. Then, N' is a network. Clearly, N' is an extension of N in which the D1 defect has been removed. N' is coherent, because N is coherent and $F\varphi$ is already in u. D2 and D3 defects can be removed in a similar way.

Suppose (u,φ) is a D4 defect. By Lemma A. 3, either $N_{\varphi,u}$ or $N_{\neg\varphi,u}$ is a coherent network. That coherent network is an extension of N that lacks the defect.

Suppose u is a D5 defect. Let t be the root of the network. Let $(u_1, \ldots, u_m)$ be the path from t to u. Let p be a propositional variable that does not occur anywhere in N. Clearly, $N_{name(p),u}$ lacks the D5 defect. We prove that $N_{name(p),u}$ is a coherent network. Coherence is direct by definition. It suffices to show that $f_{name(p),u}(u_n)$ is consistent for every $1 \leqslant n \leqslant m$. Suppose otherwise that $f_{name(p),u}(u_n)$ is inconsistent for some n. Then $\vdash_C \neg\lambda_{name(p),u}(u_n)$, that is,

$$\vdash_C \neg(\lambda(u_n) \wedge d(u_n, u_{n+1})(\lambda(u_{n+1}) \wedge \ldots \wedge d(u_{m-1}, u_m)(\lambda(u_m) \wedge name(p))\ldots).$$

Then, by the IRR rule,

$$\vdash_C \lambda(u_n) \to \neg d(u_n, u_{n+1})(\lambda(u_{n+1}) \wedge \ldots \wedge d(u_{m-1}, u_m)(\lambda(u_m))\ldots).$$

However, because N is coherent, we have

$$\vdash_C \lambda(u_n) \to d(u_n, u_{n+1})(\lambda(u_{n+1}) \wedge \ldots \wedge d(u_{m-1}, u_m)(\lambda(u_m))\ldots).$$

We obtain that $\lambda(u_n)$ is not consistent, and therefore N is not a network.

Ddfinition A. 6. *Given a consistent formula φ, we define a sequence of countably infinite networks $N_0, N_1, \ldots$ such that the following holds:*

(ⅰ) *Each network in the sequence is coherent.*

(ⅱ) *N_0 consists of a single node t with $f(t) = \{\varphi\}$.*

(ⅲ) *For any $i < j$, N_j is an extension of N_i.*

(ⅳ) *For any N_i and any defect in N_i, there is a $j > i$ such that N_j lacks this defect.*

The definition is sound by Lemma A. 5 and the fact that there are only countably infinite defects occurring in the sequence: The number of defects is upper bounded by the sum of $|\{F,P\} \times F \times \omega|$ (for D1 and D2 defects), $|F \times F \times \omega|$ (for D3 defects), $|F \times \omega|$ (for D4 defects) and $|\omega|$ (for D5 defects). Let $N = \bigcup_{i \in \omega} N_i$. Let $f(u) = \bigcup_{i \in \omega} f_i(u)$ for each $u \in N$.

Lemma A. 7. *For each $u \in N$, $f(u)$ is a maximal consistent set and is witnessing.*

Proof. If a D5 defect u is in some N_i, then there is an extension N_j that lacks the defect, i. e. $name(\psi) \in f_j(u)$ for some ψ. Then $name(\psi) \in f(u)$ and u is witnessing. Similarly, either ψ or $\neg \psi$ is in $f(u)$ for all formulas ψ.

Suppose $f(u)$ is inconsistent. Then there must be an i such that $f_i(u)$ is inconsistent. Then N_i is not a network.

Lemma A. 8. *Let $T = \{f(u) \mid u \in N\}$. Then T is saturated and witnessing.*

Proof. It is direct by Lemma A. 7 that T is witnessing. For saturatedness, let u be any member in N such that $F\psi \in f(u)$. Then $F\psi \in f_i(u)$ for some i. By Lemma A. 5, there is a j such that $\psi \in f_j(v)$ and $d_j(u,v) = F$. Then $\psi \in f(v)$. It remains to show that $f(u) <^c f(v)$. Suppose otherwise. Then there is formula χ such that $\chi \in f(v)$ and $\neg F\chi \in f(u)$. Then there is a k such that $\chi \in f_k(v)$ and $\neg F\chi \in f_k(u)$. By the coherency of N_k, $F\chi \in f_k(u)$. It follows that N_k is not a network.

The cases for P and $\Diamond_\alpha$ are similarly proved.

Countably Many Weakenings of Belnap-Dunn Logic

Minghui Ma

1. Introduction

The Belnap-Dunn four-valued logic BD is known as the logic of *De Morgan lattices* (or *De Morgan algebras* with constants 0 and 1) (cf. e. g., Belnap 1977; Dunn, 1966, 1967, 1971, 1976, 1999, 2000). This logic has been investigated in the framework of abstract algebraic logic (cf. e. g., Font 1997, 1999; Pynko 1995). From a semantical perspective, Dunn introduced a kind of "polarity semantics" for the logic of De Morgan algebras based on informational structures (cf. e. g., Dunn 1999). Let W be a set of informational states. Each proposition φ takes a pair (X^+, X^-) of subsets of W as its value. The set X^+ is the set of all states that make φ true, and the set X^- is the set of all states that make φ false. Such a pair is called a *polarity*. For any state $w \in W$, (1) φ is accepted at w, if $w \in X^+$; (2) φ is rejected at w, if $w \in X^-$; (3) φ is both accepted and rejected at w, if $w \in X^+ \cap X^-$; (4) φ is neither accepted nor rejected at w, if $w \notin X^+ \cup X^-$. The four attributes of a proposition at a state w correspond to four values T, F, B, N respectively (cf. e. g., Dunn 1999). The four-valued logic BD is sound and complete with respect to a single informational state under Dunn's polarity semantics (cf. Dunn 1999, 2000). It is remarkable that, a similar relational semantics can be obtained from canonical extensions of distributive lattices (cf. Gehrke & Harding Gehrke & Jónsson 2001, 2004), and this method is used to give relational completeness for substructural logics (cf. Allwein & Dunn 1993; Dunn, Gehrke & Palmigiano 2005). Furthermore, two-sorted generalized Kripke frames based on polarities from formal concept analysis (cf. Ganter, Stumme & Wille 2005) are introduced in Gehrke (2006).

Dunn's polarity semantics has been generalized to linearly ordered frames with persistent valuations and a deterministic weakening DW of the four-valued logic BD is established in Ma & Lin (2018). This weak logic DW is characterized by the linear frame of two states and it is indeed a 9-valued logic. In the present paper, we continue to investigate countably many weakenings of BD. These weakenings are logics of countably many subvarieties of Ockham algebras. Recall that an *Ockham algebra* is an algebra $\mathfrak{A} = (A, \wedge, \vee, 0, 1, \sim)$ where $(A, \wedge, \vee, 0, 1, \sim)$ is a bounded distributive lattice and $\sim$ is a unary operation on A (also known as a *dual endomorphism*) such that the following equations hold for all $a, b \in A$:

(01) $\sim(a \vee b) = \sim a \wedge \sim b$;

(02) $\sim(a \wedge b) = \sim a \vee \sim b$;

(03) $\sim 0 = 1$ *and* $\sim 1 = 0$.

The variety of all Ockham algebras is denoted by $\mathbb{O}$. For any $n \in \mathbb{N}$ and $a \in A$ we define $\sim^n a$ inductively by $\sim^0 a = a$ and $\sim^{n+1} a = \sim\sim^n a$. Berman's varieties are subvarieties of $\mathbb{O}$ introduced by Berman (1977). For any $p, q \in \mathbb{N}$ with $p \geqslant 1$ and $q \geqslant 0$, the *Berman's variety* $\mathbb{K}_p^q$ is the subvariety of $\mathbb{O}$ defined by the equation $\sim^{2p+q} a = \sim^q a$ Blyth and Varlet (1994: 8) pointed out that Berman's varieties are related as follows:

$$\mathbb{K}_p^q \subseteq \mathbb{K}_{p'}^{q'} \text{ if and only if } p \mid p' \text{ and } q \leqslant q'.$$

The subvarieties of $\mathbb{O}$ generated by finite members are investigated in Goldberg (1983), Priestley & Bordalo (1992), and Urquhart (1979, 1981). It is worthy to mention here that the class of algebras that characterizes the logic DW in Ma & Lin (2018) is a subvariety of $\mathbb{K}_1^2$. The smallest Berman's variety $\mathbb{K}_1^0$ determined $\sim\sim a = a$ is exactly the class of all *De Morgan algebras*. Subvarieties of Berman's varieties are widely investigated in the literature (cf. e. g., Blyth & Varlet 1983a, 1983b, 1994; Ramalho & Sequeira 1987; Urquhart 1979, 1981).

Every Berman's variety $\mathbb{K}_p^q$ determines a finitary substitution invariant consequence relation $\vdash_p^q \subseteq P(T) \times T$ where T is the set of terms and $P(T)$ is the powerset of T. Obviously $\mathbb{K}_p^q \subseteq \mathbb{K}_{p'}^{q'}$ implies $\vdash_{p'}^{q'} \subseteq \vdash_p^q$. The consequence relation $\vdash_1^0$ is the largest one among all such consequence relations and each $\vdash_p^q$ is a *weakening* of $\vdash_1^0$. The Belnap-Dunn logic BD is exactly an axiomatization of $\vdash_1^0$. For any $p \geqslant 1$ and $q \geqslant 0$ we shall introduce a sequent system S_p^q as an axiomatization of the consequence relation $\vdash_p^q$. The aim of the present paper is to develop frame semantics for S_p^q along the road taken in our previous work (Ma & Lin 2018), and we go further to show a very succinct structural-rule-free and cut-free sequent system for it.

Dunn's polarity semantics for the logic of De Morgan algebrascan be generalized to treat with S_p^q if more states are allowed in the informational frame. For any $p \geqslant 1$ and $q \geqslant 0$. we shall construct a single frame $\mathfrak{F}_p^q$ with $2p + q$ states. The interpretation of acceptance and rejection of a term (formula) at a state are given inductively as in Ma

& Lin (2018). The sequent system S_p^q will be shown to be sound and complete with respect to the single frame $\mathfrak{F}_p^q$. The completeness proof utilizes normal forms and gives a decision procedure for S_p^q. We also define the dual algebra $(\mathfrak{F}_p^q)^+$ of the frame $\mathfrak{F}_p^q$. Since the duality preserves validity of sequents, S_p^q is characterized by the algebra $(\mathfrak{F}_p^q)^+$. The algebra $(\mathfrak{F}_p^q)^+$ is a 4^{2p+q}-element distributive lattice with a unary operator. It follows that S_p^q is a 4^{2p+q}-valued logic.

The proof theory of these logics shall be explored further by giving a structural-rule-free, cut-free sequent system G_p^q for $\vdash_p^q$. Moreover, G_p^q is terminating as the backward proof-search procedure terminates in finitely many steps. Finally, by Maehara's proof-theoretic method (cf. e. g., Ono 1998), we prove that $\vdash_p^q$ has the Craig interpolation property. This proof-theoretic work goes beyond our work for the weak logic DW in Ma & Lin (2018).

The paper is structured as follows. Section 2 introduces the sequent system for any $p \geqslant 1$ and $q \geqslant 0$. Section 3 gives frame semantics for S_p^q and proves the completeness and decidability of S_p^q. Using the duality between frames and algebras, we show that S_p^q is a 4^{2p+q}-valued logic. Section 4 gives a structural-rule-free and cut-free sequent system G_p^q and proves the Craig interpolation property. Section 5 gives some concluding remarks.

2. Gentzen Sequent System

Let $\mathbb{X} = \{x_i \mid i \in \mathbb{N}\}$ be a denumerable set of variables. Let $\bot$ and $\top$ be constants, and let $\sim$ be a unary operator and $\wedge$ and $\vee$ be binary operators.

Definition 2. 1 *The set T of all terms is defined inductively as follows:*

$T \ni \varphi ::= x \mid \top \mid \bot \mid \sim \varphi \mid (\varphi \wedge \varphi) \mid (\varphi \vee \varphi)$, *where* $x \in \mathbb{X}$.

An *atomic term* is a variable or constant. Terms are denoted by φ, ψ, χ etc. with or without subscripts. For any natural number $n \geqslant 0$, we define $\sim^n \varphi$ inductively by $\sim^0 \varphi = \varphi$ and $\sim^{n+1} \varphi = \sim \sim^n \varphi$. Let $\mathfrak{T} = (T, \wedge, \vee, \top, \bot, \sim)$ be *term algebra*. For any term φ, the complexity of φ is the number $c(\varphi)$ defined inductively by:

$c(x) = c(\bot) = c(\top) = 0$, where $x \in \mathbb{X}$;

$c(\sim \varphi) = c(\varphi) + 1$

$c(\varphi \circ \psi) = \max\{c(\varphi), c(\psi)\} + 1$, where $\circ \in \{\wedge, \vee\}$.

Let Γ, Δ, Σ etc. with or without subscripts denote finite (possibly empty) multisets of terms. For any finite multiset of terms $\Gamma = \varphi_1, \ldots, \varphi_n$, we define $\sim\Gamma := \sim\varphi_1, \ldots, \sim\varphi_n$, and $\bigwedge\Gamma = \varphi_1 \wedge \ldots \wedge \varphi_n$ and $\bigvee\Gamma = \varphi_1 \vee \ldots \vee \varphi_n$. In particular, $\bigwedge\varnothing = \top$ and $\bigvee\varnothing = \bot$. A sequent is an expression $\Gamma \vdash \psi$ where Γ is a finite multiset of terms and ψ is a term. A *sequent rule* is a fraction

$$\frac{\Gamma_1 \vdash \psi_1 \quad \ldots \quad \Gamma_n \vdash \psi_n}{\Gamma_0 \vdash \psi_0}(\mathsf{r})$$

Where $\Gamma_i \vdash \psi_i (1 \leqslant i \leqslant n)$ are called the *premises* and $\Gamma_0 \vdash \psi_0$ is called the conclusion of (r).

Remark 2.2 In abstract algebraic logic (cf. Font & Jansana 2009: 45), a sequent is usually defined as $X \vdash \psi$ where X is a finite set of terms. However, in Gentzen-style proof theory for classical and some non-classical logics (cf. e.g., Ono 1998), finite sequences or multisets of terms are used to define sequents.

Definition 2.3 For any Ockham algebra $\mathfrak{A} = (A, \wedge, \vee, 0, 1, \sim)$, an *assignment* in $\mathfrak{A}$ is a function $\sigma: \mathbb{X} \to A$. Any assignment σ in $\mathfrak{A}$ can be extended homomorphically to the term algebra $\mathfrak{T}$. For any term φ, we write $\sigma(\varphi)$ as the value of φ in $\mathfrak{A}$ under the assignment σ.

Let $\mathfrak{A} = (A, \wedge, \vee, 0, 1, \sim)$ be an Ockham algebra. For any assignment σ in $\mathfrak{A}$, a sequent $\Gamma \vdash \psi$ is *true* in $\mathfrak{A}$ under σ, notation $\Gamma \models_{\mathfrak{A},\sigma} \psi$, if $\sigma(\bigwedge\Gamma) \leqslant \sigma(\psi)$. A sequent $\Gamma \vdash \psi$ is *valid* in $\mathfrak{A}$, notation $\Gamma \models_{\mathfrak{A}} \psi$, if $\Gamma \models_{\mathfrak{A},\sigma} \psi$ for any assignment σ in $\mathfrak{A}$.

Let $\mathbb{K}$ be a class of Ockham algebras. A sequent $\Gamma \vdash \psi$ is *valid* in $\mathbb{K}$, notation $\Gamma \models_{\mathbb{K}} \psi$, if $\Gamma \models_{\mathfrak{A}} \psi$, for all $\mathfrak{A} \in \mathbb{K}$. The *logic* of $\mathbb{K}$ is defined as the set of all sequents that are valid in $\mathbb{K}$. A sequent rule (r) with premises $\Gamma_i \vdash \psi_i (1 \leqslant i \leqslant n)$ and conclusion $\Gamma_0 \vdash \psi_0$ *preserves validity* in a class of Ockham algebras $\mathbb{K}$, if $\Gamma_i \models_{\mathbb{K}} \psi_i$ for all $1 \leqslant i \leqslant n$ imply $\Gamma_0 \models_{\mathbb{K}} \psi_0$.

Definition 2.4 *The Gentzen sequent system S_p^q consists of the following axioms and inference rules:*

(1) *Axioms:*

(Id) $\varphi \vdash \varphi$ ($\bot$) $\bot \vdash \varphi$ ($\top$) $\varphi \vdash \top$ ($\sim\bot$) $\varphi \vdash \sim\bot$ ($\sim\top$) $\sim\top \vdash \varphi$

(DM1) $\sim(\varphi \wedge \psi) \vdash \sim\varphi \vee \sim\psi$ (DM2) $\sim\varphi \wedge \sim\psi \vdash \sim(\varphi \vee \psi)$

(N1) $\sim^{2p+q}\varphi \vdash \sim^q\varphi$ (N2) $\sim^q\varphi \vdash \sim^{2p+q}\varphi$

(2) *Logical rules:*

$$\frac{\varphi_1, \varphi_2, \Gamma \vdash \psi}{\varphi_1 \wedge \varphi_2, \Gamma \vdash \psi}(\wedge \mathrm{L}) \quad \frac{\Gamma \vdash \psi \quad \Gamma \vdash \chi}{\Gamma \vdash \psi \wedge \chi}(\wedge \mathrm{R})$$

$$\frac{\varphi, \Gamma \vdash \chi \quad \psi, \Gamma \vdash \chi}{\varphi \vee \psi, \Gamma \vdash \chi}(\vee L) \qquad \frac{\Gamma \vdash \psi_i}{\Gamma \vdash \psi_1 \vee \psi_2}(\vee R)(i = 1, 2)$$

$$\frac{\varphi \vdash \psi}{\sim \psi \vdash \sim \varphi}(CP)$$

(3) *Structural rules*:

$$\frac{\Gamma \vdash \psi}{\varphi, \Gamma \vdash \psi}(Wk) \qquad \frac{\varphi, \psi, \Gamma \vdash \psi}{\varphi, \Gamma \vdash \psi}(Ctr)$$

(4) Cut rule:

$$\frac{\Gamma \vdash \varphi \quad \varphi, \Delta \vdash \psi}{\Gamma, \Delta \vdash \psi}(Cut)$$

A *derivation* in S_p^q is a finite tree-like structure D in which each node is either an instance of an axiom or obtained from child node(s) by an inference rule. The *height* of a derivation D is the largest length of branches in D. A sequent $\Gamma \vdash \psi$ is *provable* in S_p^q, notation $\Gamma \vdash_{S_p^q} \psi$, if there is a derivation in S_p^q with root node $\Gamma \vdash \psi$. Let $\mathrm{Thm}(S_p^q)$ denote the set of all sequents that are provable in S_p^q. Terms φ and ψ are *equivalent with respect to* S_p^q, notation $\varphi \approx_{S_p^q} \psi$, if $\varphi \vdash_{S_p^q} \psi$ and $\psi \vdash_{S_p^q} \varphi$. A sequent rule (r) with premises $\Gamma_i \vdash \psi_i (1 \leqslant i \leqslant n)$ and conclusion $\Gamma_0 \vdash \psi_0$ is *admissible* in S_p^q, if $\Gamma_0 \vdash_{S_p^q} \psi_0$ whenever $\Gamma_i \vdash_{S_p^q} \psi_i$ for all $1 \leqslant i \leqslant n$.

Lemma 2.5. *$\Gamma \vdash_{S_p^q} \psi$ if and only if $\bigwedge \Gamma \vdash_{S_p^q} \psi$.*

Proof: Assume $\Gamma \vdash_{S_p^q} \psi$. By $(\wedge L)$, $\bigwedge \Gamma \vdash_{S_p^q} \psi$. Assume $\varphi \wedge \Gamma \vdash_{S_p^q} \psi$. For any term $\varphi \in \Gamma$, we have $\Gamma \vdash_{S_p^q} \varphi$ by (Id) and (Wk). By $\Gamma \vdash_{S_p^q} \bigwedge \Gamma$. By (Cut), $\Gamma \vdash_{S_p^q} \varphi$.

Fact 2.6. The following sequent rules are admissible in S_p^q:

$$\frac{\varphi_1 \vdash \psi_1 \quad \varphi_2 \vdash \psi_2}{\varphi_1 \wedge \varphi_2 \vdash \psi_1 \wedge \psi_2}(\wedge), \qquad \frac{\varphi_1 \vdash \psi_1 \quad \varphi_2 \vdash \psi_2}{\varphi_1 \vee \varphi_2 \vdash \psi_1 \vee \psi_2}(\vee).$$

Lemma 2.7. *The following sequents are provable in S_p^q:*

(1) $\sim \varphi \vee \sim \psi \vdash \sim (\varphi \wedge \psi)$ *and* $\sim (\varphi \vee \psi) \vdash \sim \varphi \wedge \sim \psi$.

(2) $\varphi \wedge (\psi \vee \chi) \vdash (\varphi \wedge \psi) \vee (\varphi \wedge \chi)$ *and* $(\varphi \wedge \psi) \vee (\varphi \wedge \chi) \vdash \varphi \wedge (\psi \vee \chi)$.

(3) $\varphi \vee (\psi \wedge \chi) \vdash (\varphi \vee \psi) \wedge (\varphi \vee \chi)$ *and* $(\varphi \vee \psi) \wedge (\varphi \vee \chi) \vdash \varphi \vee (\psi \wedge \chi)$.

(4) $\sim^{2kp+i} \varphi \vdash \sim^i \varphi$ *and* $\sim^i \varphi \vdash \sim^{2kp+i} \varphi$, *where* $k \geqslant 0$ *and* $i \geqslant q$.

(5) $\bot \vdash \sim \top$, $\sim \top \vdash \bot$, $\top \vdash \sim \bot$ *and* $\sim \bot \vdash \top$.

(6) $\top \vdash \sim^{2n} \top$, $\sim^{2n} \top \vdash \top$, $\bot \vdash \sim^{2n} \bot$ *and* $\sim^{2n} \bot \vdash \bot$, *where* $n \geqslant 0$.

(7) $\bot \vdash \sim^{2n+1}\top$, $\sim^{2n+1}\top \vdash \bot$, $\top \vdash \sim^{2n+1} \bot$ *and* $\sim^{2n+1} \bot \vdash \top$, *where* $n \geqslant 0$.

Proof: (1) We have the following derivation:

$$\dfrac{\dfrac{\dfrac{\dfrac{\varphi \vdash \varphi}{\varphi, \psi \vdash \varphi}(\mathrm{Wk})}{\varphi \wedge \psi \vdash \varphi}(\wedge \mathrm{L})}{\sim \varphi \vdash \sim (\varphi \wedge \psi)}(\mathrm{CP}) \qquad \dfrac{\dfrac{\dfrac{\psi \vdash \psi}{\varphi, \psi \vdash \psi}(\mathrm{Wk})}{\varphi \wedge \psi \vdash \psi}(\wedge \mathrm{L})}{\sim \psi \vdash \sim (\varphi \wedge \psi)}(\mathrm{CP})}{\sim \varphi \vee \sim \psi \vdash \sim (\varphi \wedge \psi)}(\vee \mathrm{L})$$

The sequent $\sim (\varphi \wedge \psi) \vdash \sim \varphi \wedge \sim \psi$ is shown similarly. Sequents in (2) and (3) are shown easily and the proof is omitted here.

(4) We show $\sim^{2kp+i} \varphi \vdash_{S_p^q} \sim^i \varphi$ by induction on $k \geqslant 0$. The case that $k = 0$ is trivial. For the inductive step, by induction hypothesis, $\sim^{2kp+i} \varphi \vdash_{S_p^q} \sim^i \varphi$. Clearly $\sim^{2(k+1)p+i} \varphi = \sim^{2kp+i+2p} \varphi$, Then $\sim^{2kp+i+2p} \varphi \vdash_{S_p^q} \sim^{2kp+i} \varphi$ is an instance of (N1). By (Cut), $\sim^{2kp+i+2p} \varphi \vdash_{S_p^q} \sim^i \varphi$. Similarly we have $\sim^i \varphi \vdash_{S_p^q} \sim^{2kp+i} \varphi$.

The sequents in (5) are instances of axioms. For (6), we show that $\top \vdash_{S_p^q} \sim^{2n} \top$ by induction on n. The case that $n = 0$ is trivial. Consider the case for $n + 1$. By induction hypothesis, $\top \vdash_{S_p^q} \sim^{2n}\top$. Now we show that $\sim^{2n}\top \vdash_{S_p^q} \sim^{2n+2}\top$. By sequents in (5), we have the following derivation:

$$\dfrac{\dfrac{\top \vdash \sim \bot \qquad \dfrac{\sim \top \vdash \bot}{\sim \bot \vdash \sim \sim \top}(\mathrm{CP})}{\top \vdash \sim \sim \top}(\mathrm{Cut})}{\sim^{2n}\top \vdash \sim^{2n+2}\top}(\mathrm{CP})^{2n}$$

where $(\mathrm{CP})^{2n}$ means $2n$ times application of (CP). Finally, by (Cut), $\top \vdash_{S_p^q} \sim^{2n+2}\top$. The remaining sequents in (6) and (7) are shown similarly.

For any terms φ, ψ_1 and ψ_2, let $\varphi(\psi_1 / \psi_2)$ be the term obtained from φ by substituting ψ_2 for one or more occurrences of ψ_1 in φ.

Lemma 2.8. *For any terms* φ, ψ_1 *and* ψ_2, *the following hold*:

(1) if $\psi_1 \approx_{S_p^q} \psi_2$, then $\varphi \approx_{S_p^q} \varphi(\psi_1 / \psi_2)$.

(2) if $\psi_1 \vdash \psi_2$ and $\psi_2 \vdash \psi_1$ are provable in S_p^q without using (Cut), then $\varphi \vdash \varphi(\psi_1 / \psi_2)$ and $\varphi(\psi_1 / \psi_2) \vdash \varphi$ are provable in S_p^q without using (Cut).

Proof: For (1), assume $\psi_1 \approx_{S_p^q} \psi_2$. We prove $\varphi \approx_{S_p^q} \varphi(\psi_1 / \psi_2)$ by induction on the complexity of φ. The case that φ is atomic is trivial. Suppose $\varphi = \sim \varphi'$. By induction hypothesis $\varphi' \approx_{S_p^q} \varphi'(\psi_1 / \psi_2)$. By (CP), $\sim \varphi' \approx_{S_p^q} \sim \varphi'(\psi_1 / \psi_2)$.

Suppose $\varphi = \varphi_1 \circ \varphi_2$ where $\circ \in \{\wedge, \vee\}$. By induction hypothesis, $\varphi_1 \approx_{S_p^q} \varphi_1(\psi_1 / \psi_2)$ and $\varphi_2 \approx_{S_p^q} \varphi_2(\psi_1 / \psi_2)$. By ($\wedge$) and ($\vee$) in Fact 2.6, $\varphi_1 \circ \varphi_2 \approx_{S_p^q} \varphi_1(\psi_1 / \psi_2) \circ \varphi_2(\psi_1 / \psi_2)$. For (2), assume that $\psi_1 \vdash \psi_2$ and $\psi_2 \vdash \psi_2$ are provable in S_p^q

without using (Cut). It is noticed that (Cut) is not applied in the proof of (1). Hence $\varphi \vdash \varphi(\psi_1 / \psi_2)$ and $\varphi(\psi_1 / \psi_2) \vdash \varphi$ are provable in S_p^q.

Now we show the soundness and completeness of S_p^q with respect to the Berman's variety $\mathbb{K}_p^q$. Firstly, it is clear that the relation $\approx_{S_p^q}$ on the set of all terms T is an equivalence relation. Then, by (CP) and Fact 2.6, $\approx_{S_p^q}$ is a congruence relation on T. Let $|\varphi| = \{\psi \in T \mid \varphi \approx_{S_p^q} \psi\}$ be the equivalence class of φ. Let $|T|$ be the set of all equivalence classes and $\mathfrak{T}_p^q$ be the quotient algebra of the term algebra $\mathfrak{T}$ under the congruence relation $\approx S_p^q$.

Remark 2.9. *In abstract algebraic logic, the binary relation* $\approx_S q$ *is called* the *Tarskian congruence* of S_p^q (cf. Font & Moraschini 2014). The condition (1) in Lemma 2.8 is usually called *selfextensionality* (cf. Font & Moraschini 2014).

Theorem 2.10. $\Gamma \vdash_{S_p^q} \psi$ *if and only if* $\Gamma \vdash_{\mathbb{K}_p^q} \psi$.

Proof: Assume $\Gamma \vdash_{S_p^q} \psi$. It is easy to show that $\varphi \vdash_{\mathbb{K}_p^q} \psi$ by induction on the height of a derivation of $\varphi \vdash \psi$ in S_p^q. Note that all axioms are valid in $\mathbb{K}_p^q$ and all rules preserve validity in $\mathbb{K}_p^q$. Assume $\Gamma \nvdash_{S_p^q} \psi$. By Lemma 2.5, $\wedge \Gamma \nvdash_{S_p^q} \psi$. Then $|\wedge \Gamma| \nleq |\psi|$. Let $\sigma : p \mapsto |p|$ be an assignment. Then $\sigma(\chi) = |\chi|$ for any term . Then $\Gamma \nvdash_{\mathfrak{T}_p^q, \sigma} \psi$. Hence $\Gamma \vdash_{\mathbb{K}_p^q} \psi$.

Remark 2.11. *For any set of terms* $X \cup \{\psi\} \subseteq T$, *we say that* ϕ *is a consequence of* X *in* S_p^q, *if there is a finite subset* $\Gamma \subseteq X$ *such that* $\Gamma \vdash_{S_p^q} \psi$.

The logic S_p^q is indeed a *logic preserving degrees of truth* (Bou, Esteva, Font, Gil, Godo, Torrens & Verdu 2009; Bou & Font 2012; Jansana 2016) since the following conditions are satisfied for any set of terms $X \cup \{\psi\} \subseteq T$:

(1) if X is finite and non-empty, then

$X \vdash_{S_p^q} \psi \Leftrightarrow \forall \mathfrak{A} \in \mathbb{K}_p^q$, $\forall \sigma \in Hom(\mathfrak{T}, A)$, $\forall a \in A$

if $a \leqslant \sigma(\varphi)$ for all $\varphi \in X$, *then* $a \leqslant \sigma(\psi)$

where $Hom(\mathfrak{T}, A)$ is the set of all homomorphisms from the term algebra to $\mathfrak{A}$, and $\leqslant$ is the lattice order in $\mathfrak{A}$.

(2) $\varnothing \vdash_{S_p^q} \psi$ if $\sigma(\psi) = 1$ for all $\mathfrak{A} \in \mathbb{K}_p^q$ and for all $\sigma \in Hom(\mathfrak{T}, A)$.

(3) For an infinite $X \subseteq T$, $X \vdash_{S_p^q} \psi$ if there is a finite subset $\Gamma \subseteq X$ such that $\Gamma \vdash_{S_p^q} \psi$.

The condition (1) follows immediately from Theorem 2.10 and the definition of the validity of a sequent. The condition (2) is guaranteed by $\wedge \varnothing = \top$. The condition (3) is obtained by the definition. The Gentzen sequent system S_p^q is algebraizable (Jansana 2006, 2012; Raftery 2006; Rebagliato & Verdu 1995). In general, the algebraization of Gentzen sequent system expresses the equivalence of closure operations (Blok & Jónsson 2006; Font & Moraschini 2015).

3. Frame Semantics

In this section, for any $p \geqslant 1$ and $q \geqslant 0$, we shall introduce a frame $\mathfrak{F}_p^q$. And we define the frame semantics for S_p^q. The completeness of S_p^q with respect to S_p^q the frame $\mathfrak{F}_p^q$ shall be proved using normal forms. Moreover, we shall prove that S_p^q is characterized by the dual algebra of $\mathfrak{F}_p^q$.

3.1 Frames and Polarity Semantics

Now for any $p \geqslant 1$ and $q \geqslant 0$, we define a frame $\mathfrak{F}_p^q$ and give the polarity valuation of terms in this frame.

Definition 3.1 The *frame* $\mathfrak{F}_p^q = (W_p^q, R)$ is defined as below:

$W_p^q = \{s_i | 1 \leqslant i \leqslant q\} \cup \{t_j | 1 \leqslant i \leqslant 2p\}$.

$R = \{(s_i, s_{i+1}) | 1 \leqslant i \leqslant q-1\} \cup \{(s_q, t_1), (t_{2p}, t_1)\} \cup \{(t_j, t_{j+1}) | 1 \leqslant j \leqslant 2p-1\}$.

The elements in W_p^q are called *states*, and R is called *accessibility* relation.

The accessibility relation R in $\mathfrak{F}_p^q$ is indeed a function. For any $w \in W$, there is exactly one state $u \in W$ such that wRu. The image of a state w under R is denoted by $R(w)$. For any w, $u \in W_p^q$ and $n \in \mathbb{N}$, we write $w R^n u$ if there exist $w_0, \ldots, w_n \in W_p^q$ such that $w = w_0$, $w_n = u$ and $w_i R w_{i+1}$ for all $i < n$. The frame $\mathfrak{F}_p^q$ can be represented as the following directed graph:

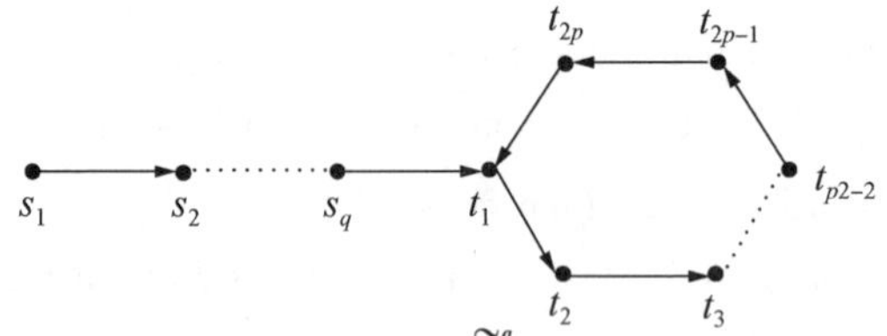

$\mathfrak{F}_p^q$

Some particular frames are represented as follows:

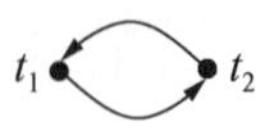

$\mathfrak{F}_1^0$

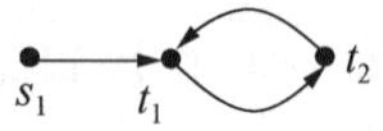

$\mathfrak{F}_1^1$

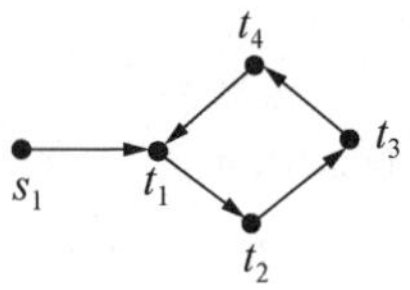

$\mathfrak{F}_2^1$

Definition 3.2 *The set of all polarities is the product $P(W_p^q) \times P(W_p^q)$ where $P(W_p^q)$ is the powerset of W_p^q. A valuation in $\mathfrak{F}_p^q$ is a function $V: \mathbb{X} \to P(W_p^q) \times P(W_p^q)$. If $V(x) = (A, B)$, we denote A by $V^+(x)$ and B by $V^-(x)$. A model is a triple $\mathfrak{M} = (W_p^q, R, V)$ where V is a valuation in $\mathfrak{F}_p^q$.*

For any model $\mathfrak{M} = (W_p^q, R, V)$, $w \in W$ and term φ, the *acceptance relation* $\mathfrak{M}, w \models^+ \varphi$ and *rejection relation* $\mathfrak{M}, w \models^- \varphi$ are defined simultaneously as follows:

- $\mathfrak{M}, w \models^+ \top$ *and* $\mathfrak{M}, w \not\models^- \top$.
- $\mathfrak{M}, w \not\models^+ \bot$ *and* $\mathfrak{M}, w \models^- \bot$.
- $\mathfrak{M}, w \models^+ x$ *if and only if* $w \in V^+(x)$.
- $\mathfrak{M}, w \models^- x$ *if and only if* $w \in V^-(x)$.
- $\mathfrak{M}, w \models^+ \varphi \wedge \psi$ *if and only if* $\mathfrak{M}, w \models^+ \varphi$ *and* $\mathfrak{M}, w \models^+ \varphi$.
- $\mathfrak{M}, w \models^- \varphi \wedge \psi$ *if and only if* $\mathfrak{M}, w \models^- \varphi$ *or* $\mathfrak{M}, w \models^- \psi$.
- $\mathfrak{M}, w \models^+ \varphi \vee \psi$ *if and only if* $\mathfrak{M}, w \models^+ \varphi$ *or* $\mathfrak{M}, w \models^+ \psi$.
- $\mathfrak{M}, w \models^- \varphi \vee \psi$ *if and only if* $\mathfrak{M}, w \models^- \varphi$ *and* $\mathfrak{M}, w \models^- \psi$.
- $\mathfrak{M}, w \models^+ \sim \varphi$ *if and only if* $\mathfrak{M}, R(w) \models^- \varphi$.
- $\mathfrak{M}, w \models^- \sim \varphi$ *if and only if* $\mathfrak{M}, R(w) \models^+ \varphi$.

A sequent $\Gamma \vdash \psi$ is *true* at w in M, notation $\Gamma \models_{M, w} \psi$, if (i) $M, w \models^+ \bigwedge \Gamma$ implies $M, w \models^+ \psi$ and (ii) $M, w \models^- \psi$ implies $M, w \models^- \bigwedge \Gamma$. A sequent $\Gamma \vdash \psi$ is *valid* in $\mathfrak{F}_p^q$, notation $\Gamma \vdash_{M, w} \psi$, if $\Gamma \models_{(\mathfrak{F}_p^q, V, w)} \psi$ for any valuation V in $\mathfrak{F}_p^q$ and $w \in W_p^q$. Let $Tau(\mathfrak{F}_p^q)$ denote the set of all sequents that are valid in $\mathfrak{F}_p^q$. A sequent rule with premisses $\Gamma_i \vdash \psi_i (1 \leqslant i \leqslant n)$ and conclusion $\Gamma_0 \vdash \psi_0$ preserves validity in $\mathfrak{F}_p^q$, if $\Gamma_0 \models_{\mathfrak{F}_p^q} \psi_0$ whenever $\Gamma_i \models_{\mathfrak{F}_p^q} \psi_i$ for all $1 \leqslant i \leqslant n$. Terms φ and ψ are called *equivalent* with respect to $\mathfrak{F}_p^q$, notation $\varphi \equiv_{\mathfrak{F}_p^q} \psi$, *if* $\varphi \models_{\mathfrak{F}_p^q} \psi$ *and* $\psi \models_{\mathfrak{F}_p^q} \varphi$.

Lemma 3.3. *The following sequents are valid in $\mathfrak{F}_p^q$:*

(1) $\varphi \vdash \varphi$, $\bot \vdash \varphi$, $\varphi \vdash \top$, $\varphi \vdash \sim \bot$ *and* $\sim \top \vdash \varphi$.

(2) $\top \vdash \sim^{2n} \top$, $\sim^{2n} \top \vdash \top$, $\bot \vdash \sim^{2n} \bot$ *and* $\sim^{2n} \bot \vdash \bot$, *where* $n \geqslant 0$.

(3) $\bot \vdash \sim^{2n+1} \top$, $\sim^{2n+1} \top \vdash \bot$, $\top \vdash \sim^{2n+1} \bot$ *and* $\sim^{2n+1} \bot \top \vdash$, *where* $n \geqslant 0$.

(4) $\varphi \wedge (\psi \vee \chi) \vdash (\varphi \wedge \psi) \vee (\varphi \wedge \chi)$ *and* $(\varphi \wedge \psi) \vee (\varphi \wedge \chi) \vdash \varphi \wedge (\psi \vee \chi)$.

(5) $\varphi \vee (\psi \wedge \chi) \vdash (\varphi \vee \psi) \wedge (\varphi \vee \chi)$ *and* $(\varphi \vee \psi) \wedge (\varphi \vee \chi) \vdash \varphi \vee (\psi \wedge \chi)$.

(6) $\sim (\varphi \wedge \psi) \vdash \sim \varphi \vee \sim \psi$ *and* $\sim \varphi \vee \sim \psi \vdash \sim (\varphi \wedge \psi)$.

(7) $\sim\varphi \wedge \sim\psi \vdash \sim(\varphi \vee \psi)$ *and* $\sim(\varphi \vee \psi) \vdash \sim\varphi \wedge \sim\psi$.

Proof: The validity of sequents in (1) – (3) is trivial. Let $\mathfrak{M} = (W_p^q, R, V)$ be any model in $\mathfrak{F}_p^q$ and $w \in W_p^q$.

For (4), assume $\mathfrak{M}, w \models^{+}\sim(\varphi \wedge \psi)$. Then $\mathfrak{M}, R(w) \models^{-} \varphi \wedge \psi$. Then $\mathfrak{M}, R(w) \models^{-} \varphi$ or $\mathfrak{M}, R(w) \models^{-} \psi$. Hence $\mathfrak{M}, w \models^{+}\sim\varphi$ or $\mathfrak{M}, w \models^{+}\sim\psi$. Then $\mathfrak{M}, w \models^{+}\sim\varphi \vee \sim\psi$. Assume $\mathfrak{M}, w \models^{-}\sim\varphi \vee \sim\psi$. Then $\mathfrak{M}, w \models^{-}\sim\varphi$ and $\mathfrak{M}, w \models^{-}\sim\psi$. Then $\mathfrak{M}, R(w) \models^{+} \varphi$ and $\mathfrak{M}, R(w) \models^{+} \psi$. Hence $\mathfrak{M}, R(w) \models^{+} \varphi \wedge \psi$. Then $\mathfrak{M}, R(w) \models^{-}\sim(\varphi \wedge \psi)$. Hence $\sim(\varphi \wedge \psi) \models_{\mathfrak{F}_p^q} \sim\varphi \vee \sim\psi$. For (5), assume $\mathfrak{M}, w \models^{+}\sim\varphi \wedge \sim\psi$. Then $\mathfrak{M}, w \models^{+}\sim\varphi$ and $\mathfrak{M}, w \models^{+}\sim\psi$. Then $\mathfrak{M}, R(w) \models^{-} \varphi$ and $\mathfrak{M}, R(w) \models^{-} \psi$. Then $\mathfrak{M}, R(w) \models^{-} \varphi \vee \psi$. Hence $\mathfrak{M}, w \models^{+}\sim(\varphi \vee \psi)$. Assume $\mathfrak{M}, w \models^{-}\sim(\varphi \vee \psi)$. Then $\mathfrak{M}$, R(w) $\models^{+} \varphi \vee \psi$. Then $\mathfrak{M}, R(w) \models^{+} \varphi$ or $\mathfrak{M}, R(w) \models^{+} \psi$. Then $\mathfrak{M}, w \models^{-}\sim\varphi$ or $\mathfrak{M}, w \models^{-}\sim\psi$. Hence $\mathfrak{M}, w \models^{-}\sim\varphi \wedge \sim\psi$.

Lemma 3.4. *Let* $k, n \geqslant 0$. *For any model* $\mathfrak{M} = (\mathfrak{F}_p^q, V)$ *and* $w, u \in W_p^q$, *the following hold*:

(1) *if* $w R^n u$ *and* $\mathfrak{M}, w \models^{+\sim^k} \varphi$ *and* $k \geqslant n$, *then* (*i*) $\mathfrak{M}, u \models^{+\sim^{k-n}} \varphi$ *whenever n is even*; (*ii*) $\mathfrak{M}, u \models^{-\sim^{k-n}} \varphi$ *whenever n is odd.*

(2) *if* $w R^n u$ *and* $\mathfrak{M}, w \models^{-\sim^k} \varphi$ *and* $k \geqslant n$, *then* (*i*) $\mathfrak{M}, u \models^{-\sim^{k-n}} \varphi$ *whene ver n is even*; (*ii*) $\mathfrak{M}, u \models^{+\sim^{k-n}} \varphi$ *whenever n is odd.*

(3) *if* $w R^n u$ *and* $\mathfrak{M}, u \models^{+\sim^k} \varphi$ *then* (*i*) $\mathfrak{M}, w \models^{+\sim^{k+n}} \varphi$ *whenever n is even*; (*ii*) $\mathfrak{M}, u \models^{-\sim^{k+n}} \varphi$ *whenever n is odd.*

(4) *if* $w R^n u$ *and* $\mathfrak{M}, u \models^{-\sim^k} \varphi$ *then* (*i*) $\mathfrak{M}, w \models^{-\sim^{k+n}} \varphi$ *whenever n is even*; (*ii*) $\mathfrak{M}, u \models^{+\sim^{k+n}} \varphi$ *whenever n is odd.*

Proof: For (1), assume that $w R^n u$ and $\mathfrak{M}, w \vdash^{+\sim^k} \varphi$ and $k \geqslant n$. The outmost negation $\sim$ is deleted along each step starting from w. If n is even, we obtain that $\mathfrak{M}, u \models^{+\sim^{k-n}} \varphi$; and if n is odd, we obtain that $\mathfrak{M}, u \models^{-\sim^{k-n}} \varphi$. The remaining items are shown easily by definition.

Lemma 3.5. *Sequents* $\sim^q \varphi \vdash \sim^{2p+q} \varphi$. *and* $\sim^{2p+q} \varphi \vdash \sim^q \varphi$ *are valid in* $\mathfrak{F}_p^q$.

Proof: We show $\sim^q \varphi \vdash_{\mathfrak{F}_p^q} \sim^{2p+q} \varphi$. The validity of $\sim^{2p+q} \varphi \vdash \sim^q \varphi$ in $\mathfrak{F}_p^q$ is shown similarly. Let V be any valuation in $\mathfrak{F}_p^q$ and $\mathfrak{M} = (\mathfrak{F}_p^q, V)$. Take any $w \in W_p^q$. We have two cases:

Case 1. $q \neq 0$ and $w \in \{s_1, \ldots, s_q\}$. Let $w = s_i$ for some $1 \leqslant i \leqslant q$. Assume $\mathfrak{M}, s_i \models^{+\sim^q} \varphi$. By Lemma 3.4, $\mathfrak{M}, s_q \models^{+\sim^i} \varphi$ whenever $q - i$ is even; and $\mathfrak{M}, s_q$

$\models^{-} \sim^{i-1} \varphi$ whenever $q-i$ is odd. Suppose that $q-i$ is even. Then $\mathfrak{M}, t_1 \models^{-} \sim^{i-1} \varphi$. Since $t_1 R^{2p} t_1$ and $2p$ is even, we have $\mathfrak{M}, t_1 \models^{-} \sim^{2p+i-1} \varphi$ by Lemma 3.4. Since $s_q R t_1$, we have $\mathfrak{M}, s_q \models^{+} \sim^{2p+i} \varphi$. Hence $\mathfrak{M}, s_i \models^{+} \sim^{2p+q} \varphi$ since $s_i R^{q-i} s_q$ and $q-i$ is even. For the case that $q-i$ is odd, by a similar argument, we get $\mathfrak{M}, s_i \models^{+} \sim^{2p+q} \varphi$.

Assume $\mathfrak{M}, s_i \models^{-} \sim^{2p+q} \varphi$. Suppose that $q-i$ is even. By Lemma 3.4, $\mathfrak{M}, s_q \models^{-} \sim^{2p+i} \varphi$. Then $\mathfrak{M}, t_1 \models^{+} \sim^{2p+i-1} \varphi$. Since $t_1 R^{2p} t_1$ and $2p$ is even, we have $\mathfrak{M}, t_1 \models^{+} \sim^{i-1} \varphi$ by Lemma 3.4. Since $s_q R t_1$, we have $\mathfrak{M}, s_q \models^{-} \sim^{i} \varphi$. Finally, since $s_i R^{q-i} s_q$, we have $\mathfrak{M}, s_i \models^{-} \sim^{q} \varphi$ by Lemma 3.4. For the case that $q-i$ is odd, by a similar argument, $\mathfrak{M}, s_i \models^{-} \sim^{q} \varphi$.

Case 2. $q = 0$ or $w \in \{t_1, \ldots, t_{2p}\}$. Let $w = t_j$ for some $1 \leqslant j \leqslant 2p$.

Assume that $\mathfrak{M}, t_j \models^{+} \sim^{q} \varphi$. Since $t_j R^{2p} t_j$ and $2p$ is even, we obtain that $\mathfrak{M}, t_j \models^{+} \sim^{2p+q} \varphi$ by Lemma 3.4. Assume $\mathfrak{M}, t_j \models^{-} \sim^{2p+q} \varphi$. Since $t_j R^{2p} t_j$ and $2p$ is even, we have $\mathfrak{M}, t_j \models^{-} \sim^{q} \varphi$ by Lemma 3.4.

Lemma 3.6. *All inference rules of S_p^q preserve validity in $\mathfrak{F}_p^q$.*

Proof. For $(\vee L)$, assume $\varphi_1, \Gamma \models_{\mathfrak{F}_p^q} \psi$ and $\varphi_2, \Gamma \models_{\mathfrak{F}_p^q} \psi$. Let $\mathfrak{M} = (\mathfrak{F}_p^q, V)$ be any model and $w \in W_p^q$. Suppose $\mathfrak{M}, w \models^{+} (\varphi_1 \vee \varphi_2) \wedge (\models \Gamma)$. Then $\mathfrak{M}, w \models^{+} \models \Gamma$, and $\mathfrak{M}, w \models^{+} \varphi_1$ or $\mathfrak{M}, w \models^{+} \varphi_2$. By the assumption, $\mathfrak{M}, w \models^{+} \psi$. Suppose $\mathfrak{M}, w \models^{-} \psi$. By the assumption, $\mathfrak{M}, w \models^{-} \models \Gamma$, or $\mathfrak{M}, w \models^{-} \varphi_1$ and $\mathfrak{M}, w \models^{-} \varphi_2$. Then $\mathfrak{M}, w \models^{-} \models \Gamma$, or $\mathfrak{M}, w \models^{-} \varphi_1 \vee \varphi_2$. In each case, we have $\mathfrak{M}, w \models^{-} (\varphi_1 \vee \varphi_2) \wedge (\models \Gamma)$. Similarly, one can show that $(\wedge L)$, $(\wedge R)$ and $(\vee R)$ preserve validity in $\mathfrak{F}_p^q$..

For (CP), assume $\varphi \models_{\mathfrak{F}_p^q} \psi$. Let $\mathfrak{M} = (\mathfrak{F}_p^q, V)$ and $w \in W_p^q$. Suppose $\mathfrak{M}, w \models^{+} \sim \psi$. Then $\mathfrak{M}, R(w) \models^{-} \psi$. By the assumption, $\mathfrak{M}, R(w) \models^{-} \varphi$. Then $\mathfrak{M}, w \models^{+} \sim \varphi$. Suppose $\mathfrak{M}, w \models^{-} \sim \varphi$. Then $\mathfrak{M}, R(w) \models^{+} \varphi$. By the assumption, $\mathfrak{M}, R(w) \models^{+} \psi$. Then $\mathfrak{M}, w \models^{-} \sim \psi$.

That the structural rules preserve validity in $\mathfrak{F}_p^q$ can be easily shown.

For (Cut), assume $\Gamma \models_{\mathfrak{F}_p^q} \psi$ and $\psi, \Delta \models_{\mathfrak{F}_p^q} \chi$. Let $\wedge \Gamma = \varphi$ and $\wedge \Delta = \xi$. Let $\mathfrak{M} = (\mathfrak{F}_p^q, V)$ and $w \in W_p^q$. Suppose $\mathfrak{M}, w \models^{+} \varphi \models \xi$. Then $\mathfrak{M}, w \models^{+} \varphi$ and $\mathfrak{M}, w \models^{+} \xi$. Then $\mathfrak{M}, w \models^{+} \psi$. Since $\psi, \Delta \models_{\mathfrak{F}_p^q} \chi$, we get $\mathfrak{M}, w \models^{+} \chi$. Suppose $\mathfrak{M}, w \models^{-} \chi$. By $\psi, \Delta \models_{\mathfrak{F}_p^q} \chi$, we get $\mathfrak{M}, w \models^{-} \psi$. or $\mathfrak{M}, w \models^{-} \xi$. If $\mathfrak{M}, w \models^{-} \xi$, then $\mathfrak{M}, w \models^{-} \varphi \models \xi$. Suppose $\mathfrak{M}, w \models^{-} \varphi$. By $\Gamma \models_{\mathfrak{F}_p^q} \psi$, we get $\mathfrak{M}, w \models^{-} \varphi$ Then $\mathfrak{M}, w \models^{-} \varphi \models \xi$.

Theorem 3.7. (*Soundness*) *If* $\Gamma \vdash_{\mathfrak{F}_p^q} \psi$, *then* $\Gamma \vdash_{\mathfrak{F}_p^q} \psi$.

Proof: Assume that $\Gamma \vdash_{\mathfrak{F}_p^q} \psi$. The proof proceeds by induction on the height of a derivation of $\Gamma \vdash \psi$ in S_p^q. By Lemmas 3.3 and 3.5, all axioms in S_p^q are valid in $\mathfrak{F}_p^q$. By Lemma 3.6, all rules in S_p^q preserve validity in $\mathfrak{F}_p^q$. Hence $\Gamma \vdash_{\mathfrak{F}_p^q} \psi$.

3.2 Completeness and Decidability

Let us continue to show the completeness of S_p^q. with respect to $\mathfrak{F}_p^q$. The proof proceeds by using norms forms. Henceforth, for any $m, n \in \mathbb{N}$, let $[m, n] = \{i \in \mathbb{N} \mid m \leqslant i \leqslant n\}$, $(m, n] = \{i \in \mathbb{N} \mid m < i \leqslant n\}$, and $[m, n) = \{i \in \mathbb{N} \mid m \leqslant i < n\}$. The normal forms are defined as follows:

Definition 3.8. *A literal is a term of the form* $\top$, $\bot$, $\sim^i x$, *where* $x \in Var$ *and* $i \in [0, 2p+q)$. *A term* φ *is in disjunction normal form (DNF), if* φ *is of the form* $\bigvee_{i\in[1,m]}(\bigwedge_{j\in[1,n]}\varphi_{ij})$ *where* φ *is a literal. A term* φ *is in conjunction normal form (CNF) if* φ *is of the form* $\bigwedge_{i\in[1,m]}(\bigvee_{j\in[1,n]}\varphi_{ij})$ *where* φ_{ij} *is a literal.*

Lemma 3.9. *If* $\psi_1 \equiv_{\mathfrak{F}_p^q} \psi_2$, *then* $\varphi \equiv_{\mathfrak{F}_p^q} \varphi(\psi_1 / \psi_2)$.

Proof: Assume $\psi_1 \equiv_{\mathfrak{F}_p^q} \psi_2$. The proof proceeds by induction on the complexity of φ. The case that φ is atomic is trivial. Assume $\varphi = \sim\chi$. By induction hypothesis, $\chi \equiv_{\mathfrak{F}_p^q} \chi(\varphi_1 / \varphi_2)$. Then we have $\sim\chi =_{\mathfrak{F}_p^q} \sim\chi(\varphi_1 / \varphi_2)$ by the fact that (CP) preserves validity in $\mathfrak{F}_p^q$ (Lemma 3.6). Assume $\varphi = \chi_1 \circ \chi_2$ for $\circ \in \{\wedge, \vee\}$. By induction hypothesis, $\chi_1 \equiv_{\mathfrak{F}_p^q} \chi_1(\varphi_1 / \varphi_2)$ and $\chi_2 \equiv_{\mathfrak{F}_p^q} \chi_2(\varphi_1 / \varphi_2)$. By Lemma 3.6, ($\wedge$) and ($\vee$) in Fact 2.6 preserves validity in $\mathfrak{F}_p^q$. Therefore $\chi_1 \circ \chi_2 \equiv_{\mathfrak{F}_p^q} \chi_1(\varphi_1 / \varphi_2) \circ \chi_2(\varphi_1 / \varphi_2)$.

Lemma 3.10. *For any term* φ, *there exist CNF term* $C(\varphi)$ *and DNF term* $D(\varphi)$ *such that the following conditions hold*:

(1) $\varphi \equiv_{\mathfrak{F}_p^q} C(\varphi)$ *and* $\varphi \equiv_{\mathfrak{F}_p^q} D(\varphi)$.

(2) $\varphi \approx_{\mathfrak{F}_p^q} C(\varphi)$ *and* $\varphi \approx_{\mathfrak{F}_p^q} D(\varphi)$.

Proof: For (1), using Lemma 3.3 (4) – (7), we get a term φ' in which all occurrences of the negation sign $\sim$ occur only before variables such that $\varphi \equiv_{\mathfrak{F}_p^q} \varphi'$. By Lemma 3.3 (1) – (3), Lemmas 3.5 and 3.9, we get a CNF term $C(\varphi)$ such that $\varphi' \equiv_{\mathfrak{F}_p^q} C(\varphi)$. Since (Cut) preserves validity in $\mathfrak{F}_p^q$, we have $\varphi \equiv_{\mathfrak{F}_p^q} C(\varphi)$. One can get an equivalent DNF term $D(\varphi)$ in a similar way. For (2), using the same consequences in (1) which are provable in S_p^q, we have $\varphi \approx_{\mathfrak{F}_p^q} \varphi'$ and all occurrences of the negation sign $\sim$ in φ' occur only before a variable. By (N1), (N2) and

Lemma 2.8, $\varphi' \approx_{S_p^q} C(\varphi)$ and $\varphi' \approx_{S_p^q} D(\varphi)$. By (Cut), $\varphi \approx_{S_p^q} C(\varphi)$ and $\varphi \approx_{S_p^q} D(\varphi)$.

Lemma 3.11. *Let φ_i and ψ_j be literals for $i \in [1, m]$ and $j \in [1, n]$. Then $\bigwedge_{i\in[1,m]}\varphi_i \vdash_{\mathfrak{F}_p^q} \bigvee_{j\in[1,n]}\psi_j$ if and only if at least of the following conditions holds:*

(C1) $\varphi_i = \bot$ for some $i \in [1, m]$.

(C2) $\psi_j = \top$ for some $j \in [1, n]$.

(C3) $\varphi_i = \psi_j$ for some $i \in [1, m]$ and $j \in [1, n]$.

Proof: Assume that one of the conditions $(C1)$ - $(C3)$ holds. It is trivial that $\bigwedge_{i\in[1,m]}\varphi_i \vDash_{\mathfrak{F}_p^q} \bigvee_{j\in[1,n]}\psi_j$. Conversely, assume that neither of the conditions $(C1)$ - $(C3)$ holds. For all $i \in [1, m]$, φ_i is $\top$ or a term of the form $\sim^k x$ for $k \in [0, 2p+q)$. For $j \in [1, n]$, ψ_j is $\bot$ or a term of the form $\sim^k x$ for $k \in [0, 2p+q)$. We define the valuation V in $\mathfrak{F}_p^q$ as follows according to q:

(Ⅰ) q is even.

(a) $s_{2k+1} \in V^+(x) \Leftrightarrow \exists i \in [1, m](\varphi_i = \sim^{2k} x)$, *where* $2k \in [0, q)$.

(b) $s_{2k+2} \in V^-(x) \Leftrightarrow \exists i \in [1, m](\varphi_i = \sim^{2k+1} x)$, *where* $2k+1 \in [0, q)$.

(c) $t_{2k+1} \in V^+(x) \Leftrightarrow \exists i \in [1, m](\varphi_i = \sim^{2k+q} x)$, *where* $2k+1 \in [1, 2p]$.

(d) $t_{2k+2} \in V^-(x) \Leftrightarrow \exists i \in [1, m](\varphi_i = \sim^{2k+q+1} x)$, *where* $2k+2 \in [1, 2p]$.

(Ⅱ) q is odd.

(a) $s_{2k+1} \in V^+(x) \Leftrightarrow \exists i \in [1, m](\varphi_i = \sim^{2k} x)$, *where* $2k \in [0, q)$.

(b) $s_{2k+2} \in V^-(x) \Leftrightarrow \exists i \in [1, m](\varphi_i = \sim^{2k+1} x)$, *where* $2k+1 \in [0, q)$.

(c) $t_{2k+1} \in V^-(x) \Leftrightarrow \exists i \in [1, m](\varphi_i = \sim^{2k+q} x)$, *where* $2k+1 \in [1, 2p]$.

(d) $t_{2k+2} \in V^+(x) \Leftrightarrow \exists i \in [1, m](\varphi_i = \sim^{2k+q+1} x)$, *where* $2k+2 \in [1, 2p]$.

Let $\mathfrak{M} = (\mathfrak{F}_p^q, V)$. Firstly, we show that $\mathfrak{M}, s_1 \vDash^+ \bigwedge_{i\in[1,m]}\varphi_i$. Suppose that q is even. If $\varphi_i = \vDash$. then $\mathfrak{M}, s_1 \vDash^+ \varphi_i$. Suppose that $\varphi_i = \sim^l x$ for some $l \in [0, 2p+q)$. We have the following cases according to φ_i:

(1.1) $\varphi_i = \sim^{2k} x$ *with* $2k \in [0, q)$. *Then* $s_{2k+1} \in V^+(x)$. By Lemma 3.4, $\mathfrak{M}$, $s_1 \vDash^+ \sim^{2k} x$.

(1.2) $\varphi_i = \sim^{2k+1} x$ *with* $2k+1 \in [0, q)$. *Then* $s_{2k+2} \in V^-(x)$. By Lemma 3.4, $\mathfrak{M}$, $s_1 \vDash^+ \sim^{2k+1} x$.

(1.3) $\varphi_i = \sim^{2k+q} x$ *with* $2k+1 \in [1, 2p)$. *Then* $t_{2k+1} \in V^+(x)$. By Lemma 3.4, $\mathfrak{M}$, $s_1 \vDash^+ \sim^{2k+q} x$. since q is even.

(1.4) $\varphi_i = \sim^{2k+q+1} x$ *with* $2k+2 \in [1, 2p]$. *Then* $t_{2k+2} \in V^-(x)$. By Lemma

3.4, $\mathfrak{M}$, $s_1 \models^{+} \sim^{2k+q+1} x$. Since q is even. The case that q is odd is shown similarly. Hence $\mathfrak{M}$, $s_1 \models^{+} \bigwedge_{i\in[1,m]}\varphi_i$.

Secondly, we show that $\mathfrak{M}$, $s_1 \not\models^{+}\psi_j$ for any $j \in [1, n]$. Obviously $\psi_j \neq \top$ since $(C2)$ does not hold. If $\psi_j = \bot$, then $\mathfrak{M}$, $s_1 \not\models^{+}\psi_j$. Suppose that $\psi_j = \sim^{l} x$ for some $l \in [0, 2p+q)$. Suppose that q is even. We have the following cases according to ψ_j:

(2.1) $\psi_j = \sim^{2k} x$ *with* $2k \in [0, q)$. *Then* $\mathfrak{M}$, $s_1 \models^{+}\psi_j$ if and only if $s_{2k+1} \in V^{+}(x)$. By definition of V, there is $i \in [1, m]$ with $\varphi_i = \sim^{2k} x$. But (C3) does not hold. Hence $\mathfrak{M}$, $s_1 \not\models^{+}\psi_j$.

(2.2) $\psi_j = \sim^{2k+1} x$ *with* $2k+1 \in [0, q)$. *Then* $\mathfrak{M}$, $s_1 \models^{+}\psi_j$ if and only if $s_{2k+2} \in V^{-}(x)$. By definition of V, there exists $i \in [1, m]$ with $\varphi_i = \sim^{2k+1} x$. Since (C3) does not hold, $\mathfrak{M}$, $s_1 \not\models^{+}\psi_j$.

(2.3) $\psi_j = \sim^{2k+q} x$ *with* $2k+1 \in [1, 2p]$. *Then* $\mathfrak{M}$, $s_1 \models^{+}\psi_j$ if and only if $t_{2k+1} \in V^{+}(x)$. By definition of V, there is $i \in [1, m]$ with $\varphi_i = \sim^{2k+q} x$. Since (C3) does not hold, $\mathfrak{M}$, $s_1 \not\models^{+}\psi_j$.

(2.4) $\psi_j = \sim^{2k+q+1} x$ *with* $2k+2 \in [1, 2p]$. *Then* $\mathfrak{M}$, $s_1 \models^{+}\psi_j$ if and only if $t_{2k+2} \in V^{-}(x)$. By definition of V, there is $i \in [1, m]$ with $\varphi_i = \sim^{2k+q+1} x$. Since (C3) does not hold, $\mathfrak{M}$, $s_1 \not\models^{+}\psi_j$.

The case that q is odd is shown similarly. Hence $\mathfrak{M}$, $s_1 \not\models^{+}\psi_j$. Hence $\bigwedge_{i\in[1,m]}\varphi_i \not\models_{\mathfrak{M}, s_1} \bigvee_{j\in[1,n]}\psi_j$. Then $\bigwedge_{i\in[1,m]}\varphi_i \not\models_{\mathfrak{F}_p^q} \bigvee_{j\in[1,n]}\psi_j$.

Lemma 3.12. *For any model* $\mathfrak{M} = (W_p^q, R, V)$ *and* $w \in W$, *the following hold*:

(1) $\varphi \vee \psi \models_{\mathfrak{M}, w} \chi$ *if and only if* $\varphi \models_{\mathfrak{M}, w} \chi$ *and* $\psi \models_{\mathfrak{M}, w} \chi$.

(2) $\varphi \models_{\mathfrak{M}, w} \psi \wedge \chi$ *if and only if* $\varphi \models_{\mathfrak{M}, w} \psi$ *and* $\varphi \models_{\mathfrak{M}, w} \chi$.

(3) $\varphi \vee \psi \models_{\mathfrak{F}_p^q} \chi$ *if and only if* $\varphi \models_{\mathfrak{F}_p^q} \chi$ *and* $\psi \models_{\mathfrak{F}_p^q} \chi$.

(4) $\varphi \models_{\mathfrak{F}_p^q} \psi \wedge \chi$ *if and only if* $\varphi \models_{\mathfrak{F}_p^q} \psi$ *and* $\varphi \models_{\mathfrak{F}_p^q} \chi$.

Proof: (1) and (2) are easily obtained by the definition. Notice that (3) and (4) follow from (1) and (2) respectively.

Theorem 3.13. (*Completeness*) *If* $\Gamma \models_{\mathfrak{F}_p^q} \psi$, *then* $\Gamma \vdash_{\mathfrak{F}_p^q} \psi$.

Proof: Assume $\Gamma \vdash_{\mathfrak{F}_p^q} \psi$. and $\bigwedge \Gamma = \varphi$. Then $\varphi \vdash_{\mathfrak{F}_p^q} \psi$. By Lemma 3.10 (1), there exist CNF term $D(\varphi)$ and DNF term $C(\psi)$ such that $\varphi \equiv_{\mathfrak{F}_p^q} D(\varphi)$ and $\psi \equiv_{\mathfrak{F}_p^q} C(\psi)$. Since (Cut) preserves validity in $\mathfrak{F}_p^q$ (Lemma 3.6), $D(\varphi) \vdash_{\mathfrak{F}_p^q} C(\psi)$. Let

$D(\varphi) = \bigvee_{i_1 \in [1, m_1]} \delta_{i_1}$ and $C(\psi) = \bigwedge_{i_2 \in [1, m_2]} \delta_{i_2}$ where $\delta_{i_1} = \bigwedge_{j_1 \in [1, n_1]} \varphi_{i_1 j_1}$ and $\delta_{i_2} = \bigvee_{j_2 \in [1, n_2]} \psi_{i_2 j_2}$. By Lemma 3. 12, for any $i_1 \in [1, m_1]$ and $i_2 \in [1, m_2]$, $\delta_{i_1} \models_{\mathfrak{F}_p^q} \delta_{i_2}$ By Lemma 3. 11, one of conditions (C1) – (C3) holds. We have three cases:

(1) $\varphi_{i_1 j_1} = \bot$ for some $j_1 \in [1, n_1]$. By ($\bot$) and ($\wedge L$), $\delta_{i_1} \vdash_{S_p^q} \delta_{i_2}$.

(2) $\psi_{i_1 j_1} = \top$ for some $j_2 \in [1, n_2]$. By ($\top$) and ($\wedge R$), $\delta_{i_1} \vdash_{S_p^q} \delta_{i_2}$.

(3) $\varphi_{i_1 j_1} = \psi_{i_1 j_1}$ for some $j_1 \in [1, n_1]$ and $j_2 \in [1, n_2]$. By (Id), ($\wedge L$) and ($\wedge R$), $\delta_{i_1} \vdash_{S_p^q} \delta_{i_2}$.

Hence $\delta_{i_1} \vdash_{S_p^q} \delta_{i_2}$ for any $i_1 \in [1, m_1]$ and $i_2 \in [1, m_2]$. By ($\wedge L$) and ($\wedge R$), we have $D(\varphi) \vdash_{S_p^q} C(\psi)$. By Lemma 3. 10 (2) and (Cut), we have $\varphi \vdash_{S_p^q} \psi$. By Lemma 2. 5, we have $\Gamma \vdash_{S_p^q} \psi$.

Corollary 3. 14. Thm (S_p^q) = Tau$(\mathfrak{F}_p^q)$

Theorem 3. 15. (*Decidability*) Tau$(\mathfrak{F}_p^q)$ *is decidable.*

Proof. Let $\Gamma \vdash \psi$ be any sequent and $\bigwedge \Gamma = \varphi$. By Lemma 3. 10, there exist a DNF term $D(\varphi) = \bigvee_{i_1 \in [1, m_1]} \bigwedge_{j_1 \in [1, n_1]} \varphi_{i_1 j_1}$ and CNF term $C(\psi) = \bigwedge_{i_2 \in [1, m_2]} \bigvee_{j_2 \in [1, n_2]} \varphi_{i_2 j_2}$ such that $\varphi \equiv_{\mathfrak{F}_p^q} D(\varphi)$ and $\psi \equiv_{\mathfrak{F}_p^q} C(\psi)$. Then $\varphi \vdash_{\mathfrak{F}_p^q} \psi$ if and only if $D(\varphi) \models_{\mathfrak{F}_p^q} C(\psi)$. By Lemma 3. 12, $D(\varphi) \models_{\mathfrak{F}_p^q} C(\psi)$. if and only if $\bigwedge_{j_1 \in [1, n_1]} \varphi_{i_1 j_1} \models_{\mathfrak{F}_p^q} \bigvee_{j_2 \in [1, n_2]} \varphi_{i_2 j_2}$ for all $i_1 \in [1, m_1]$ and $i_2 \in [1, m_2]$. By Lemma 3. 11 in order to check the validity of the sequent $\bigwedge_{j_1 \in [1, n_1]} \varphi_{i_1 j_1} \vdash \bigvee_{j_2 \in [1, n_2]} \varphi_{i_2 j_2}$, it suffices to check the conditions (C1) – (C3). There are only finitely many such sequents to check. Therefore, the validity of $\varphi \vdash \psi$ is decidable.

3. 3 Duality

Now we shall define the dual algebra of the frame $\mathfrak{F}_p^q$ which belongs to the Berman's variety $\mathbb{K}_p^q$. Then we shall prove that the duality preserves validity of sequents. It follows that the weak logic L_p^q is characterized by the dual algebra of $\mathfrak{F}_p^q$ which is a finite distributive lattice with a unary operator.

Recall that the accessibility relation R in the frame $\mathfrak{F}_p^q = (W_p^q, R)$ is a function.

For any $A \subseteq W_p^q$ and $w \subseteq W_p^q$ we define

$A\uparrow = \{R(u) | u \in A\}$, $W\downarrow = \{u \in W_p^q | R(u) \in w\}$, $A\downarrow = \bigcup_{u \in A} u\downarrow$.

For $n \geqslant 0$ we define $A\uparrow^n$ and $A\downarrow^n$ inductively by:

$A\uparrow^0 = A = A\downarrow^0$, $A\uparrow^{n+1} = (A\uparrow^n)A\uparrow^n$, $A\downarrow^{n+1} = (A\downarrow^n)$.

Definition 3. 16. Let $\mathbb{X}_p^q = W_p^q \times W_p^q$. The binary operations $\sqcup$, $\sqcap$ and the unary operation $\sim$ on $\mathbb{X}_p^q$ are defined as follows:

$$\langle A_1, B_1 \sqcup A_2, B_2\rangle = \langle A_1 \cup A_2, B_1 \cap B_2\rangle.$$
$$\langle A_1, B_1\rangle \sqcap \langle A_2, B_2\rangle = \langle A_1 \cap A_2, B_1 \cup B_2\rangle.$$
$$\sim\langle A, B\rangle = \langle B\downarrow, A\downarrow\rangle.$$

The algebra $(\mathfrak{F}_p^q)^+ = (\mathbb{X}_p^q, \sqcup, \sqcap, \sim, \langle\emptyset, W_p^q\rangle, \langle W_p^q, \emptyset\rangle)$ is called the *dual algebra* of the frame $\mathfrak{F}_p^q$.

Lemma 3.17. *For any $A, B \subseteq W_p^q$, the following hold:*

(1) If $A \subseteq B$, then $A\uparrow \subseteq B\uparrow$ and $A\downarrow \subseteq B\downarrow$.

(2) $A\uparrow^q = A\uparrow^{2p+q}$.

(3) $A\downarrow^q = A\downarrow^{2p+q}$.

(4) $(A \cup B)\uparrow = A\uparrow \cup B\uparrow$ and $(A \cup B)\downarrow = A\downarrow \cup B\downarrow$.

(5) $(A \cap B)\uparrow = A\uparrow \cap B\uparrow$ and $(A \cap B)\downarrow = A\downarrow \cap B\downarrow$.

(6) If $(A \cap B)\uparrow \neq A\uparrow \cap B\uparrow$, then $(A \cap B)\uparrow \cup \{t_1\} = A\uparrow \cap B\uparrow$, s_q, $t_{2p} \in A \cup B$ and s_q, $t_{2p} \notin A \cap B$.

(7) $W_p^q\uparrow = W_p^q s_1\}$, $\emptyset\uparrow = \emptyset$, $\emptyset\downarrow = \emptyset$ and $W_p^q\downarrow = W_p^q$.

Proof: (1) is trivial. For (2), assume that $w \in A\uparrow^q$. There exists $u \in A$ with $w \in u\uparrow^q$. Clearly $w = t_j$ for some $j \in [1, 2p]$. Then $w \in u\uparrow^{2p+q}$. Hence $w \in A\uparrow^{2p+q}$. Conversely, assume that $w \in A\uparrow^{2p+q}$. There exists $u \in A$ with $w \in u\uparrow^{2p+q}$. Then there exists $v \in W_p^q$ with $v \in u\uparrow^q$. and $w \in v\uparrow^{2p}$. Clearly $v, w \in \{t_1, \ldots, t_{2p}\}$. Since $w \in v\uparrow^{2p}$, $v = w$. Then $w \in u\uparrow^q$. Hence $w \in A\uparrow^q$. For (3), assume that $w \in A\downarrow^q$. There exists $u \in A$ with $w \in u\downarrow^q$. Clearly $u \in \{t_1, \ldots, t_{2p}\}$. If $w \in \{t_1, \ldots, t_{2p}\}$, $w \in u\downarrow^{2p+q}$. Suppose that $w \in \{s_1, \ldots, s_{2p}\}$. Then $w \in t_1\downarrow^{k_1}$ and $t_1 \in u\downarrow^{k_2}$ where $k_1 + k_2 = q$. Hence $t_1 \in u\downarrow^{2p+k_2}$ since $t_1 \in t_1\downarrow^{2p}$. Then $w \in u\downarrow^{2p+q}$. Hence $A\downarrow^q \subseteq A\downarrow^{2p+q}$. The other inclusion is shown similarly.

It is easy to show (4) and (5). For (6), assume that $(A \cap B)\uparrow \neq A\uparrow \cap B\uparrow$. By (5), there exists $w \in A\uparrow \cap B\uparrow$ with $w \notin (A \cap B)\uparrow$. Then there exist $u \in A$ and $v \in B$ with uRw and vRw. Then $u \neq v$ and $w = t_1$. Otherwise, $u = v$ and $w \in (A \cap B)\uparrow$, contradicting to $w \notin (A \cap B)\uparrow$. Then $t_1 \in A\uparrow \cap B\uparrow$ and $u, v \in \{s_q, t_{2p}\}$. Hence s_q, $t_{2p} \in A \cup B$. Suppose that $u' \in A\uparrow \cap B\uparrow$ and $u' \neq t_1$. There exist $v_1 \in A$ and $v_2 \in B$ with $v_1 Ru'$ and $v_2 R u'$. Then $v_1 = v_2$. Hence $u' \in (A \cap B)\uparrow$. Hence $A\uparrow \cap B\uparrow \subseteq (A \cap B)\uparrow \cup \{t_1\}$. Then $(A \cap B)\uparrow \cup \{t_1\} = A\uparrow \cap B\uparrow$. Since $t_1 \notin (A \cap B)\uparrow$, $s_q R t_1$ and $t_{2p} R t_1$, we have s_q, $t_{2p} \notin A \cap B$.. For (7), by $s_1\downarrow = \emptyset$, $s_1 \notin W_p^q\uparrow$. The remaining equations are shown easily.

Lemma 3.18. $(\mathfrak{F}_p^q)^+ \in \mathbb{K}_p^q$.

Proof: It is easy to show that $(\mathbb{X}_{\mathfrak{F}}, \sqcup, \sqcap \sim, \langle \emptyset, W\rangle, \langle W, \emptyset\rangle)$ is a bounded distributive lattice. Now we check the conditions (O1) – (O3) of Ockham algebras. For (O1), we calculate as follows:

$$\begin{aligned} \sim(\langle A_1, B_1\rangle \sqcup \langle A_2, B_2\rangle) &= \sim\langle A_1 \cup A_2, B_1 \cup B_2\rangle \\ &= \langle (B_1 \cap B_2)\downarrow, (A_1 \cup A_2)\downarrow\rangle \\ \text{(By Lemma 3. 17 (4) (5))} &= \langle B_1\downarrow \cap B_2\downarrow, A_1\downarrow \cup A_2\downarrow\rangle \\ &= \langle B_1\downarrow, A_1\downarrow\rangle \sqcap \langle B_2\downarrow, A_2\downarrow\rangle \\ &= \sim\langle A_1, B_1\rangle \sqcap \sim\langle A_2, B_2\rangle. \end{aligned}$$

Similarly one can show the condition (O2). The condition (O3) is easily shown by Lemma 3. 17 (7). Now we show that $\sim^{2p+q}(A, B) = \sim^{q}(A, B)$. Suppose that q is even. Then $\sim^{2p+q}\langle A, B\rangle = \langle A\downarrow^{2p+q}, B\downarrow^{2p+q}\rangle$ and $\sim^{q}(A, B) = \langle A\downarrow^{q}, B\downarrow^{q}\rangle$. By Lemma 3. 17 (3), $\sim^{2p+q}\langle A, B\rangle = \sim^{q}\langle A, B\rangle$. The case that q is odd is shown similarly. Hence $(\mathfrak{F}_p^q)^+ \in \mathbb{K}_p^q$.

The definition of $(\mathfrak{F}_p^q)^+$ is a twisted-construction which was traced back to Kalman (1958). The lattice order $\sqsubseteq$ in $(\mathfrak{F}_p^q)^+$ is defined by: $\langle A_1, B_1\rangle \sqsubseteq \langle A_2, B_2\rangle$ if and only if $\langle A_1, B_1\rangle \sqcap \langle A_2, B_2\rangle = (A_1, B_1)$. Obviously $\langle A_1, B_1\rangle \sqsubseteq \langle A_2, B_2\rangle$ if and only if $A_1 \subseteq A_2$ and $B_2 \subseteq B_1$. Then $\langle A_1, B_1\rangle = \langle A_2, B_2\rangle$ if and only if $\langle A_1, B_1\rangle \sqsubseteq \langle A_2, B_2\rangle$ and $\langle A_2, B_2\rangle \sqsubseteq \langle A_1, B_1\rangle$.

Let $\mathfrak{M} = (W_p^q, R, V)$ be a model. For any term φ, let $V^+(\varphi) = \{w \in W_p^q \mid \mathfrak{M}, w \vdash^+ \varphi\}$ and $V^-(\varphi) = \{w \in W_p^q \mid \mathfrak{M}, w \vdash^- \varphi\}$. Then $V(\varphi) = \langle V^+(\varphi), V^-(\varphi)\rangle$. One can easily show that $V(\bot) = \langle\emptyset, W\rangle$, $V(\top) = \langle W, \emptyset\rangle$, $V(\sim\varphi) = \sim V(\varphi)$, $V(\varphi \wedge \psi) = V(\varphi) \sqcap V(\psi)$, *and* $V(\varphi \vee \psi) = V(\varphi) \sqcup V(\psi)$

Lemma 3. 19. *For any model* $\mathfrak{M} = (\mathfrak{F}_p^q, V)$ *and sequent* $\Gamma \vdash \psi$, (1) $\Gamma \models_{\mathfrak{M}} \psi$ *if and only if* $\Gamma \models_{(\mathfrak{F}_p^q)^+, V} \psi$; (2) $\Gamma \models_{\mathfrak{F}_p^q} \psi$ *if and only if* $\Gamma \models_{(\mathfrak{F}_p^q)^+} \psi$.

Proof: Let $\bigwedge\Gamma = \varphi$ For (1), assume $\varphi \models_{\mathfrak{M}} \psi$. Then $V^+(\varphi) \subseteq V^+(\psi)$ and $V^-(\psi) \subseteq V^-(\varphi)$. Then $V(\varphi) \subseteq V(\psi)$. Hence $\varphi \models_{(\mathfrak{F}_p^q)^+, V} \psi$. Assume $\varphi \models_{(\mathfrak{F}_p^q)^+, V} \psi$. Then $V(\varphi) \subseteq V(\psi)$. Hence $\varphi \models_{\mathfrak{M}} \psi$. (2) follows from (1).

Theorem 3. 20. $\Gamma \vdash_{S_p^q} \psi$ *if and only if* $\Gamma \models_{(\mathfrak{F}_p^q)^+} \psi$.

Proof: By Lemma 3. 19 and Corollary 3. 14.

It follows that the logic S_p^q is characterized by the dual algebra $(\mathfrak{F}_p^q)^+$. There are $2p + q$ elements in W_p^q. It follows that there are 4^{2p+q} elements in $(\mathfrak{F}_p^q)^+$. The logic S_p^q deserves to be called a 4^{2p+q}*-valued logic*. For example, the Belnap-Dunn logic BD is

a 16-valued logic. The 16 values form a distributive lattice 16 shown in Figure 1. The definition of the unary operator $\sim$ in 16 is given in Table 2. Note that there are only two symmetric states t_1, t_2 in $\mathfrak{F}_1^0$. We write
$t_1 = 1$, $t_2 = 0$ and $R = \{(0, 1), (1, 0)\}$. To simplify notations for elements in $(\mathfrak{F}_1^0)^+$, we write 1 for $\{1\}$, 0 for $\{0\}$, and 01 for $\{0, 1\}$. The 16 values are listed in Table 1. A term assigned with the value

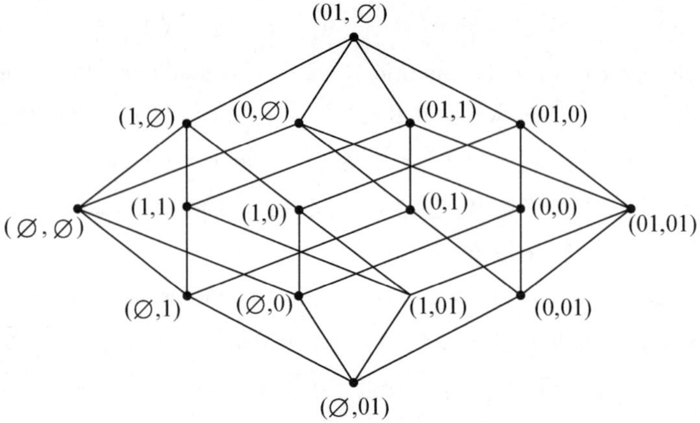

Figure 1. The distributive lattice 16

(01 , 1) is accepted at both states 0 and 1 and rejected at the state 1. A term assigned with the value ($\varnothing$, 1) is accepted at no state and rejected at the state 1. The other values are similarly explained. Although it is well-known that BD is a four-valued logic, it is indeed a 16-valued logic! The lattice 16 is isomorphic to the product 4×4.

Table 1. 16 values in $(\mathfrak{F}_1^0)^+$

Values	Abbreviations	Values	Abbreviations
$(\varnothing, \varnothing)$	$(\varnothing, \varnothing)$	$(\{1\}, \varnothing)$	$(\mathbf{1}, \varnothing)$
$(\varnothing, \{0\})$	$(\varnothing, \mathbf{0})$	$(\{1\}, \{0\})$	$(\mathbf{1}, \mathbf{0})$
$(\varnothing, \{1\})$	$(\varnothing, \mathbf{1})$	$(\{1\}, \{1\})$	$(\mathbf{1}, \mathbf{1})$
$(\varnothing, \{0,1\})$	$(\varnothing, \mathbf{01})$	$(\{1\}, \{0,1\})$	$(\mathbf{1}, \mathbf{01})$
$(\{0\}, \varnothing)$	$(\mathbf{0}, \varnothing)$	$(\{0,1\}, \varnothing)$	$(\mathbf{01}, \varnothing)$
$(\{0\}, \{0\})$	$(\mathbf{0}, \mathbf{0})$	$(\{0,1\}, \{0\})$	$(\mathbf{01}, \mathbf{0})$
$(\{0\}, \{1\})$	$(\mathbf{0}, \mathbf{1})$	$(\{0,1\}, \{1\})$	$(\mathbf{01}, \mathbf{1})$
$(\{0\}, \{0,1\})$	$(\mathbf{0}, \mathbf{01})$	$(\{0,1\}, \{0,1\})$	$(\mathbf{01}, \mathbf{01})$

4. Terminating Cut-Free Sequent System

In this section, we shall introduce a structural-rule-free and cut-free Gentzen sequent system G_p^q for $\vdash_p^q$. And G_p^q is sound and complete with respect to $\mathfrak{F}_p^q$ (and hence with respect to $\mathbb{K}_p^q$). We shall prove that G_p^q is a terminating sequent system and it is decidable. Furthermore, using Maehara's proof-theoretic method, we shall prove the Craig interpolation property of $\vdash_p^q$. In this section, let $E[0, 2p+q)$ and $O[0, 2p+q)$ be the set of all even and odd numbers in $[0, 2p+q)$ respectively.

Table 2. The operator $\sim$ in 16

a	$\sim a$	a	$\sim a$
$(\varnothing, \varnothing)$	$(\varnothing, \varnothing)$	$(1, \varnothing)$	$(\varnothing, 0)$
$(\varnothing, 0)$	$(1, \varnothing)$	$(1, 0)$	$(1, 0)$
$(\varnothing, 1)$	$(0, \varnothing)$	$(1, 1)$	$(0, 0)$
$(\varnothing, 01)$	$(01, \varnothing)$	$(1, 01)$	$(01, 0)$
$(0, \varnothing)$	$(\varnothing, 1)$	$(01, \varnothing)$	$(\varnothing, 01)$
$(0, 0)$	$(1, 1)$	$(01, 0)$	$(1, 01)$
$(0, 1)$	$(0, 1)$	$(01, 1)$	$(0, 01)$
$(0, 01)$	$(01, 1)$	$(01, 01)$	$(01, 01)$

4.1 The Sequent System G_p^q

Definition 4.1 *The sequent system G_p^q consists of the following axioms and inference rules:*

(1) **Axioms:**

(Id) $\sim^k x, \Gamma \vdash \sim^k x$ $(\bot\vdash)$ $\sim^e \bot, \Gamma \vdash \psi$ $(\vdash\sim\bot)$ $\Gamma \vdash \sim^{\circ} \bot$

$(\sim\top\vdash)$ $\sim^{\circ}\top, \Gamma \vdash \psi$ $(\vdash\top)$ $\Gamma \vdash \sim^e \top$

The numbers $k \in [0, 2p+q)$, $e \in E[0, 2p+q)$ and $o \in O[0, 2p+q)$.

(2) **Logical rules:**

$$\frac{\sim^e \varphi, \sim^e \psi, \Gamma \vdash \chi}{\sim^e(\varphi \wedge \psi), \Gamma \vdash \chi}(\wedge\vdash) \quad \frac{\Gamma \vdash \sim^e \varphi \quad \Gamma \vdash \sim^e \psi}{\Gamma \vdash \sim^e(\varphi \wedge \psi)}(\vdash\wedge)$$

$$\frac{\sim^e \varphi, \Gamma \vdash \chi \quad \sim^e \psi, \Gamma \vdash \chi}{\sim^e(\varphi \vee \psi), \Gamma \vdash \chi}(\vee\vdash) \quad \frac{\Gamma \vdash \sim^e \varphi_i}{\Gamma \vdash \sim^e(\varphi_1 \vee \varphi_2)}(\vdash\vee)(i = 1, 2)$$

$$\frac{\sim^{\circ} \varphi, \Gamma \vdash \chi \quad \sim^{\circ} \psi, \Gamma \vdash \chi}{\sim^{\circ}(\varphi \wedge \psi), \Gamma \vdash \chi}(\sim\wedge\vdash) \quad \frac{\Gamma \vdash \sim^{\circ} \varphi_i}{\Gamma \vdash \sim^{\circ}(\varphi_1 \wedge \varphi_2)}(\vdash\wedge)(i = 1, 2)$$

$$\frac{\sim^{\circ} \varphi_1, \sim^{\circ} \varphi_2, \Gamma \vdash \chi}{\sim^{\circ}(\varphi_1 \vee \varphi_2), \Gamma \vdash \chi}(\sim\vee\vdash) \quad \frac{\Gamma \vdash \sim^{\circ} \varphi \quad \Gamma \vdash \sim^{\circ} \psi}{\Gamma \vdash \sim^{\circ}(\varphi \vee \psi)}(\vdash\sim\vee)$$

$$\frac{\sim^{q}\varphi,\ \Gamma\vdash\psi}{\sim^{2p+q}\varphi,\ \Gamma\vdash\psi}(\sim^{2p+q}\top)\quad\frac{\Gamma\vdash\sim^{q}\varphi}{\Gamma\vdash\sim^{2p+q}\varphi}(\vdash\sim^{2p+q})$$

The numbers $e \in E[0, 2p+q)$ and $o \in O[0, 2p+q)$. The term with connective (s) in the below sequent of a logical rule is called *principal* .

A *derivation* in G_p^q is a finite tree-like structure $\mathfrak{D}$ in which each node is either an axiom or derived from child node (s) by a logical rule. The *height* of a derivation $\mathfrak{D}$, denoted by $|\mathfrak{D}|$, is the largest length of branches in $\mathfrak{D}$. A single node derivation has height 0. A sequent $\Gamma\vdash\psi$ is *derivable* in G_p^q, notation $\Gamma\vdash_{G_p^q}\psi$, if there is a derivation $\mathfrak{D}$. in G_p^q with root $\Gamma\vdash\psi$. Let $\Gamma\vdash_n\psi$ denote that there is a derivation $\mathfrak{D}$. of $\Gamma\vdash\psi$ in G_p^q with $|\mathfrak{D}|\leqslant n$.

A sequent rule (r) with premise $\Gamma_i\vdash\psi_i$ for $1\leqslant i\leqslant n$ and conclusion $\Gamma_0\vdash\psi_0$ is *admissible* in G_p^q, if $\Gamma_0\vdash_{G_p^q}\psi_0$ whenever $\Gamma_i\vdash_{G_p^q}\psi_i$ for all $1\leqslant i\leqslant n$. The sequent rule (r) is *height-preserving admissible* in G_p^q, if for any $k\geqslant 0$, $\Gamma_i\vdash_k\psi_i$ for $1\leqslant i\leqslant n$ imply $\Gamma_0\vdash_k\psi_0$.

Theorem 4.2. (Soundness) *If* $\Gamma\vdash_{G_p^q}\psi$. *then* $\Gamma\vdash_{\mathbb{K}_p^q}\psi$.

Proof: Assume $\Gamma\vdash_{G_p^q}\psi$. The proof proceeds by induction on the height of a derivation of $\Gamma\vdash\psi$ in G_p^q. It is trivial that all axioms G_p^q are valid in $\mathbb{K}_p^q$ It is also easy to show that all rules in G_p^q preserve validity in $\mathbb{K}_p^q$. The details of proof are omitted here.

4.2 Cut Admissibility

Now we shall prove the admissibility of structural rules of weakening and contractionin G_p^q. And then we show the admissibility of cut rule.

Lemma 4.3. The following weakening rule

$$\frac{\Gamma\vdash\psi}{\varphi,\ \Gamma\vdash\psi}(Wk)$$

is height-preserving admissible in G_p^q.

Proof: Assume $\Gamma\vdash_n\psi$. We show $\varphi,\ \Gamma\vdash_n\psi$ by induction on n. Suppose that $n=0$. Then $\Gamma\vdash\psi$ is an axiom. Then $\varphi,\ \Gamma\vdash\psi$ is also an axiom. Suppose $n>0$. Let $\Gamma\vdash\psi$ be obtained by a logical rule (r). Then we get $\varphi,\ \Gamma\vdash\psi$ by induction hypothesis and the rule (r).

Lemma 4.4. For any $n\geqslant 0$, $e\in E[0, 2p+q)$ and $o\in O[0, 2p+q)$. the following hold in G_p^q:

(1) *if* $\sim^e(\varphi\wedge\psi),\ \Gamma\vdash_n\chi$, *then* $\sim^e\varphi,\ \sim^e\psi,\ \Gamma\vdash_n\chi$.

(2) *if* $\sim^e(\varphi\vee\psi),\ \Gamma\vdash_n\chi$, *then* $\sim^e\varphi,\ \Gamma\vdash_n\chi$ *and* $\sim^e\psi,\ \Gamma\vdash_n\chi$.

(3) *if* $\sim{}^{\circ}(\varphi \wedge \psi), \Gamma \vdash_n \chi$, *then* $\sim{}^{\circ}\varphi, \Gamma \vdash_n \chi$ *and* $\sim{}^{\circ}\psi, \Gamma \vdash_n \chi$.

(4) *if* $\sim{}^{\circ}(\varphi \vee \psi), \Gamma \vdash_n \chi$, *then* $\vdash_n \sim{}^{\circ}\varphi, \sim{}^{\circ}\psi, \Gamma \vdash_n \chi$

(5) *if* $\sim^{2p+q}\varphi, \Gamma \vdash_n \psi$, *then* $\sim^{q}\varphi, \Gamma \vdash_n \psi$.

Proof: (1) Assume $\sim^{e}(\varphi \vee \psi), \Gamma \vdash_n \chi$. The proof proceeds by induction on n. The case that $n = 0$ is trivial. Suppose that $n > 0$ and $\sim^{e}(\varphi \wedge \psi), \Gamma \vdash \chi$ is obtained by a logical rule (r). If φ is not principal in (r), we obtain that $\sim^{e}\varphi, \sim^{e}\psi, \Gamma \vdash_n \chi$ by induction hypothesis and (r). If φ is principal in (r), $\sim^{e}\varphi, \sim^{e}\psi, \Gamma \vdash_{n-1} \chi$. (2) – (5) are shown similarly.

Lemma 4.5. The following contraction rule

$$\frac{\varphi, \varphi, \Gamma \vdash \psi}{\varphi, \Gamma \vdash \psi}(Ctr)$$

is height preserving-admissible in G_p^q.

Proof: Assume that $\varphi, \varphi, \Gamma \vdash_n \psi$. We show that $\varphi, \Gamma \vdash_n \psi$ by induction on n. Suppose that $n = 0$. Then $\varphi, \varphi, \Gamma \vdash \psi$ is an axiom. Hence $\varphi, \Gamma \vdash \psi$ is an axiom. Suppose that $n > 0$. Let $\varphi, \varphi, \Gamma \vdash \psi$ be obtained by a logical rule (r). If both occurrences of φ are not principal in (r), we obtain $\varphi, \Gamma \vdash_n \psi$ by induction hypothesis and the rule (r). Suppose that ϕ is principal in (r). Then (r) can only be a left logical rule. Assume that (r) is $(\wedge \varnothing)$. Let $\varphi = \sim^{e}(\chi_1 \wedge \chi_2)$ and $\Gamma = \sim^{e}(\chi_1 \wedge \chi_2), \Gamma'$ where $e \in E[0, 2p+q)$. Let the derivation end with

$$\frac{\sim^{e}\chi_1, \sim^{e}\chi_2, \sim^{e}(\chi_1 \wedge \chi_2), \Gamma' \vdash \psi}{\sim^{e}(\chi_1 \wedge \chi_2), \sim^{e}(\chi_1 \wedge \chi_2), \Gamma' \vdash \psi}(\wedge \vdash).$$

By Lemma 4.4 (1), $\sim^{e}\chi_1, \sim^{e}\chi_2, \sim^{e}\chi_1, \sim^{e}\chi_2, \Gamma' \vdash_{n-1} \psi$. By twice applications of induction hypothesis, $\sim^{e}\chi_1, \sim^{e}\chi_2, \Gamma' \vdash_{n-1} \psi$. By $(\wedge \varnothing)$, $\sim^{e}(\chi_1 \wedge \chi_2), \Gamma' \vdash_n \psi$. The remaining cases are shown similarly.

Lemma 4.6. For any $e \in E[0, 2p+q)$. and $o \in O[0, 2p+q)$. the following hold in G_p^q:

(1) *if* $\Gamma \vdash_{G_p^q} \sim^{e} \bot$, *then* $\Gamma \vdash_{G_p^q} \sim^{e} \psi$.

(2) *if* $\Gamma \vdash_{G_p^q} \sim{}^{\circ} \vdash$, *then* $\Gamma \vdash_{G_p^q} \psi$.

(3) *if* $\sim^{e}\top, \Gamma \vdash_{G_p^q} \psi$, *then* $\Gamma \vdash_{G_p^q} \psi$.

(4) *if* $\sim{}^{\circ}\bot, \Gamma \vdash_{G_p^q} \psi$, *then* $\Gamma \vdash_{G_p^q} \psi$.

Proof: (1) Assume that $\Gamma \vdash_n \sim^{e} \bot$. The proof proceeds by induction on n. Let $n = 0$. Then $\Gamma \vdash \sim^{e} \bot$ is an instance of $(\bot \top)$ or $(\sim \top \vdash)$. In each case, $\Gamma \vdash \psi$ is an axiom. Let $n > 0$ and $\Gamma \vdash \sim^{e} \bot$ be obtained by a logical rule (r). Obviously $\sim^{e}$

$\bot$ is not principal in (r). Hence (r) is a left logical rule. Then we obtain that $\Gamma \vdash_{G_p^q} \psi$ by induction hypothesis and (r). Note that (2) is shown similarly.

(3) Assume $\sim^e\top, \Gamma \vdash_n \psi$. We prove that $\Gamma \vdash_{G_p^q} \psi$ by induction on n. Let $n = 0$. Then $\sim^e\top, \Gamma \vdash \psi$ is an axiom. Suppose that $\sim^e\top, \Gamma \vdash \psi$ is an instance of (Id). Then $\psi = \sim^m x \in \Gamma$ for some $m \in [0, 2p + q)$. Hence $\Gamma \vdash \psi$ is an axiom. Suppose that $\sim^e \vdash$, $\Gamma \vdash \psi$ is an instance of $(\bot\top)$, $(\vdash\top)$, $(\sim\top\vdash)$ or $(\vdash\sim\bot)$. Then $\Gamma \vdash \psi$ is also an axiom. Now assume that $n > 0$. Let $\sim^e\top, \Gamma \vdash \psi$ be obtained by a logical rule (r). Obviously $\sim^e\top$ is not principal in (r). Then $\Gamma \vdash_{G_p^q} \psi$ by induction hypothesis and (r). Note that (4) is shown similarly.

Theorem 4.7. (Cut admissibility) *The following cut rule*

$$\frac{\Gamma \vdash \varphi \quad \varphi, \Delta \vdash \psi}{\Gamma, \Delta \vdash \psi}(\mathrm{Cut})$$

is admissible in G_p^q.

Proof: Assume that $\Gamma \vdash_m \varphi$ and $\varphi, \Delta \vdash_n \psi$. We prove that $\Gamma, \Delta \vdash_{G_p^q} \psi$ by simultaneous induction on m, n and the complexity of the cut term φ.

Assume that at least one of the premises of (Cut) is an axiom.

(1) The left premise $\Gamma \vdash \varphi$ is an axiom. We have the following cases:

(1.1) $\Gamma \vdash \varphi$ is an instance of (Id). Then $\varphi \in \Gamma$. The conclusion $\Gamma, \Delta \vdash \psi$ obtained from the right premise of (Cut) by (Wk) in Lemma 4.3.

(1.2) $\Gamma \vdash \varphi$ is an instance of $(\bot\vdash)$ or $(\sim\top\vdash)$. Then the conclusion is an instance of an axiom.

(1.3) $\Gamma \vdash \varphi$ is an instance of $(\vdash\bot)$. Let $\varphi = \sim^e\top$ where $e \in E[0, 2p + q)$. By $\sim^e\top, \Delta \vdash_{G_p^q} \psi$ and Lemma 4.6 (3), $\Delta \vdash_{G_p^q} \psi$. By (Wk), $\Gamma, \Delta \vdash_{G_p^q} \psi$.

(1.4) $\Gamma \vdash \varphi$ is an instance of $(\vdash\sim\bot)$. Let $\varphi = \sim^o\bot$ where $o \in O[0, 2p + q)$. By $\sim^o\bot, \Delta \vdash_{G_p^q} \psi$ and Lemma 4.6 (4), $\Delta \vdash_{G_p^q} \psi$. By (Wk), $\Gamma, \Delta \vdash_{G_p^q} \psi$.

(2) The right premise $\varphi, \Delta \vdash \psi$ is an axiom. We have four cases:

(2.1) $\varphi, \Delta \vdash \psi$ is an instance of (Id). If $\psi = \varphi$, the conclusion is obtained from the left premiss of (Cut) by (Wk). If $\psi \in \phi$, the conclusion is an instance of (Id).

(2.2) $\varphi, \Delta \vdash \psi$ is an instance of $(\vdash\top)$ or $(\vdash\sim\bot)$. Then the conclusion is an instance of an axiom.

(2.3) $\varphi, \Delta \vdash \psi$ is an instance of $(\bot\top)$ Let $e \in E[0, 2p+q)$. If $\sim^e \bot \in \Delta$, the conclusion is an axiom. Suppose that $\sim^e \bot \notin \Delta$. Then $\varphi = \sim^e \bot$. By $\Gamma \vdash_{G_p^q} \sim^e \top$ and Lemma 4.6 (1), $\Gamma \vdash_{G_p^q} \psi$ By (Wk), $\Gamma, \Delta \vdash_{G_p^q} \psi$.

(2.4) $\varphi, \Delta \vdash \psi$ is an instance of $(\sim\top\vdash)$. Let $o \in O[0, 2p+q)$. If $\sim{}^{o}\top \in \Delta$, the conclusion is an axiom. Suppose that $\sim{}^{o}\top \notin \Delta$, Then $\varphi = \sim{}^{o}\top$. By $\Gamma \vdash_{G_p^q} \sim{}^{o}\top$ and Lemma 4.6 (2), $\Gamma \vdash_{G_p^q} \psi$. By (Wk), $\Gamma, \Delta \vdash_{G_p^q} \psi$.

Assume that neither premises of (Cut) is an axiom. Let the left and right premises of (Cut) be obtained by (r_1) and (r_2) respectively.

(3) The cut term φ is not principal in (r_1). Then (r_1) is a left logical rule. We first apply (Cut) to the premis(es) of (r_1) and $\varphi, \Delta \vdash \psi$.. Then we have $\Gamma, \Delta \vdash_{G_p^q} \psi$. by (r_1). For example, let (r_1) be $(\sim\wedge\vdash)$ and $\Gamma = \sim{}^{o}(\chi_1 \wedge \chi_2), \Gamma'$ where $o \in [0, 2p+q)$. Let the derivation end with

$$\frac{\sim{}^{o}\chi_1, \Gamma' \vdash \varphi \quad \sim{}^{o}\chi_2, \Gamma' \vdash \varphi}{\sim{}^{o}(\chi_1 \wedge \chi_2), \Gamma' \vdash \varphi}(\sim\wedge\vdash)$$

By induction hypothesis, we have the following derivation:

$$\cfrac{\cfrac{\sim{}^{o}\chi_1, \Gamma' \vdash \varphi \quad \varphi, \Delta \vdash \psi}{\sim{}^{o}\chi_1, \Gamma', \Delta \vdash \psi}(Cut) \quad \cfrac{\sim{}^{o}\chi_2, \Gamma' \vdash \varphi \quad \varphi, \Delta \vdash \psi}{\sim{}^{o}\chi_2, \Gamma', \Delta \vdash \psi}(Cut)}{\sim{}^{o}(\chi_1 \wedge \chi_2), \Gamma', \Delta \vdash \psi}(\sim\wedge\vdash)$$

where (Cut) is applied to sequents with less height of derivation

(4) The cut term φ is principal only in (r_1). Then φ is not principal in (r_2). We first apply (Cut) to $\Gamma \vdash \varphi$ and the premiss(es) of (r_2). And then we have $\Gamma, \Delta \vdash_{G_p^q} \psi$ by (r_2). For example, let (r_2) be $(\sim\wedge\vdash)$ and $\Delta = \varphi, \sim{}^{o}(\chi_1 \wedge \chi_2), \Delta'$ where $o \in [0, 2p+q)$. Let the derivation end with

$$\frac{\varphi, \sim{}^{o}\chi_1, \vdash' \vdash \psi \quad \varphi, \sim{}^{o}\chi_2, \Delta' \vdash \psi}{\varphi, \sim{}^{o}(\chi_1 \wedge \chi_2), \Delta' \vdash \psi}(\sim\wedge\vdash)$$

By induction hypothesis, we have the following derivation:

$$\cfrac{\cfrac{\Gamma \vdash \varphi \quad \varphi, \sim{}^{o}\chi_1, \Delta' \vdash \psi}{\Gamma, \sim{}^{o}\chi_1, \Delta' \vdash \psi}(Cut) \quad \cfrac{\Gamma \vdash \varphi \quad \varphi, \sim{}^{o}\chi_2, \Delta' \vdash \psi}{\Gamma, \sim{}^{o}\chi_2, \Delta' \vdash \psi}(Cut)}{\Gamma, \sim{}^{o}(\chi_1 \wedge \chi_2), \Delta' \vdash \psi}(\sim\wedge\vdash)$$

where (Cut) is applied to sequents with less height of derivation.

(5) The cut term φ is principal in both (r_1) and (r_2). The proof proceeds by induction on the complexity of φ. We have the following cases:

(5.1) $\varphi = \sim^{e}(\varphi_1 \wedge \varphi_2)$ where $e \in E[0, 2p+q)$. Let derivations of premisses of (Cut) end with

$$\frac{\Gamma \vdash \sim^{e}\varphi_1 \quad \Gamma \vdash \sim^{e}\varphi_2}{\Gamma \vdash \sim^{e}(\varphi_1 \wedge \varphi_2)}(\vdash \wedge) \qquad \frac{\sim^{e}\varphi_1, \sim^{e}\varphi_2, \Delta \vdash \psi}{\sim^{e}(\varphi_1 \wedge \varphi_2), \Delta \vdash \psi}(\wedge \vdash)$$

We have the following derivation

$$\frac{\dfrac{\Gamma \vdash \sim^{e}\varphi_2 \quad \dfrac{\Gamma \vdash \sim^{e}\varphi_1 \quad \sim^{e}\varphi_1, \sim^{e}\varphi_2, \Delta \vdash \psi}{\Gamma, \sim^{e}\varphi_2, \Delta \vdash \psi}(\mathrm{Cut})}{\Gamma, \Gamma, \Delta \vdash \psi}(\mathrm{Cut})}{\Gamma, \Delta \vdash \psi}(\mathrm{Ctr}*)$$

where (Ctr*) means finitely many times application of (Ctr), and (Cut) is applied to sequents with cut terms of less complicated. Note that (Ctr) is height-preserving admissible in G_p^q (Lemma 4.5).

(5.2) $\varphi = \sim^{e}(\varphi_1 \wedge \varphi_2)$ where $e \in E[0, 2p+q)$. Let derivations of premisses of (Cut) end with

$$\frac{\Gamma \vdash \sim^{e}\varphi_i}{\Gamma \vdash \sim^{e}(\varphi_1 \vee \varphi_2)}(\vdash \vee) \qquad \frac{\sim^{e}\varphi_1, \Delta \vdash \psi \quad \sim^{e}\varphi_2, \Delta \vdash \psi}{\sim^{e}(\varphi_1 \vee \varphi_2), \Delta \vdash \psi}(\wedge \vdash)$$

We have the following derivation:

$$\frac{\Gamma \vdash \sim^{e}\varphi_i \quad \sim^{e}\varphi_i, \Delta \vdash \psi}{\Gamma, \Delta \vdash \psi}(\mathrm{Cut})$$

where (Cut) is applied to sequents with a cut term of less complicated.

(5.3) $\varphi = \sim{}^{o}(\varphi_1 \vee \varphi_2)$ where $o \in O[0, 2p+q)$. Let derivations of premisses of (Cut) end with

$$\frac{\Gamma \vdash \sim{}^{o}\varphi_i}{\Gamma \vdash \sim{}^{o}(\varphi_1 \wedge \varphi_2)}(\vdash \sim \wedge) \qquad \frac{\sim{}^{o}\varphi_1, \Delta \vdash \psi \quad \sim{}^{o}\varphi_2, \Delta \vdash \psi}{\sim{}^{o}(\varphi_1 \wedge \varphi_2), \Delta \vdash \psi}(\sim \wedge \vdash)$$

We have the following derivation

$$\frac{\Gamma \vdash \sim{}^{o}\varphi_i \quad \sim{}^{o}\varphi_i, \Delta \vdash \psi}{\Gamma, \Delta \vdash \psi}(\mathrm{Cut})$$

where (Cut) is applied to sequents with a cut term of less complicated.

(5.4) $\varphi = \sim{}^{o}(\varphi_1 \vee \varphi_2)$ where $o \in O[0, 2p+q)$. Let derivations of premisses of (Cut) end with

$$\frac{\Gamma \vdash \sim{}^{o}\varphi_1 \quad \Gamma \vdash \sim{}^{o}\varphi_2}{\Gamma \vdash \sim{}^{o}(\varphi_1 \vee \varphi_2)}(\vdash \sim \vee) \qquad \frac{\sim{}^{o}\varphi_1, \sim{}^{o}\varphi_2, \Delta \vdash \psi}{\sim{}^{o}(\varphi_1 \vee \varphi_2), \Delta \vdash \psi}(\sim \vee \vdash)$$

We have the following derivation

$$\dfrac{\Gamma \vdash \sim{}^{\circ}\varphi_2 \quad \dfrac{\Gamma \vdash \sim{}^{\circ}\varphi_1 \quad \sim{}^{\circ}\varphi_1, \sim{}^{\circ}\varphi_2, \Delta \vdash \psi}{\Gamma, \sim{}^{\circ}\varphi_2, \Delta \vdash \psi}(\mathrm{Cut})}{\dfrac{\Gamma, \Gamma, \Delta \vdash \psi}{\Gamma, \Delta \vdash \psi}(\mathrm{Ctr}^*)}(\mathrm{Cut})$$

where (Ctr *) means finitely many times application of (Ctr), and (Cut) is applied to sequents with cut terms of less complicated.

(5.5) $\varphi = \sim^{2p+q}\varphi'$. Let the derivations of premises of (Cut) end with

$$\dfrac{\Gamma \vdash \sim^{q}\varphi'}{\Gamma \vdash \sim^{2p+q}\varphi'}(\vdash \sim^{2p+q}) \qquad \dfrac{\sim^{q}\varphi', \Delta \vdash \psi}{\sim^{2p+q}\varphi', \Delta \vdash \psi}(\sim^{2p+q}\vdash)$$

We have the following derivation

$$\dfrac{\Gamma \vdash \sim^{q}\varphi' \quad \sim^{q}\varphi', \Delta \vdash \psi}{\Gamma, \Delta \vdash \psi}(\mathrm{Cut})$$

where (Cut) is applied to sequents with a cut term of less complicated.

4.3 Completeness and Decidability

Now we shall prove the completeness of G_p^q by establishing the equivalence between S_p^q and G_p^q. Furthermore, the sequent system G_p^q is shown to be decidable and terminating.

Lemma 4.8. *For any term φ and $n \geqslant 0$, $\sim^n \varphi, \Gamma \vdash_{G_p^q} \sim^n \varphi$.*

Proof: The proof proceeds by induction on the complexity of φ. Assume that $c(\varphi) = 0$. We have the following cases:

(1) $\varphi = x$. If $n < 2p + q$, then $\sim^n x, \Gamma \vdash \sim^n x$ is an instance of (Id). Suppose $n \geqslant 2p + q$. There are numbers $r \in [0, 2p + q)$. and $m \geqslant 1$ such that $n = 2mp + r$. Then $\sim^r x, \Gamma \vdash \sim^r x$ is an instance of (Id). By m times application of $(\sim^{2p+q}\vdash)$ and $(\vdash \sim^{2p+q})$, $\sim^n x, \Gamma \vdash_{G_p^q} \sim^n x$.

(2) $\varphi = \top$. Suppose $n < 2p + q$. If $n = 2k + 1$, then $\sim^n\top, \Gamma \vdash \sim^n\top$ is an instance of $(\sim \top \vdash)$. If $n = 2k$, then $\sim^n\top, \Gamma \vdash \sim^n\top$ is an instance of $(\vdash \top)$. Suppose $n \geqslant 2p + q$. There are numbers $r \in [0, 2p + q)$. and $m \geqslant 1$ such that $m = 2mp + r$, Since r is either even or odd, by $(\sim \top \vdash)$ or $(\vdash \top)$, $\sim^r\top, \Gamma \vdash_{G_p^q} \sim^r\top$. By m times application of $(\sim^{2p+q})$, $\sim^n\top$, $\Gamma \vdash_{G_p^q} \sim^r\top$. By m times application of $(\vdash \sim^{2p+q})$, $\sim^n\top, \Gamma \vdash_{G_p^q} \sim^n\top$.

(3) $\varphi = \bot$. The proof is similar to the case (2).

Let $c(\varphi) > 0$. Suppose that $\sim^n \varphi', \Gamma \vdash_{G_p^q} \sim^n \varphi'$ for all terms φ' such that $c(\varphi') < c(\varphi)$. Assume that $n \geqslant 2p + q$. There are numbers $r \in [0, 2p + q)$ and $m \geqslant 1$ such that $n = 2mp + r$. Clearly $c(\sim^r \varphi) < c(\sim^n \varphi)$. By induction hypothesis,

$\sim^r \varphi, \Gamma \vdash_{G_p^q} \sim^r \varphi$. By m times application of $(\sim^{2p+q}\top)$ and m times application of $(\vdash \sim^{2p+q})$, $\sim^n \varphi, \Gamma \vdash_{G_p^q} \sim^n \varphi$. Now assume $n < 2p + q$. We have the following cases:

(4) $\varphi = (\varphi_1 \wedge \varphi_1)$. Let $n = e \in E[0, 2p + q)$. By induction hypothesis, $\sim^e \varphi_1, \Gamma \vdash_{G_p^q} \sim^e \varphi_1$ and $\sim^e \varphi_2, \Gamma \vdash_{G_p^q} \sim^e \varphi_2$. By (Wk), $\sim^e \varphi_1, \sim^e \varphi_2, \Gamma \vdash_{G_p^q} \sim^e \varphi_1$ and $\sim^e \varphi_1, \sim^e \varphi_2, \Gamma \vdash_{G_p^q} \sim^e \varphi_2$. By $(\vdash \wedge)$ and $(\wedge \varnothing)$, $\sim^e (\varphi_1 \wedge \varphi_2), \Gamma \vdash_{G_p^q} \sim^e (\varphi_1 \wedge \varphi_2)$. Let $n = o \in O[0, 2p + q)$. By induction hypothesis, $\sim^\circ \varphi_1, \Gamma \vdash_{G_p^q} \sim^\circ \varphi_1$ and $\sim^\circ \varphi_2, \Gamma \vdash_{G_p^q} \sim^\circ \varphi_2$. By $(\vdash \sim \wedge)$ and $(\sim \wedge \varnothing)$, $\sim^\circ (\varphi_1 \wedge \varphi_2), \Gamma \vdash_{G_p^q} \sim^\circ (\varphi_1 \wedge \varphi_2)$.

(5) $\varphi = \varphi_1 \vee \varphi_2$. Let $n = e \in E[2p + q)$. By induction hypothesis, $\sim^e \varphi_1, \Gamma \vdash_{G_p^q} \sim^e \varphi_1$ and $\sim^e \varphi_2, \Gamma \vdash_{G_p^q} \sim^e \varphi_2$. By $(\vdash \vee)$ and $(\vee \varnothing)$, $\sim^e (\varphi_1 \vee \varphi_2), \Gamma \vdash_{G_p^q} \sim^e (\varphi_1 \vee \varphi_2)$. Let $n = o \in O[2p + q)$. By induction hypothesis, $\sim^\circ \varphi_1, \Gamma \vdash_{G_p^q} \sim^\circ \varphi_q$ and $\sim^\circ \varphi_2, \Gamma \vdash_{G_p^q} \sim^\circ \varphi_2$. By (Wk), $\sim^\circ \varphi_1, \sim^\circ \varphi_2, \Gamma \vdash_{G_p^q} \sim^\circ \varphi_1$ and $\sim^\circ \varphi_1, \sim^\circ \varphi_2, \Gamma \vdash_{G_p^q} \sim^\circ \varphi_2$. By $(\sim \vee \varnothing)$ and $(\vdash \sim \vee)$, $\sim^\circ (\varphi_1 \vee \varphi_2), \Gamma \vdash_{G_p^q} \sim^\circ (\varphi_1 \vee \varphi_2)$.

(6) $\varphi = \sim \psi$. By induction hypothesis, $\sim^{n+1} \psi, , \Gamma \vdash_{G_p^q} \sim^{n+1} \psi$.

Lemma 4.9. *The following rules are admissible in* G_p^q:

$$\frac{\varphi, \Gamma \vdash \psi}{\varphi \wedge \chi, \Gamma \vdash \psi \wedge \chi}(\wedge), \quad \frac{\varphi, \Gamma \vdash \psi}{\varphi \vee \chi, \Gamma \vdash \psi \vee \chi}(\vee).$$

Proof: By Lemma 4.8, $\varphi, \chi, \Gamma \vdash_{G_p^q} \chi$ and $\chi, \Gamma \vdash_{G_p^q} \chi$. For the admissibility of $(\wedge)$, we have the following derivation:

$$\dfrac{\dfrac{\dfrac{\varphi, \Gamma \vdash \psi}{\varphi, \chi, \Gamma \vdash \psi}(\mathrm{Wk})}{\varphi \wedge \chi, \Gamma \vdash \psi}(\wedge \vdash) \quad \dfrac{\varphi, \chi, \Gamma \vdash \chi}{\varphi \wedge \chi, \Gamma \vdash \chi}(\wedge \vdash)}{\varphi \wedge \chi, \Gamma \vdash \psi \wedge \chi}(\vdash \wedge)$$

The admissibility of $(\vee)$ is shown similarly.

Lemma 4.10. *For all* $k \geqslant 0$, *the following sequents are provable in* G_p^q:

(1) $\varphi \wedge (\psi \vee \chi) \vdash (\varphi \wedge \psi) \vee (\varphi \wedge \chi)$ *and* $(\varphi \wedge \psi) \vee (\varphi \wedge \chi) \vdash \varphi \wedge (\psi \vee \chi)$.

(2) $\varphi \vee (\psi \wedge \chi) \vdash (\varphi \vee \psi) \wedge (\varphi \vee \chi)$ *and* $(\varphi \vee \psi) \wedge (\varphi \vee \chi) \vdash \varphi \vee (\psi \wedge \chi)$.

(3) $\sim^q \varphi \vdash \sim^{2p+q} \varphi$ *and* $\sim^{2p+q} \varphi \vdash \sim^q \varphi$.

(4) $\sim^{2k} \varphi_1 \wedge \sim^{2k} \varphi_2 \vdash \sim^{2k} (\varphi_1 \wedge \varphi_2)$.

(5) $\sim^{2k}\varphi_1 \vee \sim^{2k}\varphi_2 \vdash \sim^{2k}(\varphi_1 \vee \varphi_2)$.
(6) $\sim^{2k+1}\varphi_1 \wedge \sim^{2k+1}\varphi_2 \vdash \sim^{2k+1}(\varphi_1 \vee \varphi_2)$.
(7) $\sim^{2k+1}\varphi_1 \vee \sim^{2k+1}\varphi_2 \vdash \sim^{2k+1}(\varphi_1 \wedge \varphi_2)$.

Proof: It is easy to derive sequents in (1) – (3). For (4), assume $2k < 2p + q$. By Lemma 4.8, $\sim^{2k}\varphi_1, \sim^{2k}\varphi_2 \vdash_{G_p^q} \sim^{2k}\varphi_1$ and $\sim^{2k}\varphi_1, \sim^{2k}\varphi_2 \vdash_{G_p^q} \sim^{2k}\varphi_2$. By ($\vdash \wedge$), $\sim^{2k}\varphi_1, \sim^{2k}\varphi_2 \vdash_{G_p^q} \sim^{2k}(\varphi_1 \wedge \varphi_2)$. By ($\wedge \varnothing$), $\sim^{2k}\varphi_1 \wedge \sim^{2k}\varphi_2 \vdash_{G_p^q} \sim^{2k}(\varphi_1 \wedge \varphi_2)$. Assume $2k \geqslant 2p + q$. There are numbers $r \in [0, 2p + q)$ and $m \geqslant 1$ with $2k = 2mp + r$. Then r is even. Hence $\sim^{r}\varphi_1, \sim^{r}\varphi_2 \vdash_{G_p^q} \sim^{r}(\varphi_1 \wedge \varphi_2)$. By applying ($\sim^{2p+q}\top$), $\sim^{2k}\varphi_1, \sim^{2k}\varphi_2 \vdash_{G_p^q} \sim^{2k}(\varphi_1 \wedge \varphi_2)$. By applying ($\vdash \sim^{2p+q}$), $\sim^{2k}\varphi_1, \sim^{2k}\varphi_2 \vdash_{G_p^q} \sim^{2k}(\varphi_1 \wedge \varphi_2)$. By ($\wedge \varnothing$), $\sim^{2k}\varphi_1 \wedge \sim^{2k}\varphi_2 \vdash_{G_p^q} \sim^{2k}(\varphi_1 \wedge \varphi_2)$. Sequents (5) – (7) are shown similarly.

Lemma 4.11. *The following contraposition rule is admissible in* G_p^q:

$$\frac{\Gamma \vdash \psi}{\sim \psi \vdash \bigvee \sim \Gamma}(CP).$$

Proof: Assume $\Gamma \vdash_n \psi$. The proof proceeds by induction on n.

(1) $n = 0$. Then $\Gamma \vdash \psi$ is an axiom. We have the following cases:

(1.1) $\Gamma \vdash \psi$ is an instance of (Id). Then $\psi \in \Gamma$. By Lemma 4.8, $\sim \psi \vdash_{G_p^q} \sim \psi$. By ($\vdash \vee$), $\sim \psi \vdash_{G_p^q} \bigvee \sim \Gamma$.

(1.2) $\Gamma \vdash \psi$ is an instance of ($\bot\top$). Let $\Gamma = \sim^{e}\bot, \Gamma'$ where $e \in E[0, 2p + q)$. Then $e + 1 \leqslant 2p + q$. Assume $e + 1 < 2p + q$. Then $\sim \psi \vdash \sim^{e+1}\bot$ is an instance of ($\vdash \sim \bot$). By ($\vdash \vee$), $\sim \psi \vdash_{G_p^q} \sim^{e+1}\bot \vee \bigvee \sim \Gamma'$. Assume $e + 1 = 2p + q$. Clearly $q < 2p + q$ and q is odd. Then $\sim \psi \vdash \sim^{q}\bot$ is an instance of ($\vdash \sim \bot$). By ($\vdash \sim^{2p+q}$), $\sim \psi \vdash_{G_p^q} \sim^{e+1}\bot$. By ($\vdash \vee$), $\sim \psi \vdash_{G_p^q} \sim^{e+1}\bot \vee (\bigvee \sim \Gamma')$.

(1.3) $\Gamma \vdash \psi$ is an instance of ($\vdash \sim \bot$). Let $\psi = \sim^{2k+1}\bot$ where $2k + 1 \in [0, 2p + q)$. Then $2k + 2 \leqslant 2p + q$. Assume $2k + 2 < 2p + q$. Then $\sim^{2k+2}\bot \vdash \bigvee \sim \Gamma$ is an instance of ($\bot\top$). Assume $2k + 2 = 2p + q$. Then $q < 2p + q$ and q is even. Then $\sim^{q}\bot \vdash \bigvee \sim \Gamma$ is an instance of ($\bot\top$). By ($\sim^{2p+q}\top$), $\sim^{2k+2}\bot \vdash_{G_p^q} \bigvee \sim \Gamma$.

(1.4) $\Gamma \vdash \psi$ is an instance of ($\sim \top \vdash$). The proof is similar to Case (1.2).

(1.5) $\Gamma \vdash \psi$ is an instance of ($\vdash \top$). The proof is similar to Case (1.3).

(2) $n > 0$. Then $\Gamma \vdash \psi$ is obtained by a logical rule (r).

(2.1) (r) is $(\wedge \vdash)$. Let $\Gamma = \sim^{e}(\varphi_1 \wedge \varphi_2), \Gamma'$ and the premiss of (r) be $\sim^{e}\varphi_1, \sim^{e}\varphi_2, \Gamma' \vdash \psi$ where $e \in E[0, 2p+q)$. By induction hypothesis, $\sim\psi \vdash_{G_p^q} \sim^{e+1}\varphi_1 \vee \sim^{e+1}\varphi_2 \vee (\bigvee \sim\Gamma')$. By Lemma 4.10 (7), $\sim^{e+1}\varphi_1 \vee \sim^{e+1}\varphi_2 \vdash_{G_p^q} \sim^{e+1}(\varphi_1 \wedge \varphi_2)$. By $(\vee)$ in Lemma 4.9, $\sim^{e+1}\varphi_1 \vee \sim^{e+1}\varphi_2 \vee \bigvee \sim\Gamma' \vdash_{G_p^q} \sim^{e+1}(\varphi_1 \wedge \varphi_2) \vee (\bigvee \sim\Gamma')$. By (Cut), $\sim\psi \vdash_{G_p^q} \sim^{e+1}(\varphi_1 \wedge \varphi_2) \vee (\bigvee \sim\Gamma')$.

(2.2) (r) is $(\vdash \wedge)$. Let $\psi = \sim^{e}(\psi_1 \wedge \psi_2)$ and the premises of (r) be $\Gamma \vdash \sim^{e}\psi_1$ and $\Gamma \vdash \sim^{e}\psi_2$ where $e \in E[0, 2p+q)$. By induction hypothesis, $\sim^{e+1}\psi_1 \vdash_{G_p^q} \bigvee \sim\Gamma$ and $\sim^{e+1}\psi_2 \vdash_{G_p^q} \bigvee \sim\Gamma$. Clearly $e+1 \leqslant 2p+q$. If $e+1 < 2p+q$, by $(\sim \wedge \varnothing)$, we get $\sim^{e+1}(\psi_1 \wedge \psi_2) \vdash_{G_p^q} \bigvee \sim\Gamma$. Suppose $e+1 = 2p+q$. Then $q < 2p+q$ and q is odd. Clearly $\sim^{q}\psi_1 \vdash_{G_p^q} \sim^{e+1}\psi_1$ and $\sim^{q}\psi_2 \vdash_{G_p^q} \sim^{e+1}\psi_2$. By (Cut), $\sim^{q}\psi_1 \vdash_{G_p^q} \bigvee \sim\Gamma$ and $\sim^{q}\psi_2 \vdash_{G_p^q} \bigvee \sim\Gamma$. By $(\sim \wedge \varnothing)$, $\sim^{q}(\psi_1 \wedge \psi_2) \vdash_{G_p^q} \bigvee \sim\Gamma$. By $(\sim^{2p+q}\top)$, $\sim^{e+1}(\psi_1 \wedge \psi_2) \vdash_{G_p^q} \bigvee \sim\Gamma$.

(2.3) (r) is $(\vee \varnothing)$. Let $\Gamma = \sim^{e}(\varphi_1 \vee \varphi_2), \Gamma'$ and the premises of (r) be $\sim^{e}\varphi_1, \Gamma' \vdash \psi$ and $\sim^{e}\varphi_2, \Gamma' \vdash \psi$ where $e \in E[0, 2p+q)$. By induction hypothesis, $\sim\psi \vdash_{G_p^q} \sim^{e+1}\varphi_1 \vee (\bigvee \sim\Gamma')$ and $\sim\psi \vdash_{G_p^q} \sim^{e+1}\varphi_2 \vee (\bigvee \sim\Gamma')$. By $(\vdash \wedge)$, $\sim\psi \vdash_{G_p^q} (\sim^{e+1}\varphi_1 \vee (\bigvee \sim\Gamma')) \wedge (\sim^{e+1}\varphi_2 \vee (\bigvee \sim\Gamma'))$. It is easy to show that $(\sim^{e+1}\varphi_1 \vee (\bigvee \sim\Gamma')) \wedge (\sim^{e+1}\varphi_2 \vee (\bigvee \sim\Gamma')) \vdash_{G_p^q} (\sim^{e+1}\varphi_1 \wedge \sim^{e+1}\varphi_2) \vee. (\bigvee \sim\Gamma')$ Clearly $\sim^{e+1}\varphi_1 \wedge \sim^{e+1}\varphi_2 \vdash_{G_p^q} \sim^{e+1}(\varphi_1 \vee \varphi_2)$. By $(\vee)$, $(\sim^{e+1}\varphi_1 \wedge \sim^{e+1}\varphi_2) \vee (\bigvee \sim\Gamma') \vdash_{G_p^q} \sim^{e+1}(\varphi_1 \vee \varphi_2) \bigvee \sim\Gamma'$. By (Cut), $\sim\psi \vdash_{G_p^q} \sim^{e+1}(\varphi_1 \vee \varphi_2) \bigvee \sim\Gamma'$.

(2.4) (r) is $(\vdash \vee)$. Let $\psi = \sim^{e}(\varphi_1 \vee \varphi_2)$ and the premises of (r) be $\Gamma \vdash \sim^{e}\psi_i$ where $e \in E[0, 2p+q)$. By induction hypothesis, $\sim^{e+1}\varphi_i \vdash_{G_p^q} \bigvee \sim\Gamma$. Clearly $e+1 \leqslant 2p+q$. Assume $e+1 < 2p+q$. By (Wk), $\sim^{e+1}\psi_1, \sim^{e+1}\psi_2 \vdash_{G_p^q} \bigvee \sim\Gamma$. By $(\sim \vee \varnothing)$, $\sim^{e+1}(\psi_1 \vee \psi_2) \vdash_{G_p^q} \bigvee \sim\Gamma$. Assume $e+1 = 2p+q$. Then $q < 2p+q$ and q is odd. Clearly $\sim^{q}\psi_i \vdash_{G_p^q} \sim^{e+1}\psi_i$. By (Cut) and induction hypothesis, $\sim^{q}\psi_i \vdash_{G_p^q} \bigvee \sim\Gamma$. By (Wk), $\sim^{q}\psi_1, \sim^{q}\psi_2 \vdash_{G_p^q} \bigvee \sim\Gamma$. By $(\sim \vee \varnothing)$, $\sim^{q}(\psi_1 \vee \psi_2) \vdash_{G_p^q} \bigvee \sim\Gamma$. By $(\sim^{2p+q}\top)$, $\sim^{e+1}(\psi_1 \vee \psi_2) \vdash_{G_p^q} \bigvee \sim\Gamma$.

(2.5) (r) is $(\sim\wedge\varnothing)$. Let $\Gamma=\sim^{\circ}(\varphi_1\wedge\varphi_2)$, Γ' and the premises of (r) be $\sim^{\circ}\varphi_1,\Gamma'\vdash\psi$ and $\sim^{\circ}\varphi_2,\Gamma'\vdash\psi$ where $o\in O[0,2p+q)$. By induction hypothesis, $\sim\psi\vdash_{G_p^q}\sim^{o+1}\varphi_1\vee(\bigvee\sim\Gamma')$ and $\sim\psi\vdash_{G_p^q}\sim^{o+1}\varphi_2\vee(\bigvee\sim\Gamma')$. By $(\vdash\wedge)$, $\sim\psi\vdash_{G_p^q}(\sim^{o+1}\varphi_1\vee\bigvee\sim\Gamma')\wedge(\sim^{o+1}\varphi_2\vee(\bigvee\sim\Gamma'))$. It is easy to show that $(\sim^{o+1}\varphi_1\vee(\bigvee\sim\Gamma'))\wedge(\sim^{o+1}\varphi_2\vee(\bigvee\sim\Gamma'))\vdash_{G_p^q}(\sim^{o+1}\varphi_1\wedge\sim^{o+1}\varphi_2)\vee.(\bigvee\sim\Gamma')$ Clearly $\sim^{o+1}\varphi_1\wedge\sim^{o+1}\varphi_2\vdash_{G_p^q}\sim^{o+1}(\varphi_1\wedge\varphi_2)$. By $(\vee)$ in Lemma 4.9, $(\sim^{o+1}\varphi_1\wedge\sim^{o+1}\varphi_2)\vee(\bigvee\sim\Gamma')\vdash_{G_p^q}\sim^{o+1}(\varphi_1\wedge\varphi_2)\bigvee\sim\Gamma'$. By (Cut), $\sim\psi\vdash_{G_p^q}\sim^{o+1}(\varphi_1\wedge\varphi_2)\bigvee\sim\Gamma'$.

(2.6) (r) is $(\vdash\sim\wedge)$. Let $\psi=\sim^{\circ}(\psi_1\wedge\psi_2)$ and the premises of (r) be $\Gamma\vdash\sim^{\circ}\psi_i$ where $o\in O[0,2p+q)$. By induction hypothesis, $\vdash\sim^{o+1}\psi_i\vdash\bigvee\sim\Gamma$. Clearly $o+1\leqslant 2p+q$. Assume $o+1<2p+q$. By applying $(\vee\varnothing)$ to induction hypothesis, $\vdash\sim^{o+1}(\psi_1\vee\psi_2)\vdash\bigvee\sim\Gamma$. Assume $o+1=2p+q$. Then $q<2p+q$ and q is even. Clearly $\sim^{q}\psi_i\vdash_{G_p^q}\sim^{o+1}\psi_i$. By (Cut), $\sim^{q}\psi_i\vdash_{G_p^q}\bigvee\sim\Gamma$. By (Wk), $\sim^{q}\psi_1,\sim^{q}\psi_2\vdash_{G_p^q}\bigvee\sim\Gamma$. By $(\vee\varnothing)$, $\sim^{q}(\psi_1\vee\psi_2)\vdash_{G_p^q}\bigvee\sim\Gamma$. By $(\sim^{2p+q}\mathsf{T})$, $\sim^{o+1}(\psi_1\vee\psi_2)\vdash_{G_p^q}\bigvee\sim\Gamma$.

(2.7) (r) is $(\sim\vee\vdash)$. Let $\Gamma=\sim^{\circ}(\varphi_1\vee\varphi_2)$, Γ' and the premiss of (r) be $\sim^{\circ}\varphi_1,\sim^{\circ}\varphi_2,\Gamma'\vdash\psi$ where $o\in O[0,2p+q)$. By induction hypothesis, $\sim\psi\vdash_{G_p^q}\sim^{o+1}\varphi_1\vee\sim^{o+1}\varphi_2\vee(\bigvee\sim\Gamma')$. Clearly $\sim^{o+1}\varphi_1\vee\sim^{o+1}\varphi_2\vdash_{G_p^q}\sim^{o+1}(\varphi_1\vee\varphi_2)$. By $(\vee)$ in Lemma 4.9, $\sim^{o+1}\varphi_1\vee\sim^{o+1}\varphi_2\vee(\bigvee\sim\Gamma')\vdash_{G_p^q}\sim^{o+1}(\varphi_1\vee\varphi_2)\vee(\bigvee\sim\Gamma')$. By (Cut), $\sim\psi\vdash_{G_p^q}\sim^{o+1}(\varphi_1\vee\varphi_2)\vee(\bigvee\sim\Gamma')$.

(2.8) (r) is $(\vdash\sim\wedge)$. Let $\psi=\sim^{\circ}(\psi_1\vee\psi_2)$ and the premises of (r) be $\Gamma\vdash\sim^{\circ}\psi_1$ and $\Gamma\vdash\sim^{\circ}\psi_2$ where $o\in O[0,2p+q)$. By induction hypothesis, $\sim^{o+1}\psi_1\vdash_{G_p^q}\bigvee\sim\Gamma$ and $\sim^{o+1}\psi_2\vdash_{G_p^q}\bigvee\sim\Gamma$. Clearly $o+1\leqslant 2p+q$. If $o+1<2p+q$, by $(\vee\varnothing)$, we get $\sim^{o+1}(\psi_1\vee\psi_2)\vdash_{G_p^q}\bigvee\sim\Gamma$. Suppose $o+1=2p+q$. Then $q<2p+q$ and q is even. Clearly $\sim^{q}\psi_1\vdash_{G_p^q}\sim^{o+1}\psi_1$ and $\sim^{q}\psi_2\vdash_{G_p^q}\sim^{o+1}\psi_2$. By (Cut), $\sim^{q}\psi_1\vdash_{G_p^q}\bigvee\sim\Gamma$ and $\sim^{q}\psi_2\vdash_{G_p^q}\bigvee\sim\Gamma$. By $(\vee\varnothing)$, $\sim^{q}(\psi_1\vee\psi_2)\vdash_{G_p^q}\bigvee\sim\Gamma$. By $(\sim^{2p+q}\mathsf{T})$, $\sim^{o+1}(\psi_1\vee\psi_2)\vdash_{G_p^q}\bigvee\sim\Gamma$.

(2.9) (r) is $(\sim^{2p+q}\vdash)$. Let $\Gamma = \sim^{2p+q}\varphi, \Gamma'$ and the premises of (r) be $\sim^{q}\varphi, \Gamma' \vdash \psi$. By induction hypothesis, $\sim\psi \vdash_{G_p^q} \sim^{q}\sim\varphi \vee (\bigvee \sim\Gamma')$. Clearly $\sim^{q}\sim\varphi \vdash_{G_p^q} \sim^{2p+q}\sim\varphi$. By $(\vee)$ in Lemma 4.9, $\sim^{q}\sim\varphi \vee (\bigvee \sim\Gamma') \vdash_{G_p^q} \sim^{2p+q}\sim\varphi \vee (\bigvee \sim\Gamma')'$. By (Cut), $\sim\psi \vdash_{G_p^q} \sim^{2p+q}\sim\varphi \vee (\bigvee \sim\Gamma')$.

(2.10) (r) is $(\vdash\sim^{2p+q})$. Let $\psi = \sim^{2p+q}\psi'$ and the premises of (r) be $\Gamma \vdash \sim^{q}\psi'$. By induction hypothesis, $\sim^{q}\sim\psi' \vdash_{G_p^q} \bigvee\sim\Gamma$. By $(\sim^{2p+q}\top)$, $\sim^{2p+q}\sim\psi' \vdash_{G_p^q} \bigvee\sim\Gamma$.

Lemma 4.12. *If* $\Gamma \vdash_{S_p^q} \psi$ *, then* $\Gamma \vdash_{G_p^q} \psi$.

Proof: *Assume that* $\Gamma \vdash_{S_p^q} \psi$. The proof proceeds by induction on the height of a derivation of $\Gamma \vdash \psi$ in S_p^q. Suppose that$\Gamma \vdash \psi$ is an axiom of S_p^q. By Lemmas 4.8 and 4.10, $\Gamma \vdash_{G_p^q} \psi$. Suppose that$\Gamma \vdash \psi$ is obtained by a rule (r) of S_p^q. By induction hypothesis, one can easily get that $\Gamma \vdash_{G_p^q} \psi$. By Lemmas 4.3, 4.5 and Theorem 4.7, the structural rules and the cut rule of $S_p^q$are admissible in G_p^q. The case that (r) is (CP) is treated with Lemma 4.11. The remaining rules of $S_p^q$are easily transformed into rules which are admissible in G_p^q.

Theorem 4.13. (Completeness) *If* $\Gamma \models_{\mathbb{K}_p^q} \psi$ *, then* $\Gamma \vdash_{G_p^q} \psi$.

Proof: Assume that $\Gamma \models_{\mathbb{K}_p^q} \psi$. Then $\bigwedge\Gamma \models_{\mathbb{K}_p^q} \psi$. By the completeness of S_p^q (Theorem 2.10), $\bigwedge\Gamma \vdash_{S_p^q} \psi$. By Lemma 4.12, we obtain that $\bigwedge\Gamma \vdash_{G_p^q} \psi$. It is easy to show that $\Gamma \vdash_{G_p^q} \bigwedge\Gamma$. By (Cut), $\Gamma \vdash_{G_p^q} \psi$.

Corollary 4.14. $\Gamma \vdash_{G_p^q} \psi$ *if and only if* $\Gamma \models_{\mathfrak{F}_p^q} \psi$.

Now we continue to show the termination of $G_p^q$from which the decidability of the derivability of a sequent in $G_p^q$is derived. By "terminating" we mean that every chain in the root-first backward proof search of possible derivation of a sequent, each of which is either an axiom or the premiss (es) of a rule whose conclusion matches the sequent, ends with an axiom in finitely many steps. We first define the *weight* of a sequent.

Defination 4.15. The *weight* $w(\varphi)$ of a term ϕ is defined inductively by

$w(\varphi) = 1$, where φ is atomic.

$w(\sim\varphi) = 2 \cdot w(\varphi)$

$w(\varphi \circ \psi) = 2^{w(\varphi)+w(\psi)}$, where $\circ \in \{\wedge, \vee\}$.

For anyfinite multiset of terms $\Gamma = \varphi_1, \ldots, \varphi_n$, we define $w(\Gamma) = w(\varphi_1) + \ldots$

$+ w(\varphi_n)$. In particular, let $w(\varnothing) = 0$. The weight of a sequent $\Gamma \vdash \psi$ is defined as $w(\Gamma \vdash \psi) = w(\Gamma) + w(\psi)$.

Lemma 4.16. *For any terms φ, ψ and $n \geqslant 0$, (1) $w(\sim^n(\varphi \circ \psi)) > w(\sim^n \varphi) + w(\sim^n \psi)$ where $\circ \in \{\wedge, \vee\}$; and (2) $w(\sim^{2p+q} \varphi) > w(\sim^q \varphi)$.*

Proof: For (1), $w(\sim^n(\varphi \circ \psi)) = 2^n \cdot 2^{w(\varphi)+w(\psi)}$ and $w(\sim^n \varphi) + w(\sim^n \psi) = 2^n \cdot w(\varphi) + 2^n \cdot w(\psi) = 2^n \cdot (w(\varphi) + w(\psi))$. Clearly $2^{w(\varphi)+w(\psi)} > w(\varphi) + w(\psi)$. Hence $2^n \cdot 2^{w(\varphi)+w(\psi)} > 2^n \cdot (w(\varphi) + w(\psi))$. For (2), $w(\sim^{2p+q} \varphi) = 2^{2p+q} \cdot w(\varphi) > 2^q \cdot w(\varphi) = w(\sim^q \varphi)$.

Lemma 4.17. *For any logical rule (r) of G_p^q, the weight of each premiss of (r) is strictly smaller than the weight of the conclusion of (r).*

Proof: The proof proceeds by straightforward inspection on all logical rules of G_p^q. For example, consider the rule $(\sim \wedge \varnothing)$ with premiss $\sim \circ\varphi, \sim \circ\psi, \Gamma \vdash \chi$ and conclusion $\sim \circ(\varphi \wedge \psi), \Gamma \vdash \chi$. Let $m = w(\sim \circ\varphi, \sim \circ\psi, \Gamma \vdash \chi) = w(\sim \circ\varphi) + w(\sim \circ\psi) + w(\Gamma) + w(\chi)$ and $n = w(\sim \circ(\varphi \wedge \psi), \Gamma \vdash \chi) = w(\sim \circ(\varphi \wedge \psi)) + w(\Gamma) + w(\chi)$. By Lemma 4.16 (1), $w(\sim \circ(\varphi \wedge \psi)) > w(\sim \circ\varphi) + w(\sim \circ\psi)$. Then $n > m$. The remaining cases are similar.

Theorem 4.18. *G_p^q is terminating.*

Proof: Given a sequent $\Gamma\ \psi$, the backward proof search starts from $\Gamma \vdash \psi$ and finds all possible derivations. Each step in the backward proof search allows only using one logical rule of G_p^q. By Lemma 4.17, the proof search for $\Gamma \vdash \psi$ terminates.

Corollary 4.19. *The derivability of a sequent in G_p^q is decidable.*

4.4 Craig Interpolation Property

Now we show the Craig interpolation property of the consequence relation $\vdash_p^q$ using Maehara's proof-theoretic method (cf. e. g., Ono 1998). For any term φ, let $var(\varphi)$ be the set of all variable appearing in φ. For any finite multiset of terms Γ, let $var(\Gamma) = \bigcup \{var(\varphi) \mid \varphi \in \Gamma\}$.

Definition 4.20. *A pair $(\Gamma_1;\top)(\Gamma_2;\psi)$ is a partition of a sequent $\Gamma \vdash \psi$, if the multiset union of Γ_1 and Γ_2 is equal to Γ. For any sequent $\Gamma \vdash \psi$ which is derivable in G_p^q and a partition $(\Gamma_1;\varnothing)(\Gamma_2;\psi)$ of $\Gamma \vdash \psi$, a term χ is called an interpolant of $(\Gamma_1;\varnothing)(\Gamma_2;\psi)$, if (1) $\Gamma_1 \vdash_{G_p^q} \chi$; (2) $\chi, \Gamma_2 \vdash_{G_p^q} \psi$; and (3) $var(\chi) \subseteq var(\Gamma_1) \cap var(\Gamma_2, \psi)$. The consequence relation $\vdash_p^q$ has the Craig interpolation property, if for any terms φ and ψ, $\varphi \vdash_{S_p^q} \psi$ implies that there exists a* *term* χ *such that* (1) $\varphi \vdash_{S_p^q} \chi$, (2) $\chi \vdash_{S_p^q} \psi$ *and* (3) $var(\chi) \subseteq var(\varphi) \cap var(\psi)$.

Theorem 4.21. *If* $\Gamma \vdash_{G_p^q} \psi$, *then every partition of* $\Gamma \vdash \psi$ *has an interpolant.*

Proof: Assume that $\Gamma \vdash_n \psi$. Let $(\Gamma_1;\top)(\Gamma_2;\psi)$ be any partition of $\Gamma \vdash \psi$. The proof proceeds by induction on n.

(1) $n = 0$. Then $\Gamma \vdash \psi$ is an axiom. We have the following cases:

(1.1) $\Gamma \vdash \psi$ is an instance of (Id). Let $\psi = \sim^k x$ and $\Gamma = \sim^k x, \Gamma'$ where $k \in [0, 2p+q)$. Then $\sim^k x \in \Gamma_1$ or $\sim^k x \in \Gamma_2$. Let $\sim^k x \in \Gamma_1$. Then $\Gamma_1 \vdash_{G_p^q} \sim^k x$ and $\sim^k x, \Gamma_2 \vdash_{G_p^q} \psi$. Clearly $var(\sim^k x) \subseteq var(\Gamma_1) \cap var(\Gamma_2, \psi)$. Then $\sim^k x$ is an interpolant. Let $\sim^k x \in \Gamma_2$. Then $\top, \Gamma_2 \vdash_{G_p^q} \sim^k x$. Clearly $\Gamma_1 \vdash_{G_p^q} \top$ and $var(\top) \subseteq var(\Gamma_1) \cap var(\Gamma_2, \psi)$. Then $\top$ is an interpolant.

(1.2) $\Gamma \vdash \psi$ is an instance of $(\bot\top)$. Let $\Gamma = \sim^e \bot, \Gamma'$ with $e \in E[0, 2p+q)$. Then $\sim^e \bot \in \Gamma_1$ or $\sim^e \bot \in \Gamma_2$. Let $\sim^e \bot \in \Gamma_1$. By Lemma 4.8, $\Gamma_1 \vdash_{G_p^q} \sim^e \bot$ and $\sim^e \bot, \Gamma_2 \vdash_{G_p^q} \psi$. Clearly $var(\sim^e \bot) \subseteq var(\Gamma_1) \cap var(\Gamma_2, \psi)$. Then $\sim^e \bot$ is an interpolant. Let $\sim^e \bot \in \Gamma_2$. Then $\top, \Gamma_2 \vdash_{G_p^q} \sim^e \bot$. Clearly $\Gamma_1 \vdash_{G_p^q} \top$ and $var(\top) \subseteq var(\Gamma_1) \cap var(\Gamma_2, \psi)$. Then $\top$ is an interpolant.

(1.3) $\Gamma \vdash \psi$ is an instance of $(\vdash\sim\bot)$. Let $\psi = \sim^o \bot$ with $o \in O[0, 2p+q)$. Clearly $\Gamma_1 \vdash_{G_p^q} \top$ and $\top, \Gamma_2 \vdash_{G_p^q} \sim^o \bot$. Then $\top$ as an interpolant.

(1.4) $\Gamma \vdash \psi$ is an instance of $(\sim\top\vdash)$. Let $\Gamma = \sim^e \top, \Gamma'$ with $o \in O[0, 2p+q)$. Then $\sim^o \top \in \Gamma_1$ or $\sim^o \top \in \Gamma_2$. Let $\sim^o \top \in \Gamma_1$. By Lemma 4.8, $\Gamma_1 \vdash_{G_p^q} \sim^o \top$ and $\sim^o \top, \Gamma_2 \vdash_{G_p^q} \psi$. Clearly $var(\sim^o \top) \subseteq var(\Gamma_1) \cap var(\Gamma_2, \psi)$. Then $\sim^o \top$ is an interpolant. Let $\sim^o \top \in \Gamma_2$. Then $\top, \Gamma_2 \vdash_{G_p^q} \sim^o \top$. Clearly $\Gamma_1 \vdash_{G_p^q} \top$. Then $\top$ is an interpolant.

(1.5) $\Gamma \vdash \psi$ is an instance of $(\vdash\top)$. Let $\psi = \sim^e \top$ with $e \in E[0, 2p+q)$. Clearly $\Gamma_1 \vdash_{G_p^q} \top$ and $\top, \Gamma_2 \vdash_{G_p^q} \sim^e \top$. Then $\top$ as an interpolant.

(2) $n > 0$. Let $\Gamma \vdash \psi$ be obtained by (r). We have the following cases:

(2.1) (r) is $(\wedge\varnothing)$. Let $\Gamma = \sim^e(\varphi_1 \wedge \varphi_2), \Gamma'$ and $e \in E[0, 2p+q)$. Let the premiss of (r) be $\sim^e\varphi_1, \sim^e\varphi_2, \Gamma' \vdash \psi$. Suppose $\sim^e(\varphi_1 \wedge \varphi_2) \in \Gamma_1$. Let $\Gamma' = \Gamma'_1, \Gamma'_2$ and $\Gamma_1 = \sim^e(\varphi_1 \wedge \varphi_2), \Gamma'_1$ and $\Gamma_2 = \Gamma'_2$. Consider the partition $(\sim^e\varphi_1, \sim^e\varphi_2, \Gamma'_1;\top)(\Gamma'_2;\psi)$ of $\sim^e\varphi_1, \sim^e\varphi_2, \Gamma' \vdash \psi$. By induction hypothesis, there is a term χ such that (i) $\sim^e\varphi_1$,

$\sim^e \varphi_2, \Gamma'_1 \vdash_{G_p^q} \chi$; (ii) $\chi, \Gamma'_2 \vdash_{G_p^q} \psi$; (iii) $var(\chi) \subseteq var(\sim^e\varphi_1, \sim^e\varphi_2, \Gamma'_1) \cap var(\Gamma'_2, \psi)$. By (i) and ($\wedge\varnothing$), $\sim^e(\varphi_1 \wedge \varphi_2), \Gamma'_1 \vdash_{G_p^q} \chi$. Clearly $var(\chi) \subseteq var(\sim^e\varphi_1, \sim^e\varphi_2, \Gamma'_1) \cap var(\Gamma'_2, \psi) = var(\Gamma_1) \cap var(\Gamma_2, \psi)$. Hence χ is a required interpolant.

Suppose $\sim^e(\varphi_1 \wedge \varphi_2) \in \Gamma_2$. Let $\Gamma' = \Gamma'_1, \Gamma'_2$ and $\Gamma_1 = \Gamma'_1$ and $\Gamma_2 = \sim^e(\varphi_1 \wedge \varphi_2), \Gamma'_2$. Consider the partition $(\Gamma'_1;\top)(\sim^e\varphi_1, \sim^e\varphi_2, \Gamma'_2;\psi)$ of the sequent $\sim^e\varphi_1, \sim^e\varphi_2, \Gamma' \vdash \psi$. By induction hypothesis, there is a term χ such that (i) $\Gamma'_1 \vdash_{G_p^q} \chi$; (ii) $\chi, \sim^e\varphi_1, \sim^e\varphi_2, \Gamma'_2 \vdash_{G_p^q} \psi$; (iii) $var(\chi) \subseteq var(\Gamma'_1) \cap var(\sim^e\varphi_1, \sim^e\varphi_2, \Gamma'_2, \psi)$. By (ii) and ($\wedge\varnothing$), $\chi, \sim^e(\varphi_1 \wedge \varphi_2), \Gamma'_2 \vdash_{G_p^q} \psi$. Clearly $var(\chi) \subseteq var(\Gamma'_1) \cap var(\sim^e\varphi_1, \sim^e\varphi_2, \Gamma'_2, \psi) = var(\Gamma_1) \cap var(\Gamma_2, \psi)$. Hence χ is a required interpolant.

(2.2) (r) is ($\vdash\wedge$). Let $\psi = \sim^e(\psi_1 \wedge \psi_2)$ and $e \in E[0, 2p+q)$. Let the premises (r) be $\Gamma \vdash \sim^e\psi_1$ and $\Gamma \vdash \sim^e\psi_2$. By induction hypothesis, let χ_1 and χ_2 be interpolants such that (i) $\Gamma_1 \vdash_{G_p^q} \chi_1$; (ii) $\chi_1, \Gamma_2 \vdash_{G_p^q} \sim^e\psi_1$; (iii) $var(\chi_1) \subseteq var(\Gamma_1) \cap var(\Gamma_2, \sim^e\psi_1)$; (iv) $\Gamma_1 \vdash_{G_p^q} \chi_2$; (v) $\chi_2, \Gamma_2 \vdash_{G_p^q} \sim^e\psi_2$; (vi) $var(\chi_2) \subseteq var(\Gamma_1) \cap var(\Gamma_2, \sim^e\psi_2)$. By (i), (iv) and ($\vdash\wedge$), $\Gamma_1 \vdash_{G_p^q} \chi_1 \wedge \chi_2$. By (ii), (v) and (Wk), $\chi_1, \chi_2, \Gamma_2 \vdash_{G_p^q} \sim^e\psi_1$ and $\chi_1, \chi_2, \Gamma_2 \vdash_{G_p^q} \sim^e\psi_2$. By ($\vdash\wedge$), $\chi_1, \chi_2, \Gamma_2 \vdash_{G_p^q} \sim^e(\psi_1 \wedge \psi_2)$. By ($\wedge\varnothing$), $\chi_1 \wedge \chi_2, \Gamma_2 \vdash_{G_p^q} \sim^e(\psi_1 \wedge \psi_2)$. By (iii) and (vi), $var(\chi_1) \cup var(\chi_2) \subseteq (var(\Gamma_1) \cap var(\Gamma_2, \sim^e\psi_1)) \cup (var(\Gamma_1) \cap var(\Gamma_2, \sim^e\psi_2)) = var(\Gamma_1) \cap var(\Gamma_2, \sim^e(\psi_1 \wedge \psi_2))$. Hence $\chi_1 \wedge \chi_2$ is a required interpolant.

(2.3) (r) is ($\vee\vdash$). Let $\Gamma = \sim^e(\psi_1 \vee \psi_2), \Gamma'$ and $e \in E[0, 2p+q)$. Suppose $\sim^e(\psi_1 \vee \psi_2) \in \Gamma_1$. Let $\Gamma' = \Gamma'_1, \Gamma'_2$ and $\Gamma_1 = \sim^e(\psi_1 \vee \psi_2), \Gamma'_1$ and $\Gamma_2 = \Gamma'_2$. Consider the partition $(\sim^e\varphi_1, \Gamma'_1;\top)(\Gamma'_2;\psi)$ of $\sim^e\varphi_1, \Gamma' \vdash \psi$ and the partition $(\sim^e\varphi_2, \Gamma'_1;\top)(\Gamma'_2;\psi)$ of the sequent $\sim^e\varphi_2, \Gamma' \vdash \psi$. By induction hypothesis, there are terms χ_1 and χ_2 such that (i) $\sim^e\varphi_1, \Gamma'_1 \vdash_{G_p^q} \chi_1$; (ii) $\chi_1, \Gamma'_2 \vdash_{G_p^q} \psi$; (iii) $var(\chi_1) \subseteq var(\sim^e\varphi_1, \Gamma'_1) \cap var(\Gamma'_2, \psi)$; (iv) $\sim^e\varphi_2, \Gamma'_1 \vdash_{G_p^q} \chi_2$; (v) $\chi_2, \Gamma'_2 \vdash_{G_p^q} \psi$; (vi) $var(\chi_2) \subseteq var(\sim^e\varphi_2, \Gamma'_1) \cap var(\Gamma'_2, \psi)$. By (i), (iv) and ($\vdash\vee$), $\sim^e\varphi_1, \Gamma'_1 \vdash_{G_p^q} \chi_1 \vee \chi_2$ and

$\sim^e\varphi_2, \Gamma'_1 \vdash_{G_p^q}\chi_1 \vee \chi_2$. By ($\vee\varnothing$), $\sim^e(\varphi_1 \vee \varphi_2), \Gamma'_1 \vdash_{G_p^q}\chi_1 \vee \chi_2$. By (ii), (v) and ($\vee\varnothing$), $\chi_1 \vee \chi_2, \Gamma'_2 \vdash_{G_p^q} \psi$. By (iii) and (vi), $var(\chi_1) \cup var(\chi_2) \subseteq (var(\sim^e\varphi_1, \Gamma'_1) \cap var(\Gamma'_2, \psi)) \cup (var(\sim^e\varphi_2, \Gamma'_1) \cap var(\Gamma'_2, \psi)) = var(\sim^e(\varphi_1 \vee \varphi_2), \Gamma'_1) \cap var(\Gamma'_2, \psi)$. Hence $\chi_1 \vee \chi_2$ is a required interpolant.

Suppose $\sim^e(\psi_1 \vee \psi_2) \in \Gamma_2$. Let $\Gamma' = \Gamma'_1, \Gamma'_2$ and $\Gamma_1 = \Gamma'_1$ and $\Gamma_2 = \sim^e(\psi_1 \vee \psi_2), \Gamma'_2$. Consider the partition $(\Gamma'_1;\top)(\sim^e\varphi_1, \Gamma'_2;\psi)$ of $\sim^e\varphi_1, \Gamma' \vdash \psi$ and the partition $(\Gamma'_1;\top)(\sim^e\varphi_2, \Gamma'_2;\psi)$ of $\sim^e\varphi_2, \Gamma' \vdash \psi$. By induction hypothesis, there are terms χ_1 and χ_2 such that (i) $\Gamma'_1 \vdash_{G_p^q}\chi_1$; (ii) $\chi_1, \sim^e\varphi_1, \Gamma'_2 \vdash_{G_p^q} \psi$; (iii) $var(\chi_1) \subseteq var(\Gamma'_1) \cap var(\sim^e\varphi_1, \Gamma'_2, \psi)$; (iv) $\Gamma'_1 \vdash_{G_p^q}\chi_2$; (v) $\chi_2, \sim^e\varphi_2, \Gamma'_2 \vdash_{G_p^q} \psi$; (vi) $var(\chi_2) \subseteq var(\Gamma'_1) \cap var(\sim^e\varphi_2, \Gamma'_2, \psi)$. By (i), (iv) and ($\vdash\wedge$), $\Gamma'_1 \vdash_{G_p^q}\chi_1 \wedge \chi_2$. By (ii), (v) and (Wk), $\chi_1, \chi_2, \sim^e\varphi_1, \Gamma'_2 \vdash_{G_p^q} \psi$ and $\chi_1, \chi_2, \sim^e\varphi_2, \Gamma'_2 \vdash_{G_p^q} \psi$. By ($\vee\varnothing$), $\chi_1, \chi_2, \sim^e(\varphi_1 \vee \varphi_2), \Gamma'_2 \vdash_{G_p^q} \psi$. By ($\wedge\varnothing$), $\chi_1 \wedge \chi_2, \sim^e(\varphi_1 \vee \varphi_2), \Gamma'_2 \vdash_{G_p^q} \psi$. By (iii) and (vi), $var(\chi_1) \cup var(\chi_2) \subseteq (var(\Gamma'_1) \cap var(\sim^e\varphi_1, \Gamma'_2, \psi)) \cup (var(\Gamma'_1) \cap var(\sim^e\varphi_2, \Gamma'_2, \psi)) = var(\Gamma'_1) \cap var(\sim^e(\varphi_1 \vee \varphi_2), \Gamma'_2, \psi)$. Hence $\chi_1 \wedge \chi_2$ is a required interpolant.

(2.4) (r) is ($\vdash\vee$). Let $\psi = \sim^e(\psi_1 \vee \psi_2)$ and $e \in E[0, 2p+q)$. Let the premiss be $\Gamma \vdash \sim^e\psi_i$. By induction hypothesis, there is a term χ such that (i) $\Gamma_1 \vdash_{G_p^q}\chi$; (ii) $\chi, \Gamma_2 \vdash_{G_p^q}\sim^e\psi_i$; (iii) $var(\chi) \subseteq var(\Gamma_1) \cap var(\Gamma_2, \sim^e\psi_i)$. By (ii) and ($\vdash\vee$), $\chi, \Gamma_2 \vdash_{G_p^q}(\psi_1 \vee \psi_2)$. By (iii), $var(\chi) \subseteq var(\Gamma_1) \cap var(\Gamma_2, \sim^e\psi_i) \subseteq var(\Gamma_1) \cap var(\Gamma_2, \sim^e(\psi_1 \vee \psi_2))$. Hence χ is a required interpolant.

(2.5) (r) is ($\sim\wedge\varnothing$) or ($\vdash\sim\wedge$). The proof is similar to case (2.3) or (2.4).

(2.6) (r) is ($\sim\vee\varnothing$) or ($\vdash\sim\vee$). The proof is similar to case (2.1) or (2.2).

(2.7) (r) is ($\sim^{2p+q}\top$). Let $\Gamma = \sim^{2p+q}\varphi, \Gamma'$ and the premises of (r) be $\sim^q\varphi, \Gamma' \vdash \psi$. Suppose $\sim^{2p+q}\varphi \in \Gamma_1$. Let $\Gamma' = \Gamma'_1, \Gamma'_2$ with $\Gamma_1 = \sim^{2p+q}\varphi, \Gamma'_1$ and $\Gamma_2 = \Gamma'_2$. Consider the partition

$(\sim^q \varphi, \Gamma'_1; \top)(\Gamma'_2; \psi)$ of $\sim^q \varphi, \Gamma' \vdash \psi$. By induction hypothesis, there is a term χ such that (i) $\sim^q \varphi, \Gamma'_1 \vdash_{G^q_p} \chi$, (ii) $\chi, \Gamma'_2 \vdash_{G^q_p} \psi$, (iii) $var(\chi) \subseteq var(\sim^q \varphi, \Gamma'_1) \cap var(\Gamma'_2, \psi)$. By (i) and $(\sim^{2p+q}\top)$, $\sim^{2p+q} \varphi, \Gamma'_1 \vdash_{G^q_p} \chi$. Clearly, $var(\chi) \subseteq var(\sim^q \varphi, \Gamma'_1) \cap var(\Gamma'_2, \psi) = var(\Gamma_1) \cap var(\Gamma_2, \psi)$. Hence χ is a required interpolant. Suppose $\sim^{2p+q} \varphi \in \Gamma_2$. Let $\Gamma' = \Gamma'_1, \Gamma'_2$ with $\Gamma_1 = \Gamma'_1$ and $\Gamma_2 = \sim^{2p+q} \varphi, \Gamma'_2$. Consider the partition $(\Gamma'_1; \top)(\sim^q \varphi, \Gamma'_2; \psi)$ of $\sim^q \varphi, \Gamma' \vdash \psi$. By in-duction hypothesis, there is a term χ such that (i) $\Gamma'_1 \vdash_{G^q_p} \chi$, (ii) $\chi, \sim^q \varphi, \Gamma'_2 \vdash_{G^q_p} \psi$, (iii) $var(\chi) \subseteq var(\Gamma'_1) \cap var(\sim^q \varphi, \Gamma'_2, \psi)$. By (ii) and $(\sim^{2p+q}\top)$, $\chi, \sim^{2p+q} \varphi, \Gamma'_2 \vdash_{G^q_p} \psi$. Clearly $var(\chi) \subseteq var(\Gamma'_1) \cap var(\sim^q \varphi, \Gamma'_2, \psi) = var(\Gamma_1) \cap var(\Gamma_2, \psi)$. Hence χ is a required interpolant.

(2.8) (r) is $(\vdash \sim^{2p+q})$. Let $\psi = \sim^{2p+q} \psi'$ and the premises of (r) be $\Gamma \vdash \sim^{2p+q} \psi'$. By induction hypothesis, let χ be an interpolant such that (i) $\Gamma_1 \vdash_{G^q_p} \chi$; (ii) $\chi, \Gamma_2 \vdash_{G^q_p} \sim^q \psi'$; (iii) $var(\chi) \subseteq var(\Gamma_1) \cap var(\Gamma_2, \sim^q \psi')$. By (ii) and $(\vdash \sim^{2p+q})$, $\chi, \Gamma_2 \vdash_{G^q_p} \sim^{2p+q} \psi'$. By (iii), $var(\chi) \subseteq var(\Gamma_1) \cap var(\Gamma_2, \sim^{2p+q}\psi')$. Hence χ is a required interpolant.

Corollary 4.22. $\vdash^q_p$ *has the Craig interpolation property.*

5. Concluding Remarks

The consequence relation $\vdash^q_p$ ($p \geqslant 1$ and $q \geqslant 0$) determined by Berman's variety $\mathbb{K}^q_p$ is axiomatized by the sequent system S^q. This logic is characterized by the frame $\mathfrak{F}^q_p$ under the frame semantics. And S^q_p is a 4^{2p+q}-valued logic characterized by the dual algebra $(\mathfrak{F}^q_p)^+$. Furthermore, a structural-rule-free, cut-free and terminating sequent system G^q_p for $\vdash^q_p$ is established. The Craig interpolation property of $\vdash^q_p$ is proved constructively in G^q_p.

One question about the variety $\mathbb{K}^q_p$ is if it can be generated by the finite dual algebra $(\mathfrak{F}^q_p)^+$ or not. It is known that a twist-construction between varieties of algebras is one-to-one correspondence with adjunctions (McKenzie 1996; Moraschini 2018). This fact might give a positive answer to the question. The proof is left as a future work. It is also worth to investigate these logics S^q_p in the framework of abstract algebraic logic (cf. e. g. Font 2016). The abstract algebraic logical per-spective on extensions of BD can be found in the literature (Albuquerque, Prenosil & Rivieccio 2017; Rivieccio 2012). This has not been fully explored yet for weakenings of Belnap-Dunn logic.

The polarity semantics given for S_p^q in the present paper can be generalized to talk about properties of arbitrary informational frames. The generalized frame semantics for more weakenings of Belnap-Dunn logic can be established to model inconsistency-tolerant informational scenarios. The minimal logic of arbitrary informational frames under the polarity semantics could be established. One further question is that how many logics are there between the minimal logic and Belnap-Dunn logic BD. The present work ensures that there are at least countably many such logics.

Acknowledgements

This work was supported by the key project of National Social Science Fund of China (Grant no. 18ZDA033). Thanks are given to the reviewers' insightful and helpful comments on the revision of this paper. In particular, Remark 2.2, Remark 2.11 and some facts given in the conclusion are pointed out by the first reviewer.

References

Albuquerque, H., Prenosil, A. and Rivieccio, U. An algebraic view of super-Belnap logics: Studia Logica [C]. https://doi.org/10.1007/s11225-017-9739-7, 2017.

Allwein, G. and Dunn, J. M. Kripke models for linear logic [J]. The Journal of Symbolic Logic, 1993, 58 (2): 514-545.

Belnap, N. A useful four-valued logic [C] //J. M. Dunn and G. Epstein (eds.). Modern Uses of Multiple-Valued Logic. Springer Netherlands, 1977: 5-37.

Berman, J. Distributive lattices with an additional unary operation [J]. Aequationes Mathematicae, 1977, 16: 165-171.

Blok, W. J. and Jónsson, B. Equivalence of consequence operations [J]. Studia Logica, 2006, 83 (1-3): 91-110.

Blyth, T. S. and Varlet, J. C. Ockham Algebras [M]. Oxford Science Publications, 1994.

Blyth, T. S. and Varlet, J. C. On a common abstraction of de Morgan algebras and Stone algebras [J]. Proceedings of the Royal Society of Edinburgh, 1983a, 94 (3-4): 301-308.

Blyth, T. S. and Varlet, J. C. Subvarieties of the class of MS-algebras [J]. Proceedings of the Royal Society of Edinburgh, 1983b, 95A: 157 - 169.

Bou, F. and Font, J. M. Corrigendum to the paper "Logics preserving degrees of truth from varieties of residuated lattices" [J]. Journal of Logic and Computation, 2012, 22: 661 - 665.

Bou, F., Esteva, F., Font, J. M., et al. Logics preserving degrees of truth from varieties of residuated lattices [J]. Journal of Logic and Computation, 2009, 19 (6): 1031 - 1069.

Dunn, J. M. A comparative study of various model-theoretic treatments of negation: A history of formal negation [C] //Gabbay, D. M. and Wansing, H. (eds.). What Is Negation? Kluwer Academic Publishers, 1999: 23 - 51.

Dunn, J. M. A Kripke-style semantics for first-degree relevant implications (abstract) [J]. The Journal of Symbolic Logic, 1971, 36: 362 - 363.

Dunn, J. M., Gehrke, M. and Palmigiano, A. Canonical extensions and relational completeness of some structural logics [J]. The Journal of Symbolic Logic, 2005, 70 (3): 713 - 740.

Dunn, J. M. Intuitive semantics for first-degree entailments and coupled trees [J]. Philosophical Studies, 1976, 29: 149 - 168.

Dunn, J. M. Partiality and its dual [J]. Studia Logica, 2000 65: 5 - 40.

Dunn, J. M. The Algebra of Intensional Logics [D]. Ph. D. Dissertation, University of Pittsburg, 1966.

Dunn, J. M. The effective equivalence of certain propositions about De Morgan lattices [J]. The Journal of Symbolic Logic, 1967, 32: 433 - 434.

Font, J. M. Abstract Algebraic Logic [M]. College Publications, 2016.

Font, J. M. and Moraschini, T. Logics of varieties, logics of semilattices, and conjunction [J]. Logic Journal of the IGPL, 2014, 22: 818 - 843.

Font, J. M. and Moraschini, T. M-sets and the representation problem [J]. Studia Logica, 2015, 103 (1): 21 - 51.

Font, J. M. Addendum to the paper "Belnap's four-valued logic and De Morgan lattices" [J]. Logic Journal of IGPL, 1999, 7 (5): 671 - 672.

Font, J. M. Belnaps's four-valued logic and De Morgan lattices [J]. Logic Journal of IGPL, 1997, 5 (3): 413 - 440.

Ganter, B., Stumme, G. and Wille, R. (eds.). Formal Concept Analysis: Foundations and Applications [C]. Springer, 2005.

Gehrke, M. and Harding, J. Bounded lattice expansions [J]. Journal of Algebra, 2001, 238 (1): 345 -371.

Gehrke, M. and Jónsson, B. Bounded distributive lattice expansions [J]. Mathematica Scandinavica, 2004, 94: 13 -45.

Gehrke, M. Generalized Kripke frames [J]. Studia Logica, 2006, 84 (2): 241 -275.

Goldberg, M. S. Topological duality for distributive Ockham algebras [J]. Studia Logica, 1983, 42: 23 -31.

Jansana, R. Algebraizable logics with a strong conjunction and their semi-lattice based companions [J]. Archive for Mathematical Logic, 2012, 51: 831 -861.

Jansana, R. On the deductive system of the order of an equationally orderable quasi-variety [J]. Studia Logica, 2016, 104 (3): 547 -566.

Jansana, R. Self-extensional logics with a conjunction [J]. Studia Logica, 2006, 84 (1): 63 -104.

Kalman, J. A.. Lattices with involution [J]. Transactions of the American Mathematical Society, 1958, 87: 485 -491.

Ma, M. and Lin, Y. A deterministic weakening of Belnap-Dunn logic, Studia Logica [C] https: //doi. org/10. 1007/s11225 -018 -9792 -x, 2018.

McKenzie, R. An algebraic version of categorical equivalence for varieties and more general algebraic categories [C] //Agliano, P. and Magari, R. (eds.). Logic and Algebra. New York: Dekker, 1996: 211 -243.

Moraschini, T. An algebraic characterization of adjunctions between generalized quasi-varieties [J]. The Journal of Symbolic Logic, 2018, 83 (3): 899 -919.

Ono, H. Proof-theoretic methods in non-classical logics—an introduction [C] //Taka-hashi, M., Okada, M. and Dezani-Ciancaglini, M. (eds.). Theories of Types and Proofs Mathematical Society of Japan. Tokyo, 1998: 207 -252.

Priestley, H. A. and Bordalo, G. Negation operations definable on finite distributive lattices [J]. Portugaliae Mathematica, 1992, 49 (1): 37 -49.

Pynko, A. P. Characterizing Belnap's logic via De Morgan's laws [J]. Mathematical Logic Quarterly, 1995, 41 (4): 442 -454.

Raftery, J. G. Correspondences between Gentzen and Hilbert systems [J]. The Journal of Symbolic Logic, 2006, 71 (3): 903 -95.

Ramalho, M. and Sequeira, M. On generalised MS-algebras [J]. Portugaliae Mathematica, 1987, 44 (1): 315 -328.

Rebagliato, J. and Verdu, V. Algebraizable Gentzen Systems and the Deduction Theorem for Gentzen Systems [M]. Mathematics Preprint Series 175. University of Barcelona, 1995.

Rivieccio, U. An infinity of super-Belnap logics [J]. Journal of Applied Non-Classical Logics, 2012, 22: 319 - 335.

Urquhart, A. Lattices with a dual homomorphic operation [J]. Studia Logica, 1979, 38: 201 - 209.

Urquhart, A. Lattices with a dual homomorphic operation Ⅱ [J]. Studia Logica, 1981, 40: 391 - 404.

Is Chinese Culture Dualist? An Answer to Edward Slingerland from a Medical Philosophical Viewpoint

Dawei Pan①

A recent challenge by Edward Slingerland to the conventional view of Chinese thought is that China is no exception to the recent cognitive science hypothesis that dualism is an innate cognitive universal. However, a close reexamination of Slingerland's evidence shows that it is biased. Extensive evidence across philosophy and medicine suggests that a concept of degrees of substantiality rather than a distinct barrier between mind and body underlies both early Chinese afterlife beliefs and ideas about the *xin*-body relationship. In particular, medical accounts of the *xin*'s dual role as the organ of thought and a physical organ does not reject the division between mind and body. A dualist claim, however weak, cannot explain China's traditional focus on the link between physicality and mentality, especially in medicine. The cognitive science-driven attempt to recast the conventional holist claim of Chinese thought is an overly hasty attempt to take refuge in science.

The longstanding idea of Chinese uniqueness in Chinese studies suggests that because Chinese thought gives little consideration to dichotomies such as material/immaterial and mind/body, Chinese thought has a distinctive tendency toward holistic thinking. A remarkable challenge to this uniqueness has emerged from the recent development in cognitive science regarding the universality of the distinction between mind and body, or whether humans are born Cartesians or "intuitive dualists." Proponents of intuitive dualism claim that the distinction between mind and body is an innate cognitive universal that may explain the ubiquitous existence of religious beliefs worldwide. This universalist stand-point is gaining support due to a growing body of literature in empirical studies of child development that suggests the

---

① Dawei Pan, Department of Philosophy, Center for Health and Human Development, and Center for Medical Humanities at Zhongshan Medical School, Sun Yat-sen University. This research was funded by "Three Big Constructions" of Sun Yat-sen University, the National Social Science Foundation of China (NSSFC) (Grant No. 14ZDB015), and the National Social Science Foundation of China (NSSFC) (Grant No. 15ZDB005).

universality of the mind-body dualism across cultures (Chudek et al. 2013)①. Of particular concern are two studies against Chinese holism by Edward Slingerland and his associates (Slingerland and Chudek 2011: 997 - 1007②; Slingerland et al. 2017③). These authors use quantitative analysis of texts to reveal the presence of mind-body dualism in early China with reference to the Chinese word *xin* (heart or heart-mind). In his 2013 article, Slingerland reiterates his universalist standpoint, emphasizing supplementary archeological and textual evidence about belief in the afterlife and dualist accounts of the *xin*-body relationship in the early Common Era (Slingerland 2013: 6-55).④

Although Slingerland's work adds a fresh dimension to the mind-body problem in Chinese thought, a central issue remains unclear. If it stands to reason that Chinese culture belongs in the dualist camp (though it has long been deemed outside it), "Chinese holism" might be, as Slingerland articulates, considered little more than an exotic exemplary opposite of Western thought as well as a projection of essentialist notions of cultural differences. What scholars of Chinese studies have seen as the difference distinguishing Chinese (or, more generally, Eastern) and Western thought may instead be a transcultural difference between creeping dualism and sweeping dualism.

Is this understanding correct? If it is true that dualism is a human cognitive universal that is valid worldwide, what prevents Chinese culture, or any other individual culture, from developing a similarly clear preference for dualism in the same way that Western culture has? As a corollary of the claim of the supposed universality of cognitive biases (such as mind-body dualism) (Willard and Norenzayan 2013: 379-391)⑤, the gap between these biases and myriad examples

---

① Chudek, Maciek, Rita McNamara, Susan Birch, Paul Bloom, and Joseph Henrich, Developmental and Cross Cultural Evidence for Intuitive Dualism. Working Paper. Available at http://www2.psych.ubc.ca/~henrich/pdfs/ChudekEtAl_InutiveDualism_WorkingPaper_June2014.pdf, 2013.

② Slingerland, Edward, and Maciek Chudek, The Prevalence of Mind-Body Dualism in Early China. *Cognitive Science*, 2011, 35 (5), pp. 997-1007.

③ Slingerland, Edward, Ryan Nichols, Kristoffer Neilbo, and Carson Logan, The Distant Reading of Religious Texts: A 'Big Data' Approach to Mind-Body Concepts in Early China. *Journal of the American Academy of Religion*, 2017, 85 (4), pp. 985-1016.

④ Slingerland, Edward, Body and Mind in Early China: An Integrated Humanities-Science Approach. *Journal of the American Academy of Religion*, 2013, 81 (1), pp. 6-55.

⑤ Aiyana K Willard, and Ara Norenzayan, Cognitive Biases Explain Religious Belief, Paranormal Belief, and Belief in Life's Purpose, *Cognition*, 2013, 129 (2), pp. 379-391.

of cultural diversity must not be over-looked. Instead, this gap must be addressed more seriously than ever. Specifically, in defense of the claim of a strong or weak universal dualist position underlying Chinese thought that previously held a unique position (in contrast to its European cousin) in the topography of civilizations, further accounts are needed of the specific way Chinese culture conceives of mind and body. Otherwise, any claims of cognitive biases overriding cultural heterogeneity will be of only limited explanatory power.

In this article, I examine the concepts of mind and body in early Chinese thought, highlighting their appearances in both philosophical and medical texts. There are two reasons to undertake this study in this manner. First, medicine is an area that has been largely unexplored with regard to the mind-body problem. I customarily identify four major fields within which the concepts of mind and body unfold in a given culture: religion, philosophy, science, and medicine. Whereas previous studies focused largely on the former three, the last field, medicine, has received limited attention from cognitive scientists and scholars of Chinese studies. Given the relevance of medicine to the mind-body problem, this lack of research is particularly surprising. Second, traditional Chinese medicine (TCM)① may be sufficient to represent Chinese intellectual traditions with regard to the overall view of mind and body. Because TCM served as China's orthodox medicine for almost two millennia (until the intro duction of modern medicine), it is safe to say that TCM's understanding of physiological functions and mental activities offers a useful window into the way Slingerland's supposed folk dualism was handled within the Chinese tradition, both ideologically and practically.

In the following pages, I begin with an overview of the concepts of mind and body in early China, focusing on the two major sources of evidence against strong Chinese holism provided by Slingerland: after-life beliefs in Section 2 and philosophical accounts of the *xin*-body relationship in the Section 3. In Section 4, I examine the concept of *xin* and accounts of the *xin*-body relationship in TCM. In Section 5, I discuss the traditional focus on the close link between physicality and mentality, which supports a holist rather than a dualist position. In the conclusion, I

① The term traditional Chinese medicine and the abbreviation TCM are often used to refer to traditional and indigenous medical knowledge in China to distinguish it from modern medicine. Many contemporary therapeutic practices are considered to be TCM even though they are actually affected by modern medicine. I use the term in the context of historical analysis without including its contem porary manifestations.

argue that Slingerland's claim of Chinese dualism is universalist at the cost of insight into early Chinese thought, and is therefore unsustainable.

1. Materiality of the Spirits

Let us first consider one of the two major pieces of evidence Slingerland proposes in defense of the dualist claim. As shown in his 2013 article, certain evidence from the transmitted and archeological texts in early China suggests belief in the afterlife. An initial explanation of such beliefs might be the prevalence of mind-body dualism in early Chinese thought as Slingerland proposes (Slingerland 2013: 5 - 9). ① However, in doing so, one difficulty remains: is the dualist claim the only viable explanation of early China's conception of the afterlife?

The answer might be negative. It should be noted that the underlying concepts of mind and body in such afterlife beliefs may be much subtler than Slingerland supposes. Despite the appearance of a dichotomy between a physical body and a separate or separable spirit/mind in which one's personal identity or essence is located, patterns of interaction between the dead and the living in early Chinese culture sometimes suggest the opposite.

The idea that the dead are capable of interacting with the living was not novel to the early thinkers. Since the earliest written records on the oracle bones of the Shang Dynasty, evidence exists of communicative practices with a variety of supernatural agents (ancestors of the royal line or nature deities), indicating a perennial belief in the distinct existence of nonhuman powers without physical bodies, and in the continued existence of human minds (at least of those from ruling families) after death. Although such beliefs may be supportive of the claim of Chinese dualism, it is notable that at funeral ceremonies and ancestral sacrifices, these spirits were treated with a fairly materialistic approach in which they were believed to receive nourishment from foods and drinks by absorbing the essence or rather smells of foods and drinks. Thus, the idea of homogeneity between the spirits and such essences should not be overlooked by anyone ready to exploit the issue to its fullest.

Homogeneity is suggested by this degree of materiality attributed to the spirits. The ability to travel between the divine-numinous world and the human world, or to interact with the living, coupled with the supposed need to "feed" the spirits

① Edward Slingerland, Body and Mind in Early China: An Integrated Humanities-Science Approach. *Journal of the American Academy of Religion*, 2013, 81 (1), pp. 6 - 55.

and provide for their other daily needs so that they might continue to "live" in the afterworld, makes the assumption of the quasicorporal bodies of the dead an intrinsic part of afterlife beliefs in early Chinese thought. This belief can be confirmed by the elaborate items with which the deceased are interred in Warring States (sixth to third century BCE) and Han tombs to facilitate a "life" of equal quality in the afterworld as when they were alive. That is, despite dislocation from the tangible, decaying, physical bodies that they had during life, the spirits of the deceased are not completely incorporeal but—in a strange, albeit indubitable way—material.

This poses a challenge to the claim that early Chinese thought is dualist. The claim may be defended by stressing that what is rife in early China is one particular "weak" dualism, where by mind and body are distinct from each other but overlap and interact. What would that mean? Dualism and holism are binary opposites that are traditionally juxtaposed in philosophy, allowing for no middle points; alternatively, they are presented as two opposite ends of a spectrum of views of mind and body, within which a weak dualism as well as an equally weak holism serves as little more than a signifier of some intermediate form. If one chooses to use the word *dualism* in the former sense, a reference to weak dualism seems quite untenable, and it is difficult to see the point of championing it. If one chooses to use the word dualism in the latter sense, a weak dualist claim for early Chinese thought can indicate little more than the holist claim that has been a time-honored consensus among scholars of Chinese studies, for the two amount to the same thing. At best, it requires a stronger argument than that which Slingerland has advanced to convince the reader of the advantages of a dualist (or, rather, a weak dualist) claim over the conventional holist claim used to characterize early Chinese thought or Chinese thought in general.

2. The Dual Role of the *Xin*

Another major piece of evidence for the dualism of early Chinese thought is, Slingerland proposes, the philosophical accounts of *xin*-body relations. The functions of the *xin* (heart or heart-mind) are at the core of the issue. Slingerland quotes Warring States texts as understanding the *xin* as a unique organ, namely, the only organ of thought in contrast to the other bodily organs (Slingerland 2013: 11)①. Furthermore, the *xin* is identified in these texts as the "ruler" of the kingdom

① Edward Slingerland, Body and Mind in Early China: An Integrated Humanities-Science Approach, *Journal of the American Academy of Religion*, 2013, 81 (1): 6-55.

of the body as a whole; all the senses, as well as the other physical organs, take orders from it, whereas it is subject to none (Slingerland 2013: 12 - 13)①. He concludes that these accounts reveal an underlying dualism that dominates Chinese consciousness from fairly early times.

However, this simplistic profile obscures something. First, it is not so much that scholars of early Chinese thought paid inadequate attention to the contrast of the *xin* with the senses, the other organs, or the physical body, as that they were impressed by the distinct difference between Chinese and Western thought in terms of the multiplicity of the functional role of this single organ. Cardiocentrism, or the idea that the *xin* rather than the brain serves as the organ with which one thinks and makes judgments, is not news for scholars of Western thought (least of all classicists); it immediately recalls the similar claim in Aristotelian philosophy. What merits the most attention might be the dual role that the *xin* plays in early China. The widely held perception in early China appears to be that the *xin* is the sole place where thinking is located, but *also* that it is a physical organ. Little is said about the latter role in philosophical texts, but not because the early thinkers had no ideas about it. Quite the opposite: it describes the mainstream thought of the time. As a passage from *Guanzi* notes, for the early Chinese, the idea that the *xin* was a physical organ or part of the physical body was commonplace and served as the starting point from which a physiological metaphor (which will be discussed in the next section) that is popular in Chinese political philosophy (Yu 2007: 27 -47)② emerged:

> The prince, in occupying the capital of his state, is like the *xin* in the body. When moral conduct is certain in high places, the hundred surnames will be transformed below. When a sincere mind (*xin*) takes shape within, it will be manifested without. (Rickett 1985: 418 -419, modified)③

More persuasive evidence comes from an excavated text of *Mawangdui*, *Wuxing* (lit. Five Types of Action), in which the *xin* is depicted as a crucial part of the

---

① Edward Slingerland, Body and Mind in Early China: An Integrated Humanities-Science Approach, *Journal of the American Academy of Religion*, 2013, 81 (1): 6 -55.

② Ning Yu, Heart and Cognition in Ancient Chinese Philosophy, *Journal of Cognition and Culture*, 2007, 7 (1): 27 -47.

③ W. Allyn Rickett, *Guanzi: Political, Economic and Philosophical Essays from Early China*, Princeton, NJ: Princeton University Press, 1985.

physical body, in contrast with the extremities, ears, eyes, nose, and mouth. This physical as well as functional disparity is the reason the *xin* is the ruler:

> The six (body parts), the eyes, ears, nose, mouth, hands and feet are all slaves to the *xin*.... The six (body parts), the eyes, ears, nose, mouth, hands and feet—these six are... the minor parts of the human body; the *xin* is... a major part of the human body. And this is why (the *xin*) is called the ruler. (Mawangdui Han mu Yanjiu Xiaozu 1974: 18 – 19①; Csikszentmilalyi 2004: 361, modified)②

Other organs, such as the liver or lungs, were invisible in the picture drawn by the author. However, this does not support the claim that the *xin* is qualitatively different from them. Rather, the focus is put on the physicality of the *xin*: despite its central role in cognitive activity, the *xin* is always considered not as an immaterial agent reigning the physical body but as a part of the body.

Furthermore, it is widely believed that the organ is located at the center of the physical body. Notably, in the same book of *Xunzi*, we can find explicit references to the *xin*'s role as the "lord of the body and master of its spiritual brightness" and as an organ that occupies, beyond reasonable doubt, a pivotal position in the physical body:

> The ears, the eyes, nose, mouth, and body each have the capacity to provide sense contact, but their capacities are not interchangeable. They are called the heavenly officials. The *xin* dwells in the central cavity and governs the five officials, and hence it is called the heavenly ruler. (Knoblock 1994: 105)③

The consensus on the dual role of the *xin* creates a vast domain within which a distinct barrier between mind and body is not identifiable. In this sense, the early

① Mawangdui Han Mu Yanjiu Xiaozu, *Mawangdui Han Mu Bo Shu Laozi Jia Ben Juan Hou Gu Yi Shu Wuxing* [M]. Beijing: Wenwu Chubanshe, 1974. (马王堆汉墓研究组:《马王堆汉墓帛书老子甲本卷后古佚书·五行》文物出版社 1974 年版)

② Mark Csikszentmilalyi, *Material Virtue: Ethics and the Body in Early China*. Leiden: Brill, 2004.

③ John Knoblock, *Xunzi: A Translation and Study of the Complete Work*. Stanford, CA: Stanford University Press, 1994.

Chinese could legitimately be seen as holist. This holist position does not necessarily lead to the removal of divisions between mind and body. For example, a dividing line might emerge that serves as a second-order distinction for the sake of expediency and enables one to depict and analyze mental activities specifically without having to abandon, at the first-order or fundamental level, the holist position. As a result, whereas the word holism implies the presence of a crude division between mind and body rather than a complete lack of division, that division does not imply, as Slingerland asserts, that the *xin* is qualitatively different from other organs. At best, what we can say is that it is the close integration of mind and body rather than the division between them that is emphasized by scholars of early China, to the extent that the perennial existence of that division is often unmentioned or unnoticed. Briefly, for early Chinese thinkers, the *xin* was different from the rest of the body, but not as different as Slingerland assumes.

One might call any culture with a tendency to divide a particular organ of thought (e. g., the heart or brain) and the rest of the body *dualist*. However, at least in the context of Chinese thought, it seems difficult to determine whether this overgeneralized dualist claim could provide more insight into the domain under inspection than the existing holist one. The holist claim works well to depict and explain the apparent lack of curiosity in the afterlife among the early Chinese thinkers (most notably the claims attributed to Confucius in the *Analects*①) or, in rare cases when they must refer to it, their predominant reservations toward it. In contrast, a dualist claim, despite limited success in depicting a few irrelevant characteristics of the Chinese conception of the afterlife, fails to offer an explanation that is as satisfactory as or more satisfactory than the culture-related lack of curiosity. Given this situation, claiming that early Chinese thought is dualist seems too hasty a dive into science, particularly the fads that pass therein, like the use of big data (Slingerland et al. 2017)② at the cost of the richness and depth of human consciousness that are so valued in the humanities.

---

① For instance, "When you don't yet know how to serve human beings, how can you serve the spirits?" "When you don't yet understand life, how can you understand death?" See *The Analects* 11: 12.

② Edward Slingerland, Ryan Nichols, Kristoffer Neilbo, and Carson Logan, The Distant Reading of Religious Texts: A "Big Data" Approach to Mind-Body Concepts in Early China, *Journal of the American Academy of Religion*, 2017, 85 (4) 985-1016.

3. Medical Accounts of the *Xin* and the *Xin*-Body Relation

Few resources are more indicative of the nature of the *xin* and an examination of its dual role than TCM, whose worth to studies of early Chinese thought has been underestimated. While Slingerland and his associates have recognized the significance of medical texts only recently (Slingerland et al 2017: 14 – 17)①, their remedial work seems to be locked into a position that is too important for them to abort. *Huangdi nei jing* (*the Yellow Emperor's Inner Canon*, 黄帝内经), which contains Warring States material yet was presumably assembled in the first to second centuries (Sivin 1995: 184)②, is the earliest known medical text in China and a definitive work of theories of TCM. It presents an inverse version of the physiological metaphor of the *xin* as ruler by articulating a sociopolitical metaphor in a physiological context. As *Suwen* (素问) famously remarks,

> The *xin* is the official functioning as Ruler; Spiritual light originates in it. The lung is the official functioning as Chancellor and Mentor; Order and regulation originate in it. The liver is the official functioning as General; Planning and deliberation originate in it. The gallbladder is the official functioning as Rectifier; Judgments and decision originate in it.... All these twelve officials must not lose each other. (Unschuld 2003: 133, modified)③

In another passage, the materiality of the *xin* is made clear when the anonymous author ascribes a certain pathological significance to its ruggedness: The *xin* is the grand master of the five viscera and six bowels and is where the essence-spirit dwells. Its organ is rugged so that pathogens will not invade; otherwise, the *xin* is damaged. If the *xin* is damaged, vitality (lit. spirit) will disappear; if vitality

---

① Edward Slingerland, Ryan Nichols, Kristoffer Neilbo, and Carson Logan, The Distant Reading of Religious Texts: A "Big Data" Approach to Mind-Body Concepts in Early China, *Journal of the American Academy of Religion*, 2017, 85 (4): 985 – 1016.

② The extant edition of the *Huangdi Neijing* consists of two texts: *Huangdi neijing suwen* (briefly, *Suwen* 素问) and its sister text (Unschuld 2003: ix), *Lingshu* (灵枢). Both, as Lloyd and Sivin (2002: 76) and Unschuld (2016: 1) correctly point out, are based on the accumulation of texts in the earlier period.

③ Paul U Unschuld, *Huang Di Nei Jing Su Wen: Nature, Knowledge, Imagery in an Ancient Chinese Medical Text* [M]. Berkeley: University of California Press, 2003.

disappears, the human dies (*Lingshu* 71).[①]

Hence, the superiority of the *xin* over other organs is a common view adopted by both the early thinkers and contemporary medical experts. However, this does not support a dualist claim. With the *xin* and other organs juxtaposed, the true premise is that the *xin*, like all the other organs that are enumerated or mentioned, is a physical organ or, as some modern interpreters propose, a medically functional body.[②] In either situation, the *xin* should not and cannot be identified with the mind in the Cartesian sense, either strong or weak. Medical accounts of the *xin* therefore offer a critical complement to philosophical accounts of it in defense of a holist position rather than a dualist one.

The mechanics of the *xin*-body relationship must be elaborated, which may put an end to disputes over the soundness of Chinese dualism with deciding evidence from the infiltration and integration of two realms that are often separate in the industrial West, philosophy and medicine.

In an embryological account from *Huangdi nei jing* (or, rather, *Lingshu* 54), the crucial step in the generation of a living human being is the entering of *qi* into a newly created physical body. It is the *xin* into which the *qi* enters and dwells, and this transition makes nonlife to human life possible:

> The blood and the *qi* harmonize, the nutrient and defense *qi* connect, the five viscera are formed, the shen-*qi* (lit. divine *qi*) dwells on the *xin* and therefore the *hun* (lit. celestial soul) and the *po* (lit. corporeal soul) are set; hence, it becomes a human.[③]

Of particular interest is that instead of developing something approaching Cartesian substance dualism, the strategy employed by the early Chinese physicians to explain the genesis of individual human life is quite the opposite. The word *shen* in the passage (or, more generally, in Chinese medical texts) tends to be used not as a noun referring to supernatural beings or the incorporeal soul but as an adjective to

---

① Translated by the author.

② A main motivation for adopting the functional interpretation is to manage the incompatibilities of traditional Chinese medicine with modern medicine with regard to anatomical and physiological facts and therefore to legitimate it in the modern world.

③ Translated by the author.

modify the immediately adjacent noun *qi*. The *qi* is the activating fluid in the body as well as in the atmosphere, implying an apparently holist position. The appropriate English equivalent to the word *shen-qi* might be the daimonic *qi*, suggesting that it is the *qi* that, in some subtle or quintessential form, pours into the body (which is believed to be the buildup of the *qi*) or, rather, into *xin*, the organ, and vitalizes the body, rendering it alive. In contrast with modern medicine, TCM is a distinctly holist position.

The holist position of TCM can be illustrated by its emphasis on psychosomatic diseases and corresponding treatments to address them. Emotions are believed to affect one's physiological health through the *qi*. Anger, for instance, makes the *qi* rise, whereas joy makes it relax, and sadness makes it dissipate. In particular, fright causes disorder of the *qi*, since the *shen*, whose function is to regulate the movement of the *qi* throughout the body, cannot maintain its position, namely, the *xin*, which is disturbed by the abrupt emotion: "When one is frightened, then the *xin* has nothing to lean on, the shen has nowhere to return and one's deliberations have nowhere to settle. Hence the *qi* is in disorder." (Unschuld 2003: 231, modified) ①

Pensiveness, by contrast, causes the stagnation of the *qi*, because the normal exercise of the *shen* in regulating the *qi* movement is thwarted given the failure of one's *xin* to maintain given the situation: "When one is pensive, then the *xin* has a place to be, the shen has a place to turn to and the proper *qi* stays [at one location] and does not move. Hence the *qi* lumps together." (Unschuld 2003: 231, modified) ②

The conceptual frame of TCM is built around the concept of the *qi*, which renders the immaterial/material distinction rudimentary, if not nonexistent. Moreover, although the *xin* may functionally distinguish itself from other organs and therefore the physical body as a whole, the way it functions eliminates the gap that makes it independent of the rest of the body, neutralizing any drives toward the dissociation of it from the physical body or the Cartesian mind/body distinction. This is why the *xin* should not be considered the equivalent of the brain or mind in Western thought and why the *xin*-body relation is not the same as the mind-body

---

① Paul U. Unschuld, *Huang Di Nei Jing Su Wen: Nature, Knowledge, Imagery in an Ancient Chinese Medical Text*, Berkeley: University of California Press, 2003.

② Paul U. Unschuld, *Huang Di Nei Jing Su Wen: Nature, Knowledge, Imagery in an Ancient Chinese Medical Text*, Berkeley: University of California Press, 2003.

relation in Western thought. For early Chinese thinkers and physicians, the *xin* is more the container of thought than the organ of thought; it remains inert until the injection of the *qi* at a particular moment during embryologic development. The condition presupposed for them under which conceptions of mind and body are formed is a chief concern, with an organogenesis that emphasizes the correlation of human beings and general cosmological laws and, therefore, the deprecation of human agency rather than the appreciation of it.

4. Physicality and Mentality as Two Sides of the Same Coin

The same underlying physio-psychological picture exists in early Chinese philosophy as well as in medicine. There is an intrinsic link between epistemic improvement and regimen, or the topics of self-cultivation (*xiushen* 修身) and life-nurturance (*yangsheng* 养生). The structural inevitability of this link, however, is where the dualist claim of early Chinese thought tends to fail.

Althoughit remains arguable whether Chinese philosophy is an identifiable disciplinary field in itself, it is increasingly accepted by modern scholars that many, if not all, concepts used by early Chinese thinkers do not fit into the frameworks of traditional Western philosophy (Fung 1966)①. Among those concepts characteristic of Chinese thought, the topic of self-cultivation merits attention in terms of its link with medicine. It is not unique to Confucians but rather is a common idea shared by Confucians, Daoists (both philosophical Daoism and religious Daoism), and smaller, albeit no less significant, early schools. Despite the discrepancies between their individual understandings of this concept, a close correlation between wisdom and virtue characterizes the early thinkers' ubiquitous concern with self-cultivation. The pursuit of learning is thought to contain the improvement of one's morality. (Lai 2008: 4 –5)②

However, another aspect of the topic may have not received equal attention. Although an increasing number of works on early China have provided insights

① Youlan A Fung, *Short History of Chinese Philospohy*, New York: The Free Press, 1966.

② L. Lai, *Karyn An Introduction to Chinese Philosophy*, Cambridge: Cambridge University Press, 2008.

into the embodied aspect of spiritual practice for religious (Brashier 2011[①]; Lai 2015[②]) or nonreligious purposes (Lewis 2006[③]; Harper 2015)[④], the underdeveloped state of research about the physical benefits of moral self-cultivation is conspicuous, especially in the philosophical community. The early thinkers believed that intellectual progress would not only improve one's morality but also enhance one's health. Accounts of the health benefits of epistemic improvement are echoed from the opposite direction by an ancient health concern: life-nurturance (also known as health preservation, health cultivation, or life cultivation; see World Health Organization 2007: 11)[⑤], which refers to a body of knowledge and practice in pursuit of health or an elixir of life consisting of medicine, regimen, diet, the art of sex, and so on. It is believed that life-nurturance not only leads to longevity (or even, at least for the Daoist, the immortality of the physical body) but also endows the practitioner with intel lectual and moral superiority. In turn, for the early Chinese thinkers and their successors who were affected by their enquiry, it is difficult, if not impossible, to conceive that the sage who reaches self-perfection does not necessarily appear healthy, strong, and beautiful. An accomplished person is supposed to be accomplished in every respect: mentally, morally, and physically. Self-cultivation and life-nurturance are therefore two sides of an organic whole. One is seen as originating from another, which in turn affects and shapes it, and vice versa.

Here we see the pivotal and subtlest part of this mutually generative relationship: the goal of self-perfection can only be attained, by either a mental or a physical approach, by carefully fostering and refining the *qi* from within so that the practitioner's body is ultimately filled with it. This mind-body integration and values ascribed to it are replicated across the texts of different schools. The most well-known instance is the book of *Mencius* 2: A: 2, where we read,

---

① Kenneth E Brashier, *Ancestral Memory in Ancient China*, Harvard Yenching Institute Monograph Series 72. Cambridge, MA: Harvard University Asia Center for the Harvard-Yenching Institute, distributed by Harvard University Press, 2011.

② Guolong Lai, *Excavating the Afterlife: The Archeology of Early Chinese Religion*, Seattle: University of Washington Press, 2015.

③ Mark Edward Lewis, *The Construction of Space in Early China*, Albany: SUNY Press, 2006.

④ Donald Harper, *Early Chinese Medical Literature: The Mawangdui Medical Manuscripts*, London: Routledge, 2015.

⑤ World Health Organization, *The WHO International Standard Terminologies on Traditional Medicine in the Western Pacific Region*, Manila: WHO Western Pacific Region, 2007.

> I am good at nourishing the vast, flowing *qi*... This *qi* is consummately great and consummately strong. If one nourishes it with uprightness and does not injure it, it will fill the space between Heaven and earth. This *qi* is the companion of rightness and the Way, in the absence of which it starves... If one's actions cause the *xin* to be disquieted, it starves... Always be doing something, but without fixation, with the *xin* inclined neither to forget nor to help things grow. (Bloom 2009: 30, modified)①

Although the *xin* holds a remarkable position in Mencius' instructions to "nourish the vast, flowing *qi*," it is articulated in the same discussion that this can be achieved only through mindfulness while giving a loose rein to the *qi*: "maintain the will, do no violence to the *qi*." (Bloom 2009: 30, modified)② Similarly, *Xunzi* 21: 34 emphasizes the denial of human agency, namely, the *xin* as constructively passive while performing its function:

> What do men use to know the Way? I say that it is the xin. How does the xin know? I say that by its emptiness, unity and stillness. (Knoblock 1994: vol Ⅲ, p. 104, modified)③

So it is for the Daoist. In Daoist terms, physical intactness is given a role equally indispensable to mental completeness with regard to one's *de* (potency) in accordance with *dao* (the Way). As the book of *Zhuang-zi* remarks,

> He who holds fast to the Way is complete in Virtue; being complete in Virtue, he is complete in body; being complete in body, he is complete in spirit; and to be complete in spirit is the Way of the sage. (Watson 2013, 92)④

The supposedly close alliance of mental-moral and physical development reaches

① Irene Bloom, *Mencius*, New York: Columbia University Press, 2009.

② Irene Bloom, *Mencius*, New York: Columbia University Press, 2009.

③ John Knoblock, *Xunzi: A Translation and Study of the Complete Work*, Stanford, CA: Stanford University Press, 1994.

④ Burton Watson, *The Complete Work of Zhuangzi*, New York: Columbia University Press, 2013.

such a level that it must be carefully explained that a few ideal characters in *Zhuang-zi* appear with disfigured bodies due to birth defects, illness, or mutilation penalties. Although the details of the explanation *Zhuang-zi* provides are beyond the scope of this article, the formation of one's mentality coupled with physicality that is far from intact or in good health should not threaten the Daoist ideal, for it is the way and the extent to which these characters shrug off the crippled body or even the destruction of the body that makes unnecessary a diametrical rupture between mentality and physicality at individual level. They accept—even welcome the loss of selfhood as to be one with the universe by "wandering in the *qi* of heaven and earth" (Watson 2013: 92, modified)①, or rather dissolving into the universal process of *qi* transformation: therein no hidden dualist agenda exists, "they look on life as a swelling tumor, a protruding *wen*, and on death as the draining of a sore or the bursting of a boil." (Watson 2013, 50)②

Conclusion

Although the attempt to reappraise the concepts of mind and body in early China based on the latest developments in cognitive science is, as Edward Slingerland shows, refreshing, intriguing, and impressively illuminating, it is unclear whether a new understanding of early Chinese thought can be created from such an attempt. Evidence from two major sources for Slingerland's subversive dualist claim of early Chinese thought—one of afterlife beliefs implying a substantive disparity between the living and supernatural beings such as ancestral spirits and a supposedly qualitative difference of the *xin* and the senses, other organs, and the physical body as a whole—are both largely built on the foundation of selective bias and a partial, often flattened understanding of the texts. This cherry-picking approach unfortunately undermines arguments for the claim and renders it invalid. In particular, although strong evidence from traditional Chinese medicine and Chinese philosophy suggest the concept of the dual role of a physical organ and an organ of thought in early China, it may not be deduced that a mind-body dualism, however weak, reigned in early China from the *xin*-body division involving different degrees of substantiality.

Slingerland's work is valuable in that, despite some temerity, it presents a powerful reminder of the magnitude and complexity of the links between presumably

① BurtonWatson, *The Complete Work of Zhuangzi*, New York: Columbia University Press, 2013.

② BurtonWatson, *The Complete Work of Zhuangzi*, New York: Columbia University Press, 2013.

universalist cognitive traits and cultural diversity. For instance, the idea that scholars of early China have for centuries attempted, wittingly or unwittingly, to set Chinese or Eastern thought and Western thought against each other or to create antagonism or particularism (as discussed here) with regard to Chinese holism requires more meticulous examination in a broader, yet nuanced context. In this sense, what Slingerland offers is an alternative that, despite going from one extreme to the other, demonstrates a respectable effort to give age-old issues fresh life.

维特根斯坦与新指称理论

——兼答欣迪卡问题

任　远

欣迪卡（J. Hintikka）在《综合》（*Synthese*）杂志提出的编号为36的哲学问题是：维特根斯坦是否能算作新指称理论者？欣迪卡认为，《逻辑哲学论》时期的维特根斯坦持有的逻辑－语义理论和20世纪70年代后兴起的以克里普克为主要代表的“新指称理论”之间具有显著的相似性，并指出这种相似性体现在《逻辑哲学论》的下述几个论断中：（1）每个简单名称必然地（即在所有可能事态中）指向其命名的对象；（2）简单对象之间的等同陈述要么是空的，要么是必然为假的；（3）所有简单名称（简单对象的名称）都是通过实指方式引入的；（4）名称并不是通过它们的描述性内容来被运用的。上述论题无疑与新指称理论的基本观点在表面上高度接近，那么这是否意味着维特根斯坦在《逻辑哲学论》中的观点本质上与克里普克的理论相类同？欣迪卡想要发问的是，如果两者观点类同的话，他们各自的理由是否相同？如果不同的话，差别在什么地方？①

简要言之，前期维特根斯坦在《逻辑哲学论》里追随罗素的意义的指谓观，认为名称的意义在于其指称，特别是逻辑专名指称着简单对象。这一论题与直接指称理论的下述基本立场的确是高度相似的：直接指称表达式不通过任何中介指称着对象。而后期维特根斯坦在《哲学研究》中的工作正是始于对意义的指谓观的批评，其中关于指称的主题常被概括为如下几个方面：（1）从实指的不确定性引入语言游戏的观念，（2）通过批评“名称命名简单物”来攻击意义的指谓观，（3）对指示词的直接指称理论的批评，（4）名称意义的簇描述理论。包括克里普克在内的很多哲学家认为后期维特根斯坦对于指称理论的看法，与斯特劳森和塞尔一道都属于描述理论的传统。

前后期维特根斯坦的哲学风格一般被认为是针锋相对的，分别被分析哲学运动的理想语言学派和日常语言学派奉为圭臬。如果欣迪卡所言不虚，从指称理论来看，《逻辑哲学论》时期的维特根斯坦和《哲学研究》时期的维特根斯

---

① 《综合》杂志主编、著名分析哲学家欣迪卡在1997—2002年的《综合》杂志各卷（不定期）尾页提出一个哲学问题，内容涉及语言哲学、数学和逻辑哲学、科学哲学、形而上学等领域，累计提出38个哲学问题。

坦似乎逆向对应着分析哲学中指称理论的发展，前期维特根斯坦持有名称的直接指称理论观，而后期维特根斯坦却持有名称的描述理论。就维特根斯坦本人而言，他的后期哲学对前期哲学构成了明显的批判，但就分析哲学史而言，作为新指称理论运动核心的直接指称理论则是建立在对指称的描述理论的批判上的。欣迪卡显然注意到了这里面的独特的张力。因此，欣迪卡的问题实际上对新指称理论暗含着批评：从维特根斯坦的思想发展角度，直接指称理论本身并非什么新颖洞见，而是被后来的维特根斯坦所批判和抛弃的哲学立场。当然，这里的前提是维特根斯坦版本的直接指称理论与克里普克引发晚期分析哲学运动革命的新指称理论如出一辙。这正是本文要仔细考察的地方。后文中我们将对维特根斯坦的前后期指称观分别展开解读，试图纠正一些流行的误解，并对欣迪卡的问题给出回复，在此基础上说明维特根斯坦与新指称理论的关系。

一、《逻辑哲学论》中的指称观

指称关系是指称表达式和外部世界中的对象之间的语义关系。在通常的指称理论中，指称表达式是指日常语言中的单称词项如专名、指示词和索引词、限定摹状词，或一般非单称词项如通名或理论词项等，对象则包括日常物理对象，以及自然类或理论实体。新指称理论要解释的指称关系无疑属于这种语义关系。根据新指称理论的语义学论题，一个名称对于所在语句的语义贡献就是该名称所指涉的对象。对这种语义关系的建立，可以进一步探究其认知基础。根据新指称理论的认识论论题，名称直接指向所指涉的对象而无需通过任何描述性的或非描述性的中介。但《逻辑哲学论》（Wittgenstein，1922/1961，下文简称 *TLP*）① 中论及的指称关系是否体现了上述名称和对象之间的语义关系及其认知基础呢？我们来考察 *TLP* 中的相关段落。

先考虑 *TLP* 中关于对象的论述，集中见于 *TLP* 第 2 部分。*TLP* 的第 2 部分集中给出了图像论的基本结构，主要是事态和对象之间的关系、对象的特征以及图像的性质。其中关于对象的主要论述可列举如下："基本事态是诸对象的结合"（2.01）；"对象是简单的"（2.02）；"具有相同逻辑形式的两个对象彼此间的唯一差别仅在于它们是不同的（除了它们的外在性质）"（2.0233），以及"在一幅图像中与诸对象相对应的是图像的诸元素"（2.13）。前期维特根斯坦在世界和语言之间进行同构式对应时，简单对象对应着简单名称，对象的简单性一如名称的初始性，两者都是不可分析的，分别是世界和语言的原子单位。对象是简单的，不能看作是（外在）性质的集合（2.02），在此意义上甚

① L. Wittgenstein, *Tractatus Logico-Philosophicus*, D. F. Pears and B. F. McGuinness (trans.), New York: Humanities Press, 1922/1961.

至对象是没有特定颜色的（2.0232）。另一方面，有色性是对象的形式（2.0251），与时间、空间一道构成了对象的内在性质（或逻辑形式），是稳定的，而对象的配置即对象之间的关联方式，则是变动的（2.0271），诸对象的配置构成基本事态（2.0272）。

因此，作为简单名称之指称的简单对象，并非现实世界中的具体对象，而是有待通过配置而生成基本事态的对象，因而是逻辑空间中的对象，它们仅具有逻辑形式外而不具有别的可被描述的外在性质。所谓外在性质，包括“一物具有其他物都不具有的性质，这时人们能通过某个描述将该物与其他物区别开来并指向它”（2.02331）。对于简单对象而言，它们之间的唯一差别就在于它们是不同的。这可相应于形式语言中用变元所代表的对象；不同变元指称论域中不同对象，但所指称的对象在使用变元指称这个层次上并无任何特定性质上的差异。简单对象的这个特征，使得它具有实体的地位，而实体是独立于实际情况而存在的东西（2.024）。诸对象是构成世界的实体，因此它们是简单的而不是复合的（2.021）。

对于 *TLP* 中对象的范畴地位，欣迪卡曾给出大胆解释，认为维特根斯坦在 *TLP* 中谈论的对象，可以理解成直接经验到的亲知对象。证据之一是前期维特根斯坦的思想深受同期罗素的影响，在撰写 *TLP* 时维特根斯坦与罗素正有着密切的互动。而且，*TLP* 及其他早期文本中也有若干片段似乎可以解读为 *TLP* 中的世界与生活世界或感觉材料的世界有着密切的关系。[①]然而我们容易看到，亲知对象的现象学特征与对象的简单性要求构成了明显的张力。正如欣迪卡承认的，对象的简单性意味着：对象没有结构，对象是原初的（也即不能被进一步分析成更基本的要素），对象之间是彼此合乎逻辑且独立的。另外，在 *TLP* 文本中维特根斯坦从未承诺或提及到亲知对象，即使他在 *TLP* 中考虑的对象能够追溯到现象学的世界，最终得到的对象仍是逻辑重构的结果。正如维特根斯坦在 *TLP* 接近尾声的地方说到：“物理学规律，通过其整个的逻辑手段，谈论的仍然是世界中的对象”（6.3431），并且“力学对世界的描述总是非常一般性的。比如它从不谈论世界中的特定的物质点，而总是只谈论任意的物质点”（6.3432）。因此，正如 *TLP* 中的世界是生活世界的逻辑还原，*TLP* 中的对象应当被视为亲知对象的逻辑抽象，这类似于力学中的物体与质点的关系。

TLP 中对名称的谈论集中体现在第 3 部分。*TLP* 对名称的看法总体而言可以概括成下面几点：（1）必须通过语境原则来理解名称；（2）名称具有表征

① M. Hintikka & J. Hintikka, *Investigating Wittgenstein*, New York: Basil Blackwell, 1986, pp. 51 – 63.

性，即名称的功能是指谓对象；（3）名称具有简单性或非复合性；（4）名称可以看成是变元。根据文本对这几个论题可以做如下说明。

首先在 *TLP* 中，名称是作为命题的一部分被谈论的，而且根据维特根斯坦此处设定的语境原则，离开命题谈论名称的指称是没有意义的（3.3），因此我们对名称的讨论总是要参照对命题的讨论。在讨论命题的结构时，名称在命题中的作用被清晰地刻画出来。维特根斯坦首先这样引入对名称：在一个命题中被应用的简单符号叫作名称（3.202）。其次，名称和命题都是用来表征外语言的实体的：名称如点，命题如箭，它们有指向（3.144）。紧接 *TLP* 着对名称的功能给出说明：名称指称对象。对象是其所指（3.203），名称在命题中代表对象（3.22）。因此，名称与对象的指称关系具有两个基本特征：名称在命题中出现，名称代表对象。合在一起即"名称在命题中代表对象"，这就是名称的指谓观，名称的意义就是其指谓，即名称对命题的语义贡献就是其指谓的对象。这的确与直接指称理论的语义学论题如出一辙。如果维特根斯坦所谈论的名称就是直接指称理论所讨论的名称，那么维特根斯坦的确就表达了某种直接指称论题。

维特根斯坦接下来讨论了名称的特征，特别强调了名称的简单性，名称作为初始符号是不可进一步分析的："一个名称是不能通过任何定义而进一步加以剖析的，它是一种初始符号。"（3.26）这种不可分析的简单性也可以通过非复合性来说明。"对于名称而言，所有种类的复合性都将一一证明是非本质性的。"（3.3411）如果名称是不可分析的，那么罗素关于日常专名的描述理论和摹状词理论似乎都不能在此应用。"我只能命名对象。符号表征它们。我只能谈论它们，我不能断定它们。命题只能说一个物是怎样的，而不能说它是什么。"（3.221）欣迪卡将这一点称为"对象存在的不可表达性"，由此得出"语义学的不可表达性"。[①]名称的简单性对应着对象的简单性，正如名称与其他名称的结合（得到基本命题）对应着对象之间的配置（得到基本事态）。在 *TLP* 的第 4 部分，维特根斯坦解释了基本命题与名称的关系。名称与其所在的语境的关系被更清楚地揭示。这一部分涉及名称与基本命题的关系的几个主要论述如下："基本命题是由名称构成的。它是诸名称的一种关联、链接"（4.22）；"显而易见，在对命题进行分析的时候，我们必然要达到由名称的直接结合所构成的基本命题"（4.221）；"只是在某个基本命题的关联中一个名称才出现在一个命题中"（4.23）。

值得注意的是，为了说明名称的简单性，维特根斯坦用了变元的说法来代

① M. Hintikka & J. Hintikka, *Investigating Wittgenstein*, New York: Basil Blackwell, 1986, p. 47.

替名称。“名称是简单符号，我通过使用单个的字母（‘x’‘y’‘z’）来指示它们。”（4.24）这与我们前面的分析是一致的，即简单对象是可以用变元指称的对象。这里最关键的问题是名称之间如何结合成基本命题（相应的，对象之间如何配置成基本事态）。但维特根斯坦虽然指出了这个问题，在后文中并没有给予明确的回答。维特根斯坦在接下来的段落中（第5部分）主要谈论基本事态与基本命题之间的对应关系，以及一般命题作为基本命题的函项，也即一般命题的逻辑结构。在谈论完命题形式后，维特根斯坦又回到基本命题的构成这个问题上，并且指出：“基本命题由诸名称构成。由于我们不能给出具有不同指称的名称的数目，我们也就不能给出基本命题的构成形式。”（5.55）因此，虽然基本命题是名称的链接，但是，这种链接是如何进行结合的，维特根斯坦并未指明，基本命题的构成形式从而也无法给出。在这里，基本命题的结构能否像弗雷格那样分析成用主目填充不饱和的函项那样的关系？维特根斯坦确实在4.24中写道：“我将基本命题写作如下形式的诸名称的函项：‘fx’，‘（x，y）’等等。”也就是说，诸名称被以某种方式结合在一起，但这种结合方式具有不可还原的多样性。名称虽然构成了基本命题，但并无明确的途径把基本命题进一步刻画成名称和名称之间的组合或链接方式。

二、对欣迪卡问题的回复

从前面论及的*TLP*中关于名称和对象的关系可见，就新指称理论所涉及的指称关系的认识论问题而言，维特根斯坦并未讨论日常名称和对象是如何进行认知关联的。虽然从维特根斯坦的表述的确可以推出名称直接指称对象，但是这里的名称和对象显然都是逻辑空间中的元素，与日常语言中名称的使用大异其趣。逻辑空间中的对象是简单的，其外在性质都是被忽略的，因此并不可能存在任何相关的对象的识别性质能够进入讨论中。就前述欣迪卡论及的*TLP*和新指称理论的第一点相似性（每个简单名称必然地指向其命名对象）和第四点相似性（名称并不是通过它们的描述性内容来被运用的）而言，对于维特根斯坦和直接指称论者有着全然不同的意义。维特根斯坦在名称和对象之间建立的“直接”指称关系只是建立同构映射的一种规定，这种“直接性”毋宁说是先天地被确立的，从而可以推出在每种情况下都成立。而克里普克等直接指称论者需要借助模态论证和认知错误论证来反驳描述理论的方法，在维特根斯坦这里毫无用武之地，因为逻辑空间里的情况既无须参照反事实世界中的情形来讨论，这又与日常生活中的认知情境毫无关联。

类似地，就新指称理论所涉及的指称关系的语义学问题而言，维特根斯坦自然也不可能讨论日常语言的语句所表达的命题中名称对句子的语义贡献如何。如前，逻辑空间中的名称不具有复合性及任何描述性性质。一方面，在*TLP*中尽管名称对应着对象，名称的结合形成命题，命题指称着事态，由此不难推出名称对于命题的语义贡献只能是对象，这相当于直接指称理论的结论。但另一方面，在维特根斯坦那里基本命题的构成形式并不清楚，即对名称如何构成于命题之中并未指明，在基本命题的结构并不清楚的情况下名称对于命题的语义贡献其实无法落实。

关于简单对象的等同陈述，欣迪卡指出*TLP*和新指称理论的第二点共同之处在于"简单对象之间的等同陈述要么是空的，要么是必然为假的"。但两种理论的根据并不相同。对于直接指称论者，该结论是由等同陈述中等词两边的名称的严格性造成的。名称之所以是严格的，按照克里普克的观点，是对日常语言进行经验测试的结果。相反，对于维特根斯坦，所考虑的语言是逻辑整编后的没有歧义的语言，该语言要求不同对象之间应该有不同的名称，并且每个对象只能有一个名称。也即"我用符号的同一性而不是同一性的符号来表达对象的同一性。用符号的不同来表达对象的不同"（5.53）。由于名称和对象严格地一一对应，因此任何对象不可能具有两个不同的名称。需要注意，维特根斯坦对于等同符号或等词的理解与弗雷格及罗素的传统有着很大的差别，维特根斯坦认为，"罗素关于'='的定义是不适当的"（5.5302），"同一性符号不是《概念文字》中具有本质意义的部分"（5.533）。对维特根斯坦而言，"a = b"形式的表达式不过是表现的权宜之计，并未就符号"a"和"b"的所指有所断言（4.242），但至少"a = a"这样的表达式并不是基本命题（4.243）。

因此，欣迪卡问题虽然指出了前期维特根斯坦对指称问题的表述与新指称理论的结论表面上高度类似，但我们不能就此认为半个世纪以后兴起的新指称理论不过是重复了*TLP*中的观点。新指称理论对指称关系的分析，承接的主要是日常语言学派的方法，更多地基于语用维度，着力于分析日常语言在大量生活情境中的使用。作为新指称理论发端的唐纳兰对于摹状词的指称性使用和克里普克对说话者指称的分析可作为典型的例子。也就是说，*TLP*与新指称理论对于名称与对象之关系的论述，无论从理论动机、论证过程还是一般方法论来看，两者实在是貌合神离。

再考虑欣迪卡的前述第3条"简单名称是以实指方式引入的"。这里的简单名称对应的就是逻辑专名。逻辑专名只有"这"和"那"，说是实指引入的也无可厚非，但这种实指引入的方式与新指称理论讨论的日常专名习得时的实指引入并无类似之处，后者总是伴随着知觉活动，这种知觉活动可以通过因果接触或描述性解释去刻画。这里欣迪卡的根据并不是*TLP*中的论述，而是根据维特根斯坦的《1914—1916笔记》，“下述概念似乎是先天地被给予我们的：‘这个’——与对象的概念同一”。欣迪卡在早前的论文里批评过新指称理论，认为其谬误的根源把实指性等同陈述（所谓“从物陈述”）看作是直接指称的（所谓“从物指称”）。[①] 欣迪卡认为，新指称理论正确地注意到在模态或内涵语境中不可分析的同一性标准不可还原为任何描述性条件，但是并不能由此得出存在某类特殊的词项具有直接指称的特征。欣迪卡赞成达米特对克里普克的批评，“从物”和“从言”陈述之间的差别与直接指称无关，而仅仅是模态词与量词的辖域差别。限于篇幅这里不讨论欣迪卡对于直接指称理论的批评是否合理，仅就 *TLP* 中来看，维特根斯坦没有直接讨论实指定义，而是通过“说明”（德语 Erlauterungen，英译 elucidation）来解释初始符号的所指（3.263）。这里“说明”的要点在于初始名称与对象之间的先行联系，这种联系一方面使得语言与实在发生了真实接触，另一方面是整个逻辑原子论的意义建构的出发点。

后期维特根斯坦以攻击奥古斯丁图景作为整个《哲学研究》（Wittgenstein，1953/2009，下文简称 *PI*）[②] 的开端。前期维特根斯坦的语言 - 世界图景实际上就是奥古斯丁图景的逻辑重构。根据奥古斯丁图景的语言观，指称关系是我们理解语言的出发点。实指定义是典型的引入名称和确立指称关系的活动，实指教学活动为我们提供了语言习得的基本模型。维特根斯坦在 *PI* 第28节讨论了实指定义中的不确定性。孤立的命名活动存在着解释的不确定性，任何定义都可能被误解。为了理解实指定义先必须对实指活动的场景加以说明。经过分析事实上理解实指定义离不开语境和整个说话背景，语言系统和共同体的语言实践先于个体对语词的使用，要有意义地询问一个名称的指称，就要先知道名称是用来做什么的。实指活动的不确定性意味着，不能把意义生成的活动还原成以指称的发生作为出发点，指称关系不是建构意义的原子性因素。实指关系并不能引入不可分解的简单名称。

三、后期维特根斯坦论指示词和名称

罗素曾经认为“这”“那”等指示词是真正的专名或逻辑专名，也就是真正的指称关系的支点，普通专名是缩写的摹状词，最终要还原到真正的专名上。真正的专名的一个特点就是，它只能通过实指定义来给出指称。*PI* 时期的

---

① J. Hintikka & G. Sandu, The fallacies of the new theory of reference, *Synthese*, 1995, 104 (2): 245 - 283.

② L. Wittgenstein, *Philosophical Investigations* (Rev. 4th ed.), G. Anscombe, P. Hacker and J. Schulte (trans.), Wiley-Blackwell, 1953/2009.

维特根斯坦在指出实指定义本身的不确定性后，又在第 37 节和 38 节中否认了在语词和对象之间存在着我们传统上称为指称关系的东西。在第 37 节中，维特根斯坦问“名称与被命名的事物之间的关系是什么?”维特根斯坦对这个问题的回答是提醒我们去考察各种语言游戏，因为这种关系就发生在语言游戏中。一旦我们去考察不同的语言游戏，就会发现名称和事物之间的联系不存在唯一的刻画，正如语言游戏本身背后没有本质性的定义。认为命名或指称关系内有某种深刻的本质有待揭示，这是维特根斯坦不能接受的。指称和其他语言哲学的概念一样，虽然有待澄清，但并不能作为理解意义的基础。从这个角度而言维特根斯坦可以看作是指称关系的收缩论者。

维特根斯坦进一步批评了逻辑专名是真正的名称的观点。“如果你不想制造混乱，那么你最好还是根本不要把这两个词（‘这’和‘那’）叫作名称。”（第 38 节）维特根斯坦认为，把指示词“这个”当成逻辑专名或真正的名称，把日常语言中的专名看成是逻辑专名的近似，是哲学家将语言抽离其自然历史而逻辑化造成的理论后果：命名成了一种神秘的活动，一种命名仪式，用以在名称和对象之间建立一种独一无二的联系。维特根斯坦的这种说法，与克里普克后来的因果指称理论表面上确实是背道而驰。但要注意到的是，维特根斯坦批评的是把指示词“这个”和对象之间的关系（通过实指活动建立）抽象成指称关系的本质，而克里普克刻画的则是一般日常名称的指称的社会学图景。

维特根斯坦在 *TLP* 时期所持有的指称观，认为通常的专名不是真正的名称，真正的名称或逻辑专名指称简单的事物，其意义就是其指称。而通常的专名则可以有意义而无指称。一般认为这受到了罗素的影响。为了批评早期的自己，维特根斯坦在 *PI* 第 39 节重复了罗素的论证（名称意谓着简单物），这个论证可以整理如下：

（1）尽管某个句子所谈论的对象不存在，但这个句子还是有明确的意义；

（2）仅当一个句子被分析后，这个句子所意谓的事情才变得清楚起来；

（3）在分析过程中，通常的名称被简单物的名称所替代；

（4）所有有意义的句子都必须被分析成包含“真正名称”的句子；

（5）如果名称的意义仅在于它们命名的对象，包含名称的句子要有意义，就必须真正地谈论简单对象。

这个论证的关键在步骤（3）里，注意到简单物是不可能不存在的对象。因为不是简单物的对象就可以被粉碎或不再存在，这时它们的名称就失去了承担者。真正的名称从而对应的必须是不可能被粉碎或毁灭的简单物。正如 Lugg 分析的：“整个论证的要点是，有意义的句子总是能够被转换成包含“真正名称”的句子，这种名称命名那些不能被‘粉碎’的东西”。[①] 这种不能被粉碎的东西就是前期维特根斯坦提出的必然存在于逻辑空间中的简单对象。

为使得句子“N 是 P”有意义，可以有两条路线。一种思路是：由于 N 不是真正名称（因为真正的名称总是有承担者）且承担者不会毁灭。办法是消去 N，替换成真正的名称。后期维特根斯坦没有遵循这条路线，而是采取了另一种迥然不同的思路：名称的意义不是来自它所指称的对象，而是来自名称的使用和它在语言游戏中的位置，N 本身（而不是通过承担者）就具有意义。

在 *PI* 第 40 节维特根斯坦区分了名称的“意义”和“承担者”，当后者粉碎时前者仍可以存在，名称可以有意义而不必有承担者。罗素和前期维特根斯坦都认为，真正的专名所指称的东西都必须存在，不论这种东西是罗素式的亲知对象，还是维特根斯坦式的不可毁灭的简单物。在接下来的讨论中维特根斯坦给出了众所周知的那些著名论断，表明他抛弃了他前期的形而上学立场。在 41 节中维特根斯坦提出，如果名称的意义不是其承担者，那么只能是其“在语言游戏中的位置”。名称凭借在语言中的这个位置或者功能，而不是语言外部的相联系的承担者，而具有意义。将意义理解为功能，名称就成了工具。在 42 节里维特根斯坦进一步说明作为工具的名称，即使对应的现实中的工具（承担者）破碎，其功能（在语言游戏中的位置）不会随之消失。这样 43 节里维特根斯坦顺理成章地给出了著名的“意义在于其用法”的表述。

在第 45 节中维特根斯坦再次比较了指示词和名称的差别（在第 38 节中已经指出这种差别）。名称可以没有承担者而被使用，但指示词“这个”则永远不能没有承担者。维特根斯坦对罗素的背离之处在于，维特根斯坦并不认为指示词“这个”是真正的专名。固然根据罗素，真正的专名或逻辑专名就是直接指向对象的名称，也即，真正的名称的想法来自实指定义，在这种情况下，名称和对象的联系完全是无中介的直接联系。但实指定义的不确定性使得名称和对象之间的联系无法脱离语境，因而抽象的指称关系亦无法建立起来。按照维特根斯坦，指示词“这个”是跟随指示的手势来“使用”的，而名称是通过手势来“解释”的，这正是指示词和名称的区别，解释意味着可以通过其他语词来说明。这就与罗素的观点划清了界限。根据罗素，逻辑专名“这个”是通过实指定义来直接和对象发生联系，普通专名是通过描述语为中介来和对象建立联系。如果把“解释”理解成“簇描述语”或簇摹状词，就会把后期维特根斯坦当作是名称的描述理论者，这曾经是对维特根斯坦的一种主流解读，我们将在后文讨论这个问题。

---

① A. Lugg, *Wittgenstein's Investigations* 1 – 133: *A Guide and Interpretation*, Routledge, 2004, p. 81.

在 *PI* 第 46 节里维特根斯坦分析了 39 节中的“名称命名简单物”的论题，根据这一论题，真正的名称指称着简单对象。这里的简单对象，就是不可进一步分解或还原成其他东西的对象。“名称本来标示简单对象”这种思想可以追溯至柏拉图在《泰阿泰德篇》中的论述，世界最终由不可还原的基本元素或简单对象构成，这也是作为逻辑原子主义的罗素和前期维特根斯坦的主要论题。维特根斯坦在 47 节里批评了简单性的概念，关键之处在于指出“在特定的语言游戏之外来问某个对象是否是复合的是没有意义的，对象的简单性和复合性不是抽离于语言游戏之外并奠定在世界的基本构成中的事情。诚然对某个复合物（如棋盘），可以有多种方式去理解它是如何通过简单成分构成的（比如可以通过不同颜色和单位长度为基准去分析棋盘的构成），但绝对的脱离特定视角或场合的简单性却是不存在的。正如名称的意义依赖于它在语言游戏中的位置，用绝对的方式去谈论对象的简单性也是空洞的。

不但世界中的对象不应脱离特定视角去分解成简单与否，把语言理解成名称的复合根本上也是不合适的。在 *TLP* 中维特根斯坦建立了世界 - 语言、对象 - 名称的图像对应关系，在 *PI* 中维特根斯坦瓦解了这种静止的对应关系。对象和名称的对应总是在各种语言游戏中才得以实现，无论对应（如果将之叫作指称关系的话）的直接性还是间接性都不是关键所在。维特根斯坦让我们去设想犯错的可能性。而一旦我们去考虑犯错的各种可能性，就会发现可以用图表来说明名称和对象的对应，而这无非是给出了对应关系的游戏规则说明书。因此，名称和对象的对应关系或指称关系就成了一种如何有效使用语言的规范性关系，换言之，原先那种被理解成超越特定语言游戏的静止的对应关系，应当让位于在语言游戏中被构造出来的游戏规则。而游戏规则的基本特征在于它的开放性，只能用家族类似的特征去刻画。

四、维特根斯坦是否支持簇摹状词理论

维特根斯坦在 *PI* 中论名称的最有名段落是第 79 节以“摩西”为例的一段话，这段话普遍被解释者当作是维特根斯坦在名称的指称方面所持有的一种改进的描述主义理论，即用簇摹状词理论代替了简单描述理论。①这段话因为克里普克在《命名与必然性》（下文简称为 *N&N*）里将之当作簇描述主义的典范，与塞尔的《论专名》一道进行攻击而变得更加著名。在此比较塞尔对簇描述理论的表述：“名称的功能不是用作摹状词，而是钩住一族摹状词的那个钩子。……我认为下述情况是必然的，即亚里士多德是所有通常归之于他的那

---

① 例如，Travis 主张 *PI* 第 79 节体现了描述主义的指称观，但 Traivis 对于维特根斯坦关于名称涵义和语义性质的解释不同于克里普克。

些性质的相容性析取，或逻辑和。”[①] 克里普克在 *N&N* 中对描述主义的批评，后来被直接指称论者索莫斯（S. Soames）概括为包含三个论证，即模态论证、认知论证和语义论证。这里的问题是，维特根斯坦在 79 节中的表述是否接近于塞尔式的簇描述理论？以及克里普克的批评是否对两者都适用？

索莫斯认为，对于 79 节这段话，再依据维特根斯坦在其他文本段落体现出来的思路，可以做三种解释性拓展。[②] 其一即做塞尔式的处理，把名称看作是一族不确定摹状词的逻辑和或是摹状词的挂钩。这种处理的困难在于，由于名称对应的摹状词是可变的或不确定的，如果把名称的涵义视为对应的摹状词，从而带来名称涵义的不确定性或主体间的变动，这就使得无论是通过涵义来确定指称还是通过涵义交换来实现成功交流都会面临困境。为摆脱上述困境，第二种解读方式是区分表达式的涵义和说话者的涵义。其中表达式的涵义被理解为表达式在使用过程中任何合格的说话者都能把握的公共信息，也即不同说话者涵义的公共部分。第三种解读方式，属于索莫斯用自己的立场为维特根斯坦引申，把名称在公共语言中的意义当作其指称，把包含名称的句子所表达的单称命题，看作在不同语境下断言和传达的信息中的公共部分，即该句子在语言中的意义。

从索莫斯的解读中，我们发现这段话尽管可以看作是描述主义的专名理论，但也可以理解成名称在公共语言中的涵义与不同说话者之间的涵义具有差异，后者具有不确定性和解释的开放性。这种不确定性似乎在 79 节接下来的文本得到加强：“如果要问我把‘N’理解作什么，我就得把所有这几点或其中的一些列举出来，在不同的场合给出不同的说法。……假如这种情况下我已经对这个名称给出了一个解释，现在我也会准备修正这个解释。这一点可以表达为：我没有用‘固定的’意义来使用名称‘N’”[③]。

结合这段话来看，维特根斯坦强调的重点似乎不在于克里普克所批评的描述理论的核心论题：“如果 x 存在，则 x 具有 φ的大多数特性”表达了必然真理[④]，即作为整体的簇描述中的大多数描述（名称的内容）决定了所指称的对象。如研究者 Boersema 所言，79 节文本实际强调的重心应该在“使用‘N’这个名称并没有‘固定的’意义”，即 N 的意义处于随时可修正的状态。[⑤]无独

---

① J. Searle, Proper Names, *Mind*, 1958, 67: 266: 166 – 173, here p. 171.

② S. Soames, *Philosophical Analysis in the Twentieth Century*, Princeton: Princeton University Press, 2003, pp. 20 – 22.

③ L. Wittgenstein, *Philosophical Investigations* (Rev. 4th ed.), G. Anscombe, P. Hacker and J. Schulte (trans.), Wiley-Blackwell, 1953/2009, Sec. 79.

④ S. Kripke, *Naming and Necessity*, Cambridge, MA: Harvard University Press, 1980, p. 71.

⑤ D. Boersema, Wittgenstein on names, *Essays in Philosophy*, 2000, 1 (2) Article 7, Sec. 1.

有偶，我们看到在 *PI* 的第 87 节中，维特根斯坦继续通过讨论名称“摩西”的意义的不确定性来表达这种对名称涵义的开放性理解。这种开放性是否就是名称的根本特点？回到 *PI* 第 38 节，可以发现维特根斯坦早已在对名称和指示词的区分中阐明了这一点：“我们将非常不同的东西称为‘名称’；‘名称’这个词刻画了一个词的许多不同的、以各种方式相关的用法种类……”无疑，家族类似观念才是维特根斯坦谈论指称关系的真正着眼点，虽然这对于后期维特根斯坦的哲学观而言已近乎老生常谈。

因此这里的问题就变成，维特根斯坦在第 79 节对名称“摩西”的讨论应当作为簇描述理论的标准表达，还是主要为了作为家族类似观念的表述？一种妥协的理解是两者都适用。两者的共同之处在于，与名称相联系的描述语或摹状词是可错的，没有核心的必不可少的单个摹状词能决定指称。塞尔式的簇描述理论是从正面强调簇摹状词整体构成了名称的涵义；而维特根斯坦的要点则是从反面强调涵义是不确定的，这好比“游戏”这个名称不可用某簇摹状词来下定义。但是 Cappio 试图表明：“即使为论证起见，我们可以假设维特根斯坦的家族类似的概念可以与一般词项的意义的簇理论相兼容，但对于单称词项的意义而言，这两种观念也还是无法结合起来。”[①] 这是因为，我们可以假定发现维特根斯坦从未写过 *TLP*，但却不能在类似的意义上发现篮球活动不是游戏。因此对于专名而言，簇描述理论不得不接受克里普克式模态论证的考验，但是家族类似的观念却完全不必对此有所顾忌。就此而言，克里普克把维特根斯坦关于“摩西”的谈论当作攻击专名的簇描述理论的典型似乎是脱离靶心了。

维特根斯坦并不否认可以通过描述性的内容来解释名称，但这些解释对于名称使用的作用类似于路标，目的只是在于消除误解和澄清怀疑。在 *PI* 第 49 节中，维特根斯坦写道：“命名和描述肯定并非处于一个层次上”；“命名是描述的准备。命名还根本不是语言游戏中的任何步骤，正如一个棋子的摆放不是象棋中的一个步骤一样。人们可以说，经由对一个事物的命名人们还没有做出任何事情”。因此后期维特根斯坦对于指称关系的谈论，要点显然不在于构建一种更好的描述理论，而是要通过专名含义的开放性，来说明名称的意义在于使用中体现的家族类似。正如普特南曾经指出：“维特根斯坦想要告诉我们的是，指称性的用法没有‘本质’。不存在可被称为指称的某个东西。在一种指称和相近的指称之间存在重叠的相似性，这就是问题的全部”。[②] 维特根斯坦

---

① J. Cappio, Wittgenstein on proper names or: Under the circumstances, *Philosophical Studies*, 1981, 39 (1): 87－105, here, p. 91.

② H. Putnam, *Renewing Philosophy*, Cambridge, MA: Harvard University Press, 1992, p. 167.

在*PI*的靠前部分花费大量篇幅谈论实指关系的不确定性和名称的意义，乃因为命名活动和指称关系正是语言游戏中的典型场景。克里普克在*N&N*中批评的描述主义的根本问题在于把指称关系看成是笛卡尔式的个体知识，这也正是后期维特根斯坦要批评的；根据维特根斯坦，意义是在语言的社会性使用中建构出来的。

五、结语：指称与语境

在*TLP*时期的维特根斯坦把意义的指谓观应用于逻辑空间中的指称关系，得出的结论与直接指称理论具有表面的相似性，但两者却是完全不同的意义上的表述。*PI*时期的维特根斯坦从实指活动的不确定性出发，通过对名称和指示词的对比分析，否认基于名称及其意义来谈论的指称关系具有基本的重要性，可以说是指称关系的消去论者，而并非流行认为的那样是指称的簇描述理论的支持者。在名称与对象的认知关联上，后期维特根斯坦并不否认名称可以通过因果链条或描述与对象发生关联，但认为命名没有本质。另一方面，*PI*时期的维特根斯坦仍旧大致认为指示词“这个”具有直接指称的用法，因此“这个”并不是名称。后期维特根斯坦对指示词的讨论遵循了罗素的直接指称理论传统，这一传统后来由新指称理论者做出了推进。

语境原则贯穿于从*TLP*到*PI*的论述中。仅就对指称的谈论而言，在*TLP*中，维特根斯坦强调需要在命题的语境中才能理解名称，离开命题谈论名称的指称是没有意义的；在*PI*中，则必须在语言游戏中才能理解名称的使用，使用决定意义，名称含义的不确定性正是源于语言游戏的开放性。从*TLP*到*PI*，语境由语句的逻辑形式变成了语言游戏，但对名称的谈论始终必须不能离开语境。这种对语境的重视与当代语境主义者可谓异曲同工。那么后期维特根斯坦可以算作是意义的语境主义者吗？这部分取决于我们如何刻画语境主义的观念。根据意义的语境主义的一种通常的表述，语境构成性地嵌入在语句所表达的命题之中，也即不存在独立于语境的、单纯由语词的语言学意义产生的最小命题。由于维特根斯坦主张名称的涵义随着语境变化而变化，这似乎立即可以推出包含名称的语句的内容也具有语境依赖性。激进语境主义者 Travis 因此认为后期维特根斯坦是个不折不扣的语境主义者。但近年来一些研究者如 Bridges [①]和 Voltolini[②] 都认为，从*PI*文本里非但不能得出维特根斯坦是语境主义者，还可以发现他对相反论题的辩护。而且如果后期维特根斯坦是真值条件

① J. Bridges, Wittgenstein vs. Contextualism, in Arif Ahmed (ed.), *Wittgenstein's Philosophical Investigations: A Critical Guide*, Cambridge University Press, 2010: 109 – 128.

② A. Voltolini, Is Wittgenstein a Contextualist?, *Essays in Philosophy*, 2010, 11 (2): 150 – 167.

的收缩论者，他就不太可能得出宽语境决定语句的真值条件，而当代语境主义者大都是真值条件（语义内容）的语境主义者。语境主义是晚近语言哲学中受到高度关注的立场，后期维特根斯坦与语境主义的复杂关系因此值得更深入的讨论，理解维特根斯坦与新指称理论的关系无疑也属于这项工作中的重要的一部分。

（原文删节版发表于《哲学研究》2018 年第 4 期）

Ambiguity Preference and Context Learning in Uncertain Signaling

Liping Tang

Institute of Logic and Cognition, Department of Philosophy, Sun Yat-sen University, China

1. Introduction

Natural language involves various kinds of uncertainties such as vagueness, synonymy and ambiguity. Among those uncertainties, lexical ambiguity is one of the most common features in language. Lexical ambiguity lies in the fact that a word could have more than one interpretations. For example, the word "mole" in English can be used to refer to "a dark spot on the skin", to "a burrowing mammal", to "a spy". In terms of information transaction, ambiguity does not seem an optimal choice. It is because the use of ambiguous expressions may cause the failure of information transaction and misunderstandings. We have not run out of possible words, why not invent a new word for any one of the meanings for ambiguous words? Therefore, the existence of ambiguous words needs an explanation.

In linguistics and game theory, many people have discussed this problem, and in most works, it is argued that being precise is expensive and unnecessary. Language, therefore, optimizes the balance of the benefits of precision with the costs of lexicon size (see Piantadosi et al. 2012, O'Connor 2014a and Santana 2014). The core of this argument relies on the fact that the context of the conversation can fill in information gaps left by ambiguity. According to Grice's cooperative principle (see Grice 1968), the conversational inference is based on the notion of common ground. From Stalnaker (2002), common ground is defined as the mutually recognized shared information in a situation where an act of trying to communicate takes place. In a conversation, common ground is treated as the conversational context, which plays an essential role in the pragmatic understanding of the language.

Furthermore, the influence of the context on the use of language depends on how much mutual information the interlocutors share and what kind of vocabularies is available. As the context gets clear, the more ambiguous word may be sufficient for transferring the information. However, it has not been fully investigated that where the context comes from and how the context affects the interlocutors' choice of words with different degrees of ambiguity.

The goal of this paper is to justify the existence of ambiguity from the perspective of the context dependence. We construct a context learning process in a signaling game for building the common ground of the conversation along the interactions. After that, the interlocutors' preferences of ambiguous words can be tracked as the context varies.

More specifically, we consider two interlocutors, a sender (S) and a receiver (R), are conducting a conversation for transferring information. They both have some personal beliefs about the communicating information. As the communication goes on, the interlocutors gradually infer the other's private belief from the result of each interaction. After repeated interactions, players are able to form a common ground, which serves as the context for the conversation. In addition, during the learning process, interlocutors' choices of ambiguous words may change as their beliefs about the context vary.

The following graph summarises the discussion above.

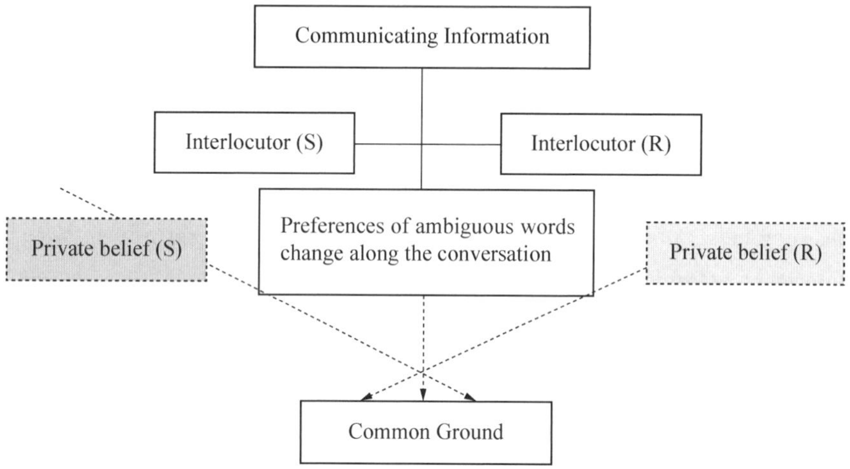

For implementing the idea above, we use Lewis's signaling game as our base model for the learning process (see Lewis 1969). Lewis's signaling game describes a very general communication scenario where a sender observes the situation (a state of the world) and then sends a signal to a receiver. The receiver takes an action based on the signal he receives. The payoff in the game depends on the state of the world and the action the receiver takes. The uncertainty of the signaling game comes from the receiver's ignorance of the true state. He can only obtain the information from the signals that the sender sends. The model has been widely used in exploring language communication (see O'Connor 2014b, Huttegger et al. 2010, Huttegger 2007, J. S. Zollman 2005, Jäger 2014).

Based on the Lewis's signaling game, we made two main changes to the model. The first change is to add players' private beliefs about the communicating information into the game. The second change is to expand the set of signals such that we can discuss ambiguous words with different degrees. With these two changes, we construct a context learning process through which the players are learning each other's beliefs during the repeated interactions. A sufficient condition is provided under which the learning is successful. After the players learned each other's private belief, they can form a mutual belief that serves as the common ground of the conversation. Furthermore, when the learning fails, though there is uncertainty about opponent's belief, we show that players still have a strong tendency to choose ambiguous expressions. We explore an uncertain signaling through the reinforcement learning mechanism.

The structure of the paper is the following. In Section 2, we first extend Lewis's signaling game such that each player has private belief about the communicating information. Then we discuss how players can learn opponent's private belief from the repeated communication. In Section 3, we establish a sufficient condition on the game under which the learning is successful. Under this condition, we discuss how the common ground of the conversation can be formed. In Section 4, we explore, when the learning fails, players' preferences of different ambiguous expressions through the reinforcement learning signaling. The paper ends with a comparison between our model and existing models on discussing uncertain signaling and pragmatic reasoning in conversation.

2. Signaling Game with Private Belief (SPB)

As the conversation goes, the interlocutors' beliefs about the communicating information change. For studying this dynamic process, we develop a new signaling game called signaling game with private belief (SPB). Based on Lewis's classical model, we assume that each player has private belief about the communicating information before the communication starts. Formally, we define players' private beliefs as partitions on the set of the states as follows.

Definition 1. *Given a set of finite states T, a private belief of player i indicated as*

B_i is defined as a partition on T. Each component of the belief partition is called an element of the partition that is indicated as B_{ik}, $k \in N$.

When the game begins, nature reveals the information to the sender. At the same time, since the receiver has private information about the state, he is also aware of relative information about the true state①. The sender then sends a signal that carries information about the true state. By combining the signal information and his private information, the receiver takes an action that decides both players' benefits. Moreover, We argue that by observing the outcome of the game, the sender can possibly infer the receiver's private belief.

States and actions can have a broad interpretation. The most obvious way to understand them is that the state is some important fact about the outside world and the action is some response to that fact. The state might be whether it is raining and the action might be to take an umbrella. But, the state might be something more internal, like the desire for the receiver to hold a certain belief. Similarly the action might be private, like coming to believe something.

Formally, SPB model is defined as follows.

Definition 2. *A signaling game with private belief (SPB) consists of the following parts:*

two players: player 1 and player 2;

- *two roles: a sender and a receiver;*
- *a set of states T: $\{1, 2, \cdots, n\}$, each state is assumed to occur with the same probability.*
- *a set of possibly ambiguous signals S with conventional meanings;*
- *each player i has private belief B_i that is unknown to their opponents;*
- *a set of actions A: $\{a_1, a_2, \cdots, a_n\}$;*
- *Sender's strategy is a function f: $T \to S$, the receiver's strategy is a function g: $S \times B_i \to \mathcal{P}(A)$, $i \in \{1, 2\}$, where $\mathcal{P}(A)$ is the power set on A;*
- *A payoff function u for both players,*

$$u(t, A, B_{i \in \{1,2\}}) = \begin{cases} \frac{1}{|A|} & \text{if } a_t \in A, |A| \text{ represents the size of the set } A, \\ 0 & \text{Otherwise.} \end{cases}$$

where $t \in T$ and $A \in \mathcal{P}(A)$.

An example (Example 1) is provided below for illustrating the concepts of the

① Similar idea appeared in Santana (2014)'s work.

game.

Example 1. The game consists of the following parts.

- Two players: player 1, player 2;
- Two roles: a sender, a receiver;
- A set of states {1,2,3,4} occuring with equal probability;
- A set of signals s_1, s_2 with commonly known conventional meanings (s_1 indicates the states {1,2}, s_2 indicates the states {3,4}).

$$1,2 \,||\, 3,4$$
$$s_1 \,||\, s_2$$

Since each signal can represent two different states, we say both signals are ambiguous. We use " || " to indicate partitions on the meaning of signals and " | " to indicate the partitions of the private belief.

Each player has a private belief about the states and does not know the opponent's belief. We assume that player 1's private belief is

$$1,2 \,|\, 3,4$$
$$B_{11} \,|\, B_{12}$$

which means that player 1 can distinguish {1,2} from {3,4} but not further. And player 2's private belief is

$$1 \,|\, 2,3,4$$
$$B_{21} \,|\, B_{22}$$

- A set of actions $\{a_1, a_2, a_3, a_4\}$

Firstly, we suppose that player 1 is the sender and player 2 is the receiver. Then, for each possible state, the game is played as follows.

Table 1. Play of the game in Example 1 (1)

state	signal	revealed information	receiver's reasoning	payoff
1	s_1	B_{21}	$B_{21} \cap S_1$	1
2	s_1	B_{22}	$B_{22} \cap S_1$	1
3	s_2	B_{22}	$B_{22} \cap S_2$	1/2
4	s_2	B_{22}	$B_{22} \cap S_2$	1/2

Table 1 shows for each state, what signal the sender sends, how the receiver reasons and what the outcome of the game is. For instance, the first row indicates that when state 1 occurs, the sender sends signal s_1 . The receiver reads the information from the signal that is {1,2}, then combines it with his private belief B_{21} that is {1}, which yields the information {1}. Because {1} is precise, the receiver is able to take the correct action which guarantees the best payoff for both players. In this example, the result holds trivially because the receiver's private belief already reveals the precise state information even without the information from the sender. Since the sender does not know the receiver's private belief, he sends the ambiguous signal anyway. But in row 3, the outcome information is {3,4}, which yields the finer information than the receiver's private belief. Hence, combining personal belief and signal information is essential in this case.

After communicating repeatedly, player 1 (sender) is able to infer player 2's (receiver) private belief by comparing the differences between the outcomes resulting from his inference and the actual outcome of the game. Player 1's inference about player 2's private belief with respect to Table 1 can be described as follows. For simplicity, we assume that both players know that players' belief partition contains two elements. ① At each stage of the inference, from the sender's point of view, all the possible configurations of the receiver's private belief are listed.

At the initial stage, since only partitions with two elements are considered, the receiver' private belief has only three possibilities. They are

1 |2,3,4　　1,2 |3,4　　1,2,3 |4

After state 1 occurs, the sender does some counterfactual reasoning. Specifically, the sender reasons that what the outcome of the game will be if he plays the game with the receiver who holds one of the three possible beliefs. It is easy to observe that only the first one yields payoff 1, which is consistent with the actual outcome in Table 1. Therefore, the other two possibilities are eliminated. Therefore, player 1 has learned that player 2's private belief is 1 |2, 3, 4.

The order of the occurrence of the states affect the learning process. If state 3 or state 4 occurs first, then the learning procedure may be different. The following analysis shows player 1's reasoning process when state 3 occurs first.

The initial stage is the same, there are three possibilities

1 |2,3,4　　1,2 |3,4　　1,2,3 |4

After state 3 is communicated, the third possibility yields payoff 1 that is

① This assumption is just for simplifying the illustration.

different from the actual payoff in Table 1. Therefore, the third possibility can be eliminated. Hence, two possibilities still remain.

1 |2,3,4   1,2 |3,4

After state 1 is communicated, applying the similar reasoning, player 1 infers player 2's private belief precisely as follows.

1 |2,3,4

Therefore, in this simple toy game, in at most two steps, namely, after communicating state 3 or state 4 and state 1 or state 2, player 1 (sender) is able to infer player 2's (receiver) private belief correctly. In addition, if player 1 is lucky enough that state 1 or state 2 occurs earlier than state 3 or state 4, then player 1 is able to learn player 2's private belief quickly.

Similarly, player 2 is also able to infer player 1's private belief by playing the role of the sender. The following part shows the reasoning process where player 2 is the sender and player 1 is the receiver.

Table 2. Play of the game in Example 1 (2)

state	signal	revealed information	receiver's reasoning	payoff
1	s_1	B_{11}	$B_{11} \cap S_1$	1/2
2	s_1	B_{11}	$B_{11} \cap S_1$	1/2
3	s_2	B_{12}	$B_{12} \cap S_2$	1/2
4	s_2	B_{12}	$B_{12} \cap S_2$	1/2

Table 2 shows the outcomes of the game for different states. Player 2's inference about player 1's private belief with respect to Table 2 is simply described as follows.

At the initial stage, there are three possible beliefs.

1 |2,3,4   1,2 |3,4   1,2,3 |4

After state 1, the first one can be eliminated.

1,2 |3,4   1,2,3 |4

After state 2, it keeps the same.

1,2 |3,4   1,2,3 |4

After state 3, only one belief remains. That is

1,2 |3,4

In this process, state 1 (or state 2) and state 3 (or state 4) are important for player 2 to learn player 1's private belief.

Therefore, after a few rounds of signaling communication with role switching, both players can learn each other's private belief. After the opponents' beliefs are learned, both players can combine their beliefs. Then a common belief 1 |2 |3,4 can be induced, which is obtained by taking the coarsest common refinement of the two belief partitions.

This common belief is important for further communication. It severs as the knowledge base for processing ambiguous expressions. For example, under this common belief, a two signal language s_1 and s_2 indicating the information {1,2,3} and {4} is sufficient to communicate precisely all the information in Example 1. Nevertheless, this kind of successful communication can not be achieved before the common belief is formed.

Moreover, if another set of signals $\{s_1, s_2, s_3\}$ (with meanings 1,2 ||3 ||4) is available as well, then the more ambiguous signal set $\{s_1, s_2\}$ (with meanings 1,2,3 ||4) is preferred given that each signal is costy.

As a result, we have built a dynamic learning process between interlocutors through the repeated SPB model. After the learning is accomplished, even by using the ambiguous language, players might be able to communicate all the information precisely.

However, the learning may not be successful in the sense that some player's private belief can not be singled out from all possible belief partitions. Therefore, it is natural to ask under what conditions players' private belief is learnable. We answer this question in details in the next section.

3. When Is Private Belief Learnable?

In the previous section, we developed a learning procedure for players to learn each other's private belief in a conversation. However, there are situations in which the learning fails. The following is an example to demonstrate that players may sometimes fail to learn their opponent's private belief.

Example 2. Suppose there are six states {1,2,3,4,5,6} occurring with equal probability, the signal structure is the following.

$$12 \,||\, 34 \,||\, 56$$

$$s_1 \,||\, s_2 \,||\, s_3$$

Assume player 1's private belief and play 2's private belie are the followings:

1,2,3 |4,5,6　　1,2 |3,4,5,6

$B_{11}|B_{12}$　　$B_{21}|B_{22}$

Firstly, we assume that player 1 is the sender and player 2 is the receiver. Then from the sender's point of view, his inference is as follows.

Table 3. Play of the game in Example 2

state	signal	revealed information	receiver's reasoning	payoff
1	s_1	B_{21}	$B_{21} \cap S_1$	1/2
2	s_1	B_{21}	$B_{21} \cap S_1$	1/2
3	s_2	B_{22}	$B_{22} \cap S_2$	1/2
4	s_2	B_{22}	$B_{22} \cap S_2$	1/2
3	s_3	B_{22}	$B_{22} \cap S_3$	1/2
4	s_3	B_{22}	$B_{22} \cap S_3$	1/2

Following Table 3, we examine player 1's learning process for player 2's private belief. Similarly, we assume that player 1 knows that player 2's belief takes the form of a two-element partition on the set of the states. Therefore, player 1's learning process can be constructed as follows. Without loss of generality, we list player 1's learning process by communicating from state 1 to state 6.

At the initial stage, there are five possibilities.

1 |2,3,4,5,6　　1,2 |3,4,5,6　　1,2,3 |4,5,6

1,2,3,4 |5,6　　1,2,3,4,5 |6

After state 1, the first possible belief can be eliminated.

1,2 |3,4,5,6　　1,2,3 |4,5,6　　1,2,3,4 |5,6　　1,2,3,4,5 |6

After state 2, it stays the same.

1,2 |3,4,5,6　　1,2,3 |4,5,6　　1,2,3,4 |5,6　　1,2,3,4,5 |6

After state 3, the second possible belief above can be eliminated.

1,2 |3,4,5,6　　1,2,3,4 |5,6　　1,2,3,4,5 |6

After state 4, it keeps the same.

1,2 |3,4,5,6　　1,2,3,4 |5,6　　1,2,3,4,5 |6

After state 5, one more possibility is eliminated.

1,2 |3,4,5,6　　1,2,3,4 |5,6

After state 6, two possibilities still remain.

1,2 |3,4,5,6　　1,2,3,4 |5,6

From this learning process, it is obvious that even though every state is communicated, player 1 still can not distinguish player 2's private belief from 1,2 |3, 4,5,6 to 1,2,3,4 |5,6. In other words, player 1 knows that player 2's private belief is one of these two, but there is no means for player 1 to figure out which one it is. Therefore, it is an example where players' private belief is not learnable. Thus, here arises a natural question that under what conditions players are able to learn each other's private belief. For answering this question, we examine more about the reason of the failure in Example 2.

We calculate the payoffs in the remaining two possible private belief under each state in Example 2.

Table 4 Payoff under each state

private belief	state 1	state 2	state 3	state 4	state 5	state 6
1,2 |3,4,5,6	1/2	1/2	1/2	1/2	1/2	1/2
1,2,3,4 |5,6	1/2	1/2	1/2	1/2	1/2	1/2

From Table 4, both possible beliefs yield the same payoffs under all the states. Recall that, in the learning process, the trigger for the sender to eliminate some private belief is the payoff differences. For example, in Example 2, from the initial stage to stage one, the private belief 1 |2,3,4,5,6 is eliminated from the possible set. It is because 1 |2,3,4,5,6 yields the payoff 1 for state 1, whereas all other possibilities yield 1/2 for state 1. Since the true payoff is 1/2, therefore, 1 |2, 3,4,5,6 should be eliminated. The essential feature here is that the payoff differences resulting from different possible private beliefs provide the sender with the opportunities to learn about the receiver's private belief. If all the possible private beliefs yield the same payoff, then the sender has no chance to learn anything.

Inspired by this phenomena, we established a sufficient condition under which the player's private belief is learnable. Before stating the condition, we first define formally what it means that two possible private belief are distinguishable.

Definition 3. *Given a SPB game with the set of states T, a set of actions and a set of signals, we say that from the player i's point of view, two possible private beliefs B^1_{-i}, B^2_{-i} are distinguishable, if there exists a state j,* such that

$u(j,A_j \mid s_j \cap B^{1j}_{-i}) \neq u(j,A_j \mid s_j \cap B^{2j}_{-i})$, where $j \in T$, s is the corresponding signal, B^{2j}_{-i} and B^{2j}_{-i} are partition elements containg state j, and $A \in \mathcal{P}(A)$

Where B_{-i} indicates player i's opponent's possible private belief $u(j,A_j \mid s_j \cap B^{1j}_{-i})$

is read as the payoff with respect to the receiver's action set A_j (indicating that $a_j \in A$) given signal and the private information B^{1j}_{-i}.

The intuition behind this definition is just saying that if there exists a state under which two belief partitions yield different payoffs, then they are distinguishable. For example, in Example 2, the belief partitions 1 | 2,3,4,5,6 and 1,2 | 3,4,5,6 are distinguishable under state 1. Moreover, the structure of the game guarantees that under state 1, at least one of the two beliefs yields the wrong payoff and can be eliminated.

Now we can present the sufficient condition under which a private belief is learnable by using Definition 3.

Theorem 1. *Given the SPB game, if any two of receiver's possible private belief partitions from the sender's point of view are distinguishable, then the receiver's private belief is learnable.*

Proof: See Appendix.

Theorem 1 tells us under what conditions receiver's private belief is learnable. The sufficient condition meets our intuition that the payoff differences provide the sender an indication of distinguishing possible private beliefs from impossible ones. An example can illustrate the intuition behind the theorem.

Conversation A:

Ann: Hi, morning! Are you going to the bank?

Bob: Yes, I go there every day.

Conversation B

Ann: Hi, morning! Are you going to the bank?

Bob: Yes, I have an appointment with the financial manager.

In the two conversations above, because of the ambiguity of the word "bank", there may be uncertainty in the conversation. In conversation A, Ann does not know which meaning of the bank that Bob is using. It is because from Bob's response, Ann can not distinguish the financial bank from the river bank. On the contrary, in conversation B, Ann can easily infer from Bob's response that Bob is using the word "bank" for the financial institute.

4. Uncertain Signaling and Ambiguity Preference

In the previous section, we provide a sufficient condition under which the players can learn opponents' private beliefs through the repeated signaling game. However, there are many situations such as Example 2 in which the learning fails.

We want to ask if the players are uncertain about each other's belief, whether ambiguous signals can be chosen. In this section, we conduct simulation studies for exploring players' preferences of ambiguous expressions when the opponent's private belief is not fully learned.

The idea is to model a communicative scenario where given a set of signaling systems with different ambiguities, players are learning which signaling system is more optimal. A signaling system is a set of signals with conventional meanings with respect to the given set of the states. In the classical signaling game and our previous discussions, we consider a game with single signaling system only. In this section, we consider multiple signaling systems simultaneously.

In Lewis's signaling game, each equilibrium can be represented as a partition on a set of states, we call it a signaling system. For example, given a set of states T: {1,2,3,4,5,6}, the separating equilibrium can be induced from the partition {1 || 2 || 3 || 4 || 5 || 6}, where we simply use || to indicate the elements in the partition. One of the possible meaningful set of signals for the partition is that signal s_i carries the meaning of state i. Apparently, in the separating equilibrium, each signal precisely represents each state information.

One the other hand, the partial pooling equilibrium involves uncertainties for the meaning of the signals. For instance, the partition {1234 || 56} can reduce a partial pooling equilibrium, in which two signals are used and each signal carries the meanings of multiple states. Therefore, ambiguous signals can appear in the partial pooling equilibrium. We say that signaling system {1 ||2 ||3 ||4 ||5 ||6} containing more signals is more precise than the signaling system {1234 ||56}. In general, for different partitions on the same set of states, the partition containing more signals is considered less ambiguity than the one with fewer signals. We assume that each signal in a partition have a cost c, then the partition with more signals is more precise but more expensive.

Assuming the existence of multiple signaling systems, we assign each signaling system a weight m by considering three factors. Firstly, the signaling system gains credences from two simultaneously occurring process: one is from the conversational information transaction, the other is from providing partial information about opponent's personal beliefs. In addition, we take into account of the cost of signals. Through keeping track of the weight of each signaling system in a reinforcement learning process, we show that ambiguous signaling systems have advantages in this uncertain signaling process.

The reinforcement learning has been widely applied in the studies of language evolution (see O'Connor 2014b, Skyrms 2010, Wagner 2009, J. S. Zollman 2005 and M. Franke and van Rooij 2011). Reinforcement learning can be described by a simple urn model with two colored balls. Every time a ball is drawn from the urn randomly. Then, the same ball and another same colored ball are returned to the urn. As a result, the probability of the ball with the same color being drawn next time is increased. When reinforcement learning is applied in the signaling game, players' strategies can be imagined as drawing the colored balls from the urns of signals and acts.

We define the reinforcement learning for only sender's choice among the signaling systems. Since we assume the signaling systems are common knowledge, once the sender's strategy is fixed, the receiver's action is also fixed. Hence, it is sufficient to consider only the sender's strategy.

The updating rule is the following.

$$wp_i(t+1) = wp_i(t) + u_j + u_l - kc$$

where wp_i is the weight for the signaling system P_i, u_j is the payoff for the result of communicating the state information j, u_l is the credence from learning the opponent's private beliefs while P_i is used. Formally, kc is the cost of the signaling system P_i in which k number of signals are contained. u_l is decided by counting how many possible belief partitions can be eliminated when P_i is used. $u_l = l$, if one possibility is eliminated. $u_l = 2l$, if two possibilities are eliminated. u_l is understood as how much impossibilities can be eliminated by using certain signals. The more impossible belief can be eliminated the more learning credences the signal can obtain. The learning here is an epistemic learning process which is also a process of reducing uncertainties.

By calculating the weight of each signaling system, we can define a response rule for the learning system to capture how frequently certain signals are used. The response rule for the reinforcement learning is defined as follows.

$$pP_i(t) = \frac{wP_i(t)}{\sum_j wP_j(t)}$$

in which the probability of P_i being chosen is calculated by the proportion of the weight of P_i among the weight of all the possible partitions. The higher the probability of certain signaling system is, the more frequently this signaling system is used and hence more advantages this signaling system obtains in the evolutionary system.

We use Example 2 for the simulation study. The signaling systems under the consideration are

$$P_1: 12 \,||\, 34 \,||\, 56 \qquad P_2: 1234 \,||\, 56 \qquad P_3: 123456$$

The costs of the signaling systems are 3 c, 2 c and c. The ambiguity increases from P_1 to P_3 .

The reinforcement learning process is the following. Firstly, the occurring state and who plays the role of the sender are decided randomly with equal probability. Then, the sender chooses the signaling system by the response rule. The results of communication and learning are reflected on the weight w. We assume the original weights for all the signaling systems are the same.

If we assume the response probability $pP_i(t) = \frac{1}{3}, i = 1,2,3$ at time $t = 0$, we can calculate the expected weights according to the following equation.

$$E_{wP_i} = \frac{1}{2}\sum_j \frac{1}{6} * \frac{1}{3}(u_j + u_l) + \frac{1}{2}\sum_j \frac{1}{6} * \frac{1}{3}(u_j + u_l) - kc$$

Therefore,

$$E_{wP_1} = \frac{7}{12} + \frac{3}{2}l \approx 0.58 + 1.5l - 3c$$

$$E_{wP_1} = \frac{4}{9} + 3l \approx 0.44 + 3l - 2c$$

$$E_{wP_1} = \frac{1}{3} + \frac{7}{2}l \approx 0.33 + 3.5l - c$$

Apparently, for comparing E_{wP_i}, we have to specify the particular values of l and c. As the proportion of P_i changes along the learning process, it becomes impossible to calculate manually. Hence we conduct simulations to explore the dynamic of this learning process.

By changing the values of l and c, we got the simulation results by conducting each trial for 2000 generations.

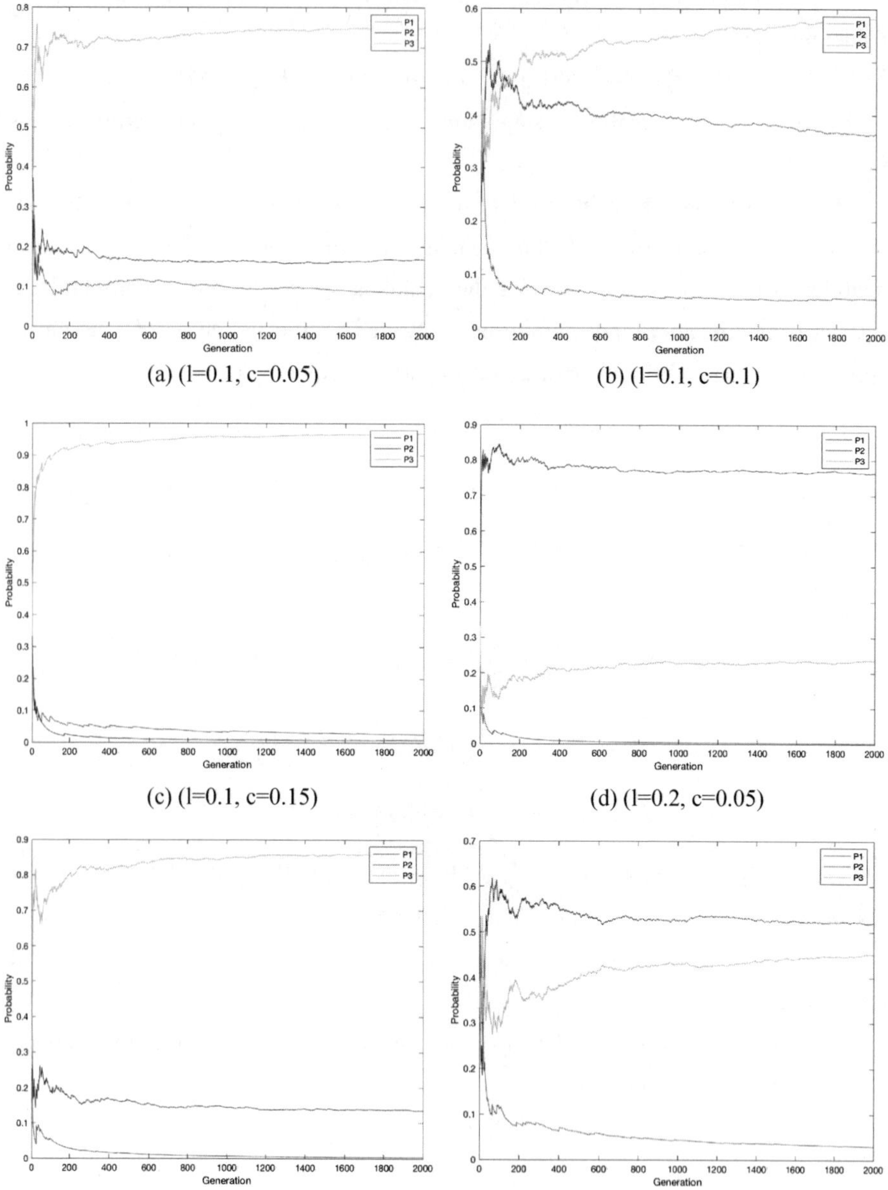

(a) (l=0.1, c=0.05)

(b) (l=0.1, c=0.1)

(c) (l=0.1, c=0.15)

(d) (l=0.2, c=0.05)

(e) (l=0.2, c=0.1)

(f) (l=0.2, c=0.15)

Fig. 1 The probability of each signaling system being chosen

Fig 1 presents one instance of simulation results for different values of l and c. The X axis shows the repeated times of communication. We repeated 2000 times for each trial. The Y axis shows the probability of each signaling system being chosen. It is obvious that in a short time of communication, the most precise signaling system P_1 still has some advantages. However, in the long run, the precise signaling system is dominated by the more ambiguous signaling systems P_2 and P_3 .

For examining the stability of the result, we also conduct simulations for 200 trials for each case. During the 200 trails, we record the frequency of each signaling system being the best among the three with respect to the best average probability in each trial. For example, when $l = 0.2$, $c = 0.15$ (case (f)), in the 200 trials, 77% times, P_3 has the best average performance, P_2 takes 22.5% of the time while P_1 takes only 0.5% of the time. When $l = 0.1$, $c = 0.05$ (case (a)), among the 200 trials, P_3 has the best average performance 45% of the time, P_2 takes 41% of the time while P_1 takes 14% of the time. Overall, the most ambiguous signaling system has the best average performance among the given three signaling systems.

The explanation of the simulation results relies on two facts. Firstly, on balancing the information transaction and the costs of signals, the ambiguous signaling systems turn out to be more optimal. Secondly, the ambiguous signaling systems have advantages in the learning process in our models. When the communication is successful through using the ambiguous expression, which means the receiver's private belief plays an important role in the information transaction, as a result, the sender can infer the receiver's private belief through the outcome of this play. On the contrary, the precise signals do not have this merit. To conclude, in this section, we use simulation studies to examine player's preference on ambiguous signals when the opponent's private belief is uncertain. Three factors are considered in the simulations: the benefits from information transactions, the partial information of opponents' belief through the learning and the cost of the signals. The simulation results show that more ambiguous signals are preferred in most of the situations.

5. Discussion and Conclusion

In the literature, there are many discussions about uncertain signaling and its communication features. We discuss the similarities and differences between our model and the established models in the literature. The models we concern are Santana's signaling model with belief context (see Santana 2014), the rational speech act model from Goodman and Frank (2016), the iterated response model by Franke and Jäger (2014) and the uncertain signaling model from Thomas (2017).

We proposed a dynamic learning procedure of private belief for communication, which differs from the models in which a common prior of beliefs is assumed. Santana's signaling model is a typical signaling game with a given context background. It studies the emergence of ambiguity in a cooperation signaling game. Based on Lewis's signaling game, a context is added to the model. Players combine both the signal information and the independent context information for making decisions. The paper argues that the evolution favors the ambiguous signaling. Our model has the similar motivation and structure as Santana's model. The major difference is that in Santana's model, the context is given as the common knowledge independent of the communication. One of the main contributions of our reseasch is building a learning process of the context belief during the communication. A dynamic perspective is taken in our model for both the context formation and the preference of ambiguities.

Our model is also different from the models built on the probabilistic (Bayesian) iterated learnings (see Goodman and Frank 2016, Franke and Jäger 2014). Rational language use is captured by a hierarchy over reasoning types in Franke and Jäger's hierarchy model. An iterated rationality reasoning is constructed on the strategy types in the model, which captures the back and forth pragmatics reasoning. Rational speech act game uses a Bayesian reasoning to predicate interlocutors' language use. Franke and Jäger's model and the Rational speech act model focus on the rationality and pragmatics in use of the language. The interlocutors' context belief is coded into the strategy types and the context information is not fully explored.

Thomas (2017)'s uncertain signaling model generates an adaptive dynamic to predicate ambiguous communication under which the players are lacking a common prior. Brochhagen's model focuses on the learning of the context belief, but only the adaptive dynamics is explored. It lacks a full analysis of whether and when a common context is possible to be established.

The investigation in this research is built on the notion of information partition that is more basic than the concept of probability. The model follows Aumann (1976)'s tradition of "Agree to Disagree". The difference is that Aumann's theorem has a common prior assumption and is based on only one random variable. In our model, we work on multiple random variables (all possible private beliefs) and different priors. Another advantage of using information partition is that we can discuss the content of the information from the signals as well as from the context beliefs instead of just posterior probabilities. From then discussion in Geanakoplos and Polemarchakis (1982), the learning of posterior probability does not equal to learning the information itself. Hence, a model built on the notion of information partition has more potential for exploring belief updating and learning. Moreover, the discussion based on information partition can be easily extended to other related fields such as other extensive games and possible world semantics in Modal Logic.

To conclude, the research tries to justify the existence of language ambiguity from the perspective of context dependence. When the context about the conversation is commonly known, the ambiguous expression is possible to communicate all the information. Furthermore, as the interlocutors' beliefs change during the repeated conversations, the interlocutors' preferences of degrees of ambiguity may change as well. The main contribution of the research is that we construct a learning process for the players to update beliefs from the result of each conversation. We also establish a testing condition under which whether the learning process is successful. In addition, we discussed players's choice of ambiguous language when the opponent's private belief is not fully known. A reinforcement learning signaling game is developed for the uncertain signaling situations.

Acknowledgements

The author wishes to thank four anonymous reviewers for commenting on the previous manuscript of this paper. The research reported in this paper was supported by the Humanity and Social Science Youth Foundation of Ministry of Education of China (No. 17YJC72040004) and the Youth Project of National Social Science Fund of China (No. 18CZX064).

Appendix

Theorem 1. *Given the SPB game, if any two of receiver's possible private belief partitions from the sender's point of view are distinguishable, then the receiver's private belief is learnable.*

Proof: This theorem can be proved from the players' reasoning process on inferring opponent's private belief by playing the SPB game repeatedly. The algorithm of this learning can be described as follows. For convenience, we eliminate the subscribe indicating the players in B in the proof.

Step 1: Since T is finite, we can list all the possible private belief partitions as a sequence $B: B^1, \ldots, B^m$;

Step 2: Calculate all the expected payoffs yielded by each $B^j, j \in \{1,2,\ldots,m\}$ for each state $i, i \in \{1,2,\ldots,n\}$;

Step 3: Pick the first two partitions in the sequence B, B^1 and B^2 , since any belief partition are distinguishable, then there exists a state k such that $u(k, A_k \mid s_k \cap B^{1k}) \neq u(k, A_k \mid s_k \cap B^{2k})$. Therefore, once state k happens (the occurrence of state k can be guaranteed because players are playing this game repeatedly and every state is possible to occur), by comparing the true payoff with the payoffs given by B^1 and B^2. There are two situations:

- One of the beliefs yields the true payoff, then the sender just return the correct partition back to the sequence B .
- Neither belief yields the true payoff, then both beliefs should be eliminated.

Step 4: Update the sequence B, then repeat from step 1.

Since for any two private belief partitions, they are distinguishable, and at least one of them is wrong, hence, the list B can be eliminated to only one element in finite steps. The remaining belief partition is receiver's true private belief. Therefore, receiver's private belief is learnable. □

References

Aumann, Robert J. Agreeing to disagree [C] //*The Annals of Statistics*, 1976, 1236 - 1239.

Geanakoplos, John D. and Polemarchakis, Heraklis M. We can't disagree forever [J]. *Journal of Economic Theory*, 1982, 28 (1): 192 - 200.

Goodman, Noah D. and Frank, Michael C. Pragmatic language interpretation as probabilistic inference [J]. *Trends in Cognitive Sciences*, 2016, 20 (11): 818 - 829.

Grice, H Paul. Utterer's meaning, sentence-meaning, and word-meaning [J]. *Foundations of language*, 1968, 4 (3): 225 - 242.

Huttegger, Simon M. Evolution and explaining of meaning [J]. *Philosophy of Science*, 2007, 74 (1): 1 - 24.

Huttegger, Simon M., Skyrms, Brian., Smead, Rory and Zollman, Kevin J.

S. Evolutionary Dynamics of Lewis Signaling Games: Signaling Systems vs Partial Pooling [J]. *Synthese*, 2010, 172 (1): 177 - 191.

Jäger, G., Franke, M. and van Rooij, R. *Vagueness, Signaling and Bounded Rationality* [M]. Berlin: Springer, 2011.

Jäger, Gerhard. Rationalizable signaling [J]. *Erkenn*, 2014, (79).

Lewis, D. *Convention: A Philosophical Study* [M]. Cambridge: Harvard University Press, 1969.

O'Connor, Cailin. Ambiguity is kinda good sometimes [J]. *Philosophy of Science*, 2014a, 82 (1): 110 - 121.

O'Connor, Cailin. The evolution of vagueness [J]. *Erkenntnis*, 2014b, 79 (4): 707 - 727.

Piantadosi, Steven T., Tily, Harry and Gibson, Edward. The communicative function of ambiguity in language [J]. *Cognition*, 2012, 122 (3): 280 - 291.

Santana, C. Ambiguity in cooperative signaling [J]. *Philosophy of Science*, 2014, 81 (3).

Skyrms, B. *Signals: Evolution, Learning and Information* [M]. New York: Oxford University Press, 2010.

Stalnaker, Robert. Common ground [J]. *Linguistics and Philosophy*, 2002, 25 (5 - 6): 701 - 721.

Thomas, Brochhagen. Signaling under uncertainty: Interpretative alignment without a common prior [J]. *The British Journal for the Philosophy of Science*, 2017.

Wagner, Elliott. Communication and structured correlation [J]. *Erkenntnis*, 2009, 71 (3): 377 - 393.

Zollman, Kevin J. S. Talking to neighbors: The evolution of regional meaning [J]. *Philosophy of Science*, 2005, (1): 69 - 85.

濠梁之辩、摩尔悖论与唯我论[①]

文学锋　何　杨

一、引言

《庄子·秋水》中有一段庄子与惠施在濠梁之上关于是否知道鱼快乐的著名辩论，抄录如下（为方便起见，用字母标记每句话对）：

> （A）庄子曰："儵鱼出游从容，是鱼之乐也。"
> （B）惠子曰："子非鱼，安知鱼之乐？"
> （C）庄子曰："子非我，安知我不知鱼之乐？"
> （D）惠子曰："我非子，固不知子矣；
> （E）（惠子曰）子固非鱼也，子之不知鱼之乐，全矣。"
> （F）庄子曰："请循其本。子曰'汝安知鱼乐'云者，既已知吾知之而问我，我知之濠上也。"

古代注解多扬庄抑惠，认为惠施已承认庄子知道鱼乐，并且基于物我合一的观点说明庄子善达物情，故知鱼乐。[②] 近现代学者则从哲学和逻辑两方面进行诠释。从哲学上看，一般认为这段辩论反映了"庄子观赏事物的艺术心态与惠子分析事物的认知心态"的区别。[③] 从逻辑上看，一般认为惠施在辩论中的表现更具逻辑性，而庄子则是靠诡辩赢得了表面上的胜利。[④]

本文不打算分析濠梁之辩在庄子哲学思想中的意义[⑤]，而是利用现代逻辑工具对这段辩论中所包含的命题和推理做更细致的分析。我们认为，惠施在论

---

① 基金项目：国家社会科学基金项目"基于范畴论的语言逻辑研究"（09CZX031）。

② 参见褚伯秀《南华真经义海纂微》，台湾商务印书馆影印文渊阁四库全书本第1057册，1986年版，第439－442页；郭庆藩撰，王孝鱼点校《庄子集释》，中华书局1961年版，第606－608页。

③ 陈鼓应：《庄子今注今译》，中华书局2007年版，第476页。

④ 参见杨向奎《惠施"历物之意"及相关诸问题》，载朱东润主编：《中华文史论丛（第八辑）》，上海古籍出版社1978年版，第209－211页。

⑤ 有关濠梁之辩的哲学意义的论著可参阅陈少明《由"鱼之乐"说及"知"之问题》，载《中山大学学报（社会科学版）》2001年第6期，第31－38页；杨国荣《他者的理解：〈庄子〉的思考——从濠梁之辩说起》，载《学术月刊》2006年第8期，第48－55页。

辩中隐含使用或承认了某种唯我论命题，该命题将导出形如“φ 且我不知道 φ”这样的摩尔句，从而产生摩尔悖论。而庄子则通过反驳和“诡辩”的方式不自觉地触及了其悖论性所在。进一步，我们利用摩尔悖论表明：在合理的预设下，认识论的唯我论即使是真的，也是不可知的。

本文结构如下：首先，我们介绍什么是摩尔句和摩尔悖论；其次，我们对濠梁之辩中的命题和推理进行逻辑分析，考察其与摩尔悖论的关系；最后我们从形式上证明，唯我论命题是不可知的。

二、摩尔悖论

摩尔悖论（Moore's paradox）是由摩尔句（Moore's sentence）引起的悖论。标准的摩尔句系指形如“φ 且我不相信 φ”这样的语句。[①] 摩尔句的奇特之处在于，它可以为真，但却无法一致地由“我”断定（assert）。它最早由摩尔提出[②]，并引起维特根斯坦等人的广泛注意，在认识论和心灵哲学等领域具有深远影响。为了和下面的知识型摩尔句相区分，我们也将标准的摩尔句称为信念型摩尔句。我们先来看断言摩尔句何以引起悖论。

摩尔本人对摩尔句的悖谬性[③]是如此解释的[④]：首先，他认为下述两个原则是合理的：

断言分配原则：断言一个合取式蕴涵断言每个合取支。

断言相信原则：断言一个命题蕴涵断言者相信该命题。

这样，由断言分配原则，我断言“φ 且我不相信 φ”蕴涵我断言了 φ 且我断言了“我不相信 φ”，再由断言相信原则，我断言 φ 蕴涵我相信 φ。如此一来，我所断言的命题（我不相信 φ）与我的断言所蕴涵的命题（我相信 φ）发生矛盾。

当然，对摩尔悖论的严格解释需要对上述断言相信原则中的“蕴涵”这个概念做出更精确的说明，因为“蕴涵”可以是逻辑蕴涵，也可以是归纳或

---

① 形如“φ 且我相信 $\neg\varphi$”的语句也被称作摩尔句的一种，它也具有某种悖论性。不过由于这种形式的摩尔句与本文关系不甚密切，故这里不作讨论。

② G. E. Moore, A Reply to My Critics, in P. Schilpp (ed.) *The Philosophy of G. E. Moore*, La Salle, Ill.: Open Court, 1942, pp. 535 - 677.

③ 摩尔区分了悖谬的（absurd）与悖论的（paradoxical）两个概念，认为后者包含矛盾而前者则未必。因为摩尔句本身可以是一致的，故有别于说谎者语句这样本身包含矛盾的语句。不过，后文将指出，在合理的预设下，断言摩尔句或相信（知道）摩尔句也将导致矛盾，故我们这里对悖谬性与悖论性这两个概念不做严格区分。

④ G. E. Moore, Russell's Theory of Descriptions, in P. Schilpp (ed.) *The Philosophy of Bertrand Russell*, La Salle, Ⅲ: Open Court, 1944, pp. 175 - 225.

概率蕴涵，还可以是语用蕴涵。① 不过，我们这里不打算讨论摩尔悖论的精确解释，而只是表明，断言摩尔句会导致某种悖论或不一致性。这种不一致性在直观上很容易察觉，但在理论上说清楚并不那么容易。

需要指出的是，摩尔句只有在以第一人称进行断言时才产生悖论。换言之，若摩尔句的第二个合取支中的信念主体是 a，而断言摩尔句的主体是 b，且 a≠b，则并不导致悖论。一般的，我们称形如 $p\wedge\neg B_a p$ 的语句为摩尔句，但它只对主体 a 的断言才产生悖论。我们称 a 为摩尔句 $p\wedge\neg B_a p$ 的相关主体，称任何形如 $p\wedge\neg B_a p$ 的语句为主体 a 的（标准）相关摩尔句。

摩尔句不但不能一致地被相关主体所断言，在合理的预设下，它也无法一致的被相关主体所相信，即 $B_a(p\wedge\neg B_a p)$ 将导致矛盾。当然，导出矛盾需要用到一些信念逻辑的原则或公理。一种导出矛盾的方法是利用如下三条经典信念逻辑的公理：

（B1）$B(\varphi\wedge\psi)\rightarrow B_\varphi\wedge B_\psi$

（B2）$B\varphi\rightarrow BB_\varphi$

（B3）$B\varphi\rightarrow\neg B\neg\varphi$

其中（B1）为信念对合取的分配原则，即如果主体相信一个合取命题，那么他（她）相信该命题的任意合取支；（B2）为信念的正反省原则，即如果主体相信一个命题，那么他（她）也相信自己相信该命题；（B3）为信念的一致性原则，它等价于 $\neg(B_\varphi\wedge B\neg\varphi)$，即主体不会同时相信一个命题和该命题的否定。② 利用这三条公理可由 $B_a(p\wedge\neg B_a p)$ 导出矛盾如下：

$B_a(p\wedge\neg B_a p)$	假设
$B_a(p\wedge\neg B_a p)\rightarrow B_a p\wedge B_a\neg B_a p$	（B1）
$B_a p\wedge B_a\neg B_a p$	（1），（2），MP
$B_a p$	（3），合取消去
$B_a\neg B_a p$	（3），合取消去
$B_a p\rightarrow B_a B_a p$	（B2）
$B_a B_a p$	（4），（6），MP
$B_a B_a p\rightarrow\neg B_a\neg B_a p$	（B3）
$\neg B_a\neg B_a p$	（7），（8），MP

① 参见 M. Green, and J. N. Williams, Introduction, in M. Green and J. N. Williams (eds.) *Moore's Paradox: New Essays on Belief, Rationality, and the First Person*, Oxford: Oxford University Press, 2007, pp. 3－36.

② Ronald Fagin, Joseph Y. Halpern, Yoram Moses, and Moshe Y. Vardi, *Reasoning about Knowledge*. 1995, The MIT Press, 1995.

$B_a\neg B_ap\wedge\neg B_a\neg B_ap$　　(5)，(9)，合取引入

除了标准的涉及信念算子的摩尔句外，还有一种非标准的涉及知道算子的摩尔句，形如“φ 且我不知道 φ”。在接受断言分配原则和如下“断言知道原则”的前提下，断言这种形式的摩尔句也将导致悖论。

断言知道原则：断言一个命题意味着断言者知道该命题。

这一原则又称作 Unger-Williamson 论题。该论题认为，一个规范的断言预设了断言者知道该命题，即只有当断言者知道一个命题时才能对其进行断言。[①] 这样，由断言分配原则，我断言“φ 且我不知道 φ”蕴涵我断言了 φ 且我断言了“我不知道 φ”，再由断言知道原则，我断言 φ 蕴涵我知道 φ。如此一来，我所断言的命题（我不知道 φ）与我的断言所蕴涵的命题（我知道 φ）发生矛盾。

一般的，我们称形如 $p\wedge\neg K_ap$ 的语句为知识型摩尔句，与信念型摩尔句一样，它只对主体 a 的断言才产生悖论。我们称 a 为摩尔句 $p\wedge\neg K_ap$ 的相关主体，称形如 $p\wedge\neg K_ap$ 的语句为主体 a 的知道型相关摩尔句。

与信念型摩尔句无法一致地被相关主体所相信类似，在合理的预设下，知识型摩尔句无法一致的被相关主体所知道，即 $Ka(p\wedge\neg K_ap)$ 将导致矛盾。这时只需用到下面两条知识逻辑的公理：

(K1) $K(\varphi\wedge\psi)\rightarrow K\varphi\wedge K\psi$

(K2) $K\varphi\rightarrow\varphi$

其中 (K1) 为知识对合取的分配公理，即如果主体知道一个合取命题，那么他（她）知道该命题的任意合取支；(K2) 为知识逻辑区别于信念逻辑的特征公理，即知识都是真命题。[②] 利用这两条公理可由 $Ka(p\wedge\neg K_ap)$ 导出矛盾如下：

$K_a(p\wedge\neg K_ap)$	假设
$K_a(p\wedge\neg K_ap)\rightarrow K_ap\wedge K_a\neg K_ap$	(K1)
$K_ap\wedge K_a\neg K_ap$	(1)，(2)，MP
K_ap	(3)，合取消去
$K_a\neg K_ap$	(3)，合取消去
$K_a\neg K_ap\rightarrow K_ap$	(K2)

① P. Unger, *Ignorance*, Oxford: Oxford University Press, 1975; T. Williamson, Knowing and Asserting, *Philosophical Review*, 1996, 105 (4): 489 – 523; T. Williamson, *Knowledge and Its Limits*, Oxford: Oxford University Press, 2000.

② Ronald Fagin, Joseph Y. Halpern, Yoram Moses, and Moshe Y. Vardi, *Reasoning about Knowledge*, the MIT Press, 1995.

$\neg K_a p$　　(5), (6), MP

$K_a p \wedge \neg K_a p$　　(4), (7), 合取引入

由上面的分析可知，在接受（K1）和（K2）的前提下，形如“φ 且 a 不知道 φ”的摩尔句无法一致地被主体 a 所知。

如果一个命题无法一致地被任何主体所知，那么我们有理由认为该命题是不可知的。显然，矛盾式是不可知的。除了矛盾式外是否还有其他的不可知命题呢？为了回答这个问题，我们先引入如下推理规则：

（K3）$\varphi \to \psi / K\varphi \to K\psi$

即知识在逻辑后承下封闭：若主体知道命题 φ，则任何 φ 的逻辑后承他（她）都知道。（K3）通常被看作是逻辑全知（logical omniscience）的某种表现[①]，但对于理想的理性主体而言，（K3）仍然是合理的。特别的，当（K3）中的知道算子被看作是隐知而不是显知时，它也是可接受的。[②] 在接受（K1）～（K3）的前提下，若对任意主体 x，$p \wedge \neg K_x p$ 都是命题 φ 的逻辑后承，则 φ 就是不可知的。因为根据（K3），任意主体知道 φ 都将导致该主体知道一个相关摩尔句，从而导致矛盾。本文第四节将指出，唯我论的某种观点即是这种意义上的不可知命题。

三、濠梁之辩与摩尔悖论

我们先给出濠梁之辩中双方断言的命题在形式语言中的翻译。初始符号及其对应的翻译如下：

z：庄子

h：惠施

f：（那只/群特指的）鱼

p：（那只/群特指的）鱼快乐

K_z：庄子知道……

K_h：惠施知道……

注意到，在（B）（C）（F）中出现了三个以“安”起始的问句。一般情况下这类问句有两种解读：一种解读为疑问句，一种解读为反问句。解读成疑问句时“安”字又至少有两种不同的解释，一种解释为“如何”或“怎样”，

---

① Ronald Fagin, Joseph Y. Halpern, Yoram Moses, and Moshe Y. Vardi, *Reasoning about Knowledge*, the MIT Press, 1995.

② H. J. Levesque, A Logic of Implicit and Explicit Belief, in *Proceedings of the National Conference on Artificial Intelligence*, 1984, pp. 198 - 202.

即询问的是方式；一种解释为“在哪里”，即询问的是处所。[1] 易见，在濠梁之辩中，（B）和（C）中的问句都是在反问句的意义上被论辩双方使用的，而（F）中庄子又忽然将（B）中的问句理解为询问处所的疑问句，这种前后不一致通常被看作是庄子的诡辩所在。下面我们将表明，当（B）中的问句作反问句理解时，其所隐含的前提将导致摩尔悖论，因而庄子的“诡辩”可以得到某种合理的解释。

反问句一般可解释为其所包含的陈述句的否定，即 φ? 意指 $\neg\varphi$。事实上，在（D）和（E）中惠施明确用否定句的形式(“固不知子矣”和“子之不知鱼之乐”）重新表达了庄子在（C）中和惠施在（B）中用反问句表达的命题。这样，（A）～（E）可以分别形式化如下：

（A′）庄子：p。

（B′）惠施：$z \neq f$（前提），$\neg K_z p$（结论）。

（C′）庄子：$h \neq z$（前提），$\neg K_h \neg K_z p$（结论）。

（D′）惠施：$h \neq z$（前提），$\neg K_h \neg K_z p$（结论）；

（E′）惠施：$z \neq f$（前提），$\neg K_z p$（结论）。

此处形式化假定了惠施和庄子在相同涵义上使用“知”这个词，该假定是合理的，因为一方面，在整个濠梁论辩过程中，两人都没有对“知”的涵义进行探讨，可以说“知”的涵义是两人的共识；另一方面，双方都是在援引对方的观点反驳对方，而并未对对方的援引是否符合本意进行辩解。

注意到在（D′）和（E′）中，惠施分别断定了 $\neg K_h \neg K_z p$ 和 $\neg K_z p$。如果用 φ 表示 $\neg K_z p$，则惠施相当于作了“φ 且我不知道 φ”这样的论断，而这正是摩尔句的形式之一。为什么会出现这种情况呢？我们分析一下惠施为何被迫说出这样的摩尔句。

首先，当庄子做出“鱼快乐”（p）的论断后，惠施通过反问的方式在（B）中指出“庄子不知道鱼快乐”（$\neg K_z p$）。在这里，惠施想反驳的并不是命题 p 本身，而是 $K_z p$。尽管庄子并未直接断言他知道 p，但根据上文提到的 Unger-Williamson 论题，只有知道 p 才能断言 p，因此惠施根据庄子的断言合理的得出 $K_z p$，并进而反对这一命题。庄子在这里其实可以反驳惠施，说自己并未声称“知道鱼快乐”，因为在最一般的情况下，断言 p 只意味着相信 p 或

[1] 参见中国社会科学院语言研究所古代汉语研究室：《古代汉语虚词词典》，商务印书馆 1999 年版，第 3－5 页。

相信知道 p 而不需要知道 p[①]。但庄子并没有这么做，而是默认了自己知道鱼快乐。换言之，论辩双方都接受了 Unger-Williamson 论题。

其次，惠施反驳 $K_z p$ 的论证是不完整的。这个论证只有一个前提，要使得该论证有效必须补充一个隐含的大前提。这个大前提可以是：

（P）任何主体都不知道其他主体的心灵状态。

根据这个大前提，因为"鱼快乐"对于庄子而言是其他主体的心灵状态，因此庄子不知道鱼快乐。庄子敏锐地发现了惠施的论证依赖于这个隐含的前提，因而利用这个隐含的前提给出了（C）中的反问：因为"庄子不知道鱼快乐"对于惠施而言是其他主体的心灵状态，因此根据（P），庄子得出"惠施不知道庄子不知道鱼快乐"。需要指出的是，"鱼快乐"和"庄子不知道鱼快乐"虽然都与心灵状态有关，但前者涉及的是情感状态，而后者涉及的是认知状态。因此，惠施本来可以就此反驳庄子，指出自己并不需要（P）而只需要如下更具体的（P_1）即可：

（P_1）任何主体都不知道其他主体的情感状态。

但惠施没有这么做，而是在（D）中通过承认庄子在（C）中通过反问给出的论证默许了（P）。这样一来，惠施不得不同时作出"庄子不知道鱼快乐"和"我不知道庄子不知道鱼快乐"这两个论断，从而断定了一个摩尔句。

当然，这里有一句话可能存在不同理解，即（D）中的"我非子，固不知子矣"。根据这句话本身，"不知"后面究竟包含关于"子"的什么内容并不明确。但从上下文和"固……矣"的语气可以推断，这句话是对庄子在（C）中通过反问方式给出的论断（论证）的承认，即"固不知子矣"是"固不知子之不知鱼之乐"的省略，也即上面的（D′）。

另一种理解是将"固不知子矣"解释为"固不知子之心"的省略，这样（D）将翻译为：

（D″）惠施：$h \neq z$（前提），h 不知道 z 的心灵状态（结论）。

易见（D″）是（P）的特例：（P）中的任意主体换成了（D″）中的特殊主体惠施和庄子。显然，（D″）成立与否与惠施和庄子的特殊性无关，它只是某个更一般命题的推论。这个一般性命题即（P）。换言之，断言（D″）即隐含承认了（P）。按照（D″）这种理解，尽管惠施并未直接断言摩尔句，但下面我们将

① 参见 J. E. Adler，and B. Armour-Garb，Moore's Paradox and the Transparency of Belief，in M. Green and J. N. Williams（eds.）*Moore's Paradox：New Essays on Belief，Rationality，and the First Person*，Oxford：Oxford University Press，2007，pp. 146－162.

证明，从（P）中仍可推出摩尔句，而（P）正是唯我论的主要观点之一[①]。下面我们证明，由（P）将导出摩尔句，进而得出（P）是不可知的。为简化问题，我们将唯我论命题中的心灵状态限定为认知状态，而不考虑情感状态，即只考虑（P）的如下推论：

（P_2）对任何主体 x，y，若 $x \neq y$，则 x 不知道 y 的认知状态。

若从（P_2）可推出摩尔句，则从（P）当然也能推出摩尔句。

四、摩尔悖论与唯我论

为了形式化（P_2），我们将（P_2）理解为

（P_3）对任何主体 x，y，若 $x \neq y$，则 x 不知道 y 知道什么。

有趣的是，在《庄子》的英译本中，对“我非子，固不知子矣”虽有若干不同的翻译，但最通行的翻译即：“I'm not you，so I certainly don't know what you know.”[②]（我不是你，所以我当然不知道你知道什么）。按照这种理解，（D）恰好是（P_3）的特例。可见将（P_2）理解为（P_3）不损害原意。

在翻译（P_3）之前，我们先看（P^+）“x 知道 y 知道什么”是什么意思。这句话可以理解为：

（a）x 知道什么是 y 的知识。

用 P 表示“y 的知识”这一谓词，则“x 知道 y 知道什么”就是“a 知道什么是 P”，即任给对象 z，x 都知道 z，x 是否具有 P 性质。因为 P 是关于命题的性质，所以（P^+）解释为：

（b）任给命题 p，x 知道 p 是否是 y 的知识。

也即

（c）对任意命题 p，x 知道 y 是否知道 p。

亦即

（d）对任意命题 p，如果 y 知道 p，那么 x 知道 y 知道 p，且如果 y 不知道 p，那么 x 知道 y 不知道 p。

用符号表示即：

（e）$\forall p\ ((K_y p \to K_x K_y p) \wedge (\neg Kyp \to Kx \neg Kyp))$

① 唯我论有本体论和认识论之分。本体论的唯我论从根本上否认他心的存在，认识论的唯我论则只否认认识他心的可能性。我们这里只考虑认识论的唯我论。

② B. Watson, *The Complete Works Of Chuang Tzu*, New York: Columbia University Press, 1968, p. 189.

注意到$K\varphi \to \varphi$，故等价的[①]，(P^+)最终翻译为：

(f) $\forall p\ (K_xK_yp \vee K_x\neg K_yp)$

现在来看(P^+)的否定(P^-)：x不知道y知道什么。由于(P^+)包含量词，故(P^-)中的否定有宽辖域(P^{-w})和窄辖域(P^{-n})两种读法：

(P^{-w}) $\neg\forall p\ (K_xK_yp \vee K_x\neg K_yp)$

(P^{-n}) $\forall p\neg\ (K_xK_yp \vee K_x\neg K_yp)$

注意到(P^{-w})等价于$\exists p\neg(K_xK_yp \vee K_x\neg K_yp)$，即按照宽辖域的读法，$(\mathrm{P}^-)$意指：

(g) 存在命题p，x不知道y是否知道p。

然而，无论惠施还是唯我论者显然都不是在这个意义上使用(P^-)的。对惠施而言，从这种存在性命题出发，惠施只能得出有一些命题是庄子不知道的，并不能得出庄子就不知道鱼快乐这个特殊命题。对唯我论者而言，其断定的也不是存在一些我的认知状态是其他主体不知道的（这是非唯我论者也承认的），而是我的所有认知状态其他主体都不知道。因此，惠施和唯我论者都是在如下更强的意义上使用(P^-)的：

(i) 对任意命题p，x不知道y是否知道p。

即(P^-)中的否定词应取窄辖域。这样，(P_3)最终翻译为：

(P') $\forall x\forall y\ (x\neq y \to \forall p\neg\ (K_xK_yp \vee K_x\neg K_yp)$

设a，b为两个不同主体。则由(P')可得（用a，b分别代入其中的x，y）

(j) $\neg\ (K_aK_bp \vee K_a\neg K_bp)$

由(j)易得

(k) $\neg K_aK_bp$

另一方面，由(P')可得（用b，a，K_bp分别代入其中的x，y，p）

(l) $\neg\ (K_bK_aK_bp \vee K_b\neg K_aK_bp)$

由(l)易得

(m) $\neg K_b\neg K_aK_bp$

记$\neg K_aK_bp$为φ，则(k)和(m)一起构成

(n) $\varphi \wedge \neg K_b\varphi$

从而得到摩尔句。当然，(n)只对主体b而言是摩尔句，其他主体可以一

① 因为$K_xK_yp \to K_xK_yp \vee K_x\neg K_yp$且$K_x\neg K_yp \to K_xK_yp \vee K_x\neg K_yp$，又$(A\to C)\ \wedge\ (\neg A\to C)$等价于$C$，故(e)蕴涵(f)；因为$K_xK_yp\to\ (K_yp\to K_xK_yp)$，又$K_xK_yp\to K_yp$且$K_yp\to\ (\neg K_yp\to K_xK_yp)$，故$K_xK_yp\to\ (K_yp\to K_xK_yp)\ \wedge\ (\neg K_yp\to Kx\neg K_yp)$，同理可得$K_x\neg K_yp\to\ (K_yp\to K_xK_yp)\ \wedge\ (\neg K_yp\to Kx\neg K_yp)$，故(f)蕴涵(e)。

致的断言（n）。但从上述推理不难看出，b 实际上是任意的，即从（P′）出发（并假定至少世界上至少存在两个主体）可以得到，对任意主体 x：

（p）$\varphi \wedge \neg K_x\varphi$

这样，根据第二节的知识，如果接受（K1）～（K3），并假定至少存在两个主体，那么（P′）就是不可知的，因为任意主体知道（P′）都将导致矛盾。

需要指出的是，从（P′）形式的唯我论导出摩尔句并未用到认知逻辑的公理或规则，只是在导出其不可知性时用到了认知逻辑，而从摩尔句导出悖论并非一定要用认知逻辑。事实上，关于摩尔句的悖论性有很多不依赖于认知逻辑的解释。[①] 因此，要想避免从唯我论中导出摩尔句，从而从根本上杜绝其导致悖论，需要对唯我论作一定的限制。例如将唯我论中的量化范围限制为事实命题，即不允许（P′）中的 p 被带认知算子的命题代入。这样或许可以避免悖论。不过，这种弱化的命题大概已经不是唯我论的初衷了。

另一方面，要得出认识论的唯我论即（P′）是不可知的，除了要假定（K1）～（K3）外，还要假定至少存在两个认知主体。因此，如果既要坚持（K1）～（K3）又要坚持唯我论的可知性，那么唯一的办法就是否定至少存在两个认知主体这一前提，而这正是本体论的唯我论所坚持的。这样看来，尽管本体论的唯我论看上去更加荒谬，但在逻辑上却比认识论的唯我论更加坚固。

五、结语

本文的分析表明，当惠施的问句“子非鱼，安知鱼之乐”作为反问句理解时，其所隐含的前提（P）具有某种不一致性。庄子通过借用这个前提迫使惠施断言摩尔句间接不自觉地触及到了其悖论性。若惠施的问句不能一致地解释为反问句，那么就只能解释为疑问句了。这样我们或许可以理解庄子最后的“诡辩”。进一步，我们表明，认识论的唯我论在某些合理的预设下是不可知的。本体论的唯我论比认识论的唯我论在逻辑上更加坚固。

---

① 参见 M. Green，and J. N. Williams，Introduction，in M. Green and J. N. Williams（eds.）*Moore's Paradox：New Essays on Belief，Rationality，and the First Person*，Oxford：Oxford University Press，2007，pp. 3－36.

作为程序与属性的论辩术[①]

——析当代论证理论中“论辩术”视角的差异解读

谢　耘

一般而言，当代论证理论以逻辑学、修辞学和论辩术为三个最主要的理论视角，但相较来看，“论辩术”之理论视角正日益强势。不但直接以“论辩术”标识自身的“形式论辩术（Formal Dialectics）”“语用论辩术（Pragma-Dialectics）”及“新论辩术（New Dialectics）”理论日臻完善，而且以修辞学和逻辑学自识的论证理论亦正展现出论辩术视角的不断渗入。

然而，纵观当代西方论证理论，不断拓展的“论辩术”视角本身却并未呈现出齐一的面貌，而是在其理论脉络中展开为多样的解读。本文将解析当前并存的两种具有实质性差异的“论辩术”视角，一种以语用论辩术理论为代表，将“论辩术”外化为论证活动的程序和规则，另一种以非形式逻辑理论（Informal Logic）[②] 为代表，将“论辩术”内化为论证成果的属性与特质。

一、引子——论辩性外层的概念

当前西方论证学界最受关注又最具争议的一本著作，当推非形式逻辑学家拉尔夫·约翰逊（R. H. Johnson）的《展示理性——一种语用的论证理论》。书中约翰逊所建构的非形式逻辑理论，因其革新性的“论辩性外层”（dialectical tier）概念而引发了旷日持久的争论。

依约翰逊对“论证”概念的语用重构，“论证是作为论证实践中之提取物的一种话语或文本，在其中论者试图通过提供理由支持来说服他人相信某个论题的真实性。除了这个推论性核心（illative core），论证还有一个论辩性外层，论者在其中履行自己的论辩性义务（dialectical obligations）”。（Johnson，2000：168）由此，一个完整的论证界定将既包括一个推论性内核，同时还具有一个论辩性外层。前者中论者以理由支持论题，后者中论者履行其相关的论辩性义务，如回应已有或可能的针对论题的批评和反对（criticisms and objections），批驳已有或可能的关于论题的可替立场（alternative positions）（ibid：165 -

---

① 本文原载于《逻辑学研究》2010 年第 4 期，第 85 - 97 页。

② 本文无意涉及关于“非形式逻辑”概念本身的理解争议，仅将之局限于指称加拿大学者约翰逊（R. H. Johnson）和布莱尔（J. A. Blair）所开创和发展的论证理论。

166）。相应地，论证评估理论也需展开为“推论性核心之评估”和“论辩性外层之评估”两个维度。前者展开为“充分性”“相关性”“可接受性及真实性”四个评估标准，后者则开启了探讨“论辩充分性”（dialectical adequacy）的全新议题。

尽管在书中约翰逊并未将其论证理论冠以“论辩术”之名，但正如语用论辩术理论学者范·里丝（M. A. van Rees）评论的那样，“该书最首要的价值在于将非形式逻辑与当前论证研究中已然显要的论辩术理论视角结合了起来”（van Rees，2001：233）。然而，在充分肯定非形式逻辑与论辩术的理论结合之外，范·里丝也补充道，以增添“论辩性外层”来“达成这两者结合的方式却留下了质疑的空间”（ibid.），甚至“根本不需要论辩性外层的概念”（van Rees，2000：258）。

既然“论辩性外层”的概念无疑地展现着“逻辑学”理论品性的非形式逻辑对于“论辩术”视角的接纳与融合，为何以“论辩术”自识的语用论辩术理论却仍会对之存有如此大的异议？换言之，是否当代论证研究之论辩术理论脉络当中，还存有不易调和的理解分歧？

二、程序与属性——当代论证理论中“论辩术”视角的差异解读

确实，纵览当代论证研究的理论与文献，冠以“论辩术”的论证理论无一不与约翰逊的“论辩性外层”迥异其趣。论证之“论辩化”（dialectification）或者指涉“一个对话过程或活动”（形式论辩术、新论辩术），或者对应“一种言语行为间的论辩性互动”（语用论辩术）；名以“论辩术”的理论或者呈现为一个涉及不同对话类型的理论框架（新论辩术），或者展开为一套导控论辩程序和行为的规则体系（形式论辩术、语用论辩术）。范·里丝对“论辩性外层”概念的质疑，正突显出语用论辩术理论与非形式逻辑对“论辩术”视角的理解歧异。

“语用论辩术”（Pragma-Dialectics）是当代论证研究之论辩术理论脉络中最具代表性的理论。“语用”（Pragma-）表征了其视论证为具有特定语用功能（即解决意见分歧）的言语活动，并致力考察其中的言语行为；而“论辩术”（Dialectics）则标识了其对“通过论辩式讨论（argumentative discussion）以批判性地评估立场”的理论侧重，以及对其实现方式和条件的理论探讨（van Eemeren & Grootendorst，2004：52）。更具体而言，在语用论辩术理论中，一个完美实现批判性评估的论辩式讨论，将以一种系统化的“批判性讨论”（critical discussion）为范型。它展开为冲突（confrontation stage）、开始（opening stage）、论辩（argumentation stage）、结论（concluding stage）四个阶

段，使理性的讨论参与者得以对有利或不利于所争议立场的各个论证进行权衡，从而批判性地评估所争议的立场，合理地解决其意见分歧。同时，这一目标的实现也需要对各个阶段中讨论参与者的言语行为进行必要的规范，因而“必须用及某些规则或程序来调控哪些（言语）行为（move）是可以被允许的”（ibid：50）。显而易见，语用论辩术理论实质上将“论辩术”视角阐发为论证活动的阶段式过程，并进而展开相关的导控性规则探讨。也正缘于此，其理论不断发展和完善的正是一系列针对讨论参与者言语行为的程序性规则（procedural rules），以规范其解决意见分歧的合作性努力，保证讨论的合理展开和分歧的成功解决。①

相比而言，约翰逊的“论辩性外层”中所蕴含的论辩术视角就显得大相径庭。它既未预设论证实践的阶段式展开，也不引发关于论辩式讨论的规则探讨，而是强调“论题总产生于争议性（controversial）论域”的现实性和具有“被挑战和质疑从而需要更多辩护”的可能性（Blair & Johnson，1987：45），以及进而“在考察和应对挑战与质疑中完善论证”的必要性（Johnson，2000：165－167）。以此观之，约翰逊实际上在其非形式逻辑理论中将“论辩术”视角解读为一个完整的、合格的论证理解与建构所应具备的特定属性。与之相应，以理性说服为目标的论证实践将是论者对论题的系统而全面的证成与辩护，在提出适当理由支持论题之外，论者仍需主动回应针对论题的既有批评与反驳，审慎考察与论题相冲突的观点及立场。这也就要求论者付出更多的理智努力，承担相应的论辩性义务。因而，依约翰逊之见，合理的论证实践必然涉及对于论辩性义务的履行，合理的论证界定必将包含论辩性外层为内容，合格的论证理论必须对论辩性内容（dialectical matters）做出充分的分析与评估。质而言之，其属性式“论辩术”视角一方面体现于论证实践的复杂结构，并蕴涵着对论证主体更多的理智要求；另一方面生发出“论辩性外层”这一论证概念中的必要要素，并展开为论证建构与评价的规范性标准（Blair & Johnson，1987：48－55；Johnson，2000：189－209）。

三、源与流——重回亚里士多德

历史地看，汉布林（C. L. Hamblin）引发了“论辩术”在当代论证研究中的复兴（Hamblin，1970），而文策尔（J. W. Wenzel）奠定了“论辩术”作为论证研究三大理论视角之一的地位（Wenzel，1980）。然而，“论辩术”自身还有其更为久远的理论历史。早在柏拉图之前，它就已经被古希腊哲学家们所

① 语用论辩术理论的程序性规则几经发展与完善，先后出现过多个体系，最新的体系见于（van Eemeren & Grootendorst，2004）中所提出的15条规则。

熟知与践行，而且亚里士多德也详细阐释过其系统的“论辩术”理论。[①] 当代论证研究中对“论辩术”视角的差异解读，无疑都有其古老的历史注脚。

就词义而言，“论辩术”（英文 dialectic，源自希腊文 *dialegesthai*）[②] 与对话和论证/反驳相关，指称一种通过与他人争辩，批判对方的观点而坚持自己立场的实践。从最一般的情形而言，与对方通过问答形式展开的论证活动即是一种论辩术的形态。以苏格拉底的对话方法为范本，柏拉图将论辩术提升为哲学家探讨真理的唯一方法。而亚里士多德则视之为人类智识活动的一种特定类型，一种从多数人接受的意见出发并以问答形式展开的特定方法。在《论题篇》中，论辩术被界定为：“一种探究的方法，通过它我们能从普遍接受的观点出发，就所面对的任何问题来进行推理；同时，在提出自己的论证时，不至于自相矛盾。”（*Topics*，100a20）实际上，亚氏的“论辩术”（dialectic）概念既呈现为与修辞学相对的一种技艺（art），又频繁地用以描述命题、论证和问题的某种属性（dialectical proposition/argument/problem）（*Topics*，100a31，104b3）。正是通过对论辩的命题、论证和问题的详尽分析，亚氏阐发了立论与驳论的论辩术技艺。

一方面，继承苏格拉底诘难法（Socratic *Elenchus*）的品性，并作为“从（正反）两方面探讨问题……在每个方面洞察出真理与谬误”的方法，亚氏论辩术具有“通过争议性观点或论证之间的对抗（pro and con argument/encounter of agonistic views）进行批判性审查”的内在特性（*Topics*，101a30，159a32 - 37；Guthrie，1981：155），从而具有探讨各门科学基础的哲学功能（*Topics*，101b3）。毕竟，对一个观点作辩驳式审查，更可能揭示其真假的特性。与之相应，对一个论题正反双方进行论争的能力，也使我们更易于做出真理与谬误的判定。因此，另一方面，作为技艺的论辩术也可以思维体操（mental gymnastics）的方式助益于哲学家敏锐思维。进而，以学园中的争辩活动为模本，亚氏论辩术亦展开为一种严格规则控制下的智识争斗的实践形式（rule-governed battles of wits）[③]。

---

① 亚氏《工具论》中《论题篇（*Topics*）》是关于“论辩术”的专论，他关于“论辩术”的探讨也散见于《辩谬篇》（Sophistikoi elenkoi）、《形而上学》及《修辞学》当中。如何全面和准确地阐释亚氏论辩术理论仍是一个争议性问题，本节并不尝试对之做出系统解读，而只限于探讨当代两种论辩术视角与亚氏遗产的理论渊源。

② 严格依词源学分析，“dia”意指“通过”（through），词根“leg-”意指“言说”（to speak），“ic”意指“技艺”（art），从而“dialectic”意为“言说/会话的技艺”（art of speaking through，i. e. the art of conversing）。

③ 《论题篇》第八卷中亚氏有大量关于这种训练式争辩活动的探讨，其规则诸如提问者只能设计以“是或否”为答案的问题，以及回答者不能提问而只能回答提问者的问题等。

同时，无论是特设性的思维体操训练，还是从正反两方面展开对于论题的批判性审查，争议性观点或论证的对抗都具体化为提问者与回应者双方之间的问答式进程。由此可见，与柏拉图一样，亚氏也将其论辩术阐释为一种“问答对话”（question-and-answer）的形式和方法。然而，何以问答对话的方式就是通达真理发现或理智进步的必由途径，无论柏拉图还是亚里士多德都没有做出明确的论证。换言之，问答对话的方法实际上只是一个公理性的预设抑或一个经验性的总结（Robinson，1953：81－83），却不是论辩术理论中一个得到证立的理论结论。从逻辑上看，由于从普遍接受而非确凿无疑的意见（*endoxa*）出发，不同甚至相对立的观点和论证成为可能；因为在争议性观点和论证间的对抗与辩驳中权衡，批判性地审查观点而达致真理得以证成；但是，何以争议性观点及论证间的对抗必然展现为问答对话的方法，却只能参照以苏格拉底对其对手的诘难，以及学园哲人相互争论的经验性范本。

由此观之，语用论辩术和非形式逻辑对“论辩术”视角的差异解读，正是在追随亚氏论辩术“以争议性观点及论证的对抗进行批判性审查”之理论特性的同时，却在“问答对话之必要性”上呈现出不同的理论传承。如前文所析，语用论辩术之“论辩术”尽管标识着对于批判性评估立场的注重，但随即这一批判性的论辩术视角就“视论证为一个通过讨论以解决观点之可接受性问题的程序（procedure）”（van Eemeren & Grootendorst，1988：280）。因而，在他们看来“亚氏论辩术正是对一个批判性讨论的指导，其中支持与反对一个特定论题的行为之间展开互动”，甚至“对话式交流形式正是亚氏论辩术的本质”（van Eemeren & Grootendorst，2004：43－48）。显然，语用论辩术理论视批判性审查之目标与对话（讨论）之方式必然结合，其“论辩术”视角自然转换为对论辩性讨论的程序及规则的探讨。与之相对，约翰逊却拆解了“争议性观点和论证之对抗”与“问答对话方法”之间的必然关联。其“论辩的论证”之理解尽管保留着“涉及至少两方之间的疑问和分歧”的特性，也体现着“在争论性观点和论证之对抗”中所蕴含的批判性审查功能，但这一对抗却只停留于自身论题与其反对意见、（竞争性的）可替立场间的相遇与互动过程，而非展开为持争议观点或论证的双方或多方之间的真实对话过程。换言之，其“论辩术”视角实质标识着“（论证实践中）一方自身的逻各斯（*logos*）（话语、推理及思考）具有被另一方所影响的可能性”（Johnson，2000：161）。从而，亚氏论辩术中的问答对话方式也只是在“强调着理解一方针对另一方所做的论证的重要性”（Blair & Johnson，1987：45）。显然，约翰逊摒弃了与“争议性观点及论证之对抗”相关联的多主体性，从而抽离了对话方式的可能性和必要性。进而，其“论辩术”视角最终展现为对相关于论题的（可能或实际）争议性观点及论证的开放性，且这一开放性所蕴涵之互动性以一种内在的理性之互动（encounter of *logos*）为特质，而不以一个外在的对话程式为表征。

四、理论与实践——规范与描述之间的当代论辩术诠释

古老的理论遗产蕴藏了当代论辩术视角不同解读的理论渊源，却并不具有历史意义之外更全面的解释力。比之于历史地追问他们对亚氏理论之正解与误读，深究其不同诠释的理论动机与缘由，更能揭示当代两种论辩术视角的深层差异。

事实上，相比于亚氏从技艺和方法的角度来阐释“论辩术”，其当代继承者们却无一不将之转换为论证理论的规范性维度。无论语用论辩术所发展的程序性规则体系，抑或论辩性外层所导出的论辩充分性标准，论辩术之理论视角最终都转变为论证理论的规范性内容，因而其解读差异也必定呈现为不同理论规范性之间的分歧。确实，当“论辩充分性”标准要求论者主动回应“标准的反对意见”（The Standard Objections）①，甚至包括那些并不为对方所知晓的反对意见时（Johnson，2000：332－333），语用论辩术学者则认定“这种要求根本不是真正基于论证实践……论者所需应对的只是他要说服的对手所知道和提出的反对意见”（van Rees，2001：234）。然而，尽管语用论辩术理论常以其“描述与规范并重的理论旨趣”自誉（van Eemeren & Grootendorst，2004：10），但非形式逻辑学家同样坚持其“规范性标准源自于对实践之审慎反思”（Johnson，2003：47）。由此，只有探问语用论辩术与非形式逻辑对于互动中的规范性理论与情境性实践的理解歧异，方能澄清两种论辩术解读的本质差异。

语用论辩术理论着眼于日常言语中的论证活动（argumentation in colloquial speech），将论证实践理解为一个言语行为（speech acts）的交换过程。它具有特定的交际性和互动性功能（communicative and interactional function），通过论辩性讨论（argumentative discussion）的形式，解决不同的语言使用者之间明确表达的观点争议（dispute of expressed opinions）（van Eemeren & Grootendorst，1984：1－4）。与之相对，非形式逻辑将论证实践理解为一种建构、表达、批评和改进论证的社会文化活动。它以争论性论题为起始背景，以合理建构论证和回应批评为展开方式，以理性说服为外在目标，以增进理性和促进理解为内在价值（Johnson，2000：154－164）。显而易见，一个解决分歧的论辩式讨论

① “标准的反对意见”指那些在论题的相关论域中频繁出现的和典型的，具有显著重要性的反对性意见（salient objections）（Johnson，2000，p. 332）。

与一个逐渐展开的论证建构和完善过程之间，既彰显出语用论辩术与非形式逻辑所理解的论证实践在形式与目标上存在重大差异，同时也注定了他们在理论建构上的不同旨趣。语用论辩术学者坚持合格的论证理论必将从对话情境中的语言使用者入手（van Eemeren & Grootendorst，1984：14），从而排斥基于独白式（monologue）论证的理论建构。于他们而言，不仅一种独白式的论证理解会妨碍对交流与互动中的论证性言语行为的探讨，甚至于一个"未能发出反对声音的被动听众"（passive listener offering no verbal opposition）都不能为其理论所接受（ibid：13－14）。相反，非形式逻辑学者却深信，建构在对话式论证理解基础上的理论成果并不能合理地应对独白式论证实践中的诸多问题，因而静态的、非对话性的论证理解更为当代论证研究之必需（Johnson，2003：183－201）。于此，对论证实践之不同理解和随之的理论建构分歧，已然部分地解释了他们面对论辩术遗产中对话方法的态度差异。对语用论辩术理论来说，继承对话方法是一个无须深究的简明抉择，但于非形式逻辑而言，它却成为一种理当慎思的理论偏见。

进一步，语用论辩术理论与非形式逻辑都以各自所辨识的最佳实践形式或构建的理想模型，架构于其实践蓝本与理论规范之间。前者构建了"批判性讨论"（critical discussion）作为论证分析与评估的理想模型（ideal model），后者选择了"哲学论证"（philosophical argument）作为理解论证的概念范式（paradigm of argument）（Johnson，2002：322）。批判性讨论的模型提供了以分歧解决为导向的程序性规范，哲学论证展示着以理性说服为目标的论证标准。进而，在语用论辩术理论中，其"分歧解决"在于使一个"理性的批判者"信服（convincing a reasonable critic）；在非形式逻辑论域里，其"理性说服"也以一个"理性的他者"（rational Other）为对象。尽管表面上"合作性的解决分歧只有通过理性说服才能得以发生"，（van Rees，2000：257）但实际上在"理性的批判者"与"理性的他者"之间，仍然深藏着理论歧异。质言之，"理性的批判者"意味着对于 reasonableness 的诉求（van Eemeren & Grootendorst，2004：2），而"理性的他者"要求着对于 rationality 的展示（Johnson，2000：163），从而，批判性讨论之模型和哲学论证的范式中，事实上潜藏着不尽相同的合理性概念。具体而言，语用论辩术所预设的 reasonableness，指涉"审慎思虑"之维度（well-thought-out aspect），指向社会生活中"人际"（interpersonal）之内涵（van Eemeren & Grootendorst，1988：272）。它追随批判理性主义（critical rationalism）之精神，进而具体为一个"批判的合理性观念"（critical reasonableness），承认人类理性的可错性（fallibility）从而推崇系统的批判性检验（systematic critical testing）（van

Eemeren & Grootendorst, 1988: 280)。与之相对，约翰逊所界定的 rationality，却归诸简单的个人内心之思考。更确切而言，它指称人类所具有的寻找、提供、接受理由的能力以及基于理由行事的特性 (Johnson, 2000: 161)。

作为论证理论最核心的规范性理想和最根本的规范性源泉，“合理性”概念的不同建构无疑将导向对转为规范性维度的论辩术视角的差异解读。一方面，一个约翰逊所界定的“理性论证者”绝不会无视于审查与论题相关的反对性理由或论证，而一个语用论辩术理论所预设的“批判理性主义者”也不会漠然于解构反对者所提出的异议和反驳。换言之，蕴含着“以争议性观点及论证的对抗进行批判性审查”的论辩术视角被融入这两种理论之规范性维度，实质上是其合理性概念建构的必然要求。另一方面，从更深层次看，承认人类理性的可错性而推崇的批判性检验，无疑是以人际间理性的对抗式互动，来最终弥补单一个体的理性之缺漏；但笃信人类理性能力而倡导的批判性审查，却是以个人理智活动中对于正反论证的主动构建与权衡，来探寻最佳之证成理由或论证方式。与此相应，语用论辩术理论中的论证参与者，都是秉承易错理性进而来相互弥补的主体，其程序性规则体系实质也是约束讨论主体的外在戒律 (commandments)，对之的遵循才能成为合格的理性讨论者 (reasonable discussants) (van Eemeren & Grootendorst, 2004: 191 - 196)。而非形式逻辑理论中的论者和他者，都是具备并且致力于展现完善理性的论证主体，其论辩充分性标准最终关联于理性论证者的内在义务 (obligation)，对之的履行以完美地展示自身所具备的理性能力 (Johnson, 2000: 163 - 164)。由此观之，论辩术视角中“争议性观点或论证之对抗”展现为多主体之间的冲突与对话，抑或单主体内心的建构与权衡，进而在论证理论中对于“对话方法”的态度是审慎地拒斥还是直接地继承，这实质上也都是其不同合理性概念建构的逻辑结论。

五、谬误界定与论证概念——两种论辩术视角的理论价值

若仅以论辩术视角之不同解读来分析语用论辩术与非形式逻辑的理论差异，则全然低估了其理论价值。事实上在当代论证理论的诸多争议问题中，它都将展现出理论潜力。本节只拟简析其中两个问题，一个显著于论证理论发展的当代情境，一个伴生于论证理论引介的中文语境。

（一）谬误研究的论辩术视角

汉布林对亚氏以来谬误之“标准解读方式”(The Standard Treatment) 的批评 (Hamblin, 1970)，催生了谬误理解方式的多样性转换，从而开启了谬误研究的当代复兴和发展。其中最具代表性的，无疑是论辩术视角下的谬误界定

转变。从“看似有效而实际无效的论证”这一标准理解到“论证实践中的不当策略（tactic）或违规行动（move）”的全新解读，论辩术视角之谬误研究既扩充了谬误界定的理论论域，也完成了谬误理论从“逻辑学视域中之论证评估”到“语用学论域中之言语行为分析”的品性变更，进而也引发了对诸多传统谬误的全新理解与评价（van Eemeren & Grootendorst，1992；Walton，1989，1992）。

然而，无论是谬误界定突破传统的“论证”之属概念，还是谬误分析相对于目标导向的语用、程序性标准，论辩术视角的谬误研究这两大理论变革都遭遇到难以应对的责难与争议。一方面，当谬误被界定为“任何使争议解决变得困难的那些对于批判性讨论规则的违反（行动）”（van Eemeren & Grootendorst，2004：162）时，一个逻辑上有说服力的论证也会因违规使用或无助于争议解决之目标而被判为谬误，而一个符合规则且助益于争议解决从而并非谬误的论证，其前提也可能并不能支持其结论（Blair & Johnson，1993）。另一方面，以某个语用目标（如解决争议）为导向的谬误分析将忽视论证中前提对于证立结论的合理保证（warrant）关系，从而导向背离合理信念证成的认识论危机（Siegel & Biro，1997）。显然，改释谬误为影响或破坏实践目标实现之不当或违规行动，解构了“谬误性”（fallaciousness）是“论证中前提对于结论的理由支持能力之不足”这一（传统）本质界定，进而也使其跃出了“（合）理性缺失（failure of rationality）”的范畴。因而，谬误理解究竟是追随一个静态的论证概念还是一个动态的言语行为过程，谬误分析是参照一种外在的语用目标还是一种内在的（合）理性品性，这些冲突将论辩术视角之谬误研究导入难以调和的争议中心。

实际上，若援以当代论辩术的不同解读方式，论辩术视角之谬误研究也蕴藏着回避前述困境的理论潜力和可能方向。当论辩术视角并不外化为论证实践的程序及规则而是内化为论证成果的属性或特质时，其谬误研究并不必然蹈入前述的争议处境。简而言之，论证实践中的不当行动可归诸于论者对其论辩性义务履行的不充分（Johnson，2000：208），进而导致论证建构的不全面，并最终被界定为其论证成果的不完整及其说服力的欠缺。从而，在保留了论辩术视角下对传统谬误理解之扩充的同时，“谬误”界定却将仍隶属于一个“不合格论证”概念，而不必然导向“不当或违规行动”的新界定；“谬误性”也仍将定性为论证中前提对于结论之理由支持能力的不足及理性说服力的缺损，而不必然突破“（合）理性缺失”之范畴以导向受制于语用目标的情境性评判①。由此而言，论辩术理论视角非但不必然导向谬误分析的语用情境标准和牺牲论证及谬误研究的认识论价值，而且也能够合理地追随传统的逻辑学理论脉络②。

（二）“论证”概念的中译问题

在“论证$_1$/论证$_2$”（O' Keefe，1977，1982）和“作为结果之论证/作为过程之论证”（argument as product/argument as process）（Brockriede，1975；Wenzel，1980）的双重区分维度下，当代论证理论中论证概念的理解和建构日趋复杂（谢耘，2007）。而纵览当代论证研究文献，“论证”概念又紧密关联于“argument”和“argumentation”两个不同语词，它们既存在不加区分的更替用法，又存在并不明晰的意义区别。大陆学者倾向于译前者为“论证”而后者为“论辩”③，由此展现出一个中文语境中的论证概念翻译问题。

首先，中文之“论证”与“论辩”显然不存在相互替换的可能性，因而此译法不当地取消了诸多论证研究语境中“argument”与“argumentation”之间的可互换性（interchangeable）。实际上，“argument”与“argumentation”之意义纠葛还具有特定的历史意义。一直以来，当“argument”被（形式）逻辑学缩减为一个“前提-结论”结构的抽象对象时，“argumentation”却保留了日常话语中论证活动的具体意义。而当代论证研究的复兴和发展，正得益于从传统“前提-结论”结构的、抽象的、命题序列式论证理解，到实践情境中动态的、活动性的论证解读这一范式转换。换言之，当代论证理论的发展进程也正是“argument”突破狭隘的（形式）逻辑学意义而向广阔的日常话语意义回归，从而重新与“argumentation”意义相通甚至等同的过程（谢耘，2008）。

其次，“论辩”一词具有“多主体之间相互争辩”的意义，它契合于“主动对话者”（active interlocutor）而非“被动听众”（passive audience）的理论预设。因而，“论辩”一译将首先依此中文语境中的亲缘关系而明确导向论辩术之理论视角，从而曲解非论辩术视角之论证理论中“argumentation”一词的

---

① 一部分论证实践中的不当行动显然可以轻易地被转换为论者对其论辩性义务履行的不充分，但能否以及如何将全部不当行动（类型）都完成这种转换，将涉及更复杂和深层的分析与探讨。限于篇幅，本文在此仅停留于揭示这一理论策略和方向。

② 事实上，“论辩术”“修辞学”与“逻辑学”三大理论视角之间的互动与融合，正成为当前论证研究中最核心的理论议题。约翰逊的属性式论辩术解读方式实质上展现出一种将“论辩术”归并于“逻辑学”的可能途径。

③ 台湾学者则有以“论点”和“论证”对译“argument”和“argumentation”的译法。但这一译法无论在佩雷尔曼新修辞学语境，还是在更广的当代论证理论论域中，都存有可商榷余地。

合法意义。① 同时，在当代论辩术视角之不同解读下，“论辩”一译在论辩术理论脉络中也非至当不移，对于属性式论辩术解读下的非对话性、独白论证（solo-argumentation）而言，“论辩”一译变得意味迥异。

实质上，在当代论证理论的视域之中，“argument”和“argumentation”都具有比“论辩”更广的外延（谢耘，2007）。在当前论证研究之语境中，更适宜将两者都取“论证”之译。② 严格而言，中文“论辩”一词只对应于“argumentative discussion”之意，它既不能合法地翻译“论证”概念，也不能合理地标识“论辩术”的理论视角。

六、结　语

尽管有着同样久远的理论传统，但相比于有着相对明确之学科建制的逻辑学与修辞学，“论辩术”的理论脉络在当代论证理论中略显扑朔迷离。在情境实践与规范理想的差异建构之间，语用论辩术与非形式逻辑将“论辩术”理论视角做出程序和属性的不同解读。古老理论遗产的批判性审查功能被齐一继承，而其对话方法却得到区别对待。两种论辩术视角既标识出两大论证理论间的实质分歧，也展现着论辩术脉络在当代论证研究中的理论潜力。面对当代论证理论中多元视角日益互动与融合的进展，清晰把握两种不同的论辩术视角，对深入展开论证研究和合理引介论证理论都具有相当重要的理论意义。

参考文献：

Blair, J. A. & Johnson, R. H. Argumentation as Dialectical [C] //Argumentation 1, 1987: 41 –56.

Blair, J. A. & Johnson, R. H. Dissent in Fallacyland, Part 1: Problems with van Eemeren and Grootendorst [C] //McKerrow, R. E. & Annandale, V. A. (eds.). Argument and the Postmodern Challenge: Proceedings of the Eighth SCA/AFA Conference on Argumentation. Speech Communication Association, 1993: 188 –190.

Blair, J. A. & Johnson, R. H. Argumentation as Dialectical [C] //Argumentation 1, 1987: 41 –56.

Brockriede, W. Where Is Argument [J]. Journal of the American Forensic

① 如戈维尔（T. Govier）以“argumentation”指称单主体所提出的“主论证 + 补充性论证”（main argument + supplementary arguments），再如佩雷尔曼新修辞学理论所界定的“argumentation”，都不适宜译为“论辩”。

② 当然，如前所析，在诸多语境中，相对于逻辑学意义上的“argument”，“argumentation”更多地指涉“论证活动”之意，然而“论证活动”也并不能简单等同于“论辩”。

Association, 1975, 11: 179 - 182.

Govier, T. The Philosophy of Argument [M]. Newport News, VA: Vale Press, 1999.

Guthrie, W. K. A History of Greek Philosophy (Vol. Ⅵ) [M]. Cambridge: Cambridge University Press, 1981.

Hamblin, C. L. Fallacies [M]. London: Methuen, 1970.

Johnson, R. H. Manifest Rationality Reconsidered [C] //Argumentation 16, 2002: 311 - 331.

Johnson, R. H. The Dialectical Tier Revisited [C] //van Eemeren, F. H., Blair, J. A., Willard, C. A. & Dorcrecht, A. F. Snoeck Henkemans. (eds.). Anyone Who has a View: Theoretical Contributions to the Study of Argumentation. Kluwer Academic Publsiers, 2003: 41 - 54.

Johnson, R. H. Manifest Rationality: A Pragmatic Theory of Argument [M]. Mahwah: Lawrence Erlbaum Associates, 2000.

O'Keefe, D. The Concepts of Argument and Arguing [C] //Cox, J. R. & Willard, C. A. (eds.). Advances in Argumentation Theory and Research. Carbondale: Southern Illinois University Press, 1982: 3 - 23.

O'Keefe, D. Two concepts of argument [J]. Journal of the American Forensic Association, 1977, 13: 121 - 128.

Robinson, R. Plato's Earlier Dialectic [M]. Oxford: Clarendon Press, 1953.

Siegel, H. & Biro, J. Epistemic Normativity, Argumentation, and Fallacies [C] // Argumentation 11, 1997: 277 - 292.

van Eemeren, F. H. & Grootendorst, R. Rationale for a Pragma-dialectical Perspective [C] // Argumentation 2, 1988: 271 - 291.

van Eemeren, F. H. & Grootendorst, R. A Systematic Theory of Argumentation: The Pragma-dialectical Approach [M]. Cambridge: Cambridge University Press, 2004

van Eemeren, F. H. & Grootendorst, R. Argumentation, Communication and Fallacies: A Pragma-dialectical Perspective [M]. Hillsdale, NJ: Erlbaum, 1992

van Eemeren, F. H. & Grootendorst, R. Speech Acts in Argumentative Discussions [M]. Dordrecht: Foris, 1984.

van Rees, M. A. Comments on Rhetoric and Dialectic in the Twenty-First Century [C] // Argumentation 14, 2000: 255 - 259.

van Rees, M. A. Book Review on Manifest Rationality [C] // Argumentation 15, 2001: 231 - 237

Walton, D. N. Informal Logic: A Handbook for Critical Discussion [M]. Cambridge University Press, 1989.

Walton, D. N. Plausible Argument in Everyday Conversation [M]. NY: State University of New York, 1992.

Wenzel, J. W. Perspectives on argument [C] /Rhodes, J. & Newell, S. (eds.). Proceedings of the 1979 Summer Conference on Argument. Falls Church: Speech Communication Association, 1980: 112 – 133.

谢耘．论证、论辩、争论——当代论证理论视域中论证概念的双重维度解读 [J]．自然辩证法研究，2007 (4).

谢耘．论证逻辑、非形式逻辑、论证理论 [J]．自然辩证法研究．2008 (3).

Legal Facts in Argumentation-Based Litigation Games

Minghui Xiong[1], **Frank Zenker**[2]

1 *Sun Yat-sen University*, *Institute of Logic and Cognition*, *Guangzhou*, *China*

2 *Philosophy*, *Konstanz University*, *Konstanz*, *Germany*

1. Introduction

Intending to further the comprehensive reform of the Chinese legal system, in early 2015, the Supreme People's Court (SPC) issued her *Opinion on Comprehensively Deepening the Reform of the People's Courts*: *Outline of the Fourth Five-Year Reform* (2014—2018), there in recognizing the need (1) to promote and strengthen the importance of argumentation in judicial judgment; (2) to implement the principle of evidence-based verdicts in courtrooms; and (3) to realize these goals through questioning evidence, identifying facts and defending opinions, and by forming reason-based verdicts.

As this opinion assigns a more important role to legal facts and legal argumentation than the legal system of mainland China (not including that of Macau and Hong Kong) had previously recognized, it is reasonable to ask: What is legal fact to begin with? Can it be as objective as the term "fact" suggests? And what makes a legal fact acceptable in judicial practice? Remarkably, some lawyers speak of "evidence-fact" as if this were a *single* concept. But failure to discriminate evidence from fact hides the argumentative or inferential relation between legal facts and evidence. We submit that a legal fact should therefore be treated as a fact-*qua*-claim, in the sense that the fact's acceptability rests on evidence and argumentation supporting it.

To explore fact-argumentation, we rely on the argumentation-based litigation game framework (ALG) presented in Xiong (2012). It provides a dynamic model of the interaction between the suitor (S), the respondent (R), and the trier (T), and distinguishes three corresponding types of fact-argumentation. We first compare how the case and the civil law systems generally constrain the parties' interaction, then detail the specific provisions applicable in mainland China [Notice that since the later years of the Qing dynasty (1644 — 1912), mainland China aligns with civil law]. Among others, we explain why parties seek to maintain a game-theoretic equilibrium, while only the civil law system makes the trier-party a *player* in the full sense.

Throughout we assume some familiarity with relevant legal concepts, but cannot hope to do justice to the intricacies that arise from *fully* problematizing terms such as "evidence", "fact", "trier", etc. Where applicable, we point to relevant literature.

2. Legal Facts as Argumentatively Supported Claims

Particularly in a legal trial, before anything can count as a legal fact a party to a litigation process must express a corresponding propositional content. But the content of what parties claim to *be* case-related facts normally differs in one and the same legal case. We therefore distinguish (1) the S-fact claimed by the suitor party; (2) the R-fact claimed by the respondent party; (3) the T-fact claimed by the trier party. (Many lawyers, judges, and jurists customarily regard these items as *facts simpliciter*, so we sometimes also use the terms "legal fact", "case fact" or "verdict fact", respectively.)

In a trial the three fact-types relate to the same overall event(s), and each party normally forwards a *set* of such facts. But at least some members of the S- and R-fact *sets* (F_S and F_R) are logically inconsistent. Otherwise a genuine dispute pivoting on these facts-*qua*-claims could hardly arise. Similarly, also T-facts may, but need not, differ from S- and R-facts. For T's foremost aim is to provide a fair and just verdict given F_S and F_R, while S and R primarily promote their narrow self-interests. Further inconsistencies may arise between T-facts presented in an initial trial and in a subsequent (re-)trial.

The jurist Zhang Baosheng contends that, although in one and the same case there is only one fact, parties to a trial may nevertheless present several legal *truths*.① Read ontologically, this may oddly suggest a multitude of truths. But *being true* is primarily another, though an important, property of natural language statements. Though a fact may be independent of human cognition (a. k. a. objective fact), the acceptability of the statement expressing its content generally

① Private conversation with Professor Zhang Baosheng at the Conference on Evidence and Fact: The Dialogue Between Philosophers and Jurists, November 2015, Shanghai, China.

isn't. Indeed, the praxis of offering reasons to support the acceptability of a fact-expressing claim would otherwise be meaningless. Rather, similar acts could be meaningful only as explanations *why* the claim expresses a fact (if it does). So if a legal must be argued for by presenting evidence, then its acceptability in a trial depends on the support the evidence set provides. A legal fact is therefore distinct from an objective fact.

One of the most important features of fact argumentation undoubtedly is its defeasibility. The renowned case Huge Jiletu (Huhhot City), for instance, pivots on three related (objective) facts. *First*, during the first and second trial, in 1996, Huge was sentenced to death, and executed in the same year. *Second*, in both instances the trier affirmed the basic judicial principle of mainland Chinese criminal law, viz., that "the case is clear and its supporting evidence set is sufficient", thus qualifying the T-fact argumentation as cogent. *Third*, however, Zhao-Zhihong was formally recognized, in 2005, as the murderer in the Huge case, effectively defeating the acceptability of the original T-fact and its argumentative basis. So a T-fact having once become acceptable may lose that feature in a retrial.

When treating argumentation that establishes a legal fact-*qua*-claim, the strategy of *maximally argumentative interpretation* (van Eemeren et al. 2002: 43) allows interpreting any utterance as an argumentative move, including simple remarks or explanations. The terms "fact argumentation" or "argumentation about facts" then simply refer to discourse moves through which judges, prosecutors, or lawmen support their respective S-, R-, and T-facts using legally admissible evidence. The more established term "fact-finding" is close in meaning to "fact-argumentation".

For instance, a judge's (T) fact-finding establishes F_T using inferential relations between F_T and its supporting evidence set E_T, and similarly for S and R. But fact-argumentation additional covers the perspectives of the prosecution (S) who files a lawsuit in a criminal (or the plaintiff in a civil or administrative) proceeding, and the perspective of the accused party (R) who is forced to join the trial. Given these three perspectives, a trial seeks to marshal the fact-argumentation by S, R, and T in the case at hand.

But what is a trial's *primary* end? According to some, its main purpose is the search for legal truth. The Canadian Supreme Court Justice Cory, for instance, submits that "[t]he ultimate aim of any trial, no matter criminal or civil, must be to seek and to ascertain the truth" (Hock Lai 2008: 52). Similarly, in *Funk versus the United States* the United States Supreme Court proclaims that "[t]he fundamental basis upon which all rules of evidence must rest—if they are to rest upon reason—is their adaptation to the successful development of the truth" (ibid.). Others, however, find that a trial primarily seeks to ensure a proper legal decision. According to Edmund M. Morgan, a lawsuit is "essentially a proceeding for the orderly settlement of a dispute between the litigants" (ibid: 52f.). Similarly, Nicholas Rescher (1977: 43) contends that a legal trial is not concerned with the truth of the matter—else why have categories of *inadmissible* evidence? —but with setting out a proper legal case.

Reflecting the basic distinction between legal truth and fact, these two opposing views entail priority-differences between procedural and substantial justice—a superficial reading of which (falsely) equates *legal* with *ontological* truth or fact. Morgan and Rescher promote the primacy of procedural justice, while Justice Cory and the United States Supreme Court advocate substantial over procedural justice. The first group includes jurists such as Chaïm Perelman or Robert Alexy, who view the rationality of justifying legal decisions as *entirely* depending on the quality of legal procedures (Feteris 1999: 92). Most members of the second group are legal practitioners such as judges and attorneys. (We return to the procedural vs. substantial justice-distinction in Sect. 6. 2.)

3. The Five-Fold Pattern of Litigation Argumentation

3. 1 Overview

We now present legal litigation as a game that agents play to secure a distinct outcome (3. 2), explain the three-part legal syllogism (3. 3), and how a more complex version there of helps understand why agents aim for a game-theoretic equilibrium (3. 4).

3. 2 Litigation as a Game

One may analytically distinguish zero-, one-, and multi-agent argumentation.① As a subtype of legal argumentation, litigation argumentation is multi-agent; its basic

① Most informal logicians focus on arguers as agents. By contrast, formal logicians (who use theories of logical syntax and semantics to evaluate arguments) did only more recently concern themselves with *who* argues, for their argument-concept has traditionally reflected the zero-agent category. But see, e. g., van Benthem (1996, 2009, 2014), and work on argumentation in AI and game theory now providing parallel tracks in argumentation and logic.

characteristics are *subjectivity*, *dynamicity*, and *interactivity*. Since "legal suit" denotes the process and product of interaction (Xiong 2010: 75), one may analyze it as an argumentation-based litigation game (ALG) with three sub-games, namely S-T, being played between suitor and trier, S-R played between suitor and respondent; and R-T between respondent and trier (Fig. 1).

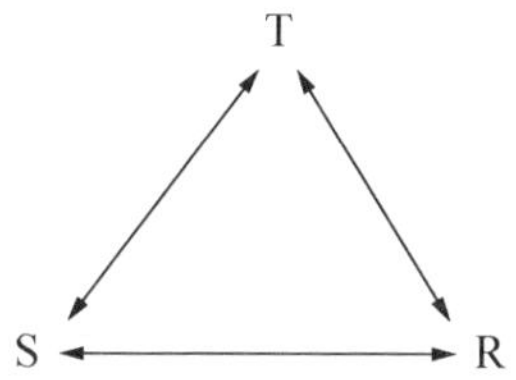

Fig. 1　Agents in an argumentation-based litigation game (ALG) playing three sub-games (S-T; S-R; R-T)

A game-theoretic perspective differs from a traditional understanding of litigation where the proper objects of litigation are *rights*, *obligations*, or *personal freedoms*. By contrast, an ALG is played for *legal interpretations* and *legal facts* or *legal conclusions*. (Legal interpretation is also known as "interpretation argumentation", referring to reasoning from legal norms to interpretations; "fact argumentation" refers to reasoning from evidence to legal facts; and "conclusion argumentation" refers to litigation argumentation as a whole.) Though one normally identifies only S or R as agents, an ALG *can* include T as a distinct player.

In the common law system, the *trier of fact* is the jury, while the *trier of law* is a collegiate bench composed of at least one judge. In the civil law system, by contrast, the collegiate bench additionally acts as a trier of fact, i.e., as a juror who participates in deciding a legal fact. Indeed, the SPC's opinion (see Sect. 1) suggests that the reformed legal system of mainland China will make it impossible for a jury to *apply* the law, rather letting it partake only in fact-finding. (For a discussion of the distinction between trier of fact and trier of law, see Article 33 of the SPC's opinion.)

3.3 The Legal Syllogism

The common and the civil law system alike have long recognized the *legal syllogism* (Fig. 2) as the basic pattern of legal argument (Gardner 1993: 3; MacCormick 2005: 32; Alexy 1989, 221; Aldisert 1997: 55). Comprising a major premise citing a law or legal norm (N), a minor premise citing a case-fact (F), and a conclusion citing a legal claim (C), this pattern reflects the principle—clearly articulated in mainland Chinese law—that *a legal trial must be based on facts and take law as the criterion*. Since judicial centrists use "judicial conclusion" rather than "legal conclusion", the pattern is also known as the *judicial syllogism*; but we prefer "legal conclusion" because S, R, and T equally apply the pattern in constructing their arguments.

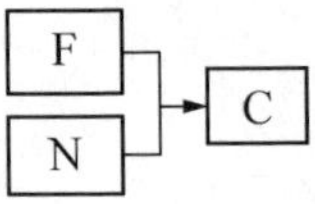

Fig. 2 The legal or judicial syllogism

Figure 2 is potentially misleading because it neither explicitly represents the *interpretative reasoning-relation* (a. k. a. interpretation-argumentation) between legal norms and their interpretation, nor the *evidential reasoning-relation* (a. k. a. fact-argumentation) between legal evidence and legal facts. To better appreciate the importance of these relations in a legal proceeding, we can turn to some major criminal grievance cases in mainland China from the past 30 years: She Xianglin (1994 – 2005; Hubei Province), Zhao Zuohai (1998 – 2010; Henan Province), Teng Xingshan (1987 – 2006; Hunan Province), Huge Jiletu (1996 – 2014; Inner Mongolia), and Nie Shubin (1994 – 2016; Hebei Province)[①]. Each case equally satisfied the requirements put forth in the legal syllogism. But the cases were nevertheless *misjudged* because T-fact argumentation here remained poor, since T-evidence failed to support T-facts.

3. 4 The Legal Five-Fold Argument Pattern

The legal five-fold argument pattern (LFA), which plays a central role among

① Familiarity with these cases may be presumed among virtually all Chinese legal scholars. Charged with murdering his wife Zhang Zaiyu, She Xianglin was, in 1994, sentenced to 15 years imprisonment. But in 2005, an unharmed Zhang Zaiyu returned to her home. In the next case, the defendant Zhao Zuohai, having, in 1999, been accused of murdering Zhao Zhenxiang, was sentenced to death, and a two-year suspension of the execution being pronounced simultaneously. But in 2010, Zhao Zhenxiang reappeared, unharmed. In the Teng Xingshan case, in 1988, Teng was sentenced to death for the murder of Shi Xiaorong, and was executed immediately. But in 2004, Shi was found to be alive. Finally, in 1996 and 1995, Huge and Nie were on independently sentenced to death for murder, and executed immediately. But it later appeared that others had committed the murders they were charged with. In present-day China similar crimes would, typically in a two-year process, lead to imprisonment for life.

others in Kelsen's (Kelsen 1991) *General Theory of Norms* (see van den Hoven 1988; Xiong 2012), remedies the representational deficits of the legal syllogism (Fig. 3). A litigation argument here consists of a legal conclusion set C, a case-fact set F, a legal evidence set E, a legal norm set N, and a legal interpretation set I. Compared with Fig. 2, the LFA manifests the relations between F and E, and between I and N, thus highlighting the relevance of interpretation and fact-argumentation for an ALG. Of course, the seeming simplicity of the LFA pattern potentially distracts from the true complexity of what the pattern models.

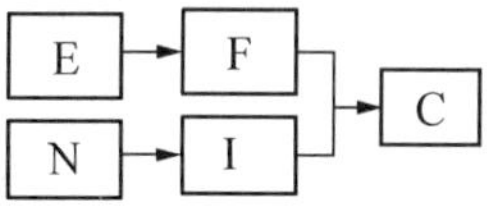

Fig. 3 The legal five-fold argument pattern (LFA), representing evidence, facts, norms, interpretations, and conclusions as sets

We already saw that not only T, but also S and R *do*—and to avoid judicial centrism *should*—engage with each other's litigation argumentation. With regard to the same party, of course, each component set of the LFA should be internally consistent (also to minimize the cost of a lawsuit). But the *mutual* inconsistencies between S- and R-facts restrict S-, R-, and T's fact-argumentation, and so give rise to a litigation game in the first place. In particular, since T's fact-argumentation interacts with S's and R's fact-argumentations, one obtains differences in allocating their burdens of proof. We now turn to the details.

4. S-Fact Argumentation

4.1 Overview

We saw that S, R, and T's construction of their fact-argumentations in an ALG is dynamic, because the original S-fact-argumentation as well as elements of S's evidence can be withdrawn. Though engaging in a lawsuit is often described as "playing the legal evidence", in an ALG framework this offers an under-description. Indeed, agents play for legal facts *and* interpretations, so that there is always a sub-game of fact-argumentation. We first turn to what is generally required of S to start an ALG (4.2), then detail the specific conditions of the legal system in mainland China (4.3).

4. 2 Starting an ALG

We saw that S and R must construct their fact-argumentation in mutually dependent ways, and that their game must be evidence-based. However, S's fact-argumentation need not necessarily presuppose argumentation-based interaction with R (e. g. , in case of a defendant *in absentia*). It may therefore seem as if only S and T properly play for legal evidence and interpretation. But since R necessarily interacts with S, who initiates the game, it is S who generally determines the starting point of an ALG.

Although a legal dispute is necessary for an ALG to start, it is by itself insufficient to initiate the game. Indeed, Teply (2005: 1) estimates that merely 5% of private disputes reach trial, with the remainder mostly terminating in negotiated settlements. Criminal disputes, by contrast, may involve bargaining, but since their ultimate purpose is to exercise justice they cannot be *settled* by negotiation. One way or another, a civil, administrative, or criminal ALG must start with a (non-empty) F_S.

A second necessary condition for an ALG to start is that S uses F_S to lodge a complaint against R, which the court subsequently places on file. This in turn depends on S's fact-argumentation being sufficiently persuasive, making cogent S-fact argumentation a necessary sub-condition. But since political reasons, national security or other concerns may prevent courts from filing a complaint, cogent S-fact-argumentation remains an insufficient sub-condition. (Notice that this goes against the principle of judicial *logos* and justice, which are therefore relative rather than absolute principles.) In the general case, then, an ALG starts *if and only if* S takes evidence-based legal action and T puts it on record.

We now turn to the specific civil and criminal provisions applicable in mainland China.

4. 3 Civil and Criminal Provisions in Mainland China

4. 3. 1 *Civil Provisions*

The *Civil Procedure Law of the People's Republic of China* (CPL) and its provisions stipulate four necessary conditions to file a case: (1) the plaintiff is a citizen, legal person, or other organization with a direct stake in the case; (2) there is at least one specific defendant and (3) at least one specific legal claim, fact, and reason; and (4) the case falls within the scope of the people's court and also comes under its jurisdiction.

Condition (3) names the applicable standard for evaluating S's fact-argumentation, which must satisfy the following conditions:

First, there is at least one concrete claim, and an associated definite purpose S seeks to achieve through litigation. Since we treat a legal claim in a LFA as a conclusion, that claim forms an S-conclusion set C_S, which is inferred from the (non-empty) set F_S using the interpretation set I_S.

Second, there is at least one fact and evidence for it, so that each item of evidence should support at least one S-fact, while irrelevant evidence fails to support some S-fact. (In case of a self-evident fact, E_S may theoretically be empty; but rather than entailing a lack of evidence, it entails being dialectically basic, so the fact does presently not *require* evidence; see Sect. 6. 3.) The link between F_S and E_S is thus one of evidential reasoning or argument. Indeed, disregarding that link may (erroneously) lead to equating evidence and fact.

Third, a complaint has at least one legal ground such as a legal norm. Legal grounds and evidence may equally serve as starting points for an ALG, and so can provide basic premises for S's argument. For this reason, a healthy legal system requires lawyers who *connect* legal grounds and evidence. ①

4. 3. 2 *Criminal Provisions*

Similarly, we find three requirements for S to institute a public prosecution: (1) the act an accusedparty is suspected to have committed does *ipso iure* constitute a crime; (2) the F_S is clear and its supporting E_S is reliable and sufficient; and (3) the accused party should be investigated for criminal responsibility in accordance with the law. Here, condition (2) provides the applicable standard to evaluate whether S's fact-argumentation is cogent. Of course, E_S may insufficiently support a relevant fact-*qua*-claim, and if F_S is empty then condition (2) fails trivially.

We can spell out condition (2) by three sub-conditions: (a) the case fact set F_S must be unambiguous; (b) the evidence set E_S must be reliable; and (c) E_S must be sufficient for F_S . While sub-condition (b) demands that each element of E_S be reliable, sub-condition (c) demands the entire E_S to sufficiently support the entire F_S, thus forming a chain of evidence. If sub-conditions (b) and (c) are individually necessary and jointly sufficient for (a), then F_S being clear *means* that E_S is both reliable and sufficient.

In each particular case, of course, the processes by which one assesses *that* an

① It is beyond the scope of this paper to discuss the legal grounds for interpretative argumentation, or reasoning, from which legal interpretation starts.

action constitutes a crime, *that* F_S is clear, *that* E_S is sufficient, and *that* transitioning from E_S to F_S is unproblematic, etc., may raise serious interpretative challenges (see, e. g., Bex 2011; Laudan 2006, esp. 117 – 124). So the forgoing and subsequently presented conditions properly express the goals such processes aim at, rather than detailing how one achieves them (if one does).

With this important caveat, we now turn to what is required of R.

5. R-Fact Argumentation: The Real Beginning of an ALG

In an ALG the context for constructing fact-argumentation is necessarily dynamic. For R must continuously consider S's fact-argumentation or will otherwise risk forgoing advantages that can arise from the specifics of how R's fact-argumentation *aligns* to S's fact-argumentation. Moreover, the fact sets may change as the ALG develops. For instance, if evidence that S produced is defeated, so is the legal fact it had supported. Consequently, R must accordingly update her fact-argumentation for the same reason.

Since R cannot decide *whether* to play the ALG, or not (but is rather forced to do so), she has a *prima facie* passive role. In a civil ALG, however, normally S and R each present at least one (mutually independent) legal fact and attendant fact-argumentation—provided the allocation principle applies that whoever raises a claim incurs a burden of proof for it (*semper necessitas probandi incumbit ei qui agit*). In fact, it holds generally that if a non-claiming party would incur unfavorable consequences from acquiescing to the other party's fact-*qua*-claim, then both S and R *should* raise claims.

Specifically in a criminal ALG, however, it can nevertheless be prudent for R to *avoid* claiming that the accused party is innocent, and instead aim to refute S's fact-argumentation (that seeks to establish the accused party's guilt). For were R to raise that claim, then she would likewise have to prove it—and so provide evidence for it—which may incur unfavorable consequences besides those arising from seeking to refute S's claim. Of course, if R can easily produce sufficient evidence, then R *should* raise an attendant claim and provide fact-argumentation. In the Huge case (see Sect. 3.3), for instance, by the time the retrial started Zhao Zhihong had been identified as the murderer. So R should have claimed that Huge is innocent.

That R can in the first place seek to merely refute S's fact-argumentation points to the status a legal system assigns to the principle of presumed innocence: R is regarded as innocent unless S can establish the claim "R is guilty" beyond reasonable doubt. The murder trial of O. J. Simpson provides a particularly infamous example of R merely disproving S's fact-argumentation, by establishing that E_S insufficiently supports F_S . R's successful advocacy here rested on character-evidence against Detective Mark Fuhrman, rather than supporting the claim that Simpson is innocent. ① It stands to reason that this led the jury to doubt the legitimacy and admissibility of *additional* evidence the prosecution presented, eventually letting S's chain of evidence collapse. Famously, on 15 May 1995, Fuhrman presented a pair of gloves as evidence, the left one being found at the victim's residence, the right one at Simpson's. But when Judge Ito asked Simpson to try on one of the gloves, it proved to be too small. Subsequently further incriminating evidence was deemed inadmissible (bloodstains, shoeprints, body fibers). Arguably, then, the jury was led to endorse that Fuhrman's bias supports that he is capable of fabricating evidence incriminating Simpson.

By contrast, the burden of proof in a civil ALG typically lies with the claimant, wherefore both parties will raise a claim. But if one party cannot shoulder their burden, then either F_S or F_R is maintained by default. In this respect, the Simpson case highlights what may appear as a paradoxical feature of the U. S. judicial system: criminal and civil ALGs *inversely* allocate the burden of proof. (Though Simpson was found *not guilty* in the criminal trial, the attendant civil trial charged him with paying 33. 5 million USD in compensation to the families of both murder victims.)

Rational agents will generally play the best response to the worst possible case that the other player's argumentative moves could induce, thus obeying the *Harsanyi Maximin* (HM) rationality principle (Harsanyi 1977): *unless player A has a reason to expect that player B will not play a strategy leading to the least preferred outcome for A, A should play the strategy that best responds to the worst case.* In stating a generalized form of pessimism, HM forces both players to reconsider their options *at each turn.* So to maintain equilibrium, R and T will both have to construct their fact-argumentation dynamically.

① When defense attorney F. Lee Bailey cross-examined Fuhrman on March 15, 1995, he denied having even once uttered the term "nigger" in the past 10 years. But on 29 August 1995, R played excerpts of interviews with Fuhrman, that screenwriter Laura H. McKinny had conducted between 1985 and 1994, in which he used the focal term 41 times. This established Fuhrman as being prone to racial bias, thus forcing him to plead his Fifth Amendment right (to withhold self-incrimination testimony). So when taking the stand on 6 September 1995, he refused to answer questions.

Having seen the constraints an ALG places on players' attempts at maintaining equilibrium, how should T construct her fact-argumentation?

6. T-Fact Argumentation: The Factual Basis for Judgment

6.1 Properties, Purpose, and Types of T-Facts

"T-fact-argumentation" refers to the argumentation by which T justifies the verdict in an ALG. In general, S- and R-fact-argumentation tend to serve S's and R's own narrow interests, and though S and R are required not to lie to the court, they can nevertheless withhold (parts of) what they know. T's fact-argumentation, by contrast, must primarily obey the principle of judicial justice and fairness.

As with S- and R-facts, a T-fact remains defeasible and so is not objective. Based on evidence presented during the first and second trial at the Court of Jingshan Court and Jingmen Intermediate People's Court, for instance, the relevant factual claim in the She Xianglin case asserted that, on 2 January 1994, She Xianglin killed his wife Zhang Zaiyu. But on 28 April 2005, Zhang Zaiyu returned unharmed to her home. Since this undermined the original T-fact-argumentation, it shows that also a T-fact is a fact-*qua*-claim.

T's argumentation in an ALG generally pursues three purposes: (1) fact-finding (i.e., identifying relevant elements of F_T); (2) application of law (i.e., identifying members of N_T and I_T applicable to F_T); and (3) decision-making (i.e., inferring members of C_T using I_T and F_T). Here being concerned with fact-argumentation, we merely address (1). Members of F_T can be divided into three types: (1) self-evident facts, (2) identified facts, and (3) facts-proven-by-a-judge. We proceed to discuss each type.

6.2 Self-evident Fact

A self-evident fact is typically free of proof, but remains defeasible if a player presents sufficient evidence to undermine it. The *Civil Procedure Law of the People's Republic of China* (CPL) stipulates different regulations concerning self-evident facts in civil, administrative, and criminal proceedings.

For a civil ALG, self-evident facts comprise natural laws and theorems, well-known or presumed facts, and effectively established ones (by a court, an arbitrating body, or a notary). Though further conditions are not placed on a self-evident fact, it does not automatically become an F_T element. In the infamous *Zhang Xueying versus Jiang Lunfang* case from 2001, for instance, T simply failed to identify (as a self-evident fact) that Zhang would inherit part of the deceased Huang Yongbin's estate, as certified by the Naxi District Notary Office. ① Being a self-evident fact is therefore neither necessary nor sufficient for F_T membership, which rather depends on whether the opponent fulfills her burden of proof, or not.

For an administrative ALG, article 68 of *the Regulation on Issues of Administrative Litigation Evidence*, issued in 2002 by the *Supreme People's Court* (SPC), determines that self-evident facts comprise natural laws and theorems, well-known facts, facts presumed by law or day-to-day experience, and facts proven in conformity with legal provisions. Administrative proceedings often compare as being similar to civil ones. But the legal system of mainland China knows significant differences with respect to self-evident facts. For instance, a fact presumable in virtue of everyday experience is self-evident in an administrative but not in a civil ALG. Nor is it perfectly clear whether a fact proven by legal provisions in an administrative ALG can be treated like an effectively established one in a civil ALG. (Such differences may merely reflect definitional shortcomings, of course.)

For a criminal ALG, article 437 of the *Regulations of Criminal Proceeding*, issued by the *Supreme People's Procuratorate* in 2012, stipulates with respect to self-evident facts that evidence need not be provided for: (a) common-sense facts known by most people; (b) facts effectively established by a court's decision not subject to trial-revision procedures; (c) facts originating with the content of laws and regulations judges should know as a matter of due diligence; (d) procedural facts not disputed in a trial; (e) facts presumed by legal provisions; and (f) natural laws and theorems. ② (The first subtype is vague, for what counts as common-sense requires interpretation.)

In a civil, administrative, or criminal ALG, since also facts besides self-evident ones may be beyond dispute, one might likewise treat them as requiring no evidence. But the legal system of mainland China currently recognizes *quasi* self-evident facts only in a criminal proceeding. In order to reduce cost and improve the efficiency of litigation, each fact that S or R do not dispute (thus falling into the intersection of F_S and F_R) is considered self-evident, and is hence treated as a F_T member.

---

① *Zhang Xueying v. Jiang Lunfang* (2001), Naxi Min Chu Shen Zi 561.

② *The Trial Regulations of Criminal Proceeding in the People's Procuratorate*, GanJian Fa Shi Zi (2012), 2 Hao.

An extreme but instructive situation arises when S and R do not dispute an alleged fact—wherefore T treats it as self-evident—which, however, fails to *be* a fact. Again demonstrating the crucial difference between a legal and an objective fact, this situation is presumably unacceptable to those who advocate the primacy of substantial over procedural justice, on grounds that the ultimate purpose of a trial is to search for (legal) truth. But it may well be acceptable to those advocating the alternative principle, viz. that the ultimate purpose of a trial is to make a legally proper case.

6. 3 Identified Facts

Besides self-evident facts, F_T may include T-facts inferred from the E_T, and identified as such by a T-judge. Identified facts always relate to the three basic steps of fact-finding: producing, questioning, and identifying evidence.

Since all players in an ALG are required to support their claims, "producing evidence" means that S, R, T each provide evidence and argue for their facts-*qua*-claims. Their burdens of proof can thus be further analyzed into a burden of production and one of justification. (Lawyers sometimes refer to the latter as the "burden of persuasion".) Indeed, to translate the term "burden of proof" into Chinese, some use "Zhengming Zeren" —the burden to prove; others prefer "Juezheng Zeren" —the burden to produce evidence. But when properly understood, each term has a unique meaning.

"Questioning evidence" specifically refers to questioning the admissibility of evidence the respondent produces (i. e., S or R), namely with regard to its probative force, authenticity, relevance, and legality. (In the broadest sense "questioning evidence" also refers to activities in *arbitration*, but here we focus on the term's narrow sense in litigation.) It is a matter of debate whether these four properties *suffice* for evidence to be admissible, and whether the latter three properties not in fact already constitute probative force. Returning to the Simpson case, for instance, the jury had neither been presented with the 911-call (reporting Simpson violently attacking Nicole Brown) nor with the 17 June 1994 TV-footage (of Simpson attempting to escape police custody). But both evidence-items nevertheless share in authenticity, relevance, legality, and probative force.

At any rate, in the legal system of mainland China only a T-judge *decides* whether evidence is admissible. (Though they are T members, the T-jury cannot do so.) In the common law system, moreover, S or R may question evidence, but T's referee role here implies no such right. In the civil system, by contrast, since T acts on behalf of justice and fairness she can produce and question evidence as much as S or R can.

Finally, "identifying evidence" means to *determine* the admissibility of evidence that S or R have produced. In both law systems, a T-jury cannot abstain from evaluating the probative force of evidence. Specifically in the common law system, the T-jury will engage in evidential reasoning (or factual argumentation) in order to determine whether elements in F_S and F_R hold up to scrutiny, as per how the collegial panel had identified E_T. But here the T-jury alone exercises factual decision-making (as per the T-judge's instruction), and hence *determines* the probative force of E_T. In the civil law system, by contrast, the jury *partakes* in this duty together with the judge.

In summary, a T-judge or a collegial panel always identifies the evidence, E_T, while fact-argumentation is partly (civil law) or entirely (common law) in the hands of a T-jury. In other words, S and R play an evidence-based game against the admissibility and probative force of the evidence set, as determined by T.

6.4 Facts-Proven-by-a-Judge

As the third and final type, in an ALG a fact-proven-by-a-judge is supported by evidence a T-judge has produced directly. This type is only known in the civil law system. As we saw, the common law system bars the T-judge at any trial stage from producing evidence to support a F_T element. T-judges here act as "second rate"-arguers, for any evidence they can identify comes from, and so belongs to, E_S or E_R. Hence, the T-judge can be a *genuine* ALG player only in the civil law system.

At the first trial stage, moreover, evidence a T-judge produces cannot be questioned and so need not be further identified. But since a T-judge at a later stage may not accept such evidence, it does remain defeasible. This explains the need for procedural restrictions on a T-judge's discretion in the civil law system, so as to prevent abuse of her unique position. As we saw for three major criminal cases in mainland China having in the last twenty years been misjudged (She-Xianglin case, Zhao Zuohai case, Huge Jiletu case), the root cause *was* the misuse of judicial discretion (see Sect. 3.3).

In the civil law system, then, a T-fact either is self-evident, identified, or proven-by-a-judge; in the common law system a T-fact either is self-evident or identified. Like S- or R-facts, also a T-fact is a fact-*qua*-claim. Unless it is self-evident, such facts must be supported by evidence and do remain defeasible. Particularly in a second trial, or at the retrial stage, T can overturn a T-fact that at the prior stage had counted as established.

7. Conclusion

Unlike an ontologically objective fact, we submit, in the context of an argument litigation game (ALG) a legal fact can be viewed as a fact-*qua*-claim. For rather than merely state it, players must in principle argue for it. Far from providing a defeating counterexample, a self-evident fact presents an exception where argumentative support is possible, but currently not needed.

In playing an ALG, the three relevant parties—the suitor, S; the respondent, R; and the trier, T—forward litigation argumentation that typically is in line with the *legal five-fold argument pattern* (LFA). But not only does their fact-argumentation react dynamically to other players' moves in order to maintain a game-theoretic equilibrium. Given each party's distinct interests, the argumentation also tends to be self-serving. Both S and R thus seek to persuade T, who in turn seeks to persuade an audience that, besides S and R, includes judges at higher courts.

We also saw that since attorneys seek to secure legal rights for their clients, they may withhold on (parts of) what they know. T's mission, by contrast, is to promote justice and fairness. This incurs distinct responsibilities in the common law and the civil law system. In the former, the T-judge carries out procedural justice and fairness by instructing the T-jury how they shall carry these values out. In the latter, it is primarily the T-judge who *together with* a T-jury balances aspects of procedural and substantial justice as well as fairness. Hence, the T-judge can be a *genuine* ALG player only in the civil law system.

Acknowledgements

The first author acknowledges funding from the Chinese MOE Projects for Key University Research in the Humanities and Social Sciences (No. 15JJD720014), the National Social Science Fund of China (No. 13AZX0017), and a Guangdong Province Pearl River Distinguished Professorship (2013). The second author acknowledges an "Understanding China"-Fellowship from the Confucius Institute (*Hanban*), and funding through the European Union's FP 7 framework program (No. 1225/02/03) as well as the Volkswagen Foundation (No. 90, 531)

References

Aldisert, Ruggero. Logic for Lawyers: A Guide to Clear Legal Thinking [M]. Boulder: National Institute for Trial Advocacy, 1997.

Alexy, Robert. A Theory of Legal Argumentation [M]. Adler, Ruth & MacCormick, Neil (Trans.) New York: Oxford University Press, 1989.

Bex, Floris J. Arguments, Stories and Criminal Evidence: A Formal Hybrid Theory [M]. Dordrecht: Springer, 2011.

Feteris, Eveline. Fundamentals of Legal Argumentation: A Survey of Theories on the Justification of Judicial Decisions. [M]. London: Kluwer Academics Publishers, 1999.

Gardner, James. A Legal Argument: The Structure of Language of Effective Advocacy [M]. Charlottesville: The Michie Company, 1993.

Harsanyi, J. Rational Behavior and Bargaining Equilibrium in Games and Social Situations [M]. Cambridge: Cambridge University Press, 1977.

Hock Lai, Ho. A Philosophy of Evidence Law: Justice in the Search for Truth [M]. Oxford: Oxford University Press, 2008.

Kelsen, Hans. General Theory of Norms [M]. Oxford: Clarendon Press, 1971, 1991.

Laudan, Larry. Truth, Error, and Criminal Law: An Essay in Legal Epistemology [M]. Cambridge: Cambridge University Press, 2006.

MacCormick, Neil. Rhetoric and the Rule of Law: A Theory of Legal Reasoning [M]. Oxford: Clarendon Press, 2005.

Rescher, Nicholas. Dialectics: A Controversy-Oriented Approach to the Theory of Knowledge [M]. New York: State University of New York Press, 1977.

Teply, Larry L. Legal Negotiation in a Nutshell [M]. 2nd ed. St. Paul: Thomson/West Publishing Co., 2005.

Van Benthem, Johan. Logic and argumentation theory [C] //van Eemeren, F., Grootendorst, R., van Benthem, J., and Veltman, F. (eds.). Proceedings Colloquium on Logic and Argumentation. Amsterdam, North-Holland, 1996: 27 -41.

The Trial Regulations of Criminal Proceeding in the People's Procuratorate, Gan Jian Fa Shi Zi, 2012, 2.

Van den Hoven, Paul. Kelsen's General Theory of Norms [J]. International

Journal for the Semiotics of Law, 1988, 1 (3): 295 – 323.

van Eemeren, Frans, Grootendorst, Rob and Snoeck-Henkemans, Francisca. Argumentation: Analaysis, Evaluation, Presentation [M]. London: Lawrence Erlbaum Associates Inc, 2002.

Xiong, Minghui. A judge's argumentation skill in judicial practice [J]. Legal Science, 2012, 370 (9): 16 – 19.

Xiong, Minghui. Litigational Argumentation: A Logical Perspective of Litigation Games [M]. Beijing: China University of Politics and Law Press, 2010.

基于形式论辩系统的滑坡论证分析[①]

——人工智能如何理解自然语言论辩

余　喆[1]　廖备水[2]

1. 中山大学哲学系，逻辑与认知研究所，广州 510275；

2. 浙江大学哲学系，语言与认知研究中心，杭州 310028

一、引言

论辩（Argumentation）是人们提出观点或主张，并对这些观点与主张给出支持，以求说服他人接受自己的看法的过程。自古希腊时期以来，论辩研究一直受到哲学、逻辑学、语用学和修辞学等领域的学者的关注。20 世纪末期，形式论辩理论开始在计算机与人工智能领域引起关注。相关研究者逐渐认识到，由于论辩是古往今来人们解决信念、观点、目标等方面冲突的一种自然而不可或缺的方式，论辩理论的研究在人工智能方面有很大的应用潜力。

根据论辩研究近几十年的发展，可将相关研究梳理为两个方向：非形式论辩和形式论辩。前者主要从语言学、修辞学和日常推理的角度，研究自然语言论辩的构造、比较和评价的规律与方法。这一方向具有代表性的研究包括图尔敏（S. E. Toulmin）的论证模型、沃尔顿（D. Walton）等人的论证图式、佩雷尔曼（Ch. Perelman）等人关于论辩评估的修辞标准，以及汗布林（C. L. Hamblin）的“形式对话”研究等。国内学者如熊明辉、谢耘等近年来也发表了诸多相关成果。其中，论证图式研究的特点是对自然语言论辩的形式进行一定的概括和提炼，建立对单个论证状态的评价机制。在大数据背景下，该类研究对于处理大规模的文本信息并从中找到有价值的论证，以及评估这些论证的可接受性，有着重要的意义。因此，把论证图式应用于论证挖掘的研究正在成为人工智能领域的研究热点之一。但从总体上看，非形式论辩与数理逻辑、人工智能逻辑等理论之间的关联较少，在人工智能领域的应用并不普遍。

后者，即形式论辩，主要受到逻辑学与人工智能领域学者的关注。这一方向致力于研究不一致情境下的推理，并以各种形式逻辑为基础，构建形式系

---

① 本文原发表于《科学技术哲学研究》2019 年第 2 期，中国人民大学《复印报刊资料（逻辑）》2019 年第 3 期转载。

统，以实现多种类型的非单调推理。形式论辩研究的迅速发展始于1995年人工智能界学者杜恩（P. M. Dung）提出的抽象论辩框架理论。其特点是抓住了不一致情景中的推理的本质特征，即如何处理各个论证之间的冲突，得出对于一个理性主体来说可接受的结论。杜恩的基本思路是通过忽略各个论证的内部结构，仅关注论证之间的冲突关系（一般称为“攻击关系”），建立用于冲突处理的数学模型，即抽象论辩框架。与非形式论辩不同的是，在抽象论辩框架中，一个论证是否可接受主要取决于其他与其相关的论证的状态。由于可建模多种类型具有的非单调推理、可使计算复杂性较低、对动态性的处理灵活等优点，近年来，形式论辩在人工智能领域引起了广泛关注，且得到了快速发展。

尽管非形式论辩与形式论辩这两个方向各自在其内部都进行了大量的研究工作，但如何结合这两方的优势，却还未得到充分的关注。非形式论辩的优点是与自然语言论证有直接关联，在人们日常生活及各类信息处理领域有着非常广泛的应用。同时，其缺点是缺乏形式化的手段来支持各种不同的人工智能应用。形式论辩研究建立在形式逻辑和数学模型的基础上，与人工智能有着天然的连接。然而，由于缺乏对自然语言论证的建模和利用，形式论辩相关理论和算法的可应用性依然存在障碍。

鉴于上述原因，如何把非形式论辩与形式论辩结合起来，正在引起逻辑与人工智能领域越来越多的关注。本文以此为出发点，关注自然语言论证，尝试借助非形式逻辑领域对论辩研究的相关方法和成果，以形式论辩方法对其进行建模。

我们发现，在形式化处理自然语言论证方面，滑坡论证（Slippery Slope Argument）作为一种常见的推理模式，尚未见相关研究报道。根据沃尔顿等人关于论证图式的研究，滑坡论证图式的形式较为复杂，是论证图式中非常有特点的一种。滑坡论证在一些早期文献中被归为谬误，但事实上却一直在日常生活及法律、政治、医药伦理语境中被应用。近年来，相关研究者开始关注滑坡论证并将其视为一种可以被合理使用的不确定性推理形式。沃尔顿指出，滑坡论证在实践推理中的一种重要情境——协商（deliberation）情境下，往往起到合理的作用。

以一段耳熟能详的诗歌为例：

例1：明日复明日，明日何其多，我生待明日，万事成蹉跎。

诗中所使用的论证方式具有滑坡论证的特征：通过一个较弱的推理链条，呈现初始事件可能的发展过程，推出令人难以接受的后果，从而达到劝说的效果，即劝服世人“最初不应‘待明日’”。

依据沃尔顿提出的滑坡论证图式，例1可以表达如下：

初始前提：主体 α在考虑采取行动 t_0（后文皆使用“t”代表“明日”）；

序列前提：采取 t_0会导致 t_1，而 t_1又会导致 t_2，继而产生一系列 t_2，…，t_x，…，t_y，…，t_n（“明日复明日”）；

不确定性前提：序列 t_0，t_1，t_2，…，t_x，…，t_y，…，t_n的子序列 t_x，…，t_y（“明日何其多”）是一个灰色区域，其中 x、y 是不确定点；

可控前提：α可以控制事态发展，直至到达灰色区域 t_x，…，t_y中的不确定点；

失控前提：一旦 α到达灰色区域 t_x，…，t_y中的不确定点，α对事态会失去控制，不得不任其继续发展（“明日”积累到一定程度，事情久拖不成就会荒废，无所事事），直到达到 t_n；

毁灭性后果前提：t_n是一个应极力避免的毁灭性后果（“万事成蹉跎”）；

结论：不应采取 t_0（“明日”）。

相应于论证图式，论辩的参与者可以提出批判性问题质疑对方的论证并据此评价论证的强度。例如：如果 t_0成立，有何证据表明后续的 t_1，t_2，…，t_x，…，t_y，…，t_n这一事件序列将会随之发生?

尽管借助滑坡论证图式可以以更严格的方式重构滑坡论证，但如何依据形式论辩相关理论和方法，从形式化角度表示滑坡论证，并在此基础上实现对相关论证状态的计算，仍是一个比较困难的问题。

针对该问题，本文尝试以形式论辩系统建模滑坡论证，并通过案例分析说明使用基于形式论辩系统刻画的滑坡论辩模型得出的结论符合推理直觉。本文的结构安排如下：第二节将介绍本文所涉及的形式论辩系统基本理论；在此基础上，第三节给出本文基于现有理论构建的滑坡论辩形式模型；在第四节通过案例，分析基于本文所给出的滑坡论辩模型的推理结果；最后，本文第五节将总结全文工作，并提出未来可能的进展思路。

二、形式论辩基本理论

抽象论辩理论的提出为形式论辩研究带来了突破性的进展，其核心概念之一是抽象论辩框架（Abstract Argumentation Framework）。如前所述，这一理念忽略了论证的内部结构，仅关注作为实心节点的论证及论证间的攻击关系。可以定义如下。

定义 1. 一个抽象论辩框架 AF 是一个二元组 $AF = \langle A, att \rangle$，其中 A 是一组论证的集合，$att \subseteq A \times A$ 是 A 中的论证之间攻击关系的集合。

根据定义，若有 A、B 两个互相攻击的论证，则论辩框架 $AF_1 = \langle \{AB\}, \{(AB), (BA)\} \rangle$如图 1 所示。

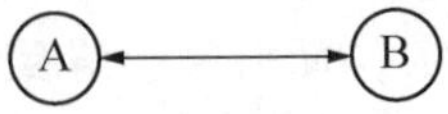

图 1　一个简单的抽象论辩框架

抽象论辩理论的核心概念之二是论辩语义（Argumentation Semantics）。给定一个抽象论辩框架，依据特定的评价标准，得到的一组集体可接受的论证集合称为它的外延。依据特定评价标准，从一个抽象论辩框架到一组外延集合的映射关系称为论辩语义。基于不同的标准和需求，现有文献中定义了多种论辩语义，本文仅介绍文中所涉及的基本语义。

一个论辩框架的外延首先应满足“无冲突”（Conflict-free）和“可防御”（Defensible）两个基本要求。满足这两个条件的论证集合可称为可相容（Admissible）集。在可相容集的基础上，可以获得几种论辩语义下外延的定义。

定义 2. 给定一个抽象论辩框架 $AF = \langle A, att \rangle$，

一组论证的集合 $E \subseteq A$ 是无冲突的，当且仅当 $\not\ni$ A，$B \in E$，使得（A，B）$\in att$；

一组论证的集合 $E \subseteq A$ 可防御论证 A，当且仅当对于任何的 $B \in A$，若（B，A）$\in att$，那么 $\exists C \in E$，使得（C，B）$\in att$；

一组论证的集合 $E \subseteq A$ 是可相容集，当且仅当 E 是无冲突的，且可防御 E 中的每个元素；

一个可相容外延 E 是优先外延，当且仅当 E 是（在集合包含意义上）极大的可相容集；

一个可相容外延 E 是完全外延，当且仅当 $\forall A \in A$，若 A 被 E 防御，那么 $A \in E$；

一个完全外延 E 是基外延，当且仅当 E 是（在集合包含意义上）最小的完全外延。

在这几种语义结果中，优先外延对应于认知主体最为宽容、轻信的态度，基外延则对应于认知主体最为怀疑、谨慎的态度。

抽象论辩理论以极简的论证与论证之间的攻击关系概念刻画了不一致情境中推理的特点，为论证评估铺平了道路，但如何构造论证和识别其中的攻击关系仍不明确。因此，在杜恩提出抽象论辩理论以后，论辩领域的研究者们结合波洛克（J. L. Pollock）等人关于论辩的早期研究，提出了多种关注论证构造与论证之间的攻击关系获取的结构化论辩系统（Structured Argumentation Systems）。包括基于假设的 ABA 框架、$ASPIC^+$ 框架，以及可废止逻辑编程

（DeLP）等。

其中，ASPIC$^+$是目前最受关注的结构化论辩理论之一，相较其他系统，ASPIC$^+$框架更适用于刻画自然语言论证，因此，本文选择以 ASPIC$^+$框架为基础来建模滑坡论证。

下面本文介绍 ASPIC$^+$框架的基本概念。要构建一个论辩系统，首先要给出一种用于知识表示的逻辑语言。此外，ASPIC$^+$框架的特点是将推理规则分为表达确定性推理的硬性规则和表达不确定性推理的可废止规则。由此，一个论辩系统可定义如下。

定义 3. 令一个论辩系统是一个三元组 $AS=(L, R, n)$，其中

L 是一种逻辑语言，它在否定符（$\neg$）下闭合；

论辩系统的规则集 $R=R_s \cup R_d$，其中 R_s是硬性规则集，R_d是可废止规则集，令 φ_i和 ψ 是 L 中的元素，使用两种规则的推理形式分别为 φ_1，…，$\varphi_n \rightarrow \psi$（如果 φ_1，…，φ_n成立，那么 ψ 必然成立）和 φ_1，…，$\varphi_n \Rightarrow \psi$（如果 φ_1，…，φ_n成立，那么 ψ 有可能成立）；且 $R_s \cap R_d=\varnothing$；

n 是一个偏函数，给每条可废止规则指派一个唯一的名称，使得 n：$R_d \rightarrow L$。

为简便起见，$\psi=\neg\varphi$ 或 $\varphi=\neg\psi$ 的情况将被记为 $\psi=-\phi$。

知识库是构建论证的前提集，其中包含两种类型的前提：表达确定性知识的公理（Axioms）和表达不确定性知识的普通前提（Ordinary Premises）。

定义 4. 一个论辩系统 $AS=(L, R, n)$ 中的知识库 $K \subseteq L$ 由公理 K_n和普通前提 K_p两个不相交的子集组成，即 $K=K_n \cup K_p$，且 $K_n \cap K_p=\varnothing$；$AT=(AS, K)$ 称为一个论辩理论。

论辩系统中的论证由知识库为起点，根据规则构建。下文用 *Prem* 表示知识库 K 中用于构建一个论证的命题集，*Conc* 表示结论集，*Sub* 表示子论证集，*DefRules* 表示用于构建论证的可废止规则集，*TopRule* 表示用于构建论证的最后一条规则。

定义 5. 基于知识库 $K \subseteq L$，论辩系统 AS 中的一个论证 A 可能为如下三种形式：

φ，如果 $\varphi \in K$；并且 $Prem(A)=\{\varphi\}$；$Conc(A)=\varphi$；$Sub(A)=\{\varphi\}$；$DefRules(A)=\varnothing$；$TopRule(A)=$未定义；

A_1，…，$A_n \rightarrow \psi$，如果 A_1，…，A_n（$n \geqslant 1$）是论证，使得 R_s中存在一条硬性规则 $Conc(A_1)$，…，$Conc(A_n) \rightarrow \psi$，并且：

$Prem(A)=Prem(A_1) \cup \cdots \cup Prem(A_n)$；$Conc(A)=\psi$；

$Sub(A)=Sub(A_1) \cup \cdots \cup Sub(A_n) \cup \{A\}$；

$DefRules(A) = DefRules(A_1) \cup \cdots \cup DefRules(A_n)$；

$TopRule(A) = Conc(A_1), \cdots, Conc(A_n) \to \psi$；

$A_1, \cdots, A_n \Rightarrow \psi$，如果 $A_1, \cdots, A_n$（$n \geq 1$）是论证，使得 R_d 中存在一条可废止规则 $Conc(A_1), \cdots, Conc(A_n) \Rightarrow \psi$，并且：

$Prem(A) = Prem(A_1) \cup \cdots \cup Prem(A_n)$；$Conc(A) = \psi$；

$Sub(A) = Sub(A_1) \cup \cdots \cup Sub(A_n) \cup \{A\}$；

$DefRules(A) = DefRules(A_1) \cup \cdots \cup DefRules(A_n) \cup \{Conc(A_1), \cdots, Conc(A_n) \Rightarrow \psi\}$；

$TopRule(A) = Conc(A_1), \cdots, Conc(A_n) \Rightarrow \psi$。

在完成论证构造后，需要识别论证之间的攻击关系。$ASPIC^+$ 框架中设定了三种攻击关系，分别为反驳（Rebutting）、底切（Undercutting）和破坏（Undermining）。其中，反驳针对一个论证的结论，底切针对一个论证中所使用的可废止规则，破坏针对一个论证的前提，可定义如下。

定义6. 若有 A、B 两个论证，A 攻击 B，当且仅当 A 反驳、底切或破坏 B。

A 反驳 B 于 B'，当且仅当 $\exists B' \in Sub(B)$，使得 $TopRule(B') \in R_d$ 且 $Conc(A) = -Conc(B')$；

A 底切 B 于 B'，当且仅当 $\exists B' \in Sub(B)$，且 $\exists r \in R_d$ 使得 $TopRule(B') = r$ 且 $Conc(A) = -n(r)$①；

A 破坏 B 于 φ，当且仅当对于 B 的任意普通前提 φ，$Conc(A) = -\varphi$。

简而言之，根据论证集合和论证之间的攻击关系，可以得到抽象论辩框架，从而可以根据论辩语义进行论证评估，获得可接受的论证外延及其结论。

三、滑坡论证形式模型

滑坡论证通常以一个预期中的行为或事件为出发点，经过渐进的推理链条，最终推出一个令人难以接受的（或十分糟糕的、灾难性的、完全荒谬的）结果。构造这样一个论证的目的通常是劝阻他人采取第一步行动，本质上与归谬法十分相似。因此，渐进的、可废止性的中间推理链条和归谬性的论证方式是滑坡论证的两大基本特点。

据此，本文在论辩系统的逻辑语言中引入一个符号“⊥”，表示“不可接受的”（或理解为“极坏的”“灾难性的”）。在推理规则上，滑坡论证中使用的推理规则可区分为滑坡规则和后果判定规则两种。前者刻画滑坡论证中的“滑坡”过程，可以视作可废止的推理链条（可能隐含多个相似的可废止中间

① “n（r）”表示规则 r 可应用。

推理过程），属于可废止规则，记为 R_{sl}；后者刻画滑坡论证最后判定（Judging）后果能否接受的步骤，记为 R_j，由于滑坡论证会极力推出一个令人无法接受的后果，因此后果判定规则一般为硬性规则，且判定结果为“⊥”。由此，论辩系统中规则的定义可由定义 3 修改如下：

定义 7. 一个论辩系统 $AS=(L, R, n)$ 中的规则集 $R=R_s\cup R_d$，其中滑坡规则 $R_{sl}\subseteq R_d$，推理形式为 $\varphi_1, \cdots, \varphi_n \Rightarrow_{sl} \psi$；后果判定规则 $R_j\subseteq R_s$，推理形式为 $\varphi_1, \cdots, \varphi_n \rightarrow_j \psi$。

一个滑坡论证中至少应包含一条滑坡规则和一条后果判定规则。

由于滑坡论证诉诸后承的特点，滑坡论证最终结论“$\neg a$”的推出实际上是基于一个逆否过程。因此，本文设定了基于可废止规则链的“弱逆否”（Weak Transposition），定义如下。

定义 8. 一个论辩系统 $AS=(L, R, n)$ 中的硬性规则 R_s 在逆否下闭合①，且滑坡规则 R_{sl} 在弱逆否下闭合，即

若存在规则 $\varphi_1, \cdots, \varphi_n \rightarrow \psi \in R_s$，那么对任意的 $i=1\cdots n$，都有其逆否规则 $\varphi_1, \cdots, \varphi_{i-1}, -\psi, \varphi_{i+1}, \cdots \varphi_n \rightarrow -\varphi_i \in R_s$；

若存在规则 $\varphi_1, \cdots, \varphi_n \Rightarrow_{sl} \psi \in R_d$，那么对任意的 $i=1\cdots n$，都有其弱逆否规则 $\varphi_1, \cdots, \varphi_{i-1}, -\psi, \varphi_{i+1}, \cdots \varphi_n \Rightarrow -\varphi_i \in R_d$。

此外，如何刻画出滑坡论证中的滑坡过程中事态从“可控”发展为“失控”的模糊地带，即沃尔顿所说的“灰色区域”，是滑坡论证形式化的一个难点。沃尔顿将促使一个滑坡论证发展的原因概括称为“驱动”（Drivers）。驱动可能是先例、公众共识、模糊不清的定义，也可能是社会舆论等其他因素。驱动使得一个滑坡论证可以合理向前推进，使行为主体（越来越）难以抗拒“滑坡”进程，对滑坡论证逐渐从可控范围发展到失控状态起到关键性的作用。

在例 1 中，驱动可能分别是如下两条经验总结：（1）不珍惜时间，久而久之养成拖延的习惯，不断浪费光阴；（2）浪费光阴造成事业/学业荒废，恶性循环，终致一无所成。将这两个驱动分别记为“d_1”和“d_2”，结合滑坡论证图式，例 1 中的滑坡论证发展过程如图 2 所示。

---

① ASPIC$^+$ 框架中，论辩系统的硬性规则在逆否（Transposition）或对置（Contraposition）下闭合是最终得到的结论外延满足一致性要求的必要条件。

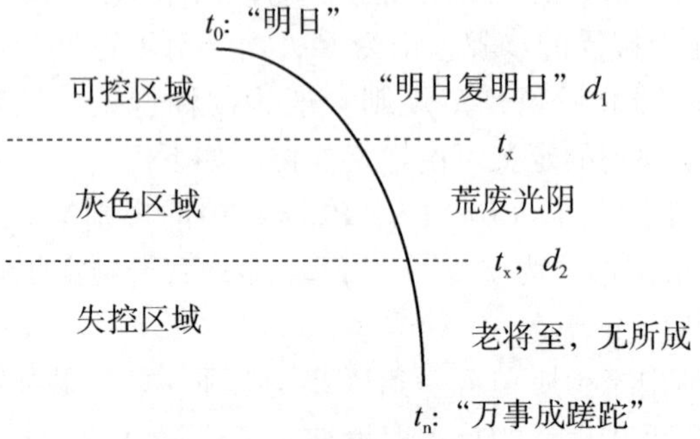

图2　滑坡论证过程

例1的论证图式中所示的几个阶段可以分别用规则表示为：

r_1：$t_0 \Rightarrow_{sl} t_{x-1}$，（"明日复明日"，尚在可控范围之中）

r_2：t_{x-1}，$d_1 \Rightarrow_{sl} t_x$，（经过可控范围，到达"灰色区域"）

r_3：$t_x \Rightarrow_{sl} t_y$，（在"灰色区域"中继续发展）

r_4：t_y，$d_2 \Rightarrow_{sl} t_n$，（经过"灰色区域"，进入失控状态，最终到了"万事成蹉跎"的一天 t_n）

后果判定规则为：

r_5：$t_n \rightarrow_j \bot$，（t_n是一个不可接受的后果）

根据定义8，上述规则的逆否及弱逆否规则有：

r_6：$\neg \bot \rightarrow \neg t_n$，

r_7：$\neg t_n\ d_2 \Rightarrow \neg t_y$，

r_8：$\neg t_n\ t_y \Rightarrow \neg d_2$，

r_9：$\neg t_y \Rightarrow \neg t_x$，

r_{10}：$\neg t_x\ d_1 \Rightarrow \neg t_{x-1}$，

r_{11}：$\neg t_x\ t_{x-1} \Rightarrow \neg d_1$，

r_{12}：$\neg t_{x-1} \Rightarrow t_0$

根据上述分析，可以在ASPIC$^+$框架的基础上构建一个滑坡论辩理论。

首先，将符号"⊥"加入ASPIC$^+$的逻辑语言。由于"⊥"一般而言不可接受，所以同时将"¬ ⊥"加入滑坡论辩理论知识库的普通前提中，表示"可接受的"，二者相互矛盾。此外，用C表示滑坡论证中的事件/行为的集合；C_0表示滑坡过程中的初始事件/行为集，这些初始事件属于可被攻击的普通前提，包含于知识库K中的普通前提K_p；用D表示滑坡论证中驱动的集合，驱动同样属于普通前提。由此可以给出一个关于滑坡论辩理论的定义。

定义9. 令$SSAT=(L, R, n, K, C, C_0, D)$是一个滑坡论辩理论，

其中：

$\bot \in L$；

$R = R_s \cup R_d$，滑坡规则 $R_{sl} \subseteq R_d$ 不为空集，且至少存在一条后果判定规则 $r_j = \varphi_1, \cdots, \varphi_n \rightarrow_j \bot \in R_s$；

L 的子集 $K = K_n \cup K_p$，$K_n \cap K_p = \varnothing$，使得 $\neg \bot \in K_p$；

$C = \{a_0, \cdots, a_n, b_0, \cdots, b_m, c_0, \cdots c_q, \cdots\} \subseteq L$，表示滑坡论证中所有事件/行为的集合，其中 a_i，b_j，c_k 是事件/行为；

$C_0 = \{a_0, b_0, c_0, \cdots\} \subseteq K_p \cap C$，表示滑坡论证中的初始事件/行为的集合，其中 a_0，b_0，c_0 是初始事件/行为；

$D = \{d_1, \cdots, d_n\} \subseteq K_p$，表示滑坡论证中的驱动集合，其中 d_i 是驱动。

四、滑坡论辩理论案例分析

根据定义 8，由例 1.1 可以构造滑坡论辩理论并获得如下 16 个论证：

A_1：t_0

A_2：$\neg\bot$

A_3：d_1

A_4：d_2

A_5：$A_2 \rightarrow \neg t_n$

A_6：$A_4 \Rightarrow_{sl} t_{x-1}$

A_7：$A_4, A_5 \Rightarrow \neg t_y$

A_8：$A_3, A_6 \Rightarrow_{sl} t_x$

A_9：$A_8 \Rightarrow_{sl} t_y$

A_{10}：$A_7 \Rightarrow \neg t_x$

A_{11}：$A_6, A_{10} \Rightarrow \neg d_1$

A_{12}：$A_4, A_9 \Rightarrow_{sl} t_n$

A_{13}：$A_{12} \rightarrow_j \bot$

A_{14}：$A_5, A_9 \Rightarrow \neg d_2$

A_{15}：$A_3, A_{10} \Rightarrow \neg t_{x-1}$

A_{16}：$A_{15} \Rightarrow \neg t_0$

根据论证之间攻击关系的定义，可以得到相应的抽象论辩框架，如图 3 所示。

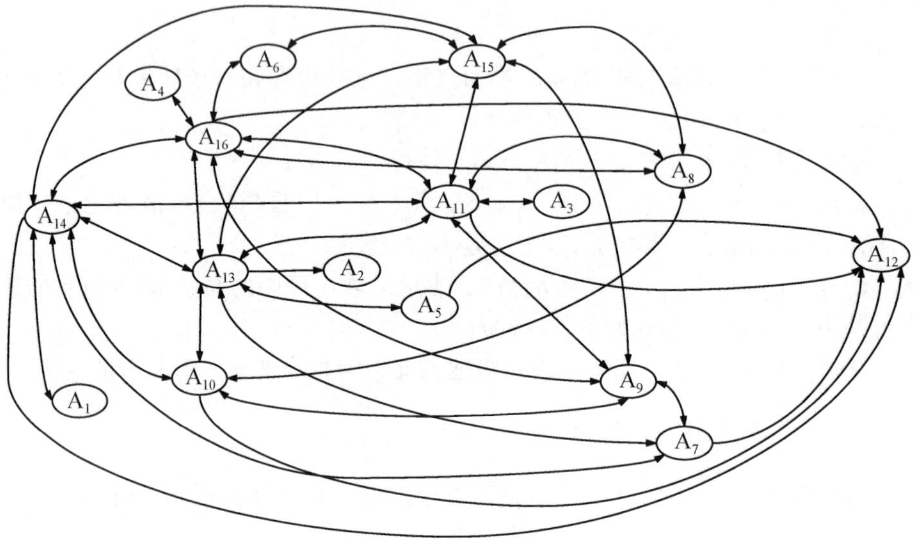

图3　抽象论辩框架

在反映轻信态度的优先语义下，由“明日复明日”案例得到的滑坡论辩理论的有 $E_1=\{A_2, A_3, A_4, A_5, A_7, A_{10}, A_{15}, A_{16}\}$、$E_2=\{A_1, A_3, A_4, A_6, A_8, A_9, A_{12}, A_{13}\}$、$E_3=\{A_1, A_2, A_3, A_4, A_5, A_6, A_7, A_{10}\}$ 等8个优先外延。

其中 E_1 对应的结论集合为 $\{d_1, d_2, \neg\bot, \neg t_n, \neg t_y, \neg t_x, \neg t_{x-1}, \neg t_0\}$，可理解为具有轻信态度的推理者认为一个滑坡论证中所有的子论证都不可接受—— 因为采取第一步行动会带来灾难性后果，所以不该采取第一步行动。E_2 对应的结论集合为 $\{t_0, d_1, d_2, t_{x-1}, t_x, t_y, t_n, \bot\}$，表示一些具有轻信态度的推理者可能认为一个滑坡论证中的所有子论证都可接受，也就是说，即便带来最坏的结果(“万事成蹉跎”)，他们此刻也要将工作推到明日。事实上这样的想法可能对应一些批判性问题的提出，例如：滑坡论证中的灾难性后果真的是最坏的结果吗？E_3 所对应的结论集合为 $\{t_0, t_{x-1}, d_1, d_2, \neg t_n, \neg t_x, \neg t_y, \neg\bot\}$，还有部分表示具有轻信态度的推理者可能认为：可以拖延几日，但要在不可收拾之前停下来，不造成太严重的后果就可以了。

由这一滑坡论辩理论得到的反映怀疑态度的基外延则为空集。

上述结果表明，面对一个滑坡论证，一个较为轻信的推理者可能会选择性地接受滑坡论证中不相冲突的一组论证及结论，而一个十分谨慎的推理者将对任一环节保持怀疑，对所有论证概不接受。

五、结论与展望

沟通非形式与形式论辩的研究，实现以自然语言呈现的实际论辩形式化表达与推理一直是语言学、逻辑学与人工智能等相关研究领域力图解决的一个难点问题，也是人工智能理解自然语言的重要基础。形式论辩与非形式论辩作为不同学科的关注点，各有所长且有互补之处。因此，虽然为二者牵线搭桥仍是一项任重道远的工作，但如果可以结合双方的优势，实现互相弥合，那么对相关领域研究发展具有非凡的意义。本文尝试运用结构化论辩框架 $ASPIC^{+}$，结合论证图式的研究，关注其中一种有特点的论证模式——滑坡论证，形成了一个可初步适用于滑坡论证的形式论辩理论。

本文目前的研究主要着眼于滑坡论证自身所包含的冲突关系，事实上滑坡论证还可能受到其他论证的攻击。参考沃尔顿论证图式中给出的相应批判性问题，可以总结滑坡论证可能受到的攻击类型。这些攻击是否将成功影响一个滑坡论辩框架中论证（及子论证）的状态，相关工作将留待未来的研究。

On the Finiteness Conjecture on Hitting Unsatisfiable Clause-sets①

Xishun Zhao

Institute of Logic and Cognition, Sun Yat-sen University, China

1 Introduction

A propositional clause-set is called minimally unsatisfiable (*MU*) if it is unsatisfiable and its any proper subset is satisfiable. Minimally unsatisfiable clause-sets have gained a substantial amount of investigations into their combinatorial and structural characterization, not only because of their theoretical interests, but also because of their application prospective. For overviews on *MU* please see the handbook article (Kleine Büning & Kullmann, 2009). An important related area of *MU* is the investigation on algorithms of extracting minimal unsatisfiable sub-clause-sets from a unsatifiable clause-sets (Marques-Silva, 2012) for a recent overview.

Fora clause-set F, the deficiency $\delta(F)$ of F is the difference between the number of clauses and the number of variables. Although MU is a D^P-complete problem (Papadimitriou & Wolfe, 1988), $MU_{\delta=k}: = \{F \mid F \in MU, \delta(F) = k\}$ is decidable in polynomial time (Fleischer, Kullmann & Szeider, 2002; Kullmann, 2000; Davydov, Davydova & Kleine Büning, 1998; Kleine Büning, 2000), where D^P is the class of decision problems which can be described as the intersection of an NP-problem and a co-NP-problem. It was also proved that $MU_{\delta=k}$ is fixed parametrized tractable (Szeider, 2004).

The combinatorial study on minimallyunsatisfiable clause-sets was opened by Aharoni & Linial (1986), showing the fundamental insight $\delta(F) \geq 1$ for any $F \in MU$. Also $SMU_{\delta=1}$ was characterized in Aharoni & Linial (1986), where $SMU \subset MU$ is the set of saturated minimally unsatisfiable clause-sets, which are also minimal w. r. t. that no clause can be further weakened. In Davydov, Davydova and Kleine Büning (1998), $MU_{\delta=1}$ was shown to be decidable in polynomial time based on an characterization.

---

① This research was partially supported by National Natural Science Foundation of China Grant 61272059, National Social Science Fund of China Grant 13&ZD186 and MOE Grant 11JJD720020.

Singular DP-reduction, which is DP-reduction restricted to singularvariables, plays a fundamental role in the investigation of $MU_{\delta=k}$, where a variable v in a clause-set $F \in MU$ is called singular if v or $\neg v$ occurs in F only once. It is shown that $MU_{\delta=k}$ is closed under singular DP reduction (see e. g. Davydov, Davydova and Kleine Büning, 1998). Thus, every clause-set in $MU_{\delta=k}$ can be reduced by applying singular DP-reduction as long as possible to a clause-set in $MU_{\delta=k}$ having no singular variable, which we call non-singular. We use MU' (resp. $MU'_{\delta=k}$) to denote the set of non-singular minimally unsatisfiable clause-sets (resp. with deficiency k). Let $sDP(F)$ be the set of non-singular clause-sets obtained from F by a sequence of singular DP-reduction. It is shown in (Kullmann & Zhao, 2013) that any two clauses F', $F'' \in SDP(F)$ have the same number of variables, in other words, F' and F'' can be obtained from F by the same number of steps of singular DP-reduction.

It is well known that for every clause-set F in $MU_{\delta=1}$, if F has at least one variable then F contains at least one singular variable (Davydov, Davydova & Kleine Büning, 1998), it follows that $MU'_{\delta=1} := \{\{\bot\}\}$, where $\bot$ denotes the empty clause, and $MU'_{\delta=2} = SMU'_{\delta=2}$. Any clause-set F in $MU'_{\delta=2}$ with n variables ($n \geq 2$) must be isomorphic to

$$F_n := \left\{\begin{matrix} x_1 & \neg x_1 & \neg x_2 & \cdots & \neg x_{n-1} & \neg x_n & \neg x_1 \\ x_2 & x_2 & x_3 & \cdots & x_n & x_1 & \neg x_2 \\ x_3 & & & & & & \neg x_3 \\ \vdots & & & & & & \vdots \\ x_n & & & & & & \neg x_n \end{matrix}\right\}$$

where each column represents a clause. Thus for any $F \in MU_{\delta=2}$, any two non-singular clause-set in $sDP(F)$ must be isomorphic (Kullmann & Zhao, 2013). More generally, we can define

$IST(k, n) :=$ the maximal number m such that there are m non-singular clause-sets in $MU'_{\delta=k}$ with n variables such that they are pairwise non-isomorphic.

$$IST(k) := \max\{IST(k, n) \mid n \in \mathbb{N}\}.$$

Clearly, we have $IST(1) = 1$ and $IST(2) = 1$. For $k \geq 3$, however, we have very limited knowledge about the structure of $MU'_{\delta=k}$, let lone $IST(k)$.

We hope that a clear characterization of $MU'_{\delta=k}$ would have applications in

- looking for hard instances for proof systems,
- developing more efficient decision algorithms for minimalunsatisability and extracting algorithms of minimally unsatisfiable sub-clause-sets.

· investigation of generalized minimal unsatisfiability such as lean clause-sets (Kullmann, 2003), minimal false quantified Boolean formulas (Kleine Büning & Zhao, 2006), and minimal unsatisfiable circuits (Belov & Marques-Silva, 2011; Schuppan, 2010).

In order to investigate MU $'\delta = k$ we at first restrict ourselves to unsatisfiable hitting clause-sets. By a hitting clause-set we mean a clause-set in which every two clauses contain a pair of complementary literals. Unsatisfiable hitting clause-sets must be minimal unsatisfiable. Hence we use $UHIT(UHIT')$ to denote the class of (non-singular) hitting minimal unsatisfiable clause-sets, likewise for $UHIT_{\delta=k}$ and $UHIT'_{\delta=k}$ Obviously, every clause-set in $UHIT'_{\delta=2}$ must be isomorphic to F_2 or F_3.

More generally, we conjecture that for any $k \geq 2$, $UNIT'_{\delta=k}$ is finite w. r. t. isomorphic. In other words, we conjecture that the number

$$N(k) := \sup\{|\mathrm{var}(F)|\,|F \in UHIT'_{\delta=k}\}$$

is finite, where $|\mathrm{var}(F)|$ is the number of all variables occurring in F Clearly $N(2) = 3$. Suppose the conjecture is true for k and we know $N(k)$, then we have a chance to construct all clause-sets in $UHIT'_{\delta=k}$ which would be much helpful for studying $MU'_{\delta=k}$

In this paper we will solve the conjecture for $k \in \{3, 4\}$ by showing $N(3) = 7$ and $N(4) = 11$. The remainder of this paper is organized as follow. Section 2 recalls the basic notions and results on (hitting) minimally clause-sets. In Section 3 we state precisely our finiteness conjecture concerning non-singular hitting unsatisfiable clause-sets. Section 4 introduces prime hitting unsatisfiable clause-sets, and studies the finiteness on non-prime hitting clause-sets with deficiency k under the assumption that $N(i)$ is finite for all $i < k$. In section 5, we at first introduce pseudo-2-subsumption resolution which replaces two clauses $(\{x, y\} \cup f)$ and $(\{\neg y\} \cup f)$ by $(\{x\} \cup f)$ and $(\{\neg x, \neg y\} \cup f)$ (where f is a clause). $UHIT$ and $UHIT_{\delta=k}$ are closed under pseudo-2-subsumption resolution. Then a prime hitting clause-set is defined to be strongly prime if it cannot be reduced to a non-prime hitting clause-set by any sequence of pseudo-2-subsumption resolution steps. Then it is proven that non-existence of strongly prime clause-sets will imply the finiteness conjecture. Finally it is shown that there are no strongly prime clause-sets with deficiency $k = 3$, 4, and as corollary, we have $N(3) = 7$ and $N(4) = 11$.

2. Preliminary

2.1 Clause-sets

In this paperwe use v, v_1, v_2, … to denote propositional variables. Literals are either propositional variables or their negations. For a variable v, we call v (resp. $\neg v$) a positive (resp. negative) literal. For a literal x, we identify $\neg\neg x$ with x. For a set K of literals, we define $K := \{\neg x \mid x \in K\}$.

We define $\text{var}(v) := v$ and $\text{var}(\neg v) := v$ for any variable v. For a set of literals we define $\text{var}(K) := \{\text{var}(x) \mid x \in K\}$.

A clause f is a finite clash-free set of literals (i. e., $f \cap f$ is empty). The empty clause is denoted as $\perp$. A clause f is called a unit clause if it contains only one literal, i. e., $|f| = 1$.

In this paper CNF formulas are considered as finite sets of clauses. So, in this paper CNF formulas are called clause-sets. Suppose F is a clause-set, we use $\text{var}(F)$ to denote the set of variables occurring in F, more precisely, $\text{var}(F) := \cup \{\text{var}(C) : C \in F\}$. And $\delta(F)$, the deficiency of F, is defined by $\delta(F) := |F| - |\text{var}(F)|$.

For a clause-set F and a literal x, the literal-degree of x in F, denoted by $ld_F(x)$, is the number of occurrences of x in F, i. e., $ld_F(x) = |\{f \in F \mid x \in f\}|$. The variable-degree of variable v in a clause-set F, denoted by $vd_F(v)$, is the number of all positive and negative occurrence of v in F, that is, $vd_F(v) = ld_F(v) + ld_F(\neg v)$. A variable v is said to be a full variable of a clause-set F if $vd_F(v) = |F|$, i. e., $v \in \text{var}(f)$ for every clause $f \in F$.

A partial truth assignment t is a mapping such that $dom(t)$ is a set of variables and $ran(t) \subseteq \{0, 1\}$. We say t satisfies a literal x if $t(x) = 1$ when x is positive or $t(\neg x) = 0$ when x is negative. If $\text{var}(x) \in dom(t)$ but t does not satisfy x then we say t falsify x. We say t satisfies a clause f if t satisfies a literal $x \in f$.

For a partial truth assignment t and a clause-set F, $t * F$ is obtained from F by deleting all clauses satisfied by t and removing all literals falsified by t. We say t satisfies F if $t * F$ is empty. We use $[v_1 \to \varepsilon_1, \ldots, v_m \to \varepsilon_m]$ to denote the partial truth assignment which assigns truth values ε_i to v_i for each $i = 1, \ldots, m$.

2.2 Minimal Unsatisfiable Clause-sets

A clause-set F is called minimal unsatisfiable if it is unsatisfiable, while removal of any clause from F will result in a satisfiable sub-clause-set. It is well-known that

$\delta(F) \geq 1$ for every $F \in MU$. By MU (resp. $MU_{\delta=k}$) we denote the set of all minimal unstisfiable clause-sets (with deficiency k). The minimally unsatisfiable clause-set without any variable is $\{\perp\}$.

A clause-set $F \in MU$ is called saturated minimally unsatisfiable if addition any literal to any clause of F will result in a satisfiable clause-set, more precisely, $(F \setminus \{f\}) \cup \{\{x\} \cup f\}$ becomes satisfiable for every clause $f \in F$ and any literal $x \notin f$.

Please note that $ld_F(v) \geq 1$ and $ld_F(\neg v) \geq 1$ for every clause-set $F \in MU$ and every variable $v \in \mathrm{var}(F)$.

The definition of min-var-degree of a clause-set F was introduced in Kullmann & Zhao (2011).

$$\mu vd(F) := \min\{vd_F(v) \mid v \in \in \mathrm{var}(F)\}.$$

$$\mu vd(MU_{\delta=k}) := \max\{\mu vd(F) \mid F \in MU_{\delta=k}\}.$$

Proposition 1. $\mu vd(MU_{\delta=1}) = 2$, $\mu vd(MU_{\delta=2}) = 4$, $\mu vd(MU_{\delta=3}) = 5$, *and* $\mu vd(MU_{\delta=4}) = 6$. (Kullmann & Zhao, 2011)

Let F be a clause-set. A literal x is called a singular literal of F if its literal-degree is one, i. e. $ld_F = 1$. A variable $v \in \mathrm{var}(F)$ is called a singular variable of F if either v or $\neg v$ occurs in F exactly once, that is, $ld_F(v) = 1$ or $ld_F(\neg v) = 1$. If both $ld_F(v) = 1$ and $ld_F(\neg v) = 1$ then v is called a 1-singular variable. More generally, a singular variable v is called m -singular if $m = vd_F(v) - 1$.

Proposition 2. *Suppose* $F \in MU_{\delta=1}$ *with* $\mathrm{var}(F) \neq \emptyset$. *Then F has at least one* 1-*singular variable.* (Davydov, Davydova and Kleine Büning, 1998)

2.3 Singular DP Reduction

We say two clauses C, D are resolvable on a variable v if $C \cap D = \{v\}$ or $C \cap D = \{\neg v\}$. If C, D are resolvable on v then we denote the resolvant $(C \cup D) \setminus \{v, \neg v\}$ by $C \diamond D$.

Let F be a clause-set, $v \in \mathrm{var}(F)$. By $DP_v(F)$ we denote the resulting clause-set obtained from F by applying DP-reduction on v, that is, adding all resolvants of resolvable clauses on v, and resolving all clauses contains v or $\neg v$. More precisely,

$$DP_v(F) := \{C \in F \mid v \notin \mathrm{var}(C)\} \cup \{C \diamond D \mid C, D \in F \text{ are resolvable on } v\}$$

In this paper we only apply DP reduction on singular variables. A step of *sDP*-reduction (for short, sDP-reduction) is a reduction from F to $DP_v(F)$, where v is a singular variable of F. We say F can be sDP-reduced to F' if $F' = F$ or F' can be obtained from F by a number of steps of sDP-reductions.

Proposition 3 *The sDP reduction preserve minimal unsatisfiability. More precisely, if v is a* singular *variable of a clause-set F then* $F \in MU_{\delta=1}$ *if and only if* $DP_v(F) \in MU_{\delta=k}$. (Kleine Büning, 2000; Kullmann & Zhao, 2013)

Thus, every clause-set $F \in MU_{\delta=1}$ can be sDP-reduced to $\{\bot\}$. And every $F \in MU_{\delta=k}$ with $k \geq 2$ can be reduced to a non-singular clause-set which has no singular variable.

2.4 Hitting Clause-sets

Given two clauses f, g, we say f, g hit each other if $f \cap g$ is non-empty, i.e., there is a literal $x \in f$ such that $\neg x \in g$. A clause-set F is said to be hitting if any two different clauses in F hit each other. For a hitting clause-set F, F is unsatisfiable if and only if $\sum_{f \in F} 2^{-|F|} = 1$ [Iwama, (1989), Büning & Zhao (2002)]. Consequently, unsatisfiable hitting clause-set must be saturated minimally unsatisfiable. We use $UNIT(UNIT_{\delta=k})$ to dente the set of all unsatisfiable hitting clause-sets (with deficiency k).

Throughout this paper, when we write $f \cup g$ for two clauses f and g, we assume implicitly that $f \cap g$ is empty. In particular, when we write $\{x\} \cup f$ we mean $x \notin f$.

Proposition 4 *Suppose*

$$F = \{(\{x\} \cup f), (\{\neg x\} \cup g_1), \ldots (\{\neg x\} \cup g_m)\}\} \cup G$$

is in *UHIT* such that G contains no occurrence of x or $\neg x$. Then $f = g_1 \cap \cdots \cap g_m$. Moreover, if $m = 1$ then $f = g_1$. (*Kullmann & Zhao*, 2013)

Corollary 1. Suppose

$$F = \{(\{x\} \cup f), (\{\neg x\} \cup g_1), \ldots (\{\neg x\} \cup g_m)\}\} \cup G$$

is given as in Proposition 4. *Let* $F' := \{g_1, \ldots g_1\} \cup G$ *which is* $DP_{\mathrm{var}(x)}(F)$. *Then*

for any literal $y \in f$, *we have* $m \leqslant ld_{F'}(y) = ld_F(y) - 1$, *and*

for any literal $y \notin f$, *we have* $ld_{F'}(y) = ld_F(y)$.

Corollary 2. Suppose *F is a clause-set in UHIT. Then each clause of F has at most one singular literal.*

Proposition 5 *Let* $F \in UNIT$, $v \in \mathrm{var}(F)$. *Suppose any variable* $u \in \mathrm{var}(F) \setminus \{v\}$ *is non-singular.*

1. *Suppose v is m-singular with* $m \geq 2$, *then* $DP_v(F)$ *is non-singular, that is, F can be sDP-reduced to a non-singular clause-set by one step singular DP reduction.*

2. *Suppose v is* 1*-singular. Then* $DP_v(F)$ *can be sDP-reduced to a non-singular clause-set by at most two steps of singular DP reduction.*

Proof:

1. Follows directly from Corollary 1.

2. Let $f_1 := (\{v\} \cup f)$, $f_2 := (\{\neg v\} \cup f)$ be the two clauses containing v or $\neg v$. If $DP_v(F)$ is non-singular, we are done. So suppose $DP_v(F)$ is singular, and let x be any singular literal in $DP_v(F)$. We remind that var(x) is non-singular in F. Please note that $DP_v(F) = \{f\} \cup (F \setminus \{f_1, f_2\})$. By Corollary 1, the number of occurrences of each literal in f decreases one in $DP_v(F)$. Thus if $DP_v(F)$ has a singular literal which is not singular in F then the new singular literal must be in f. Hence $x \in f$. By Corollary 2, f contains at most one singular literal. Thus, x is the only singular literal in $DP_v(F)$.

Since $\neg x \notin f$ we know by Corollary 1 that the number of occurrences $\neg x$ in F is the same as in $DP_v(F)$. Thus, $\neg x$ occurs in $DP_v(F)$ at least twice. Now the proposition follows item 1.

Proposition 6 *Let $F \in UHIT$, $v_1, v_2 \in var(F)$ be m_1-singular and m_2-singular, respectively. Suppose any variable $u \in var(F) \setminus \{v_1, v_2\}$ is non-singular in F.*

1. Suppose $m_1, m_2 \geq 2$.. Then F can be reduced to a non-singular clause-set by two steps of *sDP* reduction.

2. Suppose $m_1 = 1$, $m_2 \geq 2$. Then F can be reduced to a non-singular clause-set by at most three steps of *sDP* reduction.

Proof:

1. By Corollary 1 – 2, v_1 is the only singular variable in $DP_{v2}(F)$ and it is not 1-singular. Thus, $DP_{v1}(DP_{v2}(F))$ is non-singular. The assertion follows from Theorem 63 in Kullmann & Zhao (2013) which says that any two *sDP* reduction processes from F to non-singular clause-sets use the same number of *sDP* reduction steps.

2. By Corollary 1 – 2, v_1 is the only singular variable in $DP_{v2}(F)$. By Proposition 5, we know that $DP_{v2}(F)$ can be sDP-reduced to non-singular clause-set by at most two singular DP-reduction. The proposition again follows from Theorem 63 in Kullmann & Zhao (2013).

2.5 Splitting

Obviously, $[v \to \varepsilon] * F$ remains to be in *UHIT* for any $F \in UHIT$, $v \in$ var(F), and $\varepsilon \in \{0, 1\}$. Recall that $[v \to \varepsilon] * F$ is obtained from F by deleting clauses containing $v^{1-\varepsilon}$ (these clauses are satisfied by $[v \to \varepsilon]$) and removing all occurrences of v^{ε} from remaining clauses. Here, $v^0 = v$, $v^1 = \neg v$.

Proposition 7 *Suppose* $F \in UHIT(k)$ *is non-singular*, $v \in var(F)$, and $k \geqslant 2$. *Then* $\delta([v \to \varepsilon] * F) < k$ *for any* $\varepsilon \in \{0, 1\}$. (Kleine *Büning*, 2000; *Kullmann*, 2000)

2 – Subsumption Resolution

Definition 1

1. *Let* f_1, f_2 *be two clauses such that* $f_1 = (\{v\} \cup f)$, $f_2 = (\{\neg v\} \cup f)$ *for some variable* v *and clause* f. *Then we say that* f_1, f_2 *are* 2-*subsumption resolvable.*

2. *Suppose* F *is a clause-set containing two* 2-*subsumption resolvable clauses* f_1, f_2. *Let* $F' := \{f\} \cup (F \setminus \{f_1, f_2\})$, *where* $f := f_1 \cap f_2$. *We say that* F' *is obtained from* F *by a step of* 2-*subsumption resolution, and denote* F' *by* $2SR(F, f_1, f_2)$.

3. *We say* F *can be* 2*SR-reduced to* F' *if* $F' = F$ *or* F' *can be obtained from* F *by a sequence of steps of* 2-*subsumption resolution.*

Remark 1 *Let* F, f_1, f_2, v and F' be as in *the* above definition.

It is easy to see that F is in *UHIT* if and only if $F' := \{f\} \cup (F \setminus \{f_1, f_2\})$ is in *UHIT*.

- There are only two possibilities: v is either non-singular or 1-singular in F.
- If v is non-singular in F, then $\delta(2SR(F, f_1, f_2)) = \delta(F) - 1$..
- If v is 1-singular, then clearly $DP_v(F)$ is the same as $2SR(F, f_1, f_2)$.

Proposition 8 *Suppose*

$F \in UHIT_{\delta=k}$ *is non-singular, and* $k \geq 2$. *Let* $f_1 := (\{v\} \cup f)$, $f_2 := (\{\neg v\} \cup f)$ *be two* 2 – *subsumption resolvable clauses in* F. *Then* $2SR(F, f_1, f_2)$ *can be sDP-reduced to a non-singular clause-set with at most* 3 *steps of singular DP-reduction.*

Proof: In $2SR(F, f_1, f_2)$, the variable v may become singular, and some literal in f may become singular. For simplicity, let $F' := 2SR(F, f_1, f_2)$. Please note that if $x \in f$ is a singular literals in F', then $\neg x$ occurs at least twice. We shall show the assertion by case distinction.

Case 1. F' remains non-singular. Then we are done.

Case 2. In F', v is m-singular with m 2, all other variables are non-singular. Then DP $_v$ (F') is non-singular by Propositional 5.

Case 3. In F', v is m-singular with $m \geq 2$, f contains a singular literal x (then $\neg x$ occurs at least twice). By Proposition 6 (1), it is easily to see that $2SR(F, f_1, f_2)$ can be sDP-reduced to a non-singular clause-set by two steps of singular DP-reduction.

Case 4. In F', v is 1-singular, f contains a singular variable x (then $\neg x$ occurs at least twice). Please note that all other variables are non-singular. The assertion follows from Proposition 6 (2).

3. The Finiteness Conjecture

In this sectionwe state our conjectures. We denote by $UHIT'_{\delta=k}$ the class of non-singular clauses-sets in $UHIT_{\delta=k}$.

Definition 2 For $k \in \mathbb{N}$, let

$aN(k) := 4k - 5$, and let

$N(k) \in \mathbb{N} \cup \{\infty\}$ be the supremum of $|\mathrm{var}(F)|$ for $F \in UHIT'_{\delta=k}$. That is, $N(k) := \sup\{|\mathrm{var}(F)| : F \in UHIT'_{\delta=k}\}$.

Proposition 9 *Suppose* $k \geq 2$.

1. For $c \in \{1, \ldots, k-1\}$, $aN(k-c) + c \leqslant aN(k)$.
2. $aN(k-1) + 3 < aN(k)$ for $k > 2$.
3. For $k_1, k_2 \in \{2, \ldots, k-1\}$ such that $k_1 + k_2 \leqslant k+1$
$$aN(k_1) + aN(k_2) + 1 \leqslant aN(k).$$

Proof:

$$\begin{aligned} aN(k-c) + c &= 4(k-c) - 5 + c = 4k - 4c - 5 + c \\ &= 4k - 3c - 5 \\ &< 4k - 5 = aN(k). \end{aligned}$$

$$aN(k-1) + 3 = 4k - 9 + 3 = 4k - 6 < 4k - 5 = aN(k).$$

$$\begin{aligned} aN(k_1) + aN(k_2) + 1 &= 4k_1 - 5 + 4k_2 - 5 + 1 \\ &= 4(k_1 + k_2) - 9 \\ &\leqslant 4(k+1) - 9 \\ &= 4k - 5 = aN(k). \end{aligned}$$

Proposition 10 $N(1) = 0$, $N(2) = 3$, and $N(k) \geq aN(k)$ for $k \geq 2$.

Proof: Because $\{\bot\}$ is the only non-singular unsatisfiable hitting clause-set with deficiency 1, we have $N(1) = 0$.

Because every clause-set in $UHIT'_{\delta=2}$ is isomorphic to F_2 or F_3, we have $N(2) = 3$. Next we shall construct for $k \geq 2$ a clause-set in $UHIT'_{\delta=k}$ with $aN(k)$ variables. We define an operation on clause-sets.

For clause-sets F, G we denote by $F \oplus G$ the clause-set obtained as follows:

1. Obtain clause-sets F_0 isomorphic to F and G_0 isomorphic to G such that $\mathrm{var}(F_0) \cap \mathrm{var}(G_0) = \varnothing$.

2. Pick a new variable $v \notin \mathrm{var}(F_0) \cup \mathrm{var}(G_0)$.

$F \oplus G := (\{v\} \odot F_0) \cup (\{\neg v\} \odot G_0)$.

Here $\{v\} \odot F_0 = \{\{v\} \cup |f \in F_0\}$, likewise for $\{\neg v\} \odot G_0$.. Clearly,

$|F \oplus G| = |F| + |G|$,

$|\mathrm{var}(F \oplus G)| = |\mathrm{var}(F)| + |\mathrm{var}(G)| + 1$,

$\delta(F \oplus G) = \delta(F) + \delta(G) - 1$.

Now for $k \geq 2$ we define H_k as follows.

$H_2 := F_3$.

$H_{k+1} := H_k \oplus F_3$.

It is not hard to check that $H_k \in UHIT'_{\delta=k}$ and $|\mathrm{var}(H_k)| = aN(k)$.

Conjecture 1 (The Finiteness Conjecture) For every $k \geq 2$, $N(k) = aN(k) = 4k - 5$.

A weak version of the finiteness conjecture is

Conjecture 2 For every $k \geq 2$, $N(k) < \infty$, i. e. , $N(k)$ is a finite number.

4. Prime Hitting Clause-sets

To dealwith the finiteness conjecture we will introduce several subclasses of UHIT.

Definition 3 Let $F \in UHIT$.

- We say a non-empty subset $F' \subseteq F$ is a factor of F if $\cap F'$ hits all clauses in $F \setminus F''$.
- Clearly, F is a factor of itself. And $\{f\}$ is a factor of F for every $f \in F$. We call these factors trivial. In other words, a factor F' is called non-trivial if $1 < |F'| < |F|$.
- We call F prime if F has no non-trivial factor.

Example 1 The following clause-sets are prime.

$\{\{x\}, \{\neg x\}\}$,

$$\left\{\begin{array}{ccccc} x_1 & \neg x_1 & \neg x_2 & \neg x_3 & \neg x_1 \\ x_2 & x_2 & x_3 & x_1 & \neg x_2 \\ x_3 & & & & \neg x_3 \end{array}\right\},$$

$$\left\{\begin{array}{ccccccc} \neg x_1 & \neg x_1 & \neg x_1 & \neg x_3 & x_2 & x_1 & x_1 \\ x_2 & \neg x_2 & \neg x_2 & x_4 & \neg x_4 & x_3 & \neg x_2 \\ x_3 & \neg x_3 & x_3 & & & x_4 & \neg x_4 \\ \neg x_1 & \neg x_4 & & & & & \end{array}\right\},$$

$$\left\{\begin{array}{ccccccc} x_1 & x_1 & \neg x_3 & \neg x_2 & x_2 & \neg x_1 & \neg x_1 \\ \neg x_2 & x_2 & \neg x_4 & x_3 & x_3 & \neg x_3 & x_2 \\ \neg x_3 & x_4 & & & \neg x_4 & x_4 & x_3 \\ x_4 & & & & & & x_4 \end{array}\right\},$$

where every column represents a clause.

Proposition 11 *Suppose* $F \in UHIT$ *and* $v \in var(F)$. *Let* $F_v := \{C \in F \mid v \in C\}$ *and* $F_{\neg v} := \{C \in F \mid \neg v \in C\}$.

1. If v is a singular variable, then F_v, $F_{\neg v}$ and $F_v \cup F_{\neg v}$ are factors of F.

2. If v is a full variable of F (i. e. , $v \in \text{var}(f)$ for every $f \in F$, then F_v, $F_{\neg v}$ and $F_v \cup F_{\neg v}$ are factors of F.

Moreover, for every $F \in UHIT$ with $|\text{var}(F)| \geq 2$, if there is a singular or full variable in F , then F is non-prime.

Definition 4 *For* $F, G \in UHIT$ *and* $f \in F$ *with* $var(f) \cap var(G) = \varnothing$ *we define*

$comp(F, f, G) := (F \setminus \{f\}) \cup (\{f\} \odot G)$.

Where $\{f\} \odot G := \{f \cup g \mid g \in G\}$

Remark 2 Let F, f, G be as in the above definition.

$comp(F, f, G) = G$ iff $F = \{\perp\}$ and $f = \perp$.

$comp(F, f, G)$ iff $G = \{\perp\}$.

$comp(F, f, G)$ is in $UHIT$, with

$|comp(F, f, G)| = |F| + |G| - 1$

$|\text{var}(comp(F, f, G))| = |\text{var}(F)| + |\text{var}(G)| - |\text{var}(F) \cap \text{var}(G)|$

$\delta(comp(F, f, G)) = \delta(F) + \delta(G) + |\text{var}(F) \cap \text{var}(G)| - 1$

$\{f\} \odot G$ is a factor of $comp(F, f, G)$.

Proposition 12 *Suppose* $F \in UHIT$, *and* $G \subseteq F$ *is a factor of* F. *Let* $f_1 := \cap G$, $F_1 := (F \setminus G) \cup \{f_1\}$, $G_1 = \{g \setminus f_1 \mid g \in G\}$. *Then* F_1, $G_1 \in UHIT$ *and* F_1, $G_1 \in UHIT$

Proof: It is obvious that F_1, $G_1 \in UHIT$ and both F_1 and G_1 are hitting because G is a factor of F. Next we show F_1, G_1 are unsatisfiable. Please note that

$$1 = \sum_{f \in F} 2^{-|f|} = \sum_{f \in F_1 \setminus \{f_1\}} 2^{-|f|} + 2^{-|f|} \sum_{g \in G_1} 2^{-|g|} \leqslant \sum_{f \in F_1} 2^{-|f|}.$$

Then we have $\sum_{f \in F_1}{}^{-|f|} = 1$ and $\sum_{g \in G_1} 2^{-|g|} = 1$. Hence F_1, G_1 are unsatisfiable.

Corollary 3 *Suppose* $F \in UHIT$, f_1 *and* f_1 *are a two clauses of* F. *Then* $\{f_1, f_2\}$ *is a factor of* F *if and only if* f_1, f_2 *are 2-subsumption resolvable. Moreover, if* F *has at* *least two variables and contains 2-subsumption resolvable clauses then F is non-prime.*

Lemma 1 *Suppose* $F \in UHIT$. F is non-prime iff $F = comp(F_1, f_1, G_1)$ for some $F_1, G_1 \in UHIT$ and $f_1 \in F_1$ such that $F_1 \neq \{\bot\}$ and $G_1 \neq \{\bot\}$.

Proof: The direction from left to right follows from Proposition 12 in which when G is a non-trivial factor, $G_1 \neq \{\bot\}$, $F_1 \neq \{\bot\}$. For the inverse direction, suppose, $F = comp(F_1, f_1, G_1)$ and $\{f_1\} \odot G_1$ is a factor of F. In case $F_1 \neq \{\bot\}$ and $G_1 \neq \{\bot\}$, $\{f_1\} \odot G_1$ must be a non-trivial factor.

Example 2 From Proposition 11 and Corollary 3, we know that a *UHIT* clause-set F with $|\mathrm{var}(F)| > 1$ is non-prime if either F has a singular variable, or F has a full variable, or F contains 2-subsumption resolvable clauses. However, the inverse is not valid, the following is a counterexample. Let F, G be two clause-sets isomorphic to F_3. Suppose $\mathrm{var}(F) \cap \mathrm{var}(G) = \varnothing$. Pick any clause $f \in F$. Then $comp(F, f, G)$ is non-singular, has no full variable, and contains no 2-subsumption resolvable clauses.

We shall conclude this section by introducing local singular DP reduction.

4.1 Local Singular DP Reduction

Consider non-singular $comp(F, f, G) \in UHIT$. Suppose $v \in \mathrm{var}(G)$ is a m-singular variable in G. Let G_1 be $DP_v(G)$. Then $comp(F, f, G_1)$ can be obtained by applying sDP reduction on v within $\{f\} \odot G$. If v is singular in both G and F, then v becomes a singular variable in the new clause-set $comp(F_1, f, G)$.

Suppose v *is* a singular variable in F such that $v \notin \mathrm{var}(f)$. Let $F_1 := DP_v(F)$. Clearly, f still belongs to F_1. Then the clause-set $comp(F_1, f, G)$ can be obtained by applying sDP reduction on v within $F - \{f\}$. Again if v is singular in both G and F, then v becomes a singular variable in the new clause-set $comp(F_1, f, G)$.

We call v is a locally singular variable if it is singular in G or is singular in F and $v \notin \mathrm{var}(f)$. And we call the reduction from $comp(F, f, G)$ to $comp(F, f, G_1)$ or to $comp(F_1, f, G)$ local sDP reduction.

Example 3 Let $F := \{\{v_1, v_2, v_3\}, \{v_1, \neg v_2, v_3\}, \{\neg v_1, v_3\}\{\neg v_3\}\}$, $f := \{\neg v_3\}$, and $G := \{\{v_1, v_2\}, \{v_1, \neg v_2\}, \{\neg v_1\}\}$. Then $comp(F, f, G)$ is

$$\{\{v_1, v_2, v_3\}, \{v_1, \neg v_2, v_3\}, \{\neg v_1, v_3\}, \{v_1, v_2, \neg v_3\}, \{v_1, \neg v_2, \neg v_3\}, \{\neg v_1, \neg v_3\}\}$$

Clearly, v_1 is singular in G. So from $Comp(F, f, G)$ we can obtain

$$\{\{v_1, v_2, v_3\}, \{v_1, \neg v_2, v_3\}, \{\neg v_1, v_3\}, \{v_2, \neg v_3\}, \{\neg v_2, \neg v_3\}\}$$

In F, v_1 is also singular, and $v_1 \notin \mathrm{var}(f) = \{v_3\}$, hence from $Comp(F, f, G)$

we can also obtain

$$\{\{v_2, v_3\}, \{\neg v_2, v_3\}, \{v_1, v_2, \neg v_3\}, \{v_1, \neg v_2, \neg v_3\}, \{\neg v_1, \neg v_3\}\}.$$

Remark 3 Suppose $comp(F, f, G) \in UHIT$ is non-singular, $v \in \mathrm{var}(f)$ is a singular variable in F. Then $v \notin \mathrm{var}(G)$ because $\mathrm{var}(f) \cap \mathrm{var}(G) = \emptyset$. Thus if v^{ε} occurs only once in F then $v^{\varepsilon} \in f$ and $v^{1-\varepsilon}$ must occur at least twice in F (otherwise, $comp(F, f, G)$ would be singular). Recall that $v^0 = v$, $v^1 = \neg v$..

4.2 Finiteness of Non-prime Clause-sets

Proposition 13 *Let* $F := comp(F_1, f_1, G_1)$ *be in* $UHIT_{\delta=k}$ *with* $G_1 \in UHIT_{\delta=k_1}$ *and* $F_1 \in UHIT_{\delta=k_2}$. *Then*

$$k_1 + k_2 \leqslant k + 1, \text{ and}$$

$$\text{If } \mathrm{var}(F_1) \cap \mathrm{var}(G_1) \neq \emptyset \text{ then } k_1 + k_2 \leqslant k$$

$$|\mathrm{var}(F_1) \cap \mathrm{var}(G_1)| \leqslant k - 1$$

Proof: From Remark 2 (3) we have

$$k = k_1 + k_2 + |\mathrm{var}(F_1) \cap \mathrm{var}(G_1)| - 1$$

The proposition follows.

Theorem 1 *Suppose* $k \geq 3$ *and* $N(k') = aN(k')$ *for all* $k' < k$. *And suppose* $F \in UHIT_{\delta=k}$ *is non-singular non-prime. Then* $|\mathrm{var}(F)| \leqslant aN(k)$.

Proof: If F contains 2-subsumption resolvable clauses, then apply one step 2-subsumption resolution, and denote the resulting formulas as F' which is in $UHIT_{\delta=k-1}$. By Proposition 8, F' can be sDP-reduced to a non-singular formula by at most three steps singular DP-reduction. Thus, we get $|\mathrm{var}(F)| = \mathrm{var}(F') \leqslant aN(k-1) + 3 < aN(k)$.

Now we assume that F contains no 2-subsumption resolvable clauses. Let $F := comp(F_1, f_1, G_1)$ which is $(F_1 \setminus \{f_1\} \cup \{f_1\} \odot G)$. By the assumption there is no 1-singular variable in G_1 and F_1. Let $k_1 := \delta(F_1)$, $k_2 := \delta(G_1)$ and $c := |\mathrm{var}(F_1) \cap \mathrm{var}(G_1)|$.

Case 1. Both G_1, F_1 are non-singular. Then

$$|\mathrm{var}(F)| = |\mathrm{var}(F_1)| + |\mathrm{var}(G_1)| \leqslant aN(k_1) + aN(k_2) < aN(k)$$

Case 2. G_1 is non-singular, and every singular variable of F_1 is in $\mathrm{var}(f_1)$. By Remark 3, the singular literal of F_1 must occur in f_1. Since F is non-singular, for every literal $x \in f_1$, $\neg x$ must occur in $F_1 \setminus \{f_1\}$ at least twice. Then F_1 can be reduced to a non-singular clause-set by one step of singular DP reduction. Therefore, $|\mathrm{var}(F_1)| \leqslant aN(k_1) + 1$. Consequently,

$$|\mathrm{var}(F)| \leqslant |\mathrm{var}(F_1)| + |\mathrm{var}(G_1)| \leqslant aN(k_1) + aN(k_2) + 1 \leqslant aN(k)$$

Case 3. There is a variable $v \notin \text{var}(f_1)$ such that either v is singular in G_1 or is singular in F_1. In either case we can apply local singular DP reduction within $\{f_1\} \odot G_1$ or within $F_1 \setminus \{f_1\}$ to get a formula $F' \in UHIT_{\delta=k-1}$. Please note that v is not 1-singular in G_1 or F_1. Thus, in F', only v may become singular. That is, F' can be reduced to a non-singular formula by at most one step of singular DP-reduction. Please note that v must be common variable of G_1 and F_1. Thus,

$$|\text{var}(F)| \leqslant aN(k-1)+1 < aN(k).$$

The proof completes.

5. Strongly Prime Clause-sets

In this section we shall introduce a class of strongly prime *UHIT* clause-sets. For this purpose we define a new kind reduction called pseudo-2-subsumption resolution.

5.1 Pseudo-2-Subsumption Resolution

Definition 5 *Suppose* $f_1 := \{x\} \cup f'$ *and* f_2 *are two clauses such that* f', f_2 *are* 2-*subsumption resolvable. Then we say* f_1, f_2 *are pseudo-2-subsumption resolvable. Suppose F is a clause-set containing* f_1, f_2. *Let*

$$F' := (F \setminus \{f_1, f_2\}) \cup \{(\{x\} \cup f^*), (\{\neg x\} \cup f_2)\},$$

where $f^* = f' \cap f_2$. *We say that* F' *is obtained from F by one step pseudo 2-subsumption resolution on* f_1, f_2, *and we write* F' *as* $P2SR(F, f_1, f_2)$.

Lemma 2 *Let* F, $f_1 := \{x\} \cup f'$, f_2 *be as in Definition* 5. *Suppose F is in UHIT, then* $P2SR(F, f_1, f_2)$ *remains in UHIT.*

Proof: Since f', f_2 are 2-subsumption resolvable, it follows that $|f^*| = |f'| - 1 = |f_2| - 1$, where $f^* = f \cap f_2$. Hence, $|f_2| = |\{x\} \cup f^*|$ and $|f_1| = |\{x\} \cup f'| = |\{\neg x\} \cup f_2)|$. It follows that

$$\sum_{f \in F} 2^{-|f|} = \sum_{f \in P2SR(F, f_1, f_2)} 2^{-|f|} = 1.$$

Therefore, we only need to show that $P2SR(F, f_1, f_2)$ remains hitting.

Clearly, the new clauses $\{x\} \cup f^*$ and $\{\neg x\} \cup f_2$ hit each other. Since f_2 hit all other clauses in F, it follows that $\{\neg x\} \cup f_2$ hit all other clauses in $P2SR(F, f_1, f_2)$. So, we only need to show that $\{x\} \cup f^*$ hit all clauses in $F \setminus \{f_1, f_2\}$. We assume $f' = \{y\} \cup f^*$, $f_2 = \{\neg y\} \cup f^*$. Consider any clause $g \in F \setminus \{f_1, f_2\}$. If $\neg x \in g$, then $\{x\} \cup f^*$ hits g. Assume $\neg x \notin g$. If $y \in g$, then f^* must hits g because f_1 hits g and $f_1 = \{x\} \cup f' = \{x, y\} \cup f^*$, hence $\{x\} \cup f^*$ hits g. If $y \notin g$, we still can have that f^* hits g because f_2 hits g and $f_1 = \{\neg y\} \cup f^*$, hence $\{x\} \cup f^*$ hits

g.

Altogether we prove that $P2SR(F, f_1, f_2)$ belongs to $UHIT$.

Remark 4 Let F, f_1, f_2, f', f^* be as in Definition 5.

1. It is not hard tocheck that $|x \to 0| * P2SR(F, f_1, f_2) = 2SR((|x \to 0| * F), f', f_2)$, and $|x \to$

2. Suppose F has no unit clause. Then $f*$ (i. e. $f' \cap f_2$) is not the empty clause. Thus, $|x \to 0| * P2SR(F, f_1, f_2)$ and $|x \to 1| * P2SR(F, f_1, f_2)$ must have common variables.

3. Suppose $f' = \{y\} \cup f^*$, $f_2 = \{\neg y\} \cup f^*$. Then the number of occurrence of y in $P2SR(F, f_1, f_2)$ decreases one, whereas $\neg x$ has one more occurrence in $P2SR(F, f_1, f_2)$. Thus y may become a singular literal in $P2SR(F, f_1, f_2)$.

Example 4 Consider clause-set F_3

$$\left\{\begin{array}{ccccc} x_1 & \neg x_1 & \neg x_2 & x_1 & \neg x_1 \\ x_2 & x_2 & x_3 & \neg x_3 & \neg x_2 \\ x_3 & & & & \neg x_3 \end{array}\right\}$$

The clauses $\{x_1, x_2, x_3\}$ and $\{\neg x_1, x_2\}$ are pseudo-2-subsumption resolvable. Then we apply pseudo-2-subsumotion resolution on these two clauses we obtain

$$\left\{\begin{array}{ccccc} \neg x_1 & \neg x_2 & x_1 & \neg x_1 & \\ x_2 & x_2 & x_3 & \neg x_3 & \neg x_2 \\ x_3 & & & \neg x_3 \; \neg x_3 & \end{array}\right\}$$

in which x_1 is a singular variable.

Example 5 Consider the following prime clause-set in $UHIT_{\delta=3}$.

$$\left\{\begin{array}{ccccccc} \neg x_1 & \neg x_1 & \neg x_1 & \neg x_3 & x_2 & x_1 & x_1 \\ x_2 & \neg x_2 & \neg x_2 & x_4 & \neg x_4 & x_3 & \neg x_2 \\ x_3 & \neg x_3 & x_3 & & & x_4 & \neg x_4 \\ x_3 & \neg x_4 & & & & & \end{array}\right\}$$

Apply pseudo-2-subsumption resolution on clauses $\{x_1, x_3, x_4\}$ and $\{\neg x_3, x_4\}$

$$\left\{\begin{array}{ccccccc} \neg x_1 & \neg x_1 & \neg x_1 & \neg x_1 & x_2 & x_1 & x_1 \\ x_2 & \neg x_2 & \neg x_2 & \neg x_3 & \neg x_4 & x_4 & \neg x_2 \\ x_3 & \neg x_3 & x_3 & x_4 & & & \neg x_4 \\ x_3 & \neg x_4 & & & & & \end{array}\right\}$$

which remains to be prime.

Lemma 3 *Let $F \in UHIT_{\delta=k}$ be prime with $k \geq 2$, and $u \in \mathrm{var}(F)$. Suppose u occurs in F exactly twice positively and twice negatively. Then F can be reduced to a non-prime clause-set by pseudo-2-subsumption resolution.*

Proof: Suppose $f_1 := \{u\} \cup f', f_2 := \{u\} \cup f''$ are the two clauses containing u. Then f' and f'' must hit each other. So we assume $f' = \{v\} \cup g', f'' = \{\neg v\} \cup g''$. Now we can see that u occurs in $[v \to \varepsilon] * F (\varepsilon \in \{0, 1\})$ only once. Let g_1, $g_2 \in F$ be the two clauses containing $\neg u$.

Case 1. $v \notin \mathrm{var}(g_1)$ and $v \notin \mathrm{var}(g_2)$. Then $g_1, g_2 \in [v \to \varepsilon] * F$ for $\varepsilon \in \{0, 1\}$. Since u occurs only once in $[v \to \varepsilon] * F$, by Proposition 4, $g' = g'' = (g_1 \cap g_2) \setminus \{\neg u\}$. This implies f_1, f_2 are 2-subsumption resolvable, contradiction the fact that F is prime. Thus, this case cannot happen.

Case 2. $v \in g_1$ and $v \in g_2$. Then in $[v \to 1] * F$ there is no occurrence of $\neg u$. This is impossible since $[v \to 1] * F$ is *UHIT*. That is, this case cannot happen.

Case 3. $\neg v \in g_1$ an $\neg v \in g_2$. By the same argument as in Case 2, this case cannot happen.

Case 4. $\neg v \in g_1$, $\neg v \in g_2$. Then u is 1-singular in $[v \to \varepsilon] * F$, $\varepsilon \in \{0, 1\}$. Then g_1, f_1 are 2-subsumption resolvable, contradicts the fact that F is prime. Thus this case does not happen. Similarly, the case when $\neg v \in g_1$ and $v \in g_2$ does not happen, neither.

Case 5. $v \in \mathrm{var}(g_2)$ and $v \notin \mathrm{var}(g_1)$.

W. l. o. g. we assume $\neg v \in g_2$ and $v \notin \mathrm{var}(g_1)$. Then u is a 1-singular variable $[v \to 0] * F$. This implies $(f_1 \setminus \{v\})$ and g_1 are 2-subsumption resolvable.

Then f_1, g_1 are pseudo 2-subsumption resolvable in F After resolution, one occurrence of u is removed. Thus u becomes singular in the new clause-set which hence is non-prime.

Case 6. $v \in \mathrm{var}(g_1)$ and $v \notin \mathrm{var}(g_2)$. The argument is the same as Case 5. Altogether we complete the proof.

Lemma 4 *Suppose F is a prime clause-set in UHIT. Let $v \in \mathrm{var}(F)$ be such that $vd_F(v) = uvd(F)$ and $\delta([v \to 0] * F) > 1$ for some $\varepsilon \in \{0, 1\}$. Then either $[v \to \varepsilon] * F$ is non-singular, or $[v \to \varepsilon] * F$ has no 1-singular variable, or F can be reduced by one step pseudo-2-subsumption resolution to F' such that $uvd(F') < uvd(F)$.*

Proof: W. l. of. g. assume $\varepsilon = 0$. Suppose $[v \to 0] * F$ is singular and has a 1-

singular variable u. Let $f', f'' \in [v \to 0] * F$ be the two clauses containing u and $\neg u$, respectively. Since F is prime, we assume w. l. o. f that $f'' \in F$, $\{v\} \cup f' \in F$. Let $F_1 := P2SR(F, (\{v\} \cup f'), f'')$. Please note that $u \notin \mathrm{var}([v \to 0] * F_1)$ since $[v \to 0] * F_1 = 2SR([v \to 0] * F, f', f'']) = DP_u([v \to 0] * F)$. That is, in F_1 every occurrence of u and $\neg u$ occurs in some clause containing $\neg v$. Then we have

$$vd_{F_1}(u) \leqslant ld_{F_1}(\neg v) = ld_F(\neg v) + 1 < ld_F(\neg v) + ld_F(v) = \mu vd(F).$$

The proof completes.

Corollary 4 For $k \geq 2$, let m_k be the largest number m such that F can be reduced to a non-prime clause-set for every prime $F \in UHIT'_{\delta=k}$ with $2 \leqslant \mu vd(F) \leqslant m$. Suppose $F \in UHIT_{\delta=k}$ is strongly prime with $\mu vd(F) = m_k + 1$, v is a variable of F such that $vd_F(v) = m_k + 1$. Then $[v \to \varepsilon] * F$ has no 1-singular variable for $\varepsilon \in \{0, 1\}$.

5.2 Strongly Prime UHIT clause-sets

We say F can be P2SR-reduced to F' if $F = F'$ or F' can obtained from F by a number steps of pseudo-2-subsumption resolution.

Definition 6 *We say a prime clause-set is strongly prime if it cannot be P2SR-reduced to a non-prime formula. We use SPR (resp. $SPR_{\delta=k}$) to denote the class of all strongly prime UHIT clause-sets (with deficiency k).*

Theorem 2 *Suppose $N(k') = aN(k')$ for all $k' < k$. Suppose F is a prime clause-set such that $F \notin SPR_{\delta=k}$. Then $|\mathrm{var}(F)| \leqslant aN(k)$.*

Proof: Since F is not strongly prime, F can be P2SR-reduced to a non-prime clause-set by a sequence of pseudo-2-subsumption resolution. Then there are $F_0 = F$, $F_1 \dots, F_{m-1}, F_m$ satisfying the following conditions:

1. For $i = 1, \dots, m$, F_i is obtained from F_{i-1} by one step of pseudo-2-subsumption resolution.

2. For $i = 0, \dots, m-1$, F_i is prime.

F_m is non-prime.

We shall proceed by induction on m. Suppose $m = 1$, then F_1 is non-prime. Please note that $\mathrm{var}(F) = \mathrm{var}(F_1)$. If F_1 is non-singular then by Theorem 1 we have $|\mathrm{var}(F)| = |\mathrm{var}(F_1)| \leqslant aN(k)$.

So, assume that F_1 contains a singular variable. Then F_1 has only one singular variable, say v which is not 1-singular. Thus, $F' := DP_v(F_1)$ must be non-singular and non-prime.

Let $x \in \{v, \neg v\}$ be the singular literal of F_1. Then F_1 has the form

$$\{\{x\} \cup f\} \cup ((\{\neg x\} \cup f) \odot G) \cup H$$

such that $|G| \geq 2$. Then $F' = (f \odot G) \cup H$.

Since x becomes a singular literal of F_1, it must occur in F exactly twice and after a step of pseudo-2-subsumption resolution, one occurrence of x is deleted.

Thus, F must contain clauses

$$f_1 := \{y, x\} \cup f*, f_2 := \{\neg x\} \cup f*$$

such that $F_1 = P2SR(F, f_1, f_2)$. After the pseudo-2-subsumption resolution, f_1, f_2 are replaced by clauses

$$\{y\} \cup f*, \{\neg y, \neg x\} \cup f*$$

which are hence in F_1. Now we can see that $(\{y\} \cup f*) \in H$ and $\{\neg y, \neg x\} \cup f*$ lies in $(\{\neg x\} \cup f) \odot G$. Then $(\{\neg y\} \cup f*) \in (\{f\} \odot G)$. Hence $(\{\neg y\} \cup f*) \setminus f$ is a clause in G. Since $|G| \geq 2$, $(\{\neg y\} \cup f*) \setminus f$ can not be the empty clause. Please note that $(\{y\} \cup f*) \in H$. Thus, G and $\{f\} \cup H$ must have at least one common variable. Let $k_1 := \delta(G)$, $k_2 := \delta(\{f\} \cup H)$. By Remark 2 (3) we have $k_1 + k_2 \leqslant k$. Our next task is to show $|\mathrm{var}(F')| < aN(k)$.

Case 1. F' contains two 2-subsumption resolvable clauses. Then by the argument in the proof of Theorem 1, we have $\mathrm{var}(F') \leqslant aN(k-1) + 3 < aN(k)$.

Case 2. Local singular DP reduction is applicable in F'.

By the argument in Case 3 in the proof of Theorem 1 we have $|\mathrm{var}(F')| \leqslant aN(k-1) + 1 < aN(k)$.

Case 3. Not Case 1 and not Case 2. Then G is non-singular, $\{f\} \cup H$ has at most one singular literal which occur in F, and $k_1, k_2 \geq 2$. Since $k_1 + k_2 < k$, by Proposition 9 we have

$$|\mathrm{var}(F')| \leqslant aN(k_1) + aN(k_2) + 1 \leqslant aN(k-1) < aN(k).$$

Altogether, we have $|\mathrm{var}(F)| = |\mathrm{var}(F_1)| = |\mathrm{var}(F')| + 1 \leqslant aN(k)$.

Generally, suppose $m > 1$. Then $F, F_1, \ldots, F_{m-1}$ are prime and F_m is non-prime. By the above proof we have $|\mathrm{var}(F_{m-1})| \leqslant aN(k)$. Since $\mathrm{var}(F) = \mathrm{var}(F_1) = \ldots = \mathrm{var}(F_m)$. We have $|\mathrm{var}(F)| \leqslant aN(k)$.

6. The Existence of Strongly Prime Clause-sets

It is obvious that F_2 is non-prime, while F_3 are not strongly prime (see Example 4). Therefore, there is no strongly prime clause-set in $UHIT_{\delta=2}$, i. e. $SPR_{\delta=2} = \varnothing$. In this section we shall show $SPR_{\delta=3} = \varnothing$ and $SPR_{\delta=4} = \varnothing$. Then by Theorem 1 –

2 and Proposition 10 we have $N(3) = 7$ and $N(4) = 11$.

Lemma 5 *Suppose F is a non-prime clause-set in* $UHIT_{\delta=2}$ *without unit clause. Then F contains 2-subsumption resolvable clauses.*

Proof: Suppose F non-singular. It is known that F_2 and F_3 are the only two non-singular clause-sets in $UHIT_{\delta=2}$ up to isomorphism. Since F_3 is prime, F must be isomorphic to F_2. Clearly, the assertion holds.

Suppose F is singular. If F has a 1-singular variable, then the assertion is obvious. So, assume F has no 1-singular variable.

Let x be a singular literal. Then $\neg x$ occurs at least twice. Suppose $\neg x$ occurs exactly twice, then the two clauses containing $\neg x$ form a non-trivial factor of F (see Proposition 11). By Corollary 3, they must be 2-subsumption resolvable.

Next we show that F must contain a 2-singular variable. Suppose by contrary, x occurs at least three times in F for every singular literal x of F. Suppose x is a singular literal, then by the assumption the clause containing x is not a unit clause. Therefore, F can not be sDP reduced to a non-singular $UHIT_{\delta=2}$ clause-set because at any step of sDP reduction from F there always is some literal with at least three occurrences, a contradiction. Consequently, F must contain a 2-singular variable, and the proof completes.

Corollary 5 *Suppose F is a non-prime clause-set in* $UHIT_{\delta=2}$ *without 1-singular variable. Then F has a full variable.*

Proof: Suppose F contains a unit clause. Then it clearly has a full variable. Assume F has no unit clause. By Lemma 5, let $f_1 := \{v\} \cup f$, $f_2 := \{\neg v\} \cup f$ be two 2-subsumption resolvable clauses. Since v is not a 1-singular variable, $2SR(F, f_1, f_2)$ belongs to $UHIT_{\delta=1}$, hence it has a full variable which is clearly also a full variable of F.

Lemma 6 *Let F be a prime clause-set in* $UHIT_{\delta=k}$ *with* $k \geq 2$, $v \in \mathrm{var}(F)$. *Suppose for some* $\varepsilon \in \{0, 1\}$, $[v \to \varepsilon] * F$ *has deficiency 1. Then F can be P2SR-reduced to a non-prime clause-set.*

Proof: W. l. o. g. assume $[v \to 1] * F$ is in $UHIT_{\delta=1}$, then it has 1-singular variables. Thus, $[v \to 1] * F$ has two 2-subsumption resolvable clauses. This implies that there are in F clauses $\{\neg v\} \cup f'$ and f'' such that f', f'' are 2-subsumption resolvable. Now let $F' := P2SR(F, (\{\neg v\} \cup f', f''))$. By Remark 4, $[v \to 1] * F' = 2SR(([v \to 1] * F), f', f'')$. Hence the deficiency of $[v \to 1] * F'$ remains 1. If $[v \to 1] * F'$ is the clause-set $\{\bot\}$ then v is a full variable of F', hence F' is non-prime. Suppose F' is still prime, then var($[v \to 1] * F'$) is non-empty. By the same argument as above, for F' we can apply one step pseudo-2-subsumption resolution to obtain a new formula. Continue this procedure until we obtain a non-prime clause-set.

Lemma 7 *Let F be a prime clause-set in $UHIT_{\delta=k}$ with $k \geq 2$, $v \in \mathrm{var}(F)$. Suppose for some $\varepsilon \in \{0, 1\}$, $\delta([v \to \varepsilon] * F) = 2$ and $[v \to \varepsilon] * F$ has no 1-singular variable and no unit clause. Then F can be P2SR-reduced to a non-prime clause-set.*

Proof: *W. l. o. g. assume $[v \to 1] * F$ is in $UHIT_{\delta=2}$, and has no unit clause and no 1-singular variable. Then by Lemma 5, $[v \to 1] * F$ has two clauses which are 2-subsumption resolvable. This implies that there are clauses $\{\neg v\} \cup f'$ and f'' in F such that f', f'' are 2-subsumption resolvable. Now let $F' := P2SR(F, (\{\neg v\} \cup f'), f'')$. By Remark 4, $[v \to 1] * F' = 2SR([v \to 1] * F, f', f'')$. Hence the deficiency of $[v \to 1] * F'$ becomes 1. Then by Lemma 6, F' can be P2SR-reduced to a non-prime clause-set.*

Lemma 8 *$SPR_{\delta=3}$ is empty. That is, there is no strongly prime clause-set in $UHIT_{\delta=3}$.*

Proof: Consider an arbitrary prime clause-set $F \in UHIT_{\delta=3}$. Let $m := \mu vd(F)$. By Proposition 1, we have $4 \leqslant m \leqslant 5$. Pick a variable v with $vd_F(x) = m$. Let e_0, e_1 be the occurrences of v and $\neg v$. respectively. W. l. o. g. assume $e_0 \geq e_1$. If $m = 4$ then it must be that $e_0 = e_1 = 2$, by Lemma 3, F is not strongly prime. So, we assume $m = 5$. Then $e_0 = 3$, $e_1 = 2$. Therefore, $[v \to \varepsilon] * F \in UHIT_{\delta=1}$. Then by Lemma 6, F can be P2SR-reduced to a non-prime clause-set. The proof completes.

Lemma 9 *$SPR_{\delta=4}$ is empty. That is, there is no strongly prime clause-set in $UHIT_{\delta=4}$.*

Proof: Consider an arbitrary prime clause-set $F \in UHIT_{\delta=4}$. Let $m := \mu vd(F)$. By Proposition 1, we have $4 \leqslant m \leqslant 6$. Pick a variable v with $vd_F(x) = m$. Let e_0, e_1 be the occurrences of v and $\neg v$, respectively. W. l. o. g. assume $e_0 \geq e_1$. By Lemma 3 we assume $m \geq 5$.

Case 1. $m = 5$. Then $e_0 = 3$, $e_1 = 2$. Suppose $[v \to \varepsilon] * F$ contains a 1-singular variable for some $\varepsilon \in \{0, 1\}$, then by Lemma 4, F can be P2SR-reduced to a formula F' with $\mu vd(F) \leqslant 4$. Then by Lemma 3, F' can be P2SR-reduced to a non-prime formula. So, we assume that $[v \to \varepsilon] * F$ contains no 1-singular variable for each $\varepsilon \in \{0, 1\}$.

Please note that $[v \to 1] * F \in UHIT_{\delta=2}$ and has $|\mathrm{var}(F)| - 1$ variables.

If $[v \to 1] * F$ has no unit clause, then by Lemma 7, F can be P2SR-reduced to a non-prime clause-set. So we assume that $[v \to 1] * F$ has a unit clause, say $\{x\}$. Then $\neg x$ must occur in all other clauses in $[v \to 1] * F$. Since $e_1 = 2$, we see that $[x \to 0] * F$ contains at most three clauses. So, $\delta([x \to 0] * F) = 1$. It follows from Lemma 6 that F is not strongly prime.

Case 2. $m = 6$ and $e_0 = e_1 = 3$. By Corollary 4, we assume that $[v \to \varepsilon] * F$ contains no 1-singular variable for each $\varepsilon \in \{0, 1\}$. Since $\delta([v \to \varepsilon] * F) = 2$, we assume by Lemma 7 that $[v \to 1] * F$ contains a unit clause $\{x\}$. Then $\neg x$ must occur in all other clauses in $[v \to 1] * F$. Since $e_1 = 3$, we see that $[x \to 0] * F$ contains at most four clauses. So, $\delta([x \to 0] * F) \leqslant 2$. If $\delta([x \to 0] * F) = 1$. then it follows from Lemma 6 that F is not strongly prime. Suppose $[x \to 0] * F$ has deficiency 2, then it must isomorphic to F_2 because it has at most four clauses. Then by Lemma 7 again, F is not strongly prime.

Case 3. $e_0 = 4$, $e_1 = 2$. Then $[v \to 1] * F$ has deficiency 1. By Lemma 6, F can be P2SR-reduced to a non-prime clause-set.

Altogether, F is not strongly prime. The proof completes.

Theorem 3

1. *If* $SPR_{\delta=k} = \varnothing$ *and* $N(k') = aN(k')$ *for every* $k' < k$ *then* $N(k') = aN(k')$.

$N(3) = 7$, $N(4) = 11$.

Proof: Item 1 follows from Theorem 1 – 2 and Corollary 10. Item 2 follows from item 1 and Lemma 8 amd Lemma 9.

So far we have not find a strongly prime clause-set in *UHIT*. So, it is natural to conjecture the non-existence of such clause-sets.

Conjecture 3: $SPR_{\delta=k}$ for each $k \geq 2$, i. e. , there is no strongly prime clauses-set in $UHIT_{\delta=k}$.

7. Conclusion and Future Work

In this paper we have introduced the finiteness conjecture which says that for any $k \geq 2$, every non-singular unsatisifiable hitting clause-set (*UHIT*) with deficiency k has at most $4k$-5 variables. For $k = 2$ the conjecture is clearly true. To prove the conjecture for $k \in \{3, 4\}$ we have introduced prime clause-sets. Roughly speaking, a prime clause-set in *UHIT* cannot be obtained by composition of two clause-sets in *UHIT*. It has been proved that if the finiteness conjecture holds for all $k' < k$, then it holds for non-prime non-singular clause-sets in $UHIT_{\delta=k}$. Then we proposed pseudo-2-subsumption resolution. We call clauses $\{x, y\} \cup f$ and $\{\neg y\} \cup f$ are pseudo-2-subsumption resolvable. After resolution the parent clauses are replaced by $\{x\} \cup f$ and $\{\neg x, \neg y\} \cup f$. A clause-set is strongly prime if it cannot be reduced to a non-prime clause-set by any sequence of pseudo-2-subsumption resolution. We have shown that if the conjecture is true for all $k' < k$, the any prime but not strongly prime clause-set with deficiency k has at most $4k$-5 variables. Then, we proved that there are no strongly prime clause-set with deficiency 3 or 4. Consequently, the finiteness conjecture for $k \in \{3, 4\}$ is true.

In the future we shall find all non-singular clauses-sets in $UHIT_{\delta=3}$ and $UHIT_{\delta=4}$ (up to isomorphism). We hope these clause-sets would give us some hint for analysing structural properties of $MU_{\delta=3}$ and $MU_{\delta=4}$.

Our long-term future work is to prove the finiteness conjecture for all $k \geq 2$ and then investigate structures of all minimally unsatisfiable clauses-sets.

References

Aharoni, R. & Linial, N. Minimal non-two-colorable hypergraphs and minimal unsatisfiable formulas [J]. Journal of Combinatorial Theory, 1986, (43): 196 -204.

Belov, Anton, & Marques-Silva, Joao. Minimally Unsatisfiable Boolean Circuits [C] //Theory and Applications of Satisfiability Testing - SAT, 2011: 145 - 158.

Davydov, G. , Davydova, I. and Kleine Büning, Hans. An Efficient Algorithm for the Minimal Unsatisfiability problem for a subclass of CNF [J]. Annals of Mathematics and Artifficial Intelligence, 1998, 23: 229 - 245.

Fleischer, H. , Kullmann, O. and Szeider, S. Polynomial-time Recognition of Minimal Unsatisfiable Formulas with Fixed Clause-Variable Difference [J]. Theoretical Computer Science, 2002, 289 (1): 503 - 516.

Iwama, K. CNF Satisfiability Test by Counting and polynomial Average Time [J]. SIAM J Comput, 1989, 18: 385 - 391.

Kleine Büning, H. & Zhao, Xishun. On the Structure of some Classes of Minimal Unsatisfiable Formulas [J]. Discrete Applied Mathematics, 2002, 130: 185 - 207.

Kleine Büning, H. On subclasses of minimal unsatisfiable formulas [J]. Discrete Applied Mathematics, 2000, 107: 83 - 98.

Kleine Büning, H. & Kullmann O. Minimal Unsatisfiability and Autarkies [C] // Handbook of Satisfiability IOS Press, 2009 (11): 339 – 401.

Kullmann, O. An application of Matroid Theory to the SAT problem [C] // Fifteenth Annual IEEE Computational Complexity, 2000, 116 – 124.

Kullmann, O. Lean Clause-sets: Generalizations of Minimally Unsatisfiable Clause-sets [J]. Discrete Applied Mathematics, 2003, 130: 209 – 249.

Kullmann, Oliver & Zhao, Xishun. On Davis-Putanam Reduction for Minimal Unsatisfiable Clause-sets [J]. Theoretcial Computer Science, 2013, 492: 80 – 87.

Kullmann, Oliver & Zhao, Xishun. On variables with few occurrences in conjunctive normal forms [J]. Theory and Applications of Satisfiability Testing – SAT, 2011: 33 – 46.

Kullmann, Oliver, & Zhao, Xishun. On Davis-Putanam reduction for minimal unsatisfiable clause-sets [J]. Theoretical Computer Science, 2013, 492: 80 – 87.

Marques-Silva, Joao. Computing Minimally Unsatisfiable Subformulas: State of the Art and Future Directions [J]. Journal of Multiple-Valued Logic and Soft Computing, 2012, 19 (1 – 3): 163 – 183.

Papadimitriou, C. H. & Wolfe, D. The Complexity of Facets Resolved [J]. Journal of Computer System and Science, 1988, 37: 2 – 13.

Schuppan, V. Towards a notion of unsatisfiable cores for LTL [C] // Arbab, Farhad and Sirjani, Marjan. (eds.) FSEN 09, Volume 5961 of Lecture Notes in Computer Science, 2010: 129 – 145.

Szeider, S. Minimal unsatisfiable formulas with bounded clause-variable difference are fixed-parameter tractable [J]. Journal of Computer and System Science, 2004, 69 (4): 656 – 674.

宋代的数学与易学

——以秦九韶《数书九章》(1247) 第一问“蓍挂发微”为中心[①]

朱一文

一、前言

在中国古代，数学[②]为儒家六艺之一，《周易》则为重要的儒家经典，两者具有密切的联系。一方面，许多算家论述了《周易》对数学的作用。例如魏景元四年（263），刘徽注《九章算术》序云：“昔在庖牺氏始画八卦，以通神明之德，以类万物之情，作九九之术，以合六爻之变。”[③] 南宋秦九韶（1208—1261 年）更是在其传世之作《数书九章》中由《周易》引出一项世界级数学成就——大衍总数术[④]。另一方面，一些易家亦确认了两者的联系。例如，北宋邵雍（1011—1077 年）云：“大衍之数，其算法之源乎？是以算数之起，不过乎方圆曲直也。阴无一，阳无十。乘数，生数也。除数，消数也。算法虽多，不出乎此矣。”[⑤] 不过，南宋理学大家朱熹（1130—1200 年）便不同意邵雍的看法，他说“康节天资极高，其学只是术数学。后人聪明能算，亦可以推”[⑥]；而且从今人所认知的角度看，宋代象数学与传统算学还是有所不同。

学术界很早就关注到中国古代尤其是宋代数学与易学的关系。钱宝琮先生（1892—1974 年）撰文认为“宋元数学与道学之间并不存在相互促进作用。道学家的‘格物致知’说，并不涉及对客观事物及其规律的认识，不能推动自

---

① 本研究受到国家社会科学基金青年项目“儒家经典注疏中天算文献的整理与研究”（16CZS012）的资助。本文原刊于《周易研究》2019 年第 2 期，收入本文集略有改动。

② “数学”在宋代具有象数学之含义。在本文之中，根据今人的用法习惯，数学仅取 mathematics 之义，而不含有象数学之义。

③ 郭书春汇校：《汇校〈九章算术〉增补版》，辽宁教育出版社 2004 年版，第 1 页。

④ 参见罗见今：《〈数书九章〉与〈周易〉》，载吴文俊主编：《秦九韶与〈数书九章〉》，北京师范大学出版社 1986 年版，第 80 - 102 页；李继闵：《“蓍挂发微”初探》，载吴文俊主编：《秦九韶与〈数书九章〉》，北京师范大学出版社 1986 年版，第 124 - 137 页。

⑤ 〔宋〕邵雍：《皇极经世》，载郭彧、于天宝点校：《邵雍全集》第 3 册，上海古籍出版社、安徽教育出版社 2015 年版，第 1195 页。

⑥ 〔宋〕黎靖德编：《朱子语类》第 7 册，中华书局 1986 年版，第 2554 页。

然科学的进展；道学体系中的‘象数学’是一种数字神秘主义思想，也不能有助于数学的发展。”[①]由此形成一种对两者关系的负面看法。何丙郁（Ho Peng Yoke，1926—2014 年）先生则认为古代数学包括今天所谓的数学（即 mathematics）、数字学（包括所谓河图、洛书之学）以及数术[②]，实际肯定了两者的紧密关系。近来学界的研究则往往倾向于进一步肯定《周易》对中国传统数学的影响[③]。尤其是侯纲的博士学位论文专论宋代易数与数学之关系，具有较大的影响。他认为“两宋时期，一方面，数学被引入易数研究，从而有助于解释经文、阐发义理；另一方面，易数在数学研究中也有所渗透和体现，成为导致新的数学内容出现和发展的动力之一。”[④]

近年来，笔者的研究揭示出中国古代儒家独特的、与以《九章算术》为代表的传统数学不同的算法传统[⑤]，尤其朱熹也在此算法传统之中[⑥]。陈志辉与笔者的进一步研究则表明这一算法传统延续至清中叶[⑦]。这些研究提示我们必须考虑到古代不同活动中的数学实作（mathematical practice）的可能差异，易学中的数学与传统数学的关系还值得进一步研究。并且，秦九韶《数书九

① 钱宝琮：《宋元时期数学与道学的关系》，载钱宝琮主编：《宋元数学史论文集》，科学出版社 1966 年版，第 255 页。

② 何丙郁：《从科技史的观点谈易数》，载何丙郁等著、编辑委员会编：《中国科技史论文集》，联经出版事业公司 1995 年版，第 21 页。

③ 参见孙宏安：《〈周易〉与中国古代数学》，《自然辩证法研究》1991 年第 5 期，第 49 – 53 页；傅海伦：《论〈周易〉对传统数学机械化思想的影响》，《周易研究》1999 年第 2 期，第 82 – 93 页；乐爱国：《〈周易〉对中国古代数学的影响》，《周易研究》2003 年第 3 期，第 76 – 80 页；陈玲：《〈周易〉与中国传统数学》，《厦门大学学报（哲学社会科学版）》2014 年第 2 期，第 66 – 72 页；康宇：《论宋元象数思潮兴起及其对古代数学发展的影响》，《自然辩证法研究》2018 年第 9 期，第 93 – 99 页。

④ 侯钢：《两宋易数及其与数学之关系初论》，中国科学院自然科学史研究所博士学位论文，2006 年，摘要。

⑤ 参见朱一文：《儒学经典中的数学知识初探——以贾公彦对〈周礼·考工记〉“蒈氏为量”的注疏为例》，《自然科学史研究》2015 年第 2 期，第 131 – 141 页；Zhu Yiwen，“Different cultures of computation in seventh century China from the viewpoint of square root extraction”，*Historia Mathematica*，23，2016，pp. 3 – 25；朱一文：《再论中国古代数学与儒学的关系——以六至七世纪学者对礼数的不同注疏为例》，《自然辩证法通讯》2016 年第 5 期，第 81 – 87 页；朱一文，《初唐的数学与礼学——以诸家对〈礼记·投壶〉的注疏为例》，《中山大学学报（社会科学版）》2017 年第 2 期，第 60 – 68 页；朱一文，《算学、儒学与制度化——初唐数学的多样性及其与儒学的关系》，《汉学研究》2017 年第 4 期，第 109 – 134 页。

⑥ 参见朱一文：《朱熹的数学世界——兼论宋代数学与儒学的关系》，《哲学与文化》2018 年第 11 期，第 167 – 182 页。

⑦ 参见 Chen Zhihui，“Scholars recreation of two traditions of mathematical commentaries in late eighteenth-century China”，*Historia Mathematica*，44，2017，pp. 105 – 133；朱一文：《儒家开方算法之演进——以诸家对论语“道千乘之国”的注释为中心》，《自然辩证法通讯》2019 年第 2 期，第 49 – 55 页。

章》首问“蓍挂发微”往往是各家分析两者关系的重点文献，但郑诚与笔者的合作研究表明前人没有充分利用该书的一个明代版本——赵琦美（1563—1624年）钞本（1616）[①]，从而对大衍术的研究尚留有很大空间，也为我们进一步理解此议题提供了可能[②]。因此，本文先在秦书明钞本的基础上，重新分析是书“蓍挂发微”问，澄清学界之误解；进而探究宋代易家之筮法实作及其对算学之看法，重新探讨宋代数学与易学之关系，以推进学界之研究。

二、“蓍挂发微”之结构分析

秦九韶于淳祐七年（1247）完成的《数书九章》，记载了一项世界级的数学成就—— 大衍总数术。从现代数学的角度看，该术是用来求解一次同余方程组，外国学者称之为“中国剩余定理”。比利时学者李倍始（Ulrich Libbrecht，1928—2017年）认为西方数学直到欧拉（Euler，1707—1783年）、高斯（Gauss，1777—1855年）才取得与秦九韶相当的数学成就[③]。秦书总共81问，分作9类，每类9问。其中第一类“大衍”的九道问题全部用大衍总数术解决，第二类“天时”的第三问“治历演纪”则用到该术的核心程序——大衍求一术[④]。需要说明的是，秦九韶撰写大衍九问的算法都用了“术”“草”“算图”三种方式，但只有在第一问“蓍挂发微”中他用算图表达了大衍求一术[⑤]。就此而言，该书首问可以视作撰写此后八问的范例。事实上，“蓍挂发微”与大衍术之名均来源于《周易》，该术“衍母”“衍法”“衍数”等术语也与《周易》相关。因此，该问无疑处于全书的核心地位，从数学实作的角度展现了秦九韶所认为的大衍术与《周易》的关系。但是，笔者发现前人对该问的文本结构理解有误，由此影响了对秦九韶相关思想的理解。因此，本节先重新分析此问的结构，继而以此为基础，结合该书秦九韶的相关论

---

① 参见郑诚、朱一文：《〈数书九章〉流传新考——赵琦美钞本初探》，《自然科学史研究》2010年第3期，第319－328页。

② 参见朱一文：《秦九韶对大衍术的算图表达——基于〈数书九章〉赵琦美钞本（1616）的分析》，《自然科学史研究》2017年第2期，第244－257页。

③ Libbrecht Ulrich, *Chinese Mathematics in Thirteenth Century: The Shu-shu chiu-chang of Ch'in Chiu-shao*, New York: Dover Publications, 2005, p. 372.

④ 大衍总数术相当于求解一次同余方程组的总程序，其中涉及到相当于求解乘率k，使得 $ak.1\ (\mathrm{mod}\ m)$ 的算法，被称为大衍求一术。学术界时常将两者混淆，直接用求一术称呼总数术，参见郭书春：《尊重原始文献，避免以讹传讹》，《自然科学史研究》2007年第3期，第434－448页。

⑤ 另一方面，《数书九章》“治历演纪”问亦用算图书写了大衍求一术，但与“蓍挂发微”问不同。关于两者的比较，参见朱一文：《秦九韶对大衍术的算图表达——基于〈数书九章〉赵琦美钞本（1616）的分析》，《自然科学史研究》2017年第2期，第244－257页。

述，进一步分析秦氏对于《周易》和大衍总数术的看法。[①]

《数书九章》今存三个主要版本，分别是明万历四十四年（1616）的赵琦美钞本，清乾隆中叶的四库全书本与清道光二十二年（1842）宜稼堂刻本。按明钞本与宜稼堂本，“蓍挂发微”问云：

◎蓍挂发微

问《易》曰：“大衍之数五十，其用四十有九。”又曰：“分而为二以象两，挂一以象三，揲之以四以象四时。三变而成爻[②]，十有八变而成挂。”欲知所衍之术及其数各几何。

答曰：衍母一十二，衍法三[③]。一元衍数二十四，二元衍数一十二，三元衍数八，四元衍数六。已上四位衍数计五十。一揲用数一十二，二揲用数二十四，三揲用数四，四揲用数九。已上四位用数计四十九。

大衍总数术曰：置诸问数……一曰元数……二曰收数……三曰通数…… 四曰复数……大衍求一术云……

本题术曰：置诸元数……大衍求一术云……

草曰：……故《易》曰：“大衍之数五十”，算理不可以此五十为用……故《易》曰：“其用四十有九”是也……假令左手分得三十三，自一一揲之，必奇一。故不繁揲，乃径挂一。故《易》曰：“分而为二以象两，挂一以象三”……又令之以三三揲之……又令之以四四揲之……故曰：“三变而成爻。”既挂有六爻，必十八变，故曰：“十有八变而成挂。”[④]

以此观之，此问依次包括题、问、答、大衍总数术、本题术及草等六部分。四库馆臣认为：“按右大衍本法也。原书入于‘蓍策发微’题问答之后，

---

① 秦九韶认为大衍总数术来源于《周易》，属于“内算”，应被书写；而大衍求一术被历家误以为是方程，却没有被记载在属于“外算”的《九章算术》之中，其实应为一项独立的数学内容。参见朱一文《秦九韶对大衍术的算图表达——基于〈数书九章〉赵琦美钞本（1616）的分析》，《自然科学史研究》2017 年第 2 期，第 244－257 页。

② 今传本《周易》并无记载“三变而成爻”之句，《五经算术》“《周易》策数法”则有此句，因此可以推测秦九韶此问将前人注解一并纳入。2017 年 10 月 25 日笔者在法国报告相关内容时，林力娜（Karine Chemla）教授指出这一点，在此深表谢意。

③ “衍法三”，赵钞本脱“三”，依四库本、宜稼堂本校正。

④ 〔宋〕秦九韶：《数书九章》，北京中国国家图书馆藏明万历四十四年赵琦美钞本，载《四库提要著录丛书》子部 020，北京出版社 2011 年版，第 102－103 页；秦九韶：《数书九章》，清道光二十二年宜稼堂丛书本，载郭书春主编：《中国科学技术典籍通汇·数学卷》第 1 册，河南教育出版社 1993 年第 444 页。

殊失其序。今修冠于卷首。”[1]即认为大衍总数术是具有一般性的算法，不应置于此问之中，而应置于卷首，以表明统领大衍类的九问。由此，秦书四库本将“大衍总数术”部分置于卷首，即“蓍挂发微”问之前。从而使得各部分顺序调整为：大衍总数术、题、问、答、本题术及草。这一做法影响深远，许多学者如李倍始、王守义、侯钢等都接受了四库本的做法[2]。

然而，如果我们仔细阅读原文，便可知：尽管大衍总数术具有一般性，但它不应被置于卷首，它确实属于“蓍挂发微”问，进一步说是属于该问答案的一部分。笔者提出这一观点的理由有二：其一，秦九韶云“欲知所衍之术及其数各几何”，由此可知此问所求有二：所衍之术与所用之数。如果按照四库馆臣的看法，则此问的答案仅给出了所用之数（衍母、衍法、衍数及用数），但没有给出“所衍之术”。因此，“大衍总数术”应是答案的一部分，给出“所衍之术”，由此可以完整回答秦氏所求。其二，大衍总数术把问数分作四种情况，依次为元数、收数、通数与复数；而“本题术”中则直接说“置诸元数”。显然，本题术是取了大衍总数术的一种情形。“本题术”的说法在《数书九章》中仅出现这一次。只有“大衍总数术”为该问答案的一部分，我们才可以理解秦氏的用语（否则秦氏可以径称之为“术”）。

在上述分析的基础上，我们可以知道：第一，秦九韶为了表明具有一般性的大衍总数术来自于《周易》，采取了一种特殊的做法——即所设数学问题并不仅仅求某个答数，而是把大衍术也作为所要求的。这也是自四库馆臣而下许多学者对该问结构产生误解的一个重要原因。第二，“本题术”具有双重功能：一方面它是大衍总数术的一种情形或应用；另一方面，秦九韶通过用“本题术”来计算该问，从而证明了“大衍总数术”的正确性。

此问第六部分“草”的书写也极有特点。《九章算术》有术无草，唐刘孝孙为《张丘建算经》撰细草，展示出具体的计算细节。《数书九章》也安排了“草”这个形式，并添加“算图”以展示筹算过程。此问之草分成两部分：第一部分是通过大衍总数术及大衍求一数计算四元衍数及其之和（$24+12+8+6=50$）与四揲用数及其之和（$12+24+4+9=49$），由此说明《周易》“大衍之数五十，其用四十有九”之由来。第二部分从“假令左手分得三十三”开始，通过举例说明了如何利用所求得衍数和用数来进行占卜，由此说明《周

---

① 〔宋〕秦九韶：《数书九章》，载《景印文渊阁四库全书》第797册，台湾商务印书馆1985年版，第331页。

② 参见 Libbrecht Ulrich, *Chinese Mathematics in Thirteenth Century: The Shu-shu chiu-chang of Ch' in Chiu-shao*, New York: Dover Publications, 2005；王守义：《〈数书九章〉新释》，安徽科学技术出版社1992年；侯钢：《两宋易数及其与数学之关系初论》，中国科学院自然科学史研究所博士学位论文，2006年。

易》筮法语句之由来。草中亦有算图表达。因此，“草”实际也具有双重功能：一方面展示大衍总数术、衍数、用数之具体算法，通过举例说明筮法细节；另一方面，秦九韶实际也相当于用此方式注解了《周易》筮法经文[①]。

总之，四库馆臣把大衍总数术置于卷首，实际使得“蓍挂发微”问成为该术的简单应用；与之相比，秦氏原书“问”“答”的安排相当于直接从《周易》中得出大衍总数术，又立“本题术”以彰显之，撰“草”以展示计算细节并注解《周易》，从而建构了大衍总数术与《周易》筮法的紧密联系。两方对该问结构理解的差别除了受到该问特殊设问方式的影响之外，亦是由于对于大衍术与《周易》关系理解之不同。秦九韶自序云“圣有大衍，微寓于《易》。”[②]四库馆臣则认为：“此条强援蓍挂牵附衍数，致本法反晦。今以本法列于前，则其弊自见矣。”[③]显然，他们认为秦九韶的做法属于牵强附会。

从算学的角度分析，学术界一般认为大衍总数术的一般算法程序来自《孙子算经》“物不知数”问[④]，而大衍求一术则来自于历家之方程[⑤]。因此，可以说大衍术本与《周易》无关。而且，秦书内容实属算学，但是书本名却

---

① 关于秦氏草之细节见本文第三节之分析。

② 〔宋〕秦九韶：《数书九章》，北京中国国家图书馆藏明万历四十四年赵琦美钞本，载《四库提要著录丛书》子部020，北京出版社2011年版，第98页。

③ 〔宋〕秦九韶：《数书九章》，载《景印文渊阁四库全书》第797册，台湾商务印书馆1985年版，第335页。

④ 钱宝琮最先认为《孙子算经》“物不知数”与上元积年的计算有关，参见钱宝琮：《中国数学史》，科学出版社1964年版，第78－79页。李文林、袁向东同意这一看法，参见李文林，袁向东：《论汉代上元积年的计算》，载《科技史文集》第2缉，上海科学技术出版社1980年版，第70－76页。李继闵表明历家计算上元用的是演纪术，而非大衍总数术，实际否定了《孙子算经》“物不知数”问与上元纪年的关联，参见李继闵：《从“演纪之法”与“大衍总数术”看秦九韶在算法上的成就》，载吴文俊主编：《秦九韶与〈数书九章〉》，北京师范大学出版社1986年版，第203－219页；李继闵：《秦九韶关于上元积年推算的论述》，载吴文俊主编：《中国数学史论文集（四）》，山东教育出版社1996年版，第22－36页。曲安京则表明并非所有元素都参与上元的计算，参见曲安京：《中国历法与数学》，科学出版社2005年版，第24－91页。这些研究实际说明，大衍总数术的一般算法与《孙子算经》“物不知数”问有关，但并非用来求解上元积年。

⑤ 秦九韶认为历家误把大衍求一术当作方程术。严敦杰由此认为历家方程不是《九章算术》的方程，参见严敦杰：《宋金元历法中的数学知识》，载钱宝琮主编：《宋元数学史论文集》，科学出版社1966年版，第210－224页。在此基础上，王翼勋、王荣彬、徐泽林分别给出历家方程的推测，与《九章算术》方程不同，参见王翼勋：《秦九韶演纪积年法初探》，《自然科学史研究》1997年第1期，第10－20页；王翼勋：《开禧历上元积年的计算》，《天文学报》1997年1期，第94－105页；王荣彬，徐泽林：《关于“大衍术”源流的算例分析》，《自然科学史研究》1998年第1期，第47－54页。笔者则认为历家方程就是《九章算术》方程，只是计算目的不同而已，秦九韶将之优化后成为大衍求一术，参见朱一文：《秦九韶“历家虽用，用而不知”解》，《自然科学史研究》2011年第2期，第193－206页。这些研究说明，大衍求一术与历家之方程有关。

是《数术》[1]；又将“大衍”“天时”置于前两类，并“以历学荐于朝，得对，又奏稿及所稿与《数学大略》。”[2]这些事实说明，秦九韶的部分著书动机是为了参与改历[3]；并且通过与《周易》相联系的做法提升该书的重要性，贡献于数术之学。

从历史的角度看，秦九韶的做法有其渊源。北周甄鸾（6世纪）撰《五经算术》，用算学方法解答儒家经典中的数学问题。唐初李淳风等将之列为十部算经之一，并为之注释，以算书的体例重构经典。《五经算术》共38问，分别来自《尚书》《孝经》《诗经》《周易》《论语》《春秋》《周礼》《仪礼》《礼记》《汉书》等经典，“《周易》策数法”也被收入其中。通过对比该书中甄鸾、李淳风等的算法与初唐儒家对相同文本的注疏，笔者发现两者在算筹和推理的方式、算法对数与图形的运用、算法的结构等方面都有很大差别[4]。由此呈现出算学研究与经学研究中数学实作之不同。因此，甄鸾、李淳风等算家的做法实际是把算学应用于经学，并进而强调算学的基础作用[5]；孔颖达、贾公彦等儒家则认为在不同领域中应有不同的算法，与算家的看法不同。初唐的

① 参见郑诚、朱一文：《〈数书九章〉流传新考——赵琦美钞本初探》，《自然科学史研究》2010年第3期，第319-328页；李迪：《〈数书九章〉流传考》，载吴文俊主编：《秦九韶与〈数书九章〉》，北京师范大学出版社1986年版，第43-58页。

② 〔宋〕周密：《癸辛杂识续集》，载《景印文渊阁四库全书》第1040册，台湾商务印书馆1985年版，第88页。

③ 参见朱一文：《数：筭与术——以九数之方程为例》，《汉学研究》2010年第4期，第73-105页；朱一文：《秦九韶对大衍术的算图表达——基于〈数书九章〉赵琦美钞本（1616）的分析》，《自然科学史研究》2017年第2期，第244-257页。

④ 参见朱一文：《儒学经典中的数学知识初探——以贾公彦对〈周礼·考工记〉“䖍氏为量”的注疏为例》，《自然科学史研究》2015年第2期，第131-141页；Zhu Yiwen，“Different cultures of computation in seventh century China from the viewpoint of square root extraction”，*Historia Mathematica*，23，2016，pp. 3-25；朱一文：《再论中国古代数学与儒学的关系——以六至七世纪学者对礼数的不同注疏为例》，《自然辩证法通讯》2016年第5期，第81-87页；朱一文：《初唐的数学与礼学——以诸家对〈礼记·投壶〉的注疏为例》，《中山大学学报（社会科学版）》2017年第2期，第60-68页；朱一文：《算学、儒学与制度化——初唐数学的多样性及其与儒学的关系》，《汉学研究》2017年第4期，第109-134页。

⑤ 周瀚光认为《五经算术》成为辅助阅读儒家经典的工具书，参见周瀚光：《从〈算经十书〉看儒家文化对中国古代数学的影响》，《广西民族大学学报（自然科学版）》2015年第1期，第10-13页。陈巍则认为《五经算术》原书大致可以看成“经学中的算学”，并存在两次改写过程，参见陈巍：《〈五经算术〉的知识谱系初探》，《社会科学战线》2017年第10期，第104-113页。笔者不能认同这一类认为《五经算术》十具有经学性质著作的看法，并认为《五经算术》自始至终都是一本算学著作，理由有三：第一、该书作者甄鸾是中古在天文学、数学方面卓有成就的学者，而非以经学见长；第二、稍后的李淳风将之列入十部算经，并以之为国子监算学馆的教科书；第三、笔者的一系列研究表明儒家注解经典所用到的数学与《五经算术》中的不同。因此很明显该书之内容不能称之为经学中的算学，而只能是甄鸾、李淳风等算家试图将传统算学应用于经学的作品。

两种数学实作与数学观反映出儒学与算学地位的强弱关系及由此形成的张力①。以此观之，秦九韶将算学与《周易》、历法等相联系，并力图提升是书地位的做法，实际亦反映出宋代儒学与算学之间的张力。就此而言，秦九韶无疑处于算家传统之中。

三、宋代易家之筮法实作

学术界一般认为中国易学史是在象数派与义理派各领风骚、此消彼长之过程②。而《周易》大衍之数及其筮法正是象数派热衷讨论的议题，宋代易家亦对之多有讨论。在前人的基础上，本节先分析宋代具有代表性的邵雍和朱熹之说，再进而与秦九韶比较探讨宋代易家之筮法实作之特点。

邵雍云：

> 《易》之大衍何数也，圣人之倚数也。天数二十五，合之为五十。地数三十，合之为六十。故曰“五位相得而各有合”也。五十者，蓍之数也。六十者，挂数也。五者蓍之小衍也，数五十为大衍也。八者挂之小成也，六十四为大成也。蓍德圆以况天之数，故七七四十九也。五十者，存一而言也。卦德方以况地之数，故八八六十四也。六十者，去四而言之也。蓍者，用数也。卦者，体数也。用以体为基，故存一也。体以用为本，故去四也。圆者本一，方者本四，故蓍存一而卦去四也。蓍之用数七，若其余分，亦存一之义也。卦其一，亦去一之义。蓍之用数，卦一以象三，其余四十八，则一卦之策也。四其十二为四十八。十二去三而用九，四八三十二所去之策也，四九三十六所用之策也。以当乾之三十六阳爻也……③

由此，邵氏将“大衍之数五十”解释为天数之和（$1+3+5+7+9=25$）加倍（$2\times25=50$）；将“其用四十有九”解释为天数七之平方（$7\times7=49$）。他还推断（后天的）策数法与（先天的）阴阳数相合④。值得注意的是，邵雍此处之解释都用只用到简单的计算。通过算法来阐释数义，十分符合邵氏所云“大衍之数，其算法之源乎？”

---

① 参见朱一文：《算学、儒学与制度化——初唐数学的多样性及其与儒学的关系》，《汉学研究》2017 年第 4 期，第 109－134 页。

② 参见朱伯崑：《易学哲学史》第 2 卷，华夏出版社 1995 年；林忠军：《象数易学发展史》第 2 卷，齐鲁书社 1998 年。

③ 〔宋〕邵雍：《皇极经世》，载郭彧、于天宝点校：《邵雍全集》第 3 册，上海古籍出版社；安徽教育出版社 2015 年版，第 1191－1192 页。

④ 参见林忠军：《象数易学发展史》第 2 卷，齐鲁书社 1998 年版，第 232－237 页。

朱熹在《周易启蒙》中对相关问题也有具体的探讨。朱子云：“河图、洛书之中数皆五，衍之而各极其数以至于十，则合为五十矣。河图积数五十五，其五十者皆因五而后得，独五为五十所因，而自无所因，故虚之，则但为五十。又五十五之中，其四十者分为阴阳老少之数，而其五与十者无所为，则又以五乘十，以十乘五，而亦皆为五十矣。洛书积数四十五，而其四十者散布于外，而分阴阳老少之数，唯五居中而无所为，则亦自含五数，而并为五十矣。”[①] 朱熹把五称为“生数之极”，把十称为“成数之极”，两者相乘变得大衍之数五十（$5\times10=50$）[②]。朱子又云：“大衍之数五十，而蓍一根百茎，可当大衍之数者二，故揲之法，取五十茎为一握，置其一不用以象太极，而其当用之策凡四十有九。盖两仪体具而未分之象也。”[③]由此，以一象太极之说，解释“其用四十有九”（$50-1=49$）。由此可见，尽管具体的策略、数义与邵雍不同，朱熹的解释也仅用到简单的计算。

朱熹的筮法学界已有详尽的研究[④]，阐明了其内涵的数学原理。笔者在此引其第一段以说明其特色，朱子云：

> 卦者，悬于小指之间。揲者，以大指、食指间而别之。奇谓余数。扐者，扐于中三指之两间也。蓍凡四十有九，信手中分，各置一手，以象两仪，而卦右手一策于左手小指之间，以象三才。遂以四揲左手之策，以象四时，而归其余数于左手第四指间，以象闰。又以四揲右手之策，而再归其余数于左手第三指间，以象再闰。五岁之象，挂一，一也；揲左，二也；扐左，三也；揲右，四也；扐右，五也。是谓一变。其挂扐之数，不五即九。
>
> 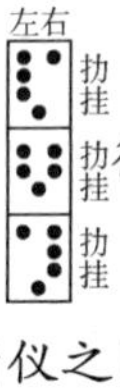
>
> 得五者三，所谓奇也。五除挂一即四，以四约之为一，故为奇，即两仪之阳数也。
>
> 
>
> 得九者一，所谓偶也。九除挂一即八，以四约之为二，故为偶，

① 〔宋〕朱熹：《周易启蒙》，载朱杰人、严佐之、刘永翔主编：《朱子全书》第 1 册，上海古籍出版社；安徽教育出版社 2002 年版，第 246 页。

② 〔宋〕黎靖德编：《朱子语类》第 5 册，中华书局 1986 年版，第 1916 页。

③ 〔宋〕朱熹：《周易启蒙》，载朱杰人、严佐之、刘永翔主编：《朱子全书》第 1 册，上海古籍出版社、安徽教育出版社 2002 年版，第 246 页。

④ 罗见今：《〈数书九章〉与〈周易〉》，载吴文俊主编：《秦九韶与〈数书九章〉》，北京师范大学出版社 1986 年版，第 92 – 96 页；侯钢：《两宋易数及其与数学之关系初论》. 中国科学院自然科学史研究所博士学位论文，2006 年，第 41 – 56 页。

即两仪之阴数也。……①

此段文献朱熹阐明了筮法的第一变。他先解释“挂”“揲”的操作含义，进而描述整个过程。简单地说，挂1之后，将48策分为左右手两部分，依次四四数之。左手之结果无非是1、2、3、4之一种；相应地，右手之结果无非是3、2、1、4之一种。两者相加再加上挂1，即得5、5、5、9之一。朱子用黑点表示数来描述一变“不五即九”的结果，体现了是宋代河图洛书之学的特点。朱熹认为得五的情况有三种，认为得九的情况只有一种，显示出对于背后之关于同余的数学原理有一定了解，但其讲述的重点在于一变之实作过程。

综上所述，我们可以看出邵雍与朱熹对于“大衍之数五十，其用四十有九”的解释都用到不出加减乘除的简单算法。侯钢博士学位论文列出自汉代以来五种大衍之数的解释，包括“合成说”（加法）、“玄数说”（加法）、“天地数虚五虚一说”（减法）、“以五乘十说”（如朱熹）、“天数加倍说”（如邵雍）等都不出简单之算法②。唐贾公彦注疏《周礼》云：“（郑玄）云‘乘犹计也’者，计者筭法，乘除之名出于此也。”③事实上，初唐贾公彦、孔颖达等都用“算法”来指出儒家之算法传统，并将之理解为乘除相关④，宋代邵雍、朱熹延续这种理解。对于筮法，邵雍依然是倾向于算法解释，反映出其将数与算相联系的观点；朱熹之解释则侧重于筮法之实作，并不试图去揭示出经文背后之数学问题。事实上，儒家算法传统起源于汉儒马融（79—166）、郑玄（127—200）等注解经文时，运用传统数学知识，却不给出计算细节，从而隐含有数学问题⑤。后世儒家为了解答汉儒之数学隐题发展出独立之算法传统。然而，虽然大衍筮法背后含有关于同余之原理⑥，却由于未被汉儒塑造为一个数学问题，因而不能充分提供运用和发展儒家算法传统之文本语境。这就显示出《周易》

---

① 〔宋〕朱熹：《周易启蒙》，载朱杰人、严佐之、刘永翔主编：《朱子全书》第1册，上海古籍出版社；安徽教育出版社2002年版，第247页。

② 参见侯钢：《两宋易数及其与数学之关系初论》，中国科学院自然科学史研究所博士学位论文，2006年版，第25－29页。

③ 郑玄注，贾公彦疏：《周礼注疏》，载阮元校刻：《十三经注疏》，中华书局1980年版，第656页。

④ 参见朱一文：《算学、儒学与制度化——初唐数学的多样性及其与儒学的关系》，《汉学研究》2017年第4期，第109－134页。

⑤ 参见朱一文：《儒家开方算法之演进——以诸家对论语“道千乘之国”的注释为中心》，《自然辩证法通讯》2019年第2期，第49－55页。

⑥ 参见罗见今：《〈数书九章〉与〈周易〉》，载吴文俊主编：《秦九韶与〈数书九章〉》，北京师范大学出版社1986年版，第80－102页；李继闵：《“蓍挂发微”初探》，载吴文俊主编：《秦九韶与〈数书九章〉》，北京师范大学出版社1986年版，第124－137页；董光璧：《大衍数与大衍术》，《自然辩证法研究》1988年第3期，第46－48页。

与其他儒经之差别。朱熹之筮法实作解释实际反映出儒家注疏筮法之传统。

与之相比，秦九韶对大衍之数及筮法之解释十分特殊。从“蓍挂发微”第六部分“草”可以看出，秦氏实际将整个筮法过程理解为以求解同余方程组

$$\begin{cases} x \equiv R_1 \pmod{1} \\ x \equiv R_2 \pmod{2} \\ x \equiv R_3 \pmod{3} \\ x \equiv R_4 \pmod{4} \end{cases}$$

为中心之过程。由此，他将“挂一”理解为“一一揲之”之余数，即蓍数除以1之余数（R_1），因必然是1，所以“乃径挂一”。他将“揲之以四”解释为依次“二二揲之”“三三揲之”“四四揲之”之余数（秦氏所谓“三变”），即蓍数分别除以2、3、4之余数（R_2，R_3，R_4）。在知道R_1，R_2，R_3，R_4的前提下，根据秦氏同余理论本因求得$2\times3\times4=24$，$1\times3\times4=12$，$1\times2\times4=8$，$1\times2\times3=6$，此四数之和为$24+12+8+6=50$，即“大衍之数五十”。然而，由于模数2与4未约化，故不可用。约化之后，四模数为1，1，3，4，故求得$1\times3\times4=12$，$1\times3\times4=12$，$1\times1\times4=4$，$1\times1\times3=3$。所求同余方程可以转化为求解乘率k_1，k_2，k_3，k_4，使得：

$$\begin{cases} 12k_1 \equiv 1 \pmod{1} \\ 12k_2 \equiv 1 \pmod{2} \\ 4k_3 \equiv 1 \pmod{3} \\ 3k_4 \equiv 1 \pmod{4} \end{cases}$$

由此，显然$k_1=k_2=k_3=1$，秦氏用算图表达“大衍求一术”求得$k_4=3$。进而求得四位用数$12k_1=12$，$12k_2=12$，$4k_3=4$，$3k_4=9$。由此，用数之和$12+12+4+9=37$。秦氏云：“但三十七无意义，兼蓍少太露，是以用四十有九。”① 因此，他将第二个12变为24（因12是1、1、3、4之公倍数，故不影响计算结果），从而得用数12、24、4、9，其和为49，即“其用四十有九”。根据“大衍总数术”计算$12R_1+24R_2+4R_3+9R_4$，再减去12的若干倍得到

① 秦九韶：《数书九章》，北京中国国家图书馆藏明万历四十四年赵琦美钞本，载《四库提要著录丛书》子部020，北京出版社2011年版，第105页。

所求同余方程的最小解 x_0（$12 > x_0 > 0$）。计算 $[\frac{x_0+2}{3}]$①必得到1、2、3、4之一，即秦氏所谓“三才衍法”。利用阴阳象数图（见图1），1、2、3、4分别对应于老阳、少阴、少阳、老阴，即可得一爻。再重复六次即“十八变”得挂。②

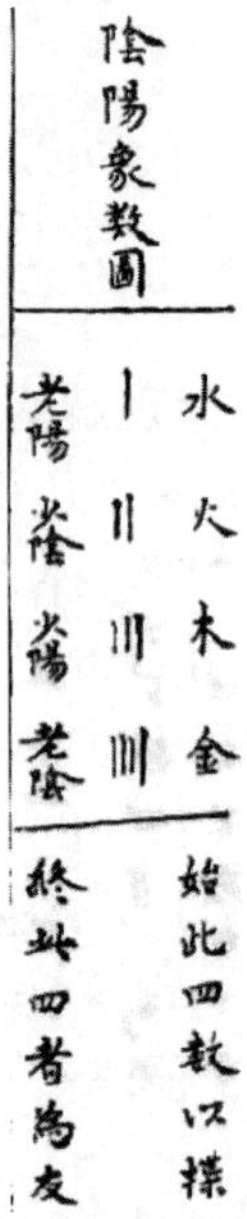

图1　秦九韶《数书九章》阴阳象数

注：秦九韶：《数书九章》，北京中国国家图书馆藏明万历四十四年赵琦美钞本，载《四库提要著录丛书》子部020，北京出版社2011年版，第103页。

---

① $[\frac{x_0+2}{3}]$ 为不超过 $[\frac{x_0+2}{3}]$ 的最大整数。此段对于秦九韶筮法解释参见李继闵《“蓍挂发微”初探》，载吴文俊主编：《秦九韶与〈数书九章〉》，北京师范大学出版社1986年版，第130页。

② 秦九韶细草举例的原文为“假令左手分得三十三，自一一揲之，必奇一，故不繁揲，乃径挂一。故《易》曰：‘分而为二以象两。挂一以象三。’次后又令筮人以二二揲之，其三十三亦奇一，故归奇于扐。又令之以三三揲之，其三十三必奇三，故又归奇于扐。又令之以四四揲之，又奇一，亦归于扐。于前挂一并三度揲，适有四扐，乃得一、一、三、一。其挂一者，乘用数图左上用数一十；其二揲扐一者，乘左副用数二十四；其三揲扐三者，乘左次用数四，得一十二；其四揲一者乘左下用数九。并此四总得五十七。问所握几何？乃满衍母一十二去之，得不满者九。[或使知其所握五十七，亦满衍母去之，亦只数九数。] 以为实用。三才衍法约之得三，乃画少阳单爻［或不满得八得七为实，皆命为三］他皆仿此。术意谓揲二、揲三、揲四者，凡三度复以三十三从头数揲之，故曰：‘三变而成爻。’既挂有六爻，必十八变，故曰：‘十有八变而成挂。’”秦九韶：《数书九章》，北京中国国家图书馆藏明万历四十四年赵琦美钞本，载《四库提要著录丛书》子部020，北京出版社2011年版，第105－106页。其中［］内为秦氏小字自注，［］为笔者所添加。此外“其三十三亦奇一”，赵钞本作“奇二”，四库全书本与宜稼堂丛书本皆作“奇一”，按算理也应为“奇一”，故校正。又“所握五十七”，赵钞本与宜稼堂本作“三十七”，四库全书本作“五十七”，按算理应为“五十七”，故亦校正。

由此可见，秦九韶将“大衍之数五十，其用四十有九”与其后之筮法统一于求解同余方程组之中。筮法之过程被理解为依次求得四个余数，而五十与四十九被理解为求解方程组过程中必然出现的四个衍数和四个用数之和。这一理解比邵雍更进一步，将数（大衍之数）与算（大衍之术）更完美地结合在一起；亦不同于朱熹等将数与算分开讨论之做法。然而，这也导致了秦氏对“挂一”“揲之以四”的解释明显与儒家传统不同，因此秦氏被四库馆臣批评为“欲以新术改《周易》，揲蓍之法殊乖故义。”①

另外，也十分重要的是，《周易》筮法所用为蓍草，朱熹以黑点表示之；秦氏以算图表示筮法，实际所用则为算筹，由此建构了“蓍草即算筹”之关系。其实，《周易》云：“乾之策二百一十六，坤之策一百四十四”②，指阴阳之蓍策数之不同。唐李淳风撰《隋书·律历志》云：“其算用竹，广二分，长三寸，正策三廉，积二百一十六枚，成六觚，乾之策也。负策四廉，积一百四十四枚，成方，坤之策也。觚方皆径十二，天地之大数也。”③此处李氏解释正算筹与负算筹之形制与数量，李俨先生认为是用 216 根郑算筹组成正六边形，用 144 根负算筹组成正方形（见图 2），而其数量与《周易》正同，从而建立了蓍草与算筹之联系。由此观之，李氏实为秦氏观点之渊源。

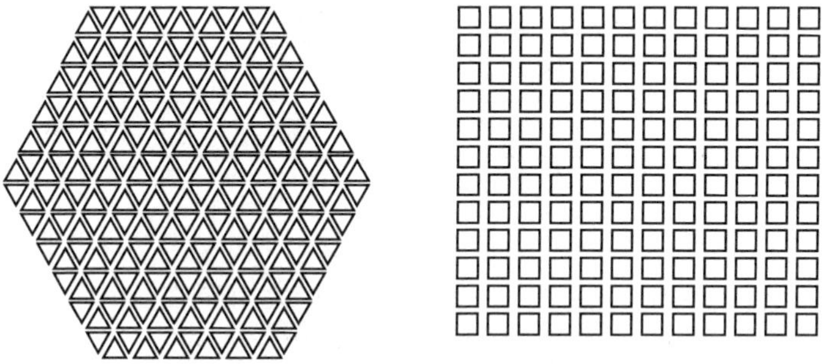

图 2　正策 216 枚，负策 144 枚

注：李俨：《筹算制度考》，载李俨：《中算史论丛》第 4 集，科学出版社 1955 年版，第 5 页。

从文本形式与数学实作的角度，笔者以大衍术为例比较了算学与历算之差别，认为传统算学经典如《孙子算经》只记载算法，而无筹算操作之过程；

① 〔宋〕秦九韶：《数书九章》，载《景印文渊阁四库全书》第 797 册，台湾商务印书馆 1985 年版，第 324 页。

② 〔唐〕李淳风：《隋书·律历志》，载魏征等：《隋书》第 2 册，中华书局 1973 年版，第 387 页。

③ 〔三国魏〕王弼注，〔唐〕孔颖达正义：《周易正义》，载〔清〕阮元校刻：《十三经注疏》，中华书局 1980 年版，第 80 页。

天文历算文献则只记载数据，而无算法与筹算过程[1]。秦九韶所建立的数术体系认为这两者之差别实际是内算与外算之别。在笔者以往对其他儒经中数学知识之研究[2]及本文对宋代易家之筮法实作之研究的基础上，可以看出：其他儒经及其注疏中记载儒家之算法，而无文本之外的操作过程；《周易》大衍经文及其注疏中记载筮法之实作，并在文本外有操作蓍草的过程。由此，从文本之书写方式、文本外之操作工具、数学问题类型等三方面比较不同活动中的数学实作，可以建立表1。

表1　不同活动中数学实作之比较

	文本之书写方式	文本外之操作工具	数学问题类型
传统算学著作	术	算筹	《孙子算经》“物不知数”问
历算文献	具体数据	算筹	求解上元积年（历家之方程）
《数书九章》	术、草、算图	算筹	《周易》筮法、上元积年及其他同余问题
《周易》大衍经文及其注疏	大衍之数、筮法、点图	蓍草	无
其他儒经及其注疏	儒家算法	无	数学隐题

总而言之，由于《周易》为儒家经典之一，故宋代易家掌握之数学实作应在儒家算法传统之中。然而，由于《周易》大衍经文及其注疏并未含有数学隐题，故其无法充分提供易家展现数学知识之文本语境。不过，由于其操作

① 参见朱一文：《秦九韶对大衍术的算图表达——基于〈数书九章〉赵琦美钞本（1616）的分析》，《自然科学史研究》2017年第2期，第244－257页。

② 参见朱一文：《儒学经典中的数学知识初探——以贾公彦对〈周礼·考工记〉“蓍氏为量”的注疏为例》，《自然科学史研究》2015年第2期，第131－141页；Zhu Yiwen，“Different cultures of computation in seventh century China from the viewpoint of square root extraction”，*Historia Mathematica*，23，2016，pp. 3－25；朱一文：《再论中国古代数学与儒学的关系——以六至七世纪学者对礼数的不同注疏为例》，《自然辩证法通讯》2016年第5期，第81－87页；朱一文，《初唐的数学与礼学——以诸家对〈礼记·投壶〉的注疏为例》，《中山大学学报（社会科学版）》2017年第2期，第60－68页；朱一文：《算学、儒学与制度化——初唐数学的多样性及其与儒学的关系》，《汉学研究》2017年第4期，第109－134页；朱一文：《朱熹的数学世界——兼论宋代数学与儒学的关系》，《哲学与文化》2018年第11期，第167－182页；朱一文：《儒家开方算法之演进——以诸家对论语“道千乘之国”的注释为中心》，《自然辩证法通讯》2019年第2期，第49－55页。

工具为蓍草，故经文注疏利用文字、点图阐发大衍之数与筮法，文本之外有蓍草之操作过程。秦九韶则在《孙子算经》“物不知数”问的基础上，发展出求解一次同余方程组的一般方法，名曰“大衍总数术”；在历家用“方程”求解上元积年的基础上，发展出该术之核心程序，名之为“大衍求一术”。继而，秦氏撰“蓍挂发微”问，创造性地在《周易》大衍经文之上提出一个数学问题，由此将数（大衍之数）与算（筮法）的解释结合在一起，并力图建立算学与易学之紧密联系。但是，其解释过程既在筮法操作层面不符合易家之传统，又并未遵循儒家算法传统中数学隐题之文本形式，故未获后世易家之认可。

四、结语

在先前的论著中①，笔者谈到中国古代数学与儒学关系之演进，认为《周礼》所载数学为六艺之一是一种理想化情形，汉儒注经所产生的数学隐题提供了发展儒家算法传统的文本语境，后世的发展导致该算法传统与算家传统形成互不隶属的局面——因此，儒家之算法传统为儒学当然之一部分，而算家之算学则是相对独立之学科。笔者进一步认为儒家之算法传统主要体现在礼学领域②，而朱熹前期倾向于将儒家与算家的两种算法都传统排除在儒学领域之外，后期则将两者一并纳入其礼学体系之中③。在这些研究的基础上，本文所探讨的宋代数学与易学之关系也应该放在数学与儒学关系的框架下来理解，并同时考虑到易学的特殊性。

朱熹是宋代儒学的代表人物，其本身处于儒家算法传统之中④，而他对《周易》筮法的注解又成为后世的定式，由此可见宋代易家之数学实作亦是儒家之算法。然而，虽然从现代数学的角度看，大衍筮法无疑与同余问题相关，但该经文在秦九韶之前从未被塑造为一个数学问题——不仅汉儒之注解未提供数学隐题，而且即使该经被甄鸾收入《五经算术》中的“《周易》策数法”，

---

① 参见朱一文：《再论中国古代数学与儒学的关系——以六至七世纪学者对礼数的不同注疏为例》，《自然辩证法通讯》2016 年第 5 期，第 81－87 页；朱一文：《算学、儒学与制度化——初唐数学的多样性及其与儒学的关系》，《汉学研究》2017 年第 4 期，第 109－134 页；朱一文：《儒家开方算法之演进——以诸家对论语“道千乘之国”的注释为中心》，《自然辩证法通讯》2019 年第 2 期，第 49－55 页。

② 参见朱一文：《初唐的数学与礼学——以诸家对〈礼记·投壶〉的注疏为例》，《中山大学学报（社会科学版）》2017 年第 2 期，第 60－68 页。

③ 参见朱一文：《朱熹的数学世界——兼论宋代数学与儒学的关系》，《哲学与文化》2018 年第 11 期，第 167－182 页。

④ 参见朱一文：《朱熹的数学世界——兼论宋代数学与儒学的关系》，《哲学与文化》2018 年第 11 期，第 167－182 页。

李淳风等也未将之重构为一个数学问题。事实上，李氏等注释云："此《五经算》一部之中多无设问及术，直据本条，略陈大数而已。今并加正术及问，仍旧数相符。其有凡说事由，不须术者，并依旧不加。"①李淳风等对《五经算术》的许多条目都添加了数学问题与术文，但对"《周易》策数法"未加注释。由此可见，李氏等认为该条甄鸾已经解释了"事由"，不需要数学问题与术文了。之后，秦九韶将《周易》筮法经文重构为一个以求解一次同余方程组为核心的数学问题，这一过程是通过给出不合易家传统的文本解释完成的。

不过，虽然在秦九韶之前《周易》筮法没有被塑造为一个数学问题，从而不提供发展数学之可能，但是历代易家对之实作解释的传统却提供了诸家将易学与数学相互联系的另一种可能性。甄鸾撰《五经算术》将《周易》筮法收入其中。李淳风撰《隋书·律历志》暗示算筹等同于蓍草。秦九韶径以算筹解释蓍草之操作，暗示两者之等价关系。朱熹以点图表达筮法结果，秦氏则以算图表达其筮法过程，暗示其学与宋代图书之学之关联。事实上，秦书原名《数术》，其数术体系分为外算与内算——外算指以《九章算术》为代表的传统算学，内算则指历法、三式（太乙、任、甲）等内容，并强调内外算"其用相通，不可歧二。"②与历法、方程、《周易》都有关系的大衍术则是沟通内外算的代表性算法③。由此，秦九韶通过扩大宋代数术的内涵将外算与内算一并包括在内，建立了两者的紧密联系。

事实上，算家向来把算学视作古代知识系统之基础，并不断扩大算学应用领域，以此提升算学之地位。李淳风撰《隋书·律历志》、注释《五经算术》，明确认为数学是音律、度量衡、历法、经学等领域的基础④。秦九韶则事实上把数术等内算也纳入算学之中。对此，儒家向来不赞同。初唐孔颖达、贾公彦等认识到儒家算法传统与算家算学之别，分别以"算法"与"九数"称呼两者，并认为前者应用于经学研究，后者应用于算学研究⑤。朱熹则根据领域不同，把数分成多种：与《周易》有关的是易数，与三式等有关的是术数，两者之学为数学，其家为数家；与历算有关的是历数，其学为历学，其家为历

---

① 〔北周〕甄鸾撰，〔唐〕李淳风等注释：《五经算术》，载钱宝琮校点：《算经十书》，中华书局1963年版，第443页。

② 〔宋〕秦九韶：《数书九章》，北京中国国家图书馆藏明万历四十四年赵琦美钞本，载《四库提要著录丛书》子部020，北京出版社2011年版，第98页。

③ 参见朱一文：《秦九韶对大衍术的算图表达——基于〈数书九章〉赵琦美钞本（1616）的分析》，《自然科学史研究》2017年第2期，第244－257页。

④ 参见朱一文：《算学、儒学与制度化——初唐数学的多样性及其与儒学的关系》，《汉学研究》2017年第4期，第109－134页。

⑤ 参见朱一文：《算学、儒学与制度化——初唐数学的多样性及其与儒学的关系》，《汉学研究》2017年第4期，第109－134页。

家；与音律有关的是律数，其学为律学，其家为律家；与算学有关的是算数，其学为算学，其家为算家；与孔颖达、贾公彦等儒家一样，他也以“算法”指出儒家的算法传统。而且，这些领域中数的表达方式有别，他注解《周易》，用点图表数；谈到司马光（1019—1086年）《潜虚》：“如《潜虚》之数用五，只似如今算位一般。其直一画则五也，下横一画则为六，横二画则为七，盖亦补凑之书。”①（《朱子语类》第7册，2546页）看来并不赞同。《仪礼经传通解》“钟律章”开篇云：“此篇凡数皆准令式借用大字。”② 全篇数字凡一至九皆用壹、贰、叁、肆、伍、陆、柒、捌、玖表示，又有拾、佰、阡、万等字表达位置。其他方面则用汉字数字表达。由此可见，秦九韶将《周易》与算学相联系的做法，实处于算家传统之中，而不符合儒家之传统。

从制度层面，我们可以进一步理解算家与儒家或易家之实作与观念之差异。唐因隋制，建立国子监算学馆。之后又编订十部算经，设立明算科，由此算学获得了很大的制度化发展。然而，与儒家算法传统所在的教授儒学的国子、太学、四门等馆相比，算学馆从师资、生源、待遇等方面皆处于下风。③这一强弱对比的情况在宋代并未获得根本性改变。北宋元丰七年（1084）秘书省刊刻了十部算经，大观三年（1109）颁布了“算学祀典”，算学几经兴废之后虽然被列入国子监，但总体而言，无法与儒家算法传统所在的儒学相抗衡。衣冠南渡以后，算学则索性被排除在制度化体制之外④，处于奄奄一息之态。然而，虽然《周易》为儒家经典之一，但因易学与数术相关，其情况有所不同。北宋末期，宋徽宗（1082—1135年）崇宁年间（1102—1106年）颁布国子监算学令云：“诸学生习《九章》《周髀》义及算问［谓假设疑数］兼通《海岛》《孙子》《五曹》《张丘建》《夏侯阳》算法并历算、三式、天文书。”⑤从而将历算、三式、天文与以《九章算术》为代表传统算学都纳入算学馆。这一做法反映出宋代以来对于算学内涵理解之变化，亦是秦九韶将《周易》筮法与大衍总数术相联系之渊源。

综上所述，宋代数学与易学的关系可以从以下两方面来理解：一方面，宋

① 〔宋〕黎靖德编：《朱子语类》第7册，中华书局1986年版，第2546页。

② 〔宋〕朱熹：《仪礼经传通解》，朱杰人、严佐之、刘永翔主编：《朱子全书》第2册，上海古籍出版社、安徽教育出版社2002年版，第484页。

③ 参见朱一文《算学、儒学与制度化——初唐数学的多样性及其与儒学的关系》，《汉学研究》2017年第4期，第109－134页。

④ 李俨：《唐宋元明清数学教育制度》，载李俨：《中算史论丛》第4集，科学出版社1955年版，第238－280页。

⑤ 〔汉〕徐岳撰，〔北周〕甄鸾注：《数术记遗·算学源流》，载《宋刻算经六种》，文物出版社1980年版，第16a页。

代儒家之算法延续唐代之传统，与以《九章算术》为代表的传统算学相对独立。由于《周易》也是儒家经典之一，并且历代儒家对其筮法的注解没有创造出可以提供发展数学之文本语境的数学隐题，因此除了简单的加减乘除之外，易学与数学实无明显之关联，但后期朱熹认为可以将算家与儒家的两种算法传统一并纳入礼学体系之内。另一方面，由于《周易》筮法的实作特性及其与数术之关联，使得甄鸾撰《五经算术》，“《周易》策数法”将之纳入算学体系，李淳风撰《隋书·律历志》暗示蓍草与算筹之等价关系，并进一步导致了宋代国家从制度化层面将历算、三式、天文纳入国子监算学馆，终至秦九韶创造“蓍挂发微”问直接建构《周易》与大衍总数术、蓍草与算筹、点图与算图之联系，从而建立了包含内算与外算两者的数术体系。总之，刘徽所论的算学与《周易》之关系可视为关于数学起源的一种理想化论述，宋代数学与易学的关系则主要体现在不同知识门类间的合并与重组，并在这一过程中扩大了传统算学的应用领域。